Metaphysics of Mystery

T&T Clark Studies in Edward Schillebeeckx

Series editors
Frederiek Depoortere
Kathleen McManus O.P.
Stephan van Erp

Metaphysics of Mystery

Revisiting the Question of Universality through Rahner and Schillebeeckx

Marijn de Jong

LONDON • NEW YORK • OXFORD • NEW DELHI • SYDNEY

T&T CLARK
Bloomsbury Publishing Plc
50 Bedford Square, London, WC1B 3DP, UK
1385 Broadway, New York, NY 10018, USA
29 Earlsfort Terrace, Dublin 2, Ireland

BLOOMSBURY, T&T CLARK and the T&T Clark logo are
trademarks of Bloomsbury Publishing Plc

First published in Great Britain 2020
Paperback edition first published 2021

Copyright © Marijn de Jong, 2020

Marijn de Jong has asserted his right under the Copyright,
Designs and Patents Act, 1988, to be identified as Author of this work.

For legal purposes the Acknowledgements on p. ix constitute
an extension of this copyright page.

Cover design: Terry Woodley

All rights reserved. No part of this publication may be reproduced or
transmitted in any form or by any means, electronic or mechanical,
including photocopying, recording, or any information storage or retrieval
system, without prior permission in writing from the publishers.

Bloomsbury Publishing Plc does not have any control over, or responsibility for,
any third-party websites referred to or in this book. All internet addresses given
in this book were correct at the time of going to press. The author and publisher
regret any inconvenience caused if addresses have changed or sites have
ceased to exist, but can accept no responsibility for any such changes.

A catalogue record for this book is available from the British Library.

Library of Congress Cataloging-in-Publication Data
Names: De Jong, Marijn, author.
Title: Metaphysics of mystery: revisiting the question of universality
through Rahner and Schillebeeckx / Marijn de Jong.
Description: London: T&T Clark, 2020. | Series: T&T Clark studies in
Edward Schillebeeckx | Includes bibliographical references and index.
Identifiers: LCCN 2019039723 (print) | LCCN 2019039724 (ebook) |
ISBN 9780567689344 (hardback) | ISBN 9780567689351 (pdf) |
ISBN 9780567689368 (epub)
Subjects: LCSH: Philosophical theology. | Rahner, Karl, 1904-1984 |
Schillebeeckx, Edward, 1914-2009
Classification: LCC BT40.D4 2020 (print) | LCC BT40 (ebook) |
DDC 230/.20922—dc23
LC record available at https://lccn.loc.gov/2019039723
LC ebook record available at https://lccn.loc.gov/2019039724

ISBN: HB: 978-0-5676-8934-4
PB: 978-0-5676-9897-1
ePDF: 978-0-5676-8935-1
eBook: 978-0-5676-8936-8

Typeset by Deanta Global Publishing Services, Chennai, India

To find out more about our authors and books visit
www.bloomsbury.com and sign up for our newsletters.

Contents

Acknowledgements ix
List of abbreviations x

Introduction 1

1 Metaphysical and hermeneutical theology: Retrieving a dialectical
   interrelation 4
   1 Introduction 4
   2 Theology and the challenges of postmodernity 4
      2.1 Sceptical theological responses to postmodernity 7
      2.2 An alternative response: Hermeneutical theology 10
   3 Francis Schüssler Fiorenza's hermeneutical turn 12
      3.1 From augmentation to critique 12
      3.2 Complementary dialectic 16
      3.3 The crisis of hermeneutical theology 19
      3.4 A reappraisal of transcendental theology 21
   4 David Tracy's hermeneutical turn 24
      4.1 Defending metaphysics 25
      4.2 Taking the hermeneutical turn 28
      4.3 The full force of postmodernity 33
   5 The rediscovery of universality 37
      5.1 The lessons of Fiorenza and Tracy 37
      5.2 A renaissance of universalism 39
   6 Going forward by stepping back 42

Part I 45

2 An eclectic theologian: The sources of Rahner's method 47
   1 Introduction 47
   2 Aggiornamento: Reading Thomas through modern philosophy 48
   3 Immanuel Kant: The destroyer of metaphysics 51
   4 Joseph Maréchal: A dynamic theological metaphysics 54
   5 Martin Heidegger: Rahner's only teacher 59
   6 Conclusion 66

3	Oscillating between heaven and earth: Human questioning as locus theologicus	68
	1 Introduction	68
	2 The phenomenon of human questioning	69
	2.1 Questionability and questionableness	71
	2.2 Materialist metaphysics of knowledge	72
	2.3 Subjectivist suspicions	75
	3 Incarnational epistemology	78
	3.1 Being with otherness	78
	3.2 Transcending otherness	80
	4 The Vorgriff of Being	82
	4.1 The scope of the Vorgriff	83
	4.2 Anticipating God	87
	5 The finite spirit: Oscillating between world and God	91
	5.1 Decentred subjectivity	91
	5.2 Modest categorical metaphysics	93
	5.3 Natural theology and the hiddenness of God	95
	6 Conclusion	97
4	Hidden hermeneutics: The history of transcendentality	98
	1 Introduction	98
	2 The threefold charge of forgetfulness	99
	2.1 Forgetful of history and suffering	99
	2.2 Forgetful of language and inter-subjectivity	101
	2.3 Forgetful of culture and community	102
	2.4 Correcting the Korrektivtheologie	104
	3 The dialectics of revelation	105
	3.1 Standing before mystery	105
	3.2 From spirit in the world to spirit in history	106
	4 The dialectics of experience	109
	4.1 The transcendental dimension of experience	110
	4.2 The categorical dimension of experience	112
	4.3 Mediated immediacy	116
	5 The dialectics of love	117
	5.1 Loving an other is realizing oneself	118
	5.2 Love of neighbour and love of God	119
	6 The dialectics of mystery	121
	6.1 The dark gate to knowledge	122
	6.2 Theological speech and silence	124
	7 Conclusion	126

5	The theological *a priori*: Transforming the transcendental method	128
	1 Introduction	128
	2 The incarnational shape of transcendental theology	129
	3 The supernatural existential	131
	3.1 Navigating between extrinsicism and immanentism	132
	3.2 The ubiquity of grace	134
	4 The contaminating effects of the supernatural existential	138
	4.1 Naturalizing the supernatural	139
	4.2 Supernaturalizing the natural	140
	4.3 Questioning purist concerns	142
	5 Philosophy within theology	144
	5.1 Ancilla or domina	145
	5.2 From purity to porosity	146
	6 Rethinking transcendentality	148
	6.1 Pluralism and gnoseological concupiscence	149
	6.2 Towards a modest transcendental theology	150
	6.3 A theological 'correction' of transcendental philosophy	154
	7 Conclusion	156

Part II		159
6	Dialogical theology: The sources of Schillebeeckx's method	161
	1 Introduction	161
	2 Phenomenological-ontological roots: Dominicus De Petter	162
	3 Understanding the past in the present	166
	3.1 Hans-Georg Gadamer's hermeneutics of history	167
	3.2 Paul Ricoeur's long route	169
	4 The future as horizon of understanding	173
	4.1 Theodor Adorno's critical negativity	174
	4.2 Jürgen Habermas's reconfiguration of theory and praxis	176
	5 Conclusion	180
7	Speculating about salvation history: The metaphysics and hermeneutics of experience	182
	1 Introduction	182
	2 Theology: Positive or speculative?	183
	3 Perspectival epistemology and relational ontology	185
	3.1 Subjective or objective dynamism: Maréchal versus De Petter	186
	3.2 Creation, the foundation of all theology	190

	4	Preambula Fidei: Transcendental or theological?		193
		4.1	The transcendental horizon	195
		4.2	The theologal horizon	197
		4.3	The theological key to transcendental anthropology	199
	5	A critical-hermeneutical turn		201
		5.1	The clear break with De Petter	201
		5.2	The dialectics of experience	203
		5.3	The dialectics of revelation	208
	6	Conclusion		210
8	A hermeneutics of living tradition: Faithful creativity and self-giving mystery			212
	1	Introduction		212
	2	Revelation: Past and present		213
		2.1	Historicity and truth	213
		2.2	The mystery which gives us to think	216
	3	Reconceptualizing correlation theology		219
		3.1	The medium co-constitutes the message	221
		3.2	Continuity in discontinuities: The criterion of proportional identity	224
	4	Evaluating the correlation of correlations		229
		4.1	Criticizing continuity: Lieven Boeve and Erik Borgman	229
		4.2	Revisiting continuity: Theological creativity as response	234
	5	Conclusion		239
9	The heuristics of grace: Natural theology and contrast experience			241
	1	Introduction		241
	2	Renewing natural theology		242
	3	Experience-oriented natural theology		245
		3.1	The critical cognitivity of recalcitrant reality	245
		3.2	The contrast experience	248
	4	Interpreting contrast experience		251
		4.1	Eschatological hope and creation faith	251
		4.2	Mediated immediacy: The nearness of mystery	254
	5	Grace perfecting nature		257
		5.1	The hermeneutics and metaphysics of contrast experience	258
		5.2	The contrast experience as heuristics of grace	260
		5.3	One reality in two languages	265
		5.4	Anonymous Christians: A real possibility?	267
	6	Conclusion		270
Conclusion				272
Bibliography				289
Index				312

Acknowledgements

Writing a dissertation asks for a monastic attitude. It is a scholarly task demanding many hours in the secluded and silent setting of a library. While there is evidently truth in this characterization, my experiences of the past couple of years taught me that the communal and relational aspects of this task are as – or perhaps even more – important as the monastic devotion. Writing this study would have been impossible without the collegiality and friendship that carried and supported me during these years.

First of all, I owe a great debt to my two doctoral supervisors. It was almost accidentally that I walked into Lieven Boeve's office at the University of Leuven in the summer of 2011. Two months later, I had moved to Leuven and started working in its famous theological library. From our very first conversation onwards, Lieven has supervised my work in a careful, critical and constructive manner. A single question raised by him was often enough to trigger key insights and new ideas. Lieven also supported my plans to conduct part of my research at the University of Oxford. During my year in Oxford, St Benet's Hall provided me with true Benedictine hospitality and in Werner Jeanrond I found a committed co-supervisor. Werner helped me to remain focused on my central questions and to avoid getting lost in Rahneriana and Schillebeeckxiana. His keen German eye for detail was invariably combined with a warm personal engagement.

Good theology requires sharing and debating one's ideas with others. I have had the pleasure and good fortune to do so often and abundantly. I want to thank the members of the Research Group in a Postmodern Context for their helpful advice and welcome conversations. I am thankful to have found good friends in my office mates Christopher Cimorelli, Dan Minch, Derrick Witherington, Justin Sands and Trevor Maine. Our coffee breaks were a welcome distraction, as well as a source of inspiration. I also want to thank Christiane Alpers, Hannah Strømmen, James Matarazzo, Stephan van Erp, Joeri Schrijvers and Tom Uytterhoeven for their generous friendship and insightful conversations. A special word of thanks goes out to Ulrich Schmiedel, for his unrivalled proofreading skills, for his friendship and for our theological sparring sessions inside and outside pubs.

I want to thank my family for their constant support throughout the years. Whenever and wherever I moved, they remained near to me. My parents Mieke and Rinus de Jong have always encouraged me in my studies, and our warm family has been my first and most important school in life. Last but not least, I am deeply grateful to Marije Marijs for her love and support. Time and again, she patiently persuaded this introvert to share his thoughts and reminded this relativizer to view things in proper perspective. I cherish the graceful gift of her loving company in my life.

Marijn de Jong
June 2019

Abbreviations

CW	*The Collected Works of Edward Schillebeeckx*
DH	Heinrich Denzinger and Helmut Hoping. *Compendium of Creeds, Definitions, and Declarations on Matters of Faith and Morals*. Ed. Peter Hünermannn, Robert Fastiggi, and Anne Englund Nash. 43rd edition. San Francisco: Ignatius Press, 2012.
NRSV	New Revised Stand Version of the Bible (1989)
SW	*Sämtliche Werke*
TI	*Theological Investigations*

Introduction

Karl Rahner (1904–84) and Edward Schillebeeckx (1914–2009) are widely considered to be two theological giants who have decisively marked theology in the twentieth century. The efforts they undertook to enter into a critical dialogue with modern thought formed a major contribution to the *aggiornamento* of Catholic theology before, during and after the Second Vatican Council. However, the rapid road to fame of these theologians has been followed more recently by a period of relative silence. This raises the question of whether their work still has any potential for dealing with the questions that confront theology today. There is an ever-increasing distance in time that now separates us from these two modern thinkers. Yet this distance in time also affords new opportunities to assess the relevance of their work for contemporary theology.

At first glance, it may seem as though Rahner and Schillebeeckx have largely fallen out of favour and risk becoming 'forgotten theologians'.[1] Russell Reno, for instance, claims unambiguously that Rahner's time has passed.[2] Reno, once himself a fervent supporter of Rahner's thought, now considers his transcendental method to be a 'muddy mediating voice' that obscures the Christian claim to truth and encourages relativism.[3] Philip Endean too observes that there are a great many commentators who judge Rahner's work to be *passé*.[4] But he contests this negative evaluation, attributing it to a refusal to grapple with the complexity of Rahner's ideas that has resulted in a flawed understanding of his work. According to Endean, 'It is not that Rahner's theology has been tried and found wanting; it has been found difficult and therefore not really tried.'[5] Schillebeeckx has suffered a strikingly similar fate. Robert Schreiter refers to his obituary in the Vatican's *L'Osservatore Romano*, which states that a 'sunset' has taken place over Schillebeeckx's work and influence.[6] He suggests that Schillebeeckx's concern with the actual questions of his own time may make him look ill-suited for our current situation. Stephan van Erp also points to this paradoxical fact that its own principles of contextuality and perspectivity may have contributed to the fact that Schillebeeckx's hermeneutical theology was so rapidly replaced by new

---

[1] See Erich Garhammer, 'Editorial', *Lebendige Seelsorge* 64 (2013): 361.
[2] Russell Reno, 'Rahner the Restorationist', *First Things* (May 2013): 45–51.
[3] Reno, 'Rahner the Restorationist', 49–50. For his earlier appreciative understanding of Rahner's work, see Russell Reno, *The Ordinary Transformed: Karl Rahner and the Vision of Transcendence* (Grand Rapids, MI: Eerdmans, 1995).
[4] Philip Endean, 'Has Rahnerian Theology a Future?' in *The Cambridge Companion to Karl Rahner*, ed. Declan Marmion and Mary E. Hines (Cambridge: Cambridge University Press, 2005), 281.
[5] Endean, 'Has Rahnerian Theology a Future?' 282.
[6] Robert J. Schreiter, 'Indicators of the Future of Theology in the Works of Edward Schillebeeckx', in *Impulse für Theologien im 21. Jahrhundert – Impetus Towards Theologies in the 21st Century*, ed. Thomas Eggensperger, Ulrich Engel, Angel F. Méndez Montoya (Mainz: Matthias Grünewald Verlag, 2012), 21.

theological models once the situation changed.[7] He criticizes this sudden break with the immediate theological past, though, and agrees with Schillebeeckx's biographer Erik Borgman that while Schillebeeckx's ideas may have become 'dated', they have not been superseded in a 'deeper sense'.[8]

This study engages in a retrieval of the theological epistemologies of Rahner and Schillebeeckx. Contesting the voices judging that the time of these modern theologians has passed, I argue that they offer us key insights into one of the most pressing theological issues of our contemporary postmodern situation, namely how to account for the universality of the truth of Christian faith in a hermeneutically responsible way. This universal aspect of Christian faith has come under pressure in the various hermeneutical theologies that have been suggested more recently in response to the challenges of postmodernity. I will develop this evaluation of the current state of fundamental theology in Chapter 1, by analysing the work of Francis Schüssler Fiorenza and David Tracy. While these theologians have enriched theology by incorporating a sharp hermeneutical awareness of the particularities that condition human understanding, the universal aspect of faith has moved out of view in their theologies. Together with Fiorenza and Tracy, I argue that theology is currently in need of a reconceptualized form of metaphysical theology to address this universal aspect of faith. I propose to return to the thought of Rahner and Schillebeeckx. The intuition motivating this retrieval is that taking a step *back* may be the way to bring the theological discussion on the universality of faith *forward*.

The thesis that I develop in this study is that the theological methodologies of Rahner and Schillebeeckx encompass a particular mediatory dialectics. Neither Rahner nor Schillebeeckx have adopted an exclusively transcendental-metaphysical or an exclusively hermeneutical approach. Instead, these two theologians employ a *dialectics* of metaphysics and hermeneutics in their methods, which enables them to think about the universality of Christian faith *from within* particularity. Rahner and Schillebeeckx have provided a major impetus for the renewed theological reconsideration of the universal presence of God's grace within this world. Dissatisfied with an inward-looking church and confronted with the challenges of secularization and religious diversity, they sought for new ways to explain the central Christian conviction that God's salvific word is addressed to all. Focusing on concrete human experience in and of the world as the locus for the encounter with God, Rahner and Schillebeeckx initiated a rethinking of the divine–human relationship as a dynamic history that continues to unfold today. This peculiar approach of thinking universality from within particularity warrants a retrieval of the work of these giants of twentieth-century theology.

---

[7] Stephan Van Erp, 'Incarnational Theology: Systematic Theology after Schillebeeckx', in *Impulse für Theologien im 21. Jahrhundert – Impetus Towards Theologies in the 21st Century*, ed. Thomas Eggensperger, Ulrich Engel, Angel F. Méndez Montoya (Mainz: Matthias Grünewald Verlag, 2012), 60. The rapid decline of Schillebeeckx's presence within theological debate is particularly striking in his own context of the Low Countries. See Stephan van Erp, 'Tussen traditie & situatie: Edward Schillebeeckx voor een volgende generatie', *Tijdschrift voor Theologie* 50 (2010): 6–8; 19.

[8] Van Erp, 'Incarnational Theology: Systematic Theology after Schillebeeckx', 59–65; Erik Borgman, *Edward Schillebeeckx: A Theologian in His History. Vol. 1: A Catholic Theology of Culture (1916–1965)*, trans. John Bowden (London: Continuum, 2003), 13–14.

Apart from the Introduction chapter, this study consists of two major parts. In Part I, which comprises Chapters 2–5, I engage in a retrieval of Rahner's theological epistemology. In order to account for my claim that his method is characterized by a dialectical interrelationship of metaphysics and hermeneutics, I will uncover the often-overlooked hermeneutical dimension of Rahner's transcendental method. Recovering this hermeneutical aspect and explaining its relation to the transcendental aspect are the key to understanding Rahner's thinking of universality from within particularity. Part II, which comprises Chapters 6–9, mirrors in a certain sense the approach of Part I. While the hermeneutical aspect of Rahner's theological epistemology remains rather implicit, Schillebeeckx takes a more explicit turn towards hermeneutics. I argue, though, that contrary to his hermeneutical successors, Schillebeeckx's hermeneutical theology retains a crucial metaphysical element. In Part II, I will recover this implicit metaphysical aspect and explain its relation to the hermeneutical aspect of Schillebeeckx's method. This retrieval of the theological epistemology of Schillebeeckx offers an insightful complementary example of the constructive dialectical interrelationship of hermeneutics and metaphysics as the key to the theological thinking of universality from within particularity.

Before I start developing the argument of this study, I must attend to two terminological issues. The first issue concerns my use of the terms 'metaphysics' and 'transcendentality'. These terms have a long and complex, partly intertwined, history. The term 'metaphysics' dates back to classical Greek philosophy, whereas the term 'transcendental' used to be part of scholastic metaphysics, but was given a decidedly new meaning by Immanuel Kant. However, for Rahner (and to a lesser degree for Schillebeeckx) these terms remain intrinsically interrelated. They both signify modes of reflection that focus on the universal trans-historical and trans-cultural aspects of human existence. Instead of sharply distinguishing between these terms, Rahner and Schillebeeckx use them interchangeably in their work, depending on the specific context of the discussion. I have decided to follow this example and will therefore not consistently speak about either metaphysics or transcendentality.

The second issue pertains to the use of the word 'Being'. Once again, this is especially important in the discussion of Rahner's work. Rahner either uses the German *Sein* or the Latin *esse* when speaking about Being. To render *Sein* or *esse* in English, one has to choose between an upper-case 'B', that is 'Being', or a lower-case 'b', that is 'being'. Capitalizing Being runs the risk of implying that Being is a metaphysical entity. However, using the lower-case formulation runs the risk of forgetting what Martin Heidegger calls the 'ontological distinction', the difference between the non-entity Being and beings understood as entities. For this reason, I have decided to render *Sein* and *esse* as Being in the subsequent discussion. This practice is followed in other instances, unless the specific author under discussion calls for a different use.

1

Metaphysical and hermeneutical theology: Retrieving a dialectical interrelation

1 Introduction

A central and long-standing tenet of the Christian tradition of faith is the conviction that the salvific truth which is revealed in history – most fully in the person of Jesus Christ – is a universal truth intended for each and every person. Theology has traditionally employed metaphysical reflection to understand and explain the content of Christian faith. However, the rise of postmodern thought has problematized all claims to universality and has, thereby, resulted in a demise of metaphysical forms of theology. Accordingly, new forms of fundamental theology have been suggested.

Two contemporary theologians, Francis Schüssler Fiorenza and David Tracy, have played a major role in the recent debates on fundamental theology. Appropriating the insights of hermeneutical theory, their theological methods are highly attentive to historicity, cultural contextuality, linguistic mediation and ideological distortion. However, as Fiorenza and Tracy have themselves noted, this focus on particularity leaves the question of how we are to account for the universal dimension of Christian faith unaddressed. As will be explained below, it is precisely this issue of universality and the question of metaphysics that have made a remarkable return in actual philosophical and theological debates. Fiorenza and Tracy suggest that a reconceptualized form of metaphysical or transcendental reflection is necessary for theology today, but they do not offer a substantial proposal for such a reconceptualization. Confronted with this lacuna in fundamental theology, I propose to retrieve the work of Rahner and Schillebeeckx.

2 Theology and the challenges of postmodernity

Theology today is confronted with the multifaceted challenges of a postmodern world. It is notoriously difficult to provide a proper definition of the concept of postmodernity. As Kevin Vanhoozer notes, one characteristic feature of postmodernity is precisely the resistance to neutral or comprehensive descriptions and definitions.[1] Following Jean-

---

[1] Kevin J. Vanhoozer, 'Theology and the Condition of Postmodernity: A Report On Knowledge (of God)', in *The Cambridge Companion to Postmodern Theology*, ed. Kevin J. Vanhoozer (Cambridge: Cambridge University Press, 2003), 3.

François Lyotard, it may be better to describe postmodernity in terms of a 'condition'.[2] This condition is 'at once intellectual/theoretical and cultural/practical' and 'affects modes of thought as well as modes of embodiment'.[3] The nature of this postmodern condition can be further clarified by contrasting it with the – equally difficult to define – notion of modernity. Thus, a series of postmodern turns can be distinguished in a variety of fields and domains, ranging from architecture and the arts to society and social organization. Particularly relevant for theology is the postmodern turn in philosophy. Postmodern philosophers are highly critical of the so-called modern Enlightenment project. The European Enlightenment sought universal human emancipation by putting considerable trust in the capacities of human reason. By contrast, postmodern thinkers reject this modern preoccupation with certainty and universality and criticize it as leading to totalitarian oppression and as being forgetful of difference.[4]

The confrontation with postmodern thought has introduced multiple challenges to theology. More concretely, it has called long accepted traditional theological understandings and methodologies into question. A particularly pertinent issue concerns the relationship between particularity and universality. The conviction that the Christian message mediates a universal truth, intended for all people of every time and place, forms a crucial and long-standing aspect of the Christian tradition of faith. Scripture attests to this fundamental belief by connecting the universality of truth to God's universal salvific will:

> This is right and is acceptable in the sight of God our Savior, who desires everyone to be saved and to come to the knowledge of the truth. For there is one God; there is also one mediator between God and humankind, Christ Jesus, himself human, who gave himself a ransom for all – this was attested at the right time.[5]

The truth to which the Christian tradition of faith bears witness is not restricted to the intellectual domain, but concerns what is theologically termed 'salvation'. This revelatory truth of Christian faith ultimately concerns the salvific and felicitous fulfilment of human life. The Second Vatican Council reaffirmed this universal dimension of the salvific truth of Christian faith in *Dei Verbum*, stating that the words and deeds of revelation are aimed at 'the salvation of all nations'.[6]

Theology has traditionally looked to metaphysics in order to explicate this universal dimension of Christian faith, thereby being faithful to its task of *fides quaerens intellectum* (faith seeking understanding). The appropriation of classical Greek philosophy by patristic theologians and the incorporation of Aristotle's philosophy into scholastic theology are examples in this instance. In his encyclical *Fides et Ratio*, Pope John Paul II elaborates on the necessary role played by philosophy in the theological reflection

---

[2] See Jean-François Lyotard, *The Postmodern Condition: A Report on Knowledge*, trans. G. Bennington and B. Massumi, foreword by F. Jameson (Minneapolis: University of Minnesota Press, 1984).
[3] Vanhoozer, 'Theology and the Condition of Postmodernity', 4.
[4] Ibid., 6–8.
[5] 1 Timothy 2, 3-5 (NSRV).
[6] Second Vatican Council, Dogmatic Constitution on Divine Revelation *Dei Verbum*, 7 (DH 4207).

on the universal truth of Christian faith.[7] This divine truth is affirmed as enjoying 'an innate intelligibility'.[8] Theology has the task of contributing to the understanding of this faith, so as to bring its salvific meaning for humankind to light.[9] Importantly, the universality of faith demands a specific mode of reflection that goes beyond the particular and concrete. Theology needs 'a philosophy of *genuinely metaphysical* range' in order to provide a coherent and plausible account of 'the universal and transcendent value of revealed truth'.[10] John Paul recognizes that such claims to universality and absoluteness prompt the question of how this can be reconciled with the unavoidable historical and cultural factors that condition the mediation of this universal truth. In order to avoid relativism and historicism, he pleads for a hermeneutics that is open to metaphysics:

> the use of a hermeneutic open to the appeal of metaphysics can show how it is possible to move from the historical and contingent circumstances in which the texts developed to the truth which they express, a truth transcending those circumstances.
>
> Human language may be conditioned by history and constricted in other ways, but the human being can still express truths which surpass the phenomenon of language. Truth can never be confined to time and culture; in history it is known, but it also reaches beyond history.[11]

In 2012, the International Theological Commission reiterated the same point in the document *Theology Today*.[12] The commission observes that the 'post-modern crisis of reason', especially the crisis of metaphysics, poses a serious challenge to contemporary theology.[13] However, the commission warns that theology should not abandon reason and philosophy in the face of these challenges. On the contrary, theology must continue to seek the dialogue with philosophy so as to give 'a scientifically and rationally argued presentation of the truths of the Christian faith'.[14] As such, theology can help to overcome the crisis of rationality and 'revitalise an authentic metaphysics'.[15] Yet, insofar as postmodern thinkers have strongly pushed for a focus on particularity, precisely the metaphysical and transcendental forms of theology that seek to account for this universal dimension of Christian faith and theology have come under pressure. This raises the question of whether it is possible to revitalize metaphysics in theology while also paying due attention to the questions and issues raised by postmodern thinkers.

---

[7] John Paul II, Encyclical *Fides et Ratio* (DH 5075-5080). Full text available at the Vatican's website www.vatican.va.
[8] *Fides et Ratio*, 66.
[9] Ibid.
[10] *Fides et Ratio*, 83.
[11] *Fides et Ratio*, 95.
[12] International Theological Commission, *Theology Today: Perspectives, Principles, and Criteria*, 2012. Full text available at the Vatican's website www.vatican.va.
[13] Ibid., 71.
[14] Ibid., 73.
[15] Ibid., 71.

Or, put differently: Are theological metaphysics and postmodernity compatible with each other?

2.1 Sceptical theological responses to postmodernity

Some theologians, such as Thomas Guarino and Saskia Wendel, argue that postmodern thought is difficult to reconcile with theology, especially with a theology that focuses on the universal aspects of Christian faith. Accordingly, they express serious doubts about the reception of postmodern ideas and intuitions into theology.

In *Foundations of Systematic Theology,* Guarino outlines his view on the challenges that postmodernism presents to theology.[16] He is interested particularly in the consequences for the understanding of Christian doctrine, more precisely the question of the continuity and universality of the doctrinal teachings of the Roman Catholic Church. How can the church maintain today that her doctrines are 'what the church has believed and continues to believe'?[17] The fact that church teachings have developed historically, and the consequent demand for continual reinterpretation, is generally recognized these days. Yet, Guarino points out that the Christian church has traditionally characterized her doctrinal teachings using notions such as 'continuity', 'perpetuity', 'objectivity' and 'universality'.[18] These claims to universality and continuity have become highly problematic due to the rise of postmodern thought, which he describes as

> a type of thinking that rebels against any totalizing understanding of reality, against any 'grand metanarrative'. It is opposed to universalization, rationalization, systematization, and the establishment of consistent criteria for the evaluation of truth-claims. It is characterized by an abiding concern for the radicalness of historicity, the pervasiveness of ideology, the decentered subject, and the rejection of transcendentalism.[19]

Falsely claiming universality and neutrality, modern appeals to reason ignore and suppress otherness and plurality, and reduce reason to instrumental and technocratic rationality. Postmodernism, instead, seeks to reintroduce notions such as 'incommensurability', 'historicity', 'fissure', 'otherness', 'finitude' and 'difference' and emphasizes the embedded and contextual nature of every rationality.[20] Consequently, metaphysical or transcendental types of thinking are rejected, because they seek to close down or to reify history and historical consciousness.

---

[16] Thomas G. Guarino, *Foundations of Systematic Theology* (London: T&T Clark, 2005).
[17] Guarino, *Foundations,* 2. This phrase refers to the traditional dictum *quod ubique, quod semper, et quod ab omnibus creditum est* (what is always, what is everywhere, and what is believed by all), attributed to Vincent of Lérins.
[18] Guarino, *Foundations,* 2–4. Guarino refers to several doctrinal documents of the Roman Catholic Church, including *Dei Verbum* (DH 4201-4235) and *Dominus Iesus* (DH 5085-5089).
[19] Ibid., 6.
[20] Ibid., 5.

According to Guarino, Martin Heidegger is the primary progenitor of postmodern thought. Heidegger's main thrust is that the Western philosophical tradition suffers from 'a complete neglect of historicity'.[21] This has led to an onto-theological metaphysics, that is a metaphysics that thinks Being in relation of God, identifies Being with God and subsequently dominates and controls all other thinking about Being. Onto-theology is concerned with the thinking of presence and, therefore, disregards the interplay between presence and absence, the tension between disclosure and concealment, which is caused by the historicity and finitude of human life. This results in a situation of *Seinsvergessenheit* (forgetfulness of Being); onto-theology has essentially lost sight of the question of Being. Heidegger seeks to overcome this way of thinking by advocating a return to the concreteness and historicity of human being in the world.[22]

Guarino considers Heidegger's deconstruction of traditional metaphysics to be the inspiration for many contemporary postmodern philosophers, including Jacques Derrida, Michel Foucault, Julia Kristeva, Jean Baudrillard, Luce Irigaray and Richard Rorty. To take an example, Rorty strongly advocates a non-foundationalism that understands truth as being socially and historically constructed. In Rorty's view, such a non-foundationalism liberates philosophy from theology and metaphysics.[23] According to Guarino, however, this position is unacceptable because it is irreconcilable with the universal claims to trans-cultural and trans-historical validity of Christian doctrine. Hence, while he agrees that theology must be 'dramatically rethought', and in so doing has much to learn from postmodern thinkers, he refuses to accept the postmodern critique fully. Instead, Guarino argues that 'some kind of (commodious) metaphysical approach' is essential for a theology that seeks to explain and defend the universal and trans-cultural claims of Christian doctrine.[24] He does not advocate any particular form of metaphysics. Instead, Guarino pleads for 'philosophies with metaphysical horizons rather than simply metaphysics *sensu strictu*'.[25] Without some theological incorporation of metaphysical and transcendental reflection, Christian faith is either reduced to fideism or forced to give up its universal claims.[26]

Saskia Wendel too has addressed the question of the relation between Christian theology and postmodern philosophy.[27] She argues that the two sides in this debate hold rather impoverished or truncated views about the respective other. On the one hand, postmodern thought is often identified with arbitrariness and relativism, and is therefore quickly dismissed. On the other hand, theology is regularly equated with metaphysical thought, resulting in equally rash verdicts.[28] Wendel, therefore, turns to

---

[21] Ibid., 9.
[22] Ibid., 9–10.
[23] Ibid., 11.
[24] Ibid., 24–5.
[25] Thomas Guarino, '*Philosophia Obscurans?* Six Theses on the Proper Relationship between Theology and Philosophy', *Nova et Vetera* 12 (2014): 389.
[26] Guarino, '*Philosophia Obscurans?*', 391.
[27] Saskia Wendel, 'Zum Verhältnis von christlicher Theologie und postmoderner Philosophie', in *Fundamentaltheologie – Fluchtlinien und gegenwärtige Herausforderungen*, ed. Klaus Müller (Regensburg: Friedrich Pustet Verlag, 1998), 193–214.
[28] Wendel, 'Zum Verhältnis von christlicher Theologie und postmoderner Philosophie', 193.

the thought of two main representatives of postmodern thought, Jean-François Lyotard and Jacques Derrida. She formulates five characteristics of postmodern thought with reference to these philosophers.

First, postmodern philosophy criticizes the search for foundations or origins, be they epistemological, ontological or ethical. This pattern of thinking, which is characteristic of Western metaphysics, assumes an illusory logic of presence (Derrida) or identity (Lyotard) that destroys plurality and negates that which does not form part of the centre or identity. The result is a hierarchical and oppositional thinking in which otherness and difference are suppressed. Second, postmodernity questions ideals of progress and representations of final ends. Lyotard, in particular, emphasizes that Utopian ideals of reconciliation must radically be done away with. Third, the modern subject philosophy is regarded as the prime representation of metaphysical thinking. The sovereign and autonomous subject is an illusion, an ideal of total identity and presence, that serves to control and oppress the objective world. Fourth, postmodernity offers an alternative way of thinking in which the dignity of the other, the different, and the plural play a central role. The absolute remains, but is unrepresentable, unnamable and undefinable according to Derrida and Lyotard. It can no longer serve a foundational role, but merely be identified as 'event' (Lyotard) or 'trace' (Derrida). Fifth, the radical absence of the absolute legitimates an ethical attitude of receptivity towards otherness, plurality and difference. This attitude cannot be mediated communicatively, because it goes beyond autonomous subjectivity, and can therefore only be accepted obediently.[29]

Wendel subsequently examines several issues that, according to her, arise when postmodern thought is brought to bear on central elements of Christian understanding. To begin with, God as origin and foundation – as creator of the world, source of truth and ethical lawgiver – is called into question. This also invalidates something like a 'universal confession', because the only absolute and universal that remains possible is beyond description and material content.[30] Postmodernity rightly criticizes the possibility to represent the absolute directly, but the alternative offered is merely its opposite extreme: radical absence and radical transcendence of the absolute. Accordingly, it becomes impossible to maintain the Christian doctrine of the incarnation. The postmodern absolute cannot 'become flesh' and must instead remain purely formal, beyond the materiality of being.[31] This leads to the further consequence that the absolute can no longer be thought of as personal, thus problematizing the Christian concept of a personal God. Personality requires the possibility of relationality and communication, but precisely these possibilities are called into question by the postmodern stress on heterogeneity and asymmetry. This also affects the understanding of human inter-subjectivity. The emphasis on absolute heterogeneity may lead to a relation-less isolationism.[32] Dialogue between different people and mutual understanding, thus, becomes impossible. Finally, the emphasis on asymmetry turns revelation into a quasi-authoritarian act of the absolute, directed at

---

[29] Ibid., 194–8.
[30] Ibid., 198.
[31] Ibid., 198–9.
[32] Ibid., 207.

people who are reduced to passive recipients. Wendel argues that this reintroduces an extrinsicist understanding of revelation, which utterly fails to connect revelation with active human self-realization in theory and praxis.[33]

In view of these considerations, it comes as no surprise that Wendel is sceptical about the reception of postmodern thought into theology. Although she agrees that postmodernity has yielded important insights for theology – the critique of excessive identity-presence thinking, critique of onto-theology and excessive ideals of autonomous subjectivity, as well as a renewed focus on the dignity of the other and of plurality – she is nonetheless more doubtful about the possibility of a wholesale theological appropriation of postmodern thought. For Wendel, there is an 'ugly broad ditch' between theology and postmodernity.[34] Theology must continue to reflect the universal claims of Christianity, without ignoring their particular context dependency. For this purpose, it is necessary to find a way to think identity-in-difference or unity-in-plurality.

2.2 An alternative response: Hermeneutical theology

This situational picture, drawn by Guarino and Wendel, helps to acquire an understanding of the predicament of theology in the postmodern condition. Put succinctly, postmodernity has introduced a thrust from identity, unity and universality towards otherness, plurality and particularity. This proves especially challenging to metaphysical and transcendental types of theological reflection, specifically those that seek to give an account of the universality of Christian truth claims. However, do these authors offer us a viable way through which to rethink theology in response to the postmodern call to particularity? It seems as if both Guarino and Wendel tend towards a rather restricted dialogue with postmodernity and, in so doing, try to evade the full force of its critique.

Guarino's plea for a 'commodious metaphysics' resorts to a so-called 'spoils from Egypt' strategy.[35] He seeks an engagement with postmodern thought that proceeds 'from the a priori truth of Christian faith itself', which 'requires some form of metaphysics or first philosophy for the sake of protecting and explicating the unity, continuity, and material identity of the gospel message'.[36] Hence, in his concern to safeguard universality, Guarino opts for a religious and metaphysical starting position in which universality is simply claimed from the outset. Wendel's argumentation exhibits a similar pattern. She evaluates the postmodern call to particularity from a prevailing commitment to traditional metaphysical concepts. For Wendel, the postmodern critique reaches its limits when the divine can no longer be thought of in universal terms such as 'origin', 'unity' or 'identity'. But, should these concepts not at least be re-examined in order to assess their appropriateness for making the Christian faith intelligible?[37] In other words, both

---

[33] Ibid., 210.
[34] Ibid., 205
[35] Guarino, *Foundations*, 320–9. For an explanation of the origins of this image in Origen of Alexandria and later patristic tradition, see 272–5.
[36] Ibid., 321–2.
[37] See Lieven Boeve, *Lyotard and Theology* (London: Bloomsbury, 2014), 112–13. Boeve criticizes Wendel's commitment to classical metaphysics, arguing that this may result in a tying down of the interruptive God of the Christian tradition.

Guarino and Wendel are reluctant to open Christianity to the postmodern challenge of particularity. Adopting a universalist perspective from the outset, the particularity and alterity that postmodern thinkers point to are no longer perceived in their own right, but always already engaged through the lens of universality. A theology that seeks to take seriously the contemporary questions and issues raised by postmodern thinkers must look for a different strategy. This study searches for another way of thinking universality that remains more attentive to the inescapable conditions of particularity.

Hermeneutical theology offers an alternative option for grappling with the questions posed by the contemporary situation. Attention to particularity has been central to the so-called hermeneutical turn in theology. Theology has a long history of hermeneutics arising from the need of Christian communities to interpret their foundational texts, most importantly the scriptures. Friedrich Schleiermacher, the father of modern hermeneutics, initiated a new stage by submitting the theological interpretation of texts to general philosophical hermeneutical principles.[38] Due to the efforts of thinkers such as Wilhelm Dilthey, Martin Heidegger, Hans-Georg Gadamer and Paul Ricoeur, hermeneutics as a theory of interpretation became a proper philosophical discipline. The twentieth century can, therefore, rightly be called 'the hermeneutical age of reason'.[39] The growing awareness of the fundamental relation between being, language and understanding and the insight into the historical situatedness of human reason has made hermeneutics central to all human understanding.[40]

The theological turn towards philosophical hermeneutics, initiated by Schleiermacher, was carried forward in Protestant theology by Rudolf Bultmann and his students Ernst Fuchs and Gerhard Ebeling.[41] Within the context of Catholic theology, however, the insights of modern hermeneutical theory only started to have a real impact on theological methodology after the Second Vatican Council. Edward Schillebeeckx belongs to the generation of Catholic theologians who first seriously considered hermeneutics in their theology. But the full impact of this Catholic turn towards hermeneutics becomes more clearly visible in the more recent work of two contemporary fundamental theologians, David Tracy and Francis Schüssler Fiorenza. Both authors have played a major role in the recent debates on theological methodology. Examining their substantive proposals for the rethinking of theological methodology will prove instructive to considering the hermeneutical turn in theology.

Both Fiorenza and Tracy started their careers at a time when Catholic theology was still significantly marked by metaphysical and transcendental styles of reflection. This influence is clearly reflected in their own early works. However, responding actively to the postmodern critique of modernity and its rationalities, they have transformed their theologies into decisively hermeneutical theologies. An important element of

---

[38] See Werner G. Jeanrond, *Theological Hermeneutics: Development and Significance* (London: SCM Press, 1994), 12–50.
[39] See Jean Greisch, *Hermeneutik und Metaphysik: Eine Problemgeschichte* (München: Wilhelm Fink Verlag, 1993), 9–28.
[40] Jim Fodor, 'Hermeneutics', in *The Oxford Handbook of Theology and Modern Thought*, 499. On the universality of hermeneutics, see Hans-Georg Gadamer, 'The Universality of the Hermeneutical Problem', in Gayle L. Ormiston and Alan D. Schrift (ed.), *The Hermeneutic Tradition: From Ast to Ricoeur* (Albany: SUNY, 1990), 147–58.
[41] Jeanrond, *Theological Hermeneutics*, 120–58.

this hermeneutical turn has been a distancing from the use of transcendental and metaphysical reflection within theology. In so doing, these thinkers have sought to provide a theological method that, by starting from particularity, seeks a more adequate response to the postmodern context and its critique than theological methods which start from universality. The question is whether their hermeneutical theology provides a viable theological alternative in view of the postmodern critique of metaphysical and transcendental theological approaches.

3 Francis Schüssler Fiorenza's hermeneutical turn

Francis Schüssler Fiorenza has played an important role in the debates on fundamental theology and theological methodology in recent decades.[42] He started with a strong interest in transcendental theology, particularly the theology of Karl Rahner.[43] Nevertheless, Fiorenza ultimately wrote his dissertation under Johann Baptist Metz, Rahner's student and critic. Both this decision and his subsequent growing engagement with hermeneutical theory may account for the fact that Fiorenza's initial appreciation of transcendental theology develops over time into a more critical and explicitly hermeneutical position. I will retrace this development by examining four phases in Fiorenza's theological career. This trajectory shows how a transcendentally minded theologian follows the hermeneutical turn, but grows increasingly aware of the limitations of an exclusively hermeneutical approach over time. Interestingly, there is a striking re-appreciation of the transcendental style of theology, especially in his later writings.

3.1 From augmentation to critique

The first phase in Fiorenza's engagement with transcendental theology begins as a complementary augmentation, but quickly develops into a more fundamentally critical stance. In the late 1970s, Fiorenza sets out his own views on theological methodology, by presenting his idea of 'political theology as foundational theology'.[44] Following Bernard Lonergan, this foundational theology analyses 'the horizon within which the

---

[42] Apart from his numerous publications in this domain, especially his book *Foundational Theology: Jesus and the Church* (New York: Crossroads, 1984), Fiorenza has also edited a number of important reference works, including Francis Schüssler Fiorenza and John P. Galvin (eds.), *Systematic Theology: Roman Catholic Perspectives*, 2nd ed. (Minneapolis: Fortress Press, 2011); and James C. Livingston and Francis Schüssler Fiorenza, with Sarah Coakley and James H. Evans Jr. (eds.), *Modern Christian Thought. Vol. 2: The Twentieth Century* (Minneapolis: Fortress Press, 2006).

[43] Francis Schüssler Fiorenza, 'Karl Rahner: A Theologian for a Cosmopolitan Twenty-First Century', in *In God's Hands. Essays on the Church and Ecumenism in Honour of Michael Fahey, S.J.*, ed. J. Z. Skira and M. S. Attridge, Bibliotheca Ephemeridum Theologicarum Lovaniensium 199 (Leuven: Peeters, 2007), 109; Francis Schüssler Fiorenza, 'Roundtable Discussion. The Influence of Feminist Theory on My Theological Work', *Journal of Feminist Studies in Religion* 7 (1991): 96. See also Fiorenza's introduction to Rahner's *Spirit in the World*: Francis P. Fiorenza, 'Introduction: Karl Rahner and the Kantian Problematic', in Karl Rahner, *Spirit in the World*, trans. William Dych (New York: Continuum, 1994), xxii–xxx.

[44] Francis Schüssler Fiorenza, 'Political Theology as Foundational Theology', *Proceedings of the Catholic Theological Society of America* 32 (1977): 142–77.

meaning of doctrines can be apprehended'.[45] Fiorenza himself opts for a focus on the political horizon of theology, but he also gives a clear warning: 'A political theology that would too readily abandon a transcendental method would fail to elaborate the complexity of issues in specifying what is rationality and how the order of human rationality and the political order are interrelated'.[46] According to Fiorenza, the political and the transcendental horizons are intrinsically interrelated. Foundational theological methods, therefore, cannot be simply hermeneutical or transcendental, but must be *reconstructive*. Reconstructive theology includes the descriptive, hermeneutical task of interpreting religious symbols. Yet it also goes beyond this interpretive task and by being normative, aiming to develop criteria for the 'correct and appropriate interrelation of religious beliefs and political patterns'.[47]

This raises the question of how these normative criteria can be established. Fiorenza's response to this matter is somewhat ambiguous. On the one hand, he repeats his concern that the essentialist (or transcendental) and the empirical (political) should not be separated but combined. On the other hand, he also argues that normative criteria cannot be developed 'simply' from a transcendental perspective, but that they require a historical reconstruction of the historical development of faith and its praxis.[48] He argues, therefore, that the transcendental method should be 'complemented and augmented by recent insights of hermeneutical theory'.[49] This use of words suggests that Fiorenza does not want to dispose of the transcendental method altogether. However, instead of elaborating this interconnection between the transcendental and the hermeneutical, he intensifies his criticism of transcendental theology in his subsequent work.

In *Foundational Theology*, published in 1984, Fiorenza presents his proposal for a new fundamental theology. His primary intention was to go beyond Karl Rahner's achievement with the help of the insights of hermeneutical thinkers.[50] The main weakness of the transcendental method, which Fiorenza articulates in this book, is that transcendental arguments fail to recognize fully the historical and hermeneutical dimension of human experience. His argument has three important elements: (1) the critique of the transcendental method as being circular, (2) the critique of transcendental theology's foundationalist appeal to human subjectivity and (3) the argument that all experience is hermeneutical. Fiorenza focuses on Karl Rahner's theology in order to illustrate the shortcomings of the transcendental method.

According to Fiorenza, Rahner's transcendental theology seeks to correlate a transcendental analysis of human experience with the Christian faith tradition in order to confirm the truth of Christian faith symbols.[51] He employs the transcendental method in a maieutic fashion in order to explicate the implicit experience of grace.

---

[45] Bernard Lonergan, *Method in Theology* (New York: Herder & Herder, 1972), 131.
[46] Fiorenza, 'Political Theology', 147.
[47] Ibid., 175.
[48] Ibid., 176.
[49] Francis Schüssler Fiorenza, 'Seminar on Rahner's Ecclesiology: Jesus and the Foundation of the Church – An Analysis of the Hermeneutical Issues', *Proceedings of the Catholic Theological Society of America* 33 (1978): 240.
[50] Fiorenza, 'Karl Rahner: A Theologian', 109–10.
[51] Fiorenza, *Foundational Theology*, 276–7.

First, he conducts a transcendental analysis of human existence, from which he concludes that all human beings have an experience of mystery. In a second move, he demonstrates how the Christian tradition explicates this human orientation to mystery as a God-given openness to, and desire for, God. This correlation between human experience and Christian tradition confirms the proof of the latter.[52] Fiorenza objects that this method of transcendental correlation overlooks the fact that tradition and experience are intrinsically interrelated. Christian tradition has deeply influenced Western society and culture and, therefore, also affects human experience and its interpretation. Rahner, thus, correlates Christian tradition with experiences already influenced by this tradition in effect. This amounts to a false universalization of specific experiences. Such a circular argument is unable to provide a convincing account of the truth of the Christian tradition to people whose experiences have not already been influenced by the Christian tradition.[53]

The second element of critique concerns foundationalism. Philosophical foundationalism presupposes certain basic truths that are either self-justified or irrefutable. These epistemological foundations are consequently used to justify all other truths. Transcendental theology seeks such a foundation in human subjectivity in order to ground Christian truth claims.[54] Foundationalism, however, has been severely criticized, primarily by analytical philosophers.[55] Linguistic philosophers have pointed out the close connection between meaning and truth conditions. In order to know the meaning of an utterance, one must know the truth conditions of an utterance.[56] Critics of foundationalism argue that it is impossible to identify one clearly recognizable truth condition that can serve to justify all other beliefs. The justification of beliefs cannot avoid a hermeneutical circle in which certain beliefs are used to justify other beliefs. Moreover, what counts as justification depends on the justificatory system of a specific person, community or culture.[57] There are no external standards that exist independent of cultural tradition and social interpretation and that can serve to provide a foundation for faith or theology.[58] Fiorenza, therefore, concludes that the transcendental appeal to a foundation of truth claims in human subjectivity is problematic.

After discussing the weakness of transcendental theology, Fiorenza offers a plea for the importance of hermeneutics for theology. In opposition to conceptions of experience as pre-linguistic immediate consciousness, he emphasizes that experience is primarily an act of interpretation; experience is itself fundamentally hermeneutical. It takes place within the context of memory and is embedded within a cultural tradition and connected with prudential and reflective judgement.[59] Fiorenza illustrates how

---

[52] Ibid., 278–80.
[53] Ibid., 281.
[54] Ibid., 286.
[55] Critics of foundationalism include philosophers such as Wilfrid Sellars, Willard Van Orman Quine and Richard Rorty. For a discussion of the critique of foundationalism and its appropriation in theology, see John Thiel, *Nonfoundationalism*, Guides to Theological Inquiry Series (Minneapolis: Fortress Press, 1994).
[56] Fiorenza, *Foundational Theology*, 292.
[57] Ibid., 287–8.
[58] Ibid., 289.
[59] Ibid., 297–8.

developments in hermeneutical theory have made manifest that abstract, universal, *a priori* structures of rationality, claimed by a Kantian transcendental philosophy, are illusionary. Martin Heidegger's concept of pre-understanding demonstrates the circular nature of human understanding. Hans-Georg Gadamer has developed this insight and points out that every human being stands within the history of a tradition of ideas and values. Human subjectivity can never be free of any prejudice, but it is always influenced by a historical tradition, especially by the classics of such a tradition.[60] Adopting this hermeneutical principle of the historical and cultural conditioning of human subjectivity, Fiorenza argues that a transcendental appeal to experience for the grounding of Christian truth claims is not possible.[61]

Fiorenza offers an alternative for foundational theology by proposing a reconstructive hermeneutical method that involves three constitutive elements. Reconstructive method starts with a hermeneutical reconstruction of 'the historical manifestation of the religious dimension of life as it is exhibited in a particular religious tradition' in order to bring to light the meaning, truth and identity of this tradition.[62] This hermeneutical reconstruction must be supplemented with two additional elements: retroductive warrants and background theories. A retroductive warrant functions as a hypothesis that has explanatory power. It warrants an argument not on the basis of logical cogency (deduction) or by generalization of data (induction), but because the hypothesis 'generates illuminative inferences'.[63] This explanatory power is grounded in the interrelation of theory and praxis. The more an idea can guide praxis, the more it is warranted. In other words, success is a warrant of validity. Background theories do not directly validate the claims of a tradition, but instead offer indirect support or constraints. A background theory can be understood to function as an auxiliary hypothesis that is used in the application of a theory to praxis. More concretely, background theories affect how experience and tradition are interpreted and interrelated.[64]

In order to avoid foundationalism, Fiorenza argues that these three elements must be brought into a 'wide reflective equilibrium', a notion he derives from the American philosopher John Rawls.[65] The method of reflective equilibrium involves a movement, first from the particular to the general and then from the general back to the particular. Thus, starting with concrete judgements or practices, universal rules or principles are reconstructed and with these reconstructed rules the concrete practice is criticized. By moving back and forth, a reflective equilibrium between practices and principles is

---

[60] Ibid., 299.
[61] Ibid., 300.
[62] Ibid., 304–6.
[63] Ibid., 307.
[64] Ibid., 310–11. Examples of such theories include ethical theories of the good, metaphysical notions of human personhood, economic and political theories on the structuring of society, scientific theories about the origin of the world and psychological theories about the human psyche. See also Francis Schüssler Fiorenza, 'Editorial Symposium. Theology: Transcendental or Hermeneutical?', *Horizons* 16 (1989): 336.
[65] See John Rawls, *A Theory of Justice*, revised edition (Cambridge, MA: Harvard University Press, 1999).

reached. This equilibrium is dynamic rather than static by revising constantly itself.⁶⁶ Crucially, in this procedure none of the three elements of reconstructive theology are accepted as foundational. Instead, reconstructive hermeneutics, retroductive warrants and background theories are brought together to support, criticize, reinforce or revise each other.⁶⁷

Whether Fiorenza's method does indeed succeed in this ambition of overcoming foundationalism cannot be evaluated here.⁶⁸ Instead, I rather focus on his position with regard to transcendental theology. Contrary to his intention, expressed earlier, to augment and complement transcendental theology, Fiorenza adopts a firmly hermeneutical approach for his foundational theology. At a review symposium devoted to his book, Fiorenza contrasts his own theological approach once again with the transcendental theology of Karl Rahner.⁶⁹ The main difference between these two approaches, in his view, concerns the starting point of theology. Transcendental theology takes *a priori* transcendental experience as its starting point, but runs the risk of minimizing the historical concreteness of religious experience in doing so. Fiorenza, therefore, opts to start with the hermeneutical reconstruction of the Christian tradition. This prompts the question as to whether Fiorenza sees a relevant role for a transcendental form of theological reflection at all.

3.2 Complementary dialectic

Fiorenza's rather sharp critique of transcendental theology makes place for a certain rapprochement in the second phase. Assessing the contemporary situation, he observes that philosophical discussions on relativity, realism and pragmatism have problematized transcendental approaches in philosophy. Modern philosophy's concept of rationality has come under critique as 'a false universality of a dominating and oppressive reason'.⁷⁰ In addition, developments in hermeneutics have led to literary-critical theories and post-structuralist philosophies that aim at reinterpreting classical texts. The result is a turn away from transcendental and metaphysical approaches and a move towards relativism.⁷¹ These postmodern critiques also affect transcendental approaches of theologians such as Karl Rahner and Bernard Lonergan. The main charge against these transcendental theologians is that they fail to take 'historicism' sufficiently into account.⁷² Interestingly, rather than joining these critics, Fiorenza defends the legitimacy, as well as the necessity, of transcendental thought.

---

⁶⁶ Fiorenza, *Foundational Theology*, 301.
⁶⁷ Ibid., 302.
⁶⁸ For a comprehensive study of Fiorenza's theological method, see Terence Bateman, *Reconstructing Theology: The Contribution of Francis Schüssler Fiorenza* (Minneapolis: Fortress Press, 2014).
⁶⁹ Fiorenza, *Foundational Theology: Review Symposium*, 418–19.
⁷⁰ Fiorenza, 'Theology: Transcendental or Hermeneutical?', 329.
⁷¹ Ibid.
⁷² Fiorenza refers to the criticisms raised by Jack Bonsor, 'Editorial Symposium. Irreducible Pluralism: The Transcendental and Hermeneutical as Theological Options', *Horizons* 16 (1989): 316–28; Fergus Kerr, *Theology after Wittgenstein* (Oxford: Blackwell, 1986); and Bruce D. Marshall, *Christology in Conflict: The Identity of a Saviour in Rahner and Barth* (New York: Blackwell, 1987).

To begin with, Fiorenza argues that the transcendental and the hermeneutical approaches must be viewed as two contrasting poles which, together, form a complementary dialectic. The two approaches provide distinct perspectives that are both necessary to interpreting the diverse structures of reality.[73] He notes that the linguistic turn has gone beyond the transcendental turn, correcting the latter's focus on pre-linguistic experience. As a result, the awareness has grown that language and culture have an independence that affects human subjectivity. However, this should not lead us to forget that language and culture are also the products of human subjectivity. Simply rejecting the transcendental approach constitutes a failure to recognize the anthropological basis of culture and language.[74]

In discussing the complementary dialectic between the transcendental and hermeneutical approaches, Fiorenza points at his own proposal of broad reflective equilibrium. The hermeneutical approach is, obviously, associated with the element of hermeneutical reconstruction. Fiorenza now also turns to the relevance of the transcendental approach:

> I would locate transcendental analysis within the range of possible retroductive warrants. Such a suggestion downplays the classic Kantian emphasis on the a priori structure of transcendental experience. It focuses instead on transcendental experience as historically mediated experience and praxis. It suggests that a transcendental analysis should not be so much deductive as it should approximate elements of Peirce's abductive reasoning and Newman's illative sense.[75]

After the previous criticisms of the shortcomings of transcendental theology, this is Fiorenza's first concrete mentioning of a constructive role of transcendental analysis within theological methodology. Two elements come to the fore, though, in this quotation. First, Fiorenza claims that the connection between retroductive warrants and transcendental analysis downplays the *a priori* character of transcendental analysis. Secondly, this connection highlights the historical and practical mediation of transcendental experience and transcendental reflection, which guards against abstract conceptions of reason and reflection. Both elements seek to correct a purely Kantian transcendental approach. However, Fiorenza leaves the issue of situating transcendental reflection within the context of retroductive warrants unresolved.[76]

Instead, he seeks to clarify the dialectical interrelationship between the transcendental and the hermeneutical approaches by relating it to a contemporary debate on the conceptions of rationality. While contextualists or historicists argue that standards of rationality are always embedded in particular cultures, and expressed in particular linguistic constructions, universalists argue that reality is

---

[73] Fiorenza, 'Theology: Transcendental or Hermeneutical?', 335–6.
[74] Ibid., 336.
[75] Ibid., 336–7.
[76] The connection between transcendental analysis and retroductive warrants recurs in Francis Schüssler Fiorenza, 'Systematic Theology: Task and Methods', in *Systematic Theology: Roman Catholic Perspectives*, 60–1. Yet here too the connection and theological appropriation is not elaborated upon.

not completely dependent upon interpretation and emphasize that truth precisely transcends contextual standards of rationality.[77] The contextualists rightly recognize that 'rationality and morality do not take place in the abstract' and that 'rationality cannot be reduced to formal structures of rationality'.[78] But the universalists correctly warn against the reduction of standards of truth to standards of assertibility. In order to enable criticism of particular customs and cultures, it is necessary to formulate counterfactual standards of rationality and morality. Fiorenza finds in Jürgen Habermas's communicative approach to rationality an insightful third position that acknowledges both the 'dependence' and the 'autonomy' of human subjects in relation to their cultural-linguistic contexts.[79]

Communicative rationality recognizes the historicity of reason, arguing that abstract or neutral starting points transcending cultural and linguistic horizons are impossible. However, it also maintains that one can adopt a critical attitude with regard to one's personal horizon. Communication can lead to agreement or disagreement, that is to affirmation or to revision and transformation of cultural-linguistic horizons. Applying these insights of communicative rationality to theology, Fiorenza arrives at the following conclusions. First, theology does not start in abstract transcendental subjectivity, but rather assumes the possibility of communication between different parties that involves the transcendence of personal horizons.[80] Second, due to the historical conditioning of our existence, a common ground for foundational theology is impossible. However, since rationality is more than contextuality, there are still partial commonalities that enable dialogue, conversation and the merging of horizons. Giving up transcendentality would entail the loss of the dimension of universal commonality required for dialogue and (self)-criticism. Interestingly, according to Fiorenza, both Rahner and Lonergan recognize that the transcendental horizon on which they reflect in their theologies is fundamentally conditioned by history.[81] Yet instead of developing this assertion, he merely repeats his plea for the complementarity between the transcendental and the hermeneutical approaches and his own decision to start with a hermeneutical retrieval.

Thus, in the second phase of his career, Fiorenza significantly retracts his harsh critique of transcendental theology. He rehabilitates transcendental arguments, situating such arguments within the context of retroductive warrants. Importantly, though, he emphasizes that these explanatory ideas are embedded in history and oriented towards praxis. Apart from these rather formal considerations, though, Fiorenza does not elaborate further on what a transcendental approach could look like and how such an approach would function in a complementary dialectic with the hermeneutical approach. Similarly, he points to the importance of partial commonalities for dialogue, thereby justifying the relevance of a transcendental approach, but does not offer any guidance on how we can fruitfully appropriate such transcendental reflections in theology.

---

[77] Fiorenza, 'Theology: Transcendental or Hermeneutical?', 338.
[78] Ibid., 339.
[79] Ibid.
[80] Ibid., 340.
[81] Ibid., 341.

3.3 The crisis of hermeneutical theology

The third phase is marked by an intensification of the hermeneutical turn, as well as by a growing awareness of the limitations of hermeneutics. This is developed throughout a number of articles reflecting on the crisis of interpretation that challenges modern theology. Due to increased historical consciousness, human subjectivity can no longer provide a certain 'foundation' for reflection.[82] The inescapable linguisticality and historicity of the subject matter of theology leads to the universality of hermeneutics. No principle of faith, dogma or human experience is free from historically conditioned human interpretation.[83] This is aptly illustrated by the feminist unmasking of transcendental appeals to experience as substitutional universality, falsely positing a particular and patriarchal experience as being a universal experience.[84] Other currents of thought, such as critical theory, liberation theology and post-structuralism, have also laid bare the limitations of human subjectivity.

Critical theory opposes the reduction of hermeneutics to the uncovering of meaning. Emphasizing the contingency and opacity of language, it argues that experience is constituted by mechanisms of power domination that are often implicit.[85] Language, therefore, mediates not only meaning, truth and freedom but also the lack of meaning, the absence of truth and the force of domination. Liberation theologies too have pointed out the critical importance of pre-understanding within the hermeneutical circle and have subsequently argued for the need to reflect critically on one's own stance and presuppositions.[86] The radicalization of hermeneutics in French post-structuralism undermines such an appeal to subjectivity even more profoundly. Authors such as Michel Foucault and Jacques Derrida argue that everything is already interpretation, including human subjectivity, and that every sign is an interpretation of other signs. Human subjectivity is not transparent to itself and, therefore, cannot be an absolute starting point for philosophical or theological reflection, either in hermeneutics or in transcendental phenomenology.[87]

Theology as hermeneutical discipline is, therefore, confronted with a crisis. Richard Bernstein's 'Cartesian anxiety' reappears: human subjectivity is unable to give a certain grounding for religious language and theological reflection.[88] Can theology get beyond the subject-centredness of the hermeneutical circle and its consequent crisis of interpretation? Theology, as creative reconstruction, may offer a solution here. However, in order to reconstruct, one must make an interpretative decision as to what constitutes the identity of the Christian tradition.[89] To address this issue, Fiorenza turns again to the notion of communicative rationality. While we always speak from somewhere, this

---

[82] Francis Schussler Fiorenza, 'The Crisis of Hermeneutics and Christian Theology', in *Theology at the End of Modernity*, ed. S. Greeve Davaney (Philadelphia, PA: Trinity Press, 1991), 117–18.
[83] Ibid., 122–3.
[84] Fiorenza, 'The Influence of Feminist Theory', 96.
[85] Francis Schüssler Fiorenza, 'The Conflict of Hermeneutical Traditions and Christian Theology', *Journal of Chinese Philosophy* 27 (2000): 21.
[86] Fiorenza, 'The Crisis of Hermeneutics', 125.
[87] Ibid., 125–7.
[88] Ibid., 127. See Richard Bernstein, *Beyond Objectivism and Relativism: Science, Hermeneutics, and Praxis* (Philadelphia, PA: University of Pennsylvania Press, 1983).
[89] Fiorenza, 'The Crisis of Hermeneutics', 133.

does not mean that we are isolated islands. Our identities are constituted out of very particular traditions and horizons that also overlap and criss-cross. This overlapping of traditions and horizons enables communication between different traditions. According to Fiorenza, authors such as George Lindbeck, John Milbank and Stanley Hauerwas, who tend to isolate the Christian tradition from modern or other religious traditions, neglect this crucial element.[90] Fiorenza searches for commonalities by criss-crossing the tradition in which he situates himself: the Christian tradition and the tradition of human rights.

In the first place, Fiorenza calls for solidarity with suffering. Suffering can cut through the hermeneutical circle because it is 'at the seam between reality and interpretation' and, therefore, 'produces a claim with negative universality'.[91] Although not without interpretation, the unmediated immediacy makes suffering a privileged hermeneutical principle. It is a retroductive warrant that moves from negative experience to challenge *status quo* justifications.[92] Referring to Emmanuel Levinas, Fiorenza argues that the response to being confronted with suffering is to take responsibility, not in an abstract universal way but as responsibility for the concrete suffering of others.[93] Such a responsibility does not simply stand above cultural particularity, but is rather rooted in particular religious traditions 'that have anchored the responsibility for the stranger and for the Other in their religious beliefs'.[94] Because suffering relates to the corporeality of life, there is also an immediate and universal dimension involved which provides support for communicative rationality.[95]

The second, and closely related, element concerns so-called communities of discourse.[96] Incorporating this element into hermeneutical conversations prevents us from conceiving of rationality and interpretation in an abstract, universalistic way. Both the interpreter and the interpreted belong to, and exist in, concrete communities of discourse. But since every discourse is influenced by power, there are both dominating and excluded discourses. Fiorenza argues that in the absence of secure foundations, and in the given situation of the plurality of interpretations, we should strive to make the community of interpretation as inclusive as possible. This implies an effort to focus on involving the neglected and repressed voices especially. As mentioned above, this connects with the previous element of taking responsibility for the suffering of others. Solidarity with the people who suffer implies giving a voice to the voiceless, so that the excluded and oppressed discourses can take part in the conversation on the interpretation of Christian identity.[97]

---

[90] Francis Schüssler Fiorenza, 'Pluralism: A Western Commodity or Justice for the Other?', in *Ethical Monotheism, Past and Present: Essays in Honor of Wendell S. Dietrich*, ed. T. Vial and M. Poster (Providence, RI: Brown Judaic Studies, 2001), 298–9.
[91] Fiorenza, 'The Crisis of Hermeneutics', 136.
[92] Ibid., 135–6. Werner G. Jeanrond, *A Theology of Love* (London: T&T Clark, 2010), 235, points out that solidarity is not free of distortions of power and alerts us to the danger of paternalism. Hence, he argues that pleas for solidarity also require a careful hermeneutics of suspicion.
[93] Fiorenza, 'Pluralism: A Western Commodity', 303.
[94] Ibid., 300–1.
[95] Ibid., 301.
[96] Fiorenza, 'The Crisis of Hermeneutics', 136–7.
[97] Ibid.

Fiorenza proposes 'integrity' as the guiding principle of reconstructive theology. The notion of integrity, developed in legal philosophy, allows room for the difference between principles or ideas, on the one hand, and conventions or concrete practices, on the other. A theology centred in integrity takes a critical stance with regard to de facto conventions and consensus, prioritizing 'neglected and excluded voices' and taking 'honestly and seriously changes in background assumptions'.[98] It involves a rationality that is piecemeal, prudential or practical rationality, rather than as *a priori*, neutral or transcendental.[99] Fiorenza's struggle with the universality of hermeneutics, and with the limitations of hermeneutics, reveals his refusal to give up the normative character of theology and on the possibility to come up with criteria for interpretation. This leads him to what could be characterized as a transcendental argumentation.

First, by putting forward the communicative concept of rationality he emphasizes a transcendental commonality between people, limited and partial though this commonality might be, that enables them to converse with each other and to transcend their own horizons. Secondly, searching for further support of such a communicative rationality, Fiorenza introduces the negative universality of suffering. Faced with the concrete suffering of others, we are all prompted to take up responsibility. He argues that suffering somehow transcends the incommensurability between different persons and their horizons. Taken together, the rationality advocated here clearly displays universal and context-transcending elements. However, Fiorenza himself explicitly refuses to characterize this rationality as transcendental.

3.4 A reappraisal of transcendental theology

The fourth, and final, phase offers additional support for the suggestion that Fiorenza has grown closer to transcendental argumentation in his most recent work. In a discussion on religious experience, he criticizes the polemical tendency of the critiques of the Enlightenment, criticizing the modern inattentiveness to the categories of gift, vulnerability and receptivity.[100] Rather than siding with these critiques, Fiorenza responds somewhat surprisingly with a defence of Rahner's theology and his transcendental approach to religious experience. While he confirms Rahner's transcendental and universal orientation, he also points to Rahner's appropriation of the hermeneutical circle and his orientation towards history.[101] Moreover, Fiorenza argues that Rahner is aware of the interconnection between language and experience and that he acknowledges the inter-subjective nature of language.[102] This is a notably different evaluation than the treatment of Rahner's theology in *Foundational Theology*. Still, despite this hermeneutical sensitivity, Rahner's starting point lies in a phenomenological analysis that emphasizes transcendental experience. Fiorenza,

---

[98] Ibid., 138.
[99] Fiorenza, 'Pluralism: A Western Commodity', 302.
[100] Francis Schüssler Fiorenza, 'The Experience of Transcendence or the Transcendence of Experience. Negotiating the Difference', in *Religious Experience and Contemporary Theological Epistemology*, ed. Lieven Boeve, Yves de Maeseneer and Stijn van den Bossche (Leuven: Peeters, 2005), 184–8; 206–7.
[101] Fiorenza, 'The Experience of Transcendence', 207–8.
[102] Ibid., 209.

therefore, also repeats his argument that the starting point should instead be located in concrete, historical, communal experience. For Christian theology, this means starting from the experience and analysis of various Christian communities' experience of God in Jesus Christ.[103]

Fiorenza points out one important danger of transcendental reflection, namely substitutional universalism that falsely universalizes the particular. This is basically the critique of the circularity of transcendental arguments, grounded in the failure to recognize the interrelatedness of experience and tradition.[104] Rather than simply repeating this critique, however, Fiorenza here also adds a clarifying distinction that signals that his own position has developed. He makes a distinction between weak and strong transcendentalism, referring to Mark Sacks's distinction between 'transcendental constraints' and 'transcendental features'.[105] Transcendental constraints refer to non-empirical *a priori* limitations or determinations of empirical knowledge and experience. Fiorenza associates this type of transcendentalism with Kant. Transcendental features, however, refer to 'limitations and possibilities that take place historically and contingently'.[106] Such transcendental features are not entirely abstract and ahistorical but actually connected to current practices. The empirical facticity of current practices determines transcendental features. So, just like current practices, transcendental features can also change over time and as such can be considered to be *a posteriori* limitations and possibilities. Fiorenza refers to Rahner's work, instead of sketching himself what such a theological appropriation of a weaker form of transcendentality could look like. He remarks that Rahner was clearly aware of the historicity of transcendental subjectivity. As a result, even when Rahner seems to search for transcendental constraints, he also 'sought to explicate in quite different ways the historicity of Christian faith'.[107]

The reappraisal of transcendental theology continues in two other publications on Rahner.[108] Here, Fiorenza expresses that he has become increasingly aware of the need to defend Karl Rahner over the years, listing three main reasons for this.[109] To begin with, criticisms raised by Johann Baptist Metz and George Lindbeck are based on a misinterpretation of Rahner. Fiorenza argues that these critics view Rahner primarily as a transcendental philosopher and theologian, whereas he himself emphasizes that Rahner is first and foremost a practical theologian.[110] In the second place, Fiorenza perceives a danger in the theological appropriation of non-foundationalism, insofar as it leads to a radical relativism and historicism in which there are no longer any

---

[103] Ibid., 215.
[104] Ibid., 216.
[105] See Mark Sacks, 'Transcendental Constraints and Transcendental Features', *International Journal of Philosophical Studies* 5 (1997): 164–86.
[106] Fiorenza, 'The Experience of Transcendence', 216.
[107] Ibid., 217.
[108] Fiorenza, 'Karl Rahner', 109–35; Francis Schüssler Fiorenza, 'Method in Theology', in *The Cambridge Companion to Karl Rahner*, ed. Declan Marmion and Mary E. Hines (Cambridge: Cambridge University Press, 2005), 65–82; Francis Schüssler Fiorenza, 'Editorial Essays. The Cosmopolitanism of Roman Catholic Theology and the Challenge of Cultural Particularity', *Horizons* 25 (2008): 298–319.
[109] Fiorenza, 'Karl Rahner', 109.
[110] Ibid., 111–18. These criticisms will be discussed in greater detail in Chapter 4.

truth criteria. Moreover, hermeneutical theory has been used in critical theory and deconstruction discourse to eliminate, rather than to complement, transcendental arguments.[111] Finally, Fiorenza states that the transcendental element of Habermas's discourse ethics brought him to appreciate the transcendental aspects of Rahner's theology.[112]

In response to these criticisms, Fiorenza maintains that Rahner's theology provides a valuable legacy for future theology and proposes three corrections to the misinterpretation of his work. First, Rahner made a more explicitly theological turn towards history and practice in his later writings and recognizes that transcendence is always historically and symbolically mediated. A proper reading of Rahner should go beyond an evaluation of his transcendental philosophical orientation and also take this theological turns and its historical-hermeneutical sensitivities into account.[113] Importantly, this requires an examination of the precise and distinct way in which Rahner employs the term 'transcendental', as well as his recognition of the inherent limitations of the transcendental method.[114] Secondly, Fiorenza characterizes Rahner as a practical theologian who responds to concrete pastoral and theological issues by writing theological essays, the *Theological Investigations*. This practical orientation is connected to his awareness of the historicity of human existence and 'further undercuts the *a priori* nature of transcendentality'.[115] Thirdly, Fiorenza retracts his own charge of foundationalism and argues that Rahner's actually does take the hermeneutical circle seriously.[116] For Fiorenza, this comes to the fore especially in Rahner's 'spiralling movement back and forth between the understanding of the self and the understanding of God'.[117]

All of these arguments basically seek to show that the theological and historical turn in Rahner's work undercut the Kantian *a priori* dimension of his transcendental method. Fiorenza, thus, clearly reassesses his own negative critique of Rahner's transcendental method. How can this changed attitude, with regard to the transcendental method in general and with regard to Rahner's theology in particular, be explained? A clarification may be found in Fiorenza's reflections on political theology in the context of human rights and cosmopolitanism. He recalls how the memory of the atrocities of the Second World War led to the United Nation's Universal Declaration of Human Rights. However, he also observes that universal rights language has become contested, being criticized as the particular masking as the universal or for failing to recognize the historical

---

[111] Ibid., 110; 120–9.
[112] Ibid., 110.
[113] Ibid., 116; Fiorenza, 'Method in Theology', 69.
[114] Fiorenza, 'Method in Theology', 77.
[115] Fiorenza, 'Karl Rahner', 117.
[116] Ibid. Jessica M. Murdoch, 'Contesting Foundations: Karl Rahner and Francis Schüssler Fiorenza's Non-Foundationalist Critique', *Philosophy & Theology* 27 (2015): 127–52, discusses Fiorenza's non-foundationalist critique of Rahner in detail. She acknowledges that Fiorenza has come to Rahner's defence more recently (135). It is, therefore, surprising to see that her discussion continues to focus on the critique that Fiorenza raised in *Foundational Theology* and fails to take Fiorenza's own correction or retraction of this critique into account. Murdoch seeks to defend Rahner's theological method in response to Fiorenza's criticism, yet conceals the fact that despite his earlier criticism, Fiorenza himself has actively contributed to this alternative vision.
[117] Fiorenza, 'Karl Rahner', 132.

ambivalence of the application of rights.[118] Still, Fiorenza finds it important to uphold a cosmopolitan vision nonetheless and refers in this regard to Jürgen Habermas:

> When asked what he considered to be the weakest element of his discourse ethics, Habermas replied that it was the transcendental aspect, especially when faced with challenge of historical and cultural diversity. Nevertheless, because of Auschwitz he could not give up the transcendental universal aspect of his ethics.[119]

Expressing his agreement with Habermas in this regard, Fiorenza states his appreciation for Rahner's vision with its transcendental elements and explains how it might provide a theological vision suitable for our pluralist age. While Rahner is aware of the particularity and historical origin of certain values, he is also convinced that some values have transcended their original context.[120] Fiorenza, thus, perceives an exemplary interplay between the transcendental and the historical perceives in Rahner's work, highly relevant for today's circumstances.

The fourth phase, then, makes clear that Fiorenza becomes increasingly aware of the need for some form of transcendental reflection within theology. Moreover, his reappraisal of Rahner also shows that he is open to a rethinking of transcendentality – one that is less confined by the Kantian paradigm and that is aware of the challenges posed by hermeneutical theory and historical consciousness. Yet, how should such a reconceptualized model of transcendental theology be developed? Before addressing this question, I now turn to a colleague and contemporary of Fiorenza's to see how he has grappled with the question of the relation between hermeneutics and transcendentality.

4 David Tracy's hermeneutical turn

David Tracy, another influential voice in the contemporary debates on theological methodology,[121] has traversed a theological path that is remarkably similar to Fiorenza's. He started firmly within the context of transcendental theology, writing a dissertation on the transcendental Thomist Bernard Lonergan. In this work, entitled *The Achievement*

---

[118] Ibid., 122–8.
[119] Fiorenza, 'Karl Rahner' 134. Unfortunately, Fiorenza does not provide a bibliographical reference in support of this assertion.
[120] Francis Schüssler Fiorenza, 'Gaudium et Spes and Human Rights: The Challenge of a Cosmopolitan World', in *The Church and Human Freedom: Forty Years after Gaudium et Spes*, ed. D. F. Weaver (Villanova, PA: Villanova University Press, 2006), 39.
[121] One of Tracy's most famous contributions to this debate is his distinction between the three 'publics' or 'audiences' of theology, that is academy, church and society, which will be discussed below. Moreover, Tracy is the best known representative of the correlational approach to theology in the debate between the so-called Chicago and Yale schools of theology. For this debate, see Werner G. Jeanrond, 'The Problem of the Starting-Point of Theological Thinking', in *The Possibilities of Theology: Studies in the Theology of Eberhard Jüngel in his Sixtieth Year*, ed. John Webster (Edinburgh: T&T Clark, 1994), 70–89; Werner G. Jeanrond, 'Correlational Theology and the Chicago School', in *Introduction to Christian Theology. Contemporary North American Perspectives*, ed. Roger A. Badham (Louisville: Westminster John Knox Press, 1998), 137–53.

of Bernard Lonergan, his interest in questions of method clearly comes to the fore.[122] Confronted with increased theological pluralism and specialization, he raises the question of whether it is possible to determine a 'fundamental theological method', one which enables theological cooperation between various theologians, but which is also grounded 'in a transcendental method which is not open to fundamental revision?'[123] Tracy's lifelong attempt to seek an adequate response to this question can be divided into three periods that roughly correspond to the publication dates of his major works.

In *Blessed Rage for Order*, he introduces a fundamental theology method that accords a crucial role to transcendental-metaphysical reflection.[124] However, by the time of *The Analogical Imagination*, Tracy makes a hermeneutical turn, which significantly alters his view on the status of transcendental-metaphysical reflection.[125] In the subsequent period, from *Plurality and Ambiguity* onwards, Tracy argues simultaneously for the indispensability and the inherent difficulty of transcendental arguments.[126] This ambivalent position on transcendental-metaphysical reflection endures in his most recent theological work, which is marked by a turn towards the fragmentary forms of apocalyptic and mystical theology. How might this theological evolution be interpreted? Werner G. Jeanrond argues that a 'fusion' occurs in Tracy's thought.[127] His transcendental questions merge with his hermeneutical questions. Other scholars have argued variously for or against the continued relevance of his original theological intuitions in his later work.[128] In this section, I will retrace the evolution of Tracy's theology and argue that despite his turn to hermeneutics, there is a vehemence of transcendental-metaphysical reflection in his work that betrays a fundamental reluctance to give up such a style of theology altogether.

4.1 Defending metaphysics

In *Blessed Rage for Order*, first published in 1975, Tracy introduces his so-called revisionist model of fundamental theology.[129] The legitimacy of theological pluralism

---

[122] See David Tracy, *The Achievement of Bernard Lonergan* (New York: Herder and Herder, 1970).
[123] Tracy, *The Achievement of Bernard Lonergan*, 238.
[124] David Tracy, *Blessed Rage for Order: The New Pluralism in Theology*, 2nd ed. with a new preface by the author (Chicago: The University of Chicago Press, 1996).
[125] David Tracy, *The Analogical Imagination: Christian Theology and the Culture of Pluralism* (New York: Crossroad, 1981).
[126] David Tracy, *Plurality and Ambiguity: Hermeneutics, Religion, Hope* (Chicago: The University of Chicago Press, 1987).
[127] Werner Jeanrond, 'Theology in the Context of Pluralism and Postmodernity: David Tracy's Theological Method', in *Postmodernism, Literature and Theology*, ed. David Jasper (London: Macmillan Press, 1993), 149; 152.
[128] William Myatt, 'Public Theology and "The Fragment": Duncan Forrester, David Tracy, and Walter Benjamin', *International Journal of Public Theology* 8 (2014): 85–106, argues that Tracy consistently applies a form of transcendent-phenomenological analysis throughout his career, thus remaining faithful to the theological approach that he introduced in *BRO*. In contrast, Younhee Kim, 'David Tracy's Postmodern Reflection on God: Towards God's Incomprehensible and Hidden Infinity', *Louvain Studies* 30 (2005): 159–79, argues that Tracy has left behind both his revisionist theological advocacy for transcendental reflection of *Blessed Rage* and his 'hermeneutical-transcendental-pragmatic' of *Analogical Imagination*.
[129] Tracy, *Blessed Rage*, 3–4.

notwithstanding, he argues that the specific nature of theology gives rise to a couple of basic shared characteristics. He discusses those characteristics by formulating five theses. Important for our discussion, one crucial characteristic concerns the need for an explicitly metaphysical or transcendental element of reflection.

The first thesis states that 'the two principal sources for theology are Christian texts and common human experience and language', and the second thesis states that 'the theological task will involve a critical correlation of the results of the two sources of theology'.[130] Following Paul Tillich, Tracy advocates a theological method that seeks to correlate the tradition with contemporary experience.[131] In the following two theses Tracy's hermeneutical orientation becomes apparent. The third thesis states that 'the principal method of investigation of the source "common human experience and language" can be described as a phenomenology of the "religious dimension" present in everyday and scientific experience and language'.[132] In view of the universalist claims of Christian self-understanding, Tracy deems it to be an imperative that theology searches for a religious dimension in the world of human experience. Given the linguistic and symbolic character of human experience, hermeneutic phenomenology, as developed by Martin Heidegger, Hans-Georg Gadamer and Paul Ricoeur, is the 'relatively adequate' method to examine these experiences.[133] The fourth thesis forms further proof of the central role of hermeneutics, stating that 'the principal method of investigation of the source "the Christian tradition" can be described as an historical and hermeneutical investigation of classical Christian texts'.[134] The Christian tradition is based on historical facts, that is experiences and actions expressed in symbols and texts. Determining the meaning of those texts and symbols is a hermeneutical task that belongs to theology.

In the fifth and final thesis, Tracy turns to the role of metaphysical or transcendental reflection. This thesis states that in order 'to determine the truth-status of the results of one's investigations into the meaning of both common human experience and Christian texts the theologian should employ an explicitly transcendental or metaphysical mode of reflection'.[135] Tracy is conscious of the fact that invoking a need for metaphysics is widely regarded with suspicion by many of his contemporaries, who deem metaphysics to be irreconcilable with a full recognition of historical consciousness.[136] His response to this anti-metaphysical stance is to claim that the very nature of religious truth claims entails a demand for metaphysical reflection.

---

[130] Ibid., 43–5.
[131] Tracy does not merely appropriate Tillich's method of correlation but rather seeks a critical revision of this method. He criticizes Tillich for juxtaposing tradition and situation like key and keyhole and instead advocates a critique of the interpretation of the situation through the tradition and a critique of the interpretation of the tradition through the situation. See Tracy, *Blessed Rage*, 45–6. This model of correlation, termed 'mutually critical correlation' by Schillebeeckx, will be discussed in more detail in Chapter 8. For a discussion of Tracy's model of correlational theology in comparison with Tillich, Schillebeeckx, and Hans Küng, see Jeanrond, 'Correlational Theology', 137–53.
[132] Tracy, *Blessed Rage*, 47.
[133] Ibid., 48.
[134] Ibid., 49.
[135] Ibid., 52.
[136] Ibid., 52.

To assess the truth status of religious truth claims, it is not sufficient to compare a hermeneutics of key Christian texts with a phenomenology of common experience. According to Tracy, a theological examination of experience discloses an 'ultimate or grounding dimension or horizon to all meaningful human activities'.[137] Since this religious horizon affects all experience, theology must consider the very conditions of the possibility of experience. This calls for a mode of reflection, traditionally known as metaphysics, which since modernity has also been called 'transcendental reflection'.[138] Such a metaphysical argument aims to demonstrate 'that certain basic beliefs must necessarily be maintained as basic conditions of the possibility of our understanding or existing at all', which is shown 'by demonstrating the self-contradictory character which their denial involves for any intelligent and rational ("reflective") inquirer'.[139] The central question of such a critical correlation is whether 'theistic language' adequately represents the 'most basic faith presupposed by all our existing and understanding'.[140] In other words, this concerns the philosophical question of God. To show the correlation between Christian truth and common human experience, theology must 'rise above' or 'go beneath' all experiential phenomena, in order to disclose that theological concepts and symbols actually express the transcendental conditions of common human experience.[141] However, this final transcendental assessment of the truth status of Christian doctrines is only possible on the basis of two preceding stages of investigating the two respective sources of theology: common human experience and Christian texts. Tracy's subsequent discussion shows that examining these two sources requires a combination of hermeneutics and transcendental reflection.

Investigating the first source – common human experience – involves two philosophical moments in effect. A phenomenological analysis of various experiential contexts, ranging from science and morality to everyday life, discloses basic 'limit experiences', which may in turn disclose a religious dimension.[142] An experience can be considered to be basic or common if it can be shown to have its ground in the very basic structures of human living and thinking, functioning as a 'basic belief' that forms the condition of possibility of all human experience.[143] Investigating these basic structures and their *a priori* conditions is the task proper to metaphysics or transcendental reflection, which is as problematic as it is inescapable:

> The accomplishment of that [transcendental] task will always remain problematic in the exact sense that it can no more be indubitably 'proved' than it can be avoided

[137] Ibid., 55–6.
[138] Ibid., 55; 159. Tracy uses metaphysical and transcendental almost interchangeably in *Blessed Rage*, seeing transcendental reflection as the more recent expression of traditional metaphysics.
[139] Ibid., 159.
[140] Ibid., 154. Tracy turns to Charles Hartshorne's theological appropriation of Alfred North Whitehead's process philosophy; see Tracy, *Blessed Rage*, 172–203. This turn to process philosophy has been received critically; see, for instance, Avery Dulles, 'Method in Fundamental Theology: Reflections on David Tracy's *Blessed Rage for Order*', *Theological Studies* 37 (1976): 312–13.
[141] See Tracy, *Blessed Rage*, 67 where he uses these metaphors of 'rising-above' and 'going-beyond' to characterize the nature of transcendental reflection in the context of a discussion on the role of philosophy within theology.
[142] Ibid., 91–118.
[143] Ibid., 71.

by any serious philosophical thinking. In the familiar dilemma posed by Aristotle to the skeptics, the choice is not really between metaphysics or no metaphysics; the only real choice is between a self-conscious and explicit metaphysics or an unconscious yet operative one.[144]

While Tracy advocates a phenomenological-transcendental approach as the proper mode of enquiry to examine the first experiential source, the second source of theology – Christian texts – demands a decisively hermeneutical approach. He seeks to distance himself from a Romanticist hermeneutics which focuses on the author's original intention or on the original reception context of a text via historical research. Instead, he engages with Hans-Georg Gadamer and Paul Ricoeur, appropriating key concepts from their hermeneutical theories, such as the fusion of horizons and the role of distanciation, in order to develop a theological hermeneutics that takes historical consciousness seriously without reducing theology to historical research.[145]

Tracy's earliest proposed model of theology, thus, involves both a hermeneutical and a transcendental component. He even explicitly states that he opposes an identification of theology with hermeneutics.[146] The hermeneutical task must be 'clearly differentiated from the further ethical and metaphysical examinations of the meanings disclosed by the interpreter', and one cannot expect hermeneutics 'to carry the impossible burden of ethical and metaphysical analysis'.[147] However, his progressive involvement in hermeneutical theory will change this, which becomes very clear in his next major publication.

4.2 Taking the hermeneutical turn

In *The Analogical Imagination*, Tracy aims to 'affirm pluralism responsibly' by including 'an affirmation of truth and public criteria for that affirmation'.[148] His assertion that theology is public discourse leads him to introduce his famous distinction of the three 'publics' or audiences of theology: academy, church and society.[149] These publics have their own internal demands of publicness. To this threefold distinction of publics corresponds a distinction of theological disciplines: fundamental theology focuses on the academy, systematic theology focuses on the church and practical theology focuses on society.[150] These theological disciplines employ distinct modes of argumentation, appropriate to their respective publics. Hence, whereas fundamental theology usually employs philosophy, systematic theology has a principally hermeneutical character and practical theology involves an orientation towards transformative praxis.[151] For Tracy,

---

[144] Ibid., 68.
[145] Ibid., 73–8.
[146] Ibid., 78–9.
[147] Ibid., 79.
[148] Tracy, *Analogical Imagination*, ix.
[149] Ibid., 3–31.
[150] Ibid., 55–6.
[151] Ibid., 56–8. Tracy uses Aristotelian terms, reformulated in 'the alternative language of transcendental reflection', to characterize the style of the theological disciplines. 'Fundamental theology is concerned principally with the "true" in the sense of metaphysics, systematic theology with the

all three theological disciplines are, to some degree, concerned with truth claims which have a metaphysical or transcendental character. Hence, the modes of argumentation these disciplines use also demand some degree of publicness.

According to Tracy, in order to avoid chaos and to affirm pluralism responsibly there must be a certain basic agreement among theologians despite their differences. He claims that there are three constants. The first constant is the interpretation of a religious tradition. Every theologian appeals to a religious tradition to warrant a theological position and, therefore, engages – implicitly or explicitly – in hermeneutics.[152] The second constant in theology involves an appeal to some analysis – either positive or negative and implicit or explicit – of the contemporary situation. This enables a public discussion within the theological community on the accuracy of this analysis of the situation.[153] The third constant involves a critical correlation between the interpretation of a tradition and the interpretation of the situation. Some theologians resist the characterization of their method as involving this third constant of correlation, yet Tracy maintains that even a Barthian *Nein* is a form a correlation.[154] Importantly, Tracy no longer elaborates on this correlation with specific reference to transcendental or metaphysical reflection. Instead, his focus on the hermeneutical nature of theology grows stronger.

The increased attention to hermeneutics becomes apparent when Tracy discusses the respective modes of argumentation of fundamental theology and systematic theology. Philosophy is affirmed to be the primary partner of fundamental theology in her role of explicating and adjudicating religious claims. In the context of the academy, personal faith cannot warrant religious truth claims. Since the warrants must be strictly public, fundamental theology resorts to philosophical arguments, which are usually either implicitly or explicitly metaphysical. However, Tracy also adds that the fundamental theologian, as theologian, also stands within the religious tradition she interprets and examines in order to assess its truth claims.[155] This situatedness is developed more fully with reference to systematic theology. Tracy defines the task of systematic theology in clearly hermeneutical terms as 'the reinterpretation of the tradition for the present situation'.[156] Accepting finitude and historicity, such a hermeneutical enterprise recognizes that 'all interpretation is a mediation of past and present, a translation carried on within the effective history of a tradition to retrieve its sometimes strange, sometimes familiar meanings'.[157] Importantly, the systematic theologian has the right and the responsibility to be formed by tradition and community in this hermeneutical task. Tracy justifies this with reference to Gadamer's critique of the Enlightenment's

---

beautiful (and, as we shall see, the beautiful *as true*) in the sense of poetics and rhetorics, practical theology with the good (and the good *as* transformatively true) in the sense of ethics and politics'. Tracy, *Analogical Imagination*, 85, n. 31.

[152] Ibid., 59.
[153] Ibid., 61.
[154] Ibid., 88, n. 44.
[155] Ibid., 62–4.
[156] Ibid., 64.
[157] Ibid., 99.

'prejudice against prejudices' and the related rehabilitation of the indispensable role of tradition in the process of historical understanding.[158]

Whereas the 'inner-Christian drive to universality' pushes the fundamental theologian towards philosophy, the 'biblical fear of idolatry' and the 'biblical insistence that philosophical wisdom cannot judge the gift of faith' lead systematic theology to a confessional position.[159] Such a confessional perspective recognizes that every claim to universality – including the claims of metaphysical systems – is subject to perspectivism. Accordingly, Tracy concludes that 'all metaphysical or general philosophical claims to universality are suspect to a historically conscious mind. All theological claims to the formulation of universal truth must be put under the strictly theological hermeneutics of suspicion of "idolatry".'[160] It is crucial to note that this argument seems to undercut Tracy's understanding of fundamental theology, discussed previously, specifically its reliance on metaphysical reflection to establish the truth of religious claims on 'strictly public grounds that are open to all rational persons'.[161] Unfortunately, however, Tracy does not discuss what consequences this insight into universality of hermeneutical conditioning has for his own understanding of fundamental theology, metaphysical, and transcendental reflection. The second question raised by the adoption of a confessional tradition-based position concerns the position of systematic theology as a public discipline. Contrary to his brevity on the subject of hermeneutical consequences for transcendental and metaphysical reflection, Tracy engages in an extensive discussion on the relation between universal truth and particular tradition. An important element of his response forms the development of the notion of the classic. Interestingly, this argument seems to assume a form of argumentation that has certain transcendental aspects.

The argument for the classic as publicly accessible particular manifestation of universal truth builds on Gadamer's understanding of conversation and on the concept of truth as disclosure. Tracy employs these insights to explain the hermeneutical nature of all understanding:

> We constantly mediate, translate, from our past understanding to our present one. We consistently find that understanding *happens* in precisely this deeply subjective yet intersubjective, shareable, public, indeed historical movement of authentic conversation. So much is this the case that we find ourselves obliged to use such transsubjective language as 'understanding happens', 'the act of understanding', the 'event' of understanding.[162]

All reflection has a hermeneutical character, insofar as understanding is happening now, as a question mediated from the past, and projected towards the future.[163] Tracy develops the notion of the classic within this hermeneutical framework of the

---

[158] Ibid., 66–7.
[159] Ibid., 65.
[160] Ibid., 66.
[161] Ibid., 64.
[162] Ibid., 101.
[163] Ibid., 102.

disclosure of truth in conversation. A classic is a text – or symbol, person, event, image and so on – that has the permanent ability to disclose meaning and truth. Classics are expressions of human culture that achieve a normative status because they disclose a normative truth about human life. They provoke, challenge and transform the horizon of understanding of the person who encounters them. Despite the fact that they are radically particular in origin and expression, classics are also public inasmuch as they disclose 'a realized experience of that which is essential, that which endures'.[164] In other words, the classic can be seen as the particular mediation of universal truth.

The notion of the classic is key to Tracy's argument for the public nature of systematic theology. Classics are found not merely in the public realm, such as philosophy or art, but also within the major religious traditions. The reinterpretation of this tradition for the contemporary situation by hermeneutical theologians therefore has a public dimension. It involves a disclosure of truth 'analogous to the philosopher's interpretation of the classics of philosophy or the literary critic's interpretation of the classics of literature'.[165] Tracy distinguishes four moments in the interpretation of classics – a distinction which can also be applied to theological hermeneutics. First, the theologian has a pre-understanding by virtue of belonging to a religious tradition and its language and history of effects. Second, she experiences some resonance or shock when encountering the religious classic, recognizing its power to disclose meaning and truth. Third, the theologian initiates a dialogue with the subject matter of the religious classic and reflects on the *Wirkungsgeschichte* (history of effects) of this classic. Fourth, the dialogue is expanded by entering into dialogue with the larger community of inquirers. Attending to the plurality of interpretations enables the theologian to initiate a critical hermeneutics of retrieval and suspicion, in which the classic is recognized not only as enriching, but also as potentially distorting.[166] It is through this reinterpretation of the tradition, by communicating the truth disclosed in religious classics, that the systematic theologian contributes to the contemporary horizon of self-understanding and, thus, has a public role.

The discussion of the religious classic leads Tracy to revisit the distinction between fundamental theology and systematic theology. Importantly, this also implies a reconfiguration of the relation between transcendental-metaphysical thought and hermeneutics. In line with his argument in *Blessed Rage for Order*, he repeats that a philosophical analysis of religion involves both a phenomenological moment, explicating the 'limit-to dimension' of human experience and in language, and a transcendental or metaphysical moment, explicating the reality that is the referent of this limit experiences.[167] Contrary to the 'softer' claim that the referent of limit experiences can only be 'displayed, disclosed, or shown', Tracy advances the 'harder' claim that it is possible 'to partly state – more exactly, to metaphysically state – the abstract, general, universal and necessary features of the reality of God as the one

---

[164] Ibid., 108; 132.
[165] Ibid., 68.
[166] Ibid., 115–24; 130–1.
[167] Ibid., 161.

necessary existent' that accounts for the reality of limit experiences.[168] Hence, his advocacy of transcendental-metaphysical argumentation remains strong. However, his use of the term 'partly' suggests that Tracy has also become more aware of the limitations of such an exercise. In his subsequent comparison of fundamental and systematic theology, a certain *weakening* of this hard claim becomes manifest. Tracy argues that the abstract metaphysical description of God as horizon of ordinary experience remains rather limited. Only within the concrete religious experiences of particular concrete religions is the 'fully concrete reality' of this horizon disclosed.[169] Accordingly, fundamental theology is, in a way, subordinate to systematic theology. It plays a 'necessary but abstract and corrective (not constitutive)' role in relation to the fuller concrete experience expressed in religious classics that is interpreted by systematic theology.[170] Hence from the perspective of systematic theology, the hard claims of fundamental theology are actually soft claims. The metaphysical and transcendental arguments serve to warrant a willingness to enter into conversation with religious classics rather than to bring the particular religions and their claims 'before the judgment seat of "metaphysics".'[171]

It seems, therefore, that there occurs a shift in the order of priority in *The Analogical Imagination*. Whereas in *Blessed Rage for Order* transcendental-metaphysical argument stands at the centre, having the task of correlating the phenomenology of experience and the hermeneutics of tradition, the philosophical arguments of fundamental theology serve a subordinate role in *The Analogical Imagination*, warranting the plausibility and reasonableness of systematic theology's hermeneutical engagement with the truth of religious classics. However, Tracy seems not to be fully aware of the consequences of this shift. As a result, there remains an ambiguity in his position on the status of transcendental-metaphysical arguments within theology. On the one hand, with the classic, Tracy introduces a transcendental element into systematic theology. His notion of the classic serves to explain that a hermeneutical engagement with a particular tradition is capable of publicly disclosing universal truth. The concept of the classic brings together permanence, publicness and particularity, and thus forms the necessary condition for the possibility of the disclosure of truth through particular religious symbols. On the other hand, arguing from the hermeneutical perspective of systematic theology, Tracy calls into the question all metaphysical or general philosophical claims to universality. To a historically conscious theologian, these claims can never be hard, but are always necessarily soft. Throughout this discussion, he maintains a rather strict distinction between fundamental and systematic theology and their respective styles of argumentation. Accordingly, he continues to argue that the transcendental thinker can provide 'strictly philosophical (and, therefore abstract) reflections on our *common*

---

[168] Ibid., 161. Tracy recounts in this regard Hegel's critique of Kant that 'the ability to state a limit means, if one reflects upon it, that the thinker is, in some manner, already beyond the limit stated'. This Hegelian correction of Kant plays an important role in Rahner's work and will be discussed in Chapter 3.
[169] Ibid., 161–2.
[170] Ibid., 183, n. 26.
[171] Ibid., 162–3.

human experience'.[172] However, is this position really viable when taking seriously the hermeneutical considerations that Tracy develops throughout *The Analogical Imagination*?

4.3 The full force of postmodernity

In *Plurality and Ambiguity*, it becomes apparent how Tracy's engagement with postmodern thought intensifies his hermeneutical turn. Having grown even more conscious of the fundamental role of language and historicity in human understanding, he now analyses these factors under the headings of plurality and ambiguity. 'Plurality' refers to the extraordinary varieties that are opened up by the study of language, and 'ambiguity' refers to the strange mixture of good and radical evil that marks history.[173] These realities fundamentally challenge and problematize all attempts at understanding.

First, the linguistic turn has made apparent the difficult relationship between language, knowledge and reality.[174] Philosophy of science and linguistic philosophy have made clear that we can only understand *in and through* language. Hence, even science and creative arts cannot escape hermeneutics. Every understanding is dependent on a plurality of particular historical, social and public languages. As such, the linguistic turn has decentred the autonomous ego, turning us away from idealism and positivism, and has forced us to focus on history and society.[175] This leads to the second major challenge to hermeneutical understanding, the contingency and ambiguity of history. 'To interpret language is to find oneself in the contingent reality named history.'[176] History as contingent and interruptive is deeply ambiguous. Every classic text comes to us with a *Wirkungsgeschichte*, an ambiguous history of effects of its production and reception. This history is not merely affected by errors, but in fact is subjected to systematic distortion.[177] Whereas the modernist optimistically believes that consciousness is a 'relatively stable and manageable affair', the postmodernist has left behind 'any belief in the transparency of consciousness to itself'.[178] Otherness is no longer only outside us represented by others, but is most radically within ourselves. Hence, there is no innocent interpretation. To uncover the distorting effects of ideology and power, a hermeneutics of retrieval must be paired with a hermeneutics

---

[172] Ibid., 183, n. 29.
[173] Tracy, *Plurality*, 69–70.
[174] Tracy distinguishes three phases in the linguistic turn. Wittgenstein's and Heidegger's emphasis on the inescapable reality of language and the pluralism of human uses of language (language games) represents the first step of 'language as use'. Structuralist thinkers, such as Ferdinand de Saussure and Lévi-Strauss, analyse language as systems. Structuralism has subsequently been radicalized by deconstructive thinkers such as Jacques Derrida, who analyse language as constituted by differential relations. This constitutes the second step of 'language as object'. The third step involves a focus on the relation between language and discourse. This phase is associated with thinkers such as Michel Foucault, Jacques Lacan, Michel de Certeau, Julia Kristeva and Paul Ricoeur. They reflect on the movement from words to sentences, to texts, and have thereby criticized Heidegger's short route to ontology and Gadamer's short route to hermeneutics via tradition. Tracy, *Plurality*, 51–65.
[175] Ibid., 48–50.
[176] Ibid., 66.
[177] Ibid., 73.
[178] Ibid., 77–8.

of suspicion.[179] This also applies to theological understanding, concerned with the interpretation of religious classics.

Classics remain key for hermeneutics because they paradoxically bring particularity and universality together. They are an example of 'radical stability become permanence and radical instability become excess of meaning through ever-changing receptions'.[180] Accordingly, Tracy maintains that hermeneutical conversation with religious classics remains a locus for theological encounters with meaning and truth. However, given the conditions of plurality and ambiguity, theological understanding resulting from such a hermeneutics of classics is never absolute or certain. At best, this understanding can claim to be 'relatively adequate'.[181] The interpretation of a classic is always 'relative to the power of disclosure and concealment of the text, relative to the skills and attentiveness of the interpreter, relative to the kind of conversation possible for the interpreter in a particular culture at a particular time'.[182] Unsurprisingly, Tracy concludes that this problematizes metaphysical and transcendental arguments.

On the one hand, Tracy maintains that transcendental arguments, such as those developed by Karl Otto Apel and Jürgen Habermas, are required to spell out the necessary conditions for communication. However, distancing himself from Cartesian ideals of indubitable truth, Tracy states that we should call them, more modestly, 'quasi-transcendental' arguments which are useful as a 'regulative ideal'.[183] Moreover, such transcendental arguments which deal with the necessary conditions of a contingent situation, that is 'the implicit claim to validity in all communication', must be distinguished from 'strictly' transcendental arguments, such as those for the existence of God or for the universe.[184] Tracy does not clarify whether he supports the latter type of strictly transcendental arguments himself. However, he asserts that an understanding of truth as manifestation results in an understanding of the 'relative, never absolute, adequacy of all metaphysical and transcendental arguments'.[185] Critics of metaphysics often fail to notice the prudent and modest way in which classical authors, like Aristotle—but also modern authors like Charles Hartshorne—put forward metaphysical claims.[186] Tracy sides with the modern attempts at reformulating metaphysical and transcendental arguments, yet he acknowledges that this task is more difficult and problematic than he realized previously. Nevertheless, 'the logically unique claims of theology on the strictly necessary individual, God' demand such transcendental analysis.[187]

Tracy reiterates his plea for the rethinking of transcendental reflection in the article 'The Uneasy Alliance Reconceived'.[188] The Christian belief in a 'radically monotheistic

---

[179] Ibid., 79.
[180] Ibid., 14.
[181] Ibid., 84–5.
[182] Ibid., 22–3.
[183] Ibid., 24–6.
[184] Ibid., 27.
[185] Ibid., 30.
[186] Ibid., 122, n. 9.
[187] Ibid., 134, n. 40.
[188] David Tracy, 'The Uneasy Alliance Reconceived: Catholic Theological Method, Modernity, and Postmodernity', *Theological Studies* 50 (1989): 548–70.

God' – a belief shared with the Jewish and the Muslim traditions – necessitates a transcendental form of analysis in order to assess its claim to truth.[189] This demand flows from the universality of this understanding of God: 'A lesser "god" for the Jew, Christian, and Muslim, is not God.'[190] Tracy suggests that this universal aspect of Christian belief could still profit from a transcendental analysis of limit questions. However, such an approach must pay greater attention to the issues of language and historicity as developed in the hermeneutical model of truth as manifestation.[191] It must, for example, take Jean-Luc Marion's critique of metaphysics and theology into account.[192] Moreover, Tracy also points to the need for a renewed focus on the 'mystical-prophetic' and the 'ethical-political' aspects of religious truth claims.[193] Rather than proposing a concrete reformulation of transcendental analysis within theology, throughout the 1990s Tracy's work increasingly focuses in this mystical-political shape of theology.

In the opening essay of *On Naming the Present*, published in 1995, Tracy describes how the contemporary time is at a loss to interpret itself:

We live in an age that cannot name itself. For some, we are still in the age of modernity and the triumph of the bourgeois subject. For others, we are in a time of the levelling of all traditions and await the return of the repressed and communal subject. For yet others, we are in a postmodern moment where the death of the subject is now upon us as the last receding wave of the death of God.[194]

Distancing himself from outright anti-modern approaches, Tracy searches for a position that oscillates between appreciation for modernity – continuing the Enlightenment ideal of emancipation, belief in the capabilities of human reason and the focus on system and continuity – and appreciation for postmodernity – learning from it the suspicion of reason and the critique of subjectivity, as well as paying ethical attention to otherness and difference.[195] This mediatory position is manifested well in his most recent reflections on the concept of God.

In one way, Tracy continues to consider natural theologies that employ metaphysical and transcendental reflection to reflect on the question of God 'fruitful exercises'.[196] Christians remain responsible for giving reasons for their hope, and this requires

---

[189] Ibid., 559
[190] Ibid., 559, n. 42.
[191] Ibid., 559; 561–4.
[192] See Tracy's foreword in Jean-Luc Marion, *God Without Being*, trans. Thomas Carlson, 2nd ed. (Chicago: The University of Chicago Press, 1991), xiv-xv: 'After Marion, every route to thinking God via Being or Becoming must be thought again (...) The need to question whether any transcendental or metaphysical reflection is the correct route forward for theology finds renewed impetus from this book'.
[193] Tracy, 'The Uneasy Alliance', 564–70.
[194] David Tracy, 'On Naming the Present', in *On Naming the Present: Reflections on God, Hermeneutics, and Church*, Concilium Series (Maryknoll: Orbis Books, 1995), 3.
[195] Tracy, 'On Naming the Present', 12–18. See also David Tracy, 'Theology and the Many Faces of Postmodernity', *Theology Today* 51 (1994): 104–14.
[196] David Tracy, 'God and Trinity: Approaching the Christian Understanding of God', in *Systematic Theology: Roman Catholic Perspectives*, 116.

developing relatively adequate arguments. Reason has many shortcomings and weaknesses, but it also has a self-correcting capacity.[197] Without claiming to comprehend the divine mystery fully, 'the antifideist character of Catholic theology encourages any reasonable attempt to find proper analogical language for understanding the divine mystery more adequately and more intelligibly'.[198] Tracy refers in this regard to *Blessed Rage for Order* as an example of such a metaphysical approach. In the new preface to this work, he reflects that despite his own hermeneutical turn, metaphysical and transcendental arguments are 'not necessarily wrong but far more complicated'.[199] However, he offers little guidance about how to reformulate and rethink such a line of transcendental argumentation. More recently, Tracy has suggested the initiation of a dialogue with 'new philosophies of event', since these are 'more akin to the principal biblical focus on God's self-revelation through historical events', but he does not develop this suggestion.[200]

Rather than exploring new ways of natural or fundamental theology, Tracy draws attention to what he calls the 'mystical-metaphysical' theologies, stressing the incomprehensibility of God, and the 'prophetic-apocalyptic' theologies, stressing the hiddenness of God. These forms of theological reflection predate modernity, but were largely forgotten when the 'modern scientific *logos* took over *theo-logia* and recast the understanding of God into properly modern (i.e., secular) terms, rationally acceptable to a modern mind'.[201] Despite its distinct achievements, the most important of which concerns solidifying relationality as a central theological category, modern theology has always risked the reductive systematizing of God into one particular 'ism', ranging from deism and theism to atheism and panentheism.[202] Postmodernity's radical disruption has revealed the inadequacies and weaknesses of all these attempts to rationalize God. Accordingly, it has also created room for new reflections of God. Drawing on the mystical and apocalyptic forms of theology, which had previously gone underground, new names of God such as the 'Impossible God' resurface:[203] a God who, first and foremost, offers hope to oppressed and marginalized people, a God who escapes the modern *logos* and presents itself as incomprehensible loving gift. This impossible God shatters the modern ambitions to control and understand God through a rational system. For this reason, the 'fragment', challenging attempts at totality and closure, can be considered the 'sign of our time'.[204]

---

[197] David Tracy, 'Religion im öffentlichen Bereich: Öffentliche Theologie', in *Im Dialog. Systematische Theologie und Religionssoziologie*, ed. Ansgar Kreutzer and Franz Gruber, Quaestiones disputatae 258 (Freiburg: Herder, 2013), 189–93. See also David Tracy, 'God, Dialogue and Solidarity: A Theologian's Refrain', *The Christian Century* 107 (1995): 902.

[198] Tracy, 'God and Trinity', 117.

[199] Tracy, *Blessed Rage*, xiv.

[200] David Tracy, 'A Hermeneutics of Orthodoxy', *Concilium: International Review of Theology – English Edition* no. 2 (2014): 78.

[201] Tracy, 'God and Trinity', 121.

[202] Ibid., 123. See also David Tracy, 'The Hermeneutics of Naming God', *Irish Theological Quarterly* 57 (1991): 254–64, for an earlier account of Tracy's critique of the various 'isms', including his own original support of panentheism.

[203] Tracy, 'God and Trinity', 124–7.

[204] David Tracy, 'Fragments: The Spiritual Situation of our Times', in *God, the Gift, and Postmodernism*, ed. John D. Caputo and Michael J. Scanlon (Bloomington: Indiana University Press, 1999), 170–84.

His keen attention to the various postmodern retrievals and suspicions that have engendered new fragmentary forms of theology notwithstanding, Tracy also acknowledges that 'eventually, it will be time again to try to gather the fragments into new orderings'.[205] However, his own relative silence on the reformulation and reconceptualization of transcendental and metaphysical forms of theology suggests that such a 'gathering of the fragments' must be carried forward by someone else. Hence, the fourth phase of Tracy's work is marked by an ambivalent position that considers transcendental-metaphysical to be necessary, but also in dire need of revision and reform.

5 The rediscovery of universality

My extensive examination of the theological trajectories of Francis Schüssler Fiorenza and David Tracy yields pertinent insights into the *status quaestionis* of Catholic discussions on theological methodology. In brief, there is a need to readdress the question of universality in fundamental theology. The insights of Fiorenza and Tracy resonate with recent developments in philosophy and theology. It is against the background of this situational picture that I return to my proposal for a retrieval of the fundamental theologies of Karl Rahner and Edward Schillebeeckx arguing that their methods are highly relevant for theology today.

5.1 The lessons of Fiorenza and Tracy

Instead of choosing the easy way to avoid a theological confrontation with postmodernity, Fiorenza and Tracy have sought new ways to account for the truth claims of Christian faith through a constructive appropriation of hermeneutical theory. Adopting such a hermeneutical perspective has enabled them to attend more properly to the particular conditions that fundamentally shape all human existence and reflective activity. Historicity, cultural contextuality, linguistic mediation and ideological distortion are not ignored or rejected, but brought to bear on their hermeneutical reconfigurations of theological method. However, Fiorenza and Tracy have also grown increasingly conscious of the fact that their hermeneutical approaches run the risk of losing sight of the crucial universal dimension of truth, and the universal dimension of Christian faith more concretely. Accordingly, they have been impelled to reassess their previous critiques of, and advocacy for, the theological use of transcendental and metaphysical reflection.

Werner G. Jeanrond, 'Thinking about God Today', in *The Concept of God in Global Dialogue*, ed. Werner G. Jeanrond and Aasulv Lande (Maryknoll, NY: Orbis, 2005), 94, remarks that this insight into the fragmentary access to God can also be expressed more positively and constructively.

[205] Tracy, 'God and Trinity', 127. Tracy has repeatedly announced to address both the fragmentation, through study of the apocalyptic and mystical forms of theology, and the gathering of fragments, through study of the classical Trinitarian forms of theology, in his new (still forthcoming) book. See, for instance, David Tracy, 'Form and Fragment. The Recovery of the Hidden and Incomprehensible God', in *The Concept of God in Global Dialogue*, 98–114.

In Fiorenza's case, the catalyst of his reappraisal of universal discourse seems to be primarily an ethical concern. Reflecting on the conflict of interpretations in contemporary pluralistic society and remembering the derailments of humanity, leading to atrocities such as the Holocaust, he raises the question about the demand for a concept of rationality that enables us to transcend the limitations of our particular and limited discourses. Fiorenza elaborates upon some of the characteristics of such a universal concept rationality. He points to Habermas's concept of communicative rationality and its key presupposition of partial commonalities that enable dialogue, conversation and the merging of horizons. Taking suffering to be another potential starting point through which to conceive of the transcendence of particular discourses, Fiorenza emphasizes that this rationality has a negative universality and can only be thematized by actively involving various – especially the often excluded – communities of discourse. All of this suggests that Fiorenza searches for a hermeneutically conditioned, or, as I have termed it, an *a posteriori* transcendental approach to universal reason. However, apart from stating that this ethical concern originates in his own belonging to the Christian tradition and commitment to the tradition of human rights, Fiorenza fails to elaborate more extensively on the contours of this universal concept of reason and does not explain its *theological* relevance. He offers little in terms of a theological argumentation to support his advocacy for a universal concept of reason and does not specifically tap into theological sources to develop this notion of a weakened *a posteriori* transcendentality.

Turning to Tracy, a similar pattern recurs in his theological trajectory. Tracy started with an unambiguous plea for the need for transcendental-metaphysical reflection within theology and has, subsequently, remained steadfast in his conviction that the logic of the Christian concept of God demands such reflection with a universal range. Christians do not believe in a particular or in a Christian God, but in the God who desires to relate to humankind as a whole. Initially, Tracy sought to explain this universal dimension with reference to the horizon of limit experiences or limit questions. However, his hermeneutical turn made him aware of the difficulty of articulating these universal aspects of experience and led him to emphasize the relative, rather than absolute, adequacy of all metaphysical and transcendental arguments. In other words, Tracy also seems to point to a softer and more modest reconceptualization of transcendental arguments. His own focus on the interpretation of the classic as an event of truth disclosure may actually be an example of such an *a posteriori* approach to universality. While the classic is never presented with express reference to transcendental or metaphysical reflection, its peculiar combination of universal permanence and stability, on the one hand, and radical instability and particularity, on the other hand, seems suggestive of a middle way between hard aprioristic claims of universality and particularism or relativism. However, Tracy does not explore this possibility and merely repeats that developing a transcendental argument in full recognition of the plural and ambiguous hermeneutical challenges is extremely difficult and complicated.

Furthermore, like Fiorenza, Tracy draws remarkably little from theological sources in his reflections on quasi-transcendental arguments. Interestingly, though, he argues in his article on the doctrine of God that the classical tradition of natural theology contains many examples of reflective attempts that aim to produce relatively adequate arguments for the intelligibility and credibility of Christian faith: 'None of the classic attempts of natural theology or apologetic theology (as distinct from some exercises in a decadent Neo-Scholasticism) can be read as deductive proofs *sensu strictu*'.[206] This comment gives a reason to expect that this tradition of natural theology may be a useful source for an investigation of *a posteriori* metaphysical and transcendental explications of Christian faith. Yet, while Tracy unambiguously affirms the need to gather the fragments, his own theology has focused mainly on the fragmentary forms.

My analysis of Fiorenza and Tracy, then, suggests that it is time for a reorientation of fundamental theology. After a period in which philosophy and theology, engendered by postmodern thought, have focused primarily on the particular, it is time to bring attention back to the universal dimension of faith as essential aspect of Christian (self-)understanding. The fact that the pendulum is indeed swinging back from particularity towards universality has been noticed more widely in academic discourse.

5.2 A renaissance of universalism

Yves De Maeseneer has more recently responded to Fiorenza's call for a historically conscious and hermeneutically attentive theology. While he does not disagree with Fiorenza's plea for a broader and hermeneutically refined concept of rationality, he observes that the contemporary situation actually poses a rather different challenge. The current generation of younger scholars no longer need to be first taught about the dangers and pitfalls of Enlightenment universalism. Rather, this new generation already departs 'from the particular as the obviously given' and is, therefore, '(tacitly) hostile towards appeals to the universal'.[207] According to De Maeseneer, the key challenge of contemporary fundamental theology is thus:

> How to convince postmodern people that there is more than the body (often reduced to its neurobiological kernel – 'I am my brains'), that there is more than culture, emotion, symbol, history. In other words, we need to demonstrate that there *is* a universal dimension, that there *is* such a thing as rationality at all.[208]

Inspired by Alain Badiou's critique of the contemporary ethical concern with the recognition of 'otherness' and his argument for a reconnecting of ethics and universal truth, De Maeseneer advocates a search for shared realities, rather than focusing merely on the things that divide us.[209] This involves an examination of modern thinkers of the Enlightenment aimed at understanding 'how Enlightenment thinkers were able to discover within their inevitably particular context ideas that bore the promise of universality'.[210]

---

[206] Tracy, 'God and Trinity', 116.
[207] Yves De Maeseneer, 'The Question of Universality. A Response to Francis Schüssler Fiorenza', *Louvain Studies* 39 (2015–2016): 144.
[208] De Maeseneer, 'The Question of Universality', 143.
[209] Ibid., 144–7.
[210] Ibid., 143.

A similar plea for a reconsideration of universality has been voiced by both Jean-Luc Marion and David C. Schindler in a scholarly exchange on the question of the universality of the university. Commenting on the increasing specialization and professionalization of university education, Marion argues for a re-examination of the hypothesis of a 'universal knowledge'.[211] Marion does not aim for a 'complete system of the sciences' or an 'absolute knowledge' and points out that it is crucial to 'know also what we do not know and can never know, and to know why we can never know it'.[212] However, in view of the growing fragmentation he suggests a modest pondering of the principle of universality and unity in relation to diversity and particularity. In constructive and critical conversation with Marion, Schindler argues for an exploration of the universality of knowledge from a 'traditional metaphysical perspective'.[213] He agrees with Marion about the need to reconsider the universality of truth. However, Schindler argues that Marion's apophatic emphasis on the unknowability of metaphysical themes such as the self or God focuses too much on the 'insurmountable limits of finitude' and, therefore, shuts down, rather than opens up, this conversation about universality.[214]

George Pattison puts forward a comparable argument and asserts that 'Christian theology's truth-claims must be brought into some kind of relation to what is sought and studies as truth elsewhere in the manifold intellectual life of the contemporary university'.[215] He argues that the commitment to truth shared by the various academic disciplines, including theology, raises the question of truth. This question of truth contains a seed of metaphysics. Without mandating any specific metaphysical system or theory, it raises, at the very least, metaphysical questions such as whether there is a common ground that enables a shared quest for truth or what truth itself actually means.[216]

This revival of the question of universality is also reflected in the recent re-emergence of metaphysics within both philosophy and theology. Eric Hall and Hartmut von Sass point to various examples of this *renaissance* of metaphysics within theological discourse, including new forms of process theology, phenomenological attempts to go beyond onto-theology and defences of the theo-ontological approach.[217] The return of metaphysics poses new questions to both proponents and critics of metaphysical thinking within theology, especially since there is little

---

[211] Jean-Luc Marion, 'The Universality of the University', *Communio* 40 (2013): 68.
[212] Marion, 'The Universality of the University', 71.
[213] David C. Schindler, 'On the Universality of the University: A Response to Jean-Luc Marion', *Communio* 40 (2013): 79. See also David C. Schindler, *The Catholicity of Reason* (Grand Rapids: Eerdmans, 2013).
[214] Schindler, 'On the Universality of the University', 97.
[215] George Pattison, 'How Much Metaphysics Can Theology Tolerate?', in *Groundless Gods. The Theological Prospects of Post-Metaphysical Thought*, ed. Eric E. Hall and Hartmut von Sass (Eugene, OR: Wipf and Stock, 2014), 63.
[216] Pattison, 'How Much Metaphysics Can Theology Tolerate?', 63; 73.
[217] Hartmut von Sass and Eric E. Hall, 'Metaphysics, Its Critique, and Post-Metaphysical Theology. An Introductory Essay', in *Groundless Gods*, 1–11.

agreement within these wide-ranging discussions on what metaphysics means and what its relation to theology might be.[218]

Nevertheless, the question of metaphysics as such has no doubt made a strong return. As George Pattison states, commenting on Heidegger's critique of ontotheology, 'Metaphysical ideas don't go away just because someone gave a lecture criticizing them. On the contrary, the more metaphysical ideas are in decline, the more their extraordinary power and impact comes into view and the more questions they provoke'.[219] Certain practices of metaphysics, based on an overly self-confident belief in the power of human reason, have been rightly put under critique.[220] However, there seems to be a growing consensus that there is a demand for new forms of metaphysical reflection. William Desmond argues in critical discussion with Kant and Heidegger that 'post-metaphysical thinking involves its own implicit orientations relative to these fundamental senses of the "to be"'.[221] Scepticism, negation and suspicion, all raise the metaphysical question of the origin and drive of this critique as such:

> Knowing itself, the human being will be also critical of itself, to be sure. But must its critique, thus understood, be anchored on some more basic understanding of being? Must not metaphysics in some fundamental sense always be in play and indeed prove to be most relevant when it is most declared to be redundant?[222]

According to Desmond, grappling with these questions opens the way for a future for metaphysics after critique.[223]

These examples confirm what my analysis of Fiorenza's and Tracy's theology has already suggested; namely, that contemporary philosophical and theological reflections are confronted with the challenge of addressing the question of universality anew. As a result, the question about the place and relevance of metaphysical and transcendental approaches within theology is put back on the table. However, while Fiorenza and Tracy clearly advocate some modest form of transcendental or metaphysical reflection within theology, they have been unable to offer a substantive proposal for such a reconceptualization of fundamental theology. For this reason, I propose in this study to take a step *back* in order to bring the discussion on the universality of Christian truth *forward*.

---

[218] See the general introduction in Ingolf U. Dalferth and Andreas Hunziker (eds.), *Gott denken – ohne Metaphysik? Zu einer aktuellen Kontroverse in Theologie und Philosophie* (Tübingen: Mohr Siebeck, 2014).

[219] George Pattison, *God and Being. An Inquiry* (Oxford: Oxford University Press, 2011), 3. Pattison criticizes philosophical attempt to 'overcome metaphysics', arguing that 'ontotheology is not an enemy to be defeated, but a trait of thinking from which we need – as the original lecture on "The Onto-theo-logical Constitution of Metaphysics" put it – to "step back" so as to come into a free and thoughtful relation to it' (9).

[220] See William Desmond, 'The Metaphysics of Modernity', in *The Oxford Handbook of Theology and Modern European Thought*, ed. Nicholas Adams, George Pattison, and Graham Ward (Oxford: Oxford University Press, 2013), 542–63.

[221] William Desmond, 'Is There Metaphysics after Critique?', *International Philosophical Quarterly* 45 (2005): 221.

[222] Desmond, 'Is There Metaphysics after Critique?', 231.

[223] Ibid., 229–31.

6 Going forward by stepping back

In order to bring the theological discussion on universality forward, I take a step back by retrieving the work of Karl Rahner and Edward Schillebeeckx. I argue that these thinkers present us with an illustrative example of a theological approach that seeks to think universality *from within* particularity. I will substantiate this claim by developing the thesis that Rahner and Schillebeeckx developed their theological ideas and methods without adopting either an exclusively metaphysical-transcendental or an exclusively hermeneutical approach. Instead, their theological methodologies are characterized by the *dialectical interplay* of hermeneutics and metaphysics. Crucially, this dialectics of hermeneutics and metaphysics offers an insight into a weakened, modest or *a posteriori* form of metaphysical reflection. Rahner and Schillebeeckx develop their theological approaches while being fully aware of their particular conditions, yet they do not rescind from thematizing and problematizing the universality of truth. Retrieving this dialectics offers important insights for the rethinking of fundamental theology. It presents a possibility to go with hermeneutical theology beyond hermeneutical theology, so as to revitalize the theological reflection on the universality of Christian faith while also remaining attentive to the crucial insights yielded by critical hermeneutical consciousness.

This decision to go back to two modern theologians in order to bring the contemporary discussion forward builds upon the insights of the theologians discussed in this chapter. Tracy has, on numerous occasions, emphatically claimed that 'a thinker today can only go through modernity, never around it, to postmodernity'.[224] Moreover, he has also gestured more concretely towards Rahner as a source for the rethinking of transcendental reflection within theology. Tracy considers Rahner's view on the 'real but limited role' of transcendental reflection within systematic theology to be 'exactly right' and also refers specifically to Rahner's attempt to seek a reasonable understanding of divine mystery without falling into rationalism.[225] Fiorenza's recent reappraisal of Rahner's transcendental theology has already been discussed earlier. Portrayals of Rahner in abstract aprioristic terms ignore the fact that Rahner acknowledges the inescapable *a posteriori* contextual nature of every discursive argumentation. A reconsideration of Rahner's transcendental method reveals a promising cosmopolitan vision that transcends particular discourses without ignoring its own particular conditions.

I will develop these insights and suggestions by offering a new reading of Rahner's transcendental theology as constituted by a *dialectics between transcendentality and hermeneutics*. Crucially, I aim to dispel the widespread notion that Rahner's transcendental theology results in a rationalist and reductive subjectivism. For this purpose, I will disclose the often-overlooked hermeneutical shape of Rahner's transcendental method. Rahner's method is, at heart, characterized by a strong incarnational theme and an Aristotelian, realist approach. He focuses on the concreteness of the historical and material world as the locus of encounter with the

---

[224] Tracy, *BRO*, xv. See also Tracy, 'Religion im öffentlichen Bereich', 203.
[225] Tracy, *Imagination*, 185, n. 31. Tracy, 'Approaching the Christian Understanding of God', 116–17.

divine mystery. Positioning himself firmly within the Christian tradition, Rahner seeks to provide with the help of transcendental and metaphysical arguments an intelligible account of the universal possibility of human encounters with this divine mystery, whom Christians call God. However, he never loses sights of the inherent limitations of this reflection on the universality of divine revelation. As I will argue in greater detail throughout this work, Rahner's joint application of transcendentality and hermeneutics actually entails a theological qualification and transformation of transcendental arguments that is highly illustrative of a weak or modest form of metaphysics, which is conscious of its particular conditions without letting itself be determined by these conditions.

The hitherto repeated references to Rahner and relative silence about Schillebeeckx now may, at this point, raise the question of why my exercise of retrieval also focuses on the latter's thought. While my retrieval of Rahner intends to draw out the hermeneutical shape of his theology, it would be too much to characterize him as an outright hermeneutical theologian. His attention to hermeneutical questions notwithstanding, Rahner's explicit engagement with hermeneutical theory has remained rather restricted. This becomes especially apparent in his relative inattention regarding the fundamental role played by language and the potentially distorting influence of ideology and power. For this reason, I suggest complementing a retrieval of Rahner with a retrieval of Schillebeeckx, so as to bring out a different yet related example of the dialectical interrelation of metaphysics and hermeneutics.

As mentioned previously, Schillebeeckx has been one of the pioneers of the appropriation of modern hermeneutical theory within Catholic theology. His work reflects an intense engagement with hermeneutical thinkers, such as Gadamer and Ricoeur, and also with critical corrections of hermeneutics as offered by thinkers such as Habermas. It is, therefore, correct to conclude that Schillebeeckx actively contributed to the hermeneutical turn in theology. However, contrary to the generation of hermeneutical theologians that succeeded him, Schillebeeckx never parted completely with metaphysics in his theology. This makes him highly relevant for a rethinking of the role of metaphysical reflection within a theology that is aware of its hermeneutical conditions.

In opposition to scholars who present Schillebeeckx's hermeneutical turn in terms of a radical break with metaphysics, I will offer a re-reading of his method that draws out a dialectical interplay between hermeneutics and metaphysics. The hermeneutical turn strengthens the incarnational dynamic that informs Schillebeeckx's methodology from the outset. His engagement with critical theory accentuates the limitation of metaphysics even further. However, a relational metaphysical framework continues to inform his theology. Hence, Schillebeeckx's critical-hermeneutical turn ultimately affects a transformation, rather than a negation, of the role played by metaphysical reflection within theology. Accordingly, his theology also offers an insightful complementary perspective on the thinking of universality from within particularity.

Part I

2

An eclectic theologian: The sources of Rahner's method

1 Introduction

In this chapter I will introduce Karl Rahner's transcendental theological method by examining his formative influences. To many scholars, the term 'transcendental' immediately calls to mind Immanuel Kant and the new meaning that he gave to this word in his *Critique of Pure Reason*.[1] Rahner is certainly well known as one of the main thinkers who appropriated Kant's transcendental philosophical approach into theology. Rahner's own description of transcendental theology contributes to this Kantian-inflected image of his method. Transcendental theology 'uses the instruments of transcendental philosophy' and focuses on 'the *a priori* conditions in the believer for the knowledge of important truths of faith' by using 'genuinely theological methods of investigation'.[2]

His use of expressions such as '*a priori* conditions' and the focus on the subject call to mind Kant's project of transcendental philosophy. However, Rahner also asserts that theology employs the instrument of transcendental philosophy from the perspective of 'genuinely theological questions'. In this chapter I will demonstrate that approaching Rahner through a narrowly Kantian lens fails to provide us with an understanding of his theological project. Many critiques and misunderstandings of Rahner's work can be traced back to these exact kinds of exclusively Kantian readings of his transcendental method.[3] In this chapter I argue instead that Rahner's appropriation of the term 'transcendental' is more complex than is often thought. As Karl Lehmann has argued, Rahner's transcendental project has a high degree of 'idiosyncracy'.[4] On the one hand,

---

[1] Immanuel Kant, *Critique of Pure Reason*, trans. and ed. Paul Guyer and Allen W. Wood (Cambridge: Cambridge University Press, 2000).
[2] Karl Rahner, 'Transcendental Theology', in *Sacramentum Mundi: An Encyclopedia of Theology*, vol. 6, ed. Karl Rahner and Adolf Darlap (New York: Herder and Herder, 1970), 287.
[3] See Nikolaus Knoepffler, *Der Begriff 'transzendental' bei Karl Rahner. Zur Frage seiner Kantischen Herkunft*, Innsbrucker theologische Studien 39 (Innsbruck: Tyrolia Verlag, 1993), for a comparison of Rahner's and Kant's understanding of the concept of transcendentality.
[4] Karl Lehmann, 'Philosophisches Denken im Werk Karl Rahners', in *Karl Rahner in Erinnerung*, ed. Albert Raffelt (Düsseldorf: Patmos Verlag, 1994), 10–27. A great many biographical accounts have been published detailing Karl Rahner's life and work. Herbert Vorgrimler, *Karl Rahner: Gotteserfahrung in Leben und Denken* (Darmstadt: Primus Verlag, 2004) offers a good introduction to Rahner's life and work. A more detailed account of Rahner's life can be found in the biography

Rahner draws upon a variety of philosophical sources and, on the other hand, he appropriates these philosophical sources in an original way with a view of developing his distinct theological transcendental methodology.

In order to present this alternative and a more balanced account of Rahner's theological approach, I will retrace the key formative influences on his work. The central thesis that I develop in the sections that follow is that Rahner's transcendental theology draws upon three intellectual sources: (1) the scholastic metaphysical tradition, (2) Kant's transcendental philosophical method and (3) Martin Heidegger's phenomenology and hermeneutics. Attending to these three different elements is crucial in ascertaining an adequate understanding of Rahner's theological method.

While Rahner seeks to remain faithful to the scholastic tradition, he does aim to do so by confronting this tradition with contemporary questions and problems. For this purpose, he brings Thomas Aquinas into dialogue with modern philosophy, particularly with the thought of Kant and Heidegger. As we will see, Rahner's confrontation of scholastic with Kantian philosophy is greatly indebted to Joseph Maréchal's groundbreaking work. Rahner follows Maréchal rethinking of metaphysics with the help of transcendental philosophy. This combination of metaphysics and transcendental philosophy comprises a crucial characteristic of Rahner's theological approach. It accounts for the confluence of the scholastic and the Kantian understandings of transcendentality in Rahner's work. At the same time, Rahner also differs markedly from Maréchal insofar as he incorporates important aspects of Heidegger's philosophy. Heidegger's phenomenological adaptation of the transcendental method, as well as his hermeneutics, provides Rahner's method with a decidedly greater historical orientation, in comparison with Kant and Maréchal. While this Heideggerian dimension of Rahner's thought has not gone unnoticed, it is not always given its due attention.

2 Aggiornamento: Reading Thomas through modern philosophy

Karl Lehmann argues that one of Karl Rahner's main merits is that he helped a dogmatics, which had become imprisoned within its own tradition, to find its original sources again.[5] Whether Rahner can or cannot be considered to be a *ressourcement*

---

published by Karl H. Neufeld on Karl Rahner and his brother Hugo, *Die Brüder Rahner: Eine Biographie*, 2nd ed. (Freiburg: Herder, 2004). Other introductory works to Rahner's life and work include Karl Lehmann, 'Karl Rahner, ein Porträt', in *SW* vol. 2, xii–lxvii; Albert Raffelt and Hansjürgen Verweyen, *Karl Rahner* (München: Beck, 1997); and Karen Kilby, *Karl Rahner: A Brief Introduction* (New York: Crossroad, 2007). Interviews with Rahner have been published as *Im Gespräch*, 2 vols., ed. Paul Imhof and Hubert Biallowons (München: Kösel Verlag, 1982–1983), and *Faith in a Wintry Season: Conversations and interviews with Karl Rahner in the Last Years of his Life*, ed. Paul Imhof and Hubert Biallowons, trans. Harvey Egan (New York: Crossroad, 1991).

[5] Lehmann, 'Karl Rahner, ein Porträt', xxx.

theologian is an oft-debated topic.[6] However, *that* he played a major role in the reform of the traditional theology of the schools is beyond a shadow of a doubt.

The starting point of Rahner's theological career was firmly rooted within the context of neo-scholastic theology, by virtue of the priestly formation of his time. Pope Leo XIII had initiated a *renaissance* of Thomism that sought to employ Thomas as an authority against modernity, with his encyclical *Aeterni Patris* (1879). Thomas's thought should be used to counter modern individualism and to defend a synthesis between reason and faith. This restorative tendency was continued by Pius X in his anti-modernist campaign.[7] As a result, Rahner's philosophical and theological formation was heavily marked by neo-scholasticism and by the thought of Francisco Suárez in particular. However, this neo-scholastic approach failed, in his own view, to engender a lively and inspirational conversation with Thomas and instead took the form of a pious admiration.[8] Importantly, Rahner considered the neo-scholastic way of thinking to be lacking because of its inward-looking orientation and its defensive avoidance of any engagement with other ideas, either from modern thinkers or from Protestant theologians. Dissatisfied with the prevailing intellectual climate of ecclesial autarky, Rahner sought to free neo-scholastic thought from its constraints by bringing it into conversation with modern thought. This transformation of neo-scholastic theology becomes central to Rahner's work. The spirit of *aggiornamento* is expressed particularly clearly in his introduction and *Begleittext* (accompanying text) to *Spirit in the World*.[9]

In the *Begleittext*, Rahner describes how the revival of neo-scholasticism has engendered a retrieval of scholastic thought and an historical, philological line of research into scholastic thinkers. However, these approaches are inadequate, insofar as they fail to enter into a lively conversation with modern philosophy. According to Rahner, philosophers such as Kant, Hegel and Heidegger share the same problems and questions with the neo-scholastic tradition and should, therefore, be taken more seriously. This can be done from *within* the scholastic point of view.[10] Recognizing the inner affinity between scholasticism and modern philosophy's concerns allows a serious mutual engagement to take place. Through this dialogue, the truth and insights of scholasticism can be introduced fruitfully into the discourse of modern philosophy.[11] Rahner explains this dialogical encounter in three steps.

---

[6] See Richard Lennan, 'The Theology of Karl Rahner: An Alternative to the *Ressourcement*?', in *Ressourcement: A Movement for Renewal in Twentieth-Century Catholic Theology*, ed. Gabriel Flynn and Paul D. Murray (Oxford: Oxford University Press, 2012), 405–22.

[7] See Roman A. Siebenrock, 'Glauben gibt zu denken: "Geist in Welt" und "Hörer des Wortes"', in *Der Denkweg Karl Rahners. Quellen – Entwicklungen – Perspektiven,* ed. Andreas R. Batlogg, Paul Rulands, Walter Schmolly, Roman A. Siebenrock, Günther Wassilowsky, Arno Zahlauer (Mainz: Matthias Grünewald Verlag, 2004), 60–2. For more information on the neo-scholastic revival, see chapter 13 in James C. Livingston, *Modern Christian Thought. Vol. 1: The Enlightenment and the Nineteenth Century* (Minneapolis: Fortress Press, 2006), 327–55.

[8] Karl Rahner, *Faith in a Wintry Season. Conversations and interviews with Karl Rahner in the Last Years of his Life*, ed. Paul Imhof and Hubert Biallowons, trans. Harvey Egan (New York: Crossroad, 1991), 42.

[9] Karl Rahner, 'Begleittext zu "Geist in Welt"', in *SW* vol. 2, 431–7.

[10] Ibid., 431–3.

[11] Ibid., 432. Rahner recognizes various other attempts at such a dialogue, for example in the works of the theologians of the Tübinger Schule or Erich Przywara. However, he deems those attempts to

First, there must be a new contemporary engagement with the old scholastic tradition. In order to become part of the tradition, a philosophical contribution must maintain its connection with the tradition. Second, this engagement with scholasticism should not be a mere repetition of the past, but must instead be shaped by an authentic and personal systematic consideration. Third, it will become apparent that scholasticism is actually not that outdated. Its problems and questions continue to live on within the thought of great thinkers, such as Kant, Hegel and Heidegger. This is what will eventually enable a lively and fruitful conversation between scholasticism and modern philosophy in which both partners actually understand their respective languages.[12] Rahner is aware of the fact that his interest in modern philosophy might make him suspicious in more traditional theological circles. Accordingly, he takes care to emphasize that he is a Thomist, faithful to the '24 theses',[13] who 'rejoices' in the fact that scholastic questions can be found in the thought of Kant, Hegel and Heidegger.[14]

In the introduction to *Spirit in the World*, Rahner explains more specifically how his work comprises his own specific contribution to the dialogue between scholasticism and modern philosophy.[15] *Spirit in the World* focuses on Thomas's metaphysics of knowledge. Rahner seeks to explain the particular character of human knowing, as being grounded in the world, as well as transcending the world, through the interpretation of one particular article from one particular *quaestio* from the *Summa Theologiae* (q. 84 a. 7). His interpretation retrieves a transcendental turn to the subject from this scholastic thinker, committed as he is to a reading of Thomas that takes contemporary philosophy into account. Importantly, Rahner qualifies his hermeneutical strategy by stating that he seeks primarily a philosophical rather than a historical engagement with Thomas's thought. In order to comprehend Thomas's ideas, Rahner seeks to philosophize *with* Thomas rather than about him.[16]

Even though he seeks to avoid an interpretative infusion of his own opinions into Thomas, Rahner admits that his personal views and concerns do condition and guide his particular reading of Thomas.[17] For Rahner, this hermeneutical strategy is not so much a shortcoming as it is an imperative, because he considers his own contemporary philosophical questions to be the only access and ground upon which to engage Thomas. While the limited scope of the work precluded an express and detailed engagement

---

be unsuccessful because either their relation to scholastic philosophy or their relation to modern philosophy was too loose (433–4).

[12] Ibid., 435.

[13] Pope Pius X ordered the publication of twenty-four philosophical propositions in order to promote 'a purer form of Thomism'. See Jean-Pierre Torrell, 'Thomism', in *Encyclopedia of Christian Theology*, vol. 3, ed. Jean-Yves Lacoste (London: Routledge: 2005), 1581.

[14] Rahner, 'Begleittext', 436–7. The thought of Thomas is more prominently present in *Spirit in the World* and in *Hearer of the Word* than in Rahner's later writings. Yet, in 1970, he still writes in 'On Recognizing the importance of Thomas Aquinas [1970]', in *TI*, vol. 13, trans. David Bourke (London: Darton, Longman and Todd, 1975), 7: 'I believe that even today Thomas still remains, in a quite special and unique sense, a theologian of such magnitude that he must not cease to have a place in our discussions'.

[15] Karl Rahner, *Spirit in the World* [1957], trans. William Dych with a foreword by Johannes B. Metz and an introduction by Francis P. Fiorenza (New York, Continuum, 1994), xlix–lv.

[16] Ibid., xlix–l.

[17] Ibid., li.

with work of Kant, Hegel and Heidegger, Rahner thinks that the connection points will be obvious to readers who are familiar with this newer philosophy. He refers, in this regard, to the Kantian formulations used in the work. However, immediately after declaring his indebtedness to Kant's thought, Rahner also differentiates himself from Kant. Contrary to Kant's epistemological critique of knowledge, Rahner maintains that he is concerned with a *metaphysics* of knowledge.[18] He does not expressly state whether he intends to proceed by way of a transcendental methodology in *Spirit in the World* or not. Instead, he acknowledges his indebtedness to the interpretation of Thomas by Pierre Rousselot and to Joseph Maréchal.[19] These two thinkers inaugurated a new approach to Thomas that became known as 'Transcendental Thomism'.[20]

Despite the clear demarcation of his goal, and the justification of his hermeneutics, the reading of Thomas which Rahner presents in *Spirit in the World* has caused a lot of debate. Karen Kilby comments that 'almost everyone who has ever examined it from this angle [as a reading of St Thomas], beginning with Rahner's own thesis director, has found it wanting'.[21] Peter Eicher points to the transcendental philosophical focus on human subjectivity, which according to some commentators disregards Thomas's primary metaphysical focus on objectivity and Thomas's participatory metaphysics.[22] However, while Eicher considers Rahner's reading of Thomas to be historically inaccurate, he maintains that Rahner still offers a legitimate philosophical anthropology that should be judged not merely on its faithfulness to either Kant or Thomas, but instead as an alternative and original theological approach in its own right.[23] In order to gain an understanding of this alternative theological approach, it will be necessary to examine Rahner's main intellectual influences: Kant, Maréchal and Heidegger.

3 Immanuel Kant: The destroyer of metaphysics

In his *Critique of Pure Reason*, Immanuel Kant sets out to reconceptualize metaphysics, the discipline which was once known as the 'queen of all the sciences'.[24] He aims to do so by way of a critique of the faculty of knowledge as such, which follows a scientific approach. His Copernican revolution proposes a revision of

---

[18] Ibid., liii.
[19] Ibid., xlvii.
[20] For more information on transcendental Thomism, see Joseph Donceel, 'Transcendental Thomism', *The Monist* 58 (1974): 67–85; Francis Schüssler Fiorenza, 'The New Theology and Transcendental Thomism', in *Modern Christian Thought. Vol. 2*, 197–232.
[21] Karen Kilby, *Karl Rahner. Theology and Philosophy* (London: Routledge, 2004), 14.
[22] Peter Eicher, *Die anthropologische Wende. Karl Rahners philosophischer Weg vom Wesen des Menschen zur personalen Existenz* (Freiburg: Universitätsverlag, 1970), 73. Well-known criticits of Rahner include Bernhard Lakebrink, *Klassische Metaphysik. Eine Auseinandersetzung mit der existenzialen Anthropozentrik* (Freiburg: Rombach, 1967) and Cornelio Fabro, *La svolta antropologica di Karl Rahner* (Milan: Rusconi, 1974). For a more extensive overview of the reception history of *Spirit in the World*, see Peter Eicher, 'Wovon spricht die transzendentale Theologie? Zur gegenwärtige Auseinandersetzung um das Denken von Karl Rahner', *Theologische Quartalschrift* 157 (1977): 285–8.
[23] Eicher, *Die anthropologische Wende*, 78. See also Eicher, 'Wovon spricht', 287–8.
[24] Kant, *Critique of Pure Reason*, A IX.

traditional metaphysics, arguing that objects conform to the knowing subject, rather than vice versa.²⁵ Kant's focus on the role of human subjectivity in knowledge has become known as the transcendental turn to the subject. In the scholastic tradition, transcendentals or *nomina transcendentia* were used as general formal concepts which go beyond individual categories and which are, therefore, applicable to all being. These transcendentals include *ens* (being), *unum* (one), *verum* (true) and *bonum* (good). In contrast to this 'old transcendental philosophy', Kant puts forward a new understanding that connects the transcendental to the subject, rather than to the object of knowledge: 'I call all cognition *transcendental* that is occupied not so much with objects but rather with our *a priori* concepts of objects in general. A system of such concepts would be called transcendental philosophy'.²⁶ Thus, transcendental philosophy asks for the conditions of the possibility of knowledge through a reflection on the knowing subject. Kant's philosophy of pure reason greatly restricts traditional metaphysical and theological claims to theoretical knowledge. For that reason, the image has arisen of Kant as the 'destroyer of metaphysics'.²⁷

In the 'Transcendental Logic' of the *Critique of Pure Reason*, Kant argues that our knowledge has two sources: receptive sensibility (*Sinnlichkeit*), that is the capacity of sense experience, and spontaneous understanding (*Verstand*), that is the capacity to form concepts. Knowledge requires the cooperation of these two faculties: 'Thoughts without content are empty, intuitions without concepts are blind.'²⁸ Kant discusses sensibility in the 'Transcendental Aesthetics' and the categories of understanding in the 'Transcendental Analytic'. Several limitations of any metaphysics result from this transcendental investigation into the conditions of the possibility of knowledge. First, there is a fundamental distinction between the *Ding an sich* (the noumenon) and the *Erscheinung* (the phenomenon). We cannot know the things as they are, only as they appear to us. Ontology as the science of things in themselves is, therefore, impossible.²⁹ Moreover, insofar as metaphysics and theology deal with realities such as God and freedom, which do not appear to us in experience as empirical phenomena, these disciplines cannot claim to provide any theoretical knowledge about these realities. Nevertheless, the *idea* of God retains an important role for Kant. As he argues in his critique of traditional metaphysics and theology in the Transcendental Dialectic, we cannot conclude or prove that God as regulative ideal of reason exists.

---

[25] Ibid., B XVI.
[26] Ibid., A 12 / B 25.
[27] The expression 'destroyer of metaphysics' goes all the way back to Moses Mendelsohn. Jean Grondin, *Introduction to Metaphysics: From Parmenides to Levinas*, trans. Lukas Soderstrom (New York: Columbia University Press, 2012), 131, notes that while Kant may be considered to be the 'gravedigger' of traditional metaphysics, the question of metaphysics continually looms over his entire philosophy. See also Otfried Höffe, *Kant's* Critique of Pure Reason*: The Foundation of Modern Philosophy*, Studies in German Idealism Vol. 10 (Dordrecht – Heidelberg – London – New York: Springer, 2010), 6–10, who similarly rejects the image of Kant as the 'destroyer of metaphysics' and instead argues that Kant transforms traditional metaphysics via a transcendental turn to the subject. Interestingly, Kant himself remarks on one of the final pages of the *Critique of Pure Reason*: 'We will always return to metaphysics as to a beloved from whom we have been estranged' (A 850/B 878).
[28] Ibid., A 51 / B 75.
[29] Ibid., B 303.

At the beginning of the *Critique of Pure Reason*, Kant concedes that human beings are naturally impelled to ask metaphysical questions.

> For human reason, without being moved by the mere vanity of knowing it all, inexorably pushes on, driven by its own need to such questions that cannot be answered by any experiential use of reason and of principles borrowed from a use; and thus a certain sort of metaphysics has actually been present in all human beings as soon as reason has extended itself to speculation in them, and it will also always remain there.[30]

According to Kant, we strive for coherence, structure and systematic unity in our knowledge. This natural inclination towards metaphysics leads us to develop the ideas of God, freedom and the immortality of the soul.[31] I will focus here on Kant's treatment of the idea of God in his critique of rational theology and the traditional metaphysical proofs for the existence of God. Kant argues that the idea of God, while necessary, is not an object of knowledge but merely a regulative transcendental ideal. The mistake of seeing an objective necessity in the subjective necessity of God amounts to what he calls a 'transcendental illusion'.[32] His argument runs as follows: the human mind has a natural drive – an inner demand for the unconditioned. Thinking individual things necessarily involves thinking a totality, an idea of all reality (*omnitudo realitatis*). Without this so-called transcendental ideal it would be impossible to know individual things as finite, limited realities.[33]

This transcendental ideal or *ens realissimum* is hypostatized and personified as God and, as such, becomes the object of transcendental theology. However, according to Kant, we cannot assume the existence of a being that corresponds to this ideal.[34] This would amount to the confusion of the real and the ideal. The critique of such a confusion lies at the heart of Kant's rejection of the traditional metaphysical proofs of God, that is the ontological, cosmological and physico-theological arguments. Summarizing his critique of the ontological proof will be sufficient here, given that he considers the latter two proofs to be dependent upon the ontological proof.

According to Kant, the ontological proof argues that God must necessarily exist, because as *ens realissimum*, it contains all realities or predicates, including the predicate of existence. Denying the existence of God would, therefore, seem self-contradictory. However, Kant objects to this way of reasoning by claiming that it involves an unjustified leap from the order of thought to the order of being. It is based upon a transcendental illusion that confuses the ideal (or logical) with the real.[35] Kant denies that being is a real predicate through which a thing can be determined or specified. To say that something 'is' does not yield a different concept of this thing than to posit it as a mere possibility. As Kant famously remarks, 'A hundred actual dollars do not contain

---

[30] Ibid., B 21.
[31] Ibid., A 798 / B 826.
[32] See Ibid., A297 / B 354.
[33] Ibid., A 575–576 /B 601–604.
[34] Ibid., A 577–579 / B 605–607.
[35] Ibid., A 598–599 / B 626–627.

the least bit more than the a hundred possible ones.'³⁶ Thus, since existence is not an element of a concept, we need something else to determine whether a thing is possible or actual. We can rely on our sensible intuition regarding empirical objects. However, the transcendental ideal is not an empirical phenomenon. Accordingly, 'For objects of pure thinking there is no means whatever for cognizing their existence, because it would have to be cognized entirely *a priori*.'³⁷

Hence, Kant argues that the existence of God, the transcendental ideal, the *ens realissimum* cannot be known or proven metaphysically. Instead, the transcendental ideas of God, soul and world have 'an excellent and indispensably necessary regulative use, namely that of directing the understanding to a certain goal'.³⁸ They provide systematic unity and coherence as imaginary focus to human knowledge, but they themselves fall beyond the domain of experience and, therefore, beyond the scope of theoretical reason. God, thus, no longer has a constitutive role in knowledge, but plays merely a regulative role. This does not mean that Kant denies the existence of God though. As he famously writes in the preface to the *Kritik der reinen Vernunft*, 'I had to deny *knowledge* in order to make room for faith.'³⁹ For Kant, reason is not merely theoretical but also practical. The ideas of reason, God, soul and world, therefore, make a return in his moral philosophy as postulates of practical reason.⁴⁰ Nevertheless, it is the banishing of God from the domain of theoretical reason that Maréchal seeks to challenge.

4 Joseph Maréchal: A dynamic theological metaphysics

Rahner himself attributes his 'transcendentally infused philosophical Thomism' to the impact that Pierre Rousselot (1878–1915) and Joseph Maréchal (1878–1944) had on his thinking.⁴¹ Both Maréchal and Rousselot seek to confront Thomas with Kant in order to restore the speculative, metaphysical function of reason. By reintroducing a dynamic notion of subjectivity, they attempt to reconceptualize Thomistic metaphysics in a transcendental key. I will focus here on Maréchal.⁴²

---

36 Ibid., A 599 / B 627.
37 Ibid., A601 / B 629.
38 Ibid., A 644 / B 672.
39 Ibid., B XXX.
40 See Immanuel Kant, *Critique of Practical Reason*, trans. Mary Gregor with an introduction by Andrew Reath (Cambridge: Cambridge University Press, 2015).
41 Rahner, *Faith in a Wintry Season*, 47.
42 Albert Raffelt has observed that Rousselot's influence on Rahner has been investigated much less often than that of Maréchal's. He emphasizes the importance of Rousselot's ontological orientation, compared to Maréchal's epistemological orientation. This influence can be seen in Rahner's discussion of the identity of Being and knowing in Rahner, *Spirit in the World*, 69, in which Rahner refers explicitly to Rousselot. See Albert Raffelt, 'Geist in Welt: einige Anmerkungen zur Interpretation', in *Die philosophische Quellen der Theologie Karl Rahners*, ed. Harald Schöndorf, Quaestiones disputatae 213 (Freiburg: Herder, 2005), 59–62. For a discussion of Rousselot's ideas and their influence on Rahner, see Thomas Sheehan, *Karl Rahner: The Philosophical Foundations* (Athens, OH: Ohio University Press, 1987), 55–73.

Maréchal's key publication *Le point de départ de la métaphysique*[43] consists of five volumes (*cahiers*) and may be considered 'the first objective and sympathetic presentation written by a Catholic philosopher, of the philosophy of Kant'.[44] The assessment of Kant's philosophy in *Cahier III* becomes a critical confrontation with Thomistic philosophy in *Cahier V*.[45] While he agrees with Kant that human beings have no intellectual intuition of noumenal reality, he maintains over and against Kant that our knowledge nevertheless extends to this noumenal order. Thus, as he explains in the Foreword, he objects to Kant's restriction of knowledge to phenomenal reality:

> We will investigate whether the initial postulates of Kant (the *phenomenal object* and the *transcendental method of analysis*) might not conceal, no matter what Kant may have thought, the implicit affirmation of a real metaphysical *object*.[46]

Thomas is Maréchal's main guide in his critical, but respectful, engagement with Kant's philosophy. His analysis of human knowledge, therefore, has a clear focus on metaphysics. For Maréchal, human beings are always already, at least implicitly, related to absolute Being. It is because of this ontological orientation that we can reach the metaphysical order.[47]

Maréchal employs Kant's transcendental method in order to establish the connection between metaphysics and transcendental philosophy.[48] In so doing he initiates his own 'Copernican revolution' – a transcendental turn in Thomistic metaphysics.[49] Maréchal recognizes that time, space and the categories of understanding form the *a priori* conditions of human understanding. However, the thrust of his argument is that a metaphysical affirmation of Being forms an additional transcendental condition of human knowing. According to Maréchal, all acts of knowing are grounded in a dynamism towards absolute Being. There is, thus, a correspondence between the metaphysical *a priori* and the transcendental *a priori*. Maréchal's intention is to show that Kant can be completed, rather than contradicted, from a scholastic point of view. He is convinced that Thomas (the ontological critique) and Kant (the transcendental critique) actually converge and that both point towards 'a dynamic metaphysics'.[50] A key

---

[43] Joseph Maréchal, *Le point de départ de la métaphysique*, 5 vols. (Louvain: Éditions du Museum Lessianum, 1926–1947). In the following discussion, I refer to the English translation of some key texts of Maréchal, which are collected in *A Maréchal Reader*, ed. and trans. Joseph Donceel (New York: Herder & Herder, 1970).

[44] Donceel, 'Transcendental Thomism', 69. See also Johannes Baptist Lotz, 'Joseph Maréchal', in *Christliche Philosophie im katholischen Denken des 19. und 20. Jahrhunderts. Band 2 Rückgriff auf scholastisches Erbe*, ed. Emerich Coreth, Walter M. Neidl, and Georg Pfligersdorffer (Graz: Styria Verlag, 1988), 454, who likewise points out the novelty of Maréchal, insofar as he initiated a thinking *with* the moderns instead of a thinking *against* them.

[45] Joseph Maréchal, *Le point de départ de la métaphysique. Cahier 5 : Le Thomisme devant la Philosophie critique* (Louvain: Éditions du Museum Lessianum, 1926).

[46] Maréchal, *A Maréchal Reader*, 66.

[47] Otto Muck, *The Transcendental Method*, trans. William D. Seidensticker (New York: Herder and Herder, 1968), 27–8.

[48] Lotz, 'Joseph Maréchal', 458.

[49] See Emerich Coreth, 'Philosophische Grundlagen der Theologie Karl Rahners', *Stimmen der Zeit* 212 (1994): 527.

[50] Maréchal, *A Maréchal Reader*, 85.

element of the dynamic metaphysics that Maréchal develops is his attempt to reconnect the domain of practical reason to the domain of theoretical reason. By elaborating the close unity between knowing and willing, he follows the example of Johann Gottlieb Fichte.[51] A finality can be discovered that opens an access to the *An-sich* and to theoretical metaphysics in the act of knowing; knowing has an inner striving towards truth. A transcendental deduction of the act of knowing reveals that this dynamism towards the absolute forms the *a priori* condition of human knowledge.[52] Maréchal's position is best explained by pointing out two important instances in which he differs from Kant. The first element is the role of affirmation in judgement, and the second element is the dynamic character of human knowledge.

To begin with, Maréchal agrees with Kant's argument that we express knowledge about objects through the formation of concepts in judgement. However, his analysis of judgement differs from Kant's insofar as he distinguishes not only a 'synthetic' element in judgement but also an 'objective' element therein.[53] The synthetic element of judgement involves the application of the *a priori* categories of understanding to the sensible intuitions; this yields a unity of subject and predicate. In scholastic terms, it is the uniting of the universal form with the particular sensible by the agent intellect.[54] In Kant's epistemology, this predicative synthesis constitutes knowledge. Maréchal argues, though, that there is another constitutive moment involved in judgement, which he terms 'objective synthesis' or affirmation. In order to objectify a predicative synthesis, it must be posited object over and against the knowing subject.[55] This happens through the positing of the copula 'is', which affirms an object as being real. However, this objective synthesis is only possible where the knowing subject in judgement somehow reaches truth or Being as such. Thus, Maréchal argues that in judgement, the *An-sich* or noumenal reality is discovered in the *für-uns* or phenomenal reality, by way of the objective synthesis which has the character of an affirmation.[56] In order to affirm a limited object as real, however, there must also be a relation to absolute Being as the ground of every finite being. Hence, every affirmation of a finite object of knowledge involves an implicit affirmation of absolute Being.[57] Maréchal explains this further by way of his argument concerning the intellectual dynamism of the human mind.

If we consider the human mind, then we discover that there is an intrinsic appetite for the absolute at the heart of human knowing. For every possible answer, every conceptual understanding formed about an object can always and immediately be put

---

[51] See ibid., 246 and Lotz, 'Joseph Maréchal', 455. Maréchal treats Fichte in *Cahier 4 : Le système idéaliste chez Kant et les postkantiens*.
[52] Lotz, 'Joseph Maréchal', 455–6.
[53] Maréchal, *A Maréchal Reader*, 115. In the secondary literature various terms are used to term these moment. Otto Muck, 'Thomas – Kant – Maréchal: Karl Rahner's transzendentale Methode', in *Die philosophischen Quellen der Theologie Karl Rahners*, 37–40, uses 'categorial synthesis' and 'affirmative synthesis', Lotz, 'Joseph Maréchal', 460, refers to 'predicative synthesis' and 'veritative synthesis', and Gerald McCool, *From Unity to Pluralism: The Internal Evolution of Thomism* (New York: Fordham University Press, 1989), 97–100, speaks of 'concretive synthesis' and 'affirmative synthesis'.
[54] See McCool, *From Unity to Pluralism*, 96–7.
[55] Maréchal, *A Maréchal Reader*, 151–2.
[56] Lotz, 'Joseph Maréchal', 460.
[57] See McCool, *From Unity to Pluralism*, 92–4.

into question. We can always learn more about finite objects and deepen our knowledge of them. The range of human knowing is potentially infinite. Thus, the human intellect is, by its very nature, something that strives for the unlimited real.[58] Following the Thomistic metaphysics of finality, the last is always first, that is the ultimate end of a movement forms the cause of its striving.[59] Hence, according to Maréchal, 'No activity of our intellect, no intellectual assimilation is possible but in virtue of the deep yearning whose saturating end would be the intuition of the absolute Real.'[60] This emphasis on finality forms another element of differentiation with Kant. Maréchal argues that Kant's concept of knowledge remained too static and, therefore, that it failed to acknowledge that knowing is an intelligibly ordered progression towards a goal. Paying proper attention to the intellectual dynamism of the human mind shows that all of our knowing activity is carried by a finality towards infinite Being and that every affirmation of a finite object, therefore, includes at least the implicit affirmation of infinite Being.[61]

Maréchal's transcendental deduction of the human orientation to absolute Being, as the *a priori* condition for the possibility of knowledge, finally opens up the way by which to re-establish the constitutive role of God within human knowledge. According to the Thomistic understanding, absolute or infinite Being is divine being or God. So, Maréchal can refer to Thomas's dictum *Omnia cognoscentia cognoscunt implicite Deum in quolibet cognito* (all knowing beings implicitly know God in everything they know).[62] As the transcendental condition of affirmative objectification, God is not merely a regulative ideal or a subjective necessity but an objective necessity because of God's constitutive importance for knowledge.[63] Individual, particular objects cannot be affirmed without at least implicitly affirming infinite Being.[64] The question of God is, therefore, intrinsically connected to the question of knowledge. However, Maréchal takes care to emphasize that our implicit affirmation of God must not be misunderstood as a simple grasping of God in objective knowing. On the contrary, it is more aptly described as a 'transcendent anticipation' which is present *within* our knowledge of finite objects.[65] Put differently, the *An-sich* which becomes apparent in the *für-uns* is never purely available. The human subject truly reaches God in the transcending movement of its intellectual dynamism, but this perspective on God remains bound to the limiting conditions of human knowing. Thus, whereas God is implicitly affirmed in all human knowledge, this affirmation can never become a total objectification or conceptualization. We have no direct knowledge of God; we know God analogously: 'We know the creatures as *relative* to an absolute Principle, as *contingent* and in this way and only in this way do we know God.'[66]

---

[58] Ibid., 99; Sheehan, *Karl Rahner*, 86.
[59] McCool, *From Unity to Pluralism*, 99; Lotz, 'Joseph Maréchal', 461.
[60] Maréchal, *A Maréchal Reader*, 248.
[61] McCool, *From Unity to Pluralism*, 108–9.
[62] Maréchal, *A Maréchal Reader*, 251.
[63] Muck, 'Thomas – Kant – Maréchal', 38–9.
[64] McCool, *From Unity to Pluralism*, 109.
[65] Maréchal, *A Maréchal Reader*, 152.
[66] Ibid., 144.

Maréchal's synthesis of Thomistic metaphysics and Kantian transcendental philosophy, while highly original, did not find broad philosophical acclaim. Richard Schaeffler notes that other transcendental philosophers deemed it an illegitimate extension of Kant's limitation of the scope of theoretical reason.[67] Within scholastic philosophical circles, on the other hand, people like Jacques Maritain and Etienne Gilson would soon inaugurate new directions of thought which were more distrustful of the compatibility of Kantian and scholastic ideas.[68] However, Maréchal's philosophy did create a new way of speaking about God as the reality to which all human persons are fundamentally oriented. This new philosophical way of speaking about God would be received more fruitfully in the work of several theologians, most importantly in Rahner.[69]

The strong influence Maréchal has had on Rahner's thought, and the affinity between their approaches, is most apparent in *Spirit in the World*. Following Maréchal's example, Rahner transposes a scholastic problem into a transcendental key. Like Maréchal, Rahner argues that experiential knowledge includes, as its condition of possibility, an implicit metaphysical understanding of Being. Thus, he derives from Maréchal a particular combination of the Kantian and the scholastic understanding of transcendentality, one which can be called a 'transcendental metaphysics'.[70] For Rahner, every 'genuine' metaphysics must employ transcendental philosophy.[71] He considers Thomas the progenitor of this combination of metaphysics and transcendentality: 'According to Thomas the reflection on that which makes metaphysics possible is already itself metaphysics, and basically is already the totality of what is accessible to human metaphysics.'[72]

However, Rahner does not simply borrow from Maréchal but instead develops his ideas further in his own work. Rahner's transcendental argument is preceded by a phenomenological analysis of human existence.[73] More concretely, Rahner begins with a phenomenological account of human questioning and proceeds then to reflect on the necessary conditions of this phenomenon of questioning. Moreover, Rahner is also more careful in making the transition from absolute Being to God. While Maréchal's account may appear to reintroduce a philosophical proof for the existence of God, Rahner rejects the suggestion that an *a priori* proof for the existence

---

[67] Richard Schaeffler, 'Philosophie und katholische Theologie', in *Christliche Philosophie im katholischen Denken des 19. und 20. Jahrhunderts. Band 3 Moderne Strömungen im 20. Jahrhundert*, ed. Emerich Coreth, Walter M. Neidl, and Georg Pfligersdorffer (Graz: Styria Verlag, 1990), 62–3.
[68] See McCool, *From Unity to Pluralism*, 110–11.
[69] Coreth, 'Philosophische Grundlagen', 528, recalls that Rahner is sometimes counted as a member of a German Maréchal school but calls into question the adequacy of this characterization. He does point out, though, that Maréchal's 'transcendental metaphysics' has been received almost exclusively by Jesuit scholars and their students, such as Lotz, Rahner and Muck. For a discussion of the German Maréchal school, see Otto Muck, 'Die deutschsprachige Maréchal-Schule – Transzendentalphilosophie als Metaphysik: J.B. Lotz, K. Rahner, W. Brugger, E. Coreth u.a.', in *Christliche Philosophie im katholischen Denken des 19. und 20. Jahrhunderts. Band 2*, 590–622.
[70] Coreth, 'Philosophische Grundlagen', 528.
[71] Karl Rahner, 'Reflections on Methodology in Theology' [1970], in *TI*, vol. 11, trans. David Bourke (London: Darton, Longman and Todd, 1974), 85.
[72] Rahner, *Spirit in the World*, 399.
[73] See Muck, *The Transcendental Method*, 195.

of God can be offered. Finally, Maréchal's more narrow focus on judgement contrasts with Rahner's broader focus on the human person's *Selbstvollzug* (self-realization). Lehmann writes that Rahner is not merely concerned with human subjectivity, but rather with the human person as temporal, worldly, historical being. For this reason, Rahner's transcendental enquiry always departs from the human experience of self-realization.[74] This connects with Rahner's own assertion that the main difference between him and Maréchal concerns the attention paid to the human orientation towards history.[75]

The various differences between Maréchal and Rahner are often explained with reference to the influence that Heidegger had on Rahner's thought. To that end, the section that follows discusses those key themes of Heidegger's thought which are relevant for understanding Rahner's method.

5 Martin Heidegger: Rahner's only teacher

The precise extent of the influence that Heidegger exerted on Rahner's thought is oft-debated in secondary literature.[76] Rahner is sometimes identified as a member of the 'Catholic Heidegger School', alongside people such as Gustav Siewerth, Max Müller, Bernhard Welte and Johannes Baptist Lotz. However, the appropriateness of that characterization has been questioned and challenged.[77] It is an undisputed fact that Rahner attended several of Heidegger's lectures and multiple seminars during his time as a doctoral student in Freiburg.[78] Yet, as Joseph Fritz has recently argued, 'It no longer suffices simply to remark that Rahner "once studied with Heidegger", or that Rahner "attended Heidegger's seminars"; the Rahner-Heidegger relationship is a complex and

---

[74] Lehmann, 'Philosophisches Denken im Werk Karl Rahners', 18.
[75] Rahner, *Faith in a Wintry Season*, 50. See also Karl H. Neufeld, 'Joseph Maréchal und Karl Rahner (K. Rahner Todestag 30.3.). Vom Umgang mit Thomas von Aquin', *Zeitschrift für katholische Theologie* 137 (2015): 127–40, for a discussion of the similarities and differences between Rahner and Maréchal.
[76] See Otto Muck, 'Heidegger und Karl Rahner', *Zeitschrift für katholische Theologie* 116 (1994): 257–69; Muck, *The Transcendental Method*, 184–6; Fiorenza, 'Introduction: Karl Rahner and the Kantian Problematic', xl–xli; Raffelt, 'Geist in Welt', 62–4; 72–4; Eicher, *Die anthropologische Wende*, 13–22; Sheehan, *Karl Rahner*, 103–32; Anne Carr, *The Theological Method of Karl Rahner* (Missoula, MT: Scholars Press, 1977), 17–35; Kreutzer, *Transzendentales versus hermeneutisches Denken*, 123–62; Coreth, 'Philosophische Grundlagen', 528–30; Jack Arthur Bonsor, *Rahner, Heidegger, and Truth: Karl Rahner's Notion of Christian Truth. The Influence of Heidegger* (Lanham, MD. University Press of America, 1987); Fritz, *Karl Rahner's Theological Aesthetics*.
[77] Coreth, 'Philosophische Grundlagen', 528–9. According to Vorgrimler, Max Müller explicitly rejected the suggestion that there was anything like a Catholic Heidegger School (Vorgrimler, *Karl Rahner*, 36). Gerald A. McCool, 'Introduction: Rahner's Philosophical Theology', in *A Rahner Reader*, ed. Gerald McCool (London: Darton, Longman and Todd, 1975), xx, on the other hand puts a rather strong emphasis on Heidegger's influence on Rahner with qualifications such as 'Rahner's Heideggerian Thomism'.
[78] See Raffelt, 'Editionsbericht', in *SW* vol. 2, xvii–xviii. The lectures include 'Hölderlin'; 'Einführung in die Metaphysik'; 'Grundfragen der Metaphysik'; and 'Schelling: Vom Wesen der menschlichen Freiheit'; and the seminars include 'Hegel: Phänomenologie des Geistes'; 'Leibnizens Weltbegriff und der deutsche Idealismus'; and 'Kant: Kritik der Urteilskraft'. Some of Rahner's lecture notes have been preserved and have been published in *SW* vol. 2, 407–64.

generative one.'[79] This already comes to the fore in Rahner's own account of Heidegger's role and influence, which is rather ambiguous. On the one hand, in a contribution to a *Festschrift* for Heidegger he honoured Heidegger by singling him out as his one and only teacher.[80] On the other hand, though, while he readily acknowledges his indebtedness to Maréchal, Rahner has warned against exaggerating the influence that Heidegger had upon his thought.[81]

While Rahner disputes a substantive dependence upon Heidegger's thought, he acknowledges that he has been inspired by Heidegger's style and method. Heidegger taught Rahner how to interpret a text, how to look out for unexpected correlations, how to bring modern problems into theology, how to synthesize dogmas into fundamental principles and so on.[82] Importantly, it must be noted that Rahner only engages with the early Heidegger.[83] To demonstrate the relevance of his thought in understanding Rahner's own method, it is insightful to draw on a short article by Rahner in which he comments on Heidegger's work *Being and Time*.[84] Three elements are particularly relevant, that is the phenomenological method, the understanding of human being as *Dasein* and the hermeneutical nature of *Dasein*'s mode of understanding.

The first important element is Heidegger's phenomenological method. Throughout his life, Heidegger remained fascinated by the question of the meaning of Being.[85] In *Being and Time*, Heidegger proposes a renewal of the question of Being that returns to the classical and scholastic question of Being, but which proceeds by way of Kant's transcendental method.[86] Any enquiry about Being must start with a consideration of how the subject precisely can ask the question of Being. In so doing, Judith Wolfe writes, Heidegger 'inherits the Scholastic's project in a decidedly post-Kantian way'.[87] Rahner characterizes Heidegger's metaphysical investigation as having a transcendental form, insofar as he seeks to examine the subjective conditions for the possibility of the

---

[79] Fritz, *Karl Rahner's Theological Aesthetics*, 262.
[80] Karl Rahner, 'Über Martin Heidegger', in *Martin Heidegger im Gespräch*, ed. Richard Wisser (Freiburg: Alber, 1970), 48.
[81] See, for instance, Karl Rahner, *I Remember. An Autobiographical Interview with Meinold Krauss*, trans. Harvey Egan (New York: Crossroad, 1985), 46.
[82] Ibid., 45; Rahner, *Im Gespräch Band I*, 31.
[83] Kreutzer, *Transzendentales versus hermeneutisches Denken*, 127–8; Lehmann, 'Philosophisches Denken', 20. Coreth, 'Philosophische Grundlagen', 529–30 also states that Rahner lost interest in Heidegger over time and did not read his later publications.
[84] Karl Rahner, 'Einführung in den Begriff der Existentialphilosophie bei Heidegger', in *SW* vol. 2, 319–46. This is a translation by Albert Raffelt of 'Introduction au concept de philosophie existentiale chez Heidegger', *Recherches de sciences religieuse* 30 (1940): 152–71, which was originally published by mistake under his brother's name, Hugo Rahner.
[85] For a more comprehensive overview of Heidegger's concern with this issue, see Dorothea Frede, 'The Question of Being: Heidegger's Project', in *The Cambridge Companion to Martin Heidegger*, ed. Charles B. Guignon (Cambridge: Cambridge University Press, 1991), 42–69.
[86] Martin Heidegger, *Being and Time*, trans. John Macquarrie and Edward Robinson (Oxford: Basil Blackwell, 1962).
[87] Judith Wolfe, *Heidegger and Theology* (London: Bloomsbury, 2014), 83.

question of Being.⁸⁸ Heidegger acknowledges that he is indebted to Edmund Husserl's philosophy in this regard:

> Edmund Husserl has not only enabled us to understand once more the meaning of any genuine philosophical empiricism; he has also given us the necessary tools. '*A-priorism*' is the method of every scientific philosophy which understands itself. There is nothing constructivistic about it. But for this very reason, *a priori* research requires that the phenomenal basis be properly prepared.⁸⁹

Hence following Husserl, a transcendental enquiry into Being or *a priori* research must be phenomenological. However, phenomena do not simply show themselves to us. The Being of beings becomes manifest in a dynamic of disclosure and concealment. It is phenomenology's task to uncover this hidden or implicit dimension and bring it to conceptual expression.⁹⁰ Heidegger also distances himself from Husserl and his ego-centred transcendental subjectivism, insofar as his phenomenology does not focus on the intentionality of consciousness, but on human existence in the context of everyday life.⁹¹

This leads us to the second theme, the concept of *Dasein*. Since the question of Being must start with the person asking this question, Heidegger proposes starting his fundamental ontological investigation with a phenomenological analysis of *Dasein*. Through this analysis he intends to show that temporality forms the transcendental horizon of the human question of Being.⁹² Heidegger introduces the term *Dasein* in order to indicate the specific form of human existence. Associated with the concept of *Dasein* is the distinction between 'ontic' or *existentiell*, on the one hand, and the 'ontological' or *existential*, on the other hand.⁹³ Ontic refers to the factual level which is open to observation. Heidegger terms any understanding of the factual level of human existence *existentiell*. The ontological level concerns the general and formal structures that underlie the ontic or *existentiell* level. Insofar as phenomenology seeks a theoretical understanding of these structures, it is ontological or, in the case of the structures of human existence, existential. An existential analysis of *Dasein* can be called transcendental because it uncovers the conditions that enable our factual being in the world. Yet rather than yielding any 'new' insights, it is an articulating or retracing of the way in which we already are.⁹⁴

Rahner analyses Heidegger's investigation of *Dasein* as having two parts: a phenomenological description of *Dasein* as being-in-the world (*In-der-Welt-sein*) and an ontological account of 'being-in-the world' as 'being in time' (*In-der-Zeit-sein*).⁹⁵ The characterization of human existence as being in the-world intends to show that

---

⁸⁸ Rahner, 'Einführung in den Begriff', 325.
⁸⁹ Heidegger, *Being and Time*, 490, n. x.
⁹⁰ Ibid., 58–61.
⁹¹ See Frede, 'The Question of Being', 52–4.
⁹² Heidegger, *Being and Time*, 63.
⁹³ Ibid., 32–3. See Frede, 'The Question of Being', 55.
⁹⁴ Frede, 'The Question of Being', 56.
⁹⁵ Rahner, 'Einführung in den Begriff', 333–4. For a more detailed discussion of Rahner's interpretation of Heidegger, which places this interpretation into the wider context of Heidegger's

human beings are not self-enclosed subjects seeking contact with the outside world, but instead are always already in the world and open (*erschlossen*) to the world. Moreover, this being-in-the-world is what Heidegger calls an 'existential'. It forms the condition for the possibility of a practical attitude that is more original than our derived theoretical attitude. As *Dasein,* we ordinarily experience worldly entities first practically, as 'ready-to-hand' (*zuhanden*), and only later in theoretical reflection as 'present-at-hand' (*vorhanden*).[96] Rahner then proceeds to discuss three existential structures of being-in-the-world that Heidegger distinguishes: 'understanding' (*Verstehen*), 'thrownness' (*Geworfenheit*) and 'fallenness' (*Verfallenheit*).[97]

Understanding is *Dasein*'s self-comprehension that takes the form of a future-oriented dynamism. Human beings live into the future, exploring possibilities in all their knowing and acting in the world. Heidegger uses the term 'thrownness' to explain that this living out of possibilities always already presumes an unchosen starting point or situation in the world. So, understanding, which reaches towards the future, is accompanied by the situatedness of thrownness Finally, *Dasein* has a necessary concern with the individual things presently available in the world, which Heidegger terms 'fallenness'.[98]

According to Rahner, temporality (*Zeitlichkeit*) is the ontological meaning of worldliness (*Weltlichkeit*). He recalls that, for Heidegger, the term or goal of the movement of *Dasein* is 'death'. Rather than some sort of last event, death is the possibility of *Dasein*'s own impossibility. We can try to evade death by fleeing into distractions and occupations, but these evasions merely confirm that we are being-unto-death (*Sein-zum-Tode*).[99] This is no chronological or linear temporality but an ontological temporality. *Dasein* as *Sein-zum-Tode* is thus fundamentally finite and limited. As we will see in the subsequent chapter, Rahner will follow Heidegger in conducting a phenomenological analysis of the question of Being, thereby showing the transcendent character of human knowing. However, when it comes to the term of this transcendence Rahner will provide a markedly different answer than Heidegger.

Something which Rahner does not touch upon explicitly, but which is no less important when considering Heidegger's influence on Rahner, is the significance of hermeneutics. Heidegger is one of the originators of the twentieth-century hermeneutical turn and has established the question of understanding as a central philosophical topic. It must be noted, though, that it is primarily Heidegger's early existential hermeneutics rather than his later philosophy of language that has exerted an influence on Rahner.[100] As we will see below, the theme of language remains somewhat underdeveloped throughout Rahner's writings.

---

work, see Kreutzer, *Transzendentales versus hermeneutisches Denken*, 127–34; and Sheehan, *Karl Rahner*, 103–32.

[96] Rahner, 'Einführung in den Begriff', 333–4.
[97] Rahner, 'Einführung in den Begriff', 334–6. Sheehan, *Karl Rahner*, 123–4, notes that *Verfallenheit* is, strictly speaking, not a third formal structure, and so the three structural moments can be reduced to two.
[98] Rahner, 'Einführung in den Begriff', 335.
[99] Ibid., 337.
[100] See Jeanrond, *Theological Hermeneutics*, 62–4, for Heidegger's philosophy of language and its reception by the theologians of 'The New Hermeneutic' (137–57).

Through the coterminous relation between world and *Dasein* developed in his phenomenological description of being-in-the-world, Heidegger extends the traditional hermeneutical circle between text and reader, and makes it a feature of human existence in general.[101] He distinguishes between interpretation as reflective, discursive and theoretical thematization and articulation, on the one hand, and a more basic, pre-predicative level of understanding, on the other. This latter pre-predicative form of understanding must be considered to be prior and always already involves a level of interpretation. Thus, we do not first purely intuit phenomena and then subsequently interpret these intuitions. On the contrary, in life we perceive something *as* something, as having a practical meaning to us. Heidegger gives everyday examples of this interpretative mode of perception. We see, for instance, something as a table, as a door or as a bridge. This unthematic seeing-as is prior to, and more original than, reflective articulations through thematic predication. For Heidegger, we human beings *are* hermeneutical before we start to reflect on it.[102] Heidegger uses the terms *Auslegung* (laying-out) and *Interpretation* (interpretation), respectively, in order to distinguish between the basic mode of interpretative understanding and the explicit reflection on this understanding.[103]

Importantly, all understanding or seeing-as takes place within a context or background. Heidegger calls this the fore-structure (*Vor-Struktur*) of understanding which involves three elements: a grasp of the whole situational background or fore-having (*Vorhabe*), a guiding perspectivity or fore-sight (*Vorsicht*) and a preliminary conceptuality or fore-conception (*Vorgriff*).[104] While Heidegger emphasizes the priority of these pre-reflective or pre-linguistic levels of understanding over explicit interpretation, he also warns that interpretation should not be broken into pieces and that the fore-structure of understanding does not function independently of explicit interpretations. He emphasizes that understanding is circular: 'Any interpretation which is to contribute understanding, must already have understood what is to be interpreted.'[105] It would be a mistake, however, to view the circular nature of human understanding as a defect that justifies any wilful interpretation.

> What is decisive is not to get out of the circle but to come in it in the right way. This circle of understanding is not an orbit in which any random kind of knowledge may move; it is the expression of the existential *fore-structure* of Dasein itself. It is not to be reduced to the level of a vicious circle, or even of a circle which is merely tolerated. In the circle is hidden a positive possibility of the most primordial kind of knowing.[106]

---

[101] David Couzens Hoy, 'Heidegger and the Hermeneutic Turn', in *The Cambridge Companion to Martin Heidegger*, 170–3.
[102] Heidegger, *Being and Time*, 188–9.
[103] Couzens Hoy, 'Heidegger and the Hermeneutic Turn', 182.
[104] Heidegger, *Being and Time*, 191.
[105] Ibid., 194.
[106] Ibid., 195.

The hermeneutical circle is unavoidable and a necessary element of all human understanding. Still, particular interpretations can be challenged, not by leaving the hermeneutical circle, but precisely by entering into it.

These three themes of Heidegger's philosophy – phenomenology, *Dasein* and hermeneutics – have all impacted upon Rahner's method. As mentioned earlier, Rahner complements Maréchal's transcendental approach with a phenomenological component.[107] His decision to begin his metaphysical investigations with an analysis of the phenomenon of human questioning confirms this.[108] Thomas Sheehan formulates it as follows: Rahner seeks 'to gather, from what man [sic] *does*, the phenomenal evidence for what he *is*'.[109] Commenting on this phenomenological aspect, he notes that Rahner seems to assume Heidegger's analysis of *Dasein* by and large, therefore moving rather quickly from the pre-predicative level of everyday experience to the predicative level that concerns the truth of judgement.[110] Michael Purcell is more positive on Rahner's phenomenology. He argues that Rahner's transcendental reduction of the '"here" of consciousness', is actually 'phenomenological and existential'.[111] Responding to the criticism that Rahner's method lacks phenomenological rigour, Purcell maintains that Rahner takes up the contemporary phenomenological problem of accounting for what Jean-Luc Marion has termed 'excess' or 'saturated phenomenon' in a very distinct way.[112] Anne Carr argues that 'where Heidegger adopts and modifies Husserl's phenomenological method and aim of a regional ontology by extending the analysis beyond the intentionality of consciousness to the intentionality of the whole experience, Rahner's analysis, for the most part, confines itself to the realm of knowledge'.[113] This narrow epistemological reading of Rahner's method has been challenged by other scholars though, who argue that Rahner follows Heidegger's concern with *Dasein*, that is with all human activities of questioning and knowing, willing and acting, with the *Vollzug* of the human person.[114] Hence, while the extent to which Rahner's appropriation of Heidegger's phenomenology is debated, the fact that this element influences his method is widely accepted.

---

[107] See Muck, 'Heidegger und Karl Rahner', 262.
[108] Eicher, *Die anthropologische Wende*, 55–64, distinguishes three steps in Rahner's transcendental procedure: (1) a phenomenological explication, (2) a transcendental reduction and (3) a transcendental deduction. So starting with the phenomenological observation that human beings are confronted with the question of Being, Rahner engages in a reduction that searches for the transcendental conditions in the subject that enable such questioning, in order to deduce, finally, the characteristics and range of the possible objects of human questioning. However, as Kilby, *Karl Rahner*, 38, points out, this distinction is of limited use, because the three steps do not always occur together or as neatly or distinctly from each other in Rahner's work.
[109] Sheehan, *Karl Rahner*, 185.
[110] Ibid., 175–6; 186.
[111] Michael Purcell, 'Rahner Amid Modernity and Post-Modernity', in *The Cambridge Companion to Karl Rahner*, ed. Declan Marmion and Mary E. Hines (Cambridge: Cambridge University Press, 2005), 198; 200–3.
[112] Purcell, 'Rahner Amid Modernity and Post-Modernity', 198. See Jean-Luc Marion, *In Excess: Studies of Saturated Phenomena*, trans. Robyn Horner and Vincent Berraud (New York: Fordham University Press, 2002).
[113] Carr, *The Theological Method*, 24–5.
[114] See Coreth, 'Philosophische Grundlagen', 531; Eicher, *Die anthropologische Wende*, 57–9; Lehmann, 'Philosophisches Denken', 18.

Heidegger's attention to historicity also resonates in Rahner's work. According to Rahner, it is only from within the world, into which we are thrown, that we can engage in metaphysics. Ultimately, the metaphysical anthropology of the human subject, as the questioner of Being, serves to show that we are oriented towards history. As spiritual beings we can reach beyond the finite world, but the realization of this movement of transcendence only takes place within the historical and material world – hence his choice of the title *Spirit in the World*. This orientation towards the world and to history is intensified when Rahner starts to shift his attention from philosophy to theology.[115] The human orientation towards Being, developed in *Spirit in the World*, becomes more explicitly an orientation towards the historical world in which God's revealing word may be found in Rahner's second major work, *Hearer of the Word*.[116] After the introduction of the supernatural existential, Rahner emphasizes that the salvific history of grace fundamentally conditions human transcendentality, and consequently transcendental philosophy and theology as well. The historical orientation of Rahner's work will remain a constant theme throughout the subsequent chapters.

Finally, Rahner also appropriates Heidegger's insight into the hermeneutical circle.[117] The best example here is Rahner's starting point with human questioning. Our questioning of Being reveals an anticipation of Being, but as finite questioners we can never achieve complete and comprehensive knowledge of Being. This reflects Heidegger's understanding of truth as the dynamic interplay of disclosure and concealment.[118] Rahner appropriates this notion of truth as disclosure and concealment to counter the critique that his transcendental approach leads to a form of idealism that absolutizes the subject and erases the difference between finite humanity and infinite divinity. The theme will also recur in his writings on God, on the human person as mystery and on theology as the science of mystery.

Apart from these parallels between Heidegger and Rahner, there are also noticeable differences.[119] Rahner's appropriation of the term *Vorgriff* is markedly different from Heidegger's use and understanding. Moreover, while Heidegger maintains an immanent notion of transcendence, arguing that the horizon of human transcendence

---

[115] Fiorenza, 'Method in theology', 69. Thomas F. O'Meara, 'The History of Being and the History of Doctrine: An Influence of Heidegger on Theology', *American Philosophical Quarterly* 12 (1995): 359–60, also specifically recognizes this Heideggerian focus on temporality in Rahner's attempt to reformulate dogmatic teachings.

[116] Karl Rahner, *Hearer of the Word: Laying the Foundation for a Philosophy of Religion* [1941], ed. and with an introduction by Andrew Tallon, trans. Joseph Donceel (New York: Continuum, 1994).

[117] Muck, 'Heidegger und Rahner', 264–5; Fiorenza, 'Kant and the Kantian Problematic', xli xlii; Fiorenza, 'Method in theology', 77; Carr, *The Theological Method*, 26.

[118] Jessica Murdoch, 'Overcoming the Foundationalist/Nonfoundationalist Divide: Karl Rahner's Transcendental Hermeneutics', *Philosophy and Theology* 22 (2010): 379; Carr, *The Theological Method*, 25; Lehmann, 'Philosophisches Denken', 20.

[119] Raffelt and Verweyen, *Karl Rahner*, 28, point out that Rahner's engagement with Heidegger is not merely theological but is also philosophical and that Rahner, despite his frequent use of Heideggerian terms, develops his own alternative to Heidegger's thought. Fritz, *Karl Rahner's Theological Aesthetics*, 16, is even more straightforward and argues that scholars all too often only focus on what Rahner took from Heidegger, rather than considering what Rahner brought to the conversation. In contrast, he argues that offers a constructive contribution because it resists Heideggerian and post-Heideggerian thought.

is pure nothingness, Rahner's notion of transcendence involves the revelation of pure Being or the mysterious God.[120] Speaking from his commitment to the Christian tradition, Rahner argues, contra Heidegger, that a phenomenological description of the human person is incomplete or distorted when the constitutive openness to divine mystery is ignored or denied.[121] These parallels and differences will become more clear in the subsequent chapters.

6 Conclusion

In this chapter I have contextualized Rahner's theological method discussing the main philosophical influences on Rahner's thought: the scholastic metaphysical tradition represented by Thomas Aquinas, Kant's transcendental turn to the subject, Maréchal's attempted reconciliation of scholastic and transcendental thought and Heidegger's phenomenological and hermeneutical philosophy. These varied influences account for the fact that Rahner's transcendental method has a high degree of idiosyncrasy. Rahner himself admits that his method is eclectic, rather than faithful to one particular school of thought.[122] I argue that this should not be considered a weakness, but actually comprises a strength of Rahner's theology which enables him to think about universality while respecting the necessary particularities of every theological position.

In the subsequent chapters, I will offer a perspective on Rahner's theological method that goes beyond a narrow Kantian conception of transcendentality. I argue instead that this method is fundamentally constituted by a *dialectics between transcendentality and hermeneutics*.[123] This is not an entirely new suggestion, considering that other

---

[120] Kreutzer, *Transzendentales versus hermeneutisches Denken*, 152–8; Sheehan, *Karl Rahner*, 128.
[121] Wolfe, *Heidegger and Theology*, 187. Sheehan, *Karl Rahner*, argues that Rahner uses Thomas 'to extort an affirmation of God out of Heidegger' (114) and that he sees Heidegger's thought as a 'propaedeutic to theological discourse' (312).
[122] Karl Rahner, 'Erfahrungen eines katholischen Theologen', in *Karl Rahner in Erinnerung*, 143.
[123] The term 'dialectic' has been used previously by others to characterize Rahner's theological method. Gerald McCool, 'Introduction: Rahner's Philosophical Theology', xxv–xxvi, argues that the dialectic in Rahner's epistemology recurs in his theology of mystery, theology of hope, eschatology, theology of the supernatural existential, theory of the anonymous Christian, moral theology and his pastoral theology. John M. McDermott, 'The Analogy of Knowing in Karl Rahner', *International Philosophical Quarterly* 36 (1996): 201–2, considers Rahner's idea of *Schwebe*, which he renders as 'dynamic oscillation', to be the central notion of his analogical understanding of human knowing. However, he is critical of Rahner because he views him as making the human intellect the 'starting point and norm for all metaphysics' (215). Not only does McDermott fear that 'objectivity is being forced into the straightjacket of subjectivity' (213) but he also criticizes Rahner's understanding of formal abstraction because it does not yield stable and conceptual knowledge (216). Patrick Burke has continued McDermott's line of critique in his book *Reinterpreting Rahner: A Critical Study of His Major Themes* (New York: Fordham University Press, 2002). Burke identifies a structure of 'dialectical analogy' at the heart of Rahner's approach, through which Rahner 'oscillated constantly between unifying dynamism and conceptual distinction' (viii). Like McDermott, however, Burke argues that the fundamental deficiency of Rahner's system is the weak role of the concept in his epistemology. Consequently, 'Rahner's dialectical analogy, and with it his entire system, fails to ground itself fully' (298). For a critical discussion of Burke's reading of Rahner, see Robert Masson, 'Interpreting Rahner's Metaphoric Logic', *Theological Studies* 71 (2010): 380–409, esp. 387–91.

scholars too have variously argued that Rahner's method can be called a 'hermeneutical transcendental Thomism'[124] or 'transcendental hermeneutics'.[125] However, up until now these assertions have been justified rather succinctly, often with primary reference only to Rahner's early work. For this reason, I intend to provide a fuller and more comprehensive substantiation of the hypothesis that Rahner's method is characterized by a dialectics between transcendentality and hermeneutics. I develop this thesis in the three subsequent chapters.

---

[124] Thomas Sheehan, 'Metaphysics and Bivalence: On Karl Rahner's *Geist in Welt*', *The Modern Schoolman* 63 (1985): 22. Sheehan, *Karl Rahner*, 180, argues that Rahner's subject matter and his method are ultimately the same, namely hermeneutics. Rahner's metaphysics is 'a hermeneutics (explication) of what man already is and knows. And the method for explicating man's condition is to cut through the surface of what he says and does, so as to unfold their hidden implications'.

[125] Murdoch, 'Overcoming the Foundationalist', 373–87; Ingolf U. Dalferth, 'Hermeneutische Theologie – heute?', in *Hermeneutische Theologie – heute?*, ed. Ingolf U. Dalferth, Pierre Bühler, and Andreas Hunziker (Tübingen: Mohr Siebeck, 2013), 23.

3

Oscillating between heaven and earth: Human questioning as locus theologicus

1 Introduction

This chapter comprises the basis of my argument that Rahner's theology is characterized by a fundamental dialectic between transcendental and hermeneutical elements. In the first step, I will examine this interrelation by retracing the central structure of Rahner's metaphysics of knowledge as developed in *Spirit in the World*. Describing and analysing this dialectic serve to dislodge the common misconception that Rahner is a transcendental idealist advocating a reductive subjectivism. While he is rightfully considered a pioneer of the turn to the subject in Catholic theology, it is fundamentally important to recognize that Rahner conceptualizes the human person as *schwebende Mitte* (suspended mid-point), oscillating between metaphysical transcendence and worldly immanence. The crux of *Spirit in the World* is that human beings are *transcending the world* precisely by virtue of their being *in the world*. Rahner explicates this ontological dialectic through his account of human knowing as an epistemological dialectic, between the faculties of sensibility and intellect. This incarnational epistemology is based upon a notion of human subjectivity which concerns the realization of (self)transcendence through the encounter with worldly otherness. The dialectic between hermeneutics and transcendentality is also instructive in explaining Rahner's understanding of categorial metaphysics and its inherent limitations. Finally, the dialectic that is characteristic of human being and knowing is appropriated theologically in the discussion of the *Vorgriff* (pre-apprehension). With the help of this concept, Rahner thematizes a dialectic between the anticipatory disclosure of God and the concealment of God, which avoids the postmodern critique of onto-theology.

The important opening reflections of *Spirit in the World* offer a good starting point to develop this argument. Over the course of these dense pages, Rahner presents in a nutshell the key features of his transcendental-hermeneutical metaphysics. I then consider several critiques that portray Rahner as a subjectivist to explain that these critiques miss certain key elements of Rahner's theory of knowledge. Re-reading Rahner's metaphysics of knowledge focusing upon the dialectic of transcendental and hermeneutical aspects the subjectivist critique is countered. This leads me to a discussion of the distinct roles played by sensibility and the intellect in Rahner's incarnational epistemology and to an investigation of Rahner's famous notion of the *Vorgriff*. Situating the *Vorgriff* within Rahner's metaphysics of knowledge shows its theological relevance. Finally, I elaborate upon the main insights yielded from this re-reading of Rahner's metaphysics of knowledge: (1) the notion of a decentred subjectivity, (2) the concept of a categorial metaphysics and (3) the tension between anticipating disclosure and the hiddenness of God in natural theology.

Before I turn to Rahner's argument, I must first tend to a methodological issue. There is considerable discussion as to whether Rahner's metaphysics of knowledge should be considered in conjunction with his theology, or whether it should rather be considered independently as a work of 'free-standing' philosophy.[1] Rahner's own remarks in response to this question are not unambiguous. In the accompanying note to *Spirit in the World*, he emphasizes the philosophical character of his work.[2] Yet, at the end of the book, he states: 'Everything that we tried to grasp of Thomas's metaphysics of knowledge is situated by Thomas within the context of a theological endeavor'.[3] In other words, the philosophical metaphysics operates in the service of a theological project. I contend that a similar interconnectedness between philosophy and theology can also be seen to operate in Rahner's own work. This matter will be discussed in greater detail in Chapter 5. In the discussion that follows here, I will refrain from approaching Rahner's work either purely as philosophical or purely as theological. Rahner has a more complicated and richer view on the question of the relation between philosophy and theology – one which does not lend itself to simple dichotomies. I have decided, therefore, to engage with Rahner's epistemology as a philosophy that finds a fuller application *within* a theological methodology.

2 The phenomenon of human questioning

The question that guides *Spirit in the World* is how metaphysics is possible in view of the fact that all human knowledge is grounded in empirical intuition of the world of time

---

[1] An important part of the debate focuses on the modifications that Johann Baptist Metz made to the second editions of *Spirit in the World* and *Hearer of the Word*. I will not go into a detailed discussion on the question of how the second editions relate to, and differ from, the first editions. Extensive studies on this topic have already appeared; see, for instance, Thomas Knieps, *Die Unvertretbarkeit von Individualität. Der wissenschafts-philosophische Ort der Theologie nach Karl Rahners 'Hörer des Wortes'*, Bonner Dogmatische Studien 19 (Würzburg: Echter, 1995); and Karsten Kreutzer, *Transzendentales versus hermeneutisches Denken. Zur Genese des religionsphilosophischen Ansatzes bei Karl Rahner und seiner Rezeption durch Johann Baptist Metz* (Regensburg: Friedrich Pustet Verlag, 2002). Examples of scholars who have emphasized the philosophical character of Rahner's argumentation in *Spirit in the World* include Eicher, *Die anthropologische Wende*, 1–13, Kilby, *Karl Rahner*, 13–17, Raffelt, 'Geist in Welt', 59, and Kreutzer, *Transzendentales versus hermeneutisches Denken*, 95–100. Conversely, other scholars such as Carr, *The Theological Method*, 60, Lehmann, 'Philosophisches Denken', 11–12, Siebenrock, 'Glauben gibt zu denken', 77, and Fritz, *Karl Rahner's Theological Aesthetics*, 27–8, stress that Rahner's philosophical argument is, ultimately, theologically informed and should, therefore, be considered in close conjunction with these theological aims and purposes.
[2] Rahner, 'Begleittext', 436.
[3] Rahner, *Spirit in the World*, 408. See also Karl Rahner, 'Thomas Aquinas on Truth', in *TI*, vol. 13, trans. David Bourke (London: Darton, Longman and Todd, 1975), 13, where Rahner strongly emphasizes that Thomas is not a philosopher but a theologian employing philosophy.

and space. Rahner searches for an adequate response to Kant's critique of metaphysics in order to defend, along with the scholastic tradition, the continuing possibility and relevance of metaphysics, without resorting to non-sensory intellectual intuition or to innate metaphysical ideas. He turns to Thomas's metaphysics of knowledge in order to address this issue, and he provides an extensive discussion of one specific passage of the *Summa Theologiae* (I q. 84, a. 7), in which Thomas discusses the following question: 'Can the intellect actually know anything through the intelligible species which it possesses, without turning to the phantasms?' For Rahner, the problem at stake is one which is at the same time epistemological and metaphysical.[4] His solution, therefore, is one which employs both metaphysical and epistemological arguments. Rahner presents a metaphysical theory of knowing that seeks to show that empirical and metaphysical knowledge mutually imply one another. For this reason, metaphysics is dependent upon, and departs from, the world of sensible and empirical intuition.[5] Faithful to this insight, Rahner starts with a very particular phenomenon: human questioning.

Rahner begins his metaphysics of knowledge with the phenomenological observation that questioning forms an inescapable feature of human life; questioning comprises an essential part of the *Vollzug* of human existence.[6] In our striving to make sense of ourselves and of our world, we call things into question, even the very act of questioning itself. Yet, every answer that we provide can also be called into question again – a process which, therefore, necessitates a new round of questioning. Heidegger's influence can be recognized in this phenomenological starting with this fact of human questioning. Moreover, the emphasis on the open-ended and circular nature of questioning also reveals that Rahner has an acute awareness of the hermeneutical nature of human being.[7] Interpretations become questions and give rise to new interpretations. This hermeneutical circle of questioning cannot be ended or closed.

Rahner moves from an examination of the phenomenon of human questioning to one specific question therein, which is concerned with the ultimate ground or with being in its totality: the question of Being. While we may ignore any other question in life, we cannot avoid the confrontation with this particular question.[8] Rahner justifies this claim indirectly by employing a so-called retorsion argument. Put succinctly, a retorsion argument aims to show that denying or doubting a principle under consideration leads the one who rejects the principle into a fundamental inconsistency.[9] Thus, Rahner

---

[4] See also Fritz, *Karl Rahner's Aesthetics*, 26–7, who contrasts his metaphysical reading of Rahner's project as the explication of 'the manifestation of being to the senses in order to elucidate the full range of being's manifestation' to Karen Kilby's more epistemologically oriented presentation of *Spirit in the World* in Kilby, *Karl Rahner*, 17–19.

[5] Fiorenza, 'Karl Rahner and the Kantian Problematic', xliii, n. 39, observes that Rahner's rejection of a metaphysical intuition acts as a major corrective to Thomistic or neo-scholastic currents of thought. In contrast to his neo-scholastic colleagues, Rahner sees a much closer proximity between the thought of Thomas and Kant. See also Rahner, 'Thomas Aquinas on Truth', 18.

[6] Rahner, *Spirit in the World*, 57.

[7] See Fiorenza, 'Method in Theology', 77.

[8] Rahner, *Spirit in the World*, 58.

[9] Otto Muck, 'The Logical Structure of the Transcendental Method', *International Philosophical Quarterly* 9 (1969): 351, explains that the argumentation style of retorsion as *reductio ad absurdum* can be traced back to Aristotle.

argues that anyone disputing this inescapability of the metaphysical question actually engages in this very activity of metaphysical questioning. An explicit rejection of the question of Being involves an implicit engagement with this question, as well as an implicit answer. To give an example, the claim that there is anything resembling truth may be contested; however, this contestation involves an unavoidable appeal to truth, insofar as it claims to be true, and thus affirms the contested proposition. Similarly, all of our ordinary dealings with, and questioning of, the world imply a certain position with regard to the question of Being.

The inescapability of the question of Being implies something about the subject who raises this question. The metaphysical question is a transcendental question – one 'which does not merely place something asked about in question, but the one questioning and his question itself, and thereby absolutely everything'.[10] *Spirit in the World* is, therefore, a transcendental epistemological project that aims to examine the human subject as a questioning, knowing subject. It is also a metaphysical project though, because the transcendental analysis of this phenomenon of questioning discloses that the human person has a primordial, ontological relation to Being.[11] In other words, this project yields a metaphysical anthropology that understands human existence *as* metaphysical questioning.[12] This ontological determination of the human person metaphysical questioner has many interesting parallels with Heidegger's ontological analysis of human persons as interpretative, hermeneutical beings, even though Rahner refrains from using any explicitly hermeneutical language here. This hermeneutical dimension comes to the fore in the 'already-but-not-yet' character of questioning in particular.

2.1 Questionability and questionableness

A closer analysis of the metaphysical question discloses a tension between 'questionability' (*Fragbarkeit*) and 'questionableness' (*Fraglichkeit*).[13] On the one hand, the fact that we are capable of asking the question of Being discloses something positive; questionability shows that human subjects are somehow in the vicinity of Being. We would not be able to call Being into question at all without some basic familiarity therewith. On the other hand, the fact that we do not straightforwardly know, but instead must ask about and question, Being also shows our distance in relation to Being. The questionableness of Being, therefore, relativizes the power of

---

[10] Rahner, *Spirit in the World*, 58.
[11] See Thomas Sheehan, 'Karl Rahner's Transcendental Project', in *The Cambridge Companion to Karl Rahner*, 30, for an examination of the co-extensiveness of Rahner transcendental philosophy and metaphysics. Knoepffler, *Der Begriff 'transzendental'*, 57, explains the connection between the epistemological and metaphysical meaning of transcendental in Rahner through the idea of participation. Following Maréchal, Rahner reasons that the *intellectus agens* is teleologically oriented to absolute being and the participation in absolute being, consequently, forms the transcendental condition for the possibility of knowledge.
[12] See Knoepffler, *Der Begriff 'transzendental'*, 47–8, who describes in greater detail how Rahner understands the metaphysical question as a transcendental question, as well as an existential question, without ever collapsing these different concepts into each other.
[13] Rahner, *Spirit in the World*, 71.

the questioning subject. It shows that, for us human beings at least, Being is ultimately 'indefinable'.[14] Alternatively, Rahner also states that Being is something we 'know of' and which is therefore *bekannt*, but which we do not really know and which is therefore not *erkannt*, in order to express the ambiguous and dialectical relation between the human knower and Being.[15]

The analysis of the metaphysical question in terms of questionability and questionableness gives rise to two concepts that play an important role in Rahner's epistemology. The element of questionability is developed with the notion of the *Vorgriff* or pre-apprehension of Being. This *Vorgriff* serves as a transcendental condition, enabling objective knowledge of limited and finite entities. The element of questionableness reappears in Rahner's reflections on the finite and limited nature of human being and knowing. It also returns in the notion of the 'non-objectivity' (*Ungegenständlichkeit*) of Being and in its function as an unthematic horizon in human knowing. Both elements will be developed below.

In view of this hermeneutical character of metaphysical questioning, Rahner concludes that human being is marked by a fundamental paradox: 'He is already with being in its totality (*beim Sein im Ganzen*); otherwise, how could he ask about it … and still he is not yet that, he is still nothing … for precisely what he does is *ask* what he means when he asks about being in its totality.'[16] Consequently, the metaphysical question entails a peculiar duality and unity. The question of Being provides the point of departure for metaphysics, but as a question it also manifests the inherent limits of any metaphysics. Rahner clarifies the human person's paradoxical constitution through a discussion of two fundamental principles that undergird his entire metaphysics of knowledge. In the first instance, he attends to the phenomenological fact that the question of Being does not come to us human beings purely or by way of some sort of intellectual intuition, but instead originates from our situatedness in the world. Human being in the world, our sensible contact with material objects, forms the condition of the possibility of our asking the question of Being. In the second instance, Rahner puts forward the scholastic principle of the unity – or convertibility – of Being and knowing. This principle serves to explain the vast scope of human knowing and the consequent ability to engage in metaphysics. Yet, Rahner also marks out the limitations of human subjectivity and reaffirms the intrinsic link that metaphysics has with sensibility through an analogical rendering of this principle.

2.2 Materialist metaphysics of knowledge

Rahner describes the human person as a metaphysical questioner. However, it would be wrong to conclude from this that his epistemology centres upon an other-worldly domain or that he discounts the empirical and historical world. Quite to the contrary, Rahner firmly holds that human beings are first and foremost *in and with the world*. All of our questioning, including metaphysical questioning, arises from 'the things of

---

[14] Ibid.
[15] Rahner, *Hearer of the Word*, 28.
[16] Rahner, *Spirit in the World*, 60.

the world, he himself with his corporeality and with all that belongs to the realm and to the environment of this corporeal life'.[17] Thomas expresses this corporeal and affective dimension of human knowing asserting that receptive corporeality and turning to the phantasms are essential to human knowledge. Hence, as Denys Turner argues, it is proper to describe Thomas as a *materialist*, contrary to his contemporaries such as Bonaventure:

> Thomas seems just a lot earthier, and in no connection does he stand out more clearly as materialistically inclined than in his account of the natural object of the human mind. Thomas thought that the mind's natural object ... is the world of material objects into which, by way of their bodies, human beings are inserted.[18]

Rahner, then, following Thomas, maintains that the human person 'dwells on earth and it is not given to him to exchange this dwelling place for a heavenly one at his own discretion'.[19] Thus, it is only through our physical contact with this world that questioning and knowing can occur. Human knowing can, therefore, be described as 'knowing being-with-the-world' (*ein wissendes Bei-der-Welt-Sein*).[20] Like Thomas, Rahner uses the term 'receptivity' to characterize this corporeal, affective dimension of human knowing. Yet, this fundamental materialist orientation notwithstanding, human knowledge is not confined to the material world. Our ability to put every material object into question shows that we are aware of the finitude and limitations of worldly material entities. It is precisely this insight into the finitude of worldly things that impels us to ask about Being.

The assertion that our being with the world also discloses Being as such rests upon the important, but not uncontroversial, metaphysical principle of the unity of being and knowing. Rahner formulates this principle in *Spirit in the World* as 'being and knowing as original unity in being-present-to-self (*Beisichsein*)'.[21] The centrality of this principle attests to the fact that Rahner expressly seeks to develop a *metaphysics* of knowledge. Peter Eicher characterizes this move as a transcendental deduction; that is Rahner deduces the ontological principle of the identity of Being and knowing from the phenomenon of human questioning.[22] This principle is then used to explain the particular mode of human knowing as it is constituted by sensibility and intellect.

Rahner argues that intelligibility is a determination of every being. Hence, it is transcendental in the scholastic sense. The scholastic dictum holds that *omne ens*

---

[17] Ibid., 62.
[18] Denys Turner, *Thomas Aquinas: A Portrait* (New Haven: Yale University Press, 2013), 52.
[19] Rahner, *Spirit in the World*, 62.
[20] Ibid., 63. Raffelt and Verweyen, *Karl Rahner*, 36, note that Rahner's use of particular terms, such as *Bei-der-Welt-Sein*, manifests Heidegger's influence, despite the fact that he refers to Thomas rather than to Heidegger.
[21] Rahner, *Spirit in the World*, 68. Bob Hurd, 'Being is Being-Present-to-Itself: Rahner's Key to Aquinas's Metaphysics', *The Thomist* 52 (1988): 63–78, argues that this understanding of Being as *Beisichsein* acts as Rahner's 'hermeneutical key' to Thomas, which explains why Rahner interprets Thomas differently than the 'conventional Neo-Scholastic'. Eicher, *Die anthropologische Wende*, 172–3, calls this principle of the identity of being and knowing the 'speculative principle' of Rahner's ontological anthropology.
[22] Eicher, *Die anthropologische Wende*, 172–3. See also Raffelt, 'Geist in Welt', 68.

est verum (everything that is, is true).²³ Consequently, every being has an intrinsic ordination towards possible knowledge and, hence, towards a possible knower.²⁴ Rahner develops this principle in a modern transcendental manner. He considers it to be the *a priori* condition for the possibility that we can know anything at all. Ordinarily, our claim to knowledge about some reality implies that this reality exists. Rahner explains the possibility of this *factual* convergence of knowing and Being by positing a more original, *essential* unity of Being and knowing. Assuming the original unity of being and knowing leads to the reciprocal determination of subjectivity and ontology:

> Knowing is the being-present-to-self of being and this being-present-to-self is the being of the existent. ... Being is the one ground which lets knowing and being-known spring out of itself as its own characteristics, and thus grounds the intrinsic possibility of an antecedent, essential, intrinsic relation of both of them to each other. Knowing is the subjectivity of being itself.²⁵

This formulation, especially the term 'being-present-to-self' (*Beisichsein*), bears an unmistakeable resemblance to German idealism.²⁶ It may call to mind the Hegelian concept of absolute subjectivity or absolute spirit. Rahner is aware of this fact and makes strides to differentiate his own position from the pantheism or idealism that others might recognize in it. The strategy by which he attempts to draw out this important difference is by emphasizing that Being has different degrees of subjectivity; Being is stratified (*gestuft*).²⁷ Insofar as beings have a higher or lower degree of Being, they also have a more or less perfect degree of subjectivity. Pure Being certainly has the capacity of 'absolute consciousness' or of 'perfect knowing'. Yet, Rahner associates this absolute or pure Being not with human subjectivity, but with God.²⁸ On the other side of the spectrum we find matter or *materia prima*. Matter cannot be present to itself and, therefore, it cannot know, but must instead be the 'being of "another"'.²⁹

These two cases, God and *materia prima*, serve as limit concepts by which to show the specific constitution of human being and knowing. The human person is a finite subject, has a finite degree of Being and therefore also has a finite capacity to know. Our metaphysical questioning shows that we have no absolute consciousness, but

---

[23] See also the passage in the *Summa Contra Gentiles*, II, 96 where Thomas asserts that *quicquid enim esse potest, intelligi potest* (whatever can be, can be known).
[24] Rahner, *Spirit in the World*, 68–9.
[25] Ibid., 69. The approach of Being from the perspective of subjectivity has been criticized by various scholars. Kreutzer succinctly summarizes several of these critiques as follows. Rahner uses the perfection of being as *Beisichsein*, as normative paradigm for all being, rather than determining the finite (human) knowing as such (Klaus Müller); Rahner's understanding of Being as subjectivity is 'monistic' or 'pan-logical' (Peter Eicher) and Rahner's subjective understanding of Being as *Beisichsein* constricts Being. See Kreutzer, *Transzendentales versus hermeneutisches Denken*, 182–3.
[26] For comparisons between Rahner and Hegel see Denis Bradley, 'Rahner's *Spirit in the World*. Aquinas or Hegel?', *The Thomist* 41 (1977): 167–99; and Winfried Corduan, 'Hegel in Rahner: A Study in Philosophical Hermeneutics', *The Harvard Theological Review* 71 (1978): 285–98.
[27] Rahner, *Spirit in the World*, 72.
[28] Rahner, 'Thomas Aquinas on Truth', 29.
[29] Rahner, *Spirit in the World*, 74.

rather a transcendental consciousness characterized by limitations. We are paradoxical finite spirits. As corporeal beings, we are fundamentally related to the material world. Yet as spiritual beings, we transcend this world and reach out towards the horizon of Being. This double orientation is reflected in the two faculties that constitute human knowledge: sensibility and intellect. Thomas, following Aristotle, speaks of the human being as *animal rationale*.[30] Just as animality and rationality are not two parts of being human, sensibility and intellect can only be understood in their co-constitutive unity. In concrete acts of knowledge, these two elements are always simultaneously present; they can neither be reduced to each other nor be deduced from each other. The subsequent discussion in *Spirit in the World* serves to explicate the peculiar mode of knowing of rational animals.

2.3 Subjectivist suspicions

This discussion of the metaphysical question, and the related metaphysical anthropology, shows that Rahner's metaphysics of knowledge revolves around a dialectic of hermeneutical and transcendental-metaphysical elements. On the one hand, Rahner acknowledges that human persons are fundamentally situated in the world, which necessitates a hermeneutical questioning through which to make sense of themselves and of their world. On the other hand, Rahner also examines and describes the transcendental and metaphysical conditions for the possibility of human questioning and knowing.

Certain commentators on Rahner's metaphysics of knowledge have focused, rather one-sidedly, upon Rahner's conceptualization of the human person as a metaphysical seeker. Their concentration on his notion of subjectivity as *Beisichsein* has resulted in the emergence of a picture of Rahner as a transcendental idealist who espouses a reductive subjectivism.[31] The complaint is that Rahner has turned *too much* towards the subject. Hence, Rahner seems rather susceptible to the postmodern critique of modern subject philosophy. Indeed, accusations of distortive idealism and subjectivism have been directed at Rahner ever since the publication of *Spirit in the World*. It is necessary to examine these critiques before engaging in a closer reading of Rahner's metaphysics of knowledge.

In *Theology after Wittgenstein*, Fergus Kerr draws upon Wittgenstein's thought to deconstruct the modern picture of a 'knowledge-seeking self'.[32] He considers Rahner's theology to be a prime example of this problematic account of human subjectivity:

> Rahner's most characteristic theological profundities are embedded in an extremely mentalist-individualist epistemology of unmistakably Cartesian provenance. Central to his whole theology, that is to say, is the possibility for the individual to occupy a standpoint beyond his immersion in the bodily, the

---

[30] Ibid., 66.
[31] Joseph S. O'Leary, 'Rahner and Metaphysics', in *Karl Rahner: Theologian for the Twenty-first Century*, ed. Pádraic Conway and Fáinche Ryan (Bern: Peter Lang, 2010), 23, argues that Rahner became 'the prisoner of the metaphysical platform he had erected'.
[32] Fergus Kerr, *Theology after Wittgenstein* (Oxford: Blackwell, 1986), 169.

historical and the institutional. Rahner's consistently individualist presentation of the self emphasizes cognition, self-reflexiveness and an unrestricted capacity to know. It rapidly leaves time and place behind.[33]

Kerr, thus, accuses Rahner of a forgetfulness of bodyliness, historicity and language, which he attributes to the legacy of Descartes, as well as to the metaphysical tradition more generally.[34] Once this Cartesian myth of human subjectivity has been dispelled, 'it becomes too awkward and embarrassing to enter into debate with Rahner about the transcendental subject.'[35] Before assessing whether Kerr's critique is justified or not, it should be noted that Rahner had already been charged with subjectivist tendencies long before the term 'postmodernism' was coined. Shortly after the publication of *Spirit in the World*, Hans Urs von Balthasar wrote a review in which he voiced his concerns about Rahner's '*a-priori* idealistic approach' and with his depiction of the human person as 'a spirit oscillating between world and God'.[36] Balthasar fears that Rahner's 'Fichtean ethos', and his focus upon the transcendental structure of the human subject, is developed at the expense of the objective metaphysical and theological order.[37] His focus on the inner potential of the subject undervalues inter-subjectivity and seems unable to affirm the fullness of Being.[38] Balthasar's initial doubts regarding Rahner's approach only grew stronger over the years and culminated in a sharp polemic against Rahner in his book *The Moment of Christian Witness*.[39]

Assessing Balthasar's disagreement with Rahner, Rowan Williams argues that the crux of Balthasar's critique comes down to Rahner's philosophical starting point of human subjectivity. In effect, Balthasar is highly critical of the mainstream philosophical tradition between Kant and Heidegger because of the obsession with 'self-constituting

---

[33] Kerr, *Theology after Wittgenstein*, 14.
[34] Ibid., 140: 'The metaphysical tradition just *is* the disavowal of the mundane world of conversation and collaboration in which human life consists.' However, Kerr also writes about metaphysics in a more nuanced way. Insofar as metaphysical commitments cannot be ignored or denied, we have 'to learn to watch our language about ourselves', because 'the only way to resist, or even recognize, the sway of the metaphysical way of thinking is to listen to things that we say about ourselves in such a way that our metaphysical inclinations are laid bare' (187). This chapter seeks precisely to engage in this type of hermeneutical 'listening' in order to examine whether Rahner's approach is indeed as metaphysically or transcendentally closed as Kerr suggests that it is.
[35] Ibid., 170.
[36] Hans Urs von Balthasar, 'Rezensionen: Karl Rahner', *Geist in Welt*', *Zeitschrift für Katholische Theologie* 63 (1939): 377–78.
[37] von Balthasar, 'Rezensionen: Karl Rahner', 375.
[38] Ibid., 378–79. It is interesting to note that Rahner himself denied the suggestion, saying that he had never read a single page of Fichte (see Rahner, *Faith in a Wintry Season*, 53–4). Since the connection between Fichte and Maréchal is generally acknowledged, Fichte might nevertheless have had an indirect influence on Rahner.
[39] Hans Urs von Balthasar, *Cordula oder der Ernstfall* (Einsiedeln: Johannes Verlag, 1966). In this work Balthasar takes aim especially at Rahner's idea of the anonymous Christian which he views as a hollowing out of the particular identity of Christianity and a negating of the aspect of wonder that he deems an indispensable element of Christian faith. For a more detailed discussion of Balthasar's critique, see Eamonn Conway, *The Anonymous Christian – A Relativized Christianity? An Evaluation of Hans Urs von Balthasar's Criticisms of Karl Rahner's Theory of the Anonymous Christian* (Frankfurt am Main: Peter Lang, 1993).

subjectivity' in this tradition that negates 'the sense of belonging in a world'.[40] This leads Williams to remark that there is a parallel between Balthasar and the post-Heidegger approach to philosophical hermeneutics, insofar as both call attention to the historical, linguistic and cultural conditions of understanding.[41] Yet, while he denies that Rahner is an 'uncritical realist', Williams does see less of this rapprochement between Rahner and hermeneutics. He arrives, therefore, at the conclusion that 'Rahner remains firmly within the limits of a transcendentalist analysis of subjectivity' who belongs 'in that world of "onto-theology" and Cartesian introspection on which Heidegger so firmly turned his back'.[42]

This brief overview shows that the critique of Rahner's subjectivism is both long-standing and persistent. However, there are good grounds upon which to challenge this subjectivist reading of Rahner. A closer look at his metaphysics shows that the situation is, in fact, much more complicated than is often thought. While Rahner does turn to the human subject, there are also important decentring moves away from the subject at work in his metaphysics. Michael Purcell and Joseph Fritz have provided alternative readings to the dominant 'transcendental anthropocentric' account of Rahner recently.[43] Purcell puts Rahner into dialogue with Levinas, so as to provide an ethical re-reading showing him to be concerned not solely with cognitive intentionality but also with 'volitional and affective intentionality'.[44] Fritz seeks to present Rahner as a 'countersubjective' theologian, arguing that Rahner's notion of subjectivity is more nuanced than is often thought, and he attributes this nuance, importantly, to his parallels with – as well as his diversions from – Heidegger. He argues for an *aesthetic* Rahner who is interested in the manifestation of being rather than in the 'absolute subject'.[45] In this regard, it is also interesting to note that Fergus Kerr has recently retracted his previous critique. He now admits, hinting at the work of Balthasar, that

---

[40] Rowan Williams, 'Balthasar and Rahner', in *The Analogy of Beauty. The Theology of Hans Urs von Balthasar*, ed. John Riches (Edinburgh: T&T Clark, 1986), 23. Karen Kilby, 'Balthasar and Karl Rahner', in *The Cambridge Companion to Hans Urs von Balthasar*, ed. Edward T. Oakes and David Moss (Cambridge: Cambridge University Press, 2004), 257, comments on the dispute between Balthasar and Rahner by drawing a parallel between Schleiermacher and Barth, on the one hand, and Rahner and Von Balthasar, on the other hand.
[41] Williams, 'Balthasar and Rahner', 28.
[42] Ibid., 29–30. Williams does not offer an extensive explanation of his claim that there is little convergence between Rahner and philosophical hermeneutics. Apart from mentioning that Rahner does not engage directly with recent hermeneutical thought, he merely repeats a generally accepted fact, namely that Rahner did not engage with the later Heidegger. In a similar vein, O'Leary criticizes Rahner for failing to develop a 'hermeneutically sophisticated theology' that takes the historical and linguistic embeddedness of ideas and experience seriously (O'Leary, 'Rahner and Metaphysics', 33).
[43] Other scholars sympathetic to this alternative reading include Ethna Regan, 'Not Merely the Cognitive Subject: Rahner's Theological Anthropology', in *Karl Rahner: Theologian for the Twenty-first Century*, 121, who argues that Rahner's 'complex exploration of human self-hood and subjectivity' enables a 'more historical and specific consideration of the self', and Kevin Hogan, 'Entering into Otherness: The Postmodern Critique of the Subject and Karl Rahner's Theological Anthropology', *Horizons* 25 (1998): 181–201, who argues that, like postmodern theory, Rahner offers an 'authentic, semi-permeable, and historically mediated subject'.
[44] Michael Purcell, *Mystery and Method. The Other in Rahner and Levinas* (Milwaukee, WI: Marquette University Press, 1998), xii–xix.
[45] Fritz, *Karl Rahner's Theological Aesthetics*, 8–11.

'there is a more "dramatic" side to Rahner's metaphysics of the human agent'.[46] In a clear revision of his former position on Rahner, Kerr argues that *Spirit in the World*, in fact, forms a 'refutation of the so-called "Cartesian" picture of a self that is wrapped up in its own consciousness, with no direct knowledge of other minds or of the supposed external world'.[47]

Drawing upon the alternative readings, I argue that Rahner's metaphysics of knowledge is characterized by a dialectical interrelationship between transcendental-metaphysical and hermeneutical elements. Crucially, this dialectics guards against subjectivism and, instead, actually decentres the subject. In order to see the decentring moves, it is necessary to take account of how Rahner conceives of sensibility and history. I argue that Rahner's incarnational approach to knowledge places his transcendental approach in a manner that is actually much closer to the hermeneutical approach than is sometimes thought.

3 Incarnational epistemology

Rahner's understanding of the unity of Being and knowing leads him to define knowing as *Beisichsein*. Yet, at the same time, Rahner also asserts that the human knower always already finds herself *in-the-world*, as a corporeal being who knows through contact with the material world first and foremost. These two assertions seem to be at odds with one another fundamentally. Knowing as *Beisichsein* seems to imply that the first object or *objectum proprium* of human knowledge is the subject's own subjectivity.[48] Yet, Rahner follows Thomas's materialist position and maintains that the *objectum proprium* of human knowing is the *other*. The human subject has always already entered into otherness, prior to any concrete apprehension. Thus, according to Rahner, human subjectivity is in the first place marked by receptivity and by an openness to the 'absolutely other' (*das schlechthin andere*).[49] In other words, the receptive character that human knowing shows us is that human *Beisichsein* is actually a 'being-with-otherness' in the first place. Michael Purcell therefore aptly remarks that, for Rahner, 'sensibility, or incarnation, is the mark of humanity and (...) as receptivity and openness to exteriority, it is the cipher of subjectivity'.[50]

3.1 Being with otherness

Rahner offers an ontological explanation to reconcile the principle of knowing, as *Beisichsein*, with the observation that the subject knows by recognizing otherness. This

---

[46] Fergus Kerr, *Immortal Longings: Versions of Transcending Humanity* (London: SPCK, 1997), 176. See also 197–9 in the Postscript of the second edition of *Theology after Wittgenstein* (London: SPCK, 1997).
[47] Fergus Kerr, *Twentieth-Century Catholic Theologians. From Neo-Scholasticism to Nuptial Mystery* (Oxford: Blackwell, 2007), 90.
[48] Rahner, *Spirit in the World*, 78.
[49] Ibid., 80.
[50] Purcell, *Mystery and Method*, 76.

explanation centres on the argument that the subject becomes in fact the 'Being' of the other in knowing. This involves a transcendental deduction of the nature of sensibility. The primary human orientation towards material otherness characterizes its mode of knowing. As mentioned earlier, *materia prima* cannot actualize a knowledge of itself, but is instead 'real and empty potency' which requires a knower to be-with-herself.[51] The human subject becomes the Being of material otherness through sensibility: 'If the world is to be the first and only intuition, then human intuition must be sensible, the being of the one intuiting must the being of the other, of matter.'[52] Thus, human *Beisichsein* is fundamentally a 'being-with-otherness' and, given that this other is material, human knowing is necessarily sensible knowing.

Rahner turns to the scholastic concept of *species* (impression) and its role in the medium of sensibility in order to explain how the receptive knower is materially related to the individual object of sensible knowing.[53] It would be a misunderstanding to view the senses through which the material things enter into the knowing subject.[54] Rather, the *species sensibilis* must be understood as something *in* the thing itself that is projected *unto* the medium of sensibility:

> The species is a determination of the object itself in a such a way that the object has it as its own property insofar as it produces in the medium of sensibility as its own, as making it manifest as its 'self-realization' (*Selbstvollzug*). Therefore, on the one hand, the species brings the object in its own self to givenness, yet on the other hand it can be understood as its 'representative effect'.[55]

Rahner reaffirms the metaphysical realism of Thomas by employing the concept of *species*. The *species sensibilis* is the self-giving of the object, through the medium of sensibility, to the knowing subject. On the one hand, it is an ontological explanation of how otherness can manifest itself to the human knower through the medium of sensibility. Through the medium of sensibility, this other material object comes to self-reflexiveness, to consciousness and to *Selbstvollzug*. On the other hand, the concept of *species* also explains that human beings realize their own subjectivity in being with the otherness of the world.[56] Rahner then explains that sensibility can only take place within the *a priori* conditions of time and space.[57] This ontological explanation of the phenomenon of receptive knowing, thus, results in an understanding of human

---

[51] Rahner, *Spirit in the World*, 80.
[52] Ibid., 82.
[53] Siebenrock, 'Glauben gibt zu denken', 81 argues that the notion of *species* forms the key ontological concept to understanding how Rahner accounts for the unity of the knower and of the known. For a more extensive discussion of the concept of *species* see Carr, *The Theological Method*, 69–73.
[54] Rahner, *Spirit in the World*, 45.
[55] Ibid., 88.
[56] Ibid., 92. James J. Conlon, 'Karl Rahner's Theory of Sensation', *The Thomist* 41 (1977): 416, considers this conjunction of the 'sensibility's self-actualization' and 'the self-realization of the sensed-object' to be the crux of Rahner's theory of sensation. For Conlon, Rahner's understanding of sensibility 'does not mutilate othernesses, but is the means for their perfection'.
[57] Rahner, *Spirit in the World*, 115.

subjectivity as being always already in the exteriority of the world by way of sensibility. It is this being-in-the-world that marks the specific form of human subjectivity.

The concept of human subjectivity as being-with-otherness opens the way by which to conceive alternatively of the traditional epistemological problematic of the gap between subject and object. Rahner is critical of an epistemological outlook that considers knowledge purely as 'intentionality', because this emphasizes the distance between subject and object.[58] By contrast, Rahner argues that human beings are always already *with* objects of cognition. Thus, he concludes:

> Thus for the Thomistic metaphysics of knowledge the problem does not lie in bridging the gap between knowing and object by a 'bridge' of some kind: such a 'gap' is merely a pseudo-problem. Rather the problem is how the known, which is identical with the knower, can stand over against the knower as other, and how there can be a knowledge which receives another as such. It is not a question of 'bridging' a gap, but of understanding how the gap is possible at all.[59]

Rahner's account of sensibility seeks to address one element of this problem, namely, the question of how receptive knowledge of *another as such* is possible. Yet, sensibility alone cannot adequately explain the workings of human knowing. If the human subject were to remain simply with the other, which she encounters through sensibility, the subject would have lost any form of consciousness and simply be lost in otherness. Human *Beisichsein* thus cannot be merely 'being with otherness'. Rather, human subjectivity is characterized as a 'suspended mid-point' (*schwebende Mitte*) which oscillates between abandonment to material otherness and intrinsic independence over against material otherness.[60] Hence, after having established sensibility in order to account for the fact that human knowledge departs from being *with* material objects, even to the extent of becoming lost in material otherness, the next question which presents itself concerns how the human knower can differentiate herself over and against material otherness in order to recognize the other *as* other. To answer this question, it is necessary to consider another element of human knowledge: the role of the intellect.

3.2 Transcending otherness

Knowing is more than sensible intuition. The unity of subject and object, which is established in sensibility, must be followed by a moment of separation, in which the

---

[58] Ibid., 69. Intentionality is, of course, the key word that the phenomenological philosophical tradition (following Husserl and Heidegger) uses to characterize the relation between human subjectivity and objects of human consciousness. See Robert Sokolowski, *Introduction to Phenomenology* (Cambridge: Cambridge University Press, 2000). It is not clear though whether Rahner's critical remark regarding intentionality exhibits a fundamental disagreement with the phenomenological approach. Vincent Holzer, 'Philosophy With[in] Theology: Rahner's Philosophy of Religion', *The Heythrop Journal* 55 (2014): 584–98, has more recently argued for a phenomenological interpretation of Rahner's transcendental approach, asserting that his notion of subjectivity shares important characteristics with Fichte's 'life philosophy' and with Michel Henry's phenomenology.

[59] Rahner, *Spirit in the World*, 75.

[60] Ibid., 81.

knowing subject distances herself from the material other and places herself *over and against* the objective world (*oppositio mundi*). The subject's ability to differentiate herself from the objective world is associated with the intellect. Through the action of the intellect the other is no longer undifferentiated otherness. In the differentiation of object and subject, the other becomes objectified and, conversely, the subject realizes her own subjectivity, thereby enabling the possibility of human experience of the objective world.[61] Thomas discusses this intellectual activity under the heading of *abstractio*. Rahner explains this abstraction, in line with the understanding of subjectivity as *Beisichsein,* as a *reditio completa in se ipsum*, a return by the subject from exteriority back to herself.[62]

Rahner's discussion of the intellect's role in knowledge builds upon Maréchal's work. Following Maréchal, he argues that the intellect performs two tasks in judgement, namely a 'concretive synthesis' and an 'affirmative synthesis'. The concretive synthesis involves the subsuming of particular things under universal concepts.[63] We can only know a 'this' (subject) in terms of having a 'what' (predicate). Thus, we apprehend a particular thing given in sensibility, such as a steel framework that has wheels, by subsuming it under the general concept of bicycle. The concept is universal because it can be applied to any number of particular things. Crucially, the ability to abstract a concept from a particular 'this', and subsequently apply it to another thing, reveals that the subject stands at a distance from the 'this'. In abstracting universal concepts from particular things, according to Rahner, the subject realizes her own subjectivity.[64]

However, this concretive synthesis alone is insufficient to constitute knowledge; the concretive synthesis remains merely as a potential and is only actualized in an affirmative synthesis.[65] Maréchal would say: the copula 'is' needs to be posited. In an affirmative synthesis, a concept is related to a thing as such (*Ansich*) and thus affirmed as really existing independently from the knower. Alternatively, as Karen Kilby puts it, 'One does not talk about one's concepts but *with* one's concepts, using the concepts to talk about something. The judgment, then, always points to something beyond itself – it intends so say something about something existing in itself, about an *Ansich*.'[66] Hence, Rahner's approach to subjectivity and knowing is fundamentally *realist*. As we will see below though, this realism has also idealistic characteristics insofar as it remains open to an infinite horizon of immanent reality. The intellect is able to differentiate subject and object, which in turn enables objective knowledge through concretive and affirmative synthesis of abstraction. Rahner then continues pursuing his transcendental line of enquiry by examining the condition for the possibility of this intellectual activity. This brings us to the crucial concept of *Vorgriff*.

---

[61] Ibid., 117–18.
[62] Ibid., 118.
[63] Ibid., 120–1.
[64] Ibid., 122–3.
[65] Ibid., 124–5.
[66] Kilby, *Karl Rahner*, 28.

4 The Vorgriff of Being

Thomas employs the notion of *agent intellect* in order to describe the intellectual activity of abstracting universal forms (concepts) from material objects, so as to make potentially intelligible matter into actually intelligible matter.[67] Rahner employs a transcendental deduction to explain that the agent intellect forms the *a priori* condition for the possibility of knowledge. First, he returns to abstraction, as the subsuming of particulars under universals, in order to demonstrate that abstraction entails knowledge of 'the confinement of form by matter' (*coarctio formae per materiam*).[68] In order to recognize a concept as being universal, it must be recognized as being limited (*begrenzt*) by the matter of the sensibly intuited 'this'. The concept must be more extensive in itself if it is to be related to other things. Crucially, the recognition of this material limitation is an experience of transcending (*Übergreifen*) in which a concomitant awareness of a broader field of possibilities emerges.[69] Rahner calls this concomitant awareness a *Vorgriff*. The term *Vorgriff*, usually translated as 'pre-apprehension' or 'anticipation', is obviously derived from Heidegger, but Rahner argues that Thomas uses an analogical concept, namely *excessus*.[70] He borrows from Maréchal the image of a spiritual dynamism to characterize the *Vorgriff*'s anticipatory movement. Accordingly, the *Vorgriff* is described as 'the dynamic movement of the intellect as such outwards towards the absolute totality of all possible objects of the human intellect'.[71]

Rahner explains his understanding of the *Vorgriff* further by using two images, namely horizon and light. He employs the term 'horizon' to characterize that to which the *Vorgriff* attains, what he calls the *Woraufhin* (whither) of human transcendence.[72] A horizon is both directional, offering us a perspectivity that enables us to navigate

[67] Rahner, *Spirit in the World*, 136.
[68] Ibid., 140.
[69] Ibid., 142.
[70] There is considerable discussion on Rahner's appropriation of this Heideggerian term in the secondary literature. Kreutzer, *Transzendentales versus hermeneutisches Denken*, 144–52, points out that Heidegger uses the term *Vorgriff* in *Being en Time* to explain the hermeneutical-existential character of human understanding, whereas Rahner uses the term in a transcendental-epistemological sense to explain the possibility of objective knowledge. Moreover, by connecting the *Vorgriff* with the scholastic agent intellect and the *excessus* Rahner also applies the notion of *Vorgriff* in an explicitly metaphysical sense. Sheehan, *Karl Rahner*, 204, too refers to Heidegger's hermeneutical use of the term arguing that Rahner's appropriation of the term is rather loose. Sheehan argues that Heidegger's term 'projection' (*Entwurf*) renders *excessus* more accurately than *Vorgriff*. However, Fritz, *Karl Rahner's Theological Aesthetics*, 72, responds to Sheehan's assessment arguing that Rahner 'recalibrates the *Vorgriff* to do something Heidegger would not have it do'. In view of the singularity of Rahner's thought, I am first and foremost concerned with how Rahner uses this term in his own metaphysics of knowledge and will, therefore, only attend to deviations from Heidegger's use of the term, insofar as these are relevant for understanding Rahner's own distinctive approach.
[71] Rahner, 'Thomas Aquinas on Truth', 24.
[72] Rahner, *Spirit in the World*, 143. Eicher, *Die anthropologische Wende*, 267, n. 7, writes that Rahner derives the image of the horizon from the philosophy of Husserl and Heidegger. A horizon here is both a border (*Grenze*) and the domain within this border. However, it is characteristic of the horizon that it always keeps moving with the one who moves it and that its borders, therefore, cannot be sharply delineated but are instead open borders that invite further searching. Rahner also uses the term 'transcendental horizon' (HW, 96). Knoepffler, *Der Begriff 'transzendental'*, 39, argues that Rahner uses the adjective 'transcendental' to explain (1) that the horizon is not empirically given as an object of experience, (2) that the horizon forms the condition for the possibility of objectifying knowledge and (3) that this horizon is only determined, as positive unlimitedness, by

it, and ever-receding and is therefore open and unreachable. The *Vorgriff* functions directionally as a transcendental condition for objective knowledge. However, the whither of this *Vorgriff* is never available to us as an object. It cannot be comprehended or grasped; it cannot become a *Begriff*, because this would imply the existence of another *Vorgriff* enabling such an objectifying grasp. This difficulty notwithstanding, when talking about this whither we cannot avoid conceiving or designating it as an object.[73] Importantly, Rahner duly recognizes and upholds the finite and fallible capacity of human knowing in emphasizing the *Ungegenständlichkeit* (non-objective nature) of the *Vorgriff*'s whither. He emphasizes that human knowledge remains marked by the restless impossibility of complete fulfilment, contrary to presenting an ideal of 'absolute' knowledge.[74]

Rahner also employs the metaphor of light in order to clarify the non-objective character of the *Vorgriff*'s whither.[75] The intellectual activity of the agent intellect (the *Vorgriff*) can be understood as the light *in which* a concrete object of knowledge becomes visible. This light should not be understood as an inborn, Platonic idea; this would give rise to ontologism – the misunderstanding that we can have a direct intuition of truth or being.[76] Instead, Rahner advocates an Aristotelian understanding of the *lumen intellectus* (intellectual light), emphasizing that all human knowledge departs from sensible intuitions.[77] The light enables us to perceive and to grasp individual objects that we intuit sensibly. However, the light itself is not an object that can be known (*gewußt*) or grasped (*erfaßt*). Instead, it is a formal *a priori* that is implicitly co-grasped (*miterfaßt*) or co-known (*miterkannt*) in every act of knowledge performed by the knowing subject.[78] This clarification of the non-objective character of the *Vorgriff*'s whither still leaves us with the question of its scope.

4.1 The scope of the Vorgriff

According to Rahner, the question of the scope of the *Vorgriff* can be answered with reference to Kant, Heidegger or scholastic philosophy:

> There are in the history of Western philosophy three typical directions in which an answer to this question has been attempted: the direction of the perennial

---

the transcendentals, that is the good and the beautiful. In the subsequent discussion I will primarily focus on the first two characteristics listed.
[73] Rahner, *Spirit in the World*, 143.
[74] Ibid., 145.
[75] Rahner traces this metaphor back to Thomas's concept of *lumen intellectus agentis* (*Spirit in the World*, 211–26), but the imagery has a much older lineage, used previously by Plato in *The Republic*, Book VI.
[76] Ontologism, or the view that we can have an 'immediate knowledge of God', was denounced by the Holy Office in 1861. See Decree of the Holy Office, *Errors of the Ontologists*, DH 2841-2847.
[77] Rahner, 'Thomas Aquinas on Truth', 24. This non-objective and formal, subjective *a priori* understanding of the *lumen intellectus* distinguishes the position of Thomas – and Aristotle, Kant and Hegel – from the position of Augustine – and Plato, Plotinus, Bonaventure and Malebranche – who, as Rahner argues, conceive of the *a priori* function of the *lumen intellectus* as an objectified idea perceptible to the senses (Ibid., 20–1).
[78] Rahner, *Spirit of the* World, 390.

philosophy which, in this case, goes from Plato to Hegel, the direction of Kant, and that of Heidegger. The first one answers: the range of the *Vorgriff* extends toward being as such, with no inner limit in itself, and therefore includes also the being of God. Kant answers: the horizon, within which our objects are conceptually given to us, is the horizon of sense intuition, which does not reach beyond space and time. Heidegger says: the transcendence which serves as the basis for man's existence, goes toward nothingness.[79]

Rahner advocates the position of the *philosophia perennis*, arguing that the *Vorgriff* attains to infinite or unlimited Being as such. The crux of his argument revolves around the assertion that a negation is always grounded in an affirmation of Being, rather than in negation or nothingness. Put differently: possibility is known from actuality, not vice versa.[80] While Rahner disagrees with Heidegger, he does use Heidegger's position to argue against Kant's position. For this reason, I will first discuss Heidegger's argument for the priority of nothingness, before turning to Rahner's critique of this position.[81]

In his inaugural Freiburg lecture, entitled *What is Metaphysics?*, Heidegger argues that the question of 'the nothing' (*das Nichts*)) is the true metaphysical question, because it is able to break the 'doctrine of logic' in metaphysical thinking.[82] It can do so because the nothing is not a being. As a result, the question of the nothing is able to resist the objectifying mode of thinking, that is the thinking of something. He explains this through a phenomenological analysis of anxiety (*Angst*). Anxiety is the event that reveals nothingness. It reveals the slipping away of beings as a whole, thereby making clear that we cannot get a hold on things.[83] The essence of nothingness is neither the annihilation (*Vernichtung*) of being nor a negation (*Verneinung*). It is instead a nihilation (*Nichtung*) that gestures towards beings by way of repulsion.[84] According to Heidegger, the nothing is prior to logical negation, as well as the transcendental

---

[79] Rahner, *Hearer of the Word*, 49. Sheehan, *Karl Rahner*, 312, argues that the attribution of these positions to Kant and Heidegger are 'dubious at best, especially in the case of Heidegger'. He maintains that Rahner wrongly attributes to Heidegger a *nihil absolutum* and that Rahner and Heidegger are actually far more in agreement, insofar as both hold that 'the *Vorgriff* does not land in an absolute negative nothing but points to something "more real" (Heidegger: *seiender*) than what is to be thematically grasped'. To support his argument for this convergence of opinion, Sheehan points out that the reference to Heidegger as the representative of this third position was dropped in the second edition of *Hearer of the Word* (Sheehan, *Karl Rahner*, 211; 214). Sheehan also argues that Rahner's introductory chapters of *Foundations* show that he came to realize that 'what Heidegger called "the Nothing" (*das Nichts*) was not a *nihil absolutum* but rather the withdrawing, self-hiding dimension of the disclosive process – i.e., the mystery'.

[80] Rahner, *Spirit in the World*, 184.

[81] Since I am primarily concerned with Rahner's position specifically, I will refrain from offering an exhaustive comparison between Heidegger and Rahner and instead merely provide a succinct overview of Heidegger's argument. For an account that focuses, in greater detail, on the convergence and divergence between these two thinkers, see Kreutzer, *Transzendentales versus hermeneutisches Denken*, 134–43; and Sheehan, *Karl Rahner*, 212–15.

[82] Martin Heidegger, 'What is Metaphysics', in *Martin Heidegger: Basic* Writings, trans. and ed. David Farrell Krell (London: Routledge, 1993), 97.

[83] Heidegger, 'What is Metaphysics', 101.

[84] Ibid., 102–3.

condition of the revelation of Being. We 'transcend' Being-as-a-whole insofar as we human beings have this fundamental orientation towards the nothing.[85]

In *Hearer of the Word*, Rahner effectively employs Heidegger's argument to counter the Kantian position, and he offers a scholastic argument to counter Heidegger's position on the scope of human transcendence by way of *Vorgriff*. According to the Kantian position, the *Vorgriff* cannot extend further than the sum of all possible sensible intuitions. Since our knowledge is limited by space and time, the *Vorgriff* can only attain to a 'relative limitlessness'.[86] To counter the Kantian position, Rahner once again resorts to a retorsive argumentation. In order to know that the totality of the sensible objects of knowledge is limited to space and time, a *Vorgriff* beyond this limitation is required to recognize it *as* limitation. This argument actually might remind of Hegel's argument in the *Enzyklopädia* that we can only know about a limit when we are already above and beyond such a limit.[87] A comparison with an idea of the totality or perfection is required to know that something is finite or limited, and this implies that the unlimited is already on our side, that is in consciousness. Kant, therefore, can only confine human knowledge to space and time if he has somehow exceeded this finite domain. But Heidegger's theory of nothingness offers an argument that shows that the scope of *Vorgriff* cannot be relative unlimitedness. Rahner, therefore, concludes that 'Heidegger is the logical outcome of Kant'.[88]

Rahner returns to the scholastic tradition in order to counter Heidegger. As we have examined earlier, the key metaphysical question for Rahner is not the question of nothingness, but the question of Being. He defends the priority of Being over nothingness through an argumentation that focuses on the element of negation in knowing. How can an individual being be recognized as finite and limited? Rahner agrees with Heidegger that negation is an essential element of human knowing, insofar as it enables us to recognize a being as finite and limited. Yet, he argues, contra Heidegger, that this negation is grounded not in nothingness, but in a *Vorgriff* towards a positive limitlessness.[89]

Rahner explains the priority of infinite Being over nothingness in a discussion of limitlessness in *Spirit in the World*. Thomas distinguishes between 'privative limitlessness' – an unlimitedness which pertains to matter – and 'negative limitlessness' – an unlimitedness which pertains to form.[90] Matter has a privative unlimitedness insofar as it is empty possibility or nothing. As long as it is deprived of form, it can be actualized in infinitely various ways. Form, on the other hand, has a negative unlimitedness, because it has an intrinsic repeatability with reference to material objects. Thomas holds that we human beings only know through actually existing things, that is through things that have form. Conversely, Heidegger maintains: 'Higher

---

[85] Ibid, 107.
[86] Rahner, *Hearer of the Word*, 50.
[87] Georg Wilhelm Friedrich Hegel, *Enzyklopädie der Philosophischen Wissenschaften im Grundrisse*, ed. Wolfgang Bonsiepen and Hans-Christian Lucas (Hamburg: Felix Meiner Verlag, 1992), 74. In 'Thomas Aquinas on Truth', 16; 21, Rahner refers to Hegel to characterize the difference between Kant's position, on the one hand, and Thomas's – or his own – position, on the other.
[88] Rahner, *Hearer of the Word*, 50.
[89] Ibid.
[90] Rahner, *Spirit of the World*, 152.

than actuality stands *possibility*'.[91] Siding with the scholastic principle of the priority of actuality over possibility, Rahner argues that knowledge of the privative unlimitedness of matter requires knowledge of the negative unlimitedness of form as its condition of possibility.

> It is always true that man knows the finiteness and limitedness of a concrete, ontological determination (of an existent) insofar as it is held in the broader 'nothing' of its potentiality; but this broader nothing itself is known only insofar as it itself is held against the infinity of the formal actuality as such (of being).[92]

Rahner concludes, therefore, that the *Vorgriff* does not merely attain to the nothing of mere possibility (privative unlimitedness), but to *negative Ungegrenztheit schlechthin* (absolute negative unlimitedness) which he identifies as infinite Being or *esse*.[93] This *Vorgriff* of infinite Being is the transcendental condition for knowing individual finite objects.

Rahner's rejection of Heidegger's argument that nothingness grounds negation is, ultimately, grounded in the postulating of the scholastic axiom that actuality takes priority over potentiality, whereas Heidegger maintains, conversely, that potentiality is higher than actuality.[94] In view of this stand-off between these two positions on the

---

[91] Heidegger, *Being and Timet*, 63. Commenting on this difference in priorities, Sheehan, *Karl Rahner*, 215–16, writes that Rahner wrongly understands Heidegger's nothingness to be the 'mere possibility of what is to be apprehended', whereas Heidegger instead considers nothingness within the context of givenness; namely, as 'the appropriation of man's excess' so as to 'allow the presentness of whatever appears'. Fritz, *Karl Rahner's Theological Aesthetics*, 60–1, attributes Rahner's disagreement with Heidegger to the former's affinity with German idealism. He points to Rahner's lecture notes on Heidegger, in which Rahner writes that he agrees with Heidegger insofar as he advocates a philosophical realism in contradistinction to idealism but that he disagrees with Heidegger's 'Apriorismus der Endlichkeit'. This position, Fritz explains, is inadequate because it 'refuses to account for the fullness of reality's scope' (61). See also Karl Rahner, 'Vortragsskizzen und Materialien – Zwischen Existentialphilosophie und Fundamentaltheologie', in SW, vol. 2, 444–5.

[92] Rahner, *Spirit of the World*, 152.

[93] Ibid., 145. Kilby, *Karl Rahner*, 29–31 criticizes Rahner for an unjustified equivocation of these two different kinds of limitations. She argues that the *Vorgriff*, as an awareness of a 'broader field of possibilities', only makes possible a recognition of the general limitation that a particular object is 'one thing and not everything' but which cannot be used to recognize a limitation of form by matter. Ryan Duns, 'Recovering Rahner's Concept of Being in *Spirit in the World*', *New Blackfriars* 91 (2010): 567–85, has responded to this critique, arguing that Kilby rightly notices that Rahner does not use the word limit univocally here. However, he responds that it is used analogically rather than equivocally: 'Form is limited by matter in a manner analogous to the way that every *ens* is a limitation of *esse*' (580). According to Duns, in order to recognize this analogical understanding of limit, it is first necessary to be attentive to the fact that 'the *Vorgriff* describes the relationship of the human knower to being, rather than giving simply a mechanistic account of cognitional processes' (581). Kilby misses this point, in his opinion, because she interprets Rahner's argument too exclusively, as an epistemology rather than as a metaphysical inquiry.

[94] See also Kreutzer, *Transzendentales versus hermeneutisches Denken*, 138–43, who similarly observes that Rahner's argument is merely supported with recourse to Thomas or the tradition more generally. Additionally, a very different and more formal contestation of Rahner's argument has been raised by Kilby, *Karl Rahner*, 44. Drawing upon analytical philosophy, she calls into question whether Rahner's transcendental argumentation actually succeeds, suggesting that it involves an 'illicit appeal to the imagination' by proposing one particular solution as 'the *only* possible one'. According to Kilby, Rahner fails to provide proof for his argument that the *Vorgriff auf esse* forms a necessary condition to explain human knowledge: 'To say "doing such and such is possible only if we

relation between actuality and possibility, it remains difficult to ascertain whether either Heidegger or Rahner presents the stronger case. However, Rahner is not merely interested in the philosophical dimension of this argument. He develops his metaphysics of knowledge with the explicit purpose of employing it within a theological argument. Hence, his philosophical account opens up into a theological direction because, by following the scholastic tradition, he connects the necessary positing of infinite Being with an argument for the affirmation of absolute Being: God.

4.2 Anticipating God

Rahner's argument that human knowing requires a *Vorgriff* of infinite Being develops into a theological argument when he starts to consider it in terms of a potential *locus* of revelation. How does Rahner move from infinite Being to God? It is crucial to note that Rahner conceives of the human affirmation of God in a very particular way; namely, as an implicit affirmation. Through this argument, he seeks to provide a reasonable explanation of the theological claim that every human person is related to God, but without wishing to claim that he has provided a proof for the existence of God.

Rahner emphasizes that Being escapes any objective grasp and is, therefore, never a first-order object of knowledge, in conjunction with the aforementioned non-objective character of the whither of the *Vorgriff*. Instead, Being is co-known in all knowledge of finite objects. Thus, it can only be a second-order object of knowledge – an attempt to express and describe the scope of the *Vorgriff*.[95] Since we are finite human beings that know receptively, we do not know Being directly, but only in conjunction with concrete acts of knowledge that involve sensible intuition. Rahner concludes that the *Vorgriff* cannot attain to *esse absolutum* (absolute Being), given this unavoidable limitation of human knowing. Once again we can see Rahner's attempt to distance himself from an ontologism that maintains the possibility of direct intuition of metaphysical realities and thereby neglects the necessary sensible and material nature of human knowing.[96] Consequently, Rahner argues that the unlimitedness, towards which we are oriented,

---

are so-and-so" is to paint a picture of what we are like, a picture within which it makes sense that we could do such-and-such, and then to issue an implicit challenge to the reader's imagination: can you think of any *other* picture which would also work. But if the possible cannot be identified with the imaginable, then even if his challenge were always successful Rahner would not have proved what he set out to do.' Kilby distinguishes Rahner's 'early' transcendental arguments in his philosophical work, that is *Spirit in the World*, from his later transcendental arguments in his theological work. She maintains that the latter are 'less radical and less ambitious than either Kantian arguments or the transcendental arguments of *Spirit in the World*, since the issue is not somehow to get behind *all possible* knowing and experiencing, but only to examine what is going on in some particular sphere or even element of our knowing – our knowing of a particular dogma' (35) Hence, she argues that while Rahner's argument for the *Vorgriff* fails philosophically, it may still function theologically (77–9).

[95] Rahner, *Spirit in the World*, 179–80.
[96] See Francis J. Caponi, 'Karl Rahner and the Metaphysics of Participation', *The Thomist* 67 (2003): 400–1, who adds that the theological reason for this rejection of ontologism is that it endangers the distinction between the natural and the supernatural orders. After all, only the beatific vision, that is grace, can fulfil an orientation towards Absolute Being or God.

is *esse commune* (common Being), rather than *esse absolutum*.⁹⁷ However, immediately after this clarification Rahner makes the controversial claim that there is a way in which the *Vorgriff* attains to God nevertheless. It is worthwhile to quote Rahner at length here:

> But in this pre-apprehension as the necessary and always already realized condition of knowledge (even in a doubt, an it-self, and thus *esse* is affirmed) the existence of an Absolute Being is also affirmed simultaneously (*mitbejaht*). For any possible object which can come to exist the breadth of the pre-apprehension is simultaneously affirmed. An Absolute Being would completely fill up the breadth of this pre-apprehension. Hence it is simultaneously affirmed as real (since it cannot be grasped as merely possible). In this sense, but only in this sense, it can be said: the pre-apprehension attains to God. Not as though it attains to the Absolute Being immediately in order to represent (*vorstellen*) it objectively in its own self, but because the reality of God as that of absolute *esse* is implicitly affirmed simultaneously by the breadth of the pre-apprehension, by *esse commune*.⁹⁸

This is a complex passage; Rahner's main assertion here is that the *Vorgriff*, which attains to *esse commune*, includes an implicit co-affirmation of the existence of *esse absolutum*. First, he argues that *esse absolutum* can potentially 'fill' the scope of the *Vorgriff*, and as such *esse absolutum* must at least be implicitly co-affirmed by the *Vorgriff* of *esse commune* as objective (or logical) possibility. However, the *Vorgriff* cannot attain to merely possible being (*bloß mögliches Sein*). The *Vorgriff* must attain to actual or real being (*wirkliches Sein*), in order to fulfil its epistemological role of negation. Hence, the *esse absolutum* that is co-affirmed in the *Vorgriff* cannot be grasped (*gefaßt*) as merely possible, but must be affirmed as real. *Esse absolutum* is a *Realmöglichkeit* (real possibility) that constitutes an implicit affirmation of the reality of God. Rahner can, therefore, say with Thomas: *omnia cognoscentia implicite cognoscunt Deum in quolibet cognito* (all knowers implicitly know God in everything they know).⁹⁹

Other scholars have reacted critically to this argumentation. Hansjürgen Verweyen accepts that human knowing requires a *Vorgriff* towards unconditioned Being. However, he argues that Rahner's move from objective or logical possibility to real or actual possibility is unjustified. God as realization of such a logical possibility is simply being presupposed here, rather than being proven.¹⁰⁰ According to Verweyen, Rahner's argument can be traced back to an Aristotelian principle that has subsequently been appropriated by scholasticism: *desiderium naturae non potest esse inane*.¹⁰¹ To argue

---

⁹⁷ Rahner, *Spirit in the World*, 181. Caponi, 'Karl Rahner and the Metaphysics of Participation', 400, notes that Rahner fails to give a detailed account of *esse commune*. Tracing the concept back to its use by Thomas, Caponi describes *esse commune* as 'the *esse* in which every *ens* logically participates, the act of existence that is common to all, considered universally rather than as received by any concrete entity. This common, created existence depends upon but does not include God' (382).
⁹⁸ Rahner, *Spirit in the World*, 181.
⁹⁹ Ibid., 226. See also Rahner, 'Thomas Aquinas on Truth', 28.
¹⁰⁰ Hansjürgen Verweyen, *Gottes letztes Wort. Grundriß der Fundamentaltheologie* (Düsseldorf: Patmos Verlag, 1991), 131.
¹⁰¹ Verweyen, *Gottes letztes Wort. Grundriß der Fundamentaltheologie*, 130–1.

that a natural desire cannot go towards emptiness or empty possibility presupposes an understanding of nature as being teleologically ordered. Invoking this principle within the context of a proof for God constitutes a *petitio principii*; God's order is presupposed to prove God's existence.[102]

Louis Dupré similarly remains unconvinced that Rahner has established a proof for the existence of God. He is willing to accept the argument that an infinite Being functions as the horizon of the affirmation of finite beings. However, this does not constitute a proof for God's existence: 'That the mind affirms Being infinitely does not imply that it affirms *an* infinite Being. Undoubtedly each affirmation of the finite as such implicitly asserts the possibility of a *more*. But must it therefore assert infinite actuality?'[103] The positing of the priority of actuality over possibility, or vice versa, provides no solution in this regard. According to Dupré, the notion of Being is neither finite nor infinite, but rather is indefinite. Hence, whether the totality of actual and possible things is termed finite or infinite depends upon 'how far one's ontological affirmation reaches'.[104] A positive understanding of transcendence, such as Rahner's, considers this totality to be finite. Yet, according to Dupré, there are no 'intrinsic grounds' to call this totality finite, and it must, therefore, be considered to be 'a choice' from a metaphysical point of view.[105] This critical note notwithstanding, Dupré remains nevertheless appreciative of Rahner's argument because it necessarily brings up the problem of transcendence and makes religious concerns meaningful and interesting for the metaphysical thinker.[106]

With the latter observation, Dupré actually provides a much fairer account of what Rahner in fact seems to be after when he speaks about God in relation to the *Vorgriff*. Let us then return to the text. Rahner stresses once more that, philosophically speaking, any direct grasp of *esse absolutum* is impossible in view of our human sensible mode of knowing, immediately after making the claim that the *Vorgriff*'s anticipation of Being also implicitly co-affirms *esse absolutum*.[107] Hence, he explicitly denies that his argument amounts to an *a priori* proof of God. The *Vorgriff*, and its whither, can only be known in *a posteriori* experience. He draws a comparison here with Thomas's five ways to demonstrate the existence of God.[108] Thomas argues that the affirmation of finite limited beings as real requires the existence of an unlimited *esse absolutum*.

---

[102] Verweyen, *Gottes letztes Wort*, 130-1. Building on Verweyen's argumentation, Kreutzer, *Transzendentales versus hermeneutisches Denken*, 196-201, too criticizes Rahner for simply equating affirmation with existence. Eicher, *Die anthropologische Wende*, 274 disagrees with Verweyen and Kreutzer, insofar as he argues that Rahner succeeds in showing that the existence of God is the condition for the possibility of human subjectivity.
[103] Louis Dupré, *The Other Dimension: A Search for the Meaning of Religious Attitudes* (Garden City, NY: Doubleday, 1972), 134.
[104] Dupré, *The Other Dimension*.
[105] Ibid., 134-5. Kreutzer, *Transzendentales versus hermeneutisches Denken*, 152-8, develops, in greater detail, the different ways in which Rahner and Heidegger understand transcendence and concludes that while Rahner views transcendence as going beyond transcendental subjectivity, Heidegger maintains a more immanent understanding of transcendence which binds Dasein more firmly to the world.
[106] Dupré, *The Other Dimension*, 135.
[107] Rahner, *Spirit in the World*, 181.
[108] See Thomas Aquinas, *Summa Theologiae*, I q. 2, a. 3.

Transposing this ontological argument into a transcendental key, Rahner argues that the affirmation of the real limitations of beings has, as its condition of possibility, a *Vorgriff* of *esse* which implies a co-affirmation of an *esse absolutum*.[109]

At first glance, it seems as though Rahner is seeking to rehabilitate the constitutive role of God for knowledge in response to Kant's argument that the idea of God can only be regulative.[110] However, in comparison with Maréchal's transcendental deduction of God's role in knowledge, Rahner's argument for the *Vorgriff* of Being and the implicit co-affirmation of God is more modest and careful. Rahner qualifies his understanding of the implicit co-affirmation of God by stating that it has the character of an 'unobjective unthematic consciousness', as opposed to a 'objective-thematic knownness'.[111] This distinction between unthematic and thematic knowledge forms an enduring insight throughout Rahner's work. It recurs, for instance, in his distinction between 'transcendental' and 'categorical'.[112] Non-objective, unthematic knowledge of the absolute is *a priori*. As pure apriority, it can never be raised entirely to thematic consciousness through categorical and reflexive interpretation. For this reason, thematic proofs of God's existence remain necessary, but the converse is also true. The absolute can never be purely *a posteriori*, because an 'absolutely unknown' would be completely unknowable.[113]

Hence, the dialectic between questionability and questionableness recurs here. Even though we always already implicitly co-affirm God, we never know God definitely by way of a comprehending grasp. Accordingly, the tacit co-affirmation of God is fundamentally affected by a hermeneutical circularity. Commenting on Rahner's use of the terms 'co-knowing' and 'co-affirming', Sheehan stresses the dynamic, anticipatory and interrogative character of these terms in Rahner's thought. Unthematic knowing, either of the being or of the affirmation of God, 'always remains *in via*', the unlimited scope of human knowing revealed in the *Vorgriff* 'remains a *docta ignorantia*, an interrogative knowing whose objective is a known unknown'.[114] Hence, Rahner's argument for God is far more elusive and careful than a simple and unwarranted move from logical possibility to real possibility. Instead of proving God's existence, Rahner points, in a philosophical manner, to an excess – a horizon upon which God may be expected to appear.

---

[109] Rahner, *Spirit in the World*, 181–2.
[110] Fiorenza, 'Karl Rahner and the Kantian Problematic', xxxvii–xliii, agrees that Maréchal and Rahner, despite their similarities, ultimately respond differently to Kant's claim that God can only play a regulative role in knowledge and points to the influence of Heidegger to explain this difference.
[111] Rahner, *Spirit in the World*, 182.
[112] Rahner's distinction between 'thematic' and 'unthematic' can be traced back to Heidegger's use of this distinction in *Being and Time*. Heidegger in turn follows Husserl, who originally distinguished between this implicit yet foundational element of explicit knowledge. See Harald Schöndorf, 'Die Bedeutung der Philosophie bei Karl Rahner', in *Die philosophischen Quellen der Theologie Karl Rahners*, 19–20. For the relation between Rahner's early reflections on 'co-consciousness' and his later distinction between transcendental and categorical, see Knoepffler, *Der Begriff 'transzendental'*, 80–1; 90–1. I will return to this important distinction in Chapter 4.
[113] Rahner, *Spirit in the World*, 182.
[114] Sheehan, *Karl Rahner*, 221. For this reason, Sheehan questions Rahner's assertion that the existence of absolute Being is 'co-affirmed' and proposes that we should speak instead of 'an ever recessive evocation of man's excess' (222).

5 The finite spirit: Oscillating between world and God

This extensive re-reading of Rahner's metaphysics of knowledge yields three important insights that are the key to understanding Rahner's project overall. First, his incarnational epistemology avoids a reductive subjectivism and, instead, advocates a decentred subjectivity which is fundamentally oriented towards otherness. Second, his reflections on the finite nature of human subjectivity lead to a reconceptualization of the possibility of metaphysics as categorical metaphysics. Third, his theological appropriation of metaphysics carefully navigates the disclosure and the hiddenness of God, without reducing God to an object of human knowledge.

5.1 Decentred subjectivity

Rahner seeks to show that human knowers are always embedded in the world, as well as transcending the concrete individualities of this world, through the elaboration of the roles of sensibility and intellect, respectively. However, by distinguishing these respective roles we must be careful not to conceal their unity. For Rahner, human knowing is essentially one; sensibility and intellect form a *unity in difference*. Contrary to the aforementioned accusations of idealist subjectivism, Rahner holds that human subjectivity is marked by the coincidence and co-dependence of abstraction and conversion, agent intellect and possible intellect, being-present-to-self and being-with-otherness, intellect and sensibility. These elements are the two sides of the same coin, which cannot act without one another, but rather require and complement each other. They attest to the fundamental dialectics between transcendentality and hermeneutics that characterizes Rahner's metaphysics of knowledge.

Converting to the sensible intuitions is an activity that Thomas associates with the intellect. To be more precise, it is an activity of the *intellectus possibilis* (possible intellect), whereas the agent intellect is associated with the intellectual activity of abstraction. Despite the fact that Rahner's discussion of abstraction is considerably more extensive and detailed than his discussion of sensibility, he states that the possible intellect forms the key word to understand human cognition.[115] Possible intellect is '*the most adequate and most simple conception for human knowledge and for human being altogether*'.[116] Conversion does not simply follow *after* abstraction, but instead forms an inner and intrinsic moment of abstraction. Abstraction is always 'rooted in the world' and involves a 'bringing along' (*Mitnahme*) of what is sensibly intuited.[117] Since the human knower, as a receptive being, needs otherness to know herself, this 'bringing along' of otherness forms the condition of the possibility of human cognition, enabling the human knower to return to herself in abstraction.[118] Human subjectivity

---

[115] Rahner, *Spirit in the World*, 240. He explains the characteristics of the possible intellect by drawing a comparison with angels. Since angels possess finite intellectual intuition, they also do not know receptively and have, therefore, no possible intellect (243).
[116] Ibid., 245 (italics in the original).
[117] Ibid., 230.
[118] Fritz, *Karl Rahner's Theological Aesthetics*, 70, concludes from the necessary moment of 'bringing along' in the *reditio* that 'the human subject actually relates to the world, not regulative, à la Kant,

is thus not realized by self-enclosed isolated reflection, but only by being in relation to otherness. Thomas Sheehan expresses it in the following way: 'Human being is an otherness that is always self-related, and a self-relatedness that cannot exist without being othered'.[119] This is the reason that Rahner's 'transcendental turn to the subject' might be more properly understood as being a 'turn to the subject-*in-relation*'.[120] This decentring orientation towards otherness is essential for understanding Rahner's notion of subjectivity.

To be fair to the subjectivist critics, Rahner's argument also contains elements that seem to distort the balance between the two faculties of knowing. His argument that the possible intellect 'creates' sensibility forms a striking case in point.[121] In order to come to herself, the finite spirit needs to have a receptive encounter with an other. To create this possibility, spirit lets sensibility 'emanate' from herself as her power. Rahner calls this process the *Versinnlichung* (sensibilization) of the possible intellect and concludes that the possible intellect must be considered to be the origin of sensibility.[122] For this reason, spirit, even though it is blind without sensible intuitions, can be considered to be more original.[123] However, it is important to read these reflections in conjunction with other instances in *Spirit in the World* in which Rahner argues for the mutuality and complementary between sensibility and intellect.[124] Thus, he also asserts that sensibility is the 'receptive origin' of intellect'.[125] Moreover, he affirms that the receptive scope of sensibility is just as broad and unlimited as the intellect's anticipating *Vorgriff*. Whereas the intellect attains to infinite Being, sensibility opens the human subject to the vast and diverse otherness of the material world.[126]

Nevertheless, Michael Purcell rightly observes that while Rahner does not simply ignore the world, his transcendental deduction of sensibility 'does lend itself, at least obliquely, to a certain Cartesian interpretation of Rahner'.[127] By awarding 'logical

---

but substantively', insofar as the subject becomes determined through what it receives from the world in sensibility. Fritz calls this the often-forgotten, 'aesthetic' element of Rahner's theory of human subjectivity.

[119] Sheehan, 'Rahner's Transcendental Project', 30. Fritz, *Karl Rahner's Theological Aesthetics*, 68–9, similarly concludes that a Cartesian understanding of subjectivity that conceives of self-knowledge – cogito ergo sum – as the *first* knowledge provides an invalid account of *human* subjectivity. Such a subjectivity 'seals itself off' from the world and fails to acknowledge that human subjectivity is precisely marked by a primordial turn towards the otherness of the world.

[120] Sheehan, 'Rahner's Transcendental Project', 32. Sheehan consequently arrives at a re-description of a transcendental first philosophy. This reconceptualized philosophy has, as its material object, the '*intrinsic relatedness* of the knower and the knowable', which requires a phenomenological reduction, and has the '*structure and source* of that correlation' as its formal object, which requires a transcendental reduction.

[121] See the critical remarks of Williams, 'Balthasar and Rahner', 25–6.

[122] Rahner, *Spirit in the World*, 247.

[123] Ibid., 240.

[124] Rahner variously describes sensibility and intellect as 'coordinate power' (*Spirit in the World*, 240) and of agent intellect and possible intellect as 'essentially complementary functions' (Ibid., 241). Commenting on the issue of emanation, Conlon, 'Karl Rahner's Theory of Sensation', 412, points out that despite the 'undeniable Hegelian overtones … for Rahner the otherness of sensibility which spirit has emanated is itself an openness to actual otherness, an otherness which is not simply a moment of spirit herself'.

[125] Rahner, *Spirit in the World*, 261.

[126] Ibid., 242.

[127] Purcell, *Mystery and Method*, 93.

secondarity' to the relationship with the world in sensibility, the world is not given 'proper significance' or 'sincerity', so that Rahner 'tends to the valuation of intellect over sense, of spirit over world'.[128] Purcell suggests a phenomenological correction, namely, to take the body's cognitive role more seriously. A sharper focus on the affective element of sensibility would also draw attention to the underdeveloped dimension of inter-subjectivity. Inspired by the thought of Emmanuel Levinas, Purcell proposes a phenomenological 'deepening' that conceptualizes human openness to the world in terms of 'vulnerability and woundedness'.[129] In any case, however, Purcell's reading of Rahner confirms that his epistemology mediates between subjectivity and objectivity, thereby avoiding a reductive subjectivism.

5.2 Modest categorical metaphysics

In the final part of *Spirit in the World*, Rahner attends to the question that has guided his investigations: the possibility of metaphysics. Rahner characterizes the human person as a *finite spirit*, based upon his elaboration of human knowledge as the unity of sensibility and intellect. As spiritual beings we are *quodammodo omnia*, capable of transcending every finite material object, capable of putting every answer into question again, oriented towards infinite Being. Yet, our subjectivity is limited, rendering our spirituality finite, given that we merely have a *Vorgriff* of infinite Being. As discussed earlier, this crucial qualification of the nature of human subjectivity goes back to Rahner's analogical understanding of Being and subjectivity.[130] Human subjectivity is intrinsically connected to the receptive nature of human knowing. Human knowledge originates in the world and is orientated towards the world. The human person 'is essentially ambivalent. He is always exiled in the world and is always already beyond it.'[131] We are finite spirits in the world.

This insight has important consequences for metaphysics and theology – two disciplines which are often regarded as 'flights' from the world to another transcendent world. Rahner's aim is to defend the legitimacy of the 'other-worldly' or metaphysical character of these disciplines by demonstrating their necessary worldly conditions.[132] For Rahner, in contradistinction to his teacher Heidegger, the fundamental

---

[128] Ibid., 89. Kreutzer, *Transzendentales versus hermeneutisches Denken*, 159–62, contrasts Rahner's understanding with Heidegger's understanding of the world. Heidegger is critical of cosmological views of the world and advocates, instead, an existential-hermeneutical perspective that views *Dasein* as transcending the world insofar as *Dasein* is hermeneutically active. Rahner, on the other hand, follows Kant's understanding of the world as the sum total of all possible objects of sensible experience and connects this with a scholastic philosophical realism. In contrast to Heidegger's hermeneutical understanding of the world, Rahner is, according to Kreutzer, primarily concerned with the 'objectification' of the world in knowledge. However, as will be demonstrated in Chapter 4, this view of knowledge as 'objectification' of the world is precisely what Rahner argues against, especially within the context of his reflections on mystery.

[129] Ibid., 94–5.

[130] Commenting on Hegel's influence on Rahner, Raffelt and Verweyen, *Karl Rahner*, 39, argue that by emphasizing the finite character of the human spirit Rahner remains closest to Kant's transcendental project.

[131] Rahner, *Spirit in the World*, 406.

[132] See also ibid., 63, in which Rahner already emphasizes that 'being-in-the-world' is the only place or *locus* for both metaphysics and theology.

Geworfenheit (thrownness) of the human person does not preclude the possibility of metaphysics and theology.[133] We are not locked into the immanent world. Granted, a metaphysics that does not depart from sensible intuition of the material world is impossible. Conversely, worldly objective knowledge is not possible either without the transcending *Vorgriff* towards the infinite horizon. Hence, worldly knowledge and metaphysics mutually require each other.

To explain this mutual relationship, Rahner reflects on the question of whether metaphysics is prior to sensible intuition or vice versa. He refers to Thomas's distinction between the 'principle of knowing' (*principium cognitionis*) and the 'object of knowledge' (*objectum cognitum*). As receptive knowers, who know through sensible intuition, the immediate or first object of human knowledge is worldly material, *ens mobile* or *physica*.[134] However, his transcendental investigation of knowledge has established that for this sensible intuition to become objective knowledge of individual concrete things, a formal *a priori* principle, namely the light of the agent intellect or *Vorgriff* of infinite Being, is required. This metaphysical principle forms the transcendental condition of *a posteriori* knowledge. A metaphysical or transcendental inquiry attempts to bring to explicit expression *a priori* principles that are always already operative in sensible knowledge of the world and are, therefore, implicitly known at first and only explicitly later after conscious reflection on concrete knowledge. Yet, by emphasizing the hermeneutical priority of *a posteriori* knowledge in this procedure, Rahner introduces an important qualification in his metaphysics of knowledge. I consider this to be a clear example of Rahner's recognition of the necessary hermeneutical and circular dimension of all metaphysical and transcendental reflection. Sheehan, who also picks up on this hermeneutical element in Rahner's method, argues that for both Thomas and Rahner, 'a second-order reflection on man [*sic*] in his fullness, a hermeneutics of his ever unresolved movement, is all there is to ontology'.[135]

This hermeneutically sophisticated understanding of metaphysics comes into focus more sharply in an important section that was added to the second edition of *Spirit in the World*. Rahner warns us about the danger of a 'formal apriorism' concerned with 'pure transcendentality'. Alternatively, he proposes the concept of a 'categorical metaphysics' – a metaphysics that is aware that her *a priori* character can only be realized through the *a posteriori*.[136]

> For every genuine, metaphysical *a priori* does not simply have the *a posteriori* 'alongside of' or 'after' itself, but holds it in itself, not of course as though once again the *a posteriori*, the 'world' in its positive content were able to be resolved

---

[133] See Purcell, *Mystery and Method*, 76, who contrasts Heidegger's 'fallenness in the world' with Rahner's view that the human person finds herself in a 'felicitous state of being declined as world, as sensibility, a declension which, as we say, opens the subject, or renders it vulnerable, to the advent of the Other'. Sheehan, *Karl Rahner*, 128, argues that 'what seems to separate Heidegger and Rahner is the question of the scope of man's transcendence and therefore the knowability or not of the term of that movement. Heidegger will be able to go only as far as man's appropriation by an unknowable recess (*lēthē*) whereas Rahner will see man claimed by the mystery of God'.
[134] Rahner, *Spirit in the World*, 390.
[135] Sheehan, *Karl Rahner*, 278.
[136] Rahner, *Spirit in the World*, 405.

adequately into pure, transcendental apriority, but in such a way that the *a priori* is *of itself* referred to the *a posteriori*, that in order to be really itself, it cannot keep itself in its pure transcendentality, but must release itself into the categorical.[137]

This notion of 'categorical metaphysics' dynamizes, while simultaneously problematizing, metaphysics as the reflection concerned with the *a priori*. As he observes in *Hearer of the Word*, metaphysics is always 'ein mühsame Sache' (a difficult thing).[138] On the one hand, metaphysics is concerned with the *a priori* – the things 'which one "always already knows and has known"'; on the other hand, metaphysics is also 'a human science. Therefore it is always and essentially burdened with the incertitude and the obscurity that belongs unavoidably to human nature.'[139] The latter remark can be read as a reference to the *a posteriori* character of human knowing, which necessitates a hermeneutical awareness of metaphysical and transcendental reflection. Insofar as we always and everywhere face the hermeneutical task of making 'sense' of our lives, by reflecting on our *Dasein* in the world through a reflection on *a posteriori* knowledge, all our attempts at metaphysical and transcendental clarification are marked by the ambiguity that is unavoidably bound up with this hermeneutical undertaking. Rahner, thus, admits the possibility of metaphysics, but it must remain a modest metaphysics which is attentive to the hermeneutical openness and limitations of human subjectivity.

In Chapter 5, I will explain how this reconceptualization of the role and the limitations of the *a priori* receive an important impetus from Rahner's theological reflections on the relationship between nature and grace. This leads to a so-called theological *a priori* or a concept of '*a posteriori* transcendentality'.

5.3 Natural theology and the hiddenness of God

In this final section I return to the question of the relation between God and metaphysics. Rahner's metaphysics of knowledge escapes easy qualification as either philosophy or theology. Even though *Spirit in the World* sets out to argue primarily in a philosophical manner, the theme of God recurs throughout Rahner's argument. Rahner associates absolute Being with God within the scholastic tradition. Insofar as the *Vorgriff* attains to Being as such (*ens commune*), Rahner argues that *esse absolutum*, or God, is at least implicitly co-affirmed in every act of knowledge. He traces the intrinsic link between metaphysics and theology back to Thomas, who argues in the *Summa contra gentiles* that 'first philosophy' is ordered towards the knowledge of God as its final end.[140] Insofar as metaphysics is concerned with 'Being as such', both 'common being' and 'first being' fall within its scope.[141] Rahner and Thomas are, therefore, onto-theological,

---

[137] Ibid., 405.
[138] Rahner, *Hearer of the Word*, 21.
[139] Ibid.
[140] Thomas Aquinas, *Summa Contra Gentiles*, III, 25.
[141] Rahner, *Spirit in the World*, 388.

inasmuch as both stress the relation between ontology and theology in metaphysics.[142] This raises the question as to whether Rahner turns God into an object in order to ground human subjectivity, with respect to the Heideggerian critique of onto-theology. The previous section has already demonstrated that Rahner's approach to metaphysics has an important hermeneutical qualification. Crucially, this hermeneutical sensitivity recurs in Rahner's view of the possible role of God within metaphysics and shows his critical distance from any onto-theological subjugation of God.

Reflections on God within the context of metaphysics are traditionally known as 'natural theology'. Rahner supports natural theology while also alerting us to its restrictions and limitations. Immediately after signalling this intrinsic relation between ontology and theology, he reminds us that for Thomas, absolute Being or God cannot be the object (*Gegenstand, subjectum*) of metaphysics: 'Metaphysics reaches God only as the ground (*prinicipium*) of its object, common being, and it is essentially impossible for it, then, to make the ground so reached another "object" in a discipline of its own.'[143] This qualified understanding of God, as 'principle' of metaphysics, was already suggested in the reflections on the non-objective character of the horizon that is opened by the *Vorgriff*. This non-objective horizon in turn presupposes a ground, an absolute Being, yet neither the horizon nor its ground can be objectified. As a result, and according to the Thomistic understanding, there cannot then be a 'special metaphysics' of God in distinction to a general metaphysics of 'common Being'. For Rahner, this entails an important limitation of metaphysics: 'Every natural theology … as a special discipline is, therefore, a repetition of general ontology or a usurpation of what can be possible only in a theology of Sacred Scripture.'[144] Natural theology, thus, can only deal with the theme of God in a very limited way, insofar as its proper object – common Being – anticipates or gestures towards God as its necessary principle. As a result, the metaphysical 'knowledge' of God remains at heart a *tenebrae ignorantiae* (darkness of ignorance).[145] Since metaphysics cannot produce a proof of God, it remains necessary to develop thematic proofs of God on the basis of positive revelation. Metaphysics is ultimately orientated towards salvation history and revealed theology.

To be clear, this is not simply a theologian's assertion of revealed theology's priority over philosophy and natural theology. Rather, it is Rahner's hermeneutical understanding of metaphysical and transcendental reflection which informs his assertion about the importance of the historical and categorical world. As receptive knowers, we start necessarily with a turn to the world. A second-order reflection on *a posteriori* knowledge discloses that our relation to this world is, in fact, sustained and enabled by a desire for Being as such. However, the term of this dynamic striving escapes our grasp; the horizon can never become an object. Rahner concludes,

---

[142] Sheehan, *Karl Rahner*, 275, observes that Rahner's transcendental approach makes him locate the unity of theology and ontology in the subject who *does* metaphysics, while Thomas roots this unity in the object of metaphysics, that is Being as such. For contestations of the claim that Thomas Aquinas's thought is onto-theological, see Jean-Luc Marion, *God without Being*, 2nd edition with a foreword by David Tracy and a new preface by Jean-Luc Marion, trans. Thomas A. Carlson (Chicago: The University of Chicago Press, 2012), 199–36.
[143] Rahner, *Spirit in the World*, 388.
[144] Ibid., 389.
[145] Ibid., 401.

therefore, that the human person is 'the mid-point suspended between the world and God, between time and eternity, and this boundary line is the point of his definition and his destiny'.[146] God is anticipated in the horizon of Being, but also remains hidden as 'the distant Unknown'.

6 Conclusion

In this chapter I have presented a re-reading of Rahner's metaphysics of knowledge, focusing on the dialectics between transcendental-metaphysical and hermeneutical aspects. I have argued that this dialectics is essential for understanding his anthropology of the finite spirit, his incarnational epistemology, his modest categorical metaphysics and his natural theology. In the subsequent chapters I will explain how this dialectic remains operative and instructive in Rahner's later work. Put succinctly, I argue that the hermeneutical dimension of his transcendental theology becomes more apparent over time. This can be illustrated with reference to the themes of history, experience, love and mystery.

The *Vorgriff* of Being discloses that humans have an extraordinary spiritual capacity of self-transcendence. However, the analogical understanding of subjectivity keeps this capacity in check and affirms its fundamental dependence on world and history for its self-realization. Rahner develops this incarnational theme in his reflection on the interrelationship between categorical and transcendental experience. Moreover, his theology of love brings to the surface the inter-subjective dimension of his anthropology. Rahner's turn to history is already prefigured in the programmatic statement on the very last page of *Spirit in the World*:

> And if Christianity is not the idea of an eternal, omnipresent spirit, but is Jesus of Nazareth, then Thomas's metaphysics of knowledge is Christian when it summons man back into the here and now of his finite world, because the Eternal has also entered into his world so that man might find Him, and in Him might find himself anew.[147]

The awareness of the limitations of metaphysics 'summons us back' to the 'here and now' of the finite world. If we are to learn more about the terms of our dynamic movement of self-transcendence, it will not occur by way of philosophical speculation or introspection, but through revelation. Crucially, as I will examine in the following chapter, Rahner develops his orientation towards the world into an orientation towards history as the locus of revelation. Still, even if this self-disclosure of mystery does occur, human knowledge remains open and incomplete. After all, Rahner's subject is a finite spirit, oscillating between transcendence and world. This is developed by bringing an analogical understanding of subjectivity into dialogue with a reflection on the mysterious and incomprehensible nature of God.

---

[146] Ibid., 407.
[147] Ibid., 408. Fritz, *Karl Rahner's Theological Aesthetics*, 211, calls the closing page of *Spirit in the World* 'the most hermeneutically determinative page of the entire text', because it shows that Rahner 'begins and ends with Jesus Christ'.

4

Hidden hermeneutics: The history of transcendentality

1 Introduction

In this chapter, I will develop the second step of my argument that Rahner's theological method is marked by a dialectical interrelation of transcendentality and hermeneutics. I begin by discussing several critiques of Rahner's transcendental approach that might seem to contradict the argument developed thus far. Rahner has been accused of being inattentive to various crucial elements that condition theological reflection, including the roles played by history, inter-subjectivity, language, culture and community. These critiques can be condensed into the claim that Rahner is *too* transcendental and *not sufficiently* hermeneutical. However, I suggest that these critiques have focused, rather one-sidedly and selectively, only on particular elements of Rahner's early work. As a result, they have missed the fundamental dialectic between transcendentality and hermeneutics that forms the heart of Rahner's method.

My alternative reading of Rahner offers a critical correction of these critiques and focuses on four themes. First, I discuss Rahner's growing attention to the historicity of revelation. His transcendental anthropology of the human person as 'spirit in the world' evolves into a view of a 'spirit in history', listening to God's historical word of revelation. Second, I analyse the distinction between transcendental and categorical experience with a view of contradicting the suggestion that Rahner was hermeneutically naive. Instead, his dialectical interrelation between experience and interpretation leads to the notion of a mediated immediacy. Third, I turn to the topics of love and inter-subjectivity and present Rahner's relational understanding of human subjectivity by exploring his argument for the unity between love of neighbour and love of God. This relational subjectivity further develops the decentring elements that are operative in Rahner's metaphysics of knowledge. Finally, I argue that reading Rahner's transcendental anthropology and theology through the lens of his reflections on mystery discloses the inherent hermeneutical dimension of his theological approach. This hermeneutical dimension transforms both the concept of human subjectivity and the theological use of metaphysical reflection.

2 The threefold charge of forgetfulness

The different criticisms levelled against Rahner are, in many ways, overlapping.[1] For this reason, it is difficult to delineate sharply these issues. However, for matters of clarity, I have chosen to discuss the various elements of critique by looking at three different theologians. Johann Baptist Metz has criticized Rahner for employing an idealist and ahistorical theological methodology. Walter Kasper deems Rahner's work to be insufficiently attentive to freedom, love and inter-subjectivity. George Lindbeck argues that Rahner fails to grasp the constitutive role played by language and community in experience. The subsequent section is dedicated to examining the aforementioned thinkers' concerns in greater detail.

2.1 Forgetful of history and suffering

Johann Baptist Metz has started his theological career as a Rahnerian scholar.[2] However, he began to diverge from his teacher in the 1960s. Influenced by other ideas, such as Ernst Bloch's philosophy of hope and Walter Benjamin's emphasis on the importance of (dangerous) memories and narratives, he chose to adopt a decisively political orientation. He presents his political theology as a critical corrective to the abstract and ahistorical nature of transcendental theology. Political theology has two main goals. First, it seeks to counter the tendency towards privatization in theology that reduces the praxis of faith to an individual decision. Second, political theology intends to overcome the purely passive hermeneutics of Christianity through a reformulation of its eschatological message. Transcendental theology focuses on the salvific question of the individual who faces death. This has made theology blind to the real salvific question, namely, to the issue of the social-historical suffering of millions of others in the world.[3]

Metz applies this general criticism more concretely to Rahner, aiming specifically at his notion of the *Vorgriff*. Transcendental theology lacks the structure of historical experience and, thus, fails to recognize that the anticipating human person exists historically. As a result, the societal contestations and antagonisms, which form the mark of painful historical experience, disappear in the transcendental account. These conflicts are undialectically resolved in the unthematic transcendental experience.[4] The failure of transcendental theology to take seriously historicity and its dependence on a 'late and atrophied metaphysics' results in a 'subjectless theology of the subject'.[5]

---

[1] For a succinct overview of the various critiques levelled against Rahner's theology over time, see Declan Marmion, 'Rahner and His Critics: Revisiting the Dialogue', *Irish Theological Quarterly* 68 (2003): 195–212; Paul Murray, 'The Lasting Significance of Karl Rahner for Contemporary Catholic Theology', *Louvain Studies* 29 (2004): 8–27.

[2] See Metz's first major work, *Christliche Anthropozentrik. Über die Denkform des Thomas von Aquin* (München: Kösel, 1962), in which he presents Thomas Aquinas as the inaugurator of an anthropocentric theology. The fact that Rahner entrusted the redaction and editing of the second editions of both *Spirit in the World* and *Hearer of the Word* to his former student is further proof of the close working relationship between both scholars.

[3] Johann Baptist Metz, *Faith in History and Society: Toward a Practical Fundamental Theology*, trans. J. Matthew Ashley (New York: Crossroad, 2011), 71–3.

[4] Metz, *Faith in History and Society*, 74.

[5] Ibid., 72.

Metz identifies two additional problematic issues. First, he fears that Rahner's elaboration of an implicit transcendental dimension of experience and faith amounts to an elitist idealism. The masses generally lack complete knowledge of the deeper structure of experience. This philosophical gnosis is the prerogative of a philosophical elite. Metz objects to this, arguing that the only possible arcane knowledge derives from the praxis of following Jesus, rather than from Socrates.[6] Second, Metz argues that Rahner views the human person as always already (*nolens, volens*) in relation to God. While Metz does not disagree with the universalization of the historical experiences that are part of the Christian faith tradition, he does criticize the 'purely intellectual-speculative path' that Rahner takes in order to perform this universalization.[7]

In order to illustrate the shortcomings of Rahner's transcendental method, Metz recounts the fairy tale about the hedgehog who challenges the hare to a footrace through a field. Before the race begins, the hedgehog makes sure that his wife posts herself at the end of the field – the place where the race finishes. So when the hedgehog and the hare start to race, to his dismay and surprise the hare runs and runs, but finds the hedgehog always already there at the end of the field. Ultimately, the hare runs himself to death. Metz identifies the racing hare with those involved in history and praxis, whereas he identifies the hedgehog with the idealist option that chooses to play a trick, thereby foregoing the threatening and dangerous experience of running. The trick illustrates idealism's universal and petrified view of history. In claiming to know the beginning and the end of history already, there is no longer any need to enter into history with its dangers and catastrophes. Moreover, the transcendental-idealist attempt to legitimize Christianity confuses identity with tautology. Just as the two hedgehogs are simply identical, so the beginning is like the end, creation is like the eschaton. Historical struggles are deprived of the possibility of intervening in this 'transcendental spell'.[8] Hence, for Metz, the transcendental-idealist account of history is all too neat and total. It cuts itself off from corrective transformative historical events and experiences.

Alternatively, Metz proposes a 'quasi-post-idealist' approach that focuses on praxis and views memory and narrative to be the key categories to legitimate and universalize historical experiences.[9] The hermeneutical force of suffering has gained a particular prominence in Metz's work, especially within the context of the question of the possibility of theology after Auschwitz. The dangerous memory of Auschwitz takes on a central role in his work, combined with his emphasis on the biblical tradition of 'anamnetic reason'.[10] Metz criticizes transcendental theology for failing to address adequately the dimension of suffering.[11]

---

[6] Ibid., 149.
[7] Ibid., 149–50.
[8] Ibid., 150–2.
[9] Ibid., 169–214.
[10] See Johann Baptist Metz, *Memoria Passionis. Ein provozierendes Gedächtnis in pluralistischer Gesellschaft* (Freiburg: Herder, 2006).
[11] Metz confronts Rahner with the question of why catastrophes, the abysses of suffering, the history of human suffering and so on were absent in his work. Why did Rahner not address the question of Auschwitz? See Dorothee Sölle and Johann Baptist Metz, *Welches Christentum hat Zukunft? Dorothee Sölle und Johann Baptist Metz im Gespräch mit Karl-Josef Kuschel* (Stuttgart: Kreuz Verlag, 1990), 23.

2.2 Forgetful of language and inter-subjectivity

The charge of excessive individualism, initiated by Metz, has also been taken up by Walter Kasper. In *Jesus the Christ*, Kasper suggests that Rahner's anthropological turn has effected a 'metaphysicizing' of historical Christianity and that the 'scandal' of Christianity's particularity has, consequently, been eliminated through philosophical speculation.[12] He attributes this to Rahner's inability to balance properly transcendentality and history, which come to the fore in the minimal attention paid to the inter-subjective and linguistic character of human subjectivity particularly. According to Kasper, we can only talk about people in the plural, because human subjectivity only exists in 'I–thou–we' relations. However, Rahner's focus on the human being as metaphysical questioner seems to overlook that the quest is necessarily social and relational. Without other people teaching us a language, we would not know how to formulate our existential questions.[13]

Kasper concedes that Rahner certainly reflected on the inter-subjective mediation of transcendental questioning in his later writings. Hence, it would be wrong to draw too sharp a contrast between his transcendental method, on the one hand, and personal-dialogical and sociopolitical methods, on the other.[14] Moreover, he also hails Rahner for elaborating the interpretative nature of truth. The transcendental approach as such is not irreconcilable with history and inter-subjectivity. After all, language and being addressed by someone also presuppose certain transcendental conditions. However, Kasper deems Rahner's rendering of this transcendental condition of *Ansprechbarkeit* (the conditions for being addressed) too formal and argues that Rahner fails to notice that historical reality determines the transcendental condition of understanding. Echoing von Balthasar and Metz, Kasper attributes this to Rahner's transcendental-idealist position.[15]

Interestingly, the differentiation that Kasper suggests seems not to be all that different from Rahner's own account. Thus, when explaining the experience of God as the basis for knowledge of God, Kasper resorts to transcendental language that seems to be clearly indebted to Rahner. He describes religious experience as the basic experience of finitude and incompleteness 'with, in, and below' our ordinary experiences, which

---

However, other scholars have suggested that Rahner actually played a catalysing role in Metz's shift towards the theme of Auschwitz and suffering. See Tiemo Rainer Peters, 'Karl Rahner und die neue Politische Theologie', in *100 Jahre Karl Rahner. Nach Rahner post et secundum*, ed. Heinrich Klauke (Cologne: Karl Rahner Akademie, 2004), 43–50; and Albert Raffelt, 'Neue politische Theologie und das Werk Karl Rahners - eine Gegenrede', in *100 Jahre Karl Rahner*, 51–62. These alternative accounts suggest that there may be a larger degree of affinity and mutual dependence between political and transcendental theology than Metz's criticism of Rahner suggests. For a more detailed analysis of Rahner's theology in the light of Metz's critique emphasizing their intrinsic interconnectedness, see Titus F. Guenther, *Rahner and Metz: Transcendental Theology as Political Theology* (Lanham, MD: University Press of America, 1994).

[12] Walter Kasper, *Jesus the Christ*, new edition, trans. Dinah Livingstone (London: Continuum, 2011), 38.
[13] Kasper, *Jesus the Christ*, 38.
[14] Walter Kasper, 'Christologie von unten? Kritik und Neuansatz gegenwärtige Christologie', in *Grundfragen der Christologie heute*, ed. Leo Scheffczyk, Quaestiones disputatae 72 (Freiburg: Herder, 1975), 156–7.
[15] Kasper, *Jesus the Christ*, 38–9.

ultimately directs us to a mysterious horizon.[16] Contra Rahner, Kasper focuses on the historical character of experience, emphasizing its inherent dialectics of experience and interpretation in words, images, symbols and concepts derived from a historical inter-subjective speech community.[17] Yet, he resorts to Rahner's terminology again when he writes thus: 'Language draws its life from a pre-apprehension of the total meaning of reality and gives expression to this meaning in metaphors and similes.'[18]

Kasper's proximity to, and difference from, Rahner recurs in his focus on freedom. He agrees that human persons have a *Vorgriff*, but also argues that this *Vorgriff* anticipates the complete realization of freedom, rather than Being. This *Vorgriff* of absolute or perfect freedom forms the transcendental condition for our free acts.[19] We become aware of this transcendental dimension through our relations with other persons. In contradistinction to Rahner's category of absolute Being, Kasper uses this personal language to speak about God as freedom in love. By receiving and giving love, we realize our personal subjectivity and, ultimately, look out for an encounter with an absolute person. The horizon of human subjectivity is, therefore, love.[20] According to Kasper, this results in a revolution in the understanding of metaphysics. Relation rather than substance is now considered 'the ultimate and highest reality'.[21] But is it correct to oppose this relational understanding of theology to Rahner's transcendental model?

2.3 Forgetful of culture and community

A third criticism of Rahner has been raised by George Lindbeck, often associated with post-liberal theology and the Yale School of theology. His main critique is that Rahner misconceives of the relation between experience and interpretation, prioritizing the former at the expense of the latter. Rahner misses the fundamental and constitutive role played by language and culture in all experience. Consequently, he views experience as shaping religion, whereas Lindbeck argues that the relation is the inverse.

In *The Nature of Doctrine*, Lindbeck presents his cultural-linguistic model as an alternative to what he calls 'propositionalist' and 'experiential-expressivist' models of religion.[22] The experiential-expressivist model assumes that there is a universally shared and pre-reflective 'common core experience'. The different religious traditions, then, are viewed as diverse symbolic and conceptual expressions of this common core experience. Lindbeck associates a host of thinkers with this experiential-expressivist model, including Friedrich Schleiermacher, Mircea Eliade, Bernard Lonergan, Karl Rahner, David Tracy and Paul Ricoeur. Conceding that this model has provided

---

[16] Walter Kasper, *The God of Jesus* Christ, new edition, trans. Dinah Livingstone (London: Continuum, 2012), 84–5.
[17] Kasper, *The God of Jesus* Christ, 82–3; 90–1.
[18] Ibid., 94.
[19] Ibid., 105.
[20] Ibid., 155.
[21] Ibid., 156.
[22] George Lindbeck, *The Nature of Doctrine. Religion and Theology in a Postliberal Age*, 25th Anniversary Edition with a new introduction by Bruce D. Marshall and a new afterword by the author (Louisville, KY: Westminster John Know Press, 2009).

brilliant and impressive accounts of religion, Lindbeck nevertheless claims that it has also created many problems. One such problem is that the core experience cannot be described in specific detail, so that the assertion of its commonality becomes 'logically and empirically vacuous'.[23] Moreover, this approach resorts to 'complicated intellectual gymnastics' in order to explain the relation between religion and experience.[24] According to Lindbeck, this can be explained much more simply.

Lindbeck's alternative argument draws upon insights derived from the linguistic turn. The linguistic turn is a particular moment within the previously described hermeneutical turn. It signifies modern philosophy's growing recognition of the fundamental role played by language and its consequent formative and de-formative powers. Paying proper attention to the role of language leads to a 'break with immediacy' in experience.[25] Alternatively, language is now seen as deeply influencing, differentiating and shaping experience itself. Lindbeck's cultural-linguistic model adopts this insight. 'It is the text so to speak, which absorbs the world, rather than the world the text.'[26] He advocates for a reversal, given that he objects to the experiential-expressivist prioritizing of experience over expression. Experience is *constituted by* culture and language. Consequently, individual subjectivity is shaped by the community, rather than vice versa. Applying these insights to theology, Lindbeck concludes that the texts of religious communities are the regulative principles of religion. Religious experiences, therefore, can be considered to be 'by-products of linguistically or conceptually structured cognitive activities'.[27]

Although Lindbeck rightly calls attention to the central role played by language and culture, his alternative cultural-linguistic models contains its own problems and weaknesses.[28] His reversal of the relation between world and text suggests that culture and language determine experience unilaterally. Lindbeck himself observes that this is dialectical or reciprocal, rather than unilateral, which leads him to conclude that 'it is

---

[23] Lindbeck, *The Nature of Doctrine*, 18.
[24] Ibid., 3. Nicholas Adams, 'Rahner's Reception in Twentieth Century Protestant Theology', in *The Cambridge Companion to Karl Rahner*, 211–24, evaluates Lindbeck's critique of Rahner in order to 'repair' Rahner. He considers such a reparation to be necessary because Rahner's theories of truth 'fail to persuade contemporary theologians' (211). However, even though Adams explains and contextualizes Rahner's philosophy, he provides no argument that supports his claim that this philosophy is no longer unpersuasive except for repeating Lindbeck's claim that 'it is more intellectually complex than the problem requires' (221).
[25] Steven Shakespeare, 'Language', in *The Oxford Handbook of Theology and Modern European Thought*, 105–26.
[26] Lindbeck, *The Nature of Doctrine*, 104.
[27] Ibid., 19–22.
[28] These concerns are well articulated by David Tracy in his review of *The Nature of Doctrine* in 'Lindbeck's New Program for Theology: A Reflection', *The Thomist* 49 (1985): 460–72. First, Tracy questions the adequacy of Lindbeck's assessment of the shortcomings of the experiential-expressive paradigm. Hermeneutical theologians belonging to this tradition have anything but ignored the linguistic turn and, yet, they strive to combine the new understandings of the role of language with a deeper and broader understanding of experience (462–4). Second, Tracy also draws attention to the fact that Lindbeck's emphasis on the inner logic of the language of a particular ecclesial community problematizes attempts to account publicly for the truth claims of any given tradition. When the only possible 'apologetics' is an 'ad-hoc apologetics', it becomes difficult to conceive of claims to truth that transcend particular cultural-linguistic discourses. As a result, the cultural-linguistic approach runs the risk of turning into relativism, confessionalism or fideism (469–70).

simplistic to say (as I earlier did) merely that religions produce experiences'.[29] However, this dialectical relationship is hardly developed in *The Nature of Doctrine*. I suggest, instead, that a reconsideration of Rahner's thought might provide a more adequate rendering of this dialectical relationship between experience and interpretation.

2.4 Correcting the Korrektivtheologie

At the risk of unduly generalizing, these three criticisms all claim that Rahner's transcendental theology pays insufficient attention to history. Rahner forgets the history of suffering, forgets historical engagements with other people and forgets the cultural-linguistic and historical conditions of experience. Put succinctly, their readings suggest that Rahner's transcendental method lacks hermeneutical awareness. Accordingly, they offer an important challenge to my claim that Rahner's theological method is characterized by a dialectics of transcendentality and hermeneutics. However, is their critical reading of Rahner fair, appropriate and complete?

It is important to note here that Metz has always maintained that his own critique of Rahner remained also indebted to him. More recently, both Metz and Kasper have acknowledged the foundational significance of Rahner's theology for their own theological projects and have, subsequently, mitigated their earlier criticisms. Metz states thus: 'My theological biography is inscribed with one name above all, Karl Rahner.'[30] Kasper now explicitly defends Rahner against charges of subjectivism and argues that he has been particularly attentive to the hermeneutical nature of truth, in clear contrast to his earlier dismissal of Rahner's transcendental-idealism.[31] Kasper also points to the fact that there is a dialectical ground structure in Rahner's work, one which proves particularly fruitful in grappling with the problematic tension between 'Christian universality and catholicity' and 'scandalising unicity, facticity, and particularity'.[32] This seems to suggest that it is incorrect to depict Rahner as an ahistorical and hermeneutically naive transcendental idealist.

Metz has expressed that his political theology intends to be a *Korrektivtheologie* (correcting theology), aimed at carrying Rahner's transcendental theology forward.[33] In response, I argue that it may be time to correct these corrections. A re-reading of Rahner's theology, in light of the aforementioned critiques, discloses that his *oeuvre* actually already addresses many of the deficiencies of which he has been

---

[29] Lindbeck, *The Nature of Doctrine*, 19.
[30] Johann Baptist Metz, 'Facing the World: A Theological and Biographical Inquiry', *Theological Studies* 75 (2014): 25. See also Johann Baptist Metz, 'Fehlt uns Karl Rahner?', in *Karl Rahner in Erinnerung*, 85–99. Matthew Lamb, 'A Response to Fr. Metz', in *Theology and Discovery: Essays in Honor of Karl Rahner, SJ*, ed. William J. Kelly (Milwaukee, WI: Marquette University Press, 1980), 179–83, argues that Metz's critique of Rahner can be interpreted dialectically. Referring to Paul Ricoeur, he terms Metz's affirmation of Rahner a 'political hermeneutics of recovery' and Metz's negation of Rahner a 'political hermeneutics of suspicion'.
[31] Walter Kasper, 'Karl Rahner. Theologe in einer Zeit des Umbruchs', in *Walter Kasper. Theologie im Diskurs*, Gesammelte Schriften vol, 6, ed. George Augustin and Klaus Krämer (Freiburg: Herder, 2014), 405.
[32] Kasper, 'Karl Rahner. Theologe in einer Zeit des Umbruchs', 408–9.
[33] Metz, *Faith in History and Society*, 30. For the personal relationship between Rahner and Metz, see Vorgrimler, *Karl Rahner*, 122–3.

accused. Rahner's transcendental theology is much more hermeneutical and open to hermeneutical considerations than his critics have suggested. The critics seem to miss the incarnational character and crucial decentring aspects in his approach. Moreover, due to their rather one-sided focus on Rahner's early work, they also seem to overlook that in his later work, Rahner develops these elements into a manifestly hermeneutical direction. This starts with his reflections on the dialectics of revelation.

3 The dialectics of revelation

Towards the end of *Spirit in the World*, it becomes apparent that Rahner's reflection on the metaphysics of knowledge serves a theological purpose. The demonstration of the interlocking of sensibility and transcendence aims to show that human beings may be able to encounter something that is beyond the world in the world. In *Hearer of the Word*, Rahner continues this line of thought so that his metaphysical anthropology transforms into a fundamental theology. A crucial element of this process is that his incarnational epistemology takes on a manifestly historical dimension. *Hearer of the Word* explains the human spirit as a being that must look out into history for a potential divine revelation. The issue at stake is no longer primarily the relation between materiality and metaphysics, but rather the perennial tension between transcendentality and history.

3.1 Standing before mystery

Gotthold Ephraim Lessing has famously formulated the problem of the 'ugly great ditch' between historical and metaphysical truths. Rahner delves into this problem by probing the relation between theology and philosophy of religion. He seeks to show that we are essentially ordered towards an historical, divine revelation by offering a metaphysical account of the human person. Despite this fundamental orientation, God's revelation remains utterly gratuitous. Rahner, thus, searches for a reasonable justification of Christian faith, without undermining historical revelation or making it redundant. His argument is organized around the previously discussed metaphysical question. Yet, whereas *Spirit in the World* demonstrated that the human spiritual capacity only exists in and through our sensible intuition of the material world, *Hearer of the Word* now attends more closely to the inextricable historical dimension of human subjectivity as spirit. This historical dimension of human subjectivity is explored in further detail in the second and third parts of *Hearer of the Word*, through a reflection on contingent human freedom in relation to its free ground.[34] This leads Rahner to a consideration of the historicity of God's revelation and of the historicity of human subjectivity, respectively.

---

[34] Coreth, 'Die philosophische Grundlagen', 532, notes that Rahner's understanding of the historicity of human subjectivity avoids the 'radical historicity' that he sees in someone like Max Müller. Moreover, he also argues that Rahner's attention to history has a theological origin, insofar as he is primarily concerned with concrete salvation history.

As discussed previously, the phenomenological observation that human beings are open to Being also leads to the awareness of the hiddenness of Being. Rahner associates this tension with the contingency of human existence. *Dasein* (human existence) is aptly described as 'purely factual' existence – an existence that is contingent or 'thrown' (*geworfen*).[35] Hence, it is only insofar as human beings recognize their own finitude and contingency that they have any notion of infinity or of absolute Being at all. Moving beyond epistemological-cognitional considerations, Rahner now argues that the affirmation of our own existence as radically contingent is an act of human freedom.[36] However, rather than confining human subjectivity to this dimension of finitude, he argues that we find here the starting point for new ontological and theological insights.[37] As limited beings, human beings lack the ground to affirm themselves absolutely. Consequently, insofar as they freely affirm themselves as *geworfen*, they affirm themselves as created and sustained by a free and creative power of absolute Being.[38]

Since this ontological ground is a free power, our knowledge of this ground remains dependent upon the free decision that this power has to reveal itself. This means that the *Vorgriff* of this sustaining ground is simultaneously a knowing that 'slips back into an unknowing', a standing before the *mysterium imperscrutabile* (inscrutable mystery).[39] Rahner puts this in more explicitly theological terms when he concludes that the human person always already stands before a God of possible revelation – one who freely chooses either to remain silent or to act and speak in history. This means that there is always some form of revelation: God's silence or God's speech. Yet, we cannot remain indifferent if God does choose to act and speak, given that we are fundamentally oriented towards a possible revelation. Importantly, the notion of freedom is intrinsically connected to history. If God chooses to break the silence, it will be through God's free actions in history.[40]

3.2 From spirit in the world to spirit in history

Rahner presents the human person primarily as spirit in relation to the material world in his previous work. In *Hearer of the Word*, he now emphasizes that this spiritual capacity of human subjectivity only exists insofar as it is historical: 'To be human is to be spirit as a historical being. The place of our transcendence is always also a historical place.'[41] Historicity is connected with spatio-temporality, but it is not reducible to the conditions of time and space. For Rahner, historicity is linked with freedom. He explains this specific understanding of history by contrasting free historical actions with natural events. Whereas the latter follow some general law of nature and are,

---

[35] Rahner, *Hearer of the Word*, 67.
[36] Ibid., 68.
[37] See Fritz, *Karl Rahner's Theological Aesthetics*, 207, who notes that Rahner shares a revelatory understanding of history with Heidegger. Yet while Heidegger sees history as revealing Being, Rahner argues that history reveals God.
[38] Rahner, *Hearer of the Word*, 69–70.
[39] Ibid., 70; 72.
[40] Ibid., 72–3.
[41] Ibid., 94.

therefore, determined to some extent, free actions are unique, original and singular. They cannot be repeated, and cannot be understood with the help of a general law, but can only be grasped in themselves. History is, thus, connected with the unicity and unpredictability of free actions.[42]

In view of the bodily constitution of human persons, free human acts are necessarily realized through encounter and in relation with the world and with other people. The collective free activity of various different people in the world becomes what we call 'human history'.[43] Hence, human beings exist historically insofar as they relate to freedom, to each other and to the world. Importantly, Rahner emphasizes that exercising our freedom through action is not merely an option for us. Rather, it is precisely through these actions that we realize (*verwirklichen*) ourselves.[44] Our spiritual capacity of transcendence towards Being is only realized when our turn to the world becomes a turn towards historical appearances, that is a turn towards human history:

> Every time we turn to the appearance, which is essential for all human knowledge, we also turn to something that is always already historical, since the appearance, at least as a fact in human life itself, is a fact that happens just once.[45]

Rahner's incarnational epistemology, therefore, takes on a historical dimension. The intellectual, spatio-temporal orientation of human subjectivity in *Spirit in the World* has been transposed and developed into a historical orientation that attends both to knowledge and to freedom. The conversion to the phantasm becomes a conversion to history; spirit in the world becomes spirit in history. As a result, the indissoluble link between history and transcendentality becomes apparent. Historicity is properly understood as a *Grundverfassung* (constitutive element) of the human being, and, consequently, the turn towards history forms an 'inner moment' of human spiritual nature.[46]

Having established the historicity of divine revelation, as well as the historicity of human subjectivity, it becomes apparent why Rahner considers history to be the locus of divine revelation. We do not encounter God's revelation in the 'interiority of the Spirit', or in a 'rapture and ecstasy of the soul', which draws us away from the realm of time and space.[47] Rather, divine revelation meets us where we find ourselves, that is in the historical world. It takes place at a specific time and at a specific point within the history of humankind, as a unique and unforeseeable gratuitous event. As a result, to encounter God's revelation we must turn to certain exceptional moments of

---

[42] Ibid., 94–5.
[43] Ibid., 112. We find here a tacit and limited acknowledgement of the importance of inter-subjectivity. Since it remains rather undeveloped though, various scholars have deemed *Hearer of the Word* to be a deficient work in this regard. For an overview of some of these criticisms see Knieps, *Die Unvertretbarkeit von Individualität*, 264–80. As we will see below, however, Rahner will develop the theme of inter-subjectivity more substantially in his later work.
[44] Rahner, *Hearer of the Word*, 112.
[45] Ibid., 138.
[46] Ibid., 95.
[47] Ibid., 91.

human history.⁴⁸ Rahner, thus, arrives at an understanding of human subjectivity that is decisively anti-rationalist. He opposes attempts to elevate human existence above history. The human person listens in history to the word of God: 'Only those who listen in this way and only to the extent that they listen in this way, are authentically what they have to be: human.'⁴⁹

In several of his early theological essays, Rahner transposes this dynamic between transcendentality and history from an anthropological context to a discussion of dogma. As expressions of revealed truth, dogmas are held to be true and binding throughout time. At the same time, however, it must be acknowledged that all human statements are inherently finite and are conditioned historically. For this reason, dogmatic formulas are incapable of expressing truth exhaustively and completely. 'Evolution within the same truth' requires a history and development of faith, dogma and theology.⁵⁰ As we will see in Chapter 7, Edward Schillebeeckx similarly grapples with the historical conditions of theological expressions of truth and introduces a perspectival epistemology to deal with this issue.

To summarize, in *Hearer of the Word* Rahner elaborates the historical dimension of his metaphysical anthropology in conjunction with the notion of freedom. Human transcendentality only exists in its relation to *historical* otherness. Importantly, an account of human subjectivity as free self-actualization in history serves to show that we are 'hearers of the word'. We know that there is a term for human self-transcendence in knowledge and action that grounds our contingent subjectivity, but in order to find out more about this inscrutable mystery we must turn to history. These reflections on the dialectical relation between the historicity and transcendentality of revelation make manifest that Rahner's transcendental approach has increasingly acquired a hermeneutical profile. Rahner gradually arrives at the conclusion that *historical experience* forms the hermeneutical key for the engagement with (transcendental, metaphysical, theological) truth. Historical experience conditions both our engagement with this truth and our reflection on this truth. Rahner's interrelation of transcendentality and history, at the anthropological level, carries over into his theological methodology.⁵¹ This becomes especially apparent in his reflections on a key hermeneutical problem: the relation between experience and interpretation.

---

⁴⁸ Ibid., 135. Werner G. Jeanrond, 'Hermeneutics and Revelation', in *Memory, Narrativity, Self and the Challenge to Think God: The Reception within Theology of the Recent Work of Paul Ricoeur*, ed. Maureen Junker-Kenny and Peter Kenny (Münster: LIT, 2004), 45–6, points out the similarity between Rahner's view of the history's revelatory capacity and Mircea Eliade's notion of 'hierophany' as the manifestation of the sacred or supernatural into the world. Rahner's concept of revelation can therefore be characterized as 'epiphanic'.

⁴⁹ Rahner, *Hearer of the Word*, 138.

⁵⁰ Karl Rahner, 'The Development of Dogma [1954], in *TI*, vol. 1, trans. Cornelius Ernst (London: Darton, Longman and Todd, 1974), 44. See also Karl Rahner, 'What is a Dogmatic Statement?' [1961], in *TI*, vol. 5, trans. Karl-H Kruger (London: Darton, Longman and Todd, 1974), 54–5.

⁵¹ See Leo J. O'Donovan, 'Orthopraxis and Theological Method: Rahner', *Proceedings of the Catholic Theological Society of America* 35 (1980): 49, who similarly points to Rahner's insistence on the reciprocal interdependence of transcendental and historical reflection in theology.

4 The dialectics of experience

The philosophical reflections on incarnational epistemology and on the intrinsic relation between transcendentality and history prepare the way for the theology of experience, which characterizes Rahner's more mature and explicitly theological work.[52] His metaphysical explorations serve to explain that historical experience, as such, is a potential place of encounter with God and therefore a *locus theologicus* (theological source).[53] I will show that Rahner employs an analytical distinction between the transcendental and the categorical dimensions of experience in order to explain the revelatory nature of concrete experiences. Introducing this distinction may appear to be an unnecessary exercise in 'intellectual gymnastics'; however, I argue that this distinction is representative of Rahner's efforts to combine transcendental reflection with a hermeneutical awareness. Crucially, I maintain that Rahner hereby succeeds in maintaining a *dialectical* relation between experience and interpretation.

While experience features prominently in Rahner's writings, he usually refrains from defining the term.[54] The short lemma in *Theological Dictionary* forms an exception to this general rule.[55] Rahner defines experience here as a form of knowledge characterized by receptivity. It originates when something which is beyond our control impresses itself upon us. Rahner then continues to define religious experience as 'inner self-attestation of supernatural reality (grace)', which is only possible 'in conjunction with objective, conceptual reflexion'.[56] So, in addition to the receptive element of experience, there is also a more active reflective or interpretative element at work in experience. L. Bruno Puntel notes that Rahner often uses experience to talk about the human self-realization with help of the terms 'transcendental' and 'categorical'.[57] The transcendental concerns a dimension that is unthematically present in every concrete experience, but which calls for conceptual interpretation and explication. The categorical dimension, then, concerns this thematic interpretation of unthematic transcendentality. Although Puntel speaks of two dimensions, rather than moments, his explanation fails to make clear that Rahner's distinction between the transcendental and categorical is never actual, but only analytical. Not noticing this crucial distinction may be the cause of various misunderstandings of the concept of transcendental experience. It contributes to the picture that exists of Rahner as being hermeneutically naive and lacking awareness of the indispensable role of interpretation. These key terms, categorical and transcendental, then, warrant a closer analysis.

---

[52] Herbert Vorgrimler, 'Gotteserfahrung im Alltag. Der Beitrag Karl Rahners zu Spiritualität und Mystik', in *Karl Rahner in Erinnerung*, 102, argues that experience of God forms the key concept of Rahner's theology.
[53] See Sheehan, *Karl Rahner*, 314.
[54] See Declan Marmion, 'Theology. Spirituality, and the Role of Experience', *Louvain Studies* 29 (2004): 59.
[55] Karl Rahner and Herbert Vorgrimler, *Theological Dictionary*, trans. Richard Strachan, ed. Cornelius Erst (New York: Herder and Herder, 1965), 162.
[56] Rahner and Vorgrimler, *Theological Dictionary*, 162.
[57] L. Bruno Puntel, 'Zu den Begriffen "transzendental" und "kategorial" bei Karl Rahner', in *Wagnis Theologie. Erfahrungen mit der Theologie Karl Rahners*, ed. Herbert Vorgrimler (Freiburg: Herder, 1979), 190–1.

4.1 The transcendental dimension of experience

Rahner's most systematic account of transcendental experience can be found in *Foundations of Christian Faith*. The term transcendental experience immediately raises questions to anyone familiar with Immanuel Kant's philosophy.[58] As discussed above, Kant employs transcendental in a strictly epistemological sense, to designate the *a priori* conditions that make concrete experience possible. Experience is bound to the empirical realm of space and time and is constituted by sensible intuition and concepts of understanding. As transcendental conditions, these concepts of understanding are prior to experience and must be deduced from concrete experiences. Hence, for Kant, a transcendental experience would be a non-sensical expression: experience cannot be transcendental, but is rather enabled by transcendental conditions. Surely Rahner must have been aware of this apparent contradiction. Why, then, does he use the expression transcendental experience? I have argued above that Rahner's transcendental method is highly idiosyncratic due to his appropriation of various sources. In order to understand Rahner's concept of transcendental experience, it is crucial to recognize both his indebtedness to, as well as his deviation from, Kant.[59] Contrary to Kant's strict epistemological focus, Rahner's understanding of transcendentality involves epistemological, ontological and theological dimensions. This can be explained by unpacking the following quotation from *Foundations* in three steps.

> We shall call *transcendental experience* the subjective, unthematic, necessary and unfailing consciousness of the knowing subject that is co-present in every spiritual act of knowledge and the subject's openness to the unlimited expanse of all reality. It is an *experience* because this knowledge, unthematic but ever-present, is a moment within and a condition of possibility for every concrete experience of any and every object. This experience is called *transcendental* experience because it belongs to the necessary and inalienable structures of the knowing subject itself, and because it consists precisely in the transcendence beyond any particular group of possible objects or categories. Transcendental experience is the experience of *transcendence*, in which experience the structure of the subject and therefore also the ultimate structure of every conceivable object of knowledge are present together and in identity. This transcendental experience, of course, is not merely an experience of pure knowledge, but also of the will and of freedom. The same character of transcendentality belongs to them, so that basically one can ask about

---

[58] The notion of transcendental experience goes back to Edmund Husserl, who uses it to describe the interior self-experience of the transcendental ego and has, subsequently, been taken up by others, including Hermann Krings, Johann Baptist Lotz, Karl Rahner and Richard Schaeffler. These latter figures have employed the notion of transcendental experience in order to explain how God can be thought of. See Bernd Irlenborn, 'Was ist eine "transzendentale Erfahrung"?', *Theologie und Philosophie* 79 (2004): 491–510.

[59] For a detailed comparison of Kant's and Rahner's understanding of transcendental experience, see Knoepffler, *Der Begriff 'transzendental'*, 173–95.

the source [*Wovonher*] and the destiny [*Woraufhin*] of the subject as a knowing being and as a free being together.⁶⁰

First, Rahner describes transcendental experience as a characteristic that belongs to the very structure of human subjectivity. He argues that there is an 'unthematic' co-consciousness of all subjective activity. It is termed unthematic because we are not ordinarily reflexively aware of this element of experience. This feature of human subjectivity can be made thematic through reflection on concrete actions. Rahner employs the term co-experience, rather than co-knowledge, in order to emphasize the elusive and ungraspable nature of this unthematic element of all experience. Importantly, this allows him to expand his earlier, primarily cognitive focus, so as to attend to the intellectual as well as to the volitional dimension of human subjectivity. His analysis of human questioning showed the unlimited transcendence of the human person towards the horizon of Being. Extending this argument, Rahner now argues that a transcendental analysis of human subjectivity must also attend to the human person as being free and responsible for her own actions.⁶¹

The second element that needs explication is Rahner's use of the term transcendental. On the one hand, he adopts the Kantian understanding of transcendentality to argue that unthematic experience is not merely co-present in all knowing and acting, but forms its transcendental condition of possibility. All cognition and freedom are exercised against the background of a horizon. Transcendental experience is what enables every concrete, ordinary experience; it is the light in which we see concrete objects and perform concrete actions. On the other hand, Rahner also employs the scholastic understanding of transcendentality, insofar as he argues that transcendental experience is 'category-transcending', going beyond every conceptual limitation. His connection of the Kantian sense of transcendental with the scholastic sense of transcendental explains why Rahner employs the 'nonsensical' expression of transcendental experience.⁶²

This leads to the third element of transcendental experience, which marks Rahner's difference with Kant even more sharply. Transcendental experience is also an experience of transcendence. As Karen Kilby explains, Rahner argues that an investigation into the formal conditions of experience discloses a material transcendence, that is an experiential openness or movement.⁶³ In concrete acts of knowing and freedom, we are aware of limitations, most importantly of our own radical finiteness. Yet, we experience ourselves as spiritual self-transcending beings, insofar as we are conscious of this radical finitude. This insight into the human capacity of self-transcendence naturally raises the question of its *Woraufhin* (destiny) and *Wovonher* (source). For Rahner, self-transcendence is ultimately an ontological concept. Finite being's

---

⁶⁰ Karl Rahner, *Foundations of Christian Faith: An Introduction to the Idea of Christianity*, trans. William Dych (New York: Crossroad, 1978), 20–1.
⁶¹ Rahner, *Foundations of Christian Faith*, 35–9.
⁶² Knoepffler, *Der Begriff 'transzendental'*, 184–95, traces the difference in understanding back to the disagreement between Rahner (and Maréchal) and Kant about the nature of judgement. Whereas Kant restricts his notion of transcendental-epistemology to the domain of knowledge, Rahner connects ontology with epistemology to address the domains of knowledge, action and being.
⁶³ Kilby, *Karl Rahner*, 34. See also Puntel, 'Zu den Begriffen "transzendental" und "kategorial"', 198.

self-transcendence is enabled by its participation in absolute Being.[64] However, he takes great care to emphasize that the horizon of transcendental experience is a holy mystery that simultaneously discloses and conceals itself. Human self-transcendence is 'a relationship which does not establish itself by its own power, but is experienced as something which was established by and is at the disposal of another, and which is grounded in the abyss of the ineffable mystery'.[65] Hence, the ground and condition of human transcendence is first of all received and escapes any full objectification or thematization.

Rahner maintains that this transcendental experience of transcendence entails an anonymous and unthematic knowledge of God. Yet this is not something which can be proven purely speculatively through transcendental reflection, but rather is an insight deriving from the events constituting the history of revelation and salvation. Transcendental experience can be viewed as transcendental revelation, but only in the light of the categorical and historical narrative revelation, as they have been handed on in the Christian tradition.[66] In other words, for Rahner the move from mystery to God is theological rather than philosophical. Rahner uses the more philosophical language of Being and mystery, rather than opting for the theological language of God, because he intends to explain this transcendental experience as a universal experience. Yet, compared with his early works, Rahner is now more prepared to acknowledge that his philosophical reflections have been informed by his specific theological perspective.[67] I will attend to this peculiar interlocking of philosophy and theology in greater detail in Chapter 5, when discussing the concept of the supernatural existential. For now, it should suffice to observe that Rahner's conceptualization of the horizon of transcendental experience as unthematic *Vorgriff* of mystery guards against the reductive objectification of this horizon.

4.2 The categorical dimension of experience

This discussion of transcendental experience could lead to a grievous misunderstanding; namely, that Rahner considers transcendental experience to be an actual experience, occurring concretely as such in our life. Although transcendental experience can be present unthematically, without reflective awareness of this experience, he forcefully maintains that every transcendental experience is always mediated historically and categorically. More concretely, it is mediated through concrete encounters with the world and especially through encounters with other people (*Mitwelt*).[68] Transcendental experience is, therefore, never available to us in a pure form, unaffected by history,

---

[64] Herbert Vorgrimler, 'Der Begriff der Selbsttranszendenz in der Theologie Karl Rahners', in *Wagnis Theologie*, 242–58 (244). See also Knoepffler, *Der Begriff 'transzendental'*, 184–95.
[65] Rahner, *Foundations*, 42.
[66] Ibid., 138–75.
[67] Vorgrimler, 'Der Begriff der Selbsttranszendenz', 250, argues that Rahner's transcendental philosophy follows the direction of his theology rather than vice versa. Knoepffler, *Der Begriff 'transzendental'*, 194, argues that Rahner does not intend to present a philosophical 'proof' for God's existence. Instead, his philosophical argument ultimately rests on positive theology, *in casu* the conviction about the universal salvific will of God.
[68] Rahner, *Foundations*, 36–7; 51–2.

world, bodyliness and language. Explaining this historical-material-inter-subjective or categorical mediation of transcendentality prompts the issue of the interpretation of experience.

According to Rahner, the categorical history of the human person as spirit is always and everywhere the historical self-interpretation of transcendental experience. This categorical mediation of transcendentality has, in itself, a dynamic towards objectification and conceptualization.[69] The distinction transcendental-categorical corresponds to Rahner's distinction between the unthematic and the thematic. The thematic element is alternatively described as interpretation, reflection, conceptualization or as objectification. So, the question of the relation between transcendental and categorical experience can then be narrowed down to the question of the relation between experience and interpretation. How does Rahner conceive of this relationship?

Rahner refrains from reflecting explicitly on the inherent interpretative aspect of experience. As we will see, Schillebeeckx is much more attentive to the fundamental hermeneutical nature of experience. Nevertheless, by closely scrutinizing his reflections on the nature of experience we can observe that his view is still much more hermeneutical than is often thought. Rahner states that there is 'an inescapable *unity in difference between one's original self-possession and reflection*'.[70] By asserting this unity in difference, he seeks to distance himself from two extreme perspectives on the relation between experience and interpretation: rationalism and modernism, respectively. While rationalism stresses conceptual reflection at the expense of experience, modernism favours experience to such an extent that it disregards the essential role played by reflection. Rahner presents an alternative position that focuses on experiences that he associates with human self-realization, that is experiences of love, sadness, anxiety, desire, trust and so on. These existential experiences are characterized by a unity that is more original than the unity between experienced reality and the concept that expresses this reality. Ontologically speaking, there is no chasm between subject and object that needs to be bridged, because the subject is directly related to reality through sensibility.[71] This original unity corresponds to the aforementioned transcendental dimension of experience.

However, while Rahner considers the transcendental dimension of experience to be more original than its conceptual (categorical) interpretation and articulation, he does acknowledge that this transcendental dimension is never experienced purely as such. On the contrary, actual and concrete experience always involves at least a primitive or incipient moment of interpretation.[72] Transcendental experience and categorical interpretation can therefore neither be separated nor be identified. Together they constitute the concrete phenomenon of experience. Rahner clarifies this further, stating that the original unity in experience can only exist 'in and through what we can call

---

[69] Ibid., 173.
[70] Ibid., 15 (emphasis in the original).
[71] Ibid., 16.
[72] Karl Rahner, 'The Experience of God Today' [1970], in *TI*, vol. 11, trans. David Bourke (London: Darton, Longman and Todd, 1974), 151–2.

language, and thus also reflection and communicability'.[73] In other words, there is no un-interpreted experience. Even very immediate experiences of pain, love or surprise involve a basic level of linguistic mediation and, therefore, an incipient moment of interpretation.

Unfortunately, Rahner hardly develops this insight into the linguistic mediation of human experience. There is relatively little attention paid to the role of language throughout his writings.[74] The essay 'Priest and Poet' is a rare exception.[75] Here, Rahner reflects on language as the incarnation of thought. Words are embodied thoughts, and it is by virtue of this embodiment that what we experience or think exists at all. For this reason, we should not understand the multiplicity of languages as various facades, behind which we can find one single thought. Linguisticality is co-constitutive of experience and, therefore, affects even the most basic experience.[76] However, as Francis Caponi argues, the reflections in 'Priest and Poet' do not yield a detailed theory of language, but rather 'some rich principles from which such a theory might be developed'.[77] As much as Rahner is affected by Heidegger's existential hermeneutics, Rahner's framework of thought clearly precedes the linguistic turn.[78]

It seems as though Rahner takes for granted that the culture and the community in which we are situated provide us with the linguistic and conceptual tools through which to interpret our experience for granted. Concrete and historical human existence involves a variety of experiences that are reflectively 'known' to various degrees.[79] In order to make sense of these experiences, we use images, concepts and horizons of understanding that derive from and are conditioned by our particular religious, cultural and historical milieus.[80] Hence, the formative role of community in experience has at least implicitly been recognized. Crucially, our attempts to interpret experience

---

[73] Rahner, *Foundations*, 16.
[74] Paul Ricoeur noted the absence of any specific attention to language in Rahner's work, yet did not judge Rahner's theory to be faulty for this reason. Instead, he advocated complementing Rahner's approach with a stronger focus on the role of language. See Paul Ricoeur, 'Response to Karl Rahner's Lecture: On the Incomprehensibility of God', *The Journal of Religion (Supplement)* 58 (1978): 126–31. Francis Caponi, 'A Speechless Grace: Karl Rahner on Religious Language', *International Journal of Systematic Theology* 9 (2007): 207, observes somewhat more critically that 'Rahner's analysis gives little attention to the relationship between "reflexive consciousness" and actual speech'. He concludes that this is 'a vexing lacuna, indicative of Rahner's lack of rigorous reflection on religious language at just those theological junctures it would be most expected'.
[75] Karl Rahner, 'Priest and Poet' [1956], in *TI*, vol. 3, trans. Karl-H. and Boniface Kruger (London: Darton, Longman and Todd, 1974), 294–317. Craig Baron, 'The Poetry of Transcendental Thomism', in *The Presence of Transcendence. Thinking 'Sacrament' in a Postmodern Age*, ed. Lieven Boeve and John C. Ries (Leuven: Peeters, 2001), 43–59, even goes as far as to assert that Rahner 'makes the postmodern turn to linguisticality' here, which seems perhaps too strong a statement in view of the brevity of Rahner's reflections on language in this essay and the relative absence of this topic in his other work.
[76] Rahner, 'Priest and Poet', 295.
[77] Caponi, 'A Speechless Grace', 209.
[78] Shakespeare, 'Language', 108–9, comments that in the Kantian project of transcendental philosophy, 'language always arrives afterwards – too late to make a difference'.
[79] Karl Rahner, 'Experience of Self and Experience of God', in *TI*, vol. 13, trans. David Bourke (London: Darton, Longman and Todd, 1975), 124.
[80] Karl Rahner, 'Experience of Transcendence from the Standpoint of Catholic Dogmatics', in *TI*, vol. 18, trans. Edward Quinn (London: Darton, Longman and Todd, 1983), 177.

also affect and change how we relate to our experiences. Interpretation leads to *different* experiences. Rahner explains this through the example of love:

> The actual *experience* of love is indeed absolutely basic and absolutely indispensable. But despite this fact the experience itself as such can in itself be accepted more profoundly, more purely, and with greater freedom when we achieve a knowledge of its true nature and its implications at the explicitly conscious level.[81]

Hence, Rahner does not advocate a complacent self-sufficiency of transcendental experience, contrary to what some commentators have argued, but argues instead that transcendental experience is always categorically mediated, carries a basic interpretation and calls for intensified interpretative clarification. Commenting on Rahner's notion of experience, Nicholas Lash points to this oft-missed hermeneutical feature of Rahner's work. However, he detects a 'problem of oversight', insofar as Rahner seems relatively inattentive to the role played by community.[82] Concrete relationships, such as the Christian community which consists of 'a network of relations defined and shaped by Christian discourse', fulfil a key role in the interpretation of experience.[83] Despite Rahner's relative silence on this subject, Lash argues that his position is open, rather than opposed, to this communal dimension in which Christian community functions as a sacrament of the relation with God.

While Rahner, then, is not as hermeneutically naive as Lindbeck suggests, important differences between their positions remain. Most importantly, Rahner insists that the transcendental experiential dimension retains a certain priority over any subsequently articulated interpretations. His recognition of the indispensable mediatory role played by interpretation is continually combined with a deep concern to retain an analytical distinction between the experiential and the interpretative dimensions. No interpretation can completely capture and articulate what is experienced. This inability to fully articulate and conceptualize the transcendental element of experience pushes us continually to revisit our experience. Consequently, just as there is a dynamism in experience towards interpretation, there is also a dynamism in interpretation that directs us back to experience.[84] Rahner already expressed this dialectical relation of experience and interpretation in an early article on the development of dogma.[85]

Yet, how far does this priority and originality of transcendental experience extend? When Rahner discusses so-called basic existential experiences, such as joy, fear, love, trust and so on, he asserts that it is more difficult to interpret and to articulate these basic experiences than it is to articulate ordinary experiences. Moreover, he also maintains that we have already achieved an understanding of these experiences before we have engaged in reflection upon them. To complicate matters further, he even states

---

[81] Karl Rahner, 'The Experience of God Today', in *TI*, vol. 11, trans. David Bourke (London: Darton, Longman and Todd, 1974), 152.
[82] Nicholas Lash, *Easter in Ordinary. Reflections on Human Experience and the Knowledge of God* (London: SCM Press, 1988), 238–9.
[83] Lash, *Easter in Ordinary*, 248–9.
[84] Rahner, *Foundations*, 17; Rahner, 'The Experience of Self', 123.
[85] Rahner, 'The Development of Dogma', 65.

that basic experiences are in principle 'independent' from conceptual clarification, because they have a lucidity that precedes reflection.[86] How can this be reconciled with the aforementioned acknowledgement of the hermeneutical nature of all experience? Does Rahner, after all, ultimately fail to take the role of language and interpretation sufficiently seriously?

4.3 Mediated immediacy

I propose to analyse Rahner's view on the relation between experience and interpretation with the help of two distinctions in order to reinforce my argument that Rahner's approach is characterized by a dialectics between transcendentality and hermeneutics. First, Rahner employs an analytical distinction between the transcendental experiential dimension and the categorical interpretative dimension. Crucially, this distinction is only used analytically in order to explain concrete experiences. As Nicholas Lash argues, 'If this distinction [between the transcendental and the categorical] is to work properly, it must not be taken as descriptive of a "division within the world".'[87] Concrete experiences always consist of a unity of this transcendental and this categorical dimension. However, Rahner introduces this distinction to show that we are ultimately not entirely controlling and determining our experience through interpretation. Experience involves a givenness that is simultaneously an orientation towards a mysterious horizon. This transcendental relation needs a categorical mediation in order to be present in concrete life. It is, therefore, latently (unthematically) co-present in every categorical experience. Conversely, every concrete experience is only possible against the background of this transcendental horizon. Consequently, the transcendental and the categorical dimension stand in a relation of mutual dependence.

A closer examination of the categorical interpretative dimension discloses a second distinction between, what we might call, original experience and reflected experience. It can be called an actual distinction because both types of experience can be encountered in real life. Strictly speaking, however, the distinction between original and reflected experience is gradual in nature. Rahner uses the concept of original or basic experience to describe experiences that entail only a very basic level of interpretation, reflection or articulation. To be sure, linguistic mediation and interpretation are operative at this level, but they are merely basic, primitive and unreflective. At this original level, the role of the unthematic experiential element is much larger than the interpretative element. Additional reflection, using categories from a specific cultural-linguistic or religious framework, increases the role played by interpretation. The subsequent articulation and conceptualization seek to clarify the original experience, thus transforming it into a reflected experience. However, reflection can never exhaust the original experience. Specific conceptualizations and articulations, therefore, always refer back to the original experience which contains a surplus of meaning. For Rahner, the origin of this surplus of meaning is located at the non-reflective, experiential level. As a result, experience retains a logical – not temporal – priority over interpretation.

---

[86] Rahner, 'The Experience of God Today', 152.
[87] Lash, *Easter in Ordinary*, 244.

Rahner employs the term 'mediated immediacy' in order to express this ability to move through language beyond language.[88]

It must be emphasized that Rahner himself does not consistently employ the distinctions I have introduced. Due to his relative inattention to the role of language and community, his own use of terms such as 'interpretation', 'articulation' and 'reflection' is rather crude. While he recognizes the essential mediating role of language and culture, the extent to which they enable, condition or determine experience remains underdeveloped. However, with the help of these two distinctions – the analytical and the actual – it becomes apparent that Rahner's understanding of experience and interpretation is anything but blind to hermeneutical considerations. For Rahner, experience and interpretation are dialectically related to each other.[89] I argue that this dialectical relation forms another demonstration of Rahner's continuous attempt in his theology to balance the transcendental with the hermeneutical. Consequently, the transcendental dimension of experience is characterized by an inescapable hermeneutical circularity. This necessitates a hermeneutical, exploratory approach to every interpretation of experience. The emphasis on the priority of the transcendental dimension of experience, therefore, turns out to be a hermeneutical reminder of the incompleteness and openness of all interpretations. Rahner's understanding of experience is open to more developed hermeneutical insights, for instance, regarding the role of prejudice or community in the process of interpretation, or with regard to the potential distortions of interpretation due to power, abuse and so on. Nevertheless, it must be recognized that Rahner himself did not extensively reflect upon these conditions of interpretation. My subsequent discussion of Schillebeeckx's approach, below, will yield important insights, necessary to fill this lacuna.

5 The dialectics of love

The preceding sections have sought to change the image of Rahner as being a transcendental idealist inattentive to hermeneutical issues such as history and interpretation. Experience implies interpretation, and interpretation requires language. However, as Ludwig Wittgenstein has pointed out, there is no such thing as a private language.[90] Thus, the discussion of the hermeneutical potential of Rahner's theology remains incomplete without a consideration of its social dimension. The current section extends its examination of the role played by inter-subjectivity in Rahner's thought, thereby responding to the critiques that his transcendental theology is overly concerned with the individual person, as levelled by Metz and Kasper. Yet, instead of looking in vain for places in which Rahner works out the inter-subjective dimension of human life through a discussion of language in his work, I propose turning to

---

[88] See Rahner, *Foundations*, 83–4. The epistemological use of the term 'mediated immediacy' to characterize the nature of human knowing goesback to Georg W. F. Hegel.
[89] Lash, *Easter in Ordinary*, 248, speaks of this dialectics in terms of a 'mutually critical correlation'.
[90] See Ludwig Wittgenstein, *Philosophical Investigations*, trans. G. E. M. Anscombe (Oxford: Basil Blackwell, 1958), 89–95.

his theology of love. This theology of love revolves around the crucial interrelation between love of God and love of neighbour.[91] Analysing Rahner's theology of love yields another instantiation of his dialectical interrelation between transcendentality and hermeneutics.

5.1 Loving an other is realizing oneself

Rahner's shift of focus from knowledge of material things to historical experience concurs with an increased attention being paid to freedom. He elaborates his understanding of freedom with reference to willing, loving and knowing.[92] Willing can be seen as an inner moment of knowing. Knowledge is not disinterested, but guided by the motivations and convictions of the free human subject. Crucially, Rahner argues that freedom has a necessary interpersonal, communicative dimension. The free affirmation of another subject is what Rahner calls love. Since knowledge is ordained towards its fulfilment in free actions of love, love can be termed the light of knowledge.[93]

Love for Rahner stands at the very centre of what he calls the human *Vollzug*, the realization of what it means to be a human person. True human personhood does not consist in unravelling scientific or philosophical questions and objects; it is in concrete loving encounters with other persons that we realize our human subjectivity. A conception of subjectivity that ignores this fundamental social relation to fellow human beings remains an 'abstract and philosophical' subjectivity.[94] Previously, Rahner explained human transcendence with reference to the encounter with the otherness of the material world. His emphasis clearly shifts then from material things to a 'thou', to the encounter with personal others. The *Sachwelt* (world of things) is, ultimately, only relevant as a moment of the relation between the human person and her *Mitwelt* (world of people).[95] We find our own personhood through loving encounters with other people. Love is the primary medium of transcendental experience as an experience of self and an experience of self-transcendence. But what does it mean to love another person? Instead of offering a phenomenological description, Rahner focuses on the recognition of the other's subjectivity.

---

[91] Lash, *Easter in Ordinary*, 238–9, argues that 'Rahner tends to underplay the indispensability of taking actual human relationships as the proper metaphor for the relation to God'. Yet, while Lash suggests that Rahner's own thought may supply the corrective required and initiates a discussion about the relation between knowledge and love, strangely enough he does not attend to the important theme of love of neighbour and, therefore, misses out on a primary part of Rahner's thought that contains this corrective that acknowledges the key role of inter-human relations for the relation with God. Another way to re-evaluate the role of inter-subjectivity and community in Rahner's work is by drawing out the ecclesial dimension of his writings. See Richard Lennan, *The Ecclesiology of Karl Rahner* (Oxford: Clarendon Press, 1995).
[92] Rahner, *Hearer of the Word*, 76–7. See Leo O'Donovan, 'Karl Rahner SJ (1904-1984). A Theologian for the Twenty-First Century', *Theology Today* 62 (2005): 354–5, who argues that Rahner's argument for the unity of knowledge and freedom introduces a 'transformational' notion of truth: human knowledge must be transformed into love.
[93] Rahner, *Foundations*, 65.
[94] Rahner, 'The Experience of Self', 127.
[95] Karl Rahner, 'Reflections on the Unity of the Love of Neighbour and the Love of God´', in *TI*, vol. 6, trans. Karl-H. and Boniface Kruger (London: Darton, Longman and Todd, 1974), 240.

Love is the affirmation and recognition of another person *as* another person, as a subject of transcendence. That means affirming the other person as such, fully recognizing her irreducible otherness, her dignity and her individuality. Loving another person means willing the other person as enduringly other. Loving them *as* other subjects is essential to realizing ourselves, rather than egoistically making fellow humans into means towards our own ends.[96] Self-realization through love is an historical process that takes place gradually, through concrete little steps and virtuous actions in life. It is, therefore, appropriate to speak of a becoming of love.[97] Yet, even an incomplete and an imperfect beginning of love must already be considered love, insofar as they are an 'implicit acceptance of the transcendental basic movement towards the foundation of all freedom'.[98] In order to explain this, we must turn to Rahner's account of the unity of love of neighbour and love of God.

5.2 Love of neighbour and love of God

The gospel of Matthew contains the famous double commandment of love:

> He said to him, 'You shall love the Lord your God with all your heart, and with all your soul, and with all your mind.' This is the greatest and first commandment. And a second is like it: 'You shall love your neighbor as yourself.'[99]

Rahner classifies the relation between these two commandments as a unity in difference. Love of God and love of neighbour are, in essence, two names for the same reality, yet they must nevertheless not be collapsed into each other.[100] He explains this with the help of the transcendental-categorical distinction. Love of neighbour, as thematically expressed categorical action, can be distinguished from the love of God, as an unthematic transcendental horizon of action. Rahner claims that every concrete and thematic act of loving a fellow human being entails, at least implicitly, love of the unthematic horizon of freedom, which Christians call God.[101] What he does not say is that God can only be loved through love of neighbour. God is also loved through prayer, trust and love. Likewise, the assertion that love of neighbour implicitly contains love of God does not seek to devalue the love of neighbour. The neighbour self is still very much the object of love, even though inter-human love is only fully realized when it is thematically identified as love of God.[102] As Werner Jeanrond observes, Rahner has

---

[96] Karl Rahner, 'Liebe', *Sacramentum* Mundi 3 (1969): 237–8.
[97] Karl Rahner, 'The "Commandment" of Love in Relation to the Other Commandments', in *TI*, vol. 5 (London: Darton, Longman and Dodd, 1966), 443–4.
[98] Ibid., 447.
[99] Mt. 22, 37–9 (NSRV).
[100] Rahner, 'Reflections on the Unity', 232. Gerald J. Beyer, 'Karl Rahner on the Radical Unity of the Love of God and Neighbour', *Irish Theological Quarterly* 68 (2003): 264–5, n. 80, points to the distinction between 'unity' and 'identity'. He notes that Rahner sometimes uses the word *Identität* but argues that unity conveys Rahner's intention better in these instances because 'unity entails internal diversity, whereas identity rules out internal diversity'.
[101] Ibid., 237–8.
[102] Ibid., 238.

an acute eye for the agency and subjectivity of both lover and beloved. The neighbour is not reduced to a means by which to achieve a higher end, namely, the love of God.[103] So, despite their interconnectedness, love of neighbour is not simply identical with love of God. Why does Rahner argue, then, that they do form a unity? The answer is that love of God comprises the transcendental condition for our love of neighbour. The same act of love can be understood as having two 'mutually inclusive objects': neighbour and God.[104]

Rahner argues that freedom can only be exercised against an infinite horizon, in close analogy to his metaphysics of knowledge. Without this horizon we would be 'locked up' in our finite self, and therefore we would not be free. A free subject is simultaneously aware of her own freedom, and therefore takes responsibility for her actions, as well as the limitations of that freedom. This recognition of having a limited, rather than an absolutely free, subjectivity requires a *Vorgriff* of a horizon of infinite freedom.[105] Rahner argues that by virtue of God's universal salvific will, this horizon has been transformed universally through God's gift of grace and now is oriented to Godself. As a result, human knowing and loving actually involve an unthematic encounter with God.[106] In other words, love of God (subject genitive) has transformed our horizon of love. It is because we are loved that we can concretely love ourselves and others.[107] When we love, we implicitly affirm the horizon which is the transcendental condition for our capacity to love. Hence, God is the 'dialogical co-partner' in every individual act of love.[108] However, it is important to realize that this unthematic presence of God in neighbourly love should not be understood in terms of an 'objective' presence. We do not encounter the transcendental horizon as an ordinary object, regardless of the fact that we can only talk about this horizon by objectifying it.[109]

Importantly, while love of God is ultimately the transcendental condition for any act of love, concrete neighbourly love is logically prior to the love of God. We are first in the world and with other persons, before we become aware of our relation to God in this relation to other persons. For this reason, Rahner terms love of neighbour to be the primary act of loving God. It is impossible to love the invisible God without loving one's visible brothers and sisters.[110] In his later writings, Rahner increasingly emphasizes that he advocates a unity in difference. He distances himself from a secular view that sees love of God as an old-fashioned and outdated term for humanistic love. Alternatively, Rahner reaffirms that 'existence towards God' belongs to the most inner core of human nature, giving human beings their value and dignity. Only by recognizing our neighbourly others as beings oriented towards God, can we love them unconditionally, without turning them into means towards our own ends.[111]

---

[103] Jeanrond, *A Theology of Love*, 146.
[104] Beyer, 'Karl Rahner on the Radical Unity', 270.
[105] Rahner, *Foundations*, 98.
[106] Rahner, 'Reflections on the Unity', 239.
[107] Jeanrond, *A Theology of Love*, 146.
[108] Rahner, 'Liebe', 243.
[109] Rahner, 'Reflections on the Unity', 244–5.
[110] Ibid., 247.
[111] Karl Rahner, *Wer ist dein Bruder?* (Freiburg: Herder, 1981), 17–18.

Rowan Williams draws an interesting parallel with Augustine's theology of love in this regard.[112] For Augustine, loving human beings independently of loving God may always prove inadequate and abusive of others, because we fail to recognize what they are. The dignity of human beings consists precisely of their being an image and sign of God. Loving another human being, therefore, means loving them as 'pointing Godwards'.[113] Williams concludes that Rahner's idea that neighbourly love is always already related to God is a version of 'Augustinian love'.[114] Importantly, both Augustine and Rahner agree that there exists a fundamental unity between the two loves. Augustine writes: 'Choose whichever love you like. You choose love of neighbor; it won't be genuine unless God is also loved. You choose love of God, it won't be genuine unless neighbor is also tacitly included.'[115] Rahner concludes that love of neighbour already contains the 'original root' of Christianity; namely, the salvific love of God. But he also remarks that while the beginning is there, it must still be unfolded to its full 'breadth' and in its 'fullness'.[116] Love of neighbour must follow its inner dynamism and seek to thematize the unthematic love of God, which is always already present as a constitutive element of inter-human relations.

The interrelation of love of neighbour and love of God comprises another illustration of the dialectical interrelationship of transcendentality and hermeneutics that characterizes Rahner's approach. His transcendental anthropology is not concerned with the human subject as isolated, self-referential individual. On the contrary, the Rahnerian human person exists by virtue of relationality. Human self-realization takes places through loving encounters with finite human others and the infinitely divine Other. These two decentring movements of love mutually imply one another; love of God is realized through love of neighbour and vice versa. Rahner's transcendental account of human subjectivity, therefore, advocates a 'surrendering' of the radically autonomous subject and the reconceptualization of subjectivity in terms of relationality.[117]

6 The dialectics of mystery

The preceding analysis of Rahner's view of the historicity of revelation, experience and interpretation and of love has sought to establish that his approach is remarkably more hermeneutical than is usually acknowledged. Throughout this discussion, the theme of mystery has recurred several times. As Philip Endean writes, Rahner's references to mystery are 'organically part of his intellectual achievement', and not 'merely pious

---

[112] Rowan Williams, 'Augustinian Love', in *Dynamics of Difference. Christianity and Alterity: A Festschrift for Werner G. Jeanrond*, ed. Ulrich Schmiedel and James M. Matarazzo Jr. (London: Bloomsbury, 2015), 189–97.
[113] Williams, 'Augustinian Love', 196.
[114] Ibid., 197.
[115] Augustine, 'Sermon 90A', in *The Works of Saint Augustine: A Translation for the 21st Century. Part III: Sermons. Vol. 11: Newly Discovered Sermons*, trans. Edmund Hill, ed. John E. Rotelle (New York: New City Press, 1997), 84.
[116] Rahner, 'Reflections on the Unity', 249.
[117] See Lash, *Easter in Ordinary*, 246.

decoration'.[118] This theme, which is suggestive of negative theology, weaves throughout Rahner's theological reflections. In this concluding section, I will explain that considering these reflections on mystery is essential to a proper understanding of his transcendental approach. The concept of mystery offers a distinct hermeneutical key by which to understand Rahner's transcendental interconnecting of both anthropology and theology. It contains a crucial safeguard against an idealist self-centred notion of subjectivity and guards against an objectifying or onto-theological understanding of divine transcendence.[119]

6.1 The dark gate to knowledge

Rahner's reconceptualization of subjectivity through mystery is best explained in connection with his reflections on the traditional teaching of the 'incomprehensibility of God'. This teaching is usually interpreted negatively; finite and created human intellects are thought to be incapable of understanding the infinite God. God remains incomprehensible, even when human reason is fulfilled in the beatific vision.[120] Alternatively, Rahner suggests an interpretation of this teaching as conveying something positive about human finitude. This alternative interpretation requires a reconsideration of a common and widespread epistemological ideal of knowledge.

A dominant model of truth presents knowledge as a quest to comprehend and control the object of knowledge. Rahner attributes this model to a combination of the Greek pursuit of absolute knowledge and the modern concept of rationality promoted by German idealism and the natural sciences.[121] Portraying rational clarity as the norm of knowledge results in a truncated and superficial understanding of mystery. A mystery is seen as something obscure and deficient, a grey or vague area which we cannot penetrate or comprehend yet. Rahner's response seeks to turn this order around radically. He argues that truth is mysterious, first and foremost, rather than rationally evident and clear. Accordingly, knowledge is characterized by its potential openness to mystery.[122] This can be explained with reference to the concept of transcendental experience.

For Rahner, mystery is not marked by deficiency and obscurity. Rather, mystery must be seen, as Nicholas Lash puts it, as a 'dark gate' to knowledge.[123] Our ordinary

---

[118] Philip Endean, 'Has Rahnerian Theology a Future?', in *The Cambridge Companion to Karl Rahner*, 289. The mystical element of Rahner's theology has been extensively studied. Klaus P. Fischer, *Der Mensch als Geheimnis: Die Anthropologie Karl Rahners* (Freiburg: Herder, 1974), initiated a reading of Rahner's work through a 'mystical' lens. Subsequent studies that continue this approach include James J. Bacik, *Apologetics and the Eclipse of Mystery: Mystagogy According to Karl Rahner* (Notre Dame, IN: Notre Dame University Press, 1980) and Philip Endean, *Karl Rahner and Ignatian Spirituality* (Oxford: Oxford University Press, 2001).
[119] See also Jessica Murdoch, 'Transcendence and Postmodernity: A Rahnerian Reading', *New Blackfriars* 92 (2011): 678–90, for an argument that defends Rahner's concept of transcendence in response to the criticisms raised by Nietzsche, Heidegger and Derrida.
[120] Karl Rahner, 'The Hidenness of God' [1974], in *TI*, vol. 16, trans. David Morland (London: Darton, Longman and Todd, 1979), 227–31.
[121] Rahner, 'The Hidenness of God', 231.
[122] Ibid., 236.
[123] See Lash, *Easter in Ordinary*, 233.

interpretative being-in-the world requires a mysterious horizon as the transcendental condition for grasping and knowing non-mysterious, finite realities. Since all acts of knowing implicitly involve an unthematic experience of this mysterious horizon, the world has a mysterious character for us at heart. Rahner strongly emphasizes the ecstatic character of our encounter with mystery.[124] We are addressed by mystery, even before we start to make sense of ourselves and of our world. Crucially, by grasping us, mystery forces human knowing to transform itself. Mystery shows that knowing involves allowing oneself to be grasped, rather than attempting a comprehensive grasp. It radically decentres human subjects and humbles their intellectual claims and pretentions. Letting ourselves be grasped by mystery teaches us the limits of human subjectivity and shows that the human person is 'not the shepherd of being' but 'the one whose being is bestowed upon him by the mystery'.[125] The recognition of the primacy of this mystery gives rise to a corresponding revaluation of our ordinary knowledge. Scientific, philosophical and existential knowledge are now seen as being 'only a tiny island in the immense ocean of the unexplored'.[126] This realization functions as a powerful critique of any given historical and societal structure, reminding us that we cannot masterfully plan our future.[127] Importantly, this also demonstrates that Rahner's notion of subjectivity is far removed from the Cartesian quest for 'certain and indubitable' knowledge.[128]

Even when we find our fulfilment in the beatific vision, God continues to be incomprehensible and mysterious to us. According to Rahner, this is actually something positive. God is our ultimate future, precisely by being an ungraspable mystery, not in spite of it. Accepting our finitude also allows us to transcend that same finitude, so that our orientation to mystery becomes a blessed participation in mystery. This idea of participation in mystery as beatitude has already been developed in the patristic literature. Authors like Pseudo-Dionysius the Areopagite, Maximus the Confessor and Gregory of Nyssa all emphasize the dimension of unknowing and entering of darkness in their reflections on the beatitude of human beings. Viewing the mysterious nature of God to be a blessing, rather than negativity, these authors are able to reconcile 'radical creatureliness' with 'radical proximity to God'.[129]

Does this mean that Rahner advocates a radically negative theology, one in which we cannot say anything about the mysterious horizon of human transcendence except that it is incomprehensible? It is quite the contrary. Rahner is convinced that the *deus absconditus* (hidden god) has chosen to reveal itself. However, as *deus revelatus* (revealed

---

[124] Karl Rahner, 'The Concept of Mystery in Catholic Theology' [1959], in *TI*, vol. 4, trans. Kevin Smith (London: Darton, Longman and Todd, 1974), 43.
[125] Rahner, 'The Hiddenness of God', 236.
[126] Rahner, 'The Concept of Mystery', 57.
[127] Rahner, 'The Hiddenness of God', 242.
[128] See Murdoch, 'Overcoming the Foundationalist', 382–4, who argues that Rahner can be considered a 'metaphysical foundationalist', insofar as he understands God to be the ground of all reality. However, Murdoch maintains that Rahner's insistence on the mysterious and unknowable nature of God demonstrates that this metaphysical foundationalism does not imply an epistemological foundationalism.
[129] Rahner, 'The Concept of Mystery', 58.

god), God communicates Godself precisely as incomprehensible mystery.[130] Through historical revelation we learn that the mystery does not remain aloof and distant. The history of revelation, culminating in Jesus Christ, discloses that the mysterious horizon is actually God who seeks to relate to humankind. Historical revelation, thus, brings to our express attention our implicit relation to the self-communicating God. However, Rahner emphasizes that historical revelation should not be viewed as a gnostic overcoming of mystery. Instead, revelation means that 'the "deus absconditus" becomes radically present as the abiding mystery'.[131] Accordingly, the beatitude of finite human beings consists not in a striving for absolute and comprehensive knowledge, but rather in a surrendering to mystery. Or, in the famous words of Thomas Aquinas: *adoro te devote, latens Deitas* (I devoutly adore you, hidden God).[132]

6.2 Theological speech and silence

Rahner's reflections on God as enduring mystery change not only the notion of subjectivity but also the task of theology. Theology must develop a 'mystagogy into the experience of grace' and use its concepts and explanations in order to demonstrate that the variety of human experiences is related to this original experience of nameless mystery. Rahner describes this task as a *reductio in mysterium* (reduction into mystery).[133] What consequences does this have for theological concepts and for language? Rahner's theology of mystery resists the temptation to stop talking at all about God. He argues that theology cannot resign itself to an attitude of silent adoration of a meditative theology and maintains the need for explicitly engaging with mystery.

Theology must, therefore, take up the hermeneutical task of interpreting and naming the mystery disclosed in experience. The theological statements resulting from this hermeneutical endeavour contain a radical reference to that which infinitely transcends them. Without this reference, theological statements would become meaningless.[134] However, Rahner also acknowledges the fundamental relativity of all theological statements, resulting from the fact that we cannot grasp and name mystery through our words and concepts. Theology must be attentive to the perpetual hermeneutical task of speaking, in perennially new ways about this unnameable mystery. Theological statements 'must be expressed in words in order that we can arrive at the authentic silence which we need'.[135]

Hence, Rahner advocates a modest and critical theology. On the one hand, theology must attempt to speak of God and cannot regard all human speech about the divine as being contaminated. On the other hand, theology cannot claim that its actual formulations in human words are ever complete and comprehensive expressions of mystery. Theologians must remain conscious of their pilgrim state, so as to avoid falling into idolatry. Rahner refers to the traditional teaching about analogy as the

---

[130] Rahner, 'The Hiddenness of God', 243.
[131] Ibid., 239.
[132] Rahner, 'The Concept of Mystery', 37.
[133] Rahner, 'Reflections on Methodology', 101; 111.
[134] Ibid., 112.
[135] Ibid.

proper mode of speaking about God, in order to maintain the precarious balance between the positive and negative dimension of theology.[136] Referring to the Fourth Lateran Council (1215), Rahner emphasizes that we cannot know anything positively about God without the concurrent realization of the radical inadequacy of every positive statement. However, both the positive and the negative dimensions are equally essential to theology. It would be wrong to let radicalized negative theologies 'conquer' God.[137] Rahner's careful reflections on the difficulty of naming God, as the whither of human transcendence, demonstrate his own attempt to maintain this balance between speaking and being silent about God.

Interpretative and clarificatory expressions about the mysterious horizon of human transcendence remain necessary, despite their inherent limitations. Rahner does not shy away from using metaphysical language in his naming of mystery. On the contrary, he claims that the theological interpretation of mystery necessarily involves an application of metaphysical reflection: 'The man who has not the courage to pursue a metaphysics (which is not the same as a closed system), a metaphysics which can be contradicted, cannot be a good theologian.'[138] However, this theological appropriation of metaphysics must be conscious of the fact that every metaphysical explanation remains, ultimately, inadequate. A proper metaphysics puts itself into question, so as to rethink itself. Moreover, theology must employ various metaphysical languages and might, for that reason, speak all those languages badly. Nevertheless, Rahner argues that it is possible to hear in those various metaphysical languages a *philosophia perennis* (perennial philosophy).[139]

Rahner's metaphysics of knowledge, and its development into a theology of revelation, serves as an example of this hermeneutical attempt to interpret mystery. His thematization of mystery, as *Vorgriff* of Being and of a self-communicating and loving God, seeks to respect the ungraspable nature of that same mystery. Rahner emphasizes that this horizon is never available to us as objects; it is anticipated rather than grasped. Moreover, his argument for the implicit co-affirmation of God in the *Vorgriff* is not intended to serve as a proof for the existence of God, but rather a *docta ignorantia* (learned ignorance). Rahner continually warns us for the misunderstanding of treating God as an ordinary object of experience. He actively opposes the onto-theological conception of God as a supreme being among all beings. No ontological or theological explication can claim to have defined or comprehended the horizon of transcendence. This horizon is, first and foremost, present in the mode of absence, as distant silence and cannot be reached directly.[140]

This emphasis on the non-objective, unnameable and mysterious character of the horizon is a negative reminder that accompanies Rahner's positive reflections on this horizon, continuously interrupting these positive statements to prevent their becoming closed. The task of naming God is, in principle, open and open-ended: 'The true

---

[136] Rahner, *Foundations*, 71–2.
[137] Karl Rahner, 'Observations on the Doctrine of God in Catholic Dogmatics' [1966], in *TI*, vol. 9, trans. Graham Harrison (London: Darton, Longman and Todd, 1972), 128.
[138] Rahner, 'Observations on the Doctrine', 138.
[139] Ibid., 143–4.
[140] Rahner, *Foundations*, 66.

radicalism in the doctrine of God can only be the continual destruction of an idol, an idol in the place of God, the idol of a theory about him.'[141] Rahner's attempt to name mystery, while remaining conscious of the inadequacies of this act of naming, eminently illustrates that his theological method encompasses a dialectics of transcendentality and hermeneutics. He seeks to foster a hermeneutically open vision of philosophy and theology, yet without wishing to rescind from the attempt to formulate the transcendental and ontological conditions which enable this searching for the mysterious God.

7 Conclusion

This chapter has established the second step of my argument for an alternative understanding of Rahner's theological method as entailing a dialectics between transcendentality and hermeneutics. Such a different perspective on Rahner's method may seem problematic in view of the various critiques raised against Rahner's method, which all in one form or another argue that his method is insufficiently hermeneutical. In critical response to these critics, I have sought to demonstrate that several aspects in Rahner's early work, which are already indicative of a dialectical interrelation between transcendentality and hermeneutics, are developed as well as modified in his later work. To justify this claim, I examined four different themes in Rahner's more mature writings that make manifest that his transcendental method acquires a more robust hermeneutical profile over time.

Rahner's reflection on revelation in *Hearer of the Word* shows that his incarnational epistemological focus on the intellectual, spatio-temporal orientation of human subjectivity is transposed and developed into a historical orientation that attends both to knowledge and to freedom. The conversion to the phantasm becomes a conversion to history; *spirit in the world* becomes *spirit in history*. This turn to history is developed by way of a turn to historical experience as the primary *locus theologicus*. Analysing the key distinction between transcendental and categorical experience as an analytical, rather than real, distinction has helped to bring to light Rahner's dialectical interrelation of experience and interpretation. Despite the fact that Rahner's 'mediated-immediacy' epistemology prioritizes the experiential dimension, it is evident that he is anything but hermeneutically naive.

Another markedly hermeneutical development of Rahner's early transcendental approach concerns his growing attention to inter-subjectivity, by way of a focus on freedom and love. With help of the transcendental-categorical distinction, Rahner sketches a vision of love as constituted by two mutually related dimensions. Loving other people is essential for realizing our lives. Yet concrete love of neighbour can only be thought of against the horizon of transcendental love of God and vice versa. This argument for the unity of love of God and love of neighbour, which avoids collapsing these loves into each other, comprises another clear example of the interconnectedness of the hermeneutical and the transcendental aspects in Rahner's work.

---

[141] Rahner, 'Observations on the Doctrine of God', 127.

Finally, reading Rahner's transcendental account of human subjectivity and transcendence through a lens of mystery demonstrates that he disavows both an idealist notion of subjectivity and reason and an onto-theological conception of God. Rahner's reflections on mystery not only offer a radically different understanding of the nature of human knowing but also introduce an important qualification to theology and the theological use of transcendental and metaphysical reflection. The discussion about mystery concluded with this tension between the need to name the mysterious horizon of experience theologically, with help of transcendental and metaphysical arguments, and the inherent limitations and perennial open-endedness of this hermeneutical exercise. For Rahner, this tension is connected to the specific relationship between philosophy and theology, which in turn cannot be seen apart from the relationship between nature and grace. This naturally invites a discussion of Rahner's concept of the supernatural existential – the topic of the next chapter.

5

The theological *a priori*: Transforming the transcendental method

1 Introduction

The question about the relationship between philosophy and theology in Rahner's work remains a bone of contention. A central discussion point within these debates revolves around the concept of the supernatural existential and its consequences for the understanding of the nature of theology and philosophy. In this chapter, I will discuss the theological background of this controversial concept, its critical reception by some theologians and its consequences for understanding Rahner's methodology. My aim is to show that the supernatural existential intensifies Rahner's hermeneutical awareness, ultimately leading to a theological metamorphosis of transcendental methodology.

First, I aim to explain how the incarnational dimension of Rahner's transcendental theology is ultimately anchored in salvation history. This incarnational orientation informs his advocacy for a new understanding of grace, which serves to explain the Christian conviction that God communicates Godself universally to humankind. Second, this new perspective on grace demands a clarification of the relationship between nature and grace. For Rahner, nature and grace are intimately connected in concrete existence. He explains this by introducing the concept of the supernatural existential into his theological anthropology. This concept, in turn, comprises the basis for the notions of both transcendental revelation and anonymous Christians. This leads me to examine two critiques of the supernatural existential. Whereas John Milbank holds that Rahner 'naturalizes the supernatural', Hansjürgen Verweyen conversely argues that he 'supernaturalizes the natural'. What unites these distinct criticisms is the desire to maintain a pure theology and a pure philosophy, respectively. Responding to these critiques, I argue that Rahner seeks to undercut the specific, sharp separation between philosophy and theology. While an autonomous philosophy is crucial for theology, the fact that concrete reality is a graced reality implies that a purely natural philosophy is impossible. This insight into the necessary 'contamination' of philosophy by salvation history makes Rahner's hermeneutical perspective on transcendental method manifest. I turn to Rahner's reflections on pluralism and gnoseological concupiscence, to disclose the intensification of this hermeneutical awareness. These insights explain Rahner's plea for a modest transcendental theology and his contribution to a theological reconfiguration of transcendentality.

2 The incarnational shape of transcendental theology

The question of the relation between philosophy and theology is a constant thread that runs through Rahner's life and work. His early philosophical formation left a distinct mark on his theological form and style, despite his later transfer to theology. However, Rahner has never cast any doubt that he identified primarily as a theologian.[1] He has firmly rejected the suggestion of the existence of a caesura between a philosophical and a theological period in his career and he has affirmed that philosophy has stood in the service of his theological work.[2] Rahner, thus, presupposes the facticity of the Christian revelation, and his use of transcendental reflection serves to establish the legitimacy and plausibility of its faith claims.[3] One particular faith conviction lies at the heart of Rahner's theology: God intends to relate to humankind through historical self-communication in grace. Beginning with this fundamental assumption, Rahner presents a vision of reality as a 'world of grace'.[4] Crucially, this concentration on grace deeply influences Rahner's transcendental methodology and leads to a fundamental reconfiguration of the relationship between philosophy and theology. Thus far, I have merely acknowledged this specific procedure, without discussing it in detail. However, Rahner's particular use of philosophy within theology is essential to understanding his idiosyncratic interrelation of hermeneutics and transcendentality.

Rahner clearly defines the agenda of theology as follows: 'Revelation is revelation of salvation and therefore theology is essentially salvation theology.'[5] What is salvation? For Rahner, this question must be answered with reference to the historical event of Jesus Christ.[6] Rahner views humankind as hoping and searching for an absolute saviour – a tangible manifestation of the healing and redemption of humankind. Standing within the Christian tradition of faith, he argues that, in the historical event of the God-man Jesus Christ, this absolute saviour has been found. In the hypostatic union, God has communicated Godself absolutely to humankind. The incarnation forms the irreversible climax and manifestation of God's self-communication, affirming and guaranteeing that God seeks to be intimately connected with humankind.[7] This particular historical event reveals 'proto-eschatologically' that God desires the salvation of everyone.[8]

---

[1] See Karl Rahner, 'Zum Geleit', in Eicher, *Die anthropologische Wende*, ix.
[2] Rahner, 'Interview', 80.
[3] Lehmann, 'Karl Rahner, ein Porträt', xli.
[4] Leo O'Donovan (ed.), *A World of Grace: An Introduction to the Themes and Foundations of Rahner's Theology* (New York: Crossroad, 1981).
[5] Karl Rahner, 'Theology and Anthropology', in *TI*, vol. 9, trans. Graham Harrison (London: Darton, Longman and Todd, 1972), 35.
[6] See also Roman Siebenrock, 'Transzendentale Offenbarung. Bedeutungsanalyse eines Begriffs im Spätwerk Rahners als Beispiel methodisch geleiteter Rahnerforschung', *Zeitschrift für katholische Theologie* 126 (2004): 45.
[7] Rahner, 'Theology and Anthropology', 36. It is important to note that despite Rahner's rather 'high' Christology, he certainly does not downplay the essential importance of Jesus Christ's human nature. See, for instance, the article 'The Eternal Significance of the Humanity of Jesus for our Relation to God' [1953], in *TI*, vol. 3, trans. Karl-H. and Boniface Kruger (London: Darton, Longman and Todd, 1974).
[8] See Thomas Peter Fössel, 'Warum ein Existential *übernatürlich* ist. Anmerkungen zur kontroversen Diskussion um Karl Rahners Theologoumenon vom "übernatürlichen Existential"', *Theologie und Philosophie* 80 (2005): 392.

Now, according to Rahner, the task of transcendental theology is to investigate the receptivity of human subjectivity for salvation (*Heilsempfänglichkeit*).[9] Importantly, Rahner warns against a potential misunderstanding of his method. The incarnation cannot be transcendentally deduced through a reflection on human subjectivity. It is only the actual encounter with the historical person of Jesus Christ that makes this transcendental reduction possible.[10] Rahner's theological focus on the human subject is, therefore, ultimately grounded in an incarnational motivation and stresses the intimate connection that exists between Christology, anthropology and theology. Jesus Christ reveals that our knowledge about human nature is intrinsically connected to our knowledge about God and vice versa. In Christ, we truly learn who God is and we truly learn what human beings are.[11]

What does a transcendental reflection on the salvific Christ event tell us about humanity and human subjectivity? Rahner responds to this question by revolutionizing the traditional understanding of grace and advocating instead for a relational understanding of grace.[12] He argues that grace *is* God's self-communication – something which fundamentally transforms human nature. Rahner pleads for a reconsideration of uncreated grace as God's presence to human beings, thereby distancing himself from the conventional scholastic emphasis on created grace. The latter is traditionally described as the 'indwelling of the Holy Spirit'.[13] God's indwelling cannot result from ontic changes, caused efficiently by created grace. This view might lead to an understanding of grace as something which is added from the outside to an already-existing human nature. This 'extrinsicist' concept of grace cannot account for the radically new relationship between creature and infinite creator which is caused by grace.[14]

Alternatively, Rahner draws attention to the self-communication of God through uncreated grace. Grace is no longer seen as a 'thing', but as the self-communication in which 'the giver is the gift'.[15] Rahner employs the Aristotelian notion of formal causality to explain that, in grace, God's very self is communicated. To be precise, however, he speaks of 'quasi-formal' causality in order to respect God's transcendence and to

---

[9] Rahner, 'Theology and Anthropology', 35.
[10] Ibid., 41. See also Rahner, *Foundations*, 177. Lennan, 'The Theology of Karl Rahner: An Alternative to the *Ressourcement*?', 414–15, emphasizes Rahner's inductive procedure over and against misconceptions of Rahner's method as the deductive construction of a model or idea.
[11] Rahner, 'Theology and Anthropology', 28; and Karl Rahner, 'On the Theology of the Incarnation' [1958], in *TI*, vol. 4, trans. Kevin Smith (London: Darton, Longman and Todd, 1974), 116. See also Ignacy Bokwa, 'Das Verhältnis zwischen Christologie und Anthropologie als Interpretationsmodell der Theologie Karl Rahners', in *Karl Rahner in der Diskussion. Erste und zweites Innsbrucker Karl-Rahner-Symposion*, ed. Roman A. Siebenrock (Innsbruck: Tyrolia Verlag, 2001), 33–43.
[12] See Roman Siebenrock, '"Draw nigh to God and He will draw nigh to you" (James 4:8) The Development of Karl Rahner's Theological Thinking in Its First Period', *Louvain Studies* 29 (2004): 39.
[13] Karl Rahner, 'Some Implications of the Scholastic Concept of Uncreated Grace' [1939], in *TI*, vol. 1, trans. Cornelius Ernst (London: Darton, Longman and Todd, 1974), 320–1. For the scholastic distinction between created and uncreated grace, see Roman Siebenrock and Walter Schmolly,'"Der Heilswille Gottes berührt uns in Christus Jesus und der Kirche": Die erste Gnadenvorlesung', in *Der Denkweg Karl Rahners*, 106–43, esp. 118–22.
[14] Rahner, 'Some Implications of the Scholastic Concept', 329.
[15] Ibid., 334–5. See also Rahner, *Foundations*, 120.

make clear the notion that his exposition of grace involves the application of an innerworldly category to God. According to Rahner, God's self-communication in grace is oriented to its ultimate fulfilment in the beatific vision, but it is already present in the human person insofar as it forms the ontological condition for this beatific vision. In other words, the eschatological union between creature and creator has already been initiated here and now.[16]

Human self-transcendence is not asymptotically oriented towards an aloof and ever-receding mysterious horizon, due to this gift of Godself in grace. Grace transforms human transcendence, so that we are invited into immediacy with the mystery of love that Christians name God. Now, in order to make this claim intelligible, an ontology of the transcendental subject is required.[17] Crucially, such an ontology must explain how God's gift of grace relates to the nature of the human person. How is the finite creature able to relate to an infinite God? When and where does self-communication take place? How can the freedom of God, as well as the freedom of the human person, be maintained in a world of grace? Rahner addresses these issues by developing his famous notion of the supernatural existential.

3 The supernatural existential

According to Fergus Kerr, 'the bitterest dispute in Roman Catholic theology this century [the twentieth century] has been over the proper way to characterize the relationship between nature and grace'.[18] Theologians of the so-called *nouvelle théologie* (new theology) opposed theologians adhering to the predominant neo-scholastic theology in this debate. Whereas the former advocated a return to the sources (*ressourcement*), in order to reconnect Christian faith with contemporary experience, the latter appealed to the intellectual force of the neo-Thomist conceptual framework in order to avoid a modernist relativization of Catholic dogma. A particularly intense battleground here concerned the question of how the supernatural (grace) is related to the natural (nature). Henri de Lubac played a key role in this debate with his publication of *Surnaturel* in 1946.[19] In this work he criticized the two-tiered, neo-scholastic structure of nature and grace. Most importantly, he attacked the notion of pure nature as invariably leading to an extrinsicist concept of grace. De Lubac sought to revive the patristic and medieval view of the human person as having a *desiderium naturale visionis beatificae* (natural desire for the beatific vision).[20] However, De Lubac's opponents feared that his proposal

---

[16] Rahner, 'Some Implications of the Scholastic Concept', 329–36.
[17] Rahner, 'Theology and Anthropology', 37.
[18] Kerr, *Immortal Longings*, 164. For a more detailed account of this debate, see Stephen Duffy, *The Graced Horizon. Nature and Grace in Modern Theological Thought* (Collegeville, MN: The Liturgical Press, 1992). This debate also found a parallel in Protestant theology, which saw an equally vigorous debate between Karl Barth and Emil Brunner on the '*Anknüpfungspunkt*' (point of contact) between human nature and the message of the Gospel.
[19] Henri de Lubac, *Surnaturel: Études historiques* (Paris: Aubier, 1946).
[20] For a succinct account of the historical and philosophical background to the natural desire, see Louis Dupré, 'On the Natural Desire of Seeing God', *Radical Orthodoxy: Theology, Philosophy, Politics* 1 (2012): 81–94. A more extensive study on the natural desire for God is provided by

would endanger the gratuity of grace and would result in immanentism. The official reaction was to follow in the form of Pope Pius XII's encyclical, *Humani Generis*, which condemned several modernist tendencies, including the attempt to 'destroy the gratuity of the supernatural order' by those who argue that 'God (…) cannot create intellectual beings without ordering and calling them to the beatific vision'.[21] While this formed an implicit rejection of the *nouvelle théologie*, it did not settle the debate about nature and grace.

Rahner enters the debate shortly after the publication of *Humani Generis*.[22] He introduces the supernatural existential in order to explain how human persons have a universal orientation towards God, while trying to steer clear of the Scylla of extrinsicism and the Charybdis of immanentism.[23] The guiding conviction that God seeks the salvation of each and every person already comprised a central element of Rahner's 1937–8 lectures on grace, *De Gratia Christi*, and continued to serve as a guiding element in his work.[24] The supernatural existential plays an essential role in explaining the possibility of such a divine universal salvific will. It serves to explain that while grace and nature are conceptually distinct, they are factually and historically indissoluble, given that they are intertwined in human existence.

3.1 Navigating between extrinsicism and immanentism

Rahner deems both opposing positions in the debate on nature and grace to be problematic, insofar as they represent two equally undesirable extremes. Although he does explicitly state his agreement with *Humani Generis*, his main object of critique is the extrinsicist conception of grace. His own position is, therefore, highly sympathetic to the *nouvelle théologie*'s concerns. According to neo-scholastic theology, the natural and the supernatural can be neatly delineated as independent domains, which have their own integrity. Consequently, it is possible to develop a comprehensive natural anthropology that explains concrete human existence, without any reference being made to the supernatural. The supernatural is conceived of as a superstructure that lies entirely beyond the capacities of human nature and the reality of human experience. Hence, grace can only be imposed on nature through the external and free decree

---

Lawrence Feingold, *The Natural Desire according to St. Thomas and his Interpreters* (Washington: The Catholic University of America Press, 2004).

[21] Pius XII, Encyclical *Humani Generis* (DH 3891).
[22] Although Rahner's first use of the supernatural existential dates from 1942, the concept is first programmatically used in the article 'On the Relationship between Nature and Grace', in *TI*, vol. 1, trans. Cornelius Ernst (London: Darton, Longman and Todd, 1974), 219–317. This article was first published in 1950 in the journal *Orientierung*. In a second essay, 'Nature and Grace' [1960], in *TI*, vol. 4, trans. Kevin Smith (London: Darton, Longman and Todd, 1974), 165–88, Rahner revisits and clarifies his theory on the supernatural existential. For the early development of the supernatural existential in Rahner's work, see Paul Rulands, *Menschsein unter dem An-Spruch der Gnade. Das übernatürliche Existential und der Begriff der natura pura bei Karl Rahners*, Innsbrucker theologische Studien 55 (Innsbruck: Tyrolia Verlag, 2000).
[23] See Stephen Duffy, 'Experience of Grace', in *The Cambridge Companion to Karl Rahner*, 50–2.
[24] See Siebenrock and Schmolly, '"Der Heilswille Gottes"', 132.

of God. It is this *duplex ordo* (dual order) of nature and grace that Rahner calls into question.²⁵

In the first place, this *duplex ordo* is problematic from an existential perspective. Rahner argues that the neo-scholastic extrinsicist conception of grace may, inadvertently, lead to naturalism and atheism. If grace has no bearing on the issues, concerns and realities of their life, why would people be interested at all in grace? Would any divine interruption not be perceived of as an unwelcome disruption of ordinary life?²⁶ In the second place, Rahner deems the epistemological and metaphysical presuppositions underlying the notion of pure nature to be problematic. How are we to distinguish between that which is solely due to nature and that which has been touched by grace in human nature and in experience? According to Rahner, revelation shows nature and grace to be far more intimately connected than the neo-scholastic *duplex ordo* structure suggests. Hence, pure nature is a questionable concept.²⁷

Rahner's alternative theological framework begins with the universal salvific will as God's 'first and last plan' for the world.²⁸ Since God seeks to share Godself in self-communication, God creates the human person in such a way that she can be the recipient of this gift of love. It is important to recognize the nuanced viewpoint that Rahner puts forward here. Alongside the *nouvelle théologie*, he argues that the natural desire for God belongs to the ontological structure of concrete human beings. We are structurally and ontologically *different* because of this orientation to God. Yet, contra the *nouvelle théologie*, he maintains that his ontological determination is not constitutive of human nature as such. This immanentist view would undermine the gratuity of grace, both from the human and from the divine perspective on freedom. If the human person is to be a real partner of God, in the human–divine relation, the offer of God's love must be accepted as unexpected wonder and free gift.²⁹ If we had been created with the desire for communion with God, God would be forced to fulfil this desire, because to do otherwise would go against the meaning of such a creation. But in this case, too, the gift of grace is no longer a free gift.

For these reasons, Rahner maintains the possibility of a human nature that does not possess a supernaturally elevated desire for God. There remains a theoretical distinction between human nature which has a natural end and human nature which has a supernatural end. Yet, Rahner affirms that concrete human beings have a supernatural orientation and are, therefore, never purely natural. How, then, are we to understand this paradoxical unexacted natural desire for personal union with God? Rahner postulates the supernatural existential in order to answer this very question.

If the human person is to be the addressee of grace, she must have a 'congeniality' or 'real potency' for such a gift.³⁰ This potency must be a permanent and abiding

---

[25] Rahner, 'On the Relationship between Nature and Grace', 298–9. Rahner, 'Nature and Grace', 167–8.
[26] Rahner, 'On the Relationship between Nature and Grace', 298–9.
[27] Ibid., 300–2.
[28] Ibid., 308. In 'Nature and Grace', 176, Rahner explains his preference for a 'Scotist' explanation of creation from the perspective of the incarnation. In other words, the world is created so that God can communicate Godself fully in Jesus Christ.
[29] Rahner, 'On the Relationship between Nature and Grace', 305–6.
[30] Ibid., 311.

ontological aspect of *Dasein*; it must be what Heidegger calls an 'existential'.[31] Rahner argues that every human person is given an existential that gives rise to an intrinsic longing for God. Through the bestowal of this gift, our natural human condition is, in effect, transformed in order to prepare us for God's self-communication in grace. However, that we are in fact created with such a desire is entirely due to God's free decision. For this reason, Rahner characterizes the human potency for grace to be a *supernatural* existential. This ensures that the eventual offer of grace is gratuitous too, given that our ontological orientation to grace is a free gift.[32]

That we are in fact supernaturally transformed creatures is something that we only learn through the word of the Gospel. So it is only in the light of revelation that a theological distinction between nature and grace can be drawn at all. The theologian, standing in the Christian faith tradition, is able to understand concretely existing human beings as de facto addressees of grace. From this revealed perspective, the theologian can reason back with the help of the transcendental method in order to gain an understanding of nature. The theologian may postulate pure nature, as a theoretical alternative for the concrete condition of humankind, in order to understand this actually graced condition. However, the effects of grace are always and everywhere at work. This significantly qualifies the role of the concept of pure nature which can only function analytically as a 'remainder concept' (*Restbegriff*).[33]

Rahner's own work in *Spirit in the World* and *Hearer of the Word* is highly illustrative of this transcendental reasoning back from the starting point of revelation. The human person can be analysed philosophically as a being of unlimited transcendence – a spiritual being whose being in the world is simultaneously oriented towards a mysterious horizon of Being. This mysterious horizon may, or may not, choose to disclose itself in history. In principle, the silence of mystery would still constitute some sort of revelation. Rahner now suggests that this silence could be connected to the concept of a purely natural human spiritual life. His reasoning here is rather hypothetical, put in the form of rhetorical questions rather than as strong assertions. Rahner questions whether a spiritual dynamism, oriented towards an asymptotic goal, must be deemed meaningless. Compared to the call to the beatific vision, this natural dynamism, which must remain eternally '*in umbris et imaginibus*' (in shadows and images), might seem less fulfilling, but must still be considered something positive.[34] Rahner expresses little interest though in expounding this natural state any further. His explanation is primarily aimed at clarifying the actual situation of graced human nature.

3.2 The ubiquity of grace

The supernatural existential takes on a crucial role within Rahner's theology in the aftermath of the first systematic treatment of the concept in 1950. However, as Rahner

---

[31] Rahner's ontological use of the term 'existential' differs from Heidegger's more phenomenological use. See Knoepffler, *Der Begriff 'transzendental'*, 61–3.
[32] Rahner, 'On the Relationship between Nature and Grace', 312–13.
[33] Ibid., 314.
[34] Ibid., 315.

himself recognized, the concept as such was still in need of further clarification and refinement, especially its relation to grace.[35] Rahner speaks of the supernatural existential as something that 'prepares' us for, or 'orders' us towards, the gift of grace, which suggests that he initially distinguished the supernatural existential more sharply from grace.[36] However, David Coffey argues that Rahner fills the gaps in his theory in his later writings without contradicting his initial position.[37] Following Coffey's suggestion, I will retrace some important elements in the development of the supernatural existential and examine how Rahner employs this concept to think about transcendental revelation and anonymous Christians.

In his second essay on the supernatural existential, Rahner argues that human transcendence is opened and carried by grace. Hence, the supernatural transformation, preparing for grace, is itself already affected by grace. Moreover, Rahner also explains that the offer of grace is always given as an offer and as a possibility to every person who has reached the age of reason. Human transcendence is said to be permanently transformed by grace, something which forms another indication that the relation between the supernatural existential and grace is much closer than was initially suggested. However, there remains a distinction between the ontological change, which is due to grace, on the one hand, and the offer of justifying grace, on the other. Whereas the former is universally present, resulting in widespread 'stirrings of grace', the acceptance of justifying grace still depends upon the free agency of each and every individual.[38] Paul Rulands observes that Rahner applies this distinction in other writings according to the traditional scholastic distinction between actual grace and justifying grace.[39] Following this logic, the supernatural existential forms a 'partial realization' of grace.[40] In another article, Rahner speaks of various 'grades' of grace.[41] Accordingly, he distinguishes between a higher grade of grace and a lower grade of grace. The supernatural existential, thus, can be regarded as a lower grade of grace, which forms the condition for the possibility of the higher grade of justifying grace.

The intimate relation between the supernatural existential and justifying grace is confirmed in *Foundations*. First, Rahner explains that God's self-communication has two basic modalities: its offer to human freedom as 'permanent existential', on the one hand, and the human reaction to this offer in terms of either acceptance or rejection, on the other. He emphasizes that God's self-communication is given to *every* human person, at least in the modality of offer. God's offer of love does not become any less miraculous because it is extended to everyone. On the contrary, the supernatural

---

[35] Ibid., 316.
[36] See Paul Rulands, 'Selbstmitteilung Gottes in Jesus Christus: Gnadentheologie', in *Der Denkweg Karl Rahners*, 171.
[37] David Coffey, 'The Whole Rahner on the Supernatural Existential', *Theological Studies* 65 (2004): 104. Coffey argues that, had Rahner used scholastic terminology to explain his understanding of the supernatural existential, his influence on De Lubac could have been more positive and fruitful.
[38] Rahner, 'Nature and Grace', 178–81.
[39] See Rulands, 'Selbstmitteilung Gottes', 171–3 for a detailed discussion of the various relevant articles in which this distinction is used.
[40] Coffey, 'The Whole Rahner', 105.
[41] Karl Rahner, 'Questions of Controversial Theology on Justification' [1958], in *TI*, vol. 4, trans. Kevin Smith (London: Darton, Longman and Todd), 215–16.

existential can be considered the 'radical realization' of grace, precisely because of this universal aspect.[42] Crucially, this universal offer of grace still requires a free response, which can be either positive or negative. We have to cooperate with the grace given in order to become truly graced. Moreover, that a positive response always and everywhere follows is anything but self-evident. In the first place, the fact that our transcendence has been supernaturally transformed is 'just as inconspicuous and can be just as much overlooked, suppressed, denied and falsely interpreted as everything else which is transcendentally spiritual in man'.[43] In the second place, Rahner also points to the distorting influence of sin in human existence, which makes neutral free responses to the offer of grace impossible and positive responses a lot more difficult.[44] These remarks form an important counterbalance to the emphasis on the universality of the offer of grace. Rahner does not argue that each and every person actually is in a state of grace, but he does maintain the universal possibility of responding positively to the offer of grace. The supernatural existential forms a key concept in the conceptual clarification of this universal possibility.

In order to explain that the universality of grace entails actually a universal revelation, Rahner connects the supernatural existential with his concept of transcendental experience.[45] Conceptualizing the supernatural existential as an inner, universal *a priori* element of human experience, he develops a theology of revelation which employs a distinction between a universal-transcendental dimension and a particular-categorical dimension. We are permanently offered God's grace by virtue of the supernatural existential. Our self-transcendence is elevated supernaturally and, thereby, ipso facto carries an unthematic revelation. Human transcendence in knowledge and freedom is no longer oriented towards an asymptotically distant mystery, but towards the self-communicating God.[46] The Christian tradition reveals that the history of humankind is permeated with the history of God's dialogical self-communication. Since the possibility of such a personal relation with God is offered to everyone, by virtue of the supernatural existential, revelation is universally present in the mode of transcendental revelation.[47]

Transcendental revelation shares the characteristics of transcendental experience. Hence, Rahner characterizes it as unreflexive and 'within the realm of consciousness' (*bewußt*), but not as objectively known (*gewußt*).[48] Moreover, transcendental revelation is mediated categorically, just like transcendental experience. It is mediated not merely through explicitly religious events and symbols, but rather through the historical material of human life. This is what Rahner calls categorical revelation.

---

[42] Rahner, *Foundations*, 118–19.
[43] Ibid., 129.
[44] Ibid., 133.
[45] Ibid., 153–4. Rulands, 'Selbstmitteilung Gottes', 173–5, notes that Rahner already in the 1950s began the development of the supernatural existential into transcendental revelation. Siebenrock, 'Transzendentale Offenbarung', 37, points to the second edition of *Hearer of the Word* as one of the earliest instances of the use of transcendental revelation in Rahner's work.
[46] See Karl Rahner, 'Bemerkungen zum Begriff der Offenbarung', in *Offenbarung und Überlieferung*, ed. Karl Rahner and Joseph Ratzinger, Quaestiones disputatae 25 (Freiburg: Herder, 1965), 14–15.
[47] Rahner, *Foundations*, 170.
[48] Ibid., 172.

He acknowledges that there are various degrees and forms of reflexive awareness of this transcendental element. Some people will ignore or deny their transcendental experience, whereas others will interpret it either religiously or non-religiously. This depends, to a significant degree, on one's particular cultural and historical context. Rahner argues that the dynamic towards reflexive clarification and interpretation of the transcendental experience gives rise to the history of religions. The various religious traditions can, therefore, be viewed as particular and distinct interpretations of transcendental revelation. All such attempts of interpretation are necessarily limited though, because of the distorting influence of sin. We can only distinguish between more and less adequate interpretations in the light of the event of Jesus Christ. This particular historical event forms the highpoint of the history of revelation, which Rahner explains through the use of a Christological argument that focuses on the hypostatic union. Put succinctly, Jesus in his human and divine nature comprises the perfect categorical mediation of divine self-communication.[49] The application of the supernatural existential within the theology of revelation leads Rahner to develop the concept of 'anonymous Christians'.

The notion of the anonymous Christian is one of Rahner's most famous ideas.[50] As we will see, though, other scholars such as Schillebeeckx have had similar intuitions. Rahner introduced this concept to explain the universal operation of grace and its various degrees of acceptance both within and outside the church. He was aware of the supernatural existential's far-ranging consequences from the outset insofar as it presupposes the presence of grace outside the church. Every human person, irrespective of whether he or she belongs to the church, is offered grace in the form of an offer and possibility. While not every person can simply be considered to be justified, this does imply that good moral acts do have potentially a supernatural significance.[51]

Rahner concludes that it is necessary to reconsider how we view other religions and the people belonging to these traditions. Outside of the church we do not merely find natural reason and sin, but instead we find a mixture of natural spirit, grace and sin. This is the case, even if we are not reflectively aware of this. Rahner describes this implicit presence of God's grace as an 'anonymous datum' and a 'secret entelechy'.[52] Yet, the fact that everyone is invited into God's salvific economy can only be

---

[49] Ibid., 172–5.
[50] For an extensive discussion of Rahner's concept of anonymous Christians see Nikolaus Schwerdtfeger, *Gnade und Welt. Zum Grundgefüge von Karl Rahners Theorie der 'anonymen Christen'* (Freiburg. Herder, 1982) and Conway, *The Anonymous Christian*. More recently, Eamonn Conway, '"So as not to Despise God's Grace". Re-assessing Rahner's Idea of the "Anonymous Christian"', *Louvain Studies* 29 (2004): 127, has argued that the 'the term "anonymous Christian" is beyond redemption. It has led to too many misunderstandings and inappropriate applications. However, its theological underpinning still has merit and provides some crucial contemporary correctives.' Stephen Bullivant, *The Salvation of Atheists and Catholic Theology* (Oxford: Oxford University Press, 2012), 59–67, has called attention to the fact that Rahner's use of the term 'anonymous Christian' is anything but exceptional. It forms part of a wider discussion in twentieth-century Catholic theology. Contemporaries such as Maurice Blondel, Jacques Maritain, Henri de Lubac, Edward Schillebeeckx, Jean Daniélou and Yves Congar were all reflecting on some form of 'implicit', 'unconscious' or 'anonymous' faith in the years preceding the Second Vatican Council.
[51] Rahner, 'Nature and Grace', 179–80.
[52] Ibid., 180.

brought to explicit reflexivity through the encounter with the Christian message. In subsequent articles, Rahner explains why non-Christian people who perform good deeds in response to grace can be called 'anonymous Christians'.[53] His explanation revolves around the argument that implicit operations of grace can be attributed to the work of the Holy Spirit. Ultimately, however, this is the grace of Christ, who is the sole mediator of salvation. Moreover, Rahner does not intend to relativize the importance of explicit Christianity. On the contrary, he insists that implicit faith is preliminary and transitory, having a historic dynamism towards explicit church membership.[54]

This brief discussion of the notion of the anonymous Christian merely serves to show the far-ranging consequences of Rahner's supernatural existential. This existential serves to explain how every human being has the possibility of accepting God's self-communication in grace. It has developed into the notion of transcendental revelation, which builds upon Rahner's understanding of human self-transcendence in knowledge and through love specifically. In the next section, I turn to the methodological consequences of Rahner's reconfiguration of the relation between nature and grace, and more specifically to the relation between philosophy and theology.

4 The contaminating effects of the supernatural existential

Rahner's introduction of the supernatural existential has been the cause of heated debates about the relationship between philosophy and theology. Interestingly though, scholars have reacted in rather different, even opposing, ways to Rahner's proposal. I will examine two examples: John Milbank and Hansjürgen Verweyen. While the former argues explicitly that Rahner 'naturalizes the supernatural', the latter's critique can be read as charging Rahner with performing a move that 'supernaturalizes the natural'. Obviously, they cannot both be right. I argue that both Milbank and Verweyen are, ultimately, misinterpreting Rahner's view on the relation between nature and grace. Both authors are overly concerned with maintaining the purity of either theology (Milbank) or philosophy (Verweyen). Rahner holds a more harmonious view on the relation between philosophy and theology – one which opposes this fear of corruption and contamination. The supernatural existential serves as a conceptual tool by which to explain that this congruity between these two disciplines goes back to a metaphysical congruity between nature and grace. Moreover, I argue that this harmonious view on the relationship between philosophy and theology contributes to the distinct interrelating of transcendentality and hermeneutics in his theological method.

---

[53] See, for instance, Karl Rahner, 'Christianity and the non-Christian Religions' [1961], in *TI*, vol. 5, trans. Karl-H. Kruger (London: Darton, Longman and Todd, 1966), and Karl Rahner, 'Anonymous Christians' [1965], in *TI*, vol. 6, trans. Karl-H. and Boniface Kruger (London: Darton, Longman and Todd, 1974), 390–8.
[54] See Conway, '"So as not to Despise God's Grace"', 124–6.

4.1 Naturalizing the supernatural

In his book *The Suspended Middle*, John Milbank revisits the debate concerning the relation between the natural and the supernatural by contrasting De Lubac's position with the positions of Hans Urs von Balthasar and Karl Rahner.[55] He prefers De Lubac's new discourse, which is 'suspended between nature and grace' and, therefore, 'does not itself belong either to philosophy or theology', over what he views to be Rahner's attempt to solve the paradox by introducing a 'third term'.[56] The reasons behind Milbank's uneasiness with Rahner are discussed more explicitly in *Theology and Social Theory*. He develops his critique as part of a critical discussion of liberation theology and political theology, which he views as building on Rahner's thought. According to Milbank, these post-conciliar theologies are marked by an 'integralist revolution', which stresses the integral unity between nature and grace. Milbank distinguishes between the French 'supernaturalizing of the natural' and the German 'naturalizing of the supernatural' as the sources of this integralist revolution.[57] The German source here is primarily associated with Rahner. His transcendentalist solution gives too much away to nature and, in so doing, relativizes grace: 'The social is an autonomous sphere which does not need to turn to theology for its self-understanding, and yet it is already a grace-imbued sphere, and therefore it is *upon* pre-theological sociology or Marxist social theory, that theology must be founded.'[58] In contrast, Milbank argues that the French version of integralism offers a theological critique of society and politics – one which focuses on historical texts, images and events as the locus of the encounter with grace instead of identifying the supernatural as a permanent area of human life.[59] The supernatural existential is both cause and illustration of these opposing solutions.

For Milbank, Rahner does not succeed in his main mission, namely, the overcoming of the neo-scholastic, two-tiered conception of nature and grace. Instead, Rahner merely reworks this *duplex ordo* in terms of transcendental philosophy and remains, therefore, indebted to neo-scholastic premises. Since Rahner preserves the notion of a pure nature in the concrete human being, his position simply results in another dual structure. For Milbank, the supernatural existential as 'another grace-given desire for grace' does 'absolutely nothing to reconcile gratuity with non-extrinsicism'.[60] The fact that human beings have a supernatural existential cannot be explained otherwise than as an arbitrary decision of God. Hence, grace remains ultimately something extrinsic.

---

[55] John Milbank, *The Suspended Middle: Henri de Lubac and the Renewed Split in Modern Catholic Theology*, (Grand Rapids: William B. Eerdmans, 2014). Milbank's critique of Rahner is rather veiled and is expressed primarily through his interpretation of De Lubac's position. He states that *Surnaturel* is 'arguably the key theological text of the twentieth century' and that De Lubac's reviving of the paradoxical question of the natural desire for God 'informed a new sensibility which stood at the heart of the Catholic cultural revival in the twentieth century' (*The Suspended Middle*, 3; xiii). See also Milbank's *Theology and Social Theory: Beyond Secular Reason* (London: Blackwell, 2006), xxv.

[56] Milbank, *The Suspended Middle*, 52; 45.

[57] Milbank, *Theology and Social*, 206–7.

[58] Ibid., 208.

[59] Ibid., 208–9.

[60] Ibid., 222–4. It must be pointed out that Milbank merely refers to Rahner's first article 'Nature and Grace'. He does not seem to take Rahner's later writings on this topic into account, for instance in *Foundations*. Moreover, his discussion lacks any concrete references to Rahner's writings.

Milbank's critique of the supernatural existential is part of a wider disagreement with Rahner's theology overall. He takes issue with Rahner's a historical metaphysics of human subjectivity and with the negative consequences of his intermingling of nature and grace. According to Milbank, this transcendental theology lacks content and is unable to account for the concrete and recognizable otherness of grace.[61]

Oddly enough, the charge that Rahner mixes the natural and the supernatural horizon of human self-transcendence seems to undercut the previous critique that Rahner re-establishes a *duplex ordo*. Now it becomes clear that Milbank's primary fear is that transcendental philosophy will usurp positive historical theology. In Milbank's view, Rahner preserves pure nature in the concrete human being, and his philosophical explanation of this natural self-transcendence dominates his theological explanation of self-transcendence, as graced orientation towards God. As a result, the concrete and historical manifestation of grace becomes redundant; revelation and Christian teachings are 'reduced to mere signs of a perfect inward self-transcendence, always humanly available'.[62] This echoes the familiar critique of Rahner's abstract transcendentalism. However, it ignores the fact that Rahner develops the transcendental dimension of grace in close connection with the categorical dimension and completely disregards Rahner's argument that the operations of grace within human transcendence can only be identified *inductively*, reasoning back from the concrete history of revelation, and most importantly from the historical event of Jesus Christ.

Milbank contrasts Rahner's selling out of theology to the domain of autonomous philosophy with his own vision for theology. When an historical philosophical account takes precedence over the historical narrative of Christianity, Christian orthodoxy is 'annexed' resulting in 'the practical rejection of Christian truth'.[63] Alternatively, Milbank criticizes the notion of the autonomous and foundationalist character of secular philosophy over and against theology. He proposes a return to the concept of theology as a master narrative. In his vision, theology must be an 'ultimate narrative' that is 'directly theological' and is not determined pre-theologically by 'transcendentalist metaphysics'.[64]

4.2 Supernaturalizing the natural

Interestingly, Milbank's critique of Rahner's supernatural existential as 'naturalizing of the supernatural' is mirrored in critiques put forward by several German theologians that Rahner 'supernaturalizes the natural'. In brief, theologians such as Hansjürgen Verweyen, Thomas Pröpper, Klaus Müller and Karsten Kreutzer argue that the supernatural existential makes so-called philosophical *Letztbegründung* (ultimate grounding) of Christian faith claims impossible.[65] To assess this alternative vision,

---

[61] Milbank, *Theology and Social*, 224.
[62] Ibid., 224.
[63] Ibid., 234.
[64] Ibid., 251–4.
[65] See Klaus Müller, 'Der Streit um Begründungsfiguren', in *Unbedingtes Verstehen?*, 9–22; Klaus Müller, 'Zur Verantwortung des Glaubens. Ein Aufriss fundamentallogischer Positionen im Streit um die Rolle der Philosophie in der Theologie – nach Rahner', in *100 Jahre Karl Rahner*, 91–113;

I will examine Verweyen's critique of the supernatural existential in greater detail. Verweyen's argument is twofold. In the first instance, he doubts whether Rahner succeeds in finding an adequate solution to the problem of nature and grace. In the second instance, Verweyen takes issue with the consequences of the supernatural existential for the relation between philosophy and theology.

Part of Rahner's argument in favour of the supernatural existential is his insistence that human beings could have been created without such an existential. The hypothetical possibility of a purely natural anthropology ensures the gratuity of our actual graced status. However, Verweyen sees the shadow of a nominalist way of thinking about God in this concern to retain pure nature as an analytical concept. He disputes that God is any less free if his decision to create humankind includes the provision of a supernatural goal. He refers, in this regard, to Saint Anselm of Canterbury, who argued that a monk who has taken vows does not live any less freely because of these vows.[66] Moreover, Verweyen also calls the rationality of Rahner's idea of such a pure nature into question. In such a situation, human transcendence would be oriented towards a silent and mysterious asymptotic goal. Verweyen does not see how such a life could be meaningful. He compares Rahner's position to the myth of Sisyphus to explain its problematic and even absurd constitution.[67] Thus, for Verweyen the supernatural existential offers no satisfactory solution to the problem of extrinsicism.

However, Verweyen's disagreement with Rahner does not so much concern the technicalities of the supernatural existential, but rather its consequences for the relation between philosophy and theology. He fears that philosophy loses its methodological autonomy in Rahner's system. According to Verweyen, there is a clear split between Rahner's early works and his later theological work. He argues that *Spirit in the World* and *Hearer of the Word* were initially conceived of within the context of a *prima philosophia* or *Erstphilosophie* (first philosophy), aiming for a purely philosophical investigation into the transcendental structure of human subjectivity.[68] However,

---

Thomas Pröpper and Magnus Striet, 'Transzendentaltheologie', in *Lexikon für Theologie und Kirche*, 3rd ed. (2001), 188–90; Kreutzer, *Transzendentales versus hermeneutisches Denken*. These approaches are all characterized by a motivation to reconnect transcendental theology to an autonomous and independent philosophical reflection. For a succinct critique of this plea for *Letztbegründung*, see Johann Baptist Metz, 'Athen versus Jerusalem? Was das Christentum dem europäischen Geist schuldig geblieben ist', in *Die Gegenwart des Holocaust. 'Erinnerung' als religionspädagogische Herausforderung*, ed. Michael Wermke (Münster: Lit Verlag, 1997), 9–14. Metz considers this concern to be a 'typically German problem' and points alternatively to the Anglo-Saxon philosophical tradition, which is more permissive of more varied forms of rationality going beyond strictly scientific or philosophical rationality.

[66] Verweyen, *Gottes letztes Wort*, 325.
[67] HansJürgen Verweyen, 'Wie wird ein Existential übernatürlich? Zu einem Grundproblem der Anthropologie K. Rahners', *Trierer Theologische Zeitschrift* 95 (1986): 127. Coffey, 'The Whole Rahner', 103, observes that Rahner leaves relatively undefined what the natural end of humanity, as opposed to the supernatural end, would involve. Filling in this lacuna, he argues that this natural end would be the knowledge of God as the 'source and end of all things', as Vatican I stated (*Dei Filius*, DH 3004). Thus, whereas Verweyen emphasizes the asymptotic and, therefore, 'absurd' character of natural human transcendence, Coffey seems more inclined to follow Rahner's argumentation in *Spirit in the World* that the asymptotic horizon of the *Vorgriff* suggests or implicitly affirms the existence of absolute Being.
[68] Verweyen, 'Wie wird ein Existential übernatürlich?', 128. Roman Siebenrock, 'Glauben gibt zu denken', 103 has challenged this assertion. Contrary to Verweyen's claim, he posits that Rahner's

Rahner's later arguments on the universal operations of the supernatural existential call the viability of such a purely philosophical account into question. Since the human person is always a *mixtum compositum* (mixed composite) of natural and supernatural transcendentality, a methodologically autonomous philosophy is no longer possible. Verweyen perceives there to be a strong connection between Rahner's supernatural existential and the rise of a hermeneutical philosophy, through the influence of Hans-Georg Gadamer, Paul Ricoeur and Ludwig Wittgenstein. The supernatural existential became the 'quasi-official' theological blessing of this hermeneutical emphasis on the circularity and indissoluble pluralism of all philosophy, resulting in a relativist conception of truth.[69]

This 'hermeneutical liquefaction of transcendental reflection', as it has been termed more recently,[70] is explained with reference to the influence Metz had upon Rahner's thinking. Verweyen illustrates this by comparing the first and second editions of *Hearer of the Word*. He points to a footnote added by Metz, which states that transcendental reflection cannot and does not want to claim to be 'purely metaphysical' because she is always historically situated.[71]

According to Verweyen, this hermeneutical intrusion, caused by the supernatural existential, undermines Rahner's transcendental approach in two ways. First, it leads to an underestimation of transcendental anthropology. Following his theological turn, Rahner restricts himself to a theological investigation of human subjectivity and its relation to Christian dogma. He fails, however, to elaborate upon how exactly Christian dogma is universally relevant with reference to a philosophical concept of *letztgültige Sinn* (ultimate meaning).[72] Second, the supernatural existential also causes an overlading of transcendental anthropology. Verweyen questions whether Rahner's concept of transcendental revelation leaves enough room for the categorical and for the historical. Rahner mixes what Verweyen considers to be two distinct methodological questions. Whereas the question of the meaning of the Christian message should be dealt with in the forum of philosophical or transcendental reason, the question of facticity is something for the forum of historical or hermeneutical reason.[73] Rahner's blurring of philosophy with theology disables these disciplines from fulfilling their distinctive tasks. But is it really possible to maintain such a sharp distinction between transcendentality and hermeneutics?

4.3 Questioning purist concerns

Milbank's and Verweyen's critiques of Rahner's supernatural existential contain interesting parallels, as well as important divergences. Both authors doubt whether Rahner succeeds in finding an adequate solution to balancing extrinsicism and

---

theology of grace has never been absent from his work.
[69] Verweyen, 'Wie wird ein Existential übernatürlich?', 128-9; Verweyen, *Gottes letztes Wort*, 168.
[70] See Kreutzer, *Transzendentales versus hermeneutisches Denken*, 17.
[71] See Karl Rahner, *Hörer des Wortes. Schriften zur Religionsphilosophie und zur Grundlegung der Theologie*, SW vol, 4 (Soloturn – Düsseldorf: Benziger / Freiburg: Herder, 1997), 19, n. 8.
[72] Verweyen, *Gottes letztes Wort*, 326-7.
[73] Ibid., 327-8.

gratuity. Moreover, they argue that Rahner remains too closely aligned to the 'old' ways of theology. While Milbank sees the supernatural existential as simply re-establishing another *duplex ordo*, Verweyen holds that Rahner's concept of pure nature is a rather absurd solution – one that reflects a nominalist theology. Both critics are concerned with purity and autonomy. The one fears that philosophy will become too dominant and will overpower theology. Too much trust in reason leads to a naturalization of grace, which results in a loss of distinctiveness and autonomy for theology. The other fears that Rahner's supernatural existential signals the end of autonomous transcendental philosophical reflection. Too little trust in reason leads to a supernaturalization of nature, which makes it impossible to ground the truth of faith in autonomous reason. Both Milbank and Verweyen argue that this, ultimately, leads to a relativization of Christian truth claims.

Instead of offering a detailed rejoinder to the critiques of Milbank and Verweyen, I would like to focus upon one particular, yet fundamental, element in their critiques.[74] Both authors interpret Rahner and his understanding of grace rather statically. Milbank, for instance, describes the supernatural existential as something which is merely added to the natural human constitution. He thereby suggests that nature and grace exist as distinct realities. Verweyen's use of the phrase *mixtum compositum* similarly gives rise to the idea that human beings are made up of natural ontic elements and supernatural ontic elements.[75] Whether we philosophize or theologize depends upon whether we choose to use either our natural faculty (reason) or our supernatural faculty (faith). Due to this static viewpoint, both authors fail to see that Rahner conceives of grace in a much more dynamic way. Rahner is not interested in applying a sharp either/or distinction. Importantly, Milbank and Verweyen ignore the fact that Rahner allows for degrees of the presence of grace in their discussions of the supernatural existential. Nature's exposure to grace ranges from the mode of offer (the supernatural existential) to acceptance in human life (justifying grace) and eventual fulfilment (beatific vision). Hence, Rahner leaves open the possibility of various levels of human consciousness of, responses to and appropriations of grace.

Milbank's and Verweyen's uneasiness with the supernatural existential stems from a concern with retaining a rigid distinction between philosophy and theology; the natural is not supposed to encroach upon the supernatural and vice versa. Once again, the view of the two respective disciplines is static, rather than dynamic. Moreover, this concern with purity is precisely what Rahner seeks to dislodge with his supernatural existential. Rahner has a much more unified and harmonious understanding of the relation between philosophy and theology. Consequently, he engages himself in philosophy and theology, without seeing the need to distinguish sharply between the two for fear of mutual contamination.

---

[74] For a more extensive engagement with Verweyen's position, see Thomas Fößel, *Gott – Begriff und Geheimnis. Hansjürgen Verweyens Fundamentaltheologie und die ihr inhärente Kritik an der Philosophie und Theologie Karl Rahners*, Innsbrucker theologische Studien 70 (Innsbruck: Tyrolia Verlag, 2004).

[75] See Fössel, 'Warum ein Existential übernatürlich ist', 401–2; 405–6.

5 Philosophy within theology

Rahner is neither concerned with keeping theology free from intrusions by secular reason nor interested in developing a purely philosophical anthropology. Rahner holds philosophy in high regard, but as a theologian he is concerned with concrete humankind as living always and everywhere under the influence of grace. As Thomas Fössel notes, Rahner is committed to the dictum that *theologia fiat in concreto, non in abstracto* (theology is conducted concretely, not abstractly).[76] He advocates mutual cooperation between philosophy and theology in the service of the self-reflection of Christian faith. This comes to the fore in his own theological metaphysics, which is informed by, and developed in close association with, his hermeneutics of the Christian tradition of revelation. On the one hand, Rahner sees no need to distrust natural reason, or to subjugate it to divine grace, because he recognizes that a free and autonomous nature is necessary for the actualization of grace. On the other hand, taking the history of revelation seriously implies a theologically qualified understanding of nature. Theology, thus, claims to know more about nature than philosophy can know herself. Theology qualifies the autonomy of philosophy insofar as theology explicitly thematizes the graced condition of nature and directs nature towards its fulfilment in grace.

'There must be "philosophising" in theology'.[77] Theology needs philosophy; it must think radically in order to avoid isolating itself by way of a 'dogmatic positivism' that denies the historicity of magisterial teachings or a 'biblicism' demanding a *sacrificium intellectus* (sacrifice of the intellect). Scripture and dogma are essential sources for any theological reflection, but these sources must be confronted with secular understanding in order to maintain the credibility of the faith convictions they express.[78] Rahner considers this intellectual engagement to be a specifically philosophical task, but one which must be performed as an inner moment of theology. The unity in difference between philosophy and theology goes back to the relation between nature and grace. Grace, as the free self-communication of God, presupposes a free addressee, a free human person. Similarly, hearing and believing revelation already comprises an elementary form of theology. Faithful acceptance of revelation implies a philosophical self-understanding – one which can have varying degrees of explicitness and reflectiveness. In other words, theology and faith build on philosophy and reason.[79]

Hence, Rahner's view on the relationship between theology and philosophy is guided by the traditional understanding that *gratia non tollit naturam, sed perficit* (grace does

---

[76] Ibid., 406.
[77] Karl Rahner, 'Philosophy and Philosophising in Theology' [1967], in *TI*, vol. 9, trans. Graham Harrison (London: Darton, Longman and Todd, 1972), 47.
[78] Rahner, 'Philosophy and Philosophising in Theology', 48–50. Rahner does not intend to minimize the importance of Scripture to theology. On the contrary, he refers explicitly to Vatican II's teaching that Scripture is the 'soul of sacred theology' (see *Dei Verbum*, DH 4226). However, Rahner also emphasizes that we have no unmediated access to Scripture, hence his plea for the indispensable role of philosophy within theology.
[79] Karl Rahner, 'Philosophy and Theology' [1962], in *TI*, vol. 6, trans. Karl-H. and Boniface Kruger (London: Darton, Longman and Todd, 1974), 71; 44.

destroy nature, but perfects it).[80] Rahner insists, as we might recall, on the theoretical possibility of distinguishing nature and grace in order to maintain the gratuity of grace. But, this distinction operates in an analytical way only. In concrete existence, grace and nature are always inextricably intertwined, so that we cannot distinguish what pertains to nature and what pertains to grace. Since there is no pure nature, there cannot be any pure philosophy either.[81] Thus, the distinction between philosophy and theology is an analytical rather than a real distinction, according to Rahner. This claim warrants further examination, especially since it seems to undermine philosophy's integrity and autonomy.

5.1 Ancilla or domina

Despite the fact that Rahner, as a theologian, accords priority to grace and theology, he also deems it essential to maintain the intrinsic value of nature and philosophy. While revelation remains the highest norm, philosophy must have its own necessary autonomy. Appropriating and transforming a classical dictum, he argues that philosophy can fulfil her role as *ancilla theologiae* (servant of theology) only when she is simultaneously a *domina* (mistress).[82] The relation between nature and grace offers, once again, the interpretative key here. God's self-communication in grace requires a spiritual nature – one which must be free if revelation is to be a dialogical encounter between two persons. Since faith requires free rational agency, theology as the reflection on faith requires free and autonomous philosophy.[83] In order to mark the difference between philosophy and theology, Rahner applies a formal methodological distinction. Philosophy differs from theology, insofar as it 'does not take any of its material contents and norms from the official, socially constituted and hence ecclesiastical, special and thematised revelation'.[84]

Karen Kilby confirms this formal distinction, but she argues that Rahner also applies a material distinction in order to differentiate philosophy from theology. Whereas philosophy is concerned with nature, theology is about grace and the supernatural.[85] She refers to the following passage in *Foundations* in which Rahner describes the 'interlocking' of philosophy and theology:

> for we are reflecting upon the concrete whole of the human self-realization of Christian. That is really 'philosophy'. We are reflecting upon a Christian existence and upon the intellectual foundation of Christian self-realization, and that is basically 'theology'.[86]

---

[80] See Thomas Aquinas, *Summa Theologiae*, I, q. 1, a. 8, ad 2.
[81] Karl Rahner, 'On the Current Relationship between Philosophy and Theology' [1972], in *TI*, vol. 13, trans. David Bourke (London: Darton, Longman and Todd, 1975), 61–2.
[82] Rahner, 'Philosophy and Theology', 75.
[83] Ibid., 75–6.
[84] Ibid., 78.
[85] Kilby, *Philosophy and Theology*, 74.
[86] Rahner, *Foundations*, 10.

Kilby interprets this passage as containing a material distinction: 'One does philosophy or theology, then, depending on whether what one is reflecting on is existence *qua* human or *qua* specifically Christian: it is the thing being reflected on and not the method of reflection that distinguishes the two.'[87] However, given the discussion above, I hold that for Rahner there are not two types of human existence, one human and one Christian. Instead, the same being is reflected upon and thematized in different manners, either with – theologically – or without – philosophically – recourse to positive revelation. Kilby is concerned with demonstrating that Rahner's theology does not require an independent philosophy, so as to avoid the trap of foundationalism. While this insight corresponds with my argument that Rahner's transcendental method is a distinct theological appropriation of philosophical sources, Kilby's suggestion that Rahner engages in 'pure theology' ultimately seems to tend towards an excluding purism, similar to that on display in the works of Milbank and Verweyen.[88] This is attested by her consistent reading of Rahner's work through the lens of an 'either-or' dichotomy between philosophy and theology.[89] Yet, as I have demonstrated, this sharp distinction makes no sense in Rahner's understanding of the unity of philosophy and theology (itself anchored in the unity of nature and grace), in which philosophy forms an inner moment of theology, rather than an independent discipline.

Hence, Rahner does not use the thesis of the supernatural existential to intervene in philosophy's own and autonomous methodology. Instead, he simply expresses a theological view on the nature of philosophy. In the eyes of the theologian, neither philosophy nor its object of reflection can ever be completely natural, regardless of any attempt or intention to proceed a-theologically in terms of method and procedure. Thus, Rahner's affirmation of philosophy's autonomy is intrinsically connected to a theological qualification of this autonomy as relative, rather than absolute, autonomy.[90] For Rahner, this is not problematic because he conceives of a porous border existing between philosophy and theology. His distinction between philosophy and theology is analytical, rather than real. The intertwinement of nature and grace in concrete human existence, thus, precludes us from drawing a sharp distinction between philosophy and theology. Although these disciplines cannot be simply equated, their mutual relation is 'extremely obscure and complex'.[91]

5.2 From purity to porosity

Rahner is very much aware that his universalizing claim about the impossibility of pure philosophy is a theological one.[92] It expresses a view on concrete human existence, and its self-reflexivity, which is informed by insights from the history of revelation.

[87] Kilby, *Philosophy and Theology*, 80.
[88] Ibid., 82.
[89] An example is her argument that the *Vorgriff* fails philosophically but that it can work theologically (Kilby, *Karl Rahner*, 76–9).
[90] See Karl H. Neufeld, *Wie "tickt" Karl Rahner?: Theologisches Erkennen und Argumentieren*, Karl Rahner Lecture 2014 (Freiburg: Universitätsbibliothek, 2015), 17, who refers to an unpublished manuscript from 1954 in which Rahner affirms this relative autonomy of philosophy.
[91] Rahner, 'On the Current Relationship', 66.
[92] Ibid., 64.

That is why Rahner, contrary to Milbank, sees no problem in affirming the autonomy of philosophy. Unlike Milbank, he views such autonomy always within the context of graced nature.[93] On the one hand, Rahner does not intend to forcefully baptize all philosophy. As Albert Raffelt notes, Rahner steers clear of theological triumphalism.[94] On the other hand, his theological conviction about the graced condition of all reality necessarily involves a qualification of the autonomy of philosophy as relative, rather than absolute. As Fössel rightly notes, such a relativization is inherent to a theological account that seeks to make universal claims, such as Rahner's.[95]

The fact that everyone is at least offered grace does not mean that everyone also accepts grace. Thus, Rahner also expressly allows for the possibility of unbelief or the rejection of grace. Nonetheless, even a rejection is no longer purely philosophical, but already a faith option and, therefore, has a theological dimension. This conscious denial of grace can be called 'culpably rejected theology'. More positively stated, philosophy can be viewed as unthematic or implicit theology – a philosophy 'that has not yet arrived at the fullness of its own nature'.[96] Importantly, this does not mean that theology is always a step ahead of philosophy. Philosophy may be on its way to becoming theology, but theology too is also still on its way, so its current state can, therefore, be a step behind in comparison with philosophy.[97] This demonstrates, once again, the porous division between philosophy and theology.

Rahner offers an interesting reinterpretation of the First Vatican Council's teaching in *Dei Filius* that 'God, the beginning and the end of all things, can be known with certainty from the things that were created through the natural light of human reason', in order to support his vision of the porous and complementary relation between philosophy and theology.[98] In Rahner's view, the crux of this teaching is that the human person already stands in a relation with the saving God, before explicit and institutionally mediated revelation.[99] The Council does not follow Blaise Pascal's stark distinction between the God of the philosophers and the God of Abraham, Isaac, Jacob and Jesus Christ.[100] On the contrary, the God known by the light of reason is affirmed to be the same as the saving God. God as the fountain of all truth unites secular, philosophical knowledge with revealed, theological knowledge. According to Rahner, the Council, thus, recognizes that there is an autonomous knowledge which

---

[93] See also Stephan van Erp, 'The Sacrament of the World. Thinking God's Presence beyond Public Theology', *ET Studies* 6 (2015): 128–9, for a similar rebuttal of Milbank's critique of Rahner's and Schillebeeckx's naturalizing of the supernatural and a defence of their complementary, integral, incarnational vision of the relation between church (theology) and world (philosophy).
[94] Albert Raffelt, 'Pluralismus – Ein Plädoyer für Rahner und eine Bemerkung zur Sache', in *Hoffnung, die Gründe nennt: Zu Hansjürgen Verweyens Projekt einer erstphilosophischen Glaubensverantwortung*, ed. Gerhard Larcher (Regensburg: Friedrich Pustet Verlag, 1996), 133.
[95] Fössel, 'Warum ein Existential übernatürlich ist', 410.
[96] Rahner, 'On the Current Relationship', 64–5.
[97] Ibid., 65.
[98] First Vatican Council, Dogmatic Constitution *Dei Filius*, chapter 2 (DH 3004).
[99] Rahner, 'On the Current Relationship', 66–7.
[100] See Blaise Pascal, *Pensées*, trans. Martin Turnell (London: Harvill, 1962). Joris Geldhof, 'Pascal's Double Mistake, or The Desirability of Sound Metaphysics', *Downside* Review 128 (2008): 235–46, 242, observes that this radical distinction has had far-ranging consequences. Pascal has been interpreted not only as espousing a radically Christocentrism, but even as a fideist who seeks to exclude philosophical reason entirely from the quest of understanding the mystery of God.

is of a decisive importance to theology.[101] He acknowledges that the autonomy of philosophy is not absolute; in matters of faith, philosophical reason is trumped by theological faith as the higher norm. However, in other matters, reason remains the competent authority. This is affirmed by the Council's express support of the human arts and sciences.[102]

Hence, *Dei Filius* confirms that reason and faith, philosophy and theology, must be considered as partners. Rahner refers to this teaching to argue that, seen from the theological perspective, these disciplines are intrinsically ordered towards each other. Both the theologian and the philosopher continually transcend their own disciplines and transgress into each other's domain.[103] Contrary to what Milbank and Verweyen advocate, Rahner argues that the boundary between philosophy and theology is characterized by porosity. Through their conversations, the philosophical and theological dialogue partners are transformed and invited to take on each other's roles. Theology must, therefore, welcome philosophy 'because everything human belongs to God, and only so is truly appropriated to man, and because in the midst of all philosophy the theologian discerns God revealing himself in his grace'.[104] This dynamic and porous understanding of the relation between philosophy and theology is crucial to understanding Rahner's own transformation of the transcendental method as involving a key hermeneutical component.

6 Rethinking transcendentality

Rahner advocates a complementary relationship between philosophy and theology – one which is based on his theological understanding of reality as graced nature. In this section, I argue that the 'hermeneutical liquefaction' of the transcendental method can be interpreted more positively than the advocates of *Letztbegründung* suggest. Rahner actually offers a reminder of the necessary self-limitation of transcendental and metaphysical reflection. At the same time, while he recognizes the limitations of human reason, Rahner avoids Milbank's 'theocratic tendency' to subjugate philosophy to theology.[105] Philosophy helps us to understand faith and, conversely, theology helps us to understand reason. Hence, his transcendental method uses philosophy in order

---

[101] Rahner, 'On the Current Relationship', 66–7.
[102] *Dei Filius*, chapter 4 (DH 3019). Joseph Fritz, 'Karl Rahner Repeated in Jean-Luc Marion?', *Theological Studies* 73 (2012): 318–38 remarks that Rahner 'may overstate his case', insofar as he interprets Vatican I 'to have opened the doors to the wisdom of the world in the way that many only see in Vatican II' (330).
[103] Rahner, 'On the Current Relationship', 78.
[104] Ibid., 79.
[105] The term 'theocratic tendency' is derived from Nicholas Lash's article 'Where does Holy Teaching Leave Philosophy? Questions on Milbank's Aquinas', *Modern Theology* 15 (1999): 433–44. In this article, Lash questions the accuracy of Milbank's interpretation of Thomas Aquinas, most importantly Milbank's claim in *The Word Made Strange. Theology, Language, Culture* (Oxford: Blackwell, 1997), 44, that for Thomas 'the domain of metaphysics is not simply subordinate to, but completely *evacuated* by theology'. Lash argues that Thomas conceives of the relationship between philosophy and theology much more constructively and positively. As I have shown, a similar Thomistic motive runs through Rahner's work.

to develop a theological understanding of the history of grace, not by insulating this transcendental method from history, but by hermeneutically confronting this method with history. The result is a hermeneutically chastized transcendental theological method. It is a method that takes history, plurality and ambiguity seriously, but without giving up on the search for universality and the unity of truth and faith. In order to demonstrate this, I turn to a selection of Rahner's later writings that are conspicuously absent from the aforementioned critical assessments.[106]

6.1 Pluralism and gnoseological concupiscence

In his reflections on the relationship between philosophy and theology, Rahner repeatedly touches upon the issue of pluralism, often drawing a contrast between the actual state of philosophy and the situation that he remembers from his youth.[107] Neo-scholasticism attempted to pursue theology with the help of one unified philosophical system. Even though the factual variety of philosophies was not ignored entirely at the time, it was still generally assumed that distilling one comprehensive philosophical system out of this plurality was possible.[108] In contrast, today's philosophical scene is marked by an irreducible pluralism. The variety of different contextual and specialized philosophies has grown enormously so that no single person is able to integrate adequately this pluralism of ideas and approaches into a single philosophical theory.[109] There is too much source material, and there are too many methods by which to interpret this enormous amount of data. The confrontation with this situation of pluralism reveals, in a movement of negative philosophy, that we are condemned to a conscious ignorance. Rahner characterizes this situation theologically as 'gnoseological concupiscence'.[110] The term 'concupiscence' denotes an interior state of pluralism, inhibiting any complete integration or systematization. We strive to make sense of what we know about ourselves, others, the world, God and so on. We desire to relate what we know rationally to what we believe in faith and what we hope for. However, ultimately we always fall short in constructing a harmonious synthesis. Our gnoseological state remains incomplete and inadequate; it is concupiscent.

Given the close relation between the two disciplines, philosophical pluralism necessarily gives rise to theological pluralism. No theologian can claim to master the diverse philosophies, ranging from scholastic philosophy to German idealism and

---

[106] The scarcity of sources to which Milbank refers in his critique of Rahner has already been mentioned. Fössel, 'Warum ein Existential übernatürlich ist', 399–400, points out that Verweyen's critique of Rahner is based on texts that do not go beyond 1963. Kreutzer's analysis of Rahner's method in *Transzendentales versus hermeneutisches Denken* is likewise constrained by focusing on the same limited period in Rahner's work.
[107] Rahner's reflections on plurality and pluralism reach back as early as 1959 and occur not solely within the context of the question of the relationship between philosophy and theology. For Rahner's varied use of the term 'pluralism', see Raffelt, 'Pluralismus – Ein Plädoyer', 128–34.
[108] Rahner, 'On the Current Relationship', 70–1.
[109] Rahner, 'Philosophy and Philosophising', 52–3.
[110] Ibid., 52. For a more extensive treatment of the idea of gnoseological concupiscence, see Karl Rahner, 'Theological Reflections on the Problem of Secularisation' [1967], in *TI*, vol. 10, trans. David Bourke (London: Darton, Longman and Todd, 1973), 341–8.

from existential philosophy to hermeneutical and linguistic philosophy.[111] Moreover, the theologian also finds herself confronted with the need to integrate the insights of biblical studies, the social sciences, the natural sciences, historical studies and so on. As a result, there is no longer either a single common philosophical or a single common theological language. The theology of the future will be a *pluralistic* theology. This has important consequences for understanding transcendental theology.

However, Rahner adds the warning that even a pluralistic theology must maintain the 'unity of the Church's creed'.[112] This remark indicates an important qualification of his views on pluralism. Rahner views the factual pluralism in philosophy and theology as being inescapable and acknowledges that we are, in our lifetimes, unable to overcome this pluralism. But this factual pluralism does not imply a principled pluralism. Despite the serious differences, he considers it false to defend that different philosophies are, as such, irreconcilable; their incommensurability is 'provisional'.[113] Hence, Rahner repeatedly emphasizes the possibility of, and the need for, dialogue between different philosophies and theologies.[114] Pluralism is not a static reality. We are not stuck and isolated in our own contextual positions but can instead, at least partially, transcend these particularities. It would be wrong, therefore, to attribute an agnostic relativism to Rahner.[115] Yet, it cannot be denied that Rahner seems to advocate a paradoxical position. He acknowledges the historicity and plurality of all theology, but does not wish to give up the aspiration for universality and common understanding. This is reflected in his later methodological reflections, which display an intensification of his hermeneutical sensitivity.

6.2 Towards a modest transcendental theology

Rahner's supernatural existential can be interpreted as demonstrating his increased attention to the fundamental historicity and hermeneutical condition of all theoretical reflection. There is no pure philosophy – a philosophy untouched by the historical influence of God's self-communication in grace. His reflections on pluralism, and the consequent gnoseological concupiscence, further attest to the historical conditions and limitations of philosophy and theology. This is especially important for the metaphysical and transcendental varieties that focus on universal *a priori* conditions.

---

[111] Rahner, 'Philosophy and Philosophising', 54–6. Lehmann, 'Karl Rahner, ein Porträt', xlvi–xlvii, notes that Rahner is fundamentally sceptical with regard to one single philosophy and becomes increasingly sceptical of the idea of philosophy as a way of thinking which is entirely independent of all theology. For Rahner, the universality of faith transcends any particular philosophy and philosophical terminology. See also Karl Lehmann, *Was bleibt von Karl Rahner? Theologische Problematik für heute und morgen*, Karl Rahner Lecture 2009 (Freiburg: Universitätsbibliothek, 2009), 20.
[112] Karl Rahner, 'Possible Courses for the Theology of the Future' [1970], in *TI*, vol. 13, trans. David Bourke (London: Darton, Longman and Todd, 1975), 38.
[113] Rahner, 'Philosophy and Philosophising', 52; Karl Rahner, 'Pluralism in Theology and the Unity of the Creed in the Church' [1969], in *TI*, vol. 11, trans. David Bourke (London: Darton, Longman and Todd, 1974), 11.
[114] Rahner, 'Pluralism in Theology', 13.
[115] Fössel, 'Warum ein Existential übernatürlich ist', 408.

These endeavours are equally contextually conditioned and must therefore be more modest in their claims and assertions.[116]

Without explicitly stating so, Rahner here basically affirms the *hermeneutical* character of all philosophical and theological reflection. This serves as further proof that Rahner's hermeneutical profile is much more pronounced than is often thought and that his understanding of the transcendental method has evolved significantly over time.[117] Moreover, the aforementioned comment is anything but an isolated remark. He affirms that all understanding depends upon a particular horizon of understanding and is, therefore, conditioned by conditions which can never be made completely transparent and reflexive.[118]

> Every point of departure of one's limited reflection (and there is always something unavoidably arbitrary about what point one chooses) is to some extent redefined and altered by the feedback which the result of one's investigations produces. It is only at the end of the path that one finds out exactly what point one stepped on the road.[119]

Rahner considers this explicit awareness of the historical or hermeneutical character of theology to be a relatively new insight.[120] The insight into the hermeneutical character of all reflection not only presents us with difficulties and challenges but also offers the opportunity of a new mode of self-critical reflexivity. We have to check our own presuppositions and relate them to the societal concerns and convictions in order to prevent subjective arbitrariness. We are reminded that truth is not the concern of isolated individuals, but involves a community and institutions. Rahner, therefore, also considers the hermeneutical dimension of theology a new opportunity to appreciate the ecclesial character of theology. If the individual theologian is not to become captured in her own subjectivity, she must relate her investigations to a concrete community of faith.[121] Yet, the ecclesial commitment of a theologian simultaneously demands critical distance regarding church and magisterium.

The emphasis on the communal and hermeneutical dimension of philosophy and theology sheds new light upon Rahner's statements regarding the impossibility of a pure philosophy. Every philosophy is embedded in a specific horizon of understanding

---

[116] Rahner, 'Philosophy and Philosophising', 57.
[117] Kreutzer, *Transzendentales versus hermeneutisches Denken*, 249, argues on the contrary that Rahner failed in adequately receiving Heidegger's hermeneutics. He claims that the hermeneutical element in his work derives primarily from Metz's editorial changes to *Spirit in the World* and *Hearer of the Word*, without considering the possibility that Rahner's transcendental method kept evolving over time. Since he does not attend to Rahner's later writings, the possibility that Rahner reconceived of his own transcendental method is not even probed.
[118] Karl Rahner, 'Reflections on a New Task for Fundamental Theology' [1972], in *TI*, vol. 16, trans. David Morland (London: Darton, Longman and Todd, 1979), 160.
[119] Karl Rahner, 'Faith between Rationality and Emotion' [1973], in *TI*, vol. 16, trans. David Morland (London: Darton, Longman and Todd, 1979), 86.
[120] Rahner, 'Reflections on Methodology', 74. Rahner fails to notice that ever since Friedrich Schleiermacher, a great many theologians have adopted a hermeneutically conscious theological approach.
[121] Ibid., 79–81.

– a historical tradition that not only enables but also limits our reflective exercises. Rahner's position effectively calls into question the project of a first philosophy seeking *Letztbegründung*. Rahner is conscious of his own indebtedness to the Christian tradition and thereby stands in contrast to Verweyen's attempt to insulate autonomous reason from the distorting influences of history and hermeneutics. In *Foundations*, Rahner explains that he is not concerned with methodologically separating philosophy and theology 'in the sharpest possible way', because 'even the most basic, self-grounded and most transcendental philosophy of human existence is always achieved only within historical experience'.[122] The distinction called for by Verweyen between philosophical reason, concerned with meaning, and hermeneutical reason, concerned with facticity, negates the fact that both forms of reason are historically and hermeneutically conditioned.

However, this critique of any self-acclaimed 'pure' transcendental philosophy does not imply either the impossibility or the danger of incorporating any form of transcendental reflection within theology. Thus, *pace* Milbank, there is no need to completely purge theology of unwarranted philosophical incursions. Philosophy plays an indispensable role in the theological self-understanding of faith. Theological reason helps to understand how revelation and faith relate to our philosophical-transcendental understanding of the human person. However, since every formulation of the transcendental structure of human subjectivity always remains dependent upon hermeneutical mediation, it is factually impossible to have one universal philosophy. Does this invalidate and disprove his earlier transcendental analysis of the human person as a being of transcendence towards a mysterious horizon? Rahner attends to this tension when he distinguishes two distinct forms of theology:

> One trying to do what it can to undercut today's cultural pluralism, making use only of that side of existence which is still common to all and which will remain so. It would work with this common experience and 'redeem' it by responding with the answers of faith, even if only able to do this in an approximate way. … On the other hand there would be the other kind of theology, with the courage to let itself disintegrate into many theologies.[123]

The first form of theology can be interpreted as corresponding to his own transcendental theology. From within the plurality of philosophies and theologies, this theology endeavours to express the common features within the wide variety of human experiences. However, the term 'approximate' makes clear that Rahner believes that every attempt to identify this ground has its limitations and cannot claim to be complete. In other words, the only possible transcendental theology is a *modest* transcendental theology. This limited and qualified understanding of transcendental theology can be explained further with reference to Rahner's plea for an indirect method.

Theology needs an indirect method in order to justify the intellectual reasonableness of faith. Rather than starting with claims that are valid always and everywhere, such

---

[122] Rahner, *Foundations*, 25.
[123] Rahner, 'Philosophy and Philosophising', 59.

an indirect method attends first to the concrete, spiritual situation of its addressee. Rahner argues that the indirect method is not a secondary theological method for the less educated, but should form an inner moment of theological methodology as such. After all, theologian and ordinary believer alike need to deal with the issues of pluralism and history.[124] Nicholas Healy recognizes this indirect method in Rahner's transcendental method at large. He argues that Rahner uses a transcendental argument that is 'more modest in intent, and recognises the logical possibility of a plurality of metaphysical schemes'.[125] Rahner is an 'ad hoc apologist', who 'appropriates the prevailing conceptuality and carefully reinterprets these categories to accord with Christian criteria'.[126] Healy perhaps puts too strong an emphasis upon the particular and local character of Rahner's transcendental argumentation, as a result of which the sight of the universal claim expressed in these arguments is put at risk. His argument that Rahner appropriates and transforms a specific philosophical concept of transcendentality, in view of his theological agenda, seems to be correct though. Karen Kilby has further developed Healy's intuition, arriving at what seems to be a more adequate formulation of Rahner's modest transcendental theology:

> The *content* of what is being affirmed, on this account, still has an ahistorical, universal character. What is affirmed is precisely that there is an aspect to our experience which transcends history and particularity and difference. The *manner* in which this is affirmed, however, is crucially different – the claim that there is something transcending history does not *itself* pretend to transcend history. What is at issue, then, is a historically rooted affirmation of the ahistorical character of an element in our experience.[127]

Without expressly using this pair of terms, Kilby's description articulates both the universal-transcendental dimension and the particular-hermeneutical dimensions of Rahner's method. Rahner insists upon the need for a type of reflection that explores the universal dimensions of the message of Christian faith, given that transcendental theology cannot claim to be immune from the effects of pluralism and history. This implies the enduring relevance of transcendental and metaphysical philosophy as sources of these universal arguments. This is supported by the fact that Rahner never distanced himself from his early works, but kept instead referring to concepts and ideas developed in these books.[128] Moreover, it must be borne in mind here that for Rahner, pluralism is a *factual* reality, which does not necessarily exclude the possibility of a unifying ground and origin. Hence, there remains the need for a metaphysical or transcendental discourse that investigates this ground and how human beings can

---

[124] Rahner, 'Reflections on Methodology', 75.
[125] Nicholas M. Healy, 'Indirect Methods in Theology: Karl Rahner as an Ad Hoc Apologist', *The Thomist* 56 (1992): 625.
[126] Healy, 'Indirect Methods in Theology', 628.
[127] Kilby, *Karl Rahner*, 97.
[128] Raffelt, 'Pluralismus – Ein Plädoyer', 132, observes that Rahner's later articles on theological pluralism appear side by side with an early article on Thomas's metaphysics of knowledge. He argues that this suggests that Rahner himself perceived no contradiction between his early and later works.

relate to it. Crucially, this transcendental and metaphysical discourse, concerned with universal characteristics and features, must be conscious of its own hermeneutical conditions and limitations. That is why Rahner, ultimately, advocates for a modest transcendental theology.

6.3 A theological 'correction' of transcendental philosophy

Rahner's increased hermeneutical sensitivity, which I have outlined earlier, leads him to advocate for a modest form of transcendental theology. Yet, his own distinct combination of transcendental reflection with hermeneutical sensitivity also entails a 'metamorphosis' of the very notion of transcendentality – one which is not afraid to go beyond the strictly philosophical understanding of transcendentality.[129] In other words, Rahner uses philosophical reason to reflect on Christian faith, but he also uses theological reason to reflect on philosophical rationality. Observing, in 1967, that modernity and transcendental philosophy were falling out of favour, Rahner insists that the transcendental-anthropological turn remains important for both contemporary and future theology.[130] It needs to make use of this philosophical tradition for a responsible intellectual engagement with faith. Serious thinking and reflection are necessary for any theology that remains committed to the dictum *fides quaerens intellectum* (faith seeking understanding). However, Rahner does not advocate a wholesale or uncritical adoption of transcendental philosophy as such, because it can be 'most profoundly un-Christian in so far as it pursues a transcendental philosophy of the autonomous subject, who stands aloof from the transcendental experience in which he experiences himself as continually dependent, with his origin in and orientation towards God'.[131] The adoption of transcendental reflection within theology demands a critical transformation of this reflection. More concretely, it demands an explicit confrontation with history, experience and hermeneutics. Rahner's own attempt to maintain a dialectics between transcendentality and hermeneutics is an example of the exact kind of a transformed transcendental method.

In his methodological reflections from the 1970s, Rahner's advocacy for a modest transcendental theology comes most clearly to the fore. He emphasizes that transcendental theology is only one particular theological method within the plurality of theologies and describes the close connection between transcendental philosophy and transcendental theology.[132] However, Rahner refuses to describe or to explain transcendental theology exclusively by way of a reference to (a specific) transcendental philosophy. He merely points out that the transcendental way of questioning focuses on 'the conditions in which knowledge of a specific subject is possible in the knowing subject'.[133] Moreover, he acknowledges that this rough description is simple and pre-

---

[129] For this use of the term 'metamorphosis' in the context of Rahner's work, see Holzer, 'Philosophy within Theology', 584–98.
[130] Rahner, 'Theology and Anthropology', 39–40.
[131] Ibid., 38–9.
[132] Rahner, 'Reflections on Methodology', 84–6.
[133] Ibid., 87.

philosophical. Yet, rather than offering a more detailed explanation, Rahner turns to the relation between transcendentality and history.

For Rahner, transcendental questioning does not imply a forgetting of history or an undervaluation of factual experience. On the contrary, a transcendental investigation precisely reveals the human person as anchored in history and *a posteriori* experience.[134] However, the inverse is also true. Affirming the historicity of human subjectivity *is* itself already a transcendental statement. Hence, transcendentality and history imply one another. This means that within the contemporary plurality of theologies, there should be room for both political theology and transcendental theology. They do not mutually exclude each other; neither of them is *the* theology of the future. Just as transcendental theology has an inherent orientation towards history, as the locus of revelation and salvation, political theology cannot avoid making transcendental claims either.[135]

Nevertheless, transcendental philosophy is often tempted to focus exclusively upon the *a priori* at the expense of history. According to Rahner, such a transcendental philosophy understands itself falsely.[136] It is precisely at this point that transcendental theology can play an important role. Pointing inherent limitations due to language, historicity and hermeneutics, theology reminds transcendental philosophy of the necessary 'self-limitation' so as to prevent it from becoming an absolutizing and totalizing discourse that 'would fall into the error of hybris and the crudity of claiming to solve all things in terms of reflective thought'.[137] There is a striking parallel here with the concluding reflections of *Spirit in the World*, in which Rahner voices the warning that a Christian metaphysics of knowledge must direct us to 'the here and now' of the historical world.[138] Yet, Rahner now seems to suggest more strongly that theology may need to fraternally correct transcendental philosophy and help it to identify blind spots. Theology, with its intrinsic orientation towards historical experience as the locus of revelation and salvation, is particularly well suited to pointing out that attending to history, language and hermeneutical experience is not something optional, something from which transcendental philosophy is exempt. Informed by salvation history, transcendental theology cannot but point out that transcendentality has a history and that the reflection on transcendentality is historically conditioned. As I have demonstrated earlier, this insight is closely connected to Rahner's reflections on the supernatural existential and its historical effects:

Insofar as Rahner applies this insight to his own method, by dialectically relating transcendentality and hermeneutics, he effectively initiates a theological transformation of the transcendental *a priori*. As Emerich Coreth notes, the theological *a priori*, as it has been pioneered by Rahner, is not a pure *a priori* but the historical *a priori,* namely the salvific Christ event,[139] It is only from the concrete historical experience of Jesus

---

[134] Ibid., 88.
[135] Rahner, 'Possible Courses', 56–60.
[136] Rahner, 'Reflections on Methodology', 99.
[137] Ibid., 99.
[138] Rahner, *Spirit in the World*, 408.
[139] Coreth, 'Philosophische Grundlagen', 534. See also Knoepffler, *Der Begriff 'transzendental'*, 123, who similarly argues that Rahner's theological use of the term 'transcendental' assumes an *a posteriori*, factual, conditioning of the *a priori*.

Christ that we can know that our transcendentality is affected by God's offer of grace. The awareness of this historical conditioning of the *a priori* transcendental structure of human subjectivity introduces a hermeneutical element into transcendental reflection. Rahner recognizes that all attempts to formulate transcendental structures and arguments are fundamentally conditioned by *a posteriori* historical experience.

Insofar as this argument in favour of the transformed and historically conditioned status of human transcendentality cannot be transcendentally deduced through philosophical reflection alone, strict transcendental philosophers may deem such an argument to be uncritical. The theological *a priori*, after all, is not strictly or purely *a priori*. Thomas Fössel notes that this may seem extremely provocative in the eyes of the transcendental philosopher. But why would transcendental theology not have the right to challenge transcendental philosophy, calling attention to the specific influence of salvation history and to the more general historical and hermeneutical conditions that affect all human reflection? Rahner is ultimately not concerned with the (im)possibility of strictly transcendental philosophy *as* philosophy. Instead, as I have demonstrated throughout my argument, his own theological encounter with transcendental philosophy appropriates this philosophy with a view to providing an intelligible account of the universal features of Christian faith, without aiming to find conclusive proof of Christian faith.

7 Conclusion

In this chapter, I have examined Rahner's concept of the supernatural existential as well as its critical reception. Rahner introduces the supernatural existential in order to explain the universal presence of God in concrete human existence. This understanding of the graced condition of actual reality leads him to an account of the relation between philosophy and theology – one which is characterized by complementarity and porosity. Rahner opposes purist positions that seek to maintain a sharp distinction between philosophy and theology. I have argued that his reflection on the intertwinement of grace and nature serves as a catalyst to bringing out the hermeneutical dimension in his own transcendental method. His harmonious view on the complementary relation between philosophy and theology finds application within his own dialectical interrelation of transcendentality and hermeneutics.

As demonstrated with reference to Rahner's later writings, the recognition of historical and hermeneutical conditions develops into a critical theological reminder of the contextual, historical, hermeneutical and limited nature of all theoretical reflection, including metaphysics and transcendental philosophy. But this fraternal correction is not aimed at theologically subjugating transcendental philosophy. Instead, Rahner continues to trust in the power of reason and remains an advocate of the use of philosophy within theology, with a view to making the Christian faith intelligible. He develops historically rooted arguments about that which transcends our particular situation and history. Importantly, Rahner acknowledges that his own transcendental arguments are fundamentally affected and informed by the history of grace. His theological *a priori* effects a transformation of the very concept of transcendentality by incorporating this hermeneutical dimension.

The dialectics between transcendental and hermeneutics explains why Rahner's transcendental theology has a fundamentally modest character. This modest transcendental theology is important for contemporary fundamental theology, because it gives an insightful example of the possibility of thinking universality from within particularity. An incarnational theological focus on the particularity can continue to reflect about the universal dimension of Christian faith without necessarily overstepping its own hermeneutical limitations and conditions. Importantly, Rahner's example shows that a theological use of philosophical rationality entails its own self-critical-hermeneutical force that recognizes the potentialities as well as the limitations of transcendental and metaphysical reflection within theology.

Uncovering the hermeneutical dimension of Rahner's transcendental theology proved to be the key to demonstrating how this theological method is attentive to particularities without giving up its universal outlook. However, as I have indicated earlier, it would be a bridge too far to label Rahner as a hermeneutical theologian. Rahner's starting point in particularity as a way to think about the universality of faith lends itself to be explicated hermeneutically, but has not been developed with explicit reference to hermeneutical theory. This can be partly explained by pointing to the fact that Rahner's exposure to hermeneutical theory has been confined to the influence of the early Heidegger. His relative inattentiveness to the specific role that language plays within interpretation attests to the largely implicit hermeneutical shape of Rahner's work and accounts for the fact that he is sometimes interpreted as being hermeneutically naive.

For this reason, I propose to complement this retrieval of Rahner with a retrieval of Edward Schillebeeckx, who is widely considered to be one of the Catholic pioneers of hermeneutical theology. Contrary to Rahner, Schillebeeckx has extensively engaged with various key hermeneutical thinkers, including Hans-Georg Gadamer and Paul Ricoeur. Accordingly, his account of interpretation is much more hermeneutically defined and is significantly more attentive to the fundamental role of language. Moreover, due to his discussion with thinkers from the Frankfurt School of Critical Theory, Schillebeeckx also develops an important insight into the distorting influence of power and ideology on experience and interpretation. These factors account for the fact that Schillebeeckx's theological method has a much more pronounced and explicitly hermeneutical profile. However, I argue that this theological turn to hermeneutics did not coincide with a complete giving up of metaphysics. I maintain instead that Schillebeeckx's hermeneutical theology remains intrinsically connected with a metaphysical framework of thought. This forms a crucial distinction between the hermeneutical turns of Schillebeeckx and his immediate successors, such as Francisc Schüssler Fiorenza and David Tracy. As a result, Schillebeeckx's theological epistemology presents an astute complementary example of the dialectical interrelation of metaphysics and hermeneutics in theology.

Part II

6

Dialogical theology:
The sources of Schillebeeckx's method

1 Introduction

Giving a brief introduction to Schillebeeckx's theological methodology is not a simple task.[1] One difficulty that immediately presents itself is that he has drawn upon such a wide variety of intellectual sources throughout his long theological career. Schillebeeckx constantly sought to enter into dialogue with contemporary intellectual developments. According to his own account of this process, he started with Thomas Aquinas's '*sacra doctrina*' and subsequently moved into the domains of hermeneutics, critical theory and structuralism.[2] However, the list of sources upon which he drew is significantly longer than this summary suggests. Philip Kennedy lists more than twenty-five sources, ranging from phenomenology and *ressourcement* to linguistics and pragmatism.[3] Discussing all of these various inspirations, one after the other, is not feasible. Instead, I have chosen to introduce Schillebeeckx's method by focusing on three distinct, yet also partially overlapping, sources: a metaphysical source, a hermeneutical source and a critical theory source.[4] I argue that the specific combination of these sources in Schillebeeckx's work accounts for his dialectical interrelation of metaphysics and hermeneutics.

The first source is connected with the philosophy of Dominicus De Petter. This philosopher exerted a formative and persistent influence on Schillebeeckx's thought.

---

[1] Erik Borgman has written a biography (Borgman, *Edward Schillebeeckx. A Theologian in his History*) that covers Schillebeeckx's life up until the conclusion of the Second Vatican Council in 1965. The second part of this biography is still forthcoming. Other, shorter biographical accounts include Maarten van den Bos and Stephan van Erp, *A Happy Theologian: A Hundred Years of Edward Schillebeeckx* (Nijmegen: Valkhof Press, 2014); Robert J. Schreiter, 'Edward Schillebeeckx', in *The Modern Theologians: An Introduction to Christian Theology in the Twentieth Century*, ed. David F. Ford, 2nd ed. (Oxford: Blackwell, 1997), 152–60; Kennedy, *Schillebeeckx*; and John Bowden, *Edward Schillebeeckx: Portrait of a Theologian* (London: SCM, 1983). Interviews with Schillebeeckx have been published as *Conversations with Francesco Strazzari*, trans. John Bowden (London: SCM, 1994), and *God is New Each Moment: In Conversation with Huub Oosterhuis en Piet Hoogeveen*, trans. David Smith (Edinburgh: T&T Clark, 1982).

[2] Schillebeeckx, *I am a Happy Theologian*, 41.

[3] Philip Kennedy, *Schillebeeckx* (Collegeville, MN: Liturgical Press, 1993), 36–7.

[4] See Daniel Speed Thompson, 'Epistemological Frameworks in the Theology of Edward Schillebeeckx', *Theological Studies* 15 (2003): 19–56, who analyses and discusses these sources as resulting in three overlapping 'epistemological frameworks' in Schillebeeckx's work.

In his early theological career, Schillebeeckx combined De Petter's epistemology with Thomas Aquinas's theology of creation in order to develop a perspectival theological epistemology. However, in the 1960s, Schillebeeckx's theological method underwent an important transformation, due to his engagement with new currents of thought. This leads to a discussion of the second source: hermeneutical theory. I will examine several key elements of the thought of both Hans-Georg Gadamer and Paul Ricoeur that inform Schillebeeckx's hermeneutical theology. Closely connected to this second influence is the third source, namely, the Frankfurt School of critical theory. The influence of Theodor W. Adorno and Jürgen Habermas, particularly, accounts for the turn in Schillebeeckx's work towards sociopolitical praxis.

My account of these three sources is primarily expository and aims to provide a broader intellectual background to Schillebeeckx's work and his theological method. A fuller discussion of Schillebeeckx's distinct theological appropriation of these sources will follow in the subsequent chapters, which engage in a more substantive discussion of Schillebeeckx's method. One important question that presents itself, though, is whether these different sources are compatible with each other. Or to put the question more concretely, 'Does the turn to hermeneutics and critical theory result in a break with the metaphysical arguments and elements of Schillebeeckx's theology?' I will address this question in the concluding section of this chapter.

2 Phenomenological-ontological roots: Dominicus De Petter

There is a striking parallel between Rahner and Schillebeeckx when it comes to their early formation.[5] Both thinkers initially started with a strong interest in philosophy but eventually turned towards theology. Both scholars were also influenced by philosophers who sought to overcome the limitations of a strict neo-Thomism. They did so by bringing Thomas Aquinas's thought into dialogue with modern philosophers and by reconsidering the role that human experience plays within theology. However, while Rahner took his inspiration from Joseph Maréchal's transcendental approach, Schillebeeckx was more influenced by Dominicus De Petter's phenomenological reading of Thomas. Understanding De Petter's philosophy is essential to understanding Schillebeeckx's early work in theological epistemology, especially his perspectival epistemology.[6]

De Petter's philosophy comprises part of the neo-Thomist response to modern philosophy, more specifically to the Kantian critique of the possibility of theoretical

---

[5] This parallel between Schillebeeckx and Rahner has also been noted by Borgman, *Edward Schillebeeckx*, 170–1. However, Borgman holds that there is also a 'fundamental difference in approach', insofar as Rahner is primarily interested in the transcendental structures of human consciousness, while Schillebeeckx focuses on the concrete content of human questions.

[6] For more information on De Petter and his philosophy, see D. Scheltens, 'De filosofie van p. D.M. De Petter', *Tijdschrift voor Filosofie* 33 (1971): 439–505. For an extensive historical and biographical discussion of De Petter, see Johan Van Wyngaerden, *Voorstudie tot het denken van E. Schillebeeckx. D.M. De Petter O.P. (1905-1971): Een inleiding tot zijn leven en denken* (unpublished licentiate thesis, Faculty of Theology, Catholic University of Leuven, 1989).

metaphysics. Contrary to Maréchal whose decision is to follow Kant's epistemological turn to the subject, De Petter advocates a phenomenological turn to deal with this problem. He employs insights drawn from Husserl, Merleau-Ponty and Heidegger to reconceptualize scholastic metaphysics in response to the modern critique. De Petter's adopts a phenomenological focus on experience and its dimension of givenness but, contrary to Husserl and other phenomenologists, he seeks to maintain a firm metaphysical realism.[7] While his philosophy is deeply rooted in the Thomistic tradition, he also criticizes that same tradition, its 'essentialist' tendency to favour abstract conceptuality at the expense of concretely existing realities particularly.[8] Alternatively, he seeks to show the relative (in)adequacy of the abstract and conceptual element of knowledge. De Petter addresses this issue in the following way.

The modern epistemological problem is described by De Petter as the antinomy between the 'conceptual-abstract' and the 'existential-concrete'.[9] Whereas idealism seeks to explain noetic contact with concrete objects, by reference to the 'pure autonomy of the spirit', Aristotelian-Thomistic realism has searched for alternative solutions. De Petter observes that these realist alternatives usually reject the possibility of a 'human intellectual intuition'.[10] As a result, they are forced to locate the point of contact with concrete realities *outside* the intellectual act as such, for instance in the 'dynamism of the intellectual activity'.[11] The aforementioned phrase is an oblique reference to Maréchal. De Petter argues that Maréchal's Aristotelian rejection of intellectual intuition and his alternative focus on the objectifying judgement suffers from an 'unnuanced abstractionism'.[12] In Maréchal's solution, the subject performs the objectifying function in knowledge through affirmative judgement, positing an object as object over and against itself. As a result, objectivity is no longer a property of the concrete thing itself but instead becomes a property of the subject's intellectual dynamism.[13] De Petter considers this epistemology to be problematic for two reasons. First, he doubts whether such an account of knowledge is not more idealist than it is realist. One characteristic of the being of a concrete being is that it exists 'really', that is independently of the knowing subject. Maréchal, however, locates the affirmation that a concrete thing really exists within a subjective moment, that is in the intellectual dynamism of the human person. According to De Petter, in so doing he fails to account for the properly independent being of concretely existing things. Second, De Petter also considers Maréchal's epistemology to be no longer strictly intellectual. Realism no longer has anything to do with knowledge as such, insofar as the affirmation of the reality of concrete beings is located within the subject's intellectual dynamism.[14]

---

[7] See Karl Schumann, 'Fragmentaire metafysiek. De metafysiek van D.M. De Petter', *Tijdschrift voor Filosofie* 36 (1974): 576–8.
[8] Schumann, 'Fragmentaire metafysiek', 582.
[9] Dominicus Maria De Petter, 'Impliciete intuïtie', *Tijdschrift voor Filosofie* 1 (1939): 84.
[10] De Petter, 'Impliciete intuïtie', 85.
[11] Ibid., 85.
[12] Dominicus Maria De Petter, 'Zin en grond van het oordeel', in *Begrip en werkelijkheid. Aan de overzijde van het conceptualisme* (Hilversum: Brand, 1964), 78–80.
[13] De Petter, 'Zin en grond van het oordeel', 78–80.
[14] Ibid., 80; De Petter, 'Impliciete intuïtie', 85.

Alternatively, De Petter seeks to rehabilitate the Platonic notion of an immediate mode of intellectual knowing. To this end, he introduces the idea of the 'implicit intuition'. Intuition here is defined as 'an intellectual, immediate grasping of the existentially-concrete'.[15] It is not something that occurs in addition to, or in preparation for, the intellectual act but something that forms an essential part of this intellectual act itself. According to De Petter, we can distinguish within the single intellectual act various elements which have varying degrees of explicitness. The intuition concerns the 'completely and essentially implicit moment'.[16] It cannot be represented directly and explicitly but can only be brought to expression through reflective analysis of the explicit moment of the intellectual act. For De Petter, this implicit intuition can be posited despite the rejection of 'ontologism' (the doctrine that defends the possibility of the unmediated experience of being) because the 'moment of intuition escapes, by definition, every immediate experiencing'.[17] In other words, implicit intuition must be understood in connection to the explicit moment of the intellectual act. How is this notion, of implicit intuition, able to resolve the antinomy of concreteness and abstractness?

In order to explain this, De Petter first discusses the explicit conceptual moment of the intellectual act. Through the formation of abstract concepts, the subject seeks to express the content of experience. However, since conceptual expression remains necessarily abstract, it also remains inadequate and deficient. The distance between subject and object cannot be bridged fully through concepts alone. Since the concept can never adequately capture the richness of a concrete reality's being, there is a fundamental relativity to all conceptual knowledge.[18] What is the origin of this consciousness of the limited capacity of concepts? According to De Petter, the awareness of the inadequacy of concepts presupposes a 'limit consciousness' of something greater.[19] It implies another non-conceptual, concrete intellectual moment. So, he argues that we must necessarily have a 'consciousness of being' (*zijnsbewustzijn*) of a concrete reality.[20] This 'consciousness of being' is complete and exhaustive, insofar as it has absolute and objective value, but it is also essentially indistinct and confused, inasmuch as it is both implicit and inexpressible. It forms the transcendental condition for conceptual expressions and, therefore, forms the constitutive element of intellectual activity as such.[21] Thus, De Petter argues that his notion of implicit intuition avoids two extremes. Knowledge is neither purely intuitive, insofar as the intuition requires conceptual expression, nor purely abstract, inasmuch as intellectual activity involves not merely abstract reflection but also concrete intellectual intuition.[22]

De Petter enumerates several characteristics that differentiate his epistemological framework from Maréchal's. First, contrary to Maréchal's dynamism, the implicit

---

[15] De Petter, 'Impliciete intuïtie', 86.
[16] Ibid., 86–7.
[17] Ibid., 87.
[18] Ibid., 87–8.
[19] Ibid., 89.
[20] Ibid., 90.
[21] Ibid., 88–91; 101.
[22] De Petter, 'Zin en grond van het oordeel', 91.

intuition is not mediated through sensory experience, but instead through a direct grasping of the concrete reality of a being.[23] It is a purely spiritual experience in which there is no distance or opposition, but it instead involves the unity between subject and object.[24] Second, the subject is, to an important extent, receptive instead of originating in intellectual activity. It is not the subjective dynamism but the implicit intuition which provides judgement with an affirmative quality. The conceptual expression has an affirmative force, yet only inasmuch as it is connected with this implicit intuition.[25] Importantly, the intuition is not produced by self-sufficient autonomous effectiveness; instead, implicit intuition as the constitutive element of knowledge depends upon the participation in God. Hence, De Petter seeks to complement the Aristotelian-Thomistic attention, paid to the role of abstraction in human knowledge, with the Augustinian doctrine of illumination.[26] However, he does not offer any justification for this turn to a human – divine participatory framework.[27] I will briefly sketch the outlines of the theological dimension of De Petter's metaphysics.

For De Petter, the plurality of concrete beings has a necessary connection to the unity of being. The implicit intuition of a concrete being implies the implicit intuition of the unity of being as the structuring principle of reality.[28] For De Petter, this unity can only be found *in* concrete beings and is, therefore, determined by this concreteness.[29] This implies that being is not static but is dynamic – an 'ever changing current of events and relations'.[30] This unity-in-plurality, confusedly present in the implicit intuition of concrete realities, can be detected by way of metaphysical reflection.[31] The argument that the unifying principle of being is determined by the concrete uniqueness of the being of each distinct being also leads De Petter to reject the scholastic notion of *esse commune*. The notion of *esse commune* leads to a forgetfulness of being.[32] Positing such a general concept of being reintroduces an abstraction which is at odds with De Petter's realist emphasis on the concreteness of being.[33] The unity of being that is present in the plurality of beings, therefore, is not a *quod* (what) of every act of knowledge but rather the *quo* (how) that enables intellectual knowledge.[34] De Petter identifies the unity of being with God. The 'ontological insufficiency' or, in other words, the contingency of concrete beings suggests a transcendent fundament.[35] The fact that concrete beings

---

[23] De Petter, 'Impliciete intuïtie', 95.
[24] Ibid., 101.
[25] Ibid., 93.
[26] Ibid., 103.
[27] Stephan van Erp, 'Implicit Faith: Philosophical Theology after Schillebeeckx', in *Edward Schillebeeckx and Contemporary Theology*, ed. Lieven Boeve, Frederiek Depoortere, and Stephan van Erp, (London: T&T Clark, 2010), 217.
[28] De Petter, 'Impliciete intuïtie', 96.
[29] Ibid., 98.
[30] Van Erp, 'Implicit Faith', 217.
[31] Stephan van Erp, 'Geïmpliceerde transcendentie. De Petter's "impliciete intuïtie" als bevestiging van het zijn van de zijnden én het Zijn zelf', in *Subliem Niemandsland. Opstellen over intersubjectiviteit, metafysica en transcendentie*, ed. W.F.C.M. Derkse, A. J. Leijen, and B. M. J. Nagel (Best: Damon, 1997), 301; Van Erp, 'Implicit Faith', 217.
[32] Schumann, 'Fragmentaire metafysiek', 582.
[33] Ibid.
[34] Van Erp, 'Implicit Faith', 217.
[35] Van Erp, 'Geïmpliceerde transcendentie', 305.

factually exist cannot be explained in a merely immanent way. De Petter, therefore, posits the necessary affirmation of a creative God who, as their very constitution, is simultaneously immanent and transcendent to the beings of the world. God is never the direct object of human experience, but instead becomes visible when we contemplate the 'gratuity' of the factual existence of contingent beings.[36]

Schillebeeckx draws heavily upon De Petter's thought in developing his early theological epistemology. Looking for a viable third way between rationalism and relativism, he proposes a *perspectival* understanding of the human relation to absolute truth. While still heavily dependent upon a metaphysical understanding of truth, this perspectival epistemology contains elements which Schillebeeckx later develops with the help of hermeneutical theory. Following De Petter, Schillebeeckx argues that our reflective conceptual knowledge of reality is based on a *pre-conceptual awareness* which cannot be brought to expression in a complete or adequate manner. He accords priority to this implicit non-conceptual consciousness, which puts us into direct contact with concrete reality. We use conceptuality to express this implicit awareness, but these abstract concepts always fall short of expressing concrete reality adequately.[37] The concreteness of reality is crucial for Schillebeeckx, just as it is for De Petter. To respect this concreteness, the implicit experiential dimension is prioritized over the explicit conceptual dimension of knowledge. In his later work, the attention devoted to concreteness becomes primarily visible in Schillebeeckx's sharp eye for the hermeneutical character of human experience and knowledge. This suggests that his hermeneutical turn must not be explained entirely with reference to the influence of key figures from the hermeneutical tradition. Finally, Schillebeeckx follows De Petter postulation of God as a necessary element of his epistemology, in order to account for the reality of objects of knowledge. Schillebeeckx develops an argument in favour of contingency, or ontological insufficiency, in explicitly theological terms with recourse to the doctrine of creation.

3 Understanding the past in the present

His engagement with hermeneutical theory comprises the second key pattern in Schillebeeckx's work. Due to hermeneutical reflections, Schillebeeckx intensified his focus on human experience. This impact of hermeneutics first becomes apparent in a series of articles published, shortly after the Second Vatican Council in the late 1960s and early 1970s.[38] Schillebeeckx observes that 'the hermeneutic question, that is, the question of how the Christian message should be interpreted nowadays, has

---

[36] Scheltens, 'De filosofie van P.D.M. De Petter', 504–5. See also Van Erp, 'Geïmpliceerde transcendentie', 304–8 for a more detailed account of De Petter's argument for the affirmation of God.
[37] Edward Schillebeeckx, 'The Concept of "Truth"' [1954-1962], in *Revelation and Theology*, trans. N.D. Smith, CW vol. 2 (London: Bloomsbury, 2014), 198 [19].
[38] Ted Schoof, 'Masters in Israel: VII. The Later Theology of Edward Schillebeeckx', *Clergy Review* 55 (1970): 943–61 (950), suggests a practical reason for Schillebeeckx's explorations of hermeneutics, namely the fact that he had to give a new lecture series on the subject.

come to assume a central position in catholic theology'.³⁹ Protestant theology had been heavily debating the need for philosophical and theological hermeneutics ever since Schleiermacher put this theme on the agenda. Theologians such as Karl Barth, Rudolf Bultmann, Ernst Fuchs and Gerhard Ebeling greatly contributed to the development of hermeneutical theology in the early twentieth century.⁴⁰ By contrast, the place of hermeneutics in pre-conciliar Catholic theology had hardly developed beyond the 'infancy' stage.⁴¹ Schillebeeckx seeks to address this lacuna in Catholic theology by initiating a critical, albeit constructive, dialogue with modern hermeneutical theory, especially with respect to the works of Hans-Georg Gadamer and Paul Ricoeur. While Rahner's engagement with hermeneutical theory remains largely limited to Heidegger, Schillebeeckx thus also draws extensively upon the later developments in hermeneutical thought. As a result, his focus on the fundamental role played by history is significantly more attentive to the role played by language in theological understanding. What insights does Schillebeeckx derive from Gadamer and Ricoeur?

3.1 Hans-Georg Gadamer's hermeneutics of history

According to Schillebeeckx, the hermeneutical problem is rooted in the historicity of human existence, which implies the historicity of human understanding and, therefore, gives rise to the hermeneutical circle:

> All understanding takes place in a circular movement – the answer is to some extent determined by the question, which is in turn confirmed, extended, or corrected by the answer. A new question then grows out of this understanding, so that the hermeneutical circle continues to develop in a never-ending spiral. Man can never escape from this circle, because he can never establish once and for all the truth or the content of the word of God. There is no definitive, timeless understanding which raises no more questions.⁴²

The circular nature of human understanding was first elaborated philosophically by Heidegger in *Being and Time*. Building upon Heidegger, Gadamer and Ricoeur have

---

[39] Edward Schillebeeckx, *The Understanding of Faith*, CW vol. 5, trans. N. D. Smith (London: Bloomsbury, 2014), xix.
[40] See Jeanrond, *Theological Hermeneutics*, 120–58, for a discussion of the appropriation of hermeneutics by these theologians.
[41] Schillebeeckx, *The Understanding of Faith*, xix. However, Schillebeeckx also maintains that the problem of the hermeneutical circle has actually been implicitly part of Catholic theology, namely, as the problem of the development of dogma. A dogma seeks to 'reinterpret' the biblical understanding of faith in Jesus Christ as the revelation of the salvific God in, and for, a new particular historical context. Changing historical circumstances challenge older formulations of faith and call for reinterpretation, which finds itself situated between the authority of the older formulations and the changed historical context with its new horizon of questioning. See Edward Schillebeeckx, 'Towards a Catholic Use of Hermeneutics' [1968], in *God the Future of Man*, CW vol. 3, trans. N. D. Smith (London: Bloomsbury, 2014), 3–4 [6–7].
[42] Schillebeeckx, 'Towards a Catholic Use of Hermeneutics', 4–5 [8].

developed this understanding of the hermeneutical circle further.⁴³ Importantly, they have demonstrated that the distance in time, between the past and the present, is not an obstacle to understanding but is instead what enables understanding; it is 'the ontological condition which makes interpretation possible'.⁴⁴ Schillebeeckx derives this insight into the positive role of temporal distance from Gadamer's hermeneutics.

Gadamer rejects the romantic idea that understanding a text involves 'transposing' oneself into the author's mind. He argues, instead, that understanding a text involves sharing in a 'common meaning', by entering into a 'conversation' with the text.⁴⁵ To enter into a conversation with the text, we must be attentive to its 'alterity'. However, this does not require the adoption of a 'neutral' perspective. Gadamer criticizes the Enlightenment's 'prejudice against prejudices' and advocates instead for a 'rehabilitation' of the positive roles played by prejudice and tradition in understanding. He stresses that prejudices form a precondition for understanding, contrary to the Enlightenment's imperative to bracket out one's own context and particular prejudices. Prejudices provide us with a horizon of understanding – a pre-understanding or pre-judgement – that enables us to engage with a text by anticipating its potential meaning(s). Because of the foundational role they play in understanding, we should strive to become conscious of our own prejudices in order to correct them when necessary, so that we can direct and improve our pre-understanding.⁴⁶

According to Gadamer, traditions are important inasmuch as they are a source of prejudices which enable understanding. Thus, he argues that understanding is not so much an individual subjective act but instead involves 'participating in an event of tradition, a process of transmission in which past and present are constantly mediated'.⁴⁷ Gadamer uses this insight into the role of prejudice and tradition to rethink the hermeneutical circle ontologically. Interpreting subjects are able to anticipate the meaning of a text, insofar as they share in a commonality through their traditions. This commonality is not static but is constantly formed and reformed through the interrelation of subject and tradition. The interplay between tradition and subject constitutes the hermeneutical circle: 'Tradition is not simply a permanent precondition; rather we produce it ourselves inasmuch as we understand, participate in the evolution of tradition, and hence further determine it ourselves.'⁴⁸

Gadamer continues his reflection on understanding and history by introducing the notion of *wirkungsgeschichtliches Bewußtsein* (consciousness of the history of effects). As historical beings, we must be conscious of the fact that our interpretative understanding is situated in, and is affected by, a web of historical effects. Insofar as we find ourselves in a particular historical situation, we have already been shaped by

---

⁴³ See Hans-Georg Gadamer, *Truth and Method*, rev. trans. Joel Weinsheimer and Donald G. Marshall (London: Continuum, 2004), 268–78, and Paul Ricoeur, 'Explanation and Understanding', in *Interpretation Theory: Discourse and the Surplus of Meaning* (Fort Worth, TX: Texas Christian University Press, 1976), 71–95.
⁴⁴ Schillebeeckx, 'Towards a Catholic Use of Hermeneutics', 3 [6]; 16 [23–4].
⁴⁵ Gadamer, *Truth and Method*, 292.
⁴⁶ Ibid., 271–7. See also Schillebeeckx, 'Towards a Catholic Use of Hermeneutics', 18 [26].
⁴⁷ Gadamer, *Truth and Method*, 291.
⁴⁸ Ibid., 293.

history and the culture which conditions our interpretive understanding.[49] However, the fact that our understanding is historically situated and conditioned does not imply that it is restricted to these particular historical conditions; perspectives can be changed or transcended. To explain this confluence of 'finite determinacy' and potential expansion, Gadamer turns to the concept of horizon. Understanding requires a historical horizon, but this horizon is not closed and actually changes continually: 'The horizon of the past, out of which all human life lives and which exists in the form of tradition, is always in motion.'[50] Accordingly, in conversations with another person or with a text, a 'fusion of horizons' (*Horizontverschmelzung*) takes place.

Schillebeeckx appropriates Gadamer's rehabilitation of tradition as a way to maintain the relevance and normativity of the Christian tradition while also taking the historicity of understanding seriously. Tradition is crucial in overcoming the distance between the past and the present.[51] Standing in a tradition forms an 'ontological pre-structure' of understanding, which simultaneously imposes the task upon us of understanding this tradition by way of reinterpretation. The reinterpretation of the past, in the light of the present situation and oriented towards the future, is necessary if the tradition is to remain a *living* tradition.[52] Gadamer explains that a living tradition makes it possible that temporal distance functions as a 'filtering process'. It allows hermeneutics to distinguish 'false' prejudices, limiting and inhibiting understanding, from 'true' prejudices that enable understanding.[53] However, this raises the question as to who exactly is doing the filtering here. Is it only the tradition that filters our prejudices, or is it also necessary that we apply the filter to the tradition? Schillebeeckx does not address this issue here, but it recurs in his engagement with critical theory.

Furthermore, Schillebeeckx builds on Gadamer's theory of *Horizontverschmelzung* in order to argue for a dialogical understanding of truth. Truth is disclosed through inter-subjectivity and is always mediated by language.[54] Understanding a text and its claim to truth requires us 'to become conscious of the other as different within the fusion of the two horizons'.[55] Schillebeeckx emphasizes that a reinterpretative understanding entails simultaneously being bound by tradition and engaging creatively and productively with tradition.[56] As we will see, this becomes particularly relevant in his hermeneutics of tradition.

3.2 Paul Ricoeur's long route

It is impossible to delineate sharply which elements of hermeneutical theory Schillebeeckx derives from Gadamer and which he derives from Ricoeur. Nevertheless,

---

[49] Ibid., 299–301.
[50] Ibid., 303.
[51] Schillebeeckx, 'Towards a Catholic Use of Hermeneutics', 14–15 [21].
[52] Ibid., 18–19 [28].
[53] Gadamer, *Truth and Method*, 298.
[54] Schillebeeckx, 'Towards a Catholic Use of Hermeneutics', 19 [29].
[55] Ibid., 19 [29]. I have slightly modified the English translation here, reintroducing the term 'horizon', used in the Dutch version, instead of 'frame of reference' and 'sphere', which are used in the translation.
[56] Ibid., 21 [31].

he does attribute certain insights to Ricoeur explicitly. He mentions Ricoeur as the one who has expressed the problem of 'understanding history historically' most clearly:

> How can human life, expressing itself, objectivize itself (for instance, in a text) and, consequently, how does human life, objectivizing itself in this way, call meanings into being which can later be taken up again and understood by another historical being in a different historical situation?[57]

Ricoeur elaborates upon the critical potential of 'alienating distanciation' in understanding, as the dialectical counterpart of Gadamer's emphasis on participatory belonging to a tradition.[58] The objectification of speech into a written text provides this text with a threefold autonomy: distance with regard to its author, its original sociocultural conditions and its original addressees. Through decontextualization or *Verfremdung* (alienation), a text receives an autonomy and, thereby, enables its future reception and appropriation 'by anyone who can read'.[59] Schillebeeckx echoes this concern for the autonomy of the text: 'A hermeneutically trained thinker must *a priori* be open to the deviation of the text from his own views, demands and expectations.'[60]

Schillebeeckx observes that the hermeneutical focus on the circularity and historicity of understanding runs the risk of placing the concept of truth on a slippery slope. Hermeneutics rightly discloses the problems of an objectivist approach to truth, which tends to disregard the subject's historicity. However, its emphasis on the unavoidable subjective perspective on truth risks losing sight of truth's objective reality. When truth is fully determined by its historical expression, it becomes merely 'authentic', something which appeals to people in a specific situation.[61] Schillebeeckx refers to Ricoeur's 'long route', in order to probe the ontological conditions of understanding.[62]

Ricoeur has criticized Heidegger for taking a 'short route' in order to develop an ontology of understanding. Heidegger analyses the ontological structures of *Dasein* without considering the role of language proper. Alternatively, Ricoeur suggests taking 'the long route which begins by analyses of language', focusing on symbols and myths. After all, it is 'in language that all ontic or ontological understanding arrives as its expression'.[63] Unveiling the ontological conditions for understanding requires investigating the semantic structure of expressions. The ontology that Ricoeur has in mind is an *ontologie brisée* (truncated ontology). It functions as a regulative idea, a

---

[57] Ibid., 16 [24]. Schillebeeckx refers to Ricoeur's text 'Existence and Hermeneutics', trans. Kathleen McLaughlin, in *The Conflict of Interpretations*, ed. Don Ihde (Evanston, IL: Northwestern University Press, 1974), 3–24.
[58] Paul Ricoeur, 'The Hermeneutical Function of Distanciation', in *From Text to Action: Essays in Hermeneutics, II*, trans. Kathleen Blamey and John B. Thompson (Evanston, IL: Northwestern University Press, 1991), 75–6.
[59] Ricoeur, 'The Hermeneutical Function of Distanciation', 84.
[60] Schillebeeckx, 'Towards a Catholic Use of Hermeneutics', 17 [26].
[61] Ibid., 6 [10].
[62] Ibid., 11 [16], n. 25.
[63] Ricoeur, 'Existence and Hermeneutics', 11.

promised land which 'like Moses, the speaking and reflecting subject can only glimpse ... before dying'.[64]

Schillebeeckx follows Ricoeur's decision to focus on the role of language, which is attested to by his intensive engagement with various philosophies of language, including structuralism and analytical language philosophy.[65] Importantly, he recognizes the insight that truth has a multidimensional character in Ricoeur's plea for the 'long route'. It is impossible to relate neutrally and abstractly to truth as such. Does this mean that there are as many truths as there are interpretations? Is any interpretation a justified and correct interpretation? Or to use Ricoeur's own expression, how are we to deal with the unavoidable 'conflict of interpretations'?[66]

The distinction between sense (*Sinn*) and reference (*Bedeutung*) has been put forward to explicate the relation between language and objective reality. This distinction was first introduced by Gottlob Frege and was appropriated by Ricoeur in his reconceptualization of hermeneutics.[67] Seeking to overcome the Romanticist hermeneutics, and its dichotomy between understanding (*verstehen*) and explanation (*erklären*), Ricoeur argues that interpretation consists of a dialectics of pre-understanding and explanation. The first naive pre-understanding moves first to explanation and then to comprehension. This comprehension, then, becomes a 'second naiveté' which forms the starting point for a new process of interpretation.[68] Importantly, explanation involves what Ricoeur terms a 'hermeneutics of suspicion'.[69] Influenced by Jürgen Habermas and drawing on what he terms the 'masters of suspicion', that is Karl Marx, Friedrich Nietzsche and Sigmund Freud, Ricoeur emphasizes the need for a critical analysis of the ideological and systematic distortions that affect understanding.[70]

The distinction between sense and reference serves to explain that interpretation has to do with the sense of text, that is the ideal object intended by the author, as well as with the reference of a text, that is the text's relation to actual reality.[71] Now, in order to understand the meaning of a text one has to follow the movement from its sense to its reference, so as to discover the possible world opened up and disclosed by the text.[72] Ricoeur emphasizes that the meaning, which is to be appropriated in the event of reading, has an objectivity: the direction of thought or the world opened up by text. Thus, the active role of the interpreting subject notwithstanding, 'It is not the reader who primarily projects himself. The reader rather is enlarged in his capacity of

---

[64] Ibid., 19; 24.
[65] See Edward Schillebeeckx, 'Linguistic Criteria' [1969], in *The Understanding of Faith*, 19–40 [20–45].
[66] See Paul Ricoeur, *The Conflict of Interpretations*.
[67] See Jeanrond, *Text and Interpretation*, 48–9.
[68] Ricoeur, 'Explanation and Understanding', 71–88.
[69] See Paul Ricoeur, *Freud and Philosophy: An Essay on Interpretation*, trans. Denis Savage (New Haven: Yale University Press, 1970).
[70] See Paul Ricoeur, 'Hermeneutics and the Critique of Ideology', in *Hermeneutics and the Human Sciences*, ed. and trans. John B. Thompson (Cambridge: Cambridge University Press, 1981), 63–100.
[71] Ricoeur, 'Hermeneutics and the Critique of Ideology', 80.
[72] Ibid., 87.

self-projection by receiving a new mode of being from the text itself.[73] Crucially, this notion of appropriation as 'dispossession' initiates a new understanding of the subject. The confrontation with the 'universal power of world disclosure' affects a decentring of the subject.[74] The narcissist ego receives a self from a text. Over and against the idealist Cartesian subject, as indubitable foundation and accomplished self, Ricoeur posits the *cogito blessé* (wounded cogito) which is engaged in a lifelong task of understanding the self.[75]

It is important to note that Ricoeur has distanced himself in his later work from the terms 'sense' and 'reference' and that he has instead adopted the terms 'application' or 'appropriation' to emphasize the practical dimension of interpretation.[76] Werner Jeanrond evaluates Ricoeur's distinction between sense and reference critically, arguing that it risks a 'relapse' into idealism.[77] He proposes a realist correction, arguing that a text's potential for sense becomes actualized only in the process of reading and points in this regard to Ricoeur's new use of the term 'refiguration'.[78] Together with 'prefiguration' and 'configuration', refiguration is part of the 'narrative arc' of understanding.[79] This narrative arc seeks to explain hermeneutical understanding as a creative imaginative process. Now in refiguration, the reader 'projects' a possible world evoked through the hermeneutical encounter with the text and thereby engages in an imaginative 'wager about what is "true" of a text'.[80]

Gadamer's and Ricoeur's rendering of the relation between the subjective and the objective dimensions of interpretation prove insightful for Schillebeeckx's own hermeneutics that he develops in his two Christological works *Jesus: An Experiment in Christology* and *Christ: The Christian Experience in the Modern World*.[81] He agrees with their insights into the historicity of human subjectivity and the conditioning consequences that this historical subjectivity has for contemporary understanding of texts from the past. Schillebeeckx applies hermeneutical theory to investigate 'what a christological belief in Jesus of Nazareth can intelligibly signify today'.[82] Importantly, throughout these critical-hermeneutical investigations he is concerned to

---

[73] Ibid., 94.
[74] Ricoeur, 'Explanation and Understanding', 94–5.
[75] For this notion of the wounded cogito, see Paul Ricoeur, *Oneself as Another*, trans. Kathleen Blamey (Chicago: The University of Chicago Press, 1992).
[76] See Ricoeur, 'Explanation and Understanding', 89–95 and Paul Ricoeur, *Time and Narrative*, vol. 3, trans. Kathleen Blamey and David Pellauer (Chicago: The University of Chicago Press, 1988), 158.
[77] Werner G. Jeanrond, *Text and Interpretation as Categories of Theological Thinking*, trans. Thomas J. Wilson (Eugene, OR: Wipf and Stock, 1986), 59–60.
[78] Jeanrond, *Theological Hermeneutics*, 76; 191–2, n. 92.
[79] Dan R. Stiver, *Ricoeur and Theology* (London: Bloomsbury, 2012), 47.
[80] Stiver, *Ricoeur and Theology*, 50.
[81] Edward Schillebeeckx, *Jesus: An Experiment in Christology* [1974], CW vol. 6, trans. Hubert Hoskins and Marcelle Manley (London: Bloomsbury, 2014), Edward Schillebeeckx, *Christ: The Christian Experience in the Modern World* [1977], CW vol. 7, trans. John Bowden (London: Bloomsbury, 2014). Whereas the focus in *Jesus* is primarily historical-critical, concerned with the 'historical Jesus', in *Christ*, Schillebeeckx analyses the New Testament text with particular attention to their literary genres, so as to take 'the texts seriously in their unity and as a whole. This means seeing them in their specific *literary* context against the background of the literature of the time' (ibid., 7 [23]).
[82] Schillebeeckx, *Jesus*, 16 [33].

maintain a balance between the subjective and the objective aspects of interpretative understanding. Schillebeeckx firmly rejects that interpretation can be reduced to subjective intentionality and argues instead that interpretation involves submitting oneself to the objective dimension of a text. He observes that the distinction between sense and reference is problematic. The questions 'what does the text say' and 'to what reality does it testify' cannot be neatly separated since 'what is said is already an interpretation of reality'.[83] The relation between sense and reference therefore is more intimate. As we will see below, Schillebeeckx develops a distinct theological-metaphysical argument to address this issue of the relation between subjectivity and objectivity in hermeneutical understanding.

4 The future as horizon of understanding

Schillebeeckx's theological appropriation of hermeneutical theory is, from the outset, attentive to its relative limitations. Theological understanding requires more than hermeneutics alone. At the end of his article on hermeneutics, he introduces the theme of the 'biblical primacy of the future' as a hermeneutical principle, aimed at the hermeneutics of Gadamer and Bultmann insofar as these are too one-sidedly oriented towards the past. In contrast, Schillebeeckx argues that our interpretation of the realized truth of the past discloses that this truth is simultaneously a *promise*. Interpretation must, therefore, be oriented towards this new reality which is still to come. Whereas Ernst Bloch has expressed this primacy of the future philosophically in *The Principle of Hope*,[84] Schillebeeckx proposes a decisively eschatological concept of God as 'the "One who is to come", the God who is *our* future'.[85] Crucially, this orientation towards the future is only possible by way of *praxis*; the future cannot be interpreted but must be realized. Schillebeeckx concludes, therefore, that 'it is only in the sphere of action – of doing the faith – that orthodox interpretation can be inwardly fulfilled … with the result that interpretation becomes a "hermeneutics of praxis"'.[86] The amount of attention Schillebeeckx paid to the dimension of the future and to the role of praxis can be explained with reference to his confrontation with the Frankfurt School of critical theory.[87] I will discuss two influences that have left a particular mark

---

[83] Schillebeeckx, 'Towards a Catholic Use of Hermeneutics', 22 [33].
[84] Ernst Bloch, *The Principle of Hope*, trans. Neville Plaice (Oxford: Blackwell, 1986).
[85] Edward Schillebeeckx, 'The New Image of God, Secularization and Man's Future on Earth' [1968], in *God the Future of Man*, 109 [181].
[86] Schillebeeckx, 'Towards a Catholic Use of Hermeneutics', 24–5 [36–7].
[87] For Schillebeeckx's engagement with critical theory, see William Portier, 'Schillebeeckx' Dialogue with Critical Theory', *The Ecumenist* 21 (1982): 20–7; William Portier, 'Edward Schillebeeckx as Critical Theorist: The Impact of Neo-Marxist Social Thought on his Recent Theology', *The Thomist* 48 (1984): 341–67; Thompson, 'Epistemological Frameworks', 45–53. Portier perceives a particularly strong influence of Heidegger in Schillebeeckx's early engagement with hermeneutical theory, which comes to light in his concern to maintain a 'permanence' in theological understanding. He argues that 'under the influence of critical theory, this Heideggerian enchantment had begun to wear off' ('Schillebeeckx' Dialogue with Critical Theory', 22).

upon Schillebeeckx's method, namely, Theodor Adorno's concept of negative dialectics and Jürgen Habermas's interrelation of theory and praxis.

4.1 Theodor Adorno's critical negativity

Nowhere in his writings does Schillebeeckx offer an extensive discussion of the thought of Theodor Adorno. He does acknowledge, though, that he has borrowed 'with gratitude' the term 'critical negativity' from this early representative of the Frankfurt School.[88] The concept of critical negativity finds an application within Schillebeeckx's notion of the contrast experience, something which turns out to be an essential element of Schillebeeckx's theological epistemology. Given the fact that this theme takes on such an important position in his theology, it is all the more striking that he scarcely discusses the thought of Adorno more specifically. To fill in this gap, I will briefly discuss how Adorno introduces the notion of 'negative dialectics' in his struggle with the hegemonic character of theoretical reason.

In the *Dialectic of Enlightenment*, Theodor Adorno and Max Horkheimer describe how, during the Enlightenment, an instrumental concept of rationality came about that can be characterized by the term 'identity thinking'.[89] Reason as systematic science uses abstraction, the instrument of Enlightenment par excellence, to establish scientific unity in the multitude of worldly objects. The result of such calculating and self-preserving thought is the subjugation of the objective world, in which differences are levelled out.[90] According to Adorno, the structure of oppressive identity thinking has culminated in the horrors of Auschwitz. The Enlightened traditions of art, philosophy and science, celebrating the subject, have utterly failed because this very same culture ended up in the violation of human subjectivity.[91] Traditionally, metaphysics has an affirmative character, inasmuch as it strives to construct a transcendent meaning and purpose in the immanent world. However, Auschwitz has made this affirmative character impossible:

> To assert that existence or being has a positive meaning constituted within itself and orientated towards the divine principle … would be, like all the principles of

---

[88] Schillebeeckx, 'The New Image of God', 116, n. 8. Apart from referring to Adorno, Schillebeeckx also mentions Ricoeur, more specifically his article 'The Tasks of the Political Educator', *Philosophy Today* 17 (1973): 142–52, as the source of inspiration behind this notion. In this article, originally published in 1965, Ricoeur argues for a dialectic between an 'ethic of conviction' and an 'ethic of responsibility'. The ethic of conviction, arising out of particular communities, should operate indirectly by exerting constant pressure upon the 'ethic of responsibility and power'. It can perform its role because such an ethic 'is not tied to the possible and the reasonable, but to what one could call the humanly desirable, the optimum ethic' (150). Schillebeeckx appropriates the idea of the indirect effect of a utopian vision to develop the positive dimension of his contrast experience.
[89] Max Horkheimer and Theodor W. Adorno, *Dialectic of Enlightenment: Philosophical Fragments*, ed. Gunzelin Schmid Noerr, trans. Edmund Jephcott (Stanford: Stanford University Press, 2002), 63–6.
[90] Horkheimer and Adorno, *Dialectic of Enlightenment*, 6.
[91] Theodor W. Adorno, *Negative Dialectics*, trans. E. B. Ashton (London: Taylor and Francis, 2004), 367.

truth, beauty and goodness which philosophers have concocted, a pure mockery in face of the victims and the infinitude of their torment.⁹²

Confronted with the horrors of the *Sho'ah*, Adorno poses the question of whether philosophy, metaphysics or poetry is still possible. Despite his strong critique, Adorno does not want to give up on metaphysics altogether. However, metaphysics must be transformed in order to remain possible: 'After Auschwitz there is no word tinged from on high, not even a theological one, that has any right unless it underwent a transformation.'⁹³ While the death camps form the horrible illustration of the derailment of traditional metaphysics, Adorno finds it impossible to think that death can have the last word. To conceive of death as the absolute means that everything is nothing, which would be the end of truth. In order to avoid such a nihilistic perspective, we need some idea of the possibility of the redemption of existence. We need a metaphysics that transcends what is immediately given – a semblance of otherness or transcendence.⁹⁴ However, Adorno is careful to distinguish his conception of transcendence from religious or theological transcendence. Theology liquidates transcendence by 'nailing it down'. In contrast, metaphysics as 'critical self-reflection of thought' remains continually open, in order to challenge status quo convictions.⁹⁵ Thinking the transcendent or the absolute, without running the risk of falling back into oppressive identitarian reasoning, requires a 'negative dialectics'.

Adorno rejects the replacement of absolute identity with absolute non-identity, or the exchange of concept for non-conceptuality.⁹⁶ Alternatively, he advocates a form of 'negative dialectics' that involves a consistent sense of non-identity. While thinking without identifying is impossible, we can nevertheless 'see through the identity principle' and think 'non-identity through identity'. We must oppose an identity thinking that is totalitarian, by 'convicting it of non-identity with itself'.⁹⁷ This critical non-identity thinking is constantly aware of the inability to grasp the object in its complex particularity through concepts. However, non-identity, in Adorno's understanding, should not be associated with absolute otherness. There is a certain tension between the presence and absence of non-identity. In that sense, the non-identical is indeed transcendent; it goes beyond the status quo. However, for Adorno the transcendence does not lie outside the historical materialistic sphere. Contrary to what traditional metaphysics usually holds, the intra-mundane and historic are crucial for metaphysics. Since the absolute appears in history, in immanence and in the particularity of human existence, it can only be expressed in categories of immanence, which do not deify this immanence. A metaphysics that proceeds by way of negative dialectics is necessarily open-ended and incomplete: 'It lies in the definition of negative dialectics that it will not come to rest in itself, as if it were total. This is its form of hope.'⁹⁸

⁹² Theodor W. Adorno, *Metaphysics. Concept and Problems*, ed. Rolf Tiedemann, trans. Edmund Jephcott (Stanford: Stanford University Press, 2001), 101–2.
⁹³ Adorno, *Negative Dialectics*, 367.
⁹⁴ Ibid., 404.
⁹⁵ Ibid., 399; Adorno, *Metaphysics*, 99.
⁹⁶ Adorno, *Negative Dialectics*, 136.
⁹⁷ Ibid., 147; 149; 189.
⁹⁸ Ibid., 361; 406; 407.

As Steven Rodenborn has observed, 'Schillebeeckx's debt to Adorno's negative dialectics is unmistakable.'[99] What Adorno says about the 'semblance of transcendence', which shines through in material immanence, finds a close parallel in Schillebeeckx's description of the revelation of universal meaning in negative experiences of contrast. Moreover, Schillebeeckx also agrees that this transcendence or 'positive horizon of meaning' cannot be conceptualized or expressed directly. However, Schillebeeckx's appropriation of Adorno is not uncritical. He concurs with Adorno's argument that negativity fulfils an essential mediatory role in our reflection on such a transcendent horizon but rejects Adorno's particular plea for a 'system of the non-system'. Whereas Adorno fears the 'nailing down' of transcendence, Schillebeeckx is convinced that we can have 'negative knowledge' of what Ricoeur calls the 'humanly desirable' and what Bloch calls the 'threatened *humanum*'.[100]

It is precisely this positive dimension that Schillebeeckx emphasizes in his appropriation of critical negativity for theological hermeneutics. Schillebeeckx insists that radical, critical negativity ultimately has a relative rather than an absolute value, in contrast to the 'tendency to make negativity itself into a new fetish and to intensify "no" until it becomes absolute'.[101] A negative dialectics that conceives absolutely of negativity loses its meaningfulness. Alternatively, Schillebeeckx presents Christian eschatological faith as comprising an example of critical negativity that does not settle for 'sterility' but rather actively contributes 'to the improvement of the condition of humankind as a whole'.[102] For Schillebeeckx, the widespread injustices and suffering in the world remain a locus for the manifestation of God's grace in all their negativity.

4.2 Jürgen Habermas's reconfiguration of theory and praxis

While Schillebeeckx's comments on Adorno are relatively scarce, he pays particular attention to the thought of Jürgen Habermas in his conversations with critical theory. He sympathizes with Habermas's constructive criticism of Gadamer's hermeneutics, as well as with his critique that earlier critical theorists such as Adorno and Horkheimer lost their critical power because of their dissociation with praxis. Gadamer famously put forward the claim of the universality of hermeneutical understanding, arguing that understanding can be successful as long as we are willing to submit to the authority of the text and the tradition which it represents.[103] Habermas calls this very confidence in the possibility of reaching mutual understanding into question. He revives the insight,

---

[99] Steven Rodenborn, *Hope in Action: Subversive Eschatology in the Theology of Edward Schillebeeckx and Johann Baptist Metz* (Minneapolis: Fortress Press, 2014), 127.
[100] Schillebeeckx, 'The New Image of God', 116 [191]; Edward Schillebeeckx, 'Theological Criteria' [1969], in *The Understanding of Faith*, 58 [65].
[101] Edward Schillebeeckx, 'The New Critical Theory and Theological Hermeneutics' [1971], in *The Understanding of Faith*, 112 [128].
[102] Schillebeeckx, 'The New Image of God', 117 [192–3].
[103] See Hans-Georg Gadamer, 'The Universality of the Hermeneutical Problem', in *The Hermeneutic Tradition: From Ast to Ricoeur*, ed. Gayle L. Ormiston and Alan D. Schrift (Albany: SUNY, 1990), 147–58.

stemming from the Enlightenment, that tradition needs to be criticized in order to disclose its potential ideological distortions of communication.

> We have good reason to suspect that the background consensus of established traditions and language games can be a consciousness forged of compulsion, a result of pseudocommunication, not only in the pathologically isolated case of disturbed familial relations, but in entire social systems as well.[104]

Schillebeeckx follows Habermas closely in this regard. Since the hermeneutic process has not merely a theoretical dimension but also social and political ones, the process of understanding is confronted with systematic obstructions and distortions by institutions of power. Hermeneutics must reconnect with the critical impulse of the Enlightenment, in order to identify these 'breakdowns of communication' that may arise from the 'despotic power of a tradition'.[105] With the help of this critique of ideology, hermeneutics can become an 'understanding of tradition *against* tradition' which recognizes that 'tradition is not only a source of truth and unanimity, but also a source of untruth, repression and violence'.[106] This plea for hermeneutical understanding as the emancipation from ideological and systemic distortion ultimately requires a reconfiguration of the relationship between theory and praxis. Schillebeeckx finds this in Habermas, especially in his works *Knowledge and Human Interest* and *Theory and Praxis*, and describes it in the following manner.[107]

Habermas's critical theory serves to rekindle an emancipatory political struggle that is indebted to the Enlightenment tradition. Crucially, in order to be able to exert a critical force, this critical theory must also be self-critical.[108] This leads Habermas to analyse theoretical reason, and scientific rationality more specifically, in order to show that no theory is free of value or interests. Empirical sciences and technical rationality cannot claim a privileged position by claiming to be neutral. On the contrary, every science is determined by a particular concern and is, therefore, characterized by a corresponding praxis. Habermas distinguishes three such concerns. First, analytical and empirical sciences are concerned with technical usability and instrumental praxis. Second, the humanities or hermeneutical sciences are concerned with the power of symbolic language with a view to communicative praxis. Third, social sciences are concerned with an explanatory understanding that has a practical and historical orientation and, therefore, with emancipative praxis.[109]

---

[104] Jürgen Habermas, 'On Hermeneutics' Claim to Universality', in *The Hermeneutics Reader: Texts of the German Tradition from the Enlightenment to the Present*, ed. Kurt Mueller-Vollmer (Oxford: Blackwell, 1986), 317.
[105] *The Understanding of Faith*, xxi [xii]; 90–1 [103–4]. See also Edward Schillebeeckx, 'The New Critical Theory' [1971], in *The Understanding of Faith*, 90 [103].
[106] Schillebeeckx, 'The New Critical Theory and Theological Hermeneutics', 114–15 [130–1].
[107] Jürgen Habermas, *Knowledge and Human Interest*, trans. Jeremy J. Shapiro (Cambridge: Polity Press, 1998); Jürgen Habermas, *Theory and Practice*, trans. John Viertel (Cambridge: Polity Press, 1986).
[108] Schillebeeckx, 'The New Critical Theory', 92 [105–6].
[109] Ibid., 93 [106–7].

The most important aspect of this analysis, according to Schillebeeckx, is its explanation of the inner synthetic unity between theory and praxis. William Portier notes that in order to stress the co-constitutive relation between theoretical and practical rationality, Schillebeeckx employs the term 'praxis' rather than 'practice'.[110] Praxis *determines* theory in all three sciences, insofar as it creates the conditions for the possibility of scientific knowledge. Critical self-reflection of theoretical sciences discloses the specific interests by which they are guided.[111] At the same time, praxis is also dependent upon theoretical reason. Praxis and theory are mutually co-constitutive and cannot, therefore, be considered in isolation from each other. Interestingly, Schillebeeckx suggests that this may betray the influence of Fichte on Habermas's thought.[112] As we will see below, Schillebeeckx initially follows De Petter's critique of Maréchal and attempts to develop an epistemology that is strictly 'intellectual'. However, in his later work he undercuts this earlier position by appropriating Habermas's interrelation of theory and praxis. Alternatively, he now argues that being faithful to the truth of faith is not simply a theoretical issue that can be solved 'idealistically, by a theory of Kantian pure reason' but necessitates a turn to Christian praxis – orthodoxy cannot do without orthopraxis.[113] The recognition of the interrelation between theory and praxis enables a critical correction of technical and communicative praxis towards emancipation. For Habermas, emancipation is the ultimate interest that underlies and informs all theoretical reason and reflection:

> The emancipative character is essential to the human consciousness and reason is a will to reason, an orientation towards emancipation. Any use of reason, even though it may be called purely theoretical, is bent towards concern, and concern is therefore not alien to reason unless there is an ideological claim for pure reason. Concern belongs to theory as well as to praxis; it precedes knowledge and is realised in knowledge.[114]

Schillebeeckx considers this outspoken practical commitment to be an improvement, in comparison with Adorno whose conception of critical negativity and deferment of meaning remains incapable of effecting practical change.[115] However, he also points out that this emancipative interest reveals the contextual and situated character of critical theory itself. Critical theory cannot claim a 'meta-theoretical' option, regarding philosophical and theological hermeneutics; it is as conditioned by its own hermeneutical circle as those disciplines are. To be more precise, critical theory's

---

[110] See Portier, 'Edward Schillebeeckx as Critical Theorist', 353. Martin G. Poulsom, *The Dialectics of Creation. Creation and the Creator in Edward Schillebeeckx and David Burrell* (London: Bloomsbury, 2014), 112–26, similarly warns against using practice and praxis interchangeably. He suggests that in Schillebeeckx's work praxis is the 'relational dialectic of theory and practice'.
[111] Schillebeeckx, 'The New Critical Theory', 94 [108].
[112] Ibid., 94 [108].
[113] Schillebeeckx, 'Theological Criteria', 59–60 [66–7].
[114] Schillebeeckx, 'The New Critical Theory', 95 [109].
[115] Rodenborn, *Hope in Action*, 142.

decision to oppose distortion and manipulation is based on an ethical and existential decision in favour of emancipation and freedom.[116]

Although Schillebeeckx is highly appreciative of this emancipative interest, his theological appropriation of Habermas's theory comes with an important qualification. According to Rodenborn, this qualified reception clearly manifests the eschatological orientation of Schillebeeckx's approach.[117] Theology not only has its own hermeneutical circle and interest but also has its own distinct impetus by which to criticize ideological elements within its tradition of understanding.[118] Christians hope for salvation, but they do not assume that the liberation and salvation of the world can be brought about by virtue of human changes of oppressive structures *alone*. Referring to the doctrine of original sin, Schillebeeckx calls such an overly optimistic trust in the powers of human reason a 'Pelagian' interpretation of emancipative praxis.[119] Christian dogma and kerygma teach us that we cannot realize the future ourselves: 'The overcoming of every form of alienation is outside the realm of human possibility.'[120] Hence, theology must draw attention to the mystical dimension of human integrity and reveal the limitations of every critical theory and of every emancipative praxis. Schillebeeckx refers, in this regard, to Johann Baptist Metz's notion of 'subversive memory' as an example of one such theological correction of the optimism of reason.[121] This critical note notwithstanding, Schillebeeckx remains highly appreciative of the value of critical theory for theology and argues that the two disciplines mutually correct each other:

> Faith is distinguished by the fact that it is faith in what is humanly impossible. Reason and myth, critical rationality and faith are indispensable to each other. They protect each other from a degeneration into a complete ideological system which is bound to lead to repression and compulsion because it is self-enclosed and totalitarian.[122]

Theology employs various forms of rational reflection, metaphysics, transcendental philosophy, hermeneutics, critical theory and so on, but it also puts these critical impulses under critique by showing their relative adequacy. In this regard, there is an interesting parallel between Schillebeeckx's and Rahner's critical and distinctly theological appropriation of their sources.

---

[116] Schillebeeckx, 'The New Critical Theory and Theological Hermeneutics', 110 [125]. Habermas develops this emancipative option later in *The Theory of Communicative Action*, 2 volumes, trans. Thomas McCarthy (Cambridge: Polity Press, 1997–1998), introducing the concept of the 'ideal speech situation' that functions as a regulative ideal in order to work towards *herrschaftsfreie Kommunikation* (communication free of power distortion).
[117] Rodenborn, *Hope in Action*, 146.
[118] Schillebeeckx, 'The New Critical Theory and Theological Hermeneutics', 123-4 [140-2].
[119] Ibid., 130 [148].
[120] Ibid., 128 [147].
[121] Ibid., 130 [148].
[122] Ibid., 129 [148].

5 Conclusion

In this chapter, I have examined three formative sources of Schillebeeckx's theological method. The variety of these sources raises the question of their relationship. Are the critical and the hermeneutical sources compatible with the phenomenological metaphysics of the earlier phase? Schillebeeckx's own views on this matter are not without ambiguities. On the one hand, he argues that the new orientation of his post-conciliar work led to a 'clear break' with the philosophy of De Petter and therefore with his own earlier theological approach.[123] This suggests that the hermeneutical aspect of his thought is incompatible with the metaphysical aspect. On the other hand, he also maintains that 'hermeneutics is not just the interpretive problem but also the science of interpretation that explores the assumptions of every exegesis'.[124] This statement lends support to the assumption that a hermeneutical turn cannot entirely sound the end of a metaphysical approach. That there have occurred significant changes in Schillebeeckx's theological approach is widely acknowledged. However, there is less agreement about the question of continuity or discontinuity between Schillebeeckx's early and later thought.

Lieven Boeve detects a duality in Schillebeeckx's project that is, in part, chronological. He argues that the thought of the early Schillebeeckx revolves around 'creation faith', whereas the later Schillebeeckx focuses on the 'hermeneutics of tradition'.[125] John Caputo adopts a more radical position, arguing that 'hermeneutics spells the end of metaphysics'.[126] He views Schillebeeckx's hermeneutical turn as an attempt to move away from an onto-theological centre, although he considers Schillebeeckx's hermeneutics to be not radical enough. Leo Scheffczyk draws a contrast between a 'pre-critical period' and a post-conciliar period marked by the influence of hermeneutics and critical theory. He argues that while Schillebeeckx remained faithful to the 'dogma of the church' in the early period, his work from the later period is marred by a 'subjectivistic principle of experience'.[127] Erik Borgman argues that Schillebeeckx entered a 'qualitatively new phase as a result of his involvement in the Council', but he also maintains that the role of Thomas and De Petter remained hugely important in Schillebeeckx's later thought.[128] Philip Kennedy has pleaded more strongly for the case of continuity. He argues that, despite the epistemological turning point in the 1960s, Schillebeeckx 'has not in any way or at any time abandoned the most basic metaphysical and epistemological fundamentals which have informed his theology

---

[123] Schillebeeckx, *Jesus*, 580 [618].
[124] Edward Schillebeeckx, 'Theological Quests' [1994], in *Essays. Ongoing Theological Quests*, 121.
[125] Lieven Boeve, 'The Enduring Significance and Relevance of Edward Schillebeeckx? Introducing the State of the Question in Medias Res', in *Edward Schillebeeckx and Contemporary Theology*, 8–9.
[126] John D. Caputo, 'Radical Hermeneutics and Religious Truth: The Case of Sheehan and Schillebeeckx', in *Phenomenology of the Truth Proper to Religion*, ed. Daniel Guerrière (Albany: State University of New York, 1990), 148–9.
[127] Leo Scheffcyzk, 'Christology in the Context of Experience: On the Interpretation of Christ by E. Schillebeeckx', *The Thomist* 48 (1984): 383–408.
[128] Borgman, *Edward Schillebeeckx*, 13; 374. Borgman's biography only covers the period of Schillebeeckx's life up until the Second Vatican Council. Even though this decision may have been made for more pragmatic reasons, this fact also lends support to the view of their being an 'early' and 'later' Schillebeeckx.

since the beginning of his career'.[129] Although the 'outer vocabulary' has changed, the 'inner syntax' has remained constant.[130] Finally, Stephan van Erp maintains that De Petter's philosophy continues to inform Schillebeeckx's later theology centred upon historical experience.[131]

It is my intention to bring this discussion on Schillebeeckx's theological method forward by introducing the following hypothesis. I argue that both the continuity and the discontinuity in Schillebeeckx's theological method can be explained by paying attention to the same dialectic that I have identified in the work of Rahner. There is a close parallel between the methods employed by Rahner and Schillebeeckx inasmuch as they both employ a dialectics between metaphysical and hermeneutical elements within their theological reflection. Commitment both to the particular and the universal dimensions of Christian faith explains his refusal to opt exclusively for either metaphysics or hermeneutics.[132] Instead, he developed a theological method in which those two approaches were kept in dialectical unity.

The hermeneutical dimension is already latently present in Schillebeeckx's early perspectivalist epistemology, even though this epistemology bears a strong mark of Thomist metaphysics. His turn towards hermeneutics and to critical theory intensifies and nourishes this incipient hermeneutical awareness. Compared to Rahner, Schillebeeckx engages more intensely with hermeneutical theory, which provides his theology with a much starker hermeneutical profile. Nevertheless, I will demonstrate in the subsequent chapters that this hermeneutical turn does not affect as clear a break with his early thought as Schillebeeckx himself suggests. While the metaphysical framework is no longer explicitly developed in his later work, it continues to play a crucial role in Schillebeeckx's theological hermeneutics nonetheless.

---

[129] Philip Kennedy, 'Continuity Underlying Discontinuity: Schillebeeckx's Philosophical Background', *New Blackfriars* 70 (1989): 265.
[130] Kennedy, 'Continuity Underlying Discontinuity', 265.
[131] Van Erp, 'Implicit Faith', 219–20.
[132] See Kennedy, *Schillebeeckx*, 121, who argues that 'there is no philosophical issue more central to his theological project than the matter of human knowledge of God or, in other words, the issue of knowledge of universality by particularity'.

7

Speculating about salvation history: The metaphysics and hermeneutics of experience

1 Introduction

Edward Schillebeeckx is widely known and acclaimed for his scholarly attention to the fundamental role that human experience plays within theology.[1] His insights into the co-constitutive roles played by experience in revelation and his intricate hermeneutics of experience are considered to be especially significant and comprise a lasting contribution to theology.[2] As a theologian of experience, Schillebeeckx endeavours to pay due attention to the concreteness and historicity of human existence. That God is revealed in concrete historical events is something pivotal to his understanding of revelation. Experiential encounters with these events are always situated in, and conditioned by, particular and historical circumstances. As a result, experience implies the need for a hermeneutics of experience. Given this focus on the concreteness of experience, the question could be raised as to whether Schillebeeckx's theology has any need for abstract exercises in metaphysical or transcendental reflection. Is this speculative undertaking helpful, given the historical character of Christian faith? Should theology be concerned with metaphysics at all?

In this chapter, I will address these questions by retracing the development of Schillebeeckx's theological epistemology and demonstrating that this epistemology is fundamentally marked by a dialectics between metaphysical and hermeneutical aspects. First, I examine why a theological focus on salvation history still implies a need for speculative reflection. This will be followed by a discussion of Schillebeeckx's metaphysics of experience, which he develops in his early period. More concretely, I will

---

[1] See Edward Schillebeeckx, 'Theologie der Erfahrung – Sackgasse oder Weg zum Glauben? Ein Gespräch mit Prof. Edward Schillebeeckx', *Herder Korrespondenz* 32 (1978): 391–7; Lieven Boeve, 'Experience according to Edward Schillebeeckx: The Driving Force of Faith and Theology', in *Divinising Experience. Essays in the History of Religious Experience from Origen to Ricoeur*, ed. Lieven Boeve and Laurence P. Hemming (Leuven: Peeters, 2004), 199–225; and Donald Gelpi, *The Turn to Experience in Contemporary Theology* (New York: Paulist, 1994), 9–23.

[2] Mary Catherine Hilkert, 'Experience and Revelation', in *The Praxis of the Reign of God. An Introduction to the Theology of Edward Schillebeeckx*, ed. Mary Catherine Hilkert and Robert J. Schreiter (New York: Fordham University Press, 2002), 60, argues that Schillebeeckx's account of revelation and experience offers a creative alternative vision to the experience-oriented theologies of Friedrich Schleiermacher and Karl Rahner, as well as the dialectical theology of revelation of Karl Barth.

examine how his combination of Thomistic metaphysics and De Petter's philosophy of the implicit intuition yields a *perspectival* epistemology. This epistemology contains metaphysical as well as (tentative) hermeneutical aspects. Subsequently, I turn to Schillebeeckx's use of a transcendental anthropology that explicates the universal intelligibility of the Christian vision of the human person. This will offer another example of his theological appropriation of transcendental and metaphysical reflection. At the same time, the growing awareness of the concrete conditions of human experience also discloses the inherent limitations of these transcendental-metaphysical explanations.

This insight becomes intensified when Schillebeeckx turns to hermeneutics. Schillebeeckx proceeds to eschew attempts to express the salvific truth of revelation purely theoretically, having grown more conscious of the fundamentally conditioning role played by history. Alternatively, he starts to develop a hermeneutical approach in order to disclose the anticipation of the meaning and truth of the concrete historical experiences of faith that mark the beginning of the Christian tradition. This hermeneutical approach to experience is attentive to the indispensable role played by interpretation within experience. However, I argue that his hermeneutics of experience remains fundamentally connected to an equally important metaphysics of experience. Demonstrating this interconnection will engender an important alternative perspective on Schillebeeckx's hermeneutical turn.

2 Theology: Positive or speculative?

In one of his earliest articles, Schillebeeckx argues that theology is concerned primarily with the interpretation of the revelation of salvation in the historical event of Jesus Christ. He formulates, programmatically, that 'the immediate basis for our analogous knowledge of God is not the created world and therefore philosophy, but the history of salvation'.[3] Although God is revealed in creation, it is the history of salvation that 'reveals to us who God really is and his wish to be really our God'.[4] God's offer of grace, God's invitation to humankind to enter into communion with God, is mediated historically. Revelation is a concrete reality – an event in which the saving God becomes historically visible to us.[5] The fullest and most complete mediation of God's grace can be found in the concrete historical person of Jesus Christ. Since revelation is a concrete historical reality, theology must focus on existential experience as the locus of encounter with the economy of salvation. In other words, it would be wrong to treat the mystery of faith as a sort of 'supra-metaphysics'.[6] However, the centrality of existential experience and concrete salvific events do not invalidate the role played by speculative theology completely.[7]

---

[3] Edward Schillebeeckx, 'Salvation History as the Basis of Theology: *Theologia* or *Oikonomia*' [1953], in *Revelation and Theology*, 281 [95].
[4] Schillebeeckx, 'Salvation History as the Basis of Theology, [90].
[5] Ibid., [93].
[6] Edward Schillebeeckx, 'The New Trends in Present-day Dogmatic Theology' [1961], in *Revelation and Theology*, 295 [115].
[7] Schillebeeckx employs the term 'speculative theology', following the classical distinction between 'positive theology', which focuses on the material content of Christian faith, and 'speculative

Instead, there remains a demand for speculative reflection within theology – a demand which stems from the structure and nature of revelation. The reality of salvation is never available to us as a pure experience. We only become consciously aware of this reality with the help of concepts. Experience and concepts, therefore, always belong together.[8] Schillebeeckx illustrates this with reference to dogma and Scripture. The salvific events of revelation have been clarified by the prophets and have found expression in Scripture and in the Church's proclamation of dogma. Taken together, 'revelation in reality' and 'revelation in word' constitute God's saving and revelatory activity.[9] The emphasis on the necessity of 'revelation-in-word' discloses an incipient awareness of the interpretative nature of experience. At this moment in time, Schillebeeckx does not yet fully acknowledge the difficulties, complexities and ambiguities involved in the interpretation and the expression of experience. In the period preceding his explicitly hermeneutical term, he explores the problematic issue of the relationship between experience and dogmatic expression, with the help of a metaphysical argumentation that focuses on the ontological reality underlying experience and concept.

Schillebeeckx refers to a dictum of Thomas: 'The act of faith does not terminate in the concepts of faith, but in reality.'[10] This implies that dogmatic formulations have a fundamentally relative value for faith. Still, even though the mysterious reality of faith cannot be fully grasped through concepts, these concepts can nevertheless orientate us towards an aspect of intelligibility within this mystery. According to Schillebeeckx, the living God of salvation is an intelligible God, whose objective reality can be known really, if only in an adequate way. Speculative reflection offers a helpful contribution in this regard. The mystery of faith is an *intelligible* mystery, begging for interpretation and explication. For this reason, 'metaphysical insights can be put in the service of theological reflection about the manifestation of God in the history of salvation' so as to prevent faith from becoming 'pseudo-mysticism, pragmatism, and subjectivism'.[11]

More concretely, Schillebeeckx mentions two important contributions that metaphysics can make to theology. First, it serves to account for the 'objective value' of our theological discourse about God. If theology is not to represent an empty 'religious projection' without content and meaning, then it must be demonstrated that theological concepts have a reference to objective reality.[12] This forms the impetus behind his perspectival epistemology. Second, metaphysics serves a transcendental function. Metaphysics explicates 'what must be assumed as a possibility' for God's

---

theology', which seeks to develop and deepen the understanding of these material elements through reflection.

[8] Schillebeeckx, 'Salvation History', 284 [99–100].
[9] Ibid. See also the article 'Revelation-in-Reality and Revelation-in-Word' [1960], in *Revelation and Theology*, 25–41 [36–62].
[10] Schillebeeckx, 'Salvation History', 284 [99]. See Thomas Aquinas, *Summa Theologiae*, II-II, q. 1, a. 2, *ad* 2. Jennifer Cooper, *Humanity in the Mystery of God: The Theological Anthropology of Edward Schillebeeckx* (London: T&T Clark, 2009), 33, notes that this emphasis on the central importance of 'salvific reality itself' for theology manifests that Schillebeeckx 'brings a historical and soteriological reference to De Petter's metaphysical realism'.
[11] Schillebeeckx, 'Salvation History', 285–7 [101–4].
[12] Schillebeeckx, 'The New Trends', 296–7 [118].

personal dialogue with humankind.[13] Schillebeeckx explains this with the help of a transcendental argumentation.

3 Perspectival epistemology and relational ontology

The relation between experience and conceptuality was a topic of intense debate in early twentieth-century Catholic theology. In Schillebeeckx's opinion, the prevailing scholastic theology focused too exclusively upon this conceptual element at the expense of the experiential element. This scholastic focus on abstract concepts was challenged by phenomenology's and existentialism's call for attention to the centrality of *'l'experience vécue'*.[14] Schillebeeckx agrees with their insight that 'human thought is not nourished by concepts, but by experience – by varying perceptive contacts with the reality of salvation'.[15] However, he considers it to be a mistake if phenomenologically informed theology 'abandons' metaphysics entirely, because then it runs the risk of becoming a relativist denial of absolute meaning and truth. Alternatively, he proposes a 'renewal' of metaphysics 'on an anthropological basis' that seeks to bring phenomenology into dialogue with the *philosophia perennis*, so as to renew the role played by scholastic metaphysics within theology.[16]

Schillebeeckx writes that the attempt to overcome the neo-scholastic emphasis on conceptuality generated two schools of thought, both seeking to call attention to the role played by the non-conceptual element of knowledge. One avenue is represented by Maurice Blondel, Maréchal and Rahner, on the one hand, and another avenue is represented by De Petter, on the other.[17] Schillebeeckx opts for the approach taken by De Petter and largely follows the latter's criticism of the route chosen by Maréchal. It is interesting to note that most of Schillebeeckx's commentators merely repeat Schillebeeckx's and De Petter's reading of Maréchal, without evaluating their critiques.[18] Yet, are these two schools of thought really as opposed to each other as Schillebeeckx suggests? Without engaging in a full comparison of Maréchal and De Petter, I will briefly consider some parallels and differences between their positions while examining Schillebeeckx's perspectival epistemology. Importantly, whereas Schillebeeckx sometimes seems to present his theory as a general epistemology, intended to explain ordinary knowledge of reality and truth in general, he effectively

---

[13] Schillebeeckx, 'Salvation History', 287 [104].
[14] Schillebeeckx, 'The Concept of "Truth"', 189–90 [6].
[15] Schillebeeckx, 'The New Trends', 297 [119].
[16] Ibid., 297–8 [119–20]; Schillebeeckx, 'The Concept of "Truth"', 189–90 [6].
[17] Ibid., 196–7 [17].
[18] See for instance Van Erp, 'Implicit Faith', 213; Poulsom, *The Dialectics of Creation*, 172–4. Carsten Barwasser, *Theologie der Kultur und Hermeneutik der Glaubenserfahrung. Zur Gottesfrage und Glaubensverantwortung bei Edward Schillebeeckx OP* (Münster: LIT Verlag, 2010), 129–31. Kennedy, *Deus Humanissimus*, 91–9, concedes that Maréchal and De Petter were in substantial agreement on several points. However, Kennedy also merely restates Schillebeeckx's critical account of Maréchal, without questioning its accuracy or persuasiveness.

only elaborates his theory with reference to the question of the knowledge of God.[19] As a result, contrary to Rahner, the distinction between Being and God is less noticeable in Schillebeeckx's epistemological discourse.

3.1 Subjective or objective dynamism: Maréchal versus De Petter

Maréchal explains the non-conceptual element of knowing with reference to the infinite dynamism of the human spirit – a dynamism which derives from the interconnection of intellect and will. This intellectual dynamism, towards infinite Being, enables the affirmation of concrete objects of knowledge as really existing. Schillebeeckx acknowledges that this is a 'strong attempt' to overcome 'purely notional knowing'.[20] However, he disagrees with Maréchal's solution of grounding the objectivity of knowledge in a 'subjective dynamism'. Firstly, Maréchal fails to explain 'the distinctive meaning of every conceptual content'.[21] This seems to imply the concern for the concrete being of every individual reality. It echoes De Petter's rejection of the notion of *esse commune* and suggests that the intellectual dynamism tends towards an abstract, rather than a concrete affirmation of objective, reality. However, Schillebeeckx does not develop this criticism in great detail.

Secondly, Schillebeeckx questions Maréchal's turn to practical reason in order to account for the dynamic finality of theoretical reason. According to Schillebeeckx, this appeal to practical reason means that knowledge is no longer grounded in a 'real intellectual element', but in a 'non-noetic', 'extra-intellectual' aspect. As a result, the 'strictly noetical value of a real, objective contact with God' is brought into question.[22] However, it remains unclear why Schillebeeckx advocates such a sharp separation between the human faculties of intellect and will. Is it correct to characterize Maréchal's intellectual dynamism as being extra-intellectual or non-noetic, for the simple reason that he argues that the activity of the human intellect cannot be understood apart from the activity of the will?[23] Both De Petter and Schillebeeckx just claim that this is the case without offering an adequate justification for this claim. As discussed earlier, Rahner emphasizes that willing forms an inner moment of knowing. However, if willing cannot be seen as an inner moment of knowing, then how do these faculties

---

[19] See Kennedy, *Deus Humanissimus*, 109, who notes that Schillebeeckx has never been concerned with developing a 'full-scale epistemological theory' and, instead, applies and appropriates elements of theories of knowledge to explain 'the meaning of the cognitivity of faith'.
[20] Edward Schillebeeckx, 'The Non-Conceptual Intellectual Dimension in our Knowledge of God according to Aquinas' [1952], in *Revelation and Theology*, 213 [162]. The English translation speaks of a 'determined effort', but the original Dutch 'sterke poging' indicates more clearly that Schillebeeckx's does not merely criticize but also appreciates Maréchal's work.
[21] Schillebeeckx, 'The Concept of "Truth"', 197–8 [18].
[22] Schillebeeckx, 'The Non-Conceptual Intellectual Dimension', 210 [162].
[23] Poulsom, *The Dialectics of Creation*, 174, simply accepts Schillebeeckx's claim that Maréchal's intellectual dynamism is non-noetic. He concludes that Maréchal 'falls onto one of the horns of the Kantian dilemma: "Thoughts without content are empty, intuitions without concepts are blind"'. Yet Poulsom fails to explain adequately why this is the case. Kant argues that knowledge always involves both sensibility (providing intuitions) and understanding (providing concepts). Maréchal's account of knowledge also involves sensible intuition and concepts but also adds the dynamism of the human spirit towards infinite being. It is not clear, therefore, why he would fall into one of the horns of the Kantian dilemma.

relate to each other? Schillebeeckx remains remarkably silent on this point. Moreover, it is striking to note that his position on this interrelationship changes radically. Schillebeeckx will come to advocate the reciprocal relationship between theory and praxis, having been influenced by insights yielded from critical theory. This later plea effectively undermines the critique that he levels here against Maréchal.[24]

The third element of critique calls into question the viability of Maréchal's Kantian turn to the subject. Locating the 'real value' of knowledge in the subject results in a projection rather than in an affirmation of the reality expressed through the use of concepts. These concepts are 'borne up by the dynamism of the spirit and, as a result, projected towards the Infinite', inasmuch as the infinite transcendence of the human spirit shows the inherent limitation of every concept.[25] This subjective act of projection, towards the infinite, serves to explain how human knowledge can know individual objects as really existing objects. Schillebeeckx agrees that our concepts contain a projection towards God. However, he questions whether a projective act can be anything more than a 'shot in the dark' if it is founded upon a *subjective* dynamism.[26] In other words, his argument must resort to 'a leap of faith' and it, therefore, fails to demonstrate that our knowledge reaches reality and, *a fortiori*, God.

Does Schillebeeckx not demand too much here? Rahner's appropriation of Maréchal's transcendental analysis of human intellectual dynamism serves a more modest end. Rahner's metaphysics of knowledge seeks to demonstrate that the human person is a relational being, simultaneously 'lost in the otherness of the objective world' and oriented by way of a *Vorgriff* towards the mysterious horizon of Being, rather than seeking to prove the existence of God philosophically. What is important here is Rahner's careful emphasis on the mysterious and ungraspable character of this horizon, which attests to his recognition of the limitations of metaphysical reflection. Schillebeeckx's objection that the subjective dynamism cannot prove the objective reality of God seems right, therefore, but only because neither Maréchal nor Rahner claims to offer such a proof in the first place. What is Schillebeeckx's alternative? Is he able to prove that theological concepts do not simply signify, but objectively reach God?

Following De Petter, Schillebeeckx argues that our conceptual mode of knowledge depends upon a non-conceptual dimension that derives from an 'objective dynamism' which originates in reality. He contrasts his own position to that of Maréchal's:

> It is therefore not an extra-intellectual dimension – the dynamism of the human spirit – that enables us to reach reality in our concepts, but a non-conceptual

---

[24] Again, the fact that Schillebeeckx fundamentally changed his view on the relation between theoretical and practical reason is not considered by other scholars when they discuss Schillebeeckx's early epistemology. Alternatively, Frans Maas, 'Stem en stilte. Waarheid en openbaring bij Schillebeeckx', *Tijdschrift voor Theologie* 50 (2010): 52–3, points out that Schillebeeckx in his article 'Humaniora en humaniora', *Biekorf* (1936–1937) no. 1, actually emphasizes that the human relation to truth involves both our intellectual and our affective faculties. This account of truth, as something which is not merely cerebral, is strikingly at odds with the purely intellectual approach that Schillebeeckx defends here.
[25] Schillebeeckx, 'The Non-Conceptual Intellectual Dimension', 210 [161].
[26] Ibid., 219 [175]; 238 [206]; Schillebeeckx, 'The Concept of "Truth"', 198 [18].

consciousness through which we become aware of the inadequacy of our concepts, and thus transcend our conceptual knowledge and approach reality, although in a manner that is no longer open to expression.[27]

The objective dynamism is found *within* concepts, but also transcends them. Just as in Maréchal and Rahner, therefore, the non-conceptual element fulfils a transcendental condition for the possibility of objective knowledge. Moreover, the non-conceptual mode of knowledge functions in close connection with the conceptual mode of knowledge. A concept is necessary in mediating the implicit objective dynamism, but no concept is able to express the implicit dynamism adequately and fully. This implicit dynamism plays a crucial role in knowledge, because it provides the concept with a reference to reality: 'The concept indicates the objective direction in which reality is to be found, and – what is more – indicates a *definite* direction – the direction which is inwardly pointed out by the abstract conceptual content.'[28] This particular combination in knowing, of the conceptual and non-conceptual elements, lies at the heart of Schillebeeckx's perspectival epistemology.

This perspectival epistemology is described as follows: 'From a finite, limited, constantly changing, and historical standpoint, we have a view of absolute truth, although we never have this in our power.'[29] On the one hand, this epistemology maintains a metaphysical conception of objective truth. It recognizes that truth is unchangeable and never at our disposal. There is such a thing as absolute truth, which norms our thinking, and we are able to relate to this truth, but only implicitly because of the implicit objective dynamism. On the other hand, this perspectivalist epistemology also acknowledges what can be called the hermeneutical dimension of truth. Since we relate to truth through concrete and historical experience, our relation to truth is conditioned by imperfect, changing and relative particular perspectives. As a result, concepts provide us with a real *perspective* on reality or truth without ever fully capturing or comprehending reality and truth.[30]

Schillebeeckx applies this theory of knowing to explicitly theological concepts, presenting a reading of Thomas's theological epistemology through the lens of De Petter's philosophy. He argues that the *transcendentalia* have a positive intellectual content which 'objectively indicates the perspective in which God is to be found'.[31] Our knowledge of God involves a dialectic between positive and negative elements. Although our concepts fail to fully 'grasp' the mystery of God notionally, they do contain a positive directionality which ensures that we know God noetically. This objective directionality towards God ensures that our knowledge of God is not 'a blind shot in the dark'.[32] How can Schillebeeckx, then, be so sure that there is indeed such an objective directionality? In other words, how does he explain the origin of this objective dynamism and how does it relate to the knowing subject?

[27] Ibid., 198 [19].
[28] Ibid.
[29] Ibid., 190 [7].
[30] Ibid., 190–1 [7–8].
[31] Schillebeeckx, 'The Non-Conceptual Intellectual Dimension', 218 [175].
[32] Ibid., 218–19 [175–6].

Schillebeeckx associates the objective dynamism with the experiential mode of human knowledge, even though he does not state it explicitly. So much is clear from statements as 'experience and conceptual thought thus together constitute our single knowledge of reality'.[33] However, we will need to delve into Schillebeeckx's understanding of experience in order to understand how experience yields this objective dynamism. To be more precise, how does he account for the relationship between the conceptual intellectual element, the non-conceptual intellectual element and the empirical element of experience? Unfortunately, Schillebeeckx is not very clear on this point and does not clarify the relation between the empirical and the intellectual elements of experience. Maréchal and Rahner follow Thomas's empirical-Aristotelian approach and, consequently, argue that the non-conceptual moment in knowledge, the subjective dynamism or *Vorgriff*, remains dependent upon and connected to sensibility. By contrast, Schillebeeckx hardly touches on the role played by sensibility. May we conclude from this silence that he agrees with De Petter and also advocates a Platonic-Augustinian intellectual intuition?

First, it is remarkable to note that, despite the clear influence of De Petter, the term 'intellectual intuition' or 'implicit intuition' is not used in the writings in which Schillebeeckx explains his theological epistemology.[34] De Petter explains implicit intuition as the participation of the human intellect in God as pure intellect.[35] How this intellectual intuition is related to empirical intuition and why it does not lead to 'ontologism' remain unclear in both De Petter's and Schillebeeckx's work. De Petter argues that the Aristotelian-Thomist account of knowledge needs to be complemented with an Augustinian doctrine of illumination. However, as Stephan van Erp points out, De Petter fails to explain adequately what this complementary role of illumination exactly entails.[36] It seems, therefore, that the focus on the objective dynamism within human knowledge has been developed without due attention to the other aspects of human knowing. Now Schillebeeckx states that the subject 'consents' to the objective dynamism through 'an act of intellectual tending or projection'.[37] He also writes that 'God is therefore situated in a projective act, in which we *reach out for* God, but do not grasp him in understanding, although we are well aware that he is found in the precise *direction* in which we are reaching'.[38] This language of 'consenting', 'tending' and 'projection' suggests a stronger role for the subject in the objective dynamism than Schillebeeckx acknowledges. It could be questioned, therefore, whether it is helpful at all to present Maréchal's subjective dynamism and De Petter's objective dynamism as being radically opposed to each other.

---

[33] Schillebeeckx, 'The Concept of "Truth"', 199 [20].
[34] In fact, in the article 'The Non-Conceptual Intellectual Dimension', De Petter's name is not mentioned at all and the position that Schillebeeckx proposes is justified primarily with reference to Thomas. In 'The Concept of Truth', he does mention De Petter and refers to his article on implicit intuition, yet once again the term 'implicit intuition' as such is not used by Schillebeeckx, who instead continues to speak of a 'non-conceptual intellectual dimension'.
[35] De Petter, 'Impliciete intuïtie', 101–3.
[36] Van Erp, 'Implicit Faith', 217.
[37] Schillebeeckx, 'The Non-Conceptual Intellectual Dimension', 238 [206].
[38] Schillebeeckx, 'The Non-Conceptual Intellectual Dimension', 219 [175].

This leaves us with the question of how Schillebeeckx accounts for the pivotal element of his theological epistemology, that is the implicit objective directionality towards God. The observation that this dynamism is associated with experience has not satisfactorily answered this question yet. What distinguishes objective dynamism from the 'blind projection' of subjective dynamism? Schillebeeckx develops an ontological argument in order to account for the non-conceptual element of his epistemology. However, instead of developing a purely philosophical ontological argument, he resorts instead to a theological 'postulate', namely, the theological view of reality as divine creation.[39]

3.2 Creation, the foundation of all theology

Philip Kennedy notes that creation forms the 'bedrock' of Schillebeeckx's theology, the 'oxygen and lifeblood' that operates as an architectonic principle throughout his writings.[40] This has been confirmed by Schillebeeckx himself: 'To me belief in creation is ultimately the foundation of all theology.'[41] How does this 'ontology of creation' inform Schillebeeckx's theological epistemology? None of Schillebeeckx's early scholarly articles are specifically devoted to the doctrine of creation. Yet, throughout his argument for the knowability of God he continuously refers to the crucial presupposition that reality is divine creation. As divine creation, reality as such is a 'theophany'.[42] Schillebeeckx accepts this view as his starting point, without offering any justification for it. He simply assumes 'the already established proof of God'.[43] Hence, the doctrine of creation must be accepted as a theological postulate in order to account for the objective value of the perspectival epistemology. Crucially, this suggests that the 'objective dynamism' does not ultimately offer a stronger philosophical argument than the 'subjective dynamism' in accounting for the reality of God. Both Rahner and Schillebeeckx use philosophical arguments to make a theological claim intelligible, rather than arriving at a theological conclusion by way of philosophy.

Two key insights, formulated by Thomas in the first *quaestio* of the *Summa Theologiae*, guide Schillebeeckx's grounding of theological epistemology in creation. First, Thomas argues that theology is dependent upon two sources in its speaking about God. It knows God as the highest cause through the created world, and it knows God 'as he alone knows himself' through God's revelatory communication.[44] Second, Thomas

---

[39] Kennedy, *Deus Humanissimus*, 103; 142, concludes that the epistemological argument is 'parasitic upon a more fundamental and overarching *ontological* postulate', a metaphysics which is turn is governed by the dogma of creation.
[40] Kennedy, *Deus Humanissimus*, 142; Philip Kennedy, 'God and Creation', in *The Praxis of the Reign of God*, 37. Other scholars have also pointed out the centrality of creation within Schillebeeckx's theology. See, for instance, Borgman, *Edward Schillebeeckx*, 374. Boeve, 'The Enduring Significance and Relevance of Edward Schillebeeckx', 10–14; Ambroos R. van de Walle, 'Theologie over de werkelijkheid. Een betekenis van het werk van Edward Schillebeeckx', *Tijdschrift voor Theologie* 14 (1974): 463–90; Poulsom, *The Dialectics of Creation*, 1–3.
[41] Schillebeeckx, 'Theological Quests', 124.
[42] Schillebeeckx, 'The Non-Conceptual Intellectual Dimension', 210 [161].
[43] Ibid., 210, n. 9 [162].
[44] Schillebeeckx, 'Salvation History', 276–7 [87–8], referring to Thomas Aquinas, *Summa Theologiae*, I, q. 1, a. 6.

holds that all of our knowledge about God is analogical. We cannot intuit or define God, but 'we appeal in theology to the intelligibility of God's natural or supernatural effects'.[45] Thomas elaborates on the positive as well as the negative consequences that 'creatureliness' has for theological epistemology by distinguishing three steps of the *analogical* mode of knowing. On the one hand, we can affirmatively speak about God because created reality exhibits the effects of a creative, divine cause.[46] On the other hand, since 'creatures are always the basis of human knowledge of God',[47] all positive knowledge of God is marked by the utter difference between creature and creator. The *via affirmationis* must, therefore, be continually corrected by the *via negationis vel remotionis*. But this negative correction, in turn, is held in check by the *via eminentiae*, which explains that the difference between creature and creator is not due to God's deficiency but rather due to God's transcendence. Creation, thus, enables us to know God as cause, as utter difference and as transcendence.[48]

This epistemological reasoning by way of creative causality is, ultimately, grounded in an ontological framework built around a participatory understanding of reality. As the effect of God's creative activity, creation participates in God and is marked by God. Every individual entity, every being, bears a *similitude* of its creator. However, insofar as creation is different from its cause, it also bears a *dissimilitudo* of God. Creation participates in the creator without being identical to the creator. Our knowledge of this cause is also marked by likeness and difference, because of this *analogical* participation.[49] The analogical relationship between creator and creature allows for a peculiar combination of an implicit, objective, positive moment and an explicit, inadequate, negative moment, resulting in an analogical mode of knowledge.[50] Schillebeeckx combines this Thomistic analogical ontology and epistemology with De Petter's philosophy in order to explain the theological knowing of God.

Intellectual knowledge of God necessitates the use of concepts. At the same time though, a 'real' knowledge of God is never purely conceptual. The only concepts at our disposal are 'creaturely' in origin. Nevertheless, these creaturely concepts can signify God 'objectively', because of the *similitudo* between creature and creator which is 'immanent *beyond*' the concept itself and refers us to an 'excess'. This *similitudo* has an intellectual content which refers us, by way of an inward dynamism, towards God.[51] In other words, since every element of reality bears the ontological mark of the creator, every being contains an epistemological pointer towards God. But this *similitudo* cannot be grasped because of the *dissimilitudo* between creature and creator. The objective reference to God is necessarily implicit. While the concept seeks to bring this reference to God to expression, no concept is able to express the reality signified either definitely or exhaustively.[52] Our knowledge of God is, therefore, marked by

---

[45] Schillebeeckx, 'Salvation History', 280 [93], referring to Thomas Aquinas, *Summa Theologiae*, I, q 1, a. 7.
[46] Thomas Aquinas, *Summa Theologiae* I, q. 1, a. 7, *ad* 2.
[47] Thomas Aquinas, *Summa Theologiae* I, q. 12, a. 12.
[48] Schillebeeckx, 'The Non-Conceptual Intellectual Dimension', 211 [162–3].
[49] Ibid.
[50] Ibid., 223 [182].
[51] Ibid., 215 [170]; 231 [195].
[52] Ibid., 215 [170].

the perspectivism that conditions all of human knowing. Or as Schillebeeckx puts it elsewhere: 'Our concepts do objectively refer us noetically (and thus not pragmatically) to God, but it is impossible to situate God more accurately within this perspective – our gaze fades in the cloud of mystery.'[53] Schillebeeckx explains this real, albeit limited, capacity to signify God through creaturely concepts by using the example of goodness. When we affirm that God is good, we necessarily start with a creaturely representation of goodness. However, creatures are only good inasmuch as they participate in God's goodness. Divine goodness is *implicitly present* in the relative goodness of the creature. In knowing the goodness of the creature, therefore, we also know God confusedly, but objectively, as good.[54]

Importantly, this participatory ontology, and its consequent analogical mode of knowing, entails both a positive and a negative aspect. It explains why the intelligibility of God is always connected to the mystery of God. While Thomas famously offers five 'proofs' to demonstrate the existence of God (*an sit Deus*), he also relativizes these proofs, arguing that we cannot know what the existence of God entails (*quid sit Deus*).[55] Schillebeeckx similarly employs the doctrine of creation not merely to ground our knowledge of God but also to chasten this knowability:

> In our natural knowledge of God, we are therefore bound to the dynamism of the world of creatures which reveals God to us, with the result that our terrestrial knowledge of God appears to be more a knowledge of the mysterious intelligibility of the creature than a knowledge of God as such.[56]

The logic of creation, thus, conditions the knowability of God as a tension between intelligibility and mystery. Schillebeeckx calls it a 'conscious unknowing', that is a 'negative knowledge of God' which is nonetheless a 'true knowledge because it is implicit in a positive knowledge'.[57] Without being able to simply attribute our creaturely concepts to God, we 'tend towards God' by virtue of the objective dynamism that inheres in the content of these concepts.[58] This 'chastizing' of our capacity to know God demonstrates, once again, that Schillebeeckx's theological epistemology is closer to Rahner's than he himself suggests. Ultimately, neither theologian offers a firm philosophical proof of God. Instead, they use philosophy to demonstrate the intelligibility of a theological datum of historical revelation.

Overall, Schillebeeckx's attempt to renew metaphysics, with the help of Thomas and De Petter, has a clearly theological agenda. He seeks to clarify and to explain the real possibility as well as the limitations of theological discourse about God with the help of his perspectival epistemology. To this end, he distinguishes between the conceptual and the non-conceptual element of knowing. Crucially, the focus on the non-conceptual objective dynamism makes room for an examination of the central role played by the

---

[53] Edward Schillebeeckx, 'What is Theology' [1958], in *Revelation and Theology*, 87 [131].
[54] Schillebeeckx, 'The Non-Conceptual Intellectual Dimension', 219 [176–7]; 237 [204].
[55] See Thomas Aquinas, *Summa Theologiae*, I, q. 2, a.3, and I, q. 3, a. 4.
[56] Schillebeeckx, 'The Non-Conceptual Intellectual Dimension', 212 [165].
[57] Schillebeeckx, 'What is Theology', 88–9 [134].
[58] Schillebeeckx, 'The Non-Conceptual Intellectual Dimension', 220 [177].

concrete existential and experiential dimension of human knowledge. This theological metaphysics of knowledge, thus, provides support for his claim for the centrality of the experiential engagement with saving reality as comprising the basis for faith and theology. Our experience of concrete reality contains an implicit objective dynamism towards God. Schillebeeckx develops a relational ontology in order to account for the objective directionality, situated within this non-conceptual aspect and mediated by the conceptual aspect. This relational ontology is, ultimately, grounded in the doctrine of creation and explicated with the help of a Thomistic metaphysics of knowledge. Hence, the relational ontology and perspectival epistemology ultimately serve to affirm 'both the absolute character of the truth of faith and the high degree of relativity and thus of growth in our reflection about faith'.[59] Metaphysics has a subordinate, albeit no less real, role within theology; it helps to create room for experience in theology without falling into relativism. But this subordinate role has its own limitations insofar as the mysterious reality of faith resists complete rationalization. As we will see below, this subordinate role of metaphysics within theology also marks Schillebeeckx's theological anthropology.

4 Preambula Fidei: Transcendental or theological?

Schillebeeckx's qualified use of metaphysics within theology recurs in those writings in which he outlines his theological anthropology.[60] With the help of a transcendental-metaphysical anthropology, he seeks to explicate that Christian anthropology logically and intelligibly builds upon what can be called a natural anthropology. The purpose of this endeavour in transcendental argumentation is to demonstrate the universal intelligibility of the Christian view of reality, as created by and oriented towards God.[61] Importantly, this theological anthropology is intrinsically connected with Schillebeeckx's view on the relationship between nature and grace. Like Rahner, Schillebeeckx maintains that 'the natural and the supernatural form only one order of salvation' and, therefore, rejects Pascal's distinction between the God of the philosophers and the God of salvation history.[62] Metaphysics and theology are complementary views of God that 'throw light on each other', because of the 'existential unity' of the natural order of creation and the supernatural order of salvation.[63] Since nature is involved within faith, reflection about faith is necessary. At the same time, this intellectual

---

[59] Schillebeeckx, 'The Concept of "Truth"', 200 [22].
[60] While Schillebeeckx has never written a theological anthropology, his focus on experience results in a complex interlocking of anthropology and theology that is similar to Rahner's theology. Thus, he writes for instance in *Christ*, 42: 'Theology is not anthropology, but a theological statement is *at the same time* an anthropological statement'. For an extensive discussion of Schillebeeckx's theological anthropology, focusing on his earlier writings, see Cooper, *Humanity in the Mystery of God*. According to Erik Borgman, '… Like a Sacrament. Towards a Theological View on the Real Existing Church', in *Edward Schillebeeckx. Impulse für Theologien im 21. Jahrhundert*, 232, Schillebeeckx's anthropology is ultimately grounded in the anthropology of Thomas Aquinas.
[61] See Borgman, *Edward Schillebeeckx*, 265–6.
[62] Schillebeeckx, 'What is Theology', 287 [104]; Schillebeeckx, 'Salvation History', 88 [133].
[63] Schillebeeckx, 'Salvation History', 88 [133].

activity cannot control faith and is, rather, 'subject to the constant correction of the divine mystery of salvation'.[64]

Schillebeeckx explains this specific role played by metaphysics within theology in his inaugural lecture, 'The Search for the Living God', where he probes the consequences of secularization for theology.[65] One particularly pressing question raised by secularization concerns the plausibility of the Christian faith as being universally intelligible. In accordance with the aforementioned priority of the history of salvation, Schillebeeckx argues that theology must have a 'christological basis', but must remain 'formally theocentric ... oriented towards the inner majesty of the living God'.[66] The particular saving history of Israel and Jesus Christ reveals a universal divine call to salvation. Explaining the universal significance and intelligibility of this particular message requires a reflection on what are traditionally referred to as the *preambula fidei* (preambles of faith). Theology must investigate the autonomous 'natural basis' of faith, demonstrating that the human person is a 'constitutive ... demand for religiousness' with the help of philosophy.[67] Importantly, Schillebeeckx considers this philosophical exercise to be a properly *theological* task. It belongs to theology's responsibility to clarify that the particular Christian faith commitment to the God revealed in salvation history has a universal 'natural theistic dimension'. Failing to do so opens the door to 'religious romanticism' and turns Christian faith into 'pure fideism'.[68] However, Schillebeeckx does not suggest that philosophy has to establish the foundations before one can engage in theological reflection. Instead, his strategy is to work in the opposite direction, from theology to philosophy, because he is confident that the anthropology revealed in salvation history complements philosophical anthropology.

Schillebeeckx employs a distinction between the natural and supernatural dimensions in his inaugural lecture. In other writings he introduces the adjectives 'transcendental' and 'theologal' to characterize these distinct, yet related, dimensions. For Schillebeeckx, the terms 'supernatural' and 'natural' are both, in fact, theological qualifications which are used to characterize the relationship of the human person to God. Every human person is able to discover, through her own particular self-interpretation, that she is related to a mysterious ground of reality. This implicit natural relationship with God can be called a 'transcendental' natural relation. The term 'theologal' is reserved to expressing the supernatural relation to God, that is the interpersonal communion with God, which we cannot ourselves attain, but to which the human person is invited through God's self-communication in grace.[69] Although

---

[64] Schillebeeckx, 'What is Theology', 87 [132].
[65] Edward Schillebeeckx, 'The Search for the Living God' [1959], in *Essays. Ongoing Theological Quests*, 35–50. Frederiek Depoortere, 'Taking Atheism Seriously: A Challenge for Theology in the 21st Century', in *Edward Schillebeeckx and Contemporary Theology*, 36–48, notes that the issue of atheism acted as a particular impetus for Schillebeeckx's concern with natural theology.
[66] Schillebeeckx, 'The Search for the Living God', 48–9.
[67] Ibid., 46–7.
[68] Ibid., 48.
[69] Edward Schillebeeckx, 'Life in God and Life in the World' [1961–1964], in *God and Man*, trans. Edward Fitzgerald and Peter Tomlinson (London: Sheed and Ward, 1969), 116; Edward Schillebeeckx, 'Faith Functioning in Human Self-Understanding', in *The Word in History: The St. Xavier Symposium*, ed. T. Patrick Burke (London: Collins, 1968), 59, n. 1; Erik Borgman, 'Van cultuurtheologie naar theologie als onderdeel van de cultuur. De toekomst van het theologische

nature and grace are two distinct realities, the natural transcendental dimension and the supernatural theologal dimension are inextricably intertwined in our concrete reality according to Schillebeeckx. In order to explain this interconnection of nature and grace, Schillebeeckx undertakes a transcendental analysis of the human person. He seeks to explain that, since *gratia supponit naturam* (grace builds on nature), the supernatural must be seen as building upon the natural as its condition of possibility. Yet, since the reverse, *natura supponit gratiam*, is also true, the natural can only be understood as being grounded in, and oriented towards, its fulfilment in grace.[70]

4.1 The transcendental horizon

Schillebeeckx argues that the human person can be characterized as a 'religious quest'.[71] This quest is materialized through the encounter with the world and with fellow human beings. To be human is to be in relationships. Like Rahner, Schillebeeckx's anthropology is marked by an incarnational theme.[72] He states that the human person is 'essentially a spirit-in-the-world', whose self-understanding and self-realization as a subject are intrinsically connected to the tangible otherness of the world. Bodiliness and perception form the basis of all human awareness.[73] Schillebeeckx also speaks, in this regard, of the human person as 'situated freedom' or 'situated openness and self-transcendence'.[74] Moreover, it is the human other who is crucial for our own self-consciousness. We become aware of ourselves in and through encounters with fellow others in this world[75] This self-awareness through the encounter with other people is, first and foremost, 'unthematic', 'indistinct' and 'pre-reflexive' and acquires clarification with the help of reflection. Even this unthematic experience already entails an interpretation and is, therefore, 'already a comprehending and clarifying perception'.[76] This observation prefigures the intrinsic interrelation between experience and interpretation that Schillebeeckx elaborates after his turn to hermeneutics in much greater detail.[77]

According to Schillebeeckx, anthropology remains incomplete as long as the human relation to God is not considered. He emphasizes more forcefully than Rahner that our relative relations are not merely founded by, but are actually *constitutive* of,

---

project van Edward Schillebeeckx', *Tijdschrift voor Theologie* 34 (1994): 335–60 (342; 345), comments that this article though written in 1968 in the aftermath of the Second Vatican Council still exhibits Schillebeeckx's line of thinking as it developed during his time in Leuven. The influence of De Petter is particularly noticeable. Nevertheless, references to theologians like Rudolf Bultmann, Thomas Altizer and John A. T. Robinson also show that Schillebeeckx sought to take part in the actual theological discussions of his time.

[70] Schillebeeckx, 'Faith Functioning', 42.
[71] Ibid.
[72] For further discussion on this 'incarnational anthropology' and its connection with phenomenology, see William J. Hill, 'A Theology in Transition', in *The Praxis and the Reign of God*, 11–2; Cooper, *Humanity in the Mystery of God*, 111–12.
[73] Schillebeeckx, 'Faith Functioning', 43–4.
[74] Schillebeeckx, 'Life in God', 117.
[75] Schillebeeckx, 'Faith Functioning', 43–4.
[76] Ibid., 44.
[77] See also Borgman, 'Van cultuurtheologie naar theologie', 351.

this absolute relation. Our transcendental relation is fundamentally shaped by the concreteness of our historical existence and 'cannot be abstracted from this without destroying itself'.[78] Horizontal and 'relative' relations to the world, and to other people, point to an 'absolute' or 'transcendental' relation to God.[79] He does not explain precisely which sense of transcendental – scholastic, Kantian, religious – he has in mind here; however, the language used to describe this transcendental relation is very much akin to Rahner's concept of transcendental experience. The 'mystery of God' is the constitutive foundation – the 'co-conscious horizon' of our conscious relations to the world and to our fellow humans. The 'inner-worldly' relations to world and to other people contain an 'objective reference toward the absolute constitutive mystery of God'.[80] This mystery is never available to us as an object, but rather manifests itself as the 'transcendent Third' in all of our relations as a 'certain orientation of conscious ignorance'.[81]

Whereas Rahner connects this transcendental experience with the wonder and surprise about the human spirit's capacity to transcend every concrete and finite limitation, Schillebeeckx instead draws our attention to the experience of contingency as being the fundamental mediation of this experience.[82] We experience reality as a question. Material things, other people, our own freedom, all of these realities are experienced as being radically contingent, unable to account for their existence. Experiencing the contingency and gratuity of one's own concrete existence is the key to the affirmation of the transcendental horizon. The question of contingency raises the metaphysical question of Being: Why is there something at all? In order to explain this radical contingency, we have to affirm an 'absolute ground of Being'.[83] It must be noted here that Schillebeeckx does not consider the possibility that contingent reality is ultimately groundless. His reasoning from contingency for the necessity of a ground seems to suggest that, like Rahner, he follows the scholastic priority of actuality over possibility.

Instead of developing a philosophical argument for the absolute ground of reality, Schillebeeckx discusses the nature of this assumed ground. He argues that our

---

[78] Schillebeeckx, 'Faith Functioning', 48.
[79] Ibid., 45.
[80] Ibid., 47.
[81] Schillebeeckx, 'Life in God', 118–19; Schillebeeckx, 'The Search for the Living God', 38.
[82] Kennedy, *Deus Humanissimus*, 107–8, considers the experience of contingency to be an 'ancillary epistemological premise' in Schillebeeckx's theological epistemology that must be viewed in connection with his creation-based relational ontology. In 'God and Creation', 48, Kennedy argues that Schillebeeckx uses finitude and contingency synonymously and that 'the single most significant of all of Schillebeeckx's many and diverse comments on creation concerns finitude'.
[83] Schillebeeckx, 'Non-Religious Humanism and Belief in God', 52–3. Barwasser, *Theologie der Kultur*, 136–43, argues that Schillebeeckx hereby situates his fundamental theology decisively within the 'modern philosophy of freedom'. Barwasser considers such a move to be necessary, because his previous argumentation based on Thomistic metaphysics has lost its persuasiveness in modernity, which no longer accepts a cosmology founded on a metaphysics of causality. However, Barwasser reads Schillebeeckx perhaps through to a too modern lens. For this reason, he fails to notice that Schillebeeckx's analysis of the experience of contingency, as the locus of revelation, remains intimately connected with his earlier Thomistic ontology. Human freedom is but one element of the whole of reality that is experienced as being contingent. Schillebeeckx's ontology includes, but also goes beyond, the individual human subject. The precise extent of his turn towards modernity, and its focus on human freedom, therefore can be debated.

experience of the contingency of reality does not merely result in the affirmation of divine mystery as a 'metaphysical condition of possibility'. An argument that restricts itself to demonstrating an anonymous 'depth dimension' remains purely anthropological.[84] Moreover, insofar as it uses the name God to signify this depth dimension, it turns God into a 'function' for our own self-understanding. Alternatively, Schillebeeckx argues that our experience of reality as *gratuitous gift*, rather than as the product of our own minds, reveals the absolute ground as a *personal* mystery.[85] God does not need us in order to be God. God remains transcendent to us, even in the very act of grounding our existence. The realization that creation is a purely gratuitous and free act breaks all 'horizontalism'. We discover that we exist by virtue of the loving, free and gratuitous decision of a personal, transcendent mystery.[86] Accordingly, the affirmation of God as metaphysical ground 'is completed only in the willing surrender to the divine mystery'.[87]

Schillebeeckx uses the category of trust to characterize our openness and surrender to this personal mysterious ground. Trust elicits a desire for an inter-subjective relation with this personal mystery. While this desire is itself already a 'beginning' (*aanzet*) of a theologal relationship with God, initiating such a relationship is beyond human capacity. The 'absolute limit' between mystery and us can only be overcome through God's grace. Referring to Levinas, Schillebeeckx argues that both the affirmation of God and ethical responsibility are intrinsically related. Human beings primarily actualize their trust in mystery ethically, through a personal commitment to, a responsibility for, or a trust in fellow humankind. Applying his metaphysics of knowledge, he argues that these inter-human relations offer us an objective perspective on the inter-subjectivity desired with God. For this reason, an affirmative trust in God, through trust in fellow humans, can be considered to be a form of 'preliminary faith'.[88] Interestingly, this close interconnection between the affirmation of God and ethics prefigures his later plea for the interrelation of theoretical and practical reason.

4.2 The theologal horizon

The transcendental analysis of human experience and self-awareness serves to demonstrate that human existence entails a religious quest. The human person is a relational being whose 'relative' relations to the world and other persons imply an 'absolute' transcendental relation of trust in a personal mystery.[89] The main thrust of this argument is to show the continuity, as well as the discontinuity, between 'natural' human experience and the religious experience of grace. Human beings have an openness to the future, 'watching for a God who is on the way', which can be termed a *capacitas gratiae* (capacity for grace).[90] Although Schillebeeckx has already used the

---

[84] Schillebeeckx, 'Life in God', 119.
[85] Schillebeeckx, 'Non-Religious Humanism and Belief in God', 54.
[86] Schillebeeckx, 'Life in God', 119; 122.
[87] Schillebeeckx, 'The Search for the Living God', 39.
[88] Schillebeeckx, 'Life in God', 124–6.
[89] Schillebeeckx, 'Faith Functioning', 46.
[90] Schillebeeckx, 'The Search for the Living God', 48; Schillebeeckx, 'Life in God', 127.

word 'God' numerous times to characterize the mystery that human beings encounter in life, he is aware of the fact that such an explicit naming of mystery is only possible in the light of a specific religious tradition. His own anthropological account is based upon the particular history of the people of Israel, culminating in the man Jesus. In this particular narrative, God has started to act 'from beyond the cloud of mystery'.[91] God has revealed God's desire for personal communion with each and every human person through the words and actions that constitute this history of salvation. In light of this divine revelation, it becomes possible to interpret secular history as salvation history.

Hence, in retrospect, 'natural' human existence takes on a much more profound dimension. Our transcendental relation to mystery is no longer an 'anonymous' revelation of God.[92] This transcendental relation escapes its 'indistinct anonymity' and breaks open into a *theologal* life-horizon through the clarifying categorical realities of salvation history.[93] To be sure, God's self-revelation does not make God directly comprehensible or signal an end to God's mystery. We continue to have a merely 'veiled' perspective on God. Yet, these persisting limitations notwithstanding, we do become aware that we can relate and experience in new ways.

> In the faith, the Absolute is no longer only 'background', but 'foreground', even though it can be experienced only in faith and thus in veiled presence through an indirect thematic expression: a theologal way of existence or communion with God, thematically expressed, however, in and through categorial factors (concepts, images, and worldly realities).[94]

Hence, God's revelation of salvation results in a radical reconfiguration of natural or philosophical anthropology. We learn the true nature of the human person in Jesus Christ; that is that humanity is invited into personal communion with God through grace. Importantly, Schillebeeckx repeats that this distinction between the natural and supernatural state of humankind is a *theological* distinction, which only becomes explicit through the Christian interpretation of revelation history.[95] Moreover, Schillebeeckx also emphasizes that this distinction is merely *formal* and does not properly correspond to existential reality. Revelation history reveals that every human person is addressed by God's graceful call to salvation. This theological insight into the pervasive influence of grace makes the entire world of human existence theologically relevant:

> By virtue of God's universally active saving will, there is no longer a purely natural human life: wherever men are found, their life is determined by a theologal life-horizon which they have (albeit implicitly) accepted or refused. Consequently,

---

[91] Schillebeeckx, 'The Search for the Living God', 39.
[92] Ibid., 39–42.
[93] Schillebeeckx, 'Faith Functioning', 50. Analogous to Rahner, Schillebeeckx employs the term 'categorial' to refer to the concepts, images and worldly realities that we use to express our unthematic experience.
[94] Ibid., 52.
[95] Ibid., 52; 55.

the concrete experience of existence is really a *locus theologicus*, because that experience unavoidably involves a Christian outlook on life – even though perhaps unthematic.[96]

Once again, there are obvious parallels with Rahner's theology here, especially with his concept of transcendental unthematic experience and the parenthetical notion of transcendental revelation. The assertion that there is no 'purely natural human life' strongly suggests that Schillebeeckx and Rahner share a congruent view on the relationship between nature and grace – a view which is reflected in their theological appropriation of philosophy.

4.3 The theological key to transcendental anthropology

Unlike De Lubac or Rahner, Schillebeeckx does not enjoy the reputation of being one of the key voices on either side of the debate on nature and grace. Instead of introducing a well-developed alternative solution, his own view on this issue remains implicitly present, to a great extent, in his writings.[97] Thus, he does touch, for instance, upon the topic of the supernatural existential in an extensive review article, albeit indirectly. Schillebeeckx critically questions what he views as the introduction by Rahner and Von Balthasar of an 'intermediary' or 'linking reality', which is neither grace nor nature.[98] It seems doubtful, however, whether this is a correct interpretation of Rahner's understanding of the supernatural existential as a graced transformation of human transcendentality rather than as another 'reality'.

More importantly, Schillebeeckx's emphasizes the primacy of the 'efficacious saving will of God' and the believer's personal inward experience of this divine initiative.[99] Schillebeeckx fails to explain adequately why this personal experience of being addressed by God's grace would be welcomed rather than rejected as a foreign intrusion into natural life. Instead, he emphasizes that this experience of grace is 'in all its aspects and dimensions, entirely bound up with our life in this world'.[100] His relative inattention to the issue of extrinsicism manifests that he is, ultimately, not really interested in speculative questions about 'pure nature'. Borgman argues that this lack of interest is precisely what affords Schillebeeckx's position 'a high degree of distinctiveness'.[101] He consistently approaches reality in its concrete state, without abstracting from the reality of grace. For Schillebeeckx, 'being human, in the fullest

---

[96] Ibid., 53.
[97] During his theological studies, Schillebeeckx engaged with the topic of nature and grace in his discussion of Karl Adam in 'Natuur en bovennatuur', *Biekorf* 1942–1943, no. 4–5. In the article 'Arabisch-Neoplatoonse achtergrond van Thomas' opvatting over de ontvankelijkheid van de mens voor de genade', *Bijdragen* 35 (1974): 298–308, he discusses the topic of the natural desire for God. However, apart from mentioning names, he does not enter into dialogue with alternative contemporary viewpoints on this issue explicitly.
[98] Edward Schillebeeckx, 'The Non-Conceptual Intellectual Element in the Act of Faith: A Reaction' [1963], in *Revelation and Theology*, 258–9 [59–62].
[99] Schillebeeckx, 'The Non-Conceptual Intellectual Element', 262 [66].
[100] Ibid., 261 [67].
[101] Borgman, *Edward Schillebeeckx*, 436–7, n. 202.

sense of the word, is only possible by virtue of God's grace'.¹⁰² This position ultimately converges materially with Rahner's vision insofar as both theologians agree that all human beings have an orientation towards God and are constantly addressed by God's grace in concrete reality.¹⁰³ As Stephen Duffy has suggested, the disagreement between Schillebeeckx and Rahner may be 'more apparent than real'.¹⁰⁴ While Schillebeeckx disagrees with Rahner on the precise technical explication, he agrees with him on the concrete intertwinement of the natural and the supernatural orders. Importantly, this interconnectedness of nature and grace fundamentally shapes Schillebeeckx's theological method and his use of philosophy particularly.

While Schillebeeckx begins his argumentation with the transcendental dimension, and then proceeds to the theologal dimension, it turns out that the transcendental horizon can only be described and explained adequately *from within* the theologal horizon.¹⁰⁵ Schillebeeckx does not develop a transcendental anthropology that serves as the foundation of a Christian anthropology. On the contrary, he seeks to explain the Christian understanding of humankind with help of transcendental and metaphysical categories. The universal human openness for God can only be articulated in light of a particular tradition. The theologian Schillebeeckx starts with Jesus Christ, the 'authorized *locus theologicus*', who reveals that all human existence can be a *locus theologicus*.¹⁰⁶ Accordingly, his analysis of human existence as absolute relation to mystery follows an inductive rather than a deductive line of reasoning. The transcendental philosophical anthropology is an abstract explanatory tool – one developed with the concrete Christian anthropology in mind.

However, Schillebeeckx also emphasizes that the transcendental relation is always experienced and interpreted within concrete historical circumstances. As a result, there is necessarily a plurality of concrete images of this transcendental relation, expressed either in religious or in non-religious terms.¹⁰⁷ This remark heralds Schillebeeckx's growing awareness of the hermeneutical nature of experience and, consequently, of the hermeneutical dimension of transcendental, metaphysical and theological argumentation. Every argument aimed at explicating a universal transcendental relation faces the difficulty of accounting for its concrete and hermeneutically conditioned manifestation and mediation. How useful and valid are universal categories, such as the 'transcendental relation', if they can only be discovered within a particular context and tradition? The Christian may recognize what she knows to be the theologal relation in the description of the transcendental relation. But does

---

¹⁰² Schillebeeckx, 'Arabisch-Neoplatoonse achtergrond', 303.
¹⁰³ Borgman, *Edward Schillebeeckx*, 436–7, n. 202, arrives at a similar conclusion.
¹⁰⁴ Stephen Duffy, *The Graced Horizon*, 135; 165; 217. Duffy does not consider Schillebeeckx's later writings, but as we will see in Chapter 9, Schillebeeckx's contrast experience builds upon his metaphysics of creation and actually forms an alternative justification of this universality and ubiquity of grace in human existence. See also Roger Haight, *The Future of Christology* (New York: Continuum, 2005), 108–9, who argues that instead of elaborating a complex theological concept, such as that of the supernatural existential, Schillebeeckx 'encompasses Rahner's view in his notion of creation'.
¹⁰⁵ Schillebeeckx, 'Faith Functioning', 55.
¹⁰⁶ Ibid., 54–5.
¹⁰⁷ Ibid., 48.

such a description in abstract terms serve a purpose when communicating with people from different traditions? Can they recognize the transcendental relation in their particular experiences? In other words, how much do context and interpretation affect the particularity of experience, and is there any room left for an analysis of experience in abstract transcendental and metaphysical terms? Does this universal discourse help to communicate Christianity's particular truth claims? These questions become increasingly pressing for Schillebeeckx when he turns to hermeneutics and to critical theory.

5 A critical-hermeneutical turn

Schillebeeckx's theological method underwent an intense transformation during the 1960s. Due to his growing awareness of the roles played by history, culture and language, his focus shifts from the issue of conceptuality to the question of interpretation. Put succinctly, while the early Schillebeeckx was concerned with the metaphysics of religious experience, the later Schillebeeckx focuses on the hermeneutics of religious experience. What are the consequences of Schillebeeckx's critical-hermeneutical turn for this theological method? I will show that Schillebeeckx's hermeneutical account of experience remains connected with his metaphysics of experience. Hermeneutics and metaphysics are both necessary in order to clarify the dialectics of object and subject that characterizes both experience and revelation.

5.1 The clear break with De Petter

In his very first reflections on hermeneutical theory, Schillebeeckx does not seem to perceive there to be a conflict between the use of hermeneutics and the use of metaphysics within theology. During this early phase of hermeneutical exploration, the question about the 'ontological conditions for understanding' the Christian message of faith appears intermittently throughout his writings.[108] Furthermore, in his essay on hermeneutics in *God the Future of Man*, he criticizes the attempts made by theologians, such as Rudolf Bultmann, Ernst Fuchs and Gerhard Ebeling, to 'overcome' or 'destroy' metaphysics in order to protect the authenticity of faith. Schillebeeckx considers this *Offenbarungspositivismus* (positivism of revelation) to be completely foreign to the Catholic understanding of revelation and faith. However, he also expresses his concern that Catholic theology runs the risk of becoming 'silted up in *essentialist* metaphysics'. Accordingly, he raises the question of whether a non-essentialist metaphysics is possible.[109]

---

[108] Schillebeeckx, 'Towards a Catholic Use of Hermeneutics', 2 [4]; 16 [24; Edward Schillebeeckx, 'Secularization and Christian Belief in God' [1968], in *God the Future of Man*, 46 [76]; 53 [87].
[109] Schillebeeckx, 'Towards a Catholic Use of Hermeneutics', 9–10, n. 20 [15]. See also Schillebeeckx, 'Theological Criteria', 52, n. 8 [58], where he also explicitly distances himself from 'anti-metaphysical presuppositions'.

However, when Schillebeeckx publishes *Jesus* in 1974, it becomes clear that his methodological interest has dramatically shifted from metaphysics to hermeneutics. In the introduction to the aforementioned work, he explains that in order to understand the Christian confession of the revelatory experience of salvation in Jesus, it is necessary first to engage in a historical-critical and hermeneutical study of the historical Jesus and his cultural context.[110] Christianity began with the specific and transformative experiential encounter with the historical person of Jesus.[111] This particular event mediates the revelation of God's universal promise. Schillebeeckx rejects the suggestion that religious experience can be identified with reference to a general core that forms the basis of religion. Such an ahistorical abstraction conceals the historical and cultural contexts of religion and results in a theoretical universality – one 'without flesh and blood'.[112] How can we, in our current time, come to understand this historical experience of revelation in Jesus Christ?

From Heidegger and Gadamer, Schillebeeckx appropriates the insight into the necessity of a historical horizon of pre-understanding for every interpretation. In the fourth part of *Jesus*, he poses the question of whether there is a 'universal horizon of understanding' for the historical interpretation of the revelation in the particular historical person of Jesus of Nazareth.[113] For Schillebeeckx, this universal horizon of understanding is connected with the human search for meaning (*zin*). He observes that the question of the universal meaning of history is both 'insuperable' and 'insoluble', thereby attempting to avoid the extremes of either a 'Hegelian unitary system' or a 'relativist pluralism'.[114] On the one hand, this universal horizon forms the condition for the possibility of interpersonal communication and understanding. Despite our varying particular pre-understandings, the fact remains that dialogue is possible. Hence, a universal horizon of understanding is, at least as a question, a necessary given.[115] On the other hand, human history presents itself as a plurality of histories characterized by ambiguity. History is marked by the co-existence of 'sense', joy and laughter, and 'non-sense', suffering and tears. This contingency cannot be rationalized or comprehended, at least not through theoretical reason alone. We are, thus, confronted with particular experiences of meaning which merely 'imply the demand for universal meaning'.[116] As Mary-Catherine Hilkert puts it more sharply: 'The question is not the meaning of the particular in relation to the whole, but whether there is any meaning to be found within some parts of history at all.'[117] Schillebeeckx argues that inasmuch as universal

---

[110] Schillebeeckx, *Jesus*, 27–56 [43–76].
[111] Edward Schillebeeckx, *Interim Report on the Books Jesus and Christ* [1978], CW vol. 8, trans. John Bowden (London: Bloomsbury, 2014), 9 [10].
[112] Schillebeeckx, *Jesus*, 551–5 [590–94].
[113] Ibid., 573 [612]; 578–9 [615–7].
[114] Ibid., 575–7 [612–15]. Schillebeeckx indicates that he derives this distinction between the 'Scylla' of the demand for totality and the 'Charybdis' of respect for historical particularity from Paul Ricoeur, *History and Truth*, trans. Charles A. Kelbley (Evanston: Northwestern University Press, 1965).
[115] Schillebeeckx, *Jesus*, 577 [615].
[116] Ibid., 579 [617].
[117] Mary-Catherine Hilkert, 'St. Thomas and the Appeal to Experience: A Response to Kenneth L. Smith', *CTSA Proceedings* 47 (1992): 23.

meaning is still to be found, it can only be detected and thematized by way of a praxis of liberation.[118]

For Schillebeeckx, the recognition of the incompleteness of every particular historical experience of meaning 'entails a clear break' with the implicit intuition of De Petter's philosophy.[119] This philosophy considers particular experiences of meaning to be implicit participations in total meaning. However, Schillebeeckx argues that this participation theory assumes a homogenous society that has a shared expectation of the beatific vision as the final destiny of humankind. This stands in sharp contrast to contemporary pluralistic society and its divergent and competing world views. For this reason, Schillebeeckx posits that 'the concept of participation has to be replaced by the idea of anticipation of total meaning in the midst of a history still in the making'.[120] Responding to the critique that this preference for anticipation is 'philosophically superficial', Schillebeeckx maintains that this term is crucial in order to realize the eschatological dimension of history. Since our history is incomplete and continues to develop towards the openness of the future, any totality of meaning can only be anticipated.[121] While he maintains that 'objective redemption' has been achieved in Jesus Christ, Schillebeeckx emphasizes the promissory nature of this salvific event. Salvation has already become a living reality in Jesus and, as such, gives us a 'certainty of faith' that there will be ultimate salvation. Yet ultimate salvation is only realized in the *eschaton*, so the promise in Jesus must reckon with actual ongoing history.[122]

Now, the turn from a concept of participation to a concept of anticipation has important consequences for how we approach the Christian tradition of faith. Schillebeeckx argues that the Christian affirmation of universal meaning in Jesus Christ must be considered a hypothesis. This hypothesis must, subsequently, be tested by confronting it with contemporary historical experience. This correlation of particular experiences must be attentive to the fact that history conditions the interpretation of experience. In short, it must have an eye for the hermeneutical nature of experience. This is precisely what Schillebeeckx deems to be lacking in De Petter.[123] For this reason, Schillebeeckx sets out to develop a concept of experience that is attentive to the hermeneutical conditions of experience.

5.2 The dialectics of experience

We cannot talk about revelation without talking about experience, because we can only perceive of revelation insofar as it is mediated by human experience.[124] 'Revelation

---

[118] Schillebeeckx, *Jesus*, 582-3 [620-2].
[119] Ibid., 580 [618]. Kennedy, *Deus Humanissimus*, 200-16, describes that Schillebeeckx's distancing from De Petter has already begun as early as 1968. He refers to transcriptions of Schillebeeckx's lectures in Nijmegen that attest to this distanciation.
[120] Schillebeeckx, *Jesus*, 581 [619].
[121] Schillebeeckx, *Interim Report*, 88 [101].
[122] Ibid., 89 [101].
[123] See Edward Schillebeeckx, 'Culture, Religion and Violence' [1996], in *Essays: Ongoing Theological Quests*, 176, n. 12, where Schillebeeckx writes that 'the word hermeneutics never crossed De Petter's lips'.
[124] Edward Schillebeeckx, 'Experience and Faith' [1980], in *Essays: Ongoing Theological Quests*, 1.

is *experience* expressed in language; it is God's saving action as experienced and communicated by *men*.'[125] This quotation makes abundantly clear the shift of attention from conceptuality to language and interpretation in Schillebeeckx's thought. Affirming the mediatory role of experience in revelation necessarily gives rise to the question of interpretation and expression. For the hermeneutical theologian, experience, context and interpretation become theologically relevant as access to, and mediation of, God's salvific activity in history.[126] Schillebeeckx elaborates a general epistemological framework that conceptualizes experience as being a dialectical process, in order to explain the interrelation between experience and revelation. Through this dialectical account, he seeks to keep the objective and the subjective elements of experience and revelation together. Schillebeeckx's use of terms is not always precise and consistent when describing the aspects that constitute this dialectics. Thus, he uses the terms 'experience', 'encounter' and 'perception' with reference to the objective aspects, while the terms 'interpretation', 'language' and 'thought' are used to describe the subjective aspect.[127] Yet, he also uses the term 'experience' to cover both of these poles, because he views experience as being constituted by the unity of the objective and the subjective.[128]

'The basic meaning of the Dutch word for experience is travelling through the country [wedervaren] and thus, through exploration – being taken up into a process of learning. Experience means learning through "direct" contact with people and things.'[129] Schillebeeckx employs the Dutch word *wedervaren* to explain the original meaning of experience in terms of a 'confrontation' with someone or something.[130] Alternatively, he also uses the term 'encounter' to convey this objective dimension of experience. Every experience originates as an encounter with reality. We experience *something* – an event in nature or history, a human person, a physical object and so on.[131] As Schillebeeckx himself puts it repeatedly: 'In experience we have an offer of reality.'[132]

---

[125] Schillebeeckx, *Christ*, 31 [46].
[126] See Stephan van Erp, 'Incessant Incarnation as the Future of Humanity: The Promise of Schillebeeckx's Sacramental Theology', *Concilium. International Review of Theology – English Edition* 1 (2012): 93–4, who characterizes this view of the revelatory dimension of experience, interpretation and history as a sacramental vision. He argues that this sacramental vision, deriving from his incarnational focus, constitutes the key motivation of Schillebeeckx's theological hermeneutics. See also Stephan van Erp, *De onvoltooide eeuw. Voorlopers van een katholieke cultuur* (Nijmegen: Valkhof Pers, 2015), 127.
[127] Schillebeeckx, *Christ*, 17 [31–2]; Schillebeeckx, 'Experience and Faith', 12.
[128] Thompson, 'Epistemological Frameworks', 36.
[129] Schillebeeckx, *Christ*, 17 [31].
[130] Bernadette Schwarz-Boenneke, 'Die Widerständigkeit der Wirklichkeit als erstes Moment des Erfahrens', in *Edward Schillebeeckx. Impulse für Theologien*, 95; 104–5, observes that both Schillebeeckx as well as commentators, such as Lieven Boeve and Louis Dupré, often simply use the terms 'experience' and 'interpretation' when discussing this dialectics. This use of terms may confuse the fact that Schillebeeckx considers interpretation to be an intrinsic aspect of experience. Alternatively, Schwarz-Boenneke suggests returning to Schillebeeckx's etymological explanation of the meaning of experience as *wedervaren*.
[131] Schillebeeckx, 'Experience and Faith', 5. The importance of the phenomenological category of 'encounter' in Schillebeeckx's incarnational approach has been mentioned earlier. Hilkert, 'Experience and Revelation', 64, notes that it conveys that experience contains a dimension of 'givenness' which is independent of, and beyond, the interpreting subject's control. See also Mary Catherine Hilkert, 'Nieuwe paden in een oude tuin. Sacramentele theologie en antropologie', *Tijdschrift voor Theologie* 50 (2010): 108–21, for Schillebeeckx's reconnecting of the fields of incarnational Christology, sacramentology and the theology of grace with the help of this phenomenological concept of encounter.
[132] Schillebeeckx, *Christ*, 19 [33].

Appropriating the insights of hermeneutical theory, Schillebeeckx continues by insisting that every encounter already contains an interpretative dimension. There are no immediate or un-interpreted experiential encounters; all experience is interpretative experience. We can only register and understand realities against a 'pre-reflective' horizon of pre-understanding.[133] An encounter, thus, requires an 'interpretative framework' – one which co-determines that which is perceived.[134] This notion of the interpretative framework elaborates and concretizes what the early Schillebeeckx termed our perspectival access to truth. An interpretative framework is itself based upon preceding cumulative experiences and can, therefore, be said to form our experiential tradition. The interpretative framework offered to us by our experiential tradition plays both a positive and a negative role in understanding. As an experiential horizon, it functions as the transcendental condition which makes experience and the understanding of experience possible. But, inasmuch as every horizon is characterized by particularity, the interpretative framework also limits our understanding.[135]

Importantly, Schillebeeckx is not concerned with experience as feeling, sensation or piety. While he considers these emotional aspects to be essential, his focus concerns the 'cognitive, critical, and productive force' of experience.[136] The role of reflexive thought is closely connected with the role of interpretative frameworks. Just like the relation between encounter and interpretation, the relation between experience and reflection is dialectical. The authority of experiences and their articulation depends upon whether these factors are critically considered and reflected upon. Critically reflected experience can become a part of a tradition and can, thereby, make new experiences possible. At the same time, 'thinking remains vacuous if it does not continually fall back on experience.'[137] A critical appeal to experience must, therefore, reflect upon several complex and interrelated factors that condition and determine all of experience. First, the interpretation and articulation of experience uses language, that is concepts, images, connotations and emotions. We receive our language from the cultural group to which we belong, and this language, having a history and context of its own, already contains certain views about the world and humankind. Moreover, an interpretation also reflects the values, interests and ideologies of the sociopolitical and socio-economic context in which we are situated. Following Ricoeur's pointing to the masters of suspicion, Schillebeeckx argues that we must critically examine whether these factors have obscured or distorted our interpretations. In other words, a hermeneutics of experience calls for a hermeneutics of suspicion. Finally, interpretation also involves the use of models and theories.[138]

How the interpretative framework and the reflexive dimension are related is not exactly apparent in Schillebeeckx's writings. Both aspects seem to elaborate the

---

[133] Ibid., 34–5 [49]. Louis Dupré, 'Experience and Interpretation: A Philosophical Reflection on Schillebeeckx' *Jesus* and *Christ*', *Theological Studies* 43 (1982): 37, notes that this differentiates Schillebeeckx's understanding of experience from a romantic concept of experience that focusses on feeling.
[134] Schillebeeckx, 'Experience and Faith', 5.
[135] Ibid.
[136] Schillebeeckx, *Christ*, 13 [29].
[137] Schillebeeckx, 'Experience and Faith', 12.
[138] Ibid., 10–11.

subjective dimension of experience, calling attention to the particular and situated factors that condition experience in distinction to the objective dimension (the encounter or perception). Moreover, Schillebeeckx warns that distinguishing sharply between the objective and the subjective dimensions of experience is impossible. The distinction between encounter, interpretation and reflection serves a useful analytical purpose, but should never obscure the fact that 'real' experience is a 'richly nuanced totality': 'We experience in the act of interpretation, without being able to draw a neat distinction between the element of experience and the element of interpretation.'[139] It is crucial to note, however, that despite his extensive discussion of the various subjective factors that are at play in interpretative experience, Schillebeeckx persists in according a certain priority to the objective aspect of experience. This priority is ontological rather than temporal, but is one which fundamentally conditions the human act of interpretation.[140]

In the book *Interim Report*, Schillebeeckx succinctly restates his view on the dialectical relationship between experience and interpretation, this time with a specific emphasis being placed on the objective aspect. This restatement is clearly indebted to (a modified version of) his perspectival epistemology. Whereas Schillebeeckx had previously emphasized the limitations of concepts and their necessary relation to implicit intuition, he now explains that subjective perception and interpretation must be seen in connection with the givenness of experience.[141] Without intending to introduce a dualism between 'events' and 'subjective experiences', it is necessary to distinguish between 'the way which things really are' and 'the way they appear' to the experiencing subject. The thing that appears within our particular perspective simultaneously transcends our observation. For this reason, our experience is determined not only by our personal perspective but also in part by 'the unique contribution' of the experienced thing itself, that is the *interpretandum*. This contribution is not restricted to the level of perception, but extends to interpretation too. The *interpretandum* itself contains *interpretaments*, or interpretative elements, which are independent of the interpreting subject, but which play an essential role in the interpretation of experience.[142]

Interpretation does not start at the moment when one begins to reflect on one's experience, but rather is an inner moment of experience itself, first unexpressed and only later reflected upon deliberately.[143] While Schillebeeckx allows for degrees of interpretation, reflexivity and expression, he does insist that there is never a raw or completely un-interpreted experience. In order to demonstrate that interpretative experience is never purely subjective, Schillebeeckx analyses the interpretative dimension of experience by distinguishing between 'inner' experiential interpretative elements – associated with the object of experience – and 'outer' reflective interpretative elements – associated with the experiencing subject. Inner interpretative elements

---

[139] Schillebeeckx, *Christ*, 18–19 [33].
[140] Dupré, 'Experience and Interpretation', 43.
[141] Interestingly, other commentators such as Boeve, Schwarz-Boenneke and Dupré do not mention this connection between Schillebeeckx's early epistemology and his hermeneutical epistemology.
[142] Schillebeeckx, *Interim Report*, 10–11. See also *Jesus*, 645 [746] and *Christ*, 18–19 [33–4] for this distinction between 'interpretament' and 'interpretative elements'.
[143] Schilebeeckx, *Interim Report*, 11 [13].

have their 'basis and source directly in what is experienced' and make this experience 'somewhat clear'.[144] The object of experience itself partially guides the direction of interpretation. There are also interpretative elements that are 'handed to us from elsewhere, outside at least this experience'.[145] These interpretative elements do not derive from the object experienced, but from cultural-linguistic elements that have constituted the experiencing subject. Once again, this is an analytical distinction. At the level of concrete experience, we cannot accurately determine which interpretative elements are 'inner' and which are 'outer'. Instead, the two interpretative dimensions mutually condition each other, which Schillebeeckx explains by giving an example of the experience of love:

> An experience of love contains interpretative elements within the experience itself, suggested by the concrete experience of love. The love that is experienced knows what love is, and it even knows more about it than it can express at the moment. This interpretative identification is therefore an intrinsic moment of the love that is experienced. Afterwards, it is possible that one may also express the experience of love in language taken from *Romeo and Juliet*, from the biblical *Song of Songs*, from St. Paul's hymn to love or from all kinds of modern poetry. This additional thematizing in no way means a nonchalant or superfluous elaboration. Interpretation and experience have a reciprocal influence on one another. Real love lives on the love experience and on its own progressive self-expression. ... However, this growing self-expression makes it possible to deepen the original experience; based on the experience, it reveals that experience more explicitly to itself.[146]

Hence the necessary attention paid to the hermeneutical condition of all experience must never lead to a forgetting of the 'reality of experience', or *interpretandum*, which exerts its own interpretative challenge *and* guidance. The indispensable role played by the 'inner interpretative elements' ensures that interpretation cannot be reduced to the level of human subjectivity. Objective reality not only offers itself as an object of experience but also conditions and guides the process of interpretation by providing what could be called a 'primary interpretation'.[147] This element of 'objective

---

[144] Ibid.
[145] Ibid.
[146] Schillebeeckx, *Interim Report*, 12 [13–14]. See also *Christ*, 622 [632], in which Schillebeeckx explains the primacy of the *interpretandum* over the *interpretaments* with reference to the gospels: 'The mere fact that various New Testament authors look for other interpretative elements and images in order to express the saving significance, say, of the death of Jesus, makes it clear that the unifying factor is provided by what is to be interpreted [the *interpretandum*] and not the interpretative element as such.'
[147] Dupré, 'Experience and Interpretation', 43–4, uses the term 'primary interpretation' to explain that there is a 'given, fundamental interpretation' in the experience of revelation which belongs to the 'original core of revelation'. He argues that this primary interpretation 'prepares and disposes' us for and to experience, contains the 'most basic interpretation' and 'guides the whole process of expression'. All of this sounds remarkably consistent with Schillebeeckx's argument in favour of the 'inner interpretative element'. It comes as something of a surprise, therefore, when Dupré criticizes Schillebeeckx for not sufficiently taking the role of primary interpretation into account. This criticism is unjustified, especially since Dupré fails to discuss Schillebeeckx's distinction between inner and outer interpretative elements.

directionality' proves to be essential when Schillebeeckx appropriates his dialectical account of experience in elaborating his understanding of revelation.

5.3 The dialectics of revelation

All experience takes place in a dialectical process of encounter and interpretation. Every experience also contains a potential element of surprise or revelation, inasmuch as reality may prove to resist our interpretation. This also applies to the religious experience of divine revelation. Yet, what is a religious experience? In *Church: The Human Story of God*, Schillebeeckx explains that an experience can become a religious experience 'with the illumination and help of a particular religious tradition in which people stand and which is thus influential as an interpretative framework which provides meaning'.[148] Hence a Christian experience is a particular human experience interpreted in the light of the Christian tradition. What implications does this have for the understanding of revelation? Does revelation belong to either the objective or the subjective dimension of experience, or to both? According to Schillebeeckx, locating the religious or revelatory element at either the experiential or the interpretative dimensions disregards the dialectical unity of experience and interpretation. Since revelation is mediated by human experience, revelation shares in the dialectics that characterizes experience.

Our particular interpretative framework always conditions how we experience. Accordingly, Schillebeeckx rejects the suggestion of a general religious experience: 'Not only does the religious man interpret in a different way from the non-believer, he lives in a different world and has different experiences.'[149] Believers and non-believers have alternative interpretative experiences. However, while there is no neutral and pre-interpretative religious experience, it would be equally mistaken to locate the religious and revelatory element entirely in the interpretative moment of experience. Ultimately, the interpretation of an experience as a religious experience is only possible insofar as there is an *offer of revelation*.

Responding to the critique of Louis Dupré that his emphasis on the interpretative dimension of experience results in a neglect of this 'offer of revelation',[150] Schillebeeckx clarifies that revelation contains its own inner interpretative element: 'The offer-from-God of course provides its own *direction* of interpretation, as the normative basis of our non-arbitrary interpretations of faith.'[151] Without this objective initiative and directionality, interpretations of faith would amount to nothing more than subjective projections. Schillebeeckx goes as far as stating that there is a 'pre-linguistic element' in experience.[152] On the one hand, we cannot express this pre-linguistic element without interpretation. On the other hand, every interpretative expression falls short of grasping

---

[148] Edward Schillebeeckx, *Church. The Human Story of God* [1989], CW vol. 10, trans. John Bowden (London: Bloomsbury, 2014), 23–4 [24].
[149] Schillebeeckx, *Christ*, 36 [50].
[150] See Dupré, 'Experience and Interpretation', 42–4.
[151] Schillebeeckx, *Church*, 37 [38].
[152] Ibid., 78 [80].

and objectifying this objective element.[153] Schillebeeckx accords primacy to this pre-linguistic dimension of encounter over and against the interpretative and reflective dimensions, without separating these aspects of the experience of revelation.[154] The reality of revelation is always richer than what human beings can experience and how it is expressed conceptually and reflectively. Revelation occurs within experience without ever becoming identical with experience.[155] This dialectical interrelation, of an objective pre-linguistic and a subjective conceptual dimension, clearly comes to the fore in the following description of revelation:

> 'Revelation' can be understood at two different levels of language. On the one hand revelation is essentially that which cannot be named, the inexpressible which lies beyond all conceptual knowledge and is the basis of experience of faith – of the praxis of faith and the thought of faith. On the other hand, revelation is also the Unnameable caught in reflection: the conceptualised, as it were 'comprehended', manifestation of the not directly comprehensible foundation of faith. At its deepest, revelation is the non-reflective, pre-theoretical givenness – or more correctly, the self-giving – of that which is always already the basis of the process of faith, that which is constitutive for faith and makes it possible. … That revelation is the foundation of experiences of faith means that faith owes neither itself nor its distinctive content to itself. It is a gift and at the same time a human choice, both in one.[156]

In 'Experience and Faith', Schillebeeckx associates this mysterious ineffable dimension, which gives itself in experiences of revelation, expressly with the work of the Holy Spirit. No experience of revelation is 'purely human' or understandable without God's initiative and work in grace.[157] As Schillebeeckx observes himself, this understanding of revelation, as the unity of an unnameable self-giving and its conceptualized reception and response, corresponds closely to Rahner's distinction between the transcendental and the categorical dimensions of revelation. Both Rahner and Schillebeeckx accord a clear primacy to the transcendental dimension of revelation.[158] But, contrary to Rahner, Schillebeeckx comes up with this description after an intensive engagement with hermeneutics and critical theory. Accordingly, his account of the categorical aspect of experience is more nuanced and attentive to the particular, and potentially distorting of the, conditions of any historical experiential encounter with revelation. Nevertheless, the directionality of non-reflective givenness in the experience of revelation – something which is crucial to avoiding a subjectivist reduction – cannot be explained

---

[153] Ibid., 37–8 [38].
[154] See also Boeve, 'Experience according to Schillebeeckx', 214–15, who describes this position as 'the primacy of experience over interpretation, in its very indissoluble bond to it'.
[155] See Hilkert, 'Experience and Revelation', 68–9.
[156] Edward Schillebeeckx, *Mensen als verhaal van God* (Baarn: Nelissen, 1989), 46–7 (my translation).
[157] Schillebeeckx, 'Experience and Faith', 30.
[158] See also Maas, 'Stem en stilte', 60, who argues that the 'transcendental' functions epistemologically primarily in Rahner and more ontologically in Schillebeeckx. However, my analysis of Rahner's understanding of transcendentality has shown that the ontological and epistemological are much more closely interrelated in his theology.

with reference to hermeneutics alone, but ultimately requires a metaphysical account. Hence, Schillebeeckx's hermeneutics of experience must be seen in connection with his metaphysics of experience.

6 Conclusion

In this chapter I have retraced the development of Schillebeeckx's theological epistemology and its focus on experience. I have argued that this epistemology revolves around a fundamental dialectic – one which can be variously expressed as a dialectic between experience and concept, between history and speculation, between mystery and intelligibility or between subjectivity and objectivity. I argued that it can be aptly characterized as a dialectical interrelation of metaphysics and hermeneutics.

In his earliest works, Schillebeeckx provides a metaphysical account of human experience and human knowledge, with a view of supporting theological claims to knowledge about God resulting from the concrete history of salvation. The incarnational approach that guides his development of a perspectival epistemology seeks to explain that the world of concrete historical experience enables real, albeit limited, knowledge of God. While the metaphysical element seems to be more dominant, the perspectival epistemology already contains the seeds of a more hermeneutical approach. Schillebeeckx is less inclined to follow the transcendental turn to the subject and focuses instead upon the revelatory aspect of the contingency and on the gratuitous givenness of reality. Nevertheless, there are significant parallels, rather than irreconcilable differences, with Rahner's approach. This became especially apparent when looking at Schillebeeckx's theological anthropology and his views on the relationship between nature and grace. Like Rahner, Schillebeeckx operates inductively, starting with the Christian account of revelation in Jesus Christ, and subsequently employs transcendental and metaphysical arguments in order to explain the universal intelligibility and significance of these salvific events. Schillebeeckx's metaphysics and transcendental argumentation are informed by – and operate in the service of – the self-interpretation of the Christian tradition of faith. However, his insight into the limitations of the explanatory power of speculative arguments, in view of the concrete nature of human historical experience, already signals the critical-hermeneutical direction his later work will take.

Schillebeeckx himself describes his hermeneutical turn as being a break with the metaphysics inspired by De Petter. The fundamental roles played by history and language accentuate the particular character of any concrete experience of truth. He starts to analyse the various factors that play a role in experience, such as interpretative frameworks and ideological distortions, all of which are informed by the insights of hermeneutical and critical theory. This can be regarded as the actualization of the hermeneutical potential of his perspectival epistemology. Instead of being concerned with the relation between concept and experience, the leading question now concerns the relation between experience and interpretation. Schillebeeckx's dialectical account of experience argues that interpretation is constitutive of experience; all experience is interpreted experience. Since revelation is mediated by experience, it is similarly marked by this dialectic. However, in order to avoid a subjectivist reduction of experience and revelation, Schillebeeckx also draws our attention to the crucial objective aspect of experience. His explication of this objective dimension shows the continued relevance of the metaphysical framework of the implicit intuition. This finds expression in the emphasis on the element of givenness in every experience, as well as in the 'inner interpretative elements' and the 'pre-linguistic element' of experience. A metaphysical framework remains key to Schillebeeckx's argument for a normative and directional dynamic in experience and revelation.

It can be concluded, therefore, that his critical-hermeneutical account of experience remains intimately connected to his metaphysics of experience. This continuity explains why Schillebeeckx describes revelation and faith, even as late as in 1994, in a manner which is highly reminiscent of his early perspectival epistemology: 'Revelation is just as much the work of searching, interpreting human beings as it is (for that very reason) the work of God. Faith has to do with the absolute, but never in an absolute manner, hence only historical, purely relative absoluteness, imperfect and open to correction.'[159] This quotation attests to the fundamental dialectic between the objective and subjective aspects – a dialectic which Schillebeeckx explicates with the help of metaphysical and hermeneutical arguments.

This dialectical interrelation of metaphysics and hermeneutics offers a crucial interpretative key to understanding Schillebeeckx's theological method. I develop this claim over the course of the following two chapters. First, Schillebeeckx uses the metaphysical account of the normative and guiding objective directionality in experience *diachronically*, in order to develop his understanding of the hermeneutics of a living tradition as a 'continuity in discontinuities'. This will be examined in Chapter 8. Second, Schillebeeckx also resorts to a *diachronic* use of the normative directionality in order to develop a new 'natural theology' of the contrast experience as a heuristic of grace. This will be the topic of discussion in Chapter 9.

---

[159] Edward Schillebeeckx, 'Discontinuities in Christian Dogmas' [1994], in *Essays. Ongoing Theological Quests*, 88.

8

A hermeneutics of living tradition: Faithful creativity and self-giving mystery

1 Introduction

In Chapter 7, I analysed Schillebeeckx's dialectical account of experience and revelation with reference to his joint application of metaphysical and hermeneutical arguments. Due to his critical-hermeneutical turn, Schillebeeckx becomes increasingly aware of the hermeneutical conditions of experience. His reflections on the crucial role of interpretative frameworks in experience attest to this transformed approach to experience. A particular human experience only becomes a Christian religious experience when it is interpreted in the light of the Christian tradition. Yet, what constitutes this Christian tradition exactly? In this chapter I discuss Schillebeeckx's hermeneutics of tradition and demonstrate that this hermeneutics only becomes intelligible when considered in connection with its metaphysical presuppositions. In brief, the dialectic between hermeneutics and metaphysics that characterizes Schillebeeckx's understanding of experience and revelation finds a *diachronic* application in his theology of correlation, which seeks to explain the possibility of a continuity of understanding throughout historical discontinuities.

First, I discuss how Schillebeeckx appropriates insights from Heidegger, Gadamer and Ricoeur with a view to explaining the hermeneutics of tradition as an understanding of the past, in the light of the present and oriented towards the future. Crucially, for Schillebeeckx, this hermeneutics of tradition is informed, but not governed solely, by general philosophical principles. It must also take the specific object of theological understanding into account. Second, I turn to Schillebeeckx's reconceptualization of correlation theology as a mutual correlation of past and present experiences. His hermeneutical insights are now translated into the recognition of the theological relevance of the particularities of context as co-constitutive of the message of faith. This leads Schillebeeckx to advocate, what I term, a 'correlation of correlations' that seeks to be attentive to historical change and to discontinuity. He introduces proportional identity as a norm for theological interpretation, in order to maintain the possibility of a continuity in discontinuities. Subsequently, I examine the critical reception of Schillebeeckx's correlation theology by Lieven Boeve and Erik Borgman, respectively. Their respective critiques are both aimed at Schillebeeckx's concern with continuity and instead elaborate upon the role of discontinuity in theological understanding.

However, their heavy emphasis on discontinuity jeopardizes Schillebeeckx's correlational project. For this reason, I propose revisiting the theme of continuity in Schillebeeckx's correlational theology. By analysing the notion of proportional identity in greater detail, I will argue that Schillebeeckx's hermeneutics of tradition must be understood in close connection with his metaphysical framework.

2 Revelation: Past and present

According to Schillebeeckx, Christianity is 'an *experience of faith which becomes message*'.[1] Christianity began with an encounter – the revelatory and salvific encounter with the historical person of Jesus Christ. The various expressions of this encounter gave rise to the Christian tradition: 'What was experience for others yesterday is tradition for us today; and what is experience for us today will again be tradition for others tomorrow. But what once was experience can only be handed down for others tomorrow, at least as living tradition, in and through renewed experiences.'[2] Hence, in order to disclose the revelatory potential of past experiences today, they must be confronted with the contemporary situation. In this *living tradition*, past revelatory experiences can become a horizon for the possibility of new revelatory experiences today.

Since historical circumstances and hermeneutical horizons constantly change, understanding biblical texts, ecclesial documents and other texts and symbols of the Christian tradition requires a *reinterpretative* effort that takes the conditions of the present and the differences with the past into account. How is it possible, then, to remain faithful to the revelatory words of the past?[3] Schillebeeckx draws extensively on general principles of hermeneutical theory to deal with this issue. He argues that since theology 'speaks the same language as every man-in-the-world', there cannot be a 'separate "theological" hermeneutics'.[4] At the same time, since theology has a distinct and unique object, it is not possible to reduce theology to 'general hermeneutics'.[5] As we will see below, Schillebeeckx's appropriation of hermeneutics remains fundamentally connected to a specific theological-ontological argumentation.

2.1 Historicity and truth

Schillebeeckx appropriates Hans-Georg Gadamer's rehabilitation of tradition and prejudices in order to explain that a contemporary lens is a necessary condition, rather

---

[1] Schillebeeckx, *Interim Report*, 43 [50].
[2] Ibid.
[3] Schillebeeckx, 'Towards a Catholic Use of Hermeneutics', 1–4 [3–7]. Schillebeeckx closely associates the issue of the 'hermeneutics of tradition' with the 'development of dogma'. See, for instance, ibid., 4 [6–7]; 12 [17–18]. See also Daniel P. Thompson, 'Schillebeeckx on the Development of Doctrine', *Theological Studies* 62 (2001): 303–21; Annekatrien Depoorter, 'Orthopraxis as a Criterion for Orthodoxy? Edward Schillebeeckx' View on the Development and the Characteristic of Religious Truth', in *Theology and the Quest for Truth: Historical- and Systematic-theological Studies*, ed. Mathijs Lambertigts, Lieven Boeve and Terrence Merrigan (Leuven: Peeters, 2006), 165–80.
[4] Schillebeeckx, 'Towards a Catholic Use of Hermeneutics', 11 [15–16].
[5] Ibid., 11 [16].

than a distortion, for the historical understanding of a tradition's truth.[6] We participate in the historical tradition that we try to understand through these prejudices. In order to understand a text of this tradition, we reconstruct the historical horizon of a text and relate this to our own contemporary horizon, so as to effect a 'fusion of horizons'.[7] We must recognize the alterity of a tradition and its texts within this dialogical engagement. As Paul Ricoeur points out, distanciation provides texts with an autonomy that contains a critical potential.[8] Schillebeeckx considers this insight to be crucial in maintaining the objective normativity of the tradition. While we cannot but approach the tradition with our own expectations and perspectives, we must also be prepared to recognize the normativity of the otherness that manifests itself in the texts of a tradition. Interpretation cannot be *eisegesis*; an interpreter must be prepared to submit herself to the otherness of a text and allow herself to be corrected by this otherness.[9] Schillebeeckx thus concludes that 'it belongs to man's very being to be within a tradition while reactivating it ... understanding is a *reinterpretative understanding of tradition*'.[10] The hermeneutics of tradition is characterized by the double aspects of belonging to, and being bound by, tradition, on the one hand, and a critical-historical distance and productive creativity regarding tradition, on the other. The concrete particularity of human subjectivity conditions understanding, but interpretation cannot be reduced to subjective intentionality without sacrificing the objectivity of a tradition.

Importantly, this tension between subjectivity and objectivity raises the question of whether there can still be a continuity in understanding at all. Put differently, given the historical conditions of all understanding, can there be an identity of faith throughout time? According to Schillebeeckx, a theological appropriation of hermeneutical theory must be attentive to this question of objective truth or 'identity of faith'.[11] Simply repeating older formulas and expressions of faith does not guarantee a fidelity to the normativity of a tradition and, therefore, offers no solution in this regard. 'Historical objectivity is the truth of the past *in the light of the present* and not a reconstruction of the past in its unrepeatable factuality.'[12] Nor is it possible to distil an unchangeable essence or kernel from the varying and changing modes of expression. While Schillebeeckx does not deny that there is such a timeless essence, he does point out that 'this "essence" is never given to us as a pure essence, but is always concealed *in* a historical mode of expression'.[13] Thus, rather than attempting to identify this pure essence in past expressions, we must strive to represent the truth of faith anew by way of reinterpretative understanding: 'If an earlier truth is to be preserved in accordance

---

[6] Gadamer, *Truth and Method*, 271–7.
[7] Schillebeeckx, 'Towards a Catholic Use of Hermeneutics', 19 [29].
[8] Ricoeur, 'The Hermeneutical Function of Distanciation', 75–6.
[9] Schillebeeckx, 'Towards a Catholic Use of Hermeneutics', 17–18 [26]. That Schillebeeckx duly acknowledges the critical and normative force, originating in the otherness of the text, is a point entirely missed by Leo Scheffcyzk, 'Christology in the Context of Experience: On the Interpretation of Christ by E. Schillebeeckx', *The Thomist* 48 (1984): 383–408, who argues that 'the crucial question as to whether the self-understanding can be questioned or even corrected radically by the text is in any case not affirmatively answered here' (390).
[10] Schillebeeckx, 'Towards a Catholic Use of Hermeneutics', 18–19 [27].
[11] Ibid., 6 [10].
[12] Ibid., 17 [25].
[13] Ibid., 8 [12].

with its original intention, it must be reformulated in the light of the present and interpreted differently.'[14] It is through historical changes that continuity, identity and objectivity manifest themselves.

Schillebeeckx's critical appropriation of hermeneutics simultaneously seeks to alert the theologian to the limitations of hermeneutics. Crucially, this reinterpretation of the past in the present remains incomplete, unless it has an orientation towards the future. Schillebeeckx calls to mind that biblical texts mediate an eschatological notion of truth. The fullness of truth belongs to the future and, therefore, 'to the extent that its content is already realized', truth 'discloses itself as essentially a *promise*'.[15] The open future dimension of truth implies that it can never be understood through theory alone – that it also involves *praxis*. In other words, orthopraxis forms an essential criterion of the authentic, 'orthodox' interpretation.[16] This emphasis on the role played by praxis reflects Jürgen Habermas's influence, as examined earlier. Schillebeeckx follows Habermas's practical correction of Gadamer's theoretical hermeneutics and points to the necessity of adopting a critical stance with regard to the actual status quo of the understanding of a tradition:

> *Traditum* is not simply a text, or existential possibilities that are simply expressed within it. It is more than a closed *depositum* on which we draw again and again in the light of the present. There certainly is a 'deposit of faith', but its content still remains, on the basis of the promise already realized in Christ (realized in fact, but nonetheless still really a *promise*), a promise-for-us, with the result that interpretation becomes 'hermeneutics of praxis'.[17]

For Schillebeeckx, Christian tradition and church are anything but exempt from elements of ideological repression and violence. Theological interpretation must, therefore, be 'permanently and consistently continued in critical thought'.[18] In other words, there is no adequate hermeneutical retrieval of the tradition without a hermeneutics of suspicion.

Apart from the necessity to expand hermeneutics with the help of critical theory, Schillebeeckx also draws attention to another limitation of hermeneutics. While a hermeneutical approach rightly discloses the problems of an overly objectivist approach to truth, which tends to disregard the subject's historicity, its emphasis on the subjective and historical access to truth risks losing sight of truth's objective reality. When truth is fully determined by its historical expression, it becomes merely 'authentic'; truth, then, is something which only 'appeals' to people in a specific situation.[19] In other words, the concept of truth is placed on a slippery slope, thereby

---

[14] Ibid., 20 [30].
[15] Ibid., 24 [36].
[16] Ibid., 24–5 [36–7]. See also Schillebeeckx, 'Theological Criteria', 57–62 [63–70], for a more extensive discussion of orthopraxis as a criterion of theological interpretation. I will attend to the role of praxis in the discussion of the contrast experience in greater detail in Chapter 9.
[17] Schillebeeckx, 'Towards a Catholic Use of Hermeneutics', 25 [37].
[18] Schillebeeckx, 'The New Critical Theory and Theological Hermeneutics', 135 [154].
[19] Schillebeeckx, 'Towards a Catholic Use of Hermeneutics', 6 [10]. According to Schillebeeckx, Bultmann's theology tends to favour a 'pure existentiality' and, therefore, risks a forgetfulness of objectivity.

losing its universal dimension. Over and against such a narrow and solipsistic notion of truth, Schillebeeckx maintains that truth 'is never found only in *my* interpretation of reality, but only in my going beyond my own historical answer'.[20] The discovery of truth is a social endeavour and involves the willingness to confront and to test one's own conception of truth with and against other notions of truth, both past and present. At the same time, Schillebeeckx also argues that this pluralism is not absolute: 'Being conscious of pluralism in fact means implicitly transcending it because, in that case, one does not regard one's own frame of thought as exclusive.'[21] We can recognize the limits of our own perspective, we can dialogue with people holding other perspectives and we can debate over different interpretations of truth. This shows that pluralism cannot have the last word. Still, this acknowledgement of pluralism raises the question of how to deal with so-called conflicts of interpretation. In order to address this issue, Schillebeeckx connects his hermeneutics of tradition with a theological metaphysics that elaborates the objective dimension of truth and understanding.

2.2 The mystery which gives us to think

Schillebeeckx views truth as being multidimensional. Our specific reading patterns and scientific models deeply influence how we relate to truth. For this reason, 'there are as many different levels of objectivity and of truth as there are scientific models of reading'.[22] Theological hermeneutics, therefore, requires a variety of analyses of language, such as the ones provided by phenomenology, structuralism and language philosophy. However, these analyses employ a 'methodological reduction; they place the reality of what is meaningfully said between brackets'.[23] Ricoeur sought to maintain the connection between ontology and hermeneutics via the distinction between 'sense' and 'reference'. Calling attention to the 'universal power of world disclosure', he decentres the interpreting subject and, thus, posits the subject as a *cogito blessé*. Schillebeeckx similarly employs an ontological argument to balance the subjective dimension of interpretation, yet chooses a different approach. Remarkably, he draws on themes and notions from his early metaphysics of knowledge in order to account for the objectivity of truth in his hermeneutics of tradition.

The fact that we cannot approach truth neutrally and abstractly does not mean that our interpretative relation to the truth of a text becomes arbitrary and completely subjective. Schillebeeckx argues that language has an inherent ontological dimension: 'Speaking is above all saying something about something, or about someone, to someone.'[24] Interpreting a text, therefore, necessitates asking about the reality to which it bears witness. Schillebeeckx turns to the later Heidegger's reflections on the

---

[20] Edward Schillebeeckx, 'The Problem of the Infallibility of the Church's Office: A Theological Reflection', *Concilium* 3, no. 9 (1973): 83.
[21] Schillebeeckx, 'Theological Criteria', 49 [54–5]. See also Schillebeeckx, 'Towards a Catholic Use of Hermeneutics', 23 [34–5].
[22] Ibid., 11 [16].
[23] Schillebeeckx, 'Linguistic Criteria', 34 [37].
[24] Ibid., 25 [27].

ontological dimension of language in order to bring this reality back to bear upon the hermeneutical discussion.[25] He is specifically interested in Heidegger's insight into the priority of listening over speaking. Echoing Ricoeur's notion of the *cogito blessé*, Schillebeeckx emphasizes that we are always first addressed by 'the event of being'.[26] This event demands to be expressed, yet simultaneously determines this linguistic expression. Language, thus, mediates and discloses the truth of being. At the same time, there is always something in language 'which is "not thought of", which *gives us to think*, but is itself never thought'.[27] Schillebeeckx incorporates this ontological priority of givenness into his theological hermeneutics of tradition. In effect, the argumentation is very similar to the dialectical account of experience and interpretation. Yet, as we will see, the ontological dimension of hermeneutics that Heidegger and Ricoeur develop philosophically finds a distinctly theological appropriation in Schillebeeckx's argument.

Schillebeeckx argues that in the act of interpretation we go 'beyond the texts and their meaning' in order to enquire about 'the *reality* to which the texts intentionally or unintentionally bear witness'.[28] The 'hermeneutical basis' that enables such a move is the fact that we ourselves have a 'living relationship' with the same reality that is mediated by the text.[29] Schillebeeckx claims that this existential connection is necessary to all human understanding. Referring to Merleau-Ponty, he argues that linguistic symbols can only have a meaning for us if they can be related to our concrete lived experience. For this reason, a hermeneutics of the Christian tradition must be confronted with a hermeneutics of experience.[30]

The outline of Schillebeeckx's method of correlation, to be discussed below, already manifests itself here. He explains this hermeneutical role of the living relationship to reality with the example of the Eucharist. We can understand a doctrine about the Eucharist, because in our celebration of the Eucharist we are related to the same reality about which this doctrine speaks.[31] At the same time, Schillebeeckx also maintains that in view of its own distinct 'object', theological understanding is not reducible to general hermeneutics.[32] Crucially, the object of theological hermeneutics, the divine mystery brought to expression in the texts of the Christian tradition, exerts its own influence in the process of understanding.

While theological understanding shares the general principles of human understanding, it ultimately deals with a particular givenness; theological hermeneutics

---

[25] Schillebeeckx discusses Heidegger's view on language as the medium of the revelation of Being and the corresponding duty for the human person to listen to this revelation in Schillebeeckx, 'Theological Criteria', 34–8 [37–42]. For Heidegger's turn to language, see Jeanrond, *Theological Hermeneutics*, 62–3.
[26] Schillebeeckx, 'Linguistic Criteria', 35 [38].
[27] Schillebeeckx, 'Towards a Catholic Use of Hermeneutics', 22 [33]. Schillebeeckx refers here specifically to Martin Heidegger, *Was heißt Denken?* (Tübingen: Niemeyer, 1954).
[28] Schillebeeckx, 'Towards a Catholic Use of Hermeneutics', 22 [33].
[29] Ibid.
[30] Edward Schillebeeckx, 'The Context and Value of Faith-Talk' [1972], in *The Understanding of Faith*, 14. No specific reference is made to the work of Merleau-Ponty by Schillebeeckx.
[31] Schillebeeckx, 'Towards a Catholic Use of Hermeneutics', 22–3 [33–4].
[32] Ibid., 11 [16].

is 'subject to God's speaking to us'.³³ At its core, Schillebeeckx's hermeneutics of tradition is grounded in his theological view of reality as continually being addressed by God's grace.³⁴ Transposing the later Heidegger's ontological understanding of language in a theological key, Schillebeeckx argues that our interpretation of tradition is, first and foremost, a response to an objective appeal to the living reality of grace. As we have observed previously, Schillebeeckx is convinced that grace presents itself universally throughout human history. The texts of the Christian tradition offer particular mediations of this revelation of grace, by way of their various attempts of interpretative expression of this reality. Even though none of these articulations are ever able to represent the truth of faith fully, they nevertheless contain 'an inexpressible *objective perspective* which is again and again meaningfully suggested from and in a changing historical outline and which makes itself felt *in* every historical outline'.³⁵

Now this objective perspective of faith can be brought to light again, precisely through the act of reinterpretation and can, thereby, become a power for transformative action. Yet, in order for such a faithful reinterpretation to succeed, it is first necessary that the interpreter opens herself to 'the mystery of promise which gives itself in history'.³⁶ Since our understanding is historically conditioned, reinterpretation involves the creative process of finding new expressions of the message mediated by the texts of the tradition. In these reinterpretative expressions, we attempt to 'suggest the mystery in a meaningful and objective way', employing language and symbols that bear a meaningful connection with our own context.³⁷ While such a reinterpretative understanding necessarily involves changes, there is an element of continuity in our theological understanding. This continuity is neither 'the result of a human plan' nor 'a destiny or a promise only existing in heaven'.³⁸ Continuity in theological understanding is an event brought about by the ineffable and absolute mystery which 'embraces us in grace, without our being able to embrace it'.³⁹ Crucially, this event happens *within* the creative theological reinterpretation and reformulations. Reinterpretative understanding, thus, consists of a dynamic interplay of creative agency and obedient submission. Importantly, it is not the individual theologian but the community of the church which sustains this theological reinterpretation of faith.⁴⁰ This explicit situating of the interpreting theologian within the community of believers attests to the social dimension of truth and its interpretation. The church as a community of interpreters can bring to light the mystery of grace and can, thereby, function as sacrament of the world.⁴¹

[33] Ibid., 18 [26].
[34] See also Hilkert, 'Hermeneutics of History in the Theology of Edward Schillebeeckx', 123–8, who similarly argues that for Schillebeeckx, 'the ultimate basis for reading the past tradition accurately is then the present experience of living in the same tradition of grace' (128).
[35] Schillebeeckx, 'Towards a Catholic Use of Hermeneutics', 27 [40].
[36] Ibid., 27–8 [39–41].
[37] Ibid., 8 [13].
[38] Ibid., 28 [42].
[39] Ibid., 27 [40].
[40] On this ecclesial dimension of theological hermeneutics, see also Schillebeeckx, 'Theological Criteria', 62–4 [70–2].
[41] Schillebeeckx, 'Towards a Catholic Use of Hermeneutics', 29 [44].

Overall, Schillebeeckx's theological hermeneutics of tradition ultimately assumes an important theological commonality between the texts of the tradition and their contemporary interpreters – a commonality that he explains with the help of a metaphysical argument. His early metaphysics, therefore, remains an intrinsic element of his new hermeneutical approach. Biblical and dogmatic texts form an expression of an existential encounter with the reality of grace that continues to offer itself in the present. These expressions are dependent upon historical conditions and, therefore, change over time; however, these varied expressions also contain an ineffable *objective perspective*. With the help of general hermeneutical principles, and through practical involvement, we are able to reinterpret past experiences mediated by the tradition. However, at a more fundamental and theological level, understanding the revelatory truth perspective of these past expressions is enabled by our own existential encounters with revelatory truth today. As we will see in Chapter 9, Schillebeeckx develops the notion of the contrast experience to explain the universal possibility of encountering salvific grace. At the same time, this reinterpretation of past experiences of grace fosters and supports our search for, and the identification of, the presence of grace in the present. This insight into the mutual dialectic between past and present experiences of revelation forms the heart of Schillebeeckx's theological hermeneutics. Its central importance for Schillebeeckx's theological method can be demonstrated by considering his reconceptualization of correlational theology.

3 Reconceptualizing correlation theology

Ted Schoof notes that the methodological reflections developed in both *God the Future of Man* and *The Understanding of Faith* formed the 'springboard' for Schillebeeckx's Christological work.[42] In the *Books Jesus* and *Christ*, Schillebeeckx applies his hermeneutical framework as a critical confrontation of past and present encounters to the historical manifestation of grace. This leads him to examine the early Christian expressions of the experience of divine grace in and through their encounter with Jesus of Nazareth.[43] In *Interim Report*, he reflects on the theological method used in these books. He now characterizes this method as a 'mutually critical correlation' between the Christian tradition of experience and contemporary experience.[44] Both sources are equally necessary to understanding the revelation in Jesus Christ. On the one hand, there is no such thing as 'the salvific significance of Jesus "in itself"', a sort of timeless, suprahistorical abstract datum'.[45] On the other hand, we also cannot 'arbitrarily make something out of Jesus or just see in him a "chiffre", a figure onto whom we can project

---

[42] Ted Mark Schoof, 'Introduction to the New Edition "God the Future of Men"', in Schillebeeckx, *God the Future of Men*, xv.
[43] See Boeve, 'Experience according to Schillebeeckx', 205, who argues that in the essays of *The Understanding of Faith* Schillebeeckx completed the preparatory work for the theological project that he develops in his Christological trilogy. Interestingly, in his discussion of Schillebeeckx's hermeneutics, Boeve does not attend to the key essay 'Towards a Catholic Use of Hermeneutics'.
[44] Schillebeeckx, *Interim Report*, 8 [9].
[45] Ibid., 43 [50].

our own human experiences'.[46] This shows that the dialectic between the subjective and the objective dimensions of revelatory truth, identified previously, informs these Christological investigations. But, how do we relate these past and present experiences precisely?

Schillebeeckx's method of mutually critical correlation can be situated within the wider circle of correlation theologians, such as Paul Tillich, Hans Küng, and David Tracy.[47] However, he also contributes to the further development of this correlational method. Tillich famously introduced the method of correlation in his *Systematic Theology*, defining correlation as the 'unity' of 'dependence and independence' between situation and tradition.[48] Through the inter-in-dependence of what the situation asks for and what the tradition answers, Tillich attempted to respond to a dilemma which has haunted theology since Friedrich Schleiermacher: the dilemma of mediation.[49] David Tracy observes in *Blessed Rage for Order* that Tillich's method merely juxtaposes instead of correlating tradition and situation. As a result, Tillich turns too quickly to the tradition and fails to take the situation sufficiently seriously.[50] Tracy argues instead for a *mutually critical correlation* as the basis for 'mutual illuminations and corrections'.[51] Emphasizing the element of mutuality, Tracy argues that a proper confrontation between tradition and situation implies that the tradition can have a critical impact upon the situation and that the situation can have a critical impact upon the tradition.

Schillebeeckx seeks to build upon the correlational method as developed by Tillich by identifying two problems.[52] First, he argues that the integrity and autonomy of the questioning human person is not duly recognized. In Tillich's account, the human question only becomes really apparent in the light of the answer of Christian revelation.[53] I will return to this critique in Chapter 9, in the discussion of the contrast experience. Second, Schillebeeckx follows Tracy and argues that such a correlational theology is too one-directional, insofar as it locates the answer to human questions exclusively in the religious tradition. Seeking to address this second issue, he introduces his own account of the concept of mutually critical correlation.[54]

---

[46] Ibid.
[47] See Fiorenza, 'Systematic Theology: Task and Methods', 42–6, for a succinct account of these correlation theologies.
[48] Paul Tillich, *Systematic Theology*, vol. 2 (Chicago: The University of Chicago Press, 1957), 13. In this second volume of his *Systematic Theology*, Tillich refines his notion of correlation by responding to the comments and the critiques of the concept of correlation developed in *Systematic Theology*, vol. 1 (Chicago: The University of Chicago Press, 1951), 59–86.
[49] See John P. Clayton, *The Concept of Correlation: Paul Tillich and the Possibility of a Mediating Theology* (Berlin: De Gruyter, 1980), 34–86; and Annekatrien Depoorter, 'Correlatie onder vuur? Bedenkingen bij de theologische methode van Paul Tillich en Edward Schillebeeckx', *Bijdragen. International Journal in Philosophy and Theology* 66 (2005): 38–44.
[50] Tracy, *Blessed Rage*, 45–6.
[51] Ibid., 32.
[52] Edward Schillebeeckx, 'Correlation between Human Question and Christian Answer' [1970], in *The Understanding of Faith*, 74–6 [84–7].
[53] Ibid., 74 [84].
[54] Ibid., 75 [85–6]. Although Schillebeeckx's essay on correlation theology dates from 1970, it was Tracy who first explicitly talks about 'mutually critical' correlation in *Blessed Rage for Order* (1975). Schillebeeckx first uses the term 'mutually critical correlation' in *Interim Report* (1978). At the same time, Tracy refers in *The Analogical Imagination*, 88, n. 4, specifically to Schillebeeckx when explaining the notion of 'mutually critical correlations'.

Examining this reconceptualization of correlation theology discloses, once again, the mutual application of hermeneutics and metaphysics in Schillebeeckx's work. Faithful to the hermeneutical reorientation of his theological method, Schillebeeckx points to the co-constitutive role the cultural-historical contexts play in any encounter with, and expression of, revelation. Every revelatory encounter of faith is, in fact, a correlation between culture and the offer of grace. While the cultural-historical medium is necessary for any encounter with revelation, no particular mediation of either the past or the present can claim to be a complete and comprehensive expression of this mystery. For this reason, Schillebeeckx advocates what I call a 'correlation of correlations', that is a critical confrontation between past and present encounters with grace that is aimed at actualizing faith and tradition today. This critical confrontation requires a criterion and in order to develop this criterion, Schillebeeckx resorts to hermeneutical as well as metaphysical arguments.

3.1 The medium co-constitutes the message

Schillebeeckx's valedictory lecture, delivered in 1982, contains the clearest presentation of his own alternative view on correlation method. Following the general structure of correlational theology, he describes Christian theology as the dialectical interrelation of two poles: tradition and situation.[55] However, contrary to other proponents of correlation theology, Schillebeeckx argues that both past tradition and present situation are in fact already correlations of two poles. Rather than comparing his model to that of Tillich, Schillebeeckx reacts to what he considers to be a misreading of his own hermeneutical theology by Hans Küng. In a discussion of Schillebeeckx's method, Küng ultimately locates the normative and definitive manifestation of revelation rather exclusively in the scriptures of the New Testament.[56] Schillebeeckx objects to this focus on tradition as the sole source of theology. It mistakenly views the situation as a 'theology-free zone' – an area that needs to be 'irrigated' by applying a normative biblical or ecclesiastical message to it.[57] Accordingly, the situation is reduced to a mere channel of revelation.

In response, Schillebeeckx argues that all of human history has 'inherent theological significance', because God's creative and liberating action extends to both past and present situations.[58] This assertion basically restates the view that every human person lives within a theologal horizon. As we will see in Chapter 9, Schillebeeckx introduces the concept of the contrast experience as a heuristic instrument that helps us to discern and identify the potential manifestations of God's universal self-revelation. Assuming that grace is a universal reality in the concrete life of people, not only the past tradition but also the present situation must be regarded as being capable of expressing this offer of grace. Schillebeeckx also refers to this offer of grace as the universal 'religious

---

[55] Edward Schillebeeckx, 'Theological Interpretation of Faith in 1983' [1983], in *Essays. Ongoing Theological Quests*, 57.
[56] See Hans Küng, 'Toward a New Consensus in Catholic (and Ecumenical) Theology', in *Consensus in Theology? A Dialogue with Hans Küng and Edward Schillebeeckx*, ed. Leonard Swidler (Philadelphia: The Westminster Press, 1980), 16–17.
[57] Schillebeeckx, 'Theological Interpretation of Faith', 57–9.
[58] Ibid., 52; 57.

substance'.[59] Crucially, particular situational expressions perform a co-constitutive role in their mediation of this religious substance. In other words, as the medium of the message, situation is co-constitutive of the message that becomes tradition. It is helpful to revisit Schillebeeckx's understanding of revelation and interpretation in order to explicate this alternative model of correlation.

There is no experience of revelation without conscious theoretical and practical interpretation and appropriation. A faithful response to revelation necessarily employs a particular interpretative framework and, therefore, takes on the cultural-historical features that are peculiar to this particular time and place. To put it very succinctly, human beings 'stamp' divine revelation.[60] This was not any different in the past than it is for us today. The apostles, gospel writers and other authors of the tradition had to take their own cultural situation into account in order to express their religious understanding and corresponding praxis. Similarly, assuming that God's self-disclosure in grace continues today, our contemporary interpretation of revelatory experiences is also a cultural embodiment of the offer of grace. Accordingly, both past tradition and current situation are, in effect, the correlation of two poles, namely, the offer of grace and the cultural-historical framework.[61] Schillebeeckx applies this general structure of revelation, as co-constituted by divine offer and human appropriation and expression, to the gospel message. The gospel is characterized by a 'perennial dialectics' between universality and particularity.[62] On the one hand, the gospel message can never be tied to, or contained within, one particular cultural expression. This universal message eludes concrete and contingent particularity, thereby transcending all particular cultures. On the other hand, the trans-cultural gospel needs concrete particularity in order to become manifest at all. In other words, cultural historical forms are constitutive of revelation as the necessary mediation of revelation. The medium *is* the message.[63]

The impossibility of any specific cultural form to mediate revelation absolutely must not disguise the positive function these concrete forms serve. It is precisely in, rather than in spite of, the particularity of his history that someone like Jesus continues to be relevant for us today. Universality or 'Christian constants' emerge in the historical transmission of this concrete history, not by abstraction from history.[64] In other words, the universality of Christian faith is always contaminated by history and is never available in its purity. The co-constitutive role played by context in revelation implies that every articulation of revelation, whether biblical, ecclesiastical or other, is necessarily contextual. The particularity of any contextual historical situation affects the universal revelation in two ways. On the one hand, it forms the condition that

---

[59] Ibid., 58.
[60] Ibid., 61.
[61] Ibid., 57–8.
[62] Ibid., 57.
[63] The English version of the valedictory lecture translates the term *bemiddeling* as 'vehicle'. I have instead chosen to render it as 'medium' or 'mediation', because it is closer to the Dutch original and also articulates the active role of the medium, while the term 'vehicle' has a rather instrumental connotation.
[64] Schillebeeckx, 'Theological Interpretation of Faith', 57; 61. In *Interim Report*, 44–7 [51–5], he provides an example of such constants by identifying four 'structural principles' that characterize the various experiences of the New Testament of grace. See also his so-called 'anthropological constants' in *Christ*, 727–37 [734–43].

makes communication and mediation of this message possible to historical people. On the other hand, it also limits and conditions that same communication. While there is an enduring religious substance, this substance is never available to us 'a-historically' or 'supra-culturally', but must be 'actualised in and acclimatised to particular cultures'.[65] This sounds strikingly similar to Schillebeeckx's early perspectival epistemology. His hermeneutical recognition of the theological relevance of context seems to build on his earlier epistemology, even though he makes no reference to it.

Recognizing the co-constitutive role of concrete contexts, on the one hand, and the elusiveness and trans-cultural character of the universal message, on the other hand, helps to avoid absolutizing either one of the poles of correlation. Traditionalists tend to focus exclusively on the past tradition and nostalgically seek a replication of the past. Modernists simply declare their own particular situation to be absolutely normative.[66] For Schillebeeckx, the truth is to be found in the middle, more precisely in the encounter between former and current cultural embodiments of revelation. In this 'correlation of correlation', the theologian's task is to actualize faith and theology in the world of today. This is performed by relating past experiences, disclosed through exegetical and historical hermeneutics of the texts of the tradition, to contemporary experiences by way of a critical analysis of the present situation. Importantly, this interrelating is a dialectical process in which both hermeneutical enterprises affect each other. While 'present-day experiences have hermeneutic, critical and productive potency for the experiential and epistemic contents of Christian tradition', conversely the Christian experiential tradition 'has its own original, critical and productive power to disclose the meaning of ordinary human experience in our world'.[67] Past and present experiences function as a hermeneutical key to understanding one another.

Drawing on the insights of critical theory, Schillebeeckx emphasizes that this interdependence of past and present experiences also includes criticism. He is particularly concerned with the effects of ideology upon understanding. The symbols and representations used to express and embody the offer of revelation always run the risk of becoming distorted, manipulated and monopolized by dominant social groups. The concrete history of human responses to God's offer of salvation, therefore, also includes 'less satisfactory, even ideological responses to the proffered grace'.[68] For this reason, hermeneutical theology must also involve a critical analysis of the hidden ideological oppressions and distortions. According to Schillebeeckx, such criticism of ideology is intrinsic to the Christian tradition of faith and is exercised primarily by way of a *praxis* of liberation.[69] This relation to praxis 'is essential for theological theory per se'.[70] Accordingly, theological understanding performed through the dialectic relating of past and present experiences also involves a critical analysis of the past through the lens of the present and a critical analysis of the present through the lens of the past.[71] The substance of faith is constantly actualized in new circumstances through this

---

[65] Schillebeeckx, 'Theological Interpretation of Faith', 57.
[66] Ibid., 58; 62.
[67] Schillebeeckx, 'Experience and Faith', 15.
[68] Schillebeeckx, 'Theological Interpretation of Faith', 65.
[69] Ibid., 67.
[70] Ibid., 55.
[71] Schillebeeckx, 'Experience and Faith', 16–21.

critical dialectics between present and past. Faith is represented in experiential and reflective categories that fit the actual historical conditions while also being faithful to past expressions.[72]

However, this 'correlation of correlations' is anything but an easy task; interrelating past and present is not always a harmonious affair. Confronted with challenges and tensions, how can we avoid the temptation to fall back upon a fundamentalist reduction of theology to tradition or a relativist reduction of theology to the actual situation?

3.2 Continuity in discontinuities: The criterion of proportional identity

Although Schillebeeckx uses the term 'correlation' to characterize the method of theology, he also points out that it is a rather ambiguous, even downright misleading term, insofar as it suggests too hastily that there is always continuity or harmony between past and present. The term 'interrelationship' would be more suitable, since that word 'permits various possible meanings, ranging from similarity and correlation to conflict and confrontation – in short, the whole broad spectrum between identity (clicking) and non-identity (clashing)'.[73] However, as David Tracy has argued, there is no reason why the term 'correlation' would not be broad enough to cover this entire spectrum of logical relation between the two sources.[74] Schillebeeckx's preference for the term 'interrelation' over the term 'correlation' therefore does not entail a substantially different position. It is important to note, though, that Schillebeeckx seeks to take the possibility and reality of discontinuity between past and present seriously. In fact, he deems discontinuities a necessary feature of a tradition that aspires to maintain a continuity throughout history. Since history proceeds not merely harmoniously but also in twists, changes in cultural interpretative frameworks are unavoidable. As a result, the Christian tradition is made up of a variety of particular expressions of faith that reflect various particular cultural eras. Biblical, patristic and medieval texts use their own, differing language and symbols of their time and place in order to express the gospel message. Is it still possible, then, to maintain that these different texts of the Christian tradition are expressions of the same faith? To address this recurring question, Schillebeeckx introduces the principle of 'proportional identity'.[75]

With a view to explaining the notion of proportional identity, it is helpful to turn briefly to Schillebeeckx's 'philosophy of history'.[76] Schillebeeckx argues that a

---

[72] Schillebeeckx, 'Theological Interpretation of Faith', 60.
[73] Ibid., 57–8.
[74] David Tracy, 'Particular Questions within General Consensus', in *Consensus in Theology?*, 35–6, has no problem with using the term 'critical correlation' and actually prefers that concept to the term 'confrontation', which is used by Küng in order to draw attention to the fact that there is often conflict between biblical sources and contemporary understanding (see Küng, 'Toward a New Consensus, 16–17). Tracy agrees that it is important to recognize these situations of conflict but argues that adopting a confrontation model runs the risk of losing sight of the continuities between these two.
[75] Schillebeeckx, 'Theological Interpretation of Faith', 63; Schillebeeckx, *Church*, 41 [42]. I have chosen to translate the Dutch *proportioneel gelijke* as 'proportional identity', as used in *Church*, rather than 'proportional equality' used in the translation of 'Theological Interpretation of Faith'.
[76] See Thompson, 'Schillebeeckx on the Development of Doctrine', 306 for this term 'philosophy of history'.

consideration of the historicity of human beings remains incomplete without attention to human consciousness of time. Although adopting a 'bird's-eye view' to escape temporality is impossible, our consciousness of time implies that we also have a certain 'transcendence of temporality'.[77] This 'real *openness* in our temporality ... could almost be called (if the phrase were not too strong) a "trans-historical" element, although this cannot be positively defined or isolated for consideration'.[78] Schillebeeckx uses this insight to argue for the possibility of a 'permanence of understanding' and to avoid a completely historicist conception of truth.[79]

Schillebeeckx continues this search for the condition of trans-historical understanding in *Jesus*. As discussed in Chapter 7, he argues that a universal historical horizon is both an 'insolulable' and 'insuperable' element of human understanding. While a universal horizon cannot be comprehensively thematized through theoretical reason, it remains, at least as a question, the necessary condition for the possibility of communication.[80] It is an inescapable fact of human existence that our understanding is conditioned by particular hermeneutical horizons. However, real differences and radical transformations notwithstanding, 'foreign hermeneutic horizons and experiential horizons are never entirely foreign to us'.[81] Schillebeeckx explains this relative difference between hermeneutical horizons by distinguishing three interpenetrating levels of history which comprise human history when taken together. This threefold division also recurs in his later writings on the role of paradigms in theology and the development of dogma.[82]

The first level is the 'factual' or 'ephemeral' history of quickly passing, day-to-day events.[83] More importantly for Schillebeeckx's purposes are the second and third levels: the 'conjunctural' and 'structural' level.[84] The conjunctural or epochal level spans a significantly longer time period and is more comprehensive than everyday events. Schillebeeckx devotes most of his attention to this level, situating the hermeneutical horizon of a specific time with its contextual concepts and models at this level.[85] A cultural conjuncture provides the interpretative framework – a paradigm that enables us to interpret ephemeral facts. Historical developments and cultural revolutions may cause a paradigm shift, which results in a changed hermeneutical horizon of understanding with new models and concepts. The concept of conjunctural history forms a crucial aspect of Schillebeeckx's hermeneutical theory of understanding. It serves to explain the 'profundity' of cultural-historical changes, the variety of

---

[77] Schillebeeckx, 'Towards a Catholic Use of Hermeneutics', 26 [39].
[78] Ibid.
[79] Ibid.
[80] Schillebeeckx, *Jesus*, 577 [615].
[81] Ibid., 539 [576].
[82] Edward Schillebeeckx, 'The Role of History in What is Called the Paradigm', in *Paradigm Change in Theology: A Symposium for the Future*, ed. Hans Küng and David Tracy, trans. Margaret Kohl (Edinburgh: T&T Clark, 1989), 307–19; Schillebeeckx, 'Discontinuities in Christian Dogmas', 94–6. See also Martin Poulsom, 'Book Essay. New Resonances in Classic Motifs. Finding Schillebeeckx's Theology in Translation', *Louvain Studies* 38 (2014): 370–81, who applies this threefold structure of history to Schillebeeckx's own work to analyse the continuities and discontinuities in his thought.
[83] Schillebeeckx, *Jesus*, 539 [577].
[84] Ibid., 539–40 [577].
[85] Ibid., 540 [577–8].

interpretative frameworks that originate due to these changes and the consequent need for a contemporary understanding of the past as a reinterpretative understanding.[86]

Schillebeeckx maintains that a fusion of hermeneutical horizons, past and present, remains possible. There is a continuity within historical discontinuities. In order to account for this possibility, he points to the third structural level of history. His explanation of this third level is rather brief. Structural history is the 'most fundamental and the least changeable' level 'which makes it possible that interpretations from different conjunctural horizons of understanding can still be made accessible once more to people who live in another cultural epoch'.[87] While he shies away from characterizing it in these terms, structural history seems to fulfil a transcendental role which is strikingly similar to that of the non-implicit intuition. This becomes particularly apparent in the interrelation of conjunctural and structural history.

While the early Schillebeeckx argues that concepts are unable to express reality fully and comprehensively, the later Schillebeeckx maintains that every hermeneutical horizon of a particular epoch has blind spots, so that 'forgotten truths' may come to light in later periods.[88] Moreover, he also repeats his argument that our time consciousness can be viewed as 'an openness to the Mystery which encompasses all history'.[89] At the same time, even structural history is not ahistorical and must not be seen as the level of timeless essences and eternally valid concepts. Our perspective on this structural level always remains coloured and conditioned by our epochal frameworks: 'The basic structure of human thinking asserts itself in conjuncturally conditioned ideas and the changing hermeneutic and experiential horizon.'[90] Schillebeeckx does not make explicit this connection between his philosophy of history and his early epistemology. Yet I argue that the same dialectical interrelation of hermeneutical and metaphysical aspects that characterize the perspectival epistemology recurs in Schillebeeckx's dialectical interrelation of conjunctural and structural history. It is against the background of this dialectical interrelation that his idea of proportional identity can be explained further.

Schillebeeckx first introduces the term 'proportional norm' in his essay on 'Theological Criteria', written in 1969, as a criterion for discerning 'continuity in the orthodox understanding of faith'.[91] Before addressing the question of continuity in understanding, he attends to the issue of what constitutes orthodox faith. According to Schillebeeckx, the act of faith, or *fides qua*, is a correlation of the intentionality of the believer with the mystery of Christ. For faith to be 'correctly orientated', it must be 'inwardly determined by the mystery of Christ'.[92] In other words, faith is constituted by both a subjective and an object aspect. Since the act of faith, *fides qua*, can never be distinguished entirely from the content of faith, or *fides quae*, this correlation with the mystery of Christ must also be found in the expressions and concepts of faith.

---

[86] Ibid., 540–1 [577–9]; Schillebeeckx, 'The Role of History', 310.
[87] Schillebeeckx, 'The Role of History', 310.
[88] Ibid.
[89] Schillebeeckx, *Jesus*, 541 [579].
[90] Ibid., 541 [578].
[91] Schillebeeckx, 'Theological Criteria', 50. Thompson, 'Schillebeeckx on the Development of Doctrine', 309 notes that this criterion of the proportional norm can be seen as being the overarching criterion, encompassing the two other criteria of interpretation that Schillebeeckx distinguishes in this essay, namely 'orthopraxis' and 'acceptance by the community of faith'.
[92] Schillebeeckx, 'Theological Criteria', 54 [60].

The cultural-historical level of conceptual expression corresponds to the subjective aspect and is, therefore, similarly a co-constitutive factor of orthodox faith. We find a plurality of different expressions of faith in the Christian tradition. How can we be certain of their continued orthodoxy and how can they help us to arrive at an orthodox interpretation of faith today?

Schillebeeckx argues that by comparing the variety of past expressions of faith, 'constant but purely proportional principles' can be deduced.[93] He accords a special position to Scripture in the search for this proportional relationship, as the 'first and normative expression of the believing community'.[94] Continuity must not be sought at the level of eternal essences, in timeless concepts or in homogenous formulas. Instead, the criterion of continuity is the constant relationship between the changing cultural-historical referential frameworks, on the one hand, and the intentionality of faith, that is the aiming at and being determined by mystery, on the other. This analogous relationship between conceptual expression and faithful orientation to mystery, which can be discerned throughout the tradition, should guide our contemporary reinterpretations of faith.[95]

Schillebeeckx's account of the *analogia fidei* in his valedictory lecture is largely continuous with his previous account of the proportional norm. He repeats that the identity of faith is to be sought 'at the level of a *corresponding relation between the original message* (tradition) and the constantly changing *situation*, then and now'.[96] The relation between the articulation of the Christian message and its historical-cultural context is *proportionally similar* to the relation of another articulation of this message and its historical-cultural context. Schillebeeckx uses the following diagram to illustrate this proportional identity:[97]

$$\frac{\text{Jesus's message}}{\text{the socio-historical context of Jesus}} = \frac{\text{the New Testament message}}{\text{the socio-historical context of the New Testament}}$$

is reproduced, for example, in the relationship:

$$\frac{\text{Patristic understanding of faith}}{\text{the socio-historical context then}} = \frac{\text{medieval understanding of faith}}{\text{the sociocultural context then}}$$

and this relationship, given and reproduced, must ultimately be reproduced once more in the following relationship or articulation:

$$\frac{\text{the present understanding of faith in the year 1990}}{\text{our social-historical and existential context in the year 1990}}$$

---

[93] Ibid., 55 [61].
[94] Ibid., 55–6 [62].
[95] Ibid., 56 [63].
[96] Schillebeeckx, 'Theological Interpretation of Faith', 62.
[97] Schillebeeckx, *Church*, 41 [42].

Throughout changing historical conditions, identity and continuity are neither found directly in the tradition nor found directly in the situation. Instead, we discover Christian identity in the relation between situation and message. This identity has remained proportionally similar throughout the successive historical phases of the tradition. The unity of these different cultural-historical interpretations of faith is a 'unity in depth'.[98] In order to reproduce this proportional identity today, our current interpretation of faith must avail itself of terms, concepts and models that are appropriate and adequate to our particular cultural context. The proportional relation of previous articulations of faith guides this new interpretative effort. Hence, being faithful to the past means *recreating* the relation between context and message of the previous phases in the Christian tradition. This contemporary 'correlation of correlations' strives for proportional identity with the past and enables the continuity of Christian identity yesterday, today and tomorrow: 'Interpretation *creates* new tradition, handing down a living religious tradition to future generations with creative piety.'[99] For Schillebeeckx, Christian identity is both a task that is given to us and a constant and perpetually new challenge. Christian identity, therefore, can never be 'perfect' or 'completed', but is constantly realized through the concrete events and encounters of human life.[100]

This concept of proportional identity also affects the traditional understanding of dogma. According to Schillebeeckx, dogmas may lose their relevance without reinterpretation and reformulation, becoming mere 'cultural relics' that remind us of the Christian past.[101] Every dogmatic pronouncement originates as an attempt to answer a question that originates from a particular cultural-historical situation. For this reason, the dogmatic answer adapts to the cultural-historical form of these questions, so as to effectively communicate the truth of faith in a particular age and day. However, this means that when the cultural-historical context changes, the effectiveness of an older dogmatic formula is put in jeopardy. Dogmas can become 'totally irrelevant' in new cultural-historical circumstances as contextually and historically conditioned expressions.[102] As a result, 'a historical break with bygone cultural forms may be the only possible way to reformulate dogma so that it remains true to the gospel and the Christian religious tradition'.[103] Schillebeeckx goes as far as to claim that without this redefinition and reformulation, dogma becomes 'untrue' and 'heretical'.[104]

However, this language might seem a bit too radical, given that Schillebeeckx also states that dogmas are 'irrevocable' and 'irreversible'.[105] We cannot simply abolish older dogmas, because they have 'always actively expressed and safeguarded the mystery of

---

[98] Schillebeeckx, 'Theological Interpretation of Faith', 17. This expression 'unity in depth' is found in the Dutch original but has been omitted from the English translation.
[99] Ibid., 64.
[100] Edward Schillebeeckx, 'Christelijke identiteit, uitdagend en uitgedaagd. Over de rakelingse nabijheid van de onervaarbare God', in *Ons Rakelings Nabij. Gedaanteveranderingen van God en geloof. Ter ere van Edward Schillebeeckx*, ed. Manuela Kalsky, André Lascaris, Leo Oosterveen, and Inez van der Spek (Zoetermeer: Meinema, 2005), 28–9.
[101] Schillebeeckx, *Church*, 43 [44].
[102] Schillebeeckx, 'Discontinuities in Christian Dogmas', 101.
[103] Ibid., 94.
[104] Ibid.
[105] Schillebeeckx, *Church*, 42 [43].

God and Jesus Christ within a particular socio-cultural system of reference'.[106] But in order for these past dogmas to remain relevant, we must find their 'different, deeper, meaning'.[107] A dogma that has become unintelligible in new circumstances, losing its direct relevance for believers, still remains theologically relevant, because in such a dogmatic statement we can discern the proportional relation that we are tasked to recreate today. Past dogmas remain normative for the understanding of faith today, as the key to the recreation of this proportional relation today.

Schillebeeckx's reconfiguration of correlation theology, thus, entrusts theology with the dynamic task of recreating continuity in discontinuities. This is a task that remains unfinished as long as history continues. Has he, hereby, found a satisfactory solution to the hermeneutical question of the theological understanding of faith?

4 Evaluating the correlation of correlations

A crucial strength of Schillebeeckx's theology of correlation is the development of Tillich's one-dimensional juxta-positioning of Christian answers and human questions into a critical model of correlation in which situation and message mutually condition each other. The situation is hereby recognized as being co-constitutive of revelation. For us, as hermeneutical and historical beings, the contextual cultural-historical medium necessarily forms part of any divine message. We can never access the divine message directly or distil its essence purely. But our own cultural-historical framework offers us a perspectival access to the revelation of the past, and informed by the tradition, we are also able to discern the revelation that presents itself to us in the present. Hence, by correlating the past correlation of revelation and situation with the present correlation of revelation and situation, we can actualize Christian faith today. Importantly, the co-constitutive role of situation for revelation means that the expression of revelation needs to change when cultural-historical frameworks change, due to evolutions at the level of conjunctural history. The criterion of the proportional norms seeks to account for the possibility of continuity in the understanding of faith, despite these historical discontinuities. Does this 'correlation of correlations' offer a plausible account of the possibility of a contemporary theological understanding of faith, which remains faithful to the past and open to the future? To address this question, I turn to two important heirs of Schillebeeckx's theology.

4.1 Criticizing continuity: Lieven Boeve and Erik Borgman

The Belgian theologian Lieven Boeve and the Dutch theologian Erik Borgman have played an important role in the reception of Schillebeeckx's thought. Although their respective theologies are clearly marked by Schillebeeckx's work and ideas, they have also raised critical questions regarding his theological methodology. I will focus here

---

[106] Schillebeeckx, 'Theological Interpretation of Faith', 63.
[107] Schillebeeckx, 'Discontinuities in Christian Dogmas', 97.

on their specific criticisms of his correlational theological project.[108] Interestingly, their critiques seem to be inversely related to each other. Boeve argues that Schillebeeckx focuses too little on the particularity of the Christian tradition, because he is too greatly concerned with establishing a synchronic continuity between Christian tradition and contemporary situation. In contrast, Borgman fears that Schillebeeckx's concern with the diachronic continuity of the tradition does not pay due theological attention to the universally present traces of God in the situation today.

The starting point of Boeve's critique is his assertion that the contemporary situation is fundamentally different than Schillebeeckx's modern context. Postmodernity has radically transformed our context, which is now marked by 'irreducible pluralism' and 'detraditionalisation'.[109] This changed context problematizes the presumed continuity at the experiential level and thereby erodes the plausibility of Schillebeeckx's correlation theology.[110] Boeve questions the extent to which Schillebeeckx's model of interrelation remains dependent on an assumed fundamental continuity and harmony between Christian tradition and context. A continuity which is grounded in a universal experience, shared by believers and non-believers in the past and the present, and which is justified with reference to pre-linguistic elements in experience.[111] This presumption of continuity and the hesitation to acknowledge the possibility of *real ruptures* 'obfuscate' the hermeneutical insight into the intrinsic connection between theological truth and history, language and context.[112] Alternatively, Boeve proposes to 'radicalise' Schillebeeckx's theological methodology.[113] He advocates a 'post-correlational' model that starts, more self-consciously, by grounding itself in the particularity of the Christian tradition.[114] In a situation of radical pluralism, the inescapable particularity of the Christian tradition is a unique resource, rather than an obstacle for a renewed encounter with the context. It is precisely this distinct particular identity and otherness that enable the Christian message to 'interrupt' history and context.[115]

Boeve's emphasis on the importance of recognizing the particularity of the Christian tradition finds support in Schillebeeckx's thought, insofar as it resonates with his concern for the concreteness of salvation history and his insistence that we

---

[108] For a more general overview of Schillebeeckx's theology and its reception by Boeve and Borgman, see Boeve, 'The Enduring Significance and Relevance of Edward Schillebeeckx?', 17–20. See also the panel discussion between Schillebeeckx, Boeve, and Borgman in Maurice Bouwens, Jacobine Geel and Frans Maas (ed.), *Jezus, een eigentijds verhaal* (Zoetermeer: Meinema, 2001).

[109] Lieven Boeve, *God Interrupts History. Theology in a Time of Upheaval* (New York: Continuum, 2007), 16–26.

[110] Boeve, 'Experience according to Edward Schillebeeckx', 221-3. See also Thompson, 'Schillebeeckx on the Development of Dogma', 320, who similarly raises the question of whether our postmodern situation, marked by 'radical non-simultaneity and non-similarity of experiences and places', invalidates the possibility of any proportional relationships.

[111] Boeve, 'Experience according to Edward Schillebeeckx', 216–17.

[112] Lieven Boeve, 'Systematic Theology, Truth and History: Recontextualisation', in *Orthodoxy, Process and Product*, 34.

[113] Ibid.

[114] Boeve, *God Interrupts History*, 109. While Boeve sketches this post-correlational model in critical dialogue with Schillebeeckx, he also states his indebtedness to the correlational theological project by refusing to term it 'anti-correlational' (40; 49).

[115] For a more detailed account of Boeve's model of theology as interruption, building on the theology of Johann Baptist Metz, see Boeve, *God Interrupts History*, esp. chapter 2.

need the past of the tradition in order to interpret the present. However, his plea for a post-correlational theology of interruption seems to conflict with the universal orientation of Schillebeeckx's theology. Boeve's particularist focus on the discontinuity between Christian tradition and situation tends to confine the locus of revelation to the Christian tradition alone. Boeve agrees with Schillebeeckx that God's revelation occurs 'independent of our knowledge thereof'.[116] But he immediately relativizes this universal dimension, arguing that 'if there were not the narratives concerning the God who makes salvation history with us, this would probably have gone unnoticed'.[117] For Boeve, recognizing and interpreting an experience as revelatory of God seems hardly possible without the particular narrative of the Christian tradition. This emphasis on the indispensable role of particular narrativity is connected with Boeve's postmodern distrust of hegemonic master narratives that suppress plurality and otherness.[118] His call for attention to particularity and his suspicion of false claims of universality result in his putting forward the concept of dialogue as a confrontation between particular differences.[119] The confrontation between the Christian tradition and other different traditions forms the starting point for the recontextualization of Christian faith today.[120]

This emphasis on the tradition becomes particularly apparent in the theological concept of interruption, which works in two ways. Not only does the particular Christian tradition interrupt the contemporary postmodern context, but the encounter with the otherness of this context also interrupts the Christian tradition. This interruption has 'the potential to become the locus in which God is revealed to Christians today'.[121] On the one hand, the acknowledgement of this revelatory capacity of otherness manifests that Boeve supports a wider scope of God's salvific activity. On the other hand, Boeve immediately reduces this scope by qualifying it as a locus of revelation for Christians. The question of whether God's revelation can be discerned and appropriated, independent of the Christian tradition by non-Christians, remains unaddressed in Boeve's theological framework.[122] This contrasts markedly with

---

[116] Boeve, 'The Enduring Significance and Relevance of Edward Schillebeeckx?', 20. Depoorter, 'Orthopraxis as a Criterion for Orthodoxy', 177, offers an interpretation of Schillebeeckx's later theology that resonates with Boeve's particularist concern. She argues that Schillebeeckx 'modifies his method of correlation towards an internal Christian correlation whereby the Christian tradition and the experiences of Christian believers (and not universal "human" experiences) are thought in a mutual relationship'. However, the correctness of this interpretation can be doubted. It is true that for Schillebeeckx, the task of correlating situation and tradition belongs to the (Christian) theologian, in particular, and to the Christian community of faith more generally. However, in view of the universality of God's salvific activity, all human experience, rather than Christian experience alone, is theologically relevant and must therefore be taken into account within the process of theological correlation. Hence, the characterization of his correlation theology as an 'internal correlation' seems misplaced.

[117] Boeve, 'The Enduring Significance and Relevance of Edward Schillebeeckx?', 20.

[118] The main inspiration behind Boeve's postmodern distrust of master narratives is Jean-François Lyotard. See Boeve, *Lyotard and Theology*.

[119] Boeve, 'The Enduring Significance and Relevance of Edward Schillebeeckx?', 20; Boeve, 'Experience according to Edward Schillebeeckx', 222.

[120] Boeve, *God Interrupts History*, 108–9.

[121] Ibid., 48.

[122] Boeve suggests a 'pluralist inclusivism' that adopts the 'mystery of Christ' to talk about (universal) salvation. However, he remains relatively silent on the specific mediation of this salvation outside the Christian tradition. See Boeve, *God Interrupts History*, 175.

Schillebeeckx's theologal perspective, which sees a trans-cultural presence of the living God in every human culture. Schillebeeckx refuses to tie the mediation of salvific revelation exclusively to the Christian tradition. Experiences of grace are conditioned, but are not determined by our interpretative framework. Crucially, the reality of grace itself also exerts its influence, even where it is not explicitly recognized as such. As a result, Schillebeeckx adopts a markedly more positive view of the non-Christian context, which is also receptive and responsive to God's grace and is, therefore, a true *locus theologicus*.[123] Boeve's postmodern correction of Schillebeeckx tends to lose sight of this universal theological intuition.

At this point, it is interesting to turn to the critique levelled by Erik Borgman. He argues that God is present throughout history and that this discernment of this divine presence takes place in secularized as well as non-Christian forms, thereby positioning himself in line with Schillebeeckx. The relevance of the Christian tradition lies in the contribution that it can make to the discovery of the traces of grace in the world. In order to perform this task, theology cannot be the mere hermeneutical retrieval of an old narrative in a contemporary form.[124] Yet, according to Borgman, this exact tendency can be detected in Schillebeeckx's theology, insofar as he remains preoccupied with the relevance and continuity of the Christian faith tradition. The result of this narrow focus is a relative neglect of contemporary culture and the concrete traces of God that it may contain. Schillebeeckx never actually manages to engage with the concrete level of human existence beyond the borders of the church, since he remains entangled in his search for the continuity and identity of the Christian tradition.[125] Moreover, Schillebeeckx ultimately presumes too easily that the Christian tradition has an underlying continuity. Schillebeeckx simply assumes the existence of a proportional identity of faith in the successive historical periods of the Christian tradition, instead of actually probing whether this is indeed the case.[126]

Borgman proposes developing Schillebeeckx's theological project in a different way than Boeve. Instead of advocating an increased hermeneutical focus on the particular shape of the Christian tradition, he pleads for an intensification of theological attention paid to the context. Borgman advocates a theological *incarnation* into the contemporary secular world and its contemporary narratives, debates and practices. The Christian tradition must be willing to renounce her 'distinct identity' and be

---

[123] Edward Schillebeeckx, 'Het gezag van de traditie in de theologie', in *Jezus, een eigentijds verhaal*, 80-4.
[124] Erik Borgman, 'Theologie als schatbewaarder of als bedelaar? In discussie met de "Onderbroken traditie" van Lieven Boeve', *Tijdschrift voor Geestelijk Leven* 56 (2000): 195. This article is, in fact, a critical discussion of Boeve's rather than Schillebeeckx's theology. Yet, insofar as Borgman considers both their theological approaches to be *too* tradition-centred, the criticism voiced here also applies to Schillebeeckx.
[125] Borgman, 'Van cultuurtheologie naar theologie als onderdeel van cultuur', 352; 357-8. As Borgman observes in 'Christelijk: een identiteit die er geen is', in *Jezus, een eigentijds verhaal*, 95, this attention to the identity of the Christian forms a shared element of the theologies of Schillebeeckx and Boeve.
[126] Borgman, 'Van cultuurtheologie naar theologie als onderdeel van cultuur', 359. See also Georges De Schrijver, 'Hertaling van het Christus-gebeuren: een onmogelijke opgave?', in *Volgens Edward Schillebeeckx*, ed. Etienne Kuypers (Leuven: Garant, 1991), 53-90, for a different but related criticism, arguing that Schillebeeckx does not recognize the possibility of 'ruptures' in historical understanding because he assumes too easily continuity between past and present.

prepared to 'incarnate' herself 'without reserve' in the contemporary situation.[127] For Borgman, the Christian tradition rediscovers her true identity precisely by way of doing this. This incarnational move is grounded in the faithful trust in the notion that traces of the saving God are already present in this secular world. Borgman considers Schillebeeckx's notion of the contrast experience to be a crucial 'key' in enabling and guiding this search for the traces of God in contemporary culture.[128]

However, at this point in his argumentation the question about the grounds of this faithful trust in the presence of divine traces in the world arises. Is this trust not based on a particular understanding of the Christian faith tradition? Moreover, another question that presents itself concerns the origin of the key that aids the theological quest for the traces of grace. As we will see in Chapter 9, the contrast experience is a theological concept which results from an extensive hermeneutical engagement with the Christian tradition. With the help of this concept, Schillebeeckx seeks to convey the original experience of salvation in Jesus Christ to a contemporary audience and to make them attentive to the possibility of these experiences in their own particular cultural and experiential context. However, arriving at this particular searchlight or interpretative key, with which to discern contemporary experiences of grace, requires substantially more tradition hermeneutics than Borgman seems to acknowledge. As Schillebeeckx himself observed, someone first has to develop the more general 'system of coordinates' at the formal level in order to enable the theological analysis at the concrete level. The latter is not possible without the former.[129]

Schillebeeckx maintains that a theological reading of the present situation is 'historically predetermined' by the past tradition, over and against Borgman's plea for a 'losing of identity' in order to 'find identity'.[130] Like Borgman, Schillebeeckx is interested in contemporary fragmentary stories that can disclose the Christian message in new and surprising ways. The many discontinuities of these fragmentary stories help to 'keep the evangelical "plot" going'.[131] Yet, it is necessary that those fragments not be detached from the 'great story' in order for those fragmentary stories to become a 'fifth gospel'.[132] To put it differently, the willingness to lose one's identity in the confrontation with new experiences still presumes some understanding of the identity that is put at risk. For Schillebeeckx, Christian identity only becomes a living identity in relation to contemporary experience, which involves the exposure to new and potentially estranging experiencing that transforms identity. Theological actualization of faith in the present is only possible in the light of the past. Without the continuity that links us to the past, talking about rediscovering a specifically Christian identity in the present becomes meaningless. After all, is it not our standing in the tradition that impels and enables the theologian to look for traces of God in the world of today? Hence, it seems

---

[127] Borgman, 'Christelijk: een identiteit die er geen is', 94.
[128] Borgman, 'Van cultuurtheologie naar theologie als onderdeel van cultuur', 358; Borgman, 'Christelijk: een identiteit die er geen is', 91–2.
[129] Schillebeeckx, 'Culture, Religion and Violence', 175–6; Schillebeeckx, 'Het gezag van de traditie in de theologie', 85.
[130] Schillebeeckx, 'Culture, Religion and Violence', 175.
[131] Ibid., 176.
[132] Ibid.

that Borgman's correction of Schillebeeckx risks losing sight of the importance of the particular identity of the Christian tradition throughout history.

The discussion of the critical reception of Schillebeeckx's work by Boeve and Borgman shows that his correlational theology is open to being developed in rather divergent directions. Whereas Boeve deems the intensification of the theological focus on the tradition to be necessary, Borgman advocates a fuller consideration of the theological possibilities of the situation. Both theologians are able to claim that their critical corrections build upon key theological intuitions of Schillebeeckx, so as to advance his theological project. Boeve rightly recognizes that the theological engagement with the context is grounded in and motivated by the theological tradition of the past. However, his advocacy for a radicalized hermeneutics of tradition tends to lose sight of the effective operations of grace in the situation at large and, thus, puts the universal dimension of Christian faith at risk. This conflicts with Schillebeeckx's firm conviction that 'God's grace and mercy are at work ... transcendently accommodating our finite human culture from the depth dimension of all cultures'.[133] For Schillebeeckx, due consideration for particularity cannot come at the cost of universality. Borgman is much more attentive to this universal element. However, his critique of the concern about the continuity of the Christian tradition throughout history tends to underestimate the distinct contribution that the particular lens of the Christian tradition offers when it comes to discerning new fragmentary manifestations of God's grace. A hermeneutics of the universality of grace remains indebted to the particular identity of the Christian tradition as its source and inspiration. A reconsideration of these criticisms is called for, given that both critical corrections run the risk of distorting Schillebeeckx's attempt to balance particularity and universality in his critical correlation of correlation.

4.2 Revisiting continuity: Theological creativity as response

One particular strength of Schillebeeckx's model of correlation is its recognition that altered socio-historical circumstances demand changes in theological understanding and expression. His proposal to situate continuity and identity at the level of proportional relations responds to the challenges of historical understandings that have been identified by hermeneutical thinkers. Part of this keen eye for historical discontinuity is an emphasis on the active role played by the interpreter. Perceiving the revelatory meaning of the tradition and recognizing the contemporary presence of grace involve a *creative* attribution of meaning. Hermeneutical theology aims at keeping a tradition alive, re-reads the tradition in the light of the present and introduces new conceptual expressions and practices. In brief, actualizing the tradition of faith, thus, entails the creation of new tradition. Both Boeve's plea for recontextualizing the interruptive force of tradition and Borgman's search for new fragmentary traces of God outside the tradition can, in fact, be seen as further developments of this appraisal of dynamic change and creative agency as key elements in theological interpretation. Hence, these theologians have fruitfully appropriated the room for discontinuities and changes in theological understandings that has been opened up by Schillebeeckx.

---

[133] Ibid., 175.

However, Boeve and Borgman pay less attention to the issue of continuity and unity in theological understanding. What guarantees that a contemporary theological reinterpretation of the tradition remains in continuity with the past tradition? How do we avoid that new interpretations of tradition become pure projection or reinvention? How do we know that newly found practices and convictions are indeed traces of the living God? Can radically different expressions of faith still be regarded as representations of the same truth? Or, as Martin Poulsom phrases the question, is Schillebeeckx's correlation 'compatible with realism', that is is there 'something beyond history, beyond the situational, to which the Christian faith refers?'[134] I argue that in order to find a response to these pressing questions, it is necessary first to reconsider the notion of proportional identity and, more specifically, the metaphysical presuppositions underlying this concept.

It is relevant to note, in this regard, that Borgman seems to have grown more sympathetic to Schillebeeckx's concern for the continuity of the tradition. In a more recent publication, he praises Schillebeeckx's argument in favour of a continuity by way of discontinuity. This proportional continuity offers a promising alternative to views of continuity as something which 'the Church owns or could define as a characteristic belonging to its identity' or as a 'holding on to what is said before'.[135] Yet, what exactly enables this proportional continuity? Borgman's answer is very brief. He merely states that 'continuity is given to the Church through God's faithfulness to human history'.[136] This essential aspect of Schillebeeckx's correlation of correlations surely demands a more elaborate clarification. I argue that this explication ought to revisit certain key metaphysical presuppositions developed by Schillebeeckx previously. In other words, hermeneutics must be reconnected with metaphysics in order to develop an intelligible account of continuity through discontinuities. This interconnection between hermeneutics and metaphysics has already come to the fore in this chapter several times.

To begin with, Schillebeeck's philosophy of history and its distinction between structural and conjunctural history forms an application of this interrelation of hermeneutics and metaphysics. The concept of structural history explains how there can be an aspect of continuity that ensures that different cultural-historical contexts are never radically different. Different historical epochs and their interpretative frameworks are never *absolutely* different. Schillebeeckx points to this element of continuity when he states that 'three paradigmatically divergent periods', such as the patristic, medieval and reformation paradigms, may still 'display an underlying unity'.[137] Hence, the contemporary postmodern situation is characterized by many conjunctural differences, but is not radically different in comparison with modernity and other preceding historical epochs. The continuity at the structural level is a key metaphysical

---

[134] Poulsom, 'The Dialectics of Creation', 110. Poulsom actually repeats a question which was raised by Bernard McGinn in 'Response to Edward Schillebeeckx and Jürgen Moltmann', in *Paradigm Change in Theology*, 347–8.
[135] Borgman, 'Retrieving God's Contemporary Presence', 250.
[136] Ibid., 249.
[137] Schillebeeckx, 'Discontinuities in Christian Dogmas', 95.

assumption for explaining the possibility of a continuity of understanding throughout history.

This fundamental conviction about an underlying continuity in historical changes also comes to the fore in Schillebeeckx's view on pluralism and truth. For Schillebeeckx, it is manifest that plurality can never be absolute and that interpretative frameworks can never be radically different. To be sure, truth has a multidimensional character, and our only access to truth is limited and conditioned by cultural-historical perspectivity. But truth also has an objective dimension, which equally conditions the plural human relations to truth. Crucially, this objective dimension entails a directionality that ultimately ensures a unity in plurality of diverse interpretations and expressions of truth. Our relation to truth is, thus, characterized by both creative activity and obedient listening to the self-manifestation of truth. Now, while it is true that the later Schillebeeckx no longer explicitly elaborates these metaphysical views on history, pluralism and truth, I argue that they remain a crucial element of his hermeneutical theology. This becomes most clearly apparent in his reflections on the objective directionality of the theological interpretation of faith.

In both the first essay on hermeneutics and in the first discussion of the proportional norm, Schillebeeckx devotes considerable attention to the essential role of the self-giving mystery in the process of theological interpretation. The mystery which embraces us in grace inwardly determines faith and objectively orientates its various interpretations and expressions. This objective directionality of the mysterious object of faith is the ultimate guarantor of orthodoxy and continuity in the understanding of faith. As Kennedy rightly observes, at this stage in his theological thinking, the continuity between past and present reinterpretations of faith is warranted by the fundamental relational theological ontology that he developed earlier.[138] Unfortunately, however, Kennedy does not address the question whether this relational ontology remains as relevant and important in Schillebeeckx's later hermeneutics of tradition, especially in his reconceptualized correlation theology.[139] Judged by the relative silence on this metaphysical theme in the reception of Schillebeeckx's hermeneutics by Boeve and Borgman, it may seem as though metaphysics loses its central importance for his hermeneutics. At first glance, Schillebeeckx's argument in his valedictory lecture and in *Church* seems to confirm this suggestion, insofar as the emphasis on historicity and the consequent stress on the creative agency of the interpreter occupy the centre stage. However, a closer analysis of the argumentation reveals that the hermeneutical search for proportional unity remains dependent upon a metaphysical frame of thought. This can be demonstrated when we compare the original text of the valedictory lecture with the revised edition included in *Church*.

In the valedictory lecture, tradition as the interpretation of faith is presented as a correlation between the universal substance of faith (message) and particular interpretative frameworks (context). Since this trans-cultural and universal religious substance is only accessible through concrete particularity, and also transcends all

---

[138] Kennedy, *Deus Humanissimus*, 189.
[139] Neither in *Deus Humanissimus*, 381–2, nor in *Schillebeeckx*, 64–5, does Kennedy bring Schillebeeckx's method of mutually critical correlation into the discussion with his ontology.

particularity, it remains a necessarily elusive concept.[140] But what consequences does this elusiveness, and the dependence upon concrete mediation, have for the role of this religious substance in theological hermeneutics? Schillebeeckx is remarkably silent on this issue in the valedictory lecture. Contrary to the early essay on hermeneutics, the valedictory lecture omits references made to a directive force of the substance of faith as guiding our interpretations. Although he mentions that the substance of faith is 'given' or 'received', he merely emphasizes that this gift has always a 'culturally specific form' and he fails to address the question of whether this element of givenness plays a hermeneutical role.[141]

When turning to *Church*, we see that Schillebeeckx undertakes an attempt to clarify some ambiguities connected to the concept of religious substance. Ellen van Wolde has criticized his use of the term 'religious substance', arguing that it is suggestive of an 'objectivist principle of revelation' which exists independently of the interpreting subject and concrete reality.[142] Responding to this critique, Schillebeeckx decides to change his terminology. He now introduces the term 'offer of revelation', because he fears that the term 'substance of faith' contains misleading reminiscences of Aristotelianism or scholasticism.[143] According to Boeve, this change of terms signals a radicalization of his hermeneutical insights, which would suggest that he has moved away further from his metaphysical past.[144] However, immediately after conceding the potential misunderstanding connected to the term 'substance of faith', Schillebeeckx emphasizes that the offer of revelation is not 'an empty cipher', but has a 'meaningful' or 'objective' content.[145] Although this content can never be grasped or objectified, it nonetheless 'provides its own *direction* of interpretation, as the normative basis of our non-arbitrary interpretations of faith'.[146] Remarkably, the attempt to show his distance from a specific metaphysical framework of thought is combined with the reintroduction of his own alternative metaphysics, as they were developed previously. We have seen that the argument in favour of the objective directionality serves to guard against reductions of interpretation to subjective projection or arbitrary interpretations. However, Schillebeeckx requires a metaphysical argument in order to account for such an objective dynamism. Even though he omits such an argumentation here and also does not refer explicitly to his own previous work, Schillebeeckx's clarification of religious substance as an offer of revelation demonstrates the continuous relevance of his metaphysics for his hermeneutics of faith.

In view of this correction, it comes as something of a surprise that when the concept 'offer of revelation' recurs in the discussion of theological correlation, no further refinement or clarification is provided about the specific role of this element within the

---

[140] Schillebeeckx, 'Theological Interpretation of Faith', 57.
[141] Ibid., 63.
[142] See Ellen van Wolde, 'Semiotiek en haar betekenis voor de theologie', *Tijdschrift voor Theologie* 24 (1984): 159.
[143] Schillebeeckx, *Church*, 35-8.
[144] As suggested by Boeve, 'The Enduring Significance and Relevance of Edward Schillebeeckx', 17.
[145] Schillebeeckx, *Church*, 37 [38].
[146] Ibid.

concept of proportional continuity.¹⁴⁷ Instead, the account of the proportional remains heavily focused on the subjective creative dimension of interpretation. Accordingly, it may appear as though the subject has become solely responsible for the hermeneutical recreation of proportional identity of faith throughout changing historical-cultural epochs. Nevertheless, there are some clues that Schillebeeckx associates continuity with the objective reality of revelation and its directive force. One example is the fact that Schillebeeckx refers to the tradition as the 'original message', while he calls the situation 'constantly changing'.¹⁴⁸ Although he affirms that the tradition always includes the situation of the time, the adjective 'original' suggests that it also contains a more permanent aspect. Another oblique reference can be found in the assertion that different figures from the Christian tradition, such as Jesus, Paul, Augustine, Pope Gregory, Thomas, Bonaventure, Bellarmine, Luther, Calvin, Theresa of Avila or Romero, have expressed 'the same fundamental view of God and humankind and their interrelationship'.¹⁴⁹ The boundaries and divisions between these different cultural-historical expressions of faith 'were and are nonetheless obliterated and transcended in a specifically Christian way'.¹⁵⁰ But the precise way in which these differences are transcended 'is difficult to conceptualize', so Schillebeeckx adds in *Church*, without offering any further explication.¹⁵¹

In order to solve this aporia, I suggest that this specifically Christian way of 'transcending' historical differences throughout history can be explained with reference to the dialectical interrelation of human subjectivity and the objective reality of revelation in the theological interpretation of faith. This dialectical relationship offers an interpretative key to theological hermeneutics as a continuity in discontinuities. Metaphysical assumptions about history and truth remain indispensable for his theological hermeneutics and are analogous to the persisting relevance of a metaphysical dimension in Schillebeeckx's understanding of experience and revelation. Our reinterpretation of faith today can be proportionally similar to past expressions of faith, because these two interpretations share a structural similarity; they are both responding to the same divine self-giving mystery. As we noted earlier, this conviction that God continues to be actively present today forms the main impetus for Schillebeeckx's recognition of the theological significance of the contemporary cultural-historical context. Hilkert speaks more concretely about the work of the Holy Spirit as the common basis of various different interpretations of faith. The Spirit ultimately initiates, sustains and orientates all new interpretations of faith, so that they become faithful expressions of 'the living mystery of Christ'.¹⁵² Schillebeeckx has sought to make this theological claim of the priority of God's speaking over human listening

---

¹⁴⁷ Except for some minor details, there are no major differences in the discussion of proportional identity in 'Theological Interpretation of Faith' and *Church*.
¹⁴⁸ Schillebeeckx, 'Theological Interpretation of Faith', 62; Schillebeeckx, *Church*, 41 [41].
¹⁴⁹ Schillebeeckx, 'Theological Interpretation of Faith', 64; Schillebeeckx, *Church*, 43 [44].
¹⁵⁰ Schillebeeckx, 'Theological Interpretation of Faith', 64.
¹⁵¹ Schillebeeckx, *Church*, 44 [44].
¹⁵² Hilkert, 'Hermeneutics of History in Schillebeeckx', 131. For Hilkert's argument on the centrality of Schillebeeckx's 'profound belief in grace' for his theological project, see also Mary Catherine Hilkert, '"Grace-Optimism": The Spirituality at the Heart of Schillebeeckx's Theology', *Spirituality Today* 44 (1991): 220–39.

intelligible with the help of metaphysical arguments about the nature of history and truth. Most important, however, is his argument that the mystery of faith exerts an objective directionality in our particular interpretations of faith. A theological account of the interpretation of faith, therefore, cannot be reduced to hermeneutics alone, but it also involves necessarily a metaphysics.

It is fair to say, however, that this metaphysical aspect becomes increasingly implicit in Schillebeeckx's later work and tends to be overshadowed by the emphasis on the particular cultural-historical conditions of any contextual interpretation. Thus, the terminology changes from divine mystery to religious substance and, once again, to the offer of revelation. Moreover, the objective directionality is no longer explicitly mentioned in his later writings. However, I argue that his clarification in *Church*, regarding the concept of revelation, can be applied analogously to the issue of interpreting the tradition. The metaphysical priority and directionality of the object of interpretation remains crucial to accounting for proportional identity when the relation between tradition and situation changes at both levels. Changes at the level of the situation (changed interpretative frameworks) necessitate creative changes at the level of tradition (changed conceptual expressions and symbols). But a continuity with the past remains possible only inasmuch as these creative transformations remain connected to the objective directionality of the self-offering divine mystery. In other words, without this metaphysical argumentation in favour of the objective guidance of mystery in the interpretation of faith, Schillebeeckx cannot intelligibly claim that there is a theological continuity in discontinuities throughout consecutive historical periods. A theological reception of Schillebeeckx's correlation theology remains committed to the aspect of identity and continuity of Christian faith and must be attentive to this metaphysical argumentation supporting his hermeneutics of faith.

5 Conclusion

This chapter has elaborated how the dialectics between hermeneutics and metaphysics underlying Schillebeeckx's theological epistemology finds diachronic application within this hermeneutics of tradition. Rejecting any sharp distinction between philosophical and theological hermeneutics, Schillebeeckx engages intensively with hermeneutical theory with a view of explaining how we can understand the texts of the Christian tradition today. Nevertheless, theological understanding cannot be reduced to general philosophical hermeneutics. In view of the many ideological distortions that affect understanding, theoretical hermeneutics must be expanded critically and practically. Schillebeeckx is particularly concerned to avoid a narrow existentialist approach to theological hermeneutics which loses sight of the objective dimension of truth. Attempting to balance the objective and subjective dimensions of theological understanding, he draws attention to givenness of mystery in the understanding of faith. Our creative reinterpretative understanding of faith is first and foremost a *response* to the gift of grace that manifests itself to us in existential experience. Schillebeeckx employs an ontological-theological argumentation, which is heavily indebted to his earlier epistemology, in order to explain this objective facet of theological understanding.

The hermeneutical attention to the cultural-historical conditions of understanding is developed further in Schillebeeckx's reworking of correlation theology. Recognizing the co-constitutive role of the situation in revelation, both past and present, yields an understanding of theology as involving a 'correlation of correlations'. The offer of grace is never available purely to us, but continually finds new embodiments throughout history. Still, Schillebeeck maintains that within these various different cultural-historical expressions there is an element of continuity. However, this continuity must be sought at the level of the proportional relation between various expressions of faith. In other words, there is a continuity *in* discontinuities. Critical discussions of Schillebeeckx's correlation theology have primarily focused on this element of *discontinuity* in Christian understanding. However, I have argued that this has led to a relative neglect on the equally important role of *continuity* in Schillebeeckx's hermeneutics of tradition.

Revisiting the theme of continuity raises the question of the possibility of a proportional identity. I have argued that this must be explicated with reference to Schillebeeckx's metaphysical framework of thought. Analysing Schillebeeckx's reflections on the proportional norm with attention to his philosophy of history and his theology of revelation demonstrates the persisting relevance of the metaphysical arguments that he developed previously. It is the mystery of faith, exerting an objective directionality within the various creative interpretative expressions, that guarantees the possibility of a continuity in discontinuities. Even though Schillebeeckx does not explicitly discuss these arguments anymore, they remain fundamental to understanding his hermeneutics of tradition. This insight confirms my argument that Schillebeeckx's theological method entails a dialectics of metaphysics and hermeneutics.

This chapter has already touched upon a key assumption of Schillebeeckx's correlation theology, namely the conviction that God universally presents Godself throughout history. Given the centrality of this assumption, this claim warrants further examination. In Chapter 9, I will examine how Schillebeeckx seeks to justify this belief in the universal presence of grace with a reworked natural theology that revolves around the notion of the contrast experience. This natural theology comprises, in effect, a *synchronic* application of the dialectics between metaphysics and hermeneutics.

9

The heuristics of grace:
Natural theology and contrast experience

1 Introduction

The correlation of correlations, analysed in Chapter 8, comprises Schillebeeckx's account of a reinterpretative understanding of faith – an understanding that is connected with the past, informed by the present and oriented towards the future. Crucially, this hermeneutics of faith argues that understanding past experiences of grace, meditated by the Christian tradition, is made possible because we continue to experience God's grace today. In other words, the world of human experience at large, both past and present, is considered to be a *locus theologicus*. The central assumption that God's salvific activity is universally operative warrants closer scrutiny.

In this chapter, I examine how Schillebeeckx seeks to account for the universal possibility of the experience of God through his notion of the contrast experience. The contrast experience functions not only *ad intra*, that is as an element of the mutual dialectic between past and present that correlation theology thematizes, but also *ad extra*. I argue that Schillebeeckx develops this concept in service of a new natural theology that seeks to demonstrate the universal plausibility and intelligibility of the Christian faith. The contrast experience can be analysed as the *synchronic* application of the dialectics between metaphysics and hermeneutics which characterizes Schillebeeckx's theological method. Importantly, examining this concept also sheds new light on Schillebeeckx's theological appropriation of philosophy.

First, I explain how Schillebeeckx's critical-hermeneutical explorations do not sound the end of his commitment to the justification of faith, but instead impel him to search for a new experience-oriented natural theology. For this purpose, he employs his dialectical understanding of experience in order to elaborate the critical cognitivity of both recalcitrant reality and ethical praxis. This leads, second, to the notion of the contrast experience as a universal and basic human experience. A closer analysis of the contrast experience reveals that it is constituted by a dialectical interrelation of negativity and positivity. Contrast experiences involve a practical response to suffering that is sustained by hope. Third, I examine Schillebeeckx's account of the different interpretations of contrast experiences and his explanation for the Christian interpretation in terms of eschatological proviso and creation faith. This also brings into focus the special nature of this Christian articulation of grace by way of mystical speaking about silence and Christ-like praxis.

In the final section, I explain that the contrast experience epitomizes the joint application of metaphysics and hermeneutics in Schillebeeckx's theological method and how this affects the theological use of philosophy. Analysing the key aspects of the notion of the contrast reveals the persistent relevance of the metaphysical framework that Schillebeeckx developed in his earlier work. But Schillebeeckx's critical-hermeneutical turn also marks and influences his specific use of metaphysical arguments. It brings to the fore the inductive *a posteriori* logic of his metaphysics even more sharply – a metaphysics developed on the basis of the tradition of concrete Christian experience, rather than being purely speculative. Accordingly, the contrast experience must be seen as a philosophical heuristic that serves to explain the concrete Christian interpretation of reality as graced reality. This heuristic use of the contrast experience reveals Schillebeeckx's qualified understanding of philosophical rationality. Schillebeeckx's view on the notion of the anonymous Christian offers an apt illustration of this theological vision.

2 Renewing natural theology

Assessing the contemporary situation in 1989, Schillebeeckx observes that pluralistic society with its many competing and conflicting truth claims urgently calls for a justification of Christian faith.[1] At the same time, the Christian tradition maintains that faith is a 'gift of grace'.[2] Schillebeeckx argues, therefore, that finding philosophical proofs for God is neither possible nor desirable. Faith and the knowledge of God are not based on rational arguments, but are instead developed in response to a specific history of salvation. An apologetics that strives to show that Christian faith is 'more rational' than atheism or other religions fails to understand the specific nature of faith.[3] A healthy dose of *scepsis* regarding the possibility of proving the existence of God has been a constant element throughout Schillebeeckx's theology. His recognition of the need for *preambula fidei* has always been combined with an attentiveness to the fact that the nature of Christian faith is not only marked by intelligibility but also by mystery. The newly acquired insights into the ambiguities of history and its consequent resistance to theoretical rationalization have only strengthened his view on the fundamentally subordinate role of speculative theology regarding salvation history.

Nevertheless, two decades of intense critical-hermeneutical investigations did not extinguish Schillebeeckx's concern with the universal intelligibility and communicability of Christian faith. Yet he now advocates an alternative and more modest justification of faith. Schillebeeckx proposes searching for a reasonable argument that aims to 'uncover the "intelligibility" or the comprehensibility of faith', acknowledging openly that he reasons from within a religious faith perspective.[4] A refusal to engage in this kind of critical and self-critical examination into the nature

---

[1] Schillebeeckx, *Church*, 80 [82].
[2] Ibid., 78 [80].
[3] Ibid., 80 [82].
[4] Ibid., 78–80 [80–3].

of Christian faith runs the risk of making faith convictions ideologically immune to criticism. Schillebeeckx derives inspiration for a religiously grounded uncovering of the intelligibility of Christian faith from the examples of Immanuel Kant and Thomas Aquinas. These thinkers developed philosophical arguments in order to demonstrate the point at which religious discourse becomes intelligible.[5] Committing himself to this tradition of thought, Schillebeeckx initiates a rethinking of natural theology, which focuses specifically on human experience.

Schillebeeckx addresses the actual demand for natural theology in his article on correlation theology, written in 1970. Faced with the challenges of secularization, he argues that it is necessary to find a 'sensitive point of resonance' between the Christian faith and the world of human experience.[6] He observes that Protestant and Catholic theology have, in recent years, converged in their attempts to offer a response to the hermeneutical problem of the universal intelligibility of Christian revelation. This comes particularly to the fore in the various ways in which theologians like Paul Tillich, Karl Barth and Rudolf Bultmann deal with the 'question-answer correlation'.[7] Schillebeeckx argues that the different accounts of this 'question-answer correlation' can be considered as exercises in natural theology.

While Schillebeeckx welcomes the ecumenical convergence that has resulted from this common search for the universal pre-understanding of Christian faith, he deems the theological answers which have been offered by these theologians to be inadequate. Protestant theologians fail to recognize the distinct integrity and autonomy of the realm of non-religious experience and questions, insofar as they maintain that human questions only become clear in the light of the Christian answer of revelation. Consequently, they resort to a theological *deduction* of human questions from Christian revelation. This strategy results in what linguistic philosophers, such as Ludwig Wittgenstein and Ian Ramsey, have called a 'category mistake'.[8] Since the non-religious question and the religious answer belong to different language games, they cannot be meaningfully correlated. Following this insight from linguistic philosophy, Schillebeeckx concludes that 'if the question is asked philosophically, the answer must also be given within the philosophical language game, if it is to be universally meaningful'.[9] Dialectical theologians have attempted to solve this issue of meaning by arguing that revelation brings its own intelligibility through conversion. Yet according to Schillebeeckx, this solution ultimately results in a fideist position that undermines the universal dimension of faith:

> Both the Barthian and the Bultmannian versions of this theology do have the disadvantage of placing such strong emphasis on the transcendent reality of God,

---

[5] Ibid., 62–3.
[6] Schillebeeckx, 'Correlation between Human Question', 70–1 [80]; 86 [99].
[7] Ibid., 70–3 [79–83]. By subsuming these various theologians under the label of 'correlation theology', Schillebeeckx seems to assume that even anti-correlational theologies necessarily engage in a correlation of context and tradition. For a similar argument, see David Tracy, 'The Uneasy Alliance Reconceived', 556–60.
[8] Schillebeeckx, 'Correlation between Human Question', 75 [85].
[9] Ibid.

the 'wholly other', that faith has become an unintelligible decision and the factual discrepancy between faith and the context of man's experience has been almost canonised.[10]

Schillebeeckx is rather brief on the alternatives offered in Catholic theology. Without mentioning any names, he merely points out that purely metaphysical natural theologies are all equally unintelligible. These theologies fail to convey that the God of Christian faith is a meaningful mystery that resonates with lived experience, due to their 'rigid and abstractly metaphysical standpoint'.[11] This can be interpreted as being an implicit critique of his own earlier attempt to formulate a natural theology through a transcendental-metaphysical analysis of the human person. Schillebeeckx does not explicitly discard his former theological anthropology, but his insistence on the need to attend to the concreteness of lived historical experience shows that it needs to be complemented with a critical-hermeneutical approach, at the very least.

Schillebeeckx proposes a different form of natural theology that takes the non-religious context of human experience fully seriously. Instead of offering a Christian response directly, we must first explore the human answers given to human questions. A meaningful correlation between human question and human answer forms the pre-understanding for an understanding of the relation between human question and divine answer. Natural theology must, therefore, first focus its attention on human answers and clarify their relation to the religious answer only subsequently. Apart from avoiding a category mistake, this approach also safeguards the true meaning of the religious answer. Christian revelation is not a 'stop-gap' – a functional solution to existential and social problems.[12] Rather, God's revelation is true gift, complete gratuity, an unexpected and surprising answer, which not only deepens and clarifies human questions but also transcends these questions. Schillebeeckx accords a significant role to philosophy, in order to elaborate this human question and answer:

> Philosophy can demonstrate that talk about God is at the limit of all meaningful speech and that it is to be found where language becomes speechless and therefore reaches a limit, but also speaks about the limit of man in this world. Philosophy itself cannot fill this speechless space – only religion, the believer, can do that – but it can certainly show where religious talk has a meaningful place in our world and in our experience.[13]

Philosophy, thus, helps us to find the place where religion becomes meaningful, yet it does so without determining the content of potentially meaningful answers. After all, according to Schillebeeckx, philosophical arguments stand in the service of theology. They help to demonstrate the intelligibility of faith, but cannot arrive

---

[10] Schillebeeckx, 'Correlation between Human Question', 77 [87]. See also 'Secularization and Christian Belief', 44–5 [73], in which Schillebeeckx similarly advances an argument for a new natural theology to stave off fideism.
[11] Schillebeeckx, 'Correlation between Human Question', 77 [88].
[12] Ibid., 79 [90].
[13] Ibid., 78 [89].

at firm conclusions about the rationality of faith. However, this acknowledgement that his philosophical argumentation is motivated and informed by a theological rationale seems to problematize his earlier criticism that dialectical theologians deduce human questions from religious answers. I have already explained in Chapter 7 that Schillebeeckx's analysis of the human person as a transcendental relation to mystery is ultimately guided by his Christian faith conviction that all human beings are invited into theologal communion with the living God. The specific nature of his earlier natural theology and this more recent insistence on the limited role played by theoretical reason in the justification of faith suggest that Schillebeeckx might be less far removed from his Protestant colleagues than he acknowledges himself.

3 Experience-oriented natural theology

In order to develop his alternative natural theology, Schillebeeckx draws extensively upon his dialectical account of experience. His goal is to find a universally shared experience that is open to either religious or non-religious interpretations.[14] Two interrelated steps can be distinguished in this procedure. First, he engages in a philosophical analysis of 'secular experience' so as to disclose 'elements which inwardly *refer* to an absolute mystery'.[15] More concretely, this involves an examination of the critical and revelatory dimensions of contingency and negativity. Schillebeeckx develops the concept of the contrast experience by combining these elements with a consideration of the crucial role played by praxis. The contrast experience is the paradoxical confluence of a practical resistance, motivated by hope, in the confrontation with the negativity of suffering. In a second step, he seeks to demonstrate that a religious interpretation of experiences of contrast has a 'distinctive comprehensibility' in comparison to non-religious interpretations.[16] Crucially, the distinctive argumentative force of the religious interpretation only becomes apparent in the intersection of theoretical and practical reason. It is the movement beyond the purely speculative theoretical level that distinguishes his new natural theology from traditional forms of natural theology.[17]

3.1 The critical cognitivity of recalcitrant reality

Following his hermeneutical turn, Schillebeeckx views the human person as an interpretative being. The human person is a 'projecting existence' that employs interpretative frameworks, critical rationality and theoretical models in order to make sense of her experiences.[18] However, despite the essential role played by human subjectivity, Schillebeeckx still considers objective reality to be the 'final criterion'.[19] Refractory reality puts our interpretations and projections under critique and

---

[14] Schillebeeckx, *Church*, 82 [84].
[15] Schillebeeckx, 'Secularization and Christian Belief', 43 [71].
[16] Schillebeeckx, *Church*, 82 [84].
[17] Schillebeeckx, 'Secularization and Christian Belief', 44–5 [73].
[18] Schillebeeckx, *Christ*, 20 [34].
[19] Ibid.

correction. In all of our attempts to grasp, to understand and to control reality through theoretical models and frameworks, we experience that reality resists and escapes these complete rationalizations. Our models never completely work; reality keeps escaping us, because reality is always more than what humans can imagine and articulate.[20]

The central importance of the element of the otherness and refractoriness of experience comes particularly to the fore in Schillebeeckx's explanation of experience as *wedervaren*, which was already mentioned in Chapter 7. Experience involves risky and dangerous encounters with objective realities that may prove to be hindrances and obstacles. But this possibility of failure and this encountering of resistance also make new and positive experiences possible. In other words, the recalcitrance of experience has a revelatory potential.[21] The new is never 'radically other' in new experiences, but is rather a matter of recognition through alienation.[22] Revelatory experiences operate as a conversion process; they move from integration via disintegration to new and different reintegration, so that the 'old, always unspoken "familiar" reality' is revealed to us in a new way.[23]

According to Schillebeeckx, every experience is, in principle, characterized by this coincidence of positive familiarity and negative alienation. Every experience is, therefore, marked by a revelatory dynamic. However, negative experiences of failure and recalcitrance have a particular revelatory density and significance. These scandalous confrontations with the refractoriness of reality function as the hermeneutical principle par excellence of the disclosure of reality:

> Where reality offers resistance to such outlines and implicitly therefore guides them in an indirect way, we come into contact with a reality which is *independent* of us, which is not thought of, made or projected by men. At this point we have a revelation of that which cannot be manipulated, a 'transcendent' power, something that comes 'from elsewhere', which asserts its validity in the face of our projects and nevertheless makes all human plans, products, and considerations possible, by virtue of its critical and negative orientation.[24]

When interpretation and rationalization fail or fall short, revelation may occur. Reality reorients us as a 'hidden magnet', in manifesting its autonomy and surprising otherness.[25] Negative experiences are therefore *productive*; they disclose that our experience is 'supported and propelled by a permanent reference to the inexhaustibility of the real'.[26] From the religious point of view, this experience of the fundamental contingency and givenness of reality is an experience of grace. Schillebeeckx considers it to be the root of all religion, even though it is not necessarily interpreted in religious terms.[27] At

---

[20] Schillebeeckx, *Christ*, 20 [35].
[21] See also Schwarz-Boenneke, 'Die Widerständigkeit der Wirklichkeit', 96–8.
[22] Schillebeeckx, *Christ*, 25–6 [40].
[23] Schillebeeckx, 'Experience and Faith', 1–2.
[24] Schillebeeckx, *Christ*, 20 [34–5].
[25] Ibid., 21 [35].
[26] Schillebeeckx, *Christ*, 21 [36] (slightly adapted translation).
[27] Ibid., 806–7 [811].

this point in his argumentation, the influence of Schillebeeckx's early metaphysics of knowledge can be clearly recognized. The critical force of negative experiences is explained by reference to an objective reference or dynamism that was previously associated with the implicit intuition as a way to explain the knowledge of God.

Schillebeeckx further elaborates the revelatory potential of experiences of negativity through a discussion of the theme of contingency. Contingency already formed an important building block of his relational ontology of creation. Schillebeeckx claims that the diverse variety of human experience shares one basic and universal element, namely an 'experience of an absolute limit'.[28] Importantly, this experience of the absolute limit is not an abstract generalization of particular experiences of concrete limit situations. Nor should it be understood as an immediate religious experience, such as Schleiermacher's feeling of absolute dependence. Rather, the experience of the absolute limit is 'mediated through all kinds of experiences of relative limits in our life', the realization of 'radical contingency or finitude at any moment of life' that occurs *in* these concrete experiences.[29] In the experience of our own radical finitude, we come to recognize we are not 'lords and masters' of ourselves, nature or history. To put it in the words of Heidegger, as finite beings we are fundamentally thrown into the world. Referring to Jean-Paul Sartre's analysis of existential experience in terms of radical contingency, Schillebeeckx argues that the 'recognition of radical finitude as such is no longer a religious concept, as it used to be, but is usually a generally recognized reality of human experience'.[30] The experience of absolute limit is, therefore, a 'real fact' or 'basic condition' of human existence that demands interpretation, either in religious or in non-religious terms.[31]

However, Schillebeeckx rejects the notion of a general religious experience, because this fails to respect the concreteness of all human experience. Particular backgrounds and perspectives colour all experience inasmuch as interpretation forms an *intrinsic* part of experience. It is, therefore, correct to say that the believer experiences contingency *fundamentally differently* than the agnostic. But this crucial hermeneutical insight must be seen in connection with an equally important metaphysical consideration:

> But it in no way follows from this that one cannot speak meaningfully of the same sort of experience with two possible interpretations. It does not mean that there is a neutral common experience which is simply interpreted in two ways. It means that there is no uninterpreted experience of contingency, but in the whole of this interpretative experience there is a pre-linguistic element of experience which is universally human.[32]

---

[28] Schillebeeckx, *Church*, 75 [77].
[29] Ibid., 76 [78].
[30] Ibid. Schillebeeckx omits a specific reference to any of Sartre's work. Kennedy, *Schillebeeckx*, 80–1, points to Sartre's *Being and Nothingness: An Essay on Phenomenological Ontology*, trans. Hazel E. Barne (London: Methuen, 1958), arguing that Schillebeeckx studied this text intensively during his time in Paris.
[31] Schillebeeckx, *Church*, 77 [79].
[32] Ibis., 78 [80].

Schillebeeckx, thus, argues that there is an 'experiential aspect of contingency *qua* contingency'[33] – an aspect which is pre-linguistic and universal, even though we can only talk about it by way of particular linguistic interpretations. This commonly shared element means that specific interpretations of human experience, such as the Christian interpretation, can be related to other interpretations of experience. It provides the possibility of demonstrating the universal relevance and intelligibility of the Christian tradition of faith, and of its particular interpretation of human experience, as containing a revelation of the saving God. However, this universal element of experience cannot simply be distilled from human experience through theoretical reflection. For Schillebeeckx, the universal dimension of experience, as a revelatory reference to God, only becomes intelligible within the context of praxis. This practical element and the critical force of contingency are brought together in the concept of the contrast experience.

3.2 The contrast experience

The theme of the contrast experience continues to appear throughout Schillebeeckx's subsequent writings after its first introduction in 1968 in *God the Future of Man*.[34] The development of this concept is indebted to Theodor W. Adorno's negative dialectics and to other critical theorists.[35] Schillebeeckx specifically mentions that he considers the contrast experience to be an element of natural theology in different places.[36] He employs this concept to explain why human experience has an intrinsic religious significance: 'For "the human" is the medium of the possible revelation of God'.[37] The contrast experience serves to identify a specific reference point within the variety of human experience to explain this universal dimension of God's salvific revelation. Crucially, this universal presence of grace only becomes realized within *conscious ethical activity*. This ethical dimension was not entirely absent from Schillebeeckx's earlier natural theology, but now it comes much more prominently to the fore.

Schillebeeckx argues that the experience of absolute contingency finds its most radical realization in the confrontation with human suffering, evil, unhappiness and oppression. Our world is marred by 'the rule of evil' which seems 'universal and

---

[33] Ibid., 78 [80].
[34] For the first occurrence of the term, see Schillebeeckx, *God the Future of Man*, 83 [136]; 92–4 [153–6]; 116 [191]. Schillebeeckx refers to Joseph Cardijn, an important figure in the Catholic Worker Movement, as having coined the term 'contrast-experience'. In *The Understanding of Faith* Schillebeeckx discusses the notion of contrast experience and negative dialectics in various places, including 58 [65]; 112 [117–18]; 80–6 [91–9]. The concept recurs in *Jesus*, 583–4 [622]; *Christ*, 786–34, esp. 813–17 [790–821]; *Church*, 5–6 [5–6]; and 'Theological Quests', 154–5.
[35] Borgman, 'Van cultuurtheologie naar theologie', 350, n. 61, comments that the origin of the term 'contrast experience' is not entirely clear. Borgman mentions that Schillebeeckx himself refers to Adorno and to Ricoeur, but he suggests that the insight into the critical cognitivity of the human resistance to suffering actually seems to be derived from Albert Camus. He also considers Johann Baptist Metz's and Jürgen Moltmann's appropriation of Ernst Bloch's theory of hope a formative influence.
[36] Schillebeeckx, 'Correlation between Human Question', esp. 86 [99]; and Schillebeeckx, *Church*, 6 [6].
[37] Ibid., 10 [10].

ineradicable in our history'.[38] However, there is something which binds us human beings universally. According to Schillebeeckx, our encounters with suffering are marked by a contrastive ambiguity:

> I now want to radicalize what I have previously, indeed repeatedly, called important human experiences, namely negative experiences of contrast: they form a basic human experience which as such I regard as being pre-religious experience and thus a basic experience accessible to all human beings, namely that of a 'no' to the world as it is.[39]

These universal encounters with suffering reveal to us that there is something *fundamentally wrong* in reality – that reality is scarred by an unexplainable mixture of good and evil. To be sure, there are many manifestations of goodness, beauty and happiness, but these positive fragments are constantly overshadowed, violated and contradicted by abuse, oppression and suffering. A closer analysis of this universal experience of suffering and evil, however, discloses a particular human response to suffering, namely 'indignation'.[40] The confrontation with suffering elicits a *no* – a refusal to simply accept the wretched reality of suffering. Human experiences of negativity are, in this way, marked by a revelatory dialectic; they mediate something *positive*. What is this positive element?

Schillebeeckx describes this positivity somewhat elusively as the 'common search to realise the constantly threatened *humanum*' as a universal element in the human search for meaning.[41] The term *humanum*, derived from the philosophy of Ernst Bloch, resists a single and clear definition.[42] Its positive content only comes to the fore indirectly and in contrast to the experience of negativity and can, therefore, only be articulated in fragmentary and contradictory ways. Schillebeeckx describes it variously as 'an obscure consciousness of what must be confessed positively by human integrity' or as an 'openness to another situation which has the right to our affirmative "yes"'.[43] While every positive expression of the *humanum* remains incomplete, all expressions share an important common characteristic, namely its 'resistance to the threat to humanity'.[44] Resistance implies action. The positive vision of the *humanum* is only disclosed within practical resistance to the violation of humanity, in 'a praxis of liberation and reconciliation'.[45] This emphasis on the necessity of praxis is connected to Schillebeeckx's

---

[38] Ibid., 88 [90].
[39] Ibid., 5 [5]. See also Schillebeeckx, 'Theological Quests', 154–6 for another succinct outline of the contrast experience. Borgman, 'Theologie tussen universiteit en emancipatie. De weg van Edward Schillebeeckx', *Tijdschrift voor Theologie* 26 (1986): 240–58 (255), argues that Schillebeeckx gradually begins to view the contrast experience as the central human experience, due to his engagement with liberation theologies.
[40] Schillebeeckx, *Church*, 6 [6].
[41] Schillebeeckx, 'Correlation between Human Question', 80 [91].
[42] See Helen Bergin, 'Edward Schillebeeckx and the Suffering Human Being', *International Journal of Public Theology* 4 (2010): 466–82 (467–70), for a more detailed discussion of Schillebeeckx's use of the term *humanum*.
[43] Schillebeeckx, *Church*, 6 [6]; Schillebeeckx, 'Correlation between Human Question', 80 [92].
[44] Schillebeeckx, 'Correlation between Human Question', 80 [92].
[45] Schillebeeckx, *Church*, 29 [29].

argument that our historical situation incapacitates the theoretical rationalization of universal meaning. As a future promise, something that still needs to be realized within history, the *humanum* can only be anticipated in the praxis of liberation.[46] This emphasis on anticipatory praxis marks the difference with his previous participatory metaphysical account of the human person. The universal revelatory power of contrast experience originates in this future-oriented praxis: 'The particular epistemological value of the experience of contrast in suffering is a knowledge which looks for the *future* and opens it up.'[47]

However, the central role accorded to praxis should not obfuscate the role played by theory. On the contrary, the contrast experience assumes a dialectics of theory and praxis. On the one hand, praxis is key for any theoretical anticipation of universal meaning. On the other hand, this praxis of liberation also reveals a hope that sustains and motivates this praxis. Human resistance to suffering reveals an 'illuminating perspective' – a basic form of '"underground" existential trust' which gives us hope that a different world is indeed possible.[48] Despite this mutual dependence of theory and praxis, the 'open yes' is stronger than the 'no', because it is what makes the practical opposition to suffering possible.[49] In other words, practical anticipation requires hope as its condition of possibility. Schillebeeckx argues that this hope contains an 'element of knowledge' and that it can be 'formulated into a theory'.[50] This raises the question of the interpretation and articulation of the hope which sustains a praxis of liberation.

Schillebeeckx insists that the hope that lies at the heart of indignation, and which sustains the praxis of liberation, is a universal element of human experience shared by believers and non-believers alike. At the same time, and remaining faithful to his hermeneutical insights, he also acknowledges that this universal basic experience is never experienced without interpretation. Contrast experiences are always concrete experiences, interpreted and expressed in either religious or non-religious terms.[51] Accordingly, the basic trust and hope that sustain our praxis towards a better future is given various names. In light of the historical in Jesus Christ, Christians recognize in the contrast experience the self-revelation of God. According to Schillebeeckx, this religious interpretation gives the open yes more 'direction' and 'deepness' (*'reliëf'*).[52] However, such a religious interpretation is not the only possible interpretation available. Non-religious people can just as well respond ethically to violations of the *humanum*. Schillebeeckx maintains that there is an *autonomous ethics* – an ethics without a belief in God.[53] Does this recognition relativize the religious interpretation or make it redundant? Can religion simply be reduced to ethics? It is quite the contrary. Schillebeeckx maintains that the Christian interpretation offers a unique and valuable

---

[46] Ibid., 788 [791–2]; Schillebeeckx, 'Theological Criteria', 59 [66]; Schillebeeckx, 'Correlation between Human Question', 80 [92].
[47] Schillebeeckx, *Christ*, 814 [819].
[48] Ibid., 6 [6]; Schillebeeckx, 'Secularization and Christian Belief', 45 [74].
[49] Schillebeeckx, *Church*, 6 [6].
[50] Schillebeeckx, 'Correlation between Human Question', 80 [92].
[51] Schillebeeckx, *Church*, 6 [6]; 76–7 [78–9].
[52] Ibid., 6 [6].
[53] Ibid., 29 [29–30].

perspective on human contrast experience – one which finds its expression in the eschatological hope for redemption and faith in creation.[54]

4 Interpreting contrast experience

The universal contrast experience revolves around an appeal to a praxis of liberation that is motivated by hope. According to Schillebeeckx, the question of the origin of this hope is pertinent to both the believer and the non-believer alike. He refers in this regard to Bloch, who argues that there must be an 'objective hope' which corresponds to 'subjective hope' and makes this 'subjective hope' possible.[55] Who or what can guarantee us that evil does not have the final word? Or to put it more theologically, what grounds our hope that liberation and salvation (or *heil*) are a real possibility?[56] Schillebeeckx discusses two interpretative options: the humanistic and the religious points of view. Importantly, while he acknowledges that one cannot rationally decide which of the two offers the 'better' point of view, Schillebeeckx clearly presents the Christian account as having a distinct intelligibility. He is aware, though, that this distinct intelligibility cannot be established by rational argumentation alone. Ultimately, the thematization of the contrast experience as an experience of grace occurs primarily by way of mystical negative theology and by way of a concrete praxis of liberation. For Schillebeeckx this is peculiar to the *concrete universality* that is mediated by the Christian tradition of faith.

4.1 Eschatological hope and creation faith

To begin with, Schillebeeckx asserts that a gratuitous heroic actions 'for the sake of the *humanum*' are performed by religious and non-religious people alike.[57] These heroic actions are concrete manifestations of hope for the ultimate victory of the good. But what is the ground of this hope? Schillebeeckx argues that this hope lacks an historical or anthropological ground, but he insists that it is not merely 'postulary'.[58] The argument supporting this claim is rather weak though. Schillebeeckx's justification of this humanistic hope relies heavily on the example of the agnostic Jean-Paul Sartre's refusal to lose trust in the 'humanity of humankind'.[59] Humanistic hope has its own autonomous foundation. It is founded on 'the rights of justice', 'the human conviction that justice is superior to injustice, despite the fact that the experiencable world is constantly an empirical contradiction of this'.[60] Instead of offering an

---

[54] See also Edward Schillebeeckx, 'Theologie als bevrijdingskunde. Enkele noodzakelijke beschouwingen vooraf', *Tijdschrift voor Theologie* 24 (1984): 397.
[55] Schillebeeckx, 'Correlation between Human Question', 83 [95].
[56] Schillebeeckx argues that this is one of the main tasks of theology, namely 'to safeguard belief in and this hope for a liberating saving power which loves men and women and which will over-come this evil' (*Church*, 4 [4]).
[57] Ibid., 92–3 [94–6].
[58] Ibid., 93 [95].
[59] Ibid., 94 [96].
[60] Ibid.

extensive philosophical account, Schillebeeckx merely points to examples of non-religious manifestations of hope and thereby concludes that hope can exist universally, independent of religious convictions.

Despite his acknowledgement that ethical praxis is realized outside and independent of explicitly religious discourses, Schillebeeckx voices several doubts about an ethics without God. As Poulsom notes, Schillebeeckx affirms the humanist position critically. He aims to show that secular humanism is 'less fully justified' than Christian humanism, but without intending to contradict or negate secular humanism *tout court*.[61] The religious conviction that God is the deepest foundation and source of all human ethics only accords ethics a 'relative independence'.[62] By contrasting the Christian understanding of hope with the secular understanding of hope, Schillebeeckx seeks to demonstrate that the religious perspective offers a critical and productive improvement upon the humanistic ethical outlook.

Hilkert has pointed out that past examples, such as Auschwitz, as well as ongoing global atrocities, problematize Schillebeeckx's rather optimistic view of humankind. She suggests that this trust in human agency must be complemented with a more thorough analysis of the distorting influence of bias and (social) sin.[63] Schillebeeckx's alternative theological account of hope actually seeks to address the shadow side of human history. His strong assertion that the contrast experience is a universal experience implies that the demand for liberation and salvation is also, in principle, universally recognized. However, Schillebeeckx continues more critically that 'without spirituality of the perspective of faith in God, ethics is often merciless: intent on vengeance and retribution'.[64] Human reason alone always risks being distorted. There is always the tendency to posit a 'secular principle of unity' that seeks to organize and coordinate the praxis of liberation, but its good intentions notwithstanding, it may end up becoming the totalitarian rule of one particular group.[65]

As mentioned in Chapter 6, Schillebeeckx explains this critical evaluation of secular ethics with reference to the doctrine of original sin. He employs this doctrine in order to simultaneously affirm and correct secular reason.[66] The doctrine of original sin teaches us that human beings are ultimately incapable of bringing about salvation and peace purely by human means, either at the collective or at the personal level. Thus, it exerts a critical hermeneutics of suspicion that calls into question an overly confident 'optimism of reason'.[67] Yet this optimism of reason is not rejected *tout court*. Rather, the pessimism of original sin transforms the optimism of reason into an 'optimism

---

[61] Poulsom, *The Dialectics of Creation*, 131–4.
[62] Schillebeeckx, *Church*, 29–31 [30–2]. See also Bradford E. Hinze, 'Eschatology and Ethics', in *The Praxis of the Reign of God*, 178.
[63] Mary Catherine Hilkert, 'The Threatened *Humanum* as *Imago Dei*: Anthropology and Christian Ethics', in *Edward Schillebeeckx and Contemporary Theology*, 132–3. See also Rodenborn, *Hope in Action*, 326, for a similar call for a 'critical re-evaluation of the fragility and, thus, universality of that [contrast] experience under the pressure of historical conditions'.
[64] Schillebeeckx, *Church*, 31 [31].
[65] Schillebeeckx, 'Correlation between Human Question', 81 [93].
[66] For a more extensive discussion of Schillebeeckx's use of the doctrine of original as a source for the structural and ideological distortions in society, see Daniel Minch, '"Dat jullie dan als God zullen zijn." Erfzonde en ideologiekritiek', *Tijdschrift voor Theologie* 54 (2014): 350–64.
[67] Schillebeeckx, 'The New Critical Theory and Theological Hermeneutics', 130 [148–9].

of grace'.⁶⁸ Schillebeeckx emphasizes that the full extent of human sinfulness, and consequent limitations of human reason and ethics, only came to light in Christ's *redemption*. This revelation of sin therefore also contains a promise; 'God continues to be present in redemption and forgiveness.'⁶⁹ Taken together, the doctrine of original sin and the promise of redemption offer a distinctly theological view on salvation.

Christian faith and hope are historically mediated in the 'eschatological recollection of the death and the resurrection of Jesus'.⁷⁰ Once again, the faith entails both affirmation and critique.⁷¹ The life, death and resurrection of Jesus Christ fully reveal God's promise of salvation. What is impossible for human beings is possible for God. Christian faith, thus, criticizes the view that human persons alone are responsible for, and the guarantor of, liberation. It affirms instead that only God is the 'universal subject of history'.⁷² The promise of universal salvation is revealed in Jesus, but also awaits realization in our ongoing and open history. This eschatological proviso prevents any definitive identifications of the *humanum* and ensures that we remain critical and self-critical of every substantive articulation of the *humanum* and about any concrete praxis of liberation.⁷³ Moreover, contrary to humanistic accounts of hope, eschatological faith offers hope for the countless historical victims who have fallen without experiencing liberation or redemption. Entrusting the absurdity of human suffering to God gives hope to these and other victims who are at risk of being forgotten. Without arguing away or understanding absurd situations of suffering, believers find a mystical source for an eschatological hope in God – one which can sustain an ethical commitment which goes as far as risking self-sacrificial martyrdom.⁷⁴

However, the eschatological proviso alone is not sufficient to explain the Christian understanding of hope. Christian faith cannot be reduced to 'pure eschatology'.⁷⁵ Apart from the negative critique exerted by this eschatological proviso, Christian faith is also 'consolidating and confessing'.⁷⁶ It can be so because Christian hope is ultimately anchored in the 'eschatological abundance' that is inherent in reality as the effect of God's creation.⁷⁷ Jesus Christ not only reveals God's eschatological promise of universal salvation but also affirms the essential goodness of creation. Salvation is only comprehensible through creation and vice versa. In Jesus we learn God's unconditional

---

[68] Ibid.
[69] Schillebeeckx, *Church*, 88 [91].
[70] Ibid., 96 [99]. Schillebeeckx develops his Christological image of Jesus as the 'eschatological prophet' who mediates God's salvation in great detail in the books *Jesus* and *Christ*. For a succinct discussion, see Rodenborn, *Hope in Action*, 156–65; Hinze, 'Eschatology and Ethics', 170–2.
[71] Schillebeeckx, *Church*, 97 [99].
[72] Schillebeeckx, 'Correlation between Human Question', 81 [93].
[73] Ibid., 81–2 [93–4].
[74] Schillebeeckx, *Church*, 94–5 [96–7].
[75] Edward Schillebeeckx, 'The Crisis in the Language of Faith as a Hermeneutical Problem', *Concilium* 5, no. 9 (1973): 38.
[76] Schillebeeckx, *Church*, 97 [99].
[77] For this term 'eschatological abundance', see Edward Schillebeeckx, 'Terugblik vanuit de tijd na Vaticanum II. De gebroken ideologieën van de moderniteit', in *Tussen openheid en isolement. Het voorbeeld van de katholieke theologie in de negentiende eeuw*, ed. Erik Borgman and Anton van Harskamp (Kampen: Kok, 1992), 171. For a more detailed discussion of the eschatological proviso and of the eschatological surplus, see Derek Simon, 'Salvation and Liberation in the Practical-Critical Soteriology of Schillebeeckx', *Theological Studies* 63 (2002): 494–520.

trust in humankind. The creator's saving presence abides in reality, in spite of human sinfulness and despite the atrocities such as Auschwitz.[78] This basic trust in this gracious presence grounds the universal human experience of the surplus of hope that motivates and sustains our praxis of justice. The Christian tradition offers a compelling account that this hope that lives within us is a gift of grace:

> Human reality, which can, despite everything, be meaningfully interpreted in secular terms and especially by realising meaning in praxis within a history of meaninglessness, receives from Christianity meaning in abundance: the living God himself, who is ultimately the abundance to which all secular meaning is indebted for its own secular significance.[79]

Schillebeeckx emphasizes that this basic trust is open to non-religious interpretation but that it cannot be completely secularized. He maintains that the contingency of reality and the manifestation of hope-inspired action in response to suffering contain an inexhaustible reference towards a source that transcends all secularity. They contain a 'latent religious depth dimension'.[80] Yet how can this dimension be adequately expressed?

4.2 Mediated immediacy: The nearness of mystery

Christians identify the ground of the hope that sustains the praxis of liberation as God's salvific grace. In light of the revelation in Jesus Christ, finitude and contingency are no longer left by themselves in solitude, but instead are viewed as being 'supported by the absolute, saving presence of the living God'.[81]

> In its changing historical forms, the experience of creation is the foundation which supports everything. It might equally well be called a fundamental 'experience of grace', or rather more neutrally, an experience of the reality which prepares us and is therefore a norm for us – in other words, an experience of ourselves, our fellow men and the world in which we feel as a norm something which transcends at least our arbitrary control of ourselves. It is an experience of givenness, which is also

---

[78] Schillebeeckx, 'Correlation between Human Question', 85 [97–8]; Schillebeeckx, *Interim Report*, 96–8 [109–12]. There is considerable scholarly debate about the relation between creation and salvation in Schillebeeckx's thought. Whereas Kennedy, 'God and Creation', 37–41, and Rodenborn, *Hope in Action*, 176; 197, emphasize the priority of creation, Schreiter, 'Edward Schillebeeckx: His Continuing Relevance', 191–3, argues that Schillebeeckx's emphasis on creation is best viewed 'in light of his larger soteriological plan'. Attempting to reconcile these positions, Poulsom, *The Dialectics of Creation*, 182–90, puts forward the thesis that a 'relational dialectic' characterizes the relation between creation and salvation in Schillebeeckx's thought. However, insofar as he derives this relational characteristic from Schillebeeckx's theology of creation primarily, he too seems to favour creation over salvation.

[79] Schillebeeckx, 'Correlation between Human Question', 86 [98–9].
[80] Schillebeeckx, *Church*, 231 [233].
[81] Ibid.

the root of all religion as a mediated immediate relationship with what believers call the Creator God.[82]

Importantly, Schillebeeckx takes great care to qualify this Christian interpretation of the contrast experience, so as to avoid the suggestion of Christian imperialism or absolutism. By employing the term 'mediated immediacy' – a term also used by Rahner – he seeks to explain that the nearness of God in creation is immediate from God's side, but is always dependent upon mediation from the human side.[83] This has important consequences for every attempt to name and thematize the traces of grace in reality.

The Christian understanding of the contrast experience as an experience of grace does not imply that it is an ordinary experience of a reality among other realities. According to Schillebeeckx, God is never available to us as an objective reality and only comes into our view through horizontal experiences. We paradoxically experience God as the 'inexperiencable', as a mystery which comes indirectly into view through our experience of the world.[84] This sounds strikingly similar to Rahner's understanding of the interconnection between transcendental and categorical experience. Rather than explicating the paradoxical 'non-objectivity' of God in greater detail, Schillebeeckx explores the consequences of this peculiar experience for theological discourse. Since we never have the reality of God 'at our disposal', all our projective images and concepts about God continually fall short; our language about God is 'broken time and again'.[85] The awareness of the limitations of theological concepts, being creaturely rather than divine, has been a constant theme throughout Schillebeeckx's work, but always in conjunction with the conviction that the divine mystery is an intelligible mystery. Drawing on his dialectics of hermeneutics and metaphysics, he explains how the mediated immediacy of God can be thematized theologically, despite the inherent limitations of all theological speech.

Schillebeeckx seeks to navigate between empty apophaticism and the idolatrous objectification of God. While human beings are 'by nature idolaters', he firmly rejects the concept of God as 'wholly Other', 'philosophical agnosticism', 'postmodern silence' or a 'religion without God'.[86] The necessary awareness of the inadequacy of our theological speaking must not turn into an idolatry of silence; instead, we need a 'dialectic of speaking and being silent'.[87] Speaking about God is possible because we continually stumble upon mystery as something which *surprises* us. In our dealings with the world and with other people, we experience that our projects and plans are smashed by an uncontrollable projection coming from elsewhere.[88] 'God is new each moment' – a mystery that always offers itself in revelation and concealment.[89]

---

[82] Schillebeeckx, *Christ*, 807 [811].
[83] Ibid., 68 [70].
[84] Ibid., 70-2 [72–4].
[85] Ibid., 72 [74].
[86] Edward Schillebeeckx, 'Prologue: Human God-Talk and God's Silence' [2002], in *The Praxis of the Reign of God*, xi–xiv; *Church*, 56 [57]; Schillebeeckx, 'Christelijke identiteit, uitdagend en uitgedaagd', 18.
[87] Schillebeeckx, 'Prologue', xi; Schillebeeckx, *Christ*, 41 [55].
[88] Schillebeeckx, *Church*, 72 [74].
[89] Schillebeeckx, *God is New Each Moment*, 29.

Crucially, this element of concealment and darkness remains part of our relation to God, even when the silence is interrupted by the voice that speaks in Jesus Christ. The revelation in Jesus Christ does not in any way end the hiddenness of God.[90] Rather, Schillebeeckx points out that the incarnational shape of Christian revelation fundamentally affects and conditions Christian understanding and self-understanding. As a concrete, particular, historical human being, even Jesus remains a limited manifestation of God and, therefore, cannot be used to justify any absolute claim to truth. At the same time, the concrete particularity of Jesus discloses that there are many and varied ways of relating to the universal truth revealed in Jesus Christ:

> We learn from the revelation of God in Jesus that non individual historical particularity can be said to be absolute, and that therefore through the relativity present in Jesus anyone can encounter God even outside Jesus, especially in our worldly history and in the many religions which have arisen in its. The risen Jesus of Nazareth also continues to *point to* God beyond himself. One could say: God points via Jesus Christ in the Spirit to himself as creator and redeemer, as a God of men and women, of *all* men and women.[91]

This express emphasis on the particular and limited nature of the revelation in Jesus Christ forces Christians to be attentive to other manifestations of grace throughout the world, especially in the other religions.[92] Moreover, Christians, thus, always speak *through* darkness in response to the revelation of mystery. It is the 'absolute priority of grace' which elicits a response of trust and hope that does not go against reason, but at the same time *transcends* reason which can be called a 'conscious ignorance'.[93]

For Schillebeeckx, the mystical thematization of grace is closely connected with praxis. The mystical tradition has developed the dialectics between speaking and being silent about God in terms of the *triplex viae*: the *via affirmativa*, *via negativa* and *via eminentiae*. As discussed in Chapter 7, Schillebeeckx employed this analogical mode of knowledge in order to explain the dialectics between the conceptual and the non-conceptual elements in our knowledge of God. Following his turn to praxis, Schillebeeckx now emphasizes that, for Christians, the origins of this dialectical naming of God are not purely philosophical, but go back to a *concrete praxis*: 'We do not learn to know the *via eminentiae* beyond affirmation and negation in and through a conceptual interplay of thought, but in and from the history of solidarity, justice and love made by men and women in a world of egotism, injustice and love.'[94] This insight stems from the *concrete universality* of the revelation in Jesus Christ. It is by following the concrete example of practical commitment to the poor and the oppressed that

---

[90] Schillebeeckx, *Church*, 9 [9].
[91] Ibid., 164 [166].
[92] Ibid., 165 [166]. See also 'Prologue', ix, where Schillebeeckx refers to the other religions as 'schools of wisdom' which liberate us from idolatry and which trace a way of life that discloses truth.
[93] Schillebeeckx, 'Prologue', xiii; Schillebeeckx, 'Christelijke identiteit, uitdagend en uitgedaagd', 17; Schillebeeckx, *Christ*, 42–3 [57].
[94] Schillebeeckx, *Church*, 75 [77].

the revelation in Jesus takes on a universal significance.[95] This implies that a natural theology attempting to demonstrate the universal intelligibility of Christian faith must involve the mediation of a Christ-like praxis of liberation.

In view of the concrete universality of Christian revelation, the truth of Christian faith cannot be communicated purely rationally to the non-believer with the help of a 'metaphysic of being' or through a transcendental account of free subjectivity.[96] Instead, it is the combination of an ethical commitment, which dares to go as far as risking martyrdom, and the mystical thematization of this praxis, as being anchored in a theologal relation to God, which together comprises the justification of the intelligibility of Christian faith to non-believers. Offering a well-grounded hope for a more human future, this creation faith has an 'inexhaustible potential' to inspire and to convince people.[97] Confronted with this combination of silent speech and liberative praxis, non-believers may find a resonance with this Christian interpretation of the contrast experience as a locus of grace.

> Whether this Christian answer is accepted or rejected, it cannot be denied that it is, as an answer in the form of a promise, possibility, perspective, strength and criticism, historically relevant and meaningful to any man who is seeking the meaning of human life, whether individually or collectively, personally or politically and socially. In this way, the Christian message can be made intelligible.[98]

5 Grace perfecting nature

In this chapter, I have examined how Schillebeeckx employs his dialectical account of experience with the aim of providing a natural theology that is anchored in human experience. This natural theology does not claim to offer a firm philosophical proof of God, but aims to make Christian faith intelligible by pointing to an element in human experience which is *open* to a religious interpretation: the contrast experience. I argue that Schillebeeckx draws upon both metaphysical and hermeneutical arguments in order to develop the contrast experience. The concept demonstrates the *synchronic* application of the dialectics between metaphysics and hermeneutics that marks his theological method. A closer analysis of the contrast experience also brings to light the particular use of philosophical rationality within Schillebeeckx's theology. As a

---

[95] Ibid., 167–8 [168–9].
[96] Schillebeeckx, *Church*, 96 [98]. Barwasser, *Theologie der Kultur*, 300–23, criticizes this lack of a firm philosophical justification of the contrast experience as an experience of God. Alternatively, he advocates an investigation into the transcendental-anthropological conditions of the contrast experience through an examination of human freedom. Barwasser acknowledges that the philosophical grounding of theological hermeneutics goes beyond Schillebeeckx's project. It seems difficult to reconcile this strong focus on philosophical-transcendental subjectivity with Schillebeeckx's own argument in favour of the priority of the theological-ontological dimension. Moreover, I would argue that this approach misses Schillebeeckx's transformed understanding of the hermeneutically conditioned nature of all transcendental and metaphysical reflection.
[97] Schillebeeckx, *Church*, 230 [233].
[98] Schillebeeckx, 'Correlation between Human Question', 82–3 [95].

metaphysical or transcendental concept that is elaborated *a posteriori*, the contrast experience serves primarily as a philosophical heuristic to present and explain the concrete Christian interpretation of reality as graced reality.

5.1 The hermeneutics and metaphysics of contrast experience

The contrast experience reflects the new direction taken in Schillebeeckx's theology, following his turn to hermeneutical thought and critical theory. Factors such as the historicity of experience, the refractoriness of reality and the variety of self-interpretations problematize any particular theoretical identification of universal meaning. As Philip Kennedy observes, impelled by these insights Schillebeeckx exchanges 'an aprioristic theory of knowledge for an *a posteriori* theory of knowledge'.[99] He deems it necessary to go beyond a purely speculative justification of faith. This leads him to consider the cognitive force of the ethical praxis that responds to suffering. At the same time, in order to retain the intelligibility of Christian faith there must be a universal horizon of understanding. The contrast experience is an attempt to sketch the contours of such a universal horizon, with due attention being paid to its inescapable concrete manifestation and particular interpretation. In Schillebeeckx's own opinion, the new critical-hermeneutical direction implied a radical break with his earlier metaphysical approach. However, I argue that the contrast experience actually reveals the continuing relevance of his metaphysical line of thought. At the same time, the critical-hermeneutical turn also affects and transforms his particular theological appropriation of philosophical rationality and metaphysical speculation. There are several instances in Schillebeeckx's natural theology of experience where the dialectical interrelation between metaphysics and hermeneutics becomes manifest.

To begin with, his designation of contingency as the hermeneutical principle for the disclosure of reality builds on his earlier epistemology of implicit intuition. Schillebeeckx now elaborates the objective directionality that forms a key component of his metaphysics of experience in more explicitly hermeneutical terms. Schillebeeckx argues that our failures to comprehend or to grasp reality do not end in resignation, but have a revelatory potential. Something positive becomes manifest in these negative experiences of contingency and recalcitrance. Our inadequate attempts at understanding confront us with a hidden magnet, which shapes and guides our knowledge. It forms the catalyst and directive force of every new effort of interpretation and clarification. This hermeneutical quest is in principle open-ended. At the same time, this quest for understanding is also anchored in and enabled by the independent objective reality that we encounter in experience. In order to explain the hermeneutical force of the hidden magnet, Schillebeeckx needs a metaphysical argument that establishes the priority of objective reality in experience and explains how it affects the hermeneutical process of interpretation. Affirming the critical-hermeneutical cognitivity of the refractoriness of reality presupposes a larger metaphysical framework that explains the relation between subjectivity and objectivity in experience.

---

[99] See Kennedy, *Schillebeeckx*, 127.

This metaphysical thread also remains visible when the hermeneutical force of negativity is combined with the critical cognitivity of praxis in the contrast experience. Although he never explicitly discusses this question, Schillebeeckx seems to agree with Rahner (and with the scholastic tradition at large) on the metaphysical principle that upholds the primacy of actuality over possibility. His focus on the reality of suffering and radical contingency manifests his intention not to ignore or lose sight of the negativity that fundamentally characterizes human existence. Nevertheless, contra Adorno, he refuses to absolutize this negativity and argues instead that negativity reveals positivity. The negativity of contrast experiences does not end in despair, but gives rise to an indignation that triggers a praxis of liberation. This fundamental conviction that negativity is ultimately grounded in, and revelatory of, positivity goes back to his earlier argumentation that contingency is ontologically insufficient and, therefore, contains a reference to a constitutive ground. It shows the abiding influence of his relational metaphysics of creation.

Schillebeeckx argues that the praxis of justice mediates a vision of the *humanum*. As a future promise, any theoretical expression of this perspective on the *humanum* remains fragmented and incomplete. That is why Schillebeeckx speaks of an obscure consciousness and prefers to speak of anticipation, rather than of participation. However, the possibility of this universal practical anticipation can only be posited in conjunction with a metaphysical claim. Crucially, the practical veto to suffering requires as its transcendental condition of possibility some form of existential trust and hope. For Schillebeeckx, the universal manifestation of this trust and hope raises the question of their ground. Practical anticipation, it seems after all, is impossible without a theoretical source or foundation. Schillebeeckx emphasizes that this metaphysical source of hope can be hermeneutically named in various ways, either religious or non-religious. But instead of articulating this source philosophically in secular terms, he elaborates the characteristic elements of the Christian view of hope. Once again, this reveals the dynamic between hermeneutics and metaphysics.

The Christian naming of hope is marked by an eschatological proviso that emphasizes the promissory nature of hope. All articulations of the *humanum* are subjected to a permanent hermeneutics of suspicion, thereby reminding us that history is unfinished and that only God can bring ultimate salvation. But this promise of universal salvation becomes believable, because the Christian discovers in reality as creation a surplus of meaning, goodness and trust that refers to its creative ground. The goodness of creation gives us reason to believe that salvation can become fully realized. This dynamic tension between creation faith and eschatological proviso comprises another illustration of the dialectics between metaphysics and hermeneutics.

Finally, the impossibility of articulating the *humanum* positively recurs in Schillebeeckx's negative theology. Praxis may be the primary mediation of the God's immediate nearness to creation, but for Schillebeeckx the ground sustaining this praxis must also be named. Despite our inherent limitations and notwithstanding the perennial danger of idolatry, Schillebeeckx rejects a complete silence about God. Instead, he advocates a dialectics of being silent and speaking about God. Theology can never adequately grasp and comprehend God. The mysterious ground of contingent reality continually manifests itself anew and keeps surprising us. For Schillebeeckx, the givennes of reality (to put it metaphysically) or the absolute priority of grace (to put it theologically) sustains our hermeneutical theological efforts. The divine mystery challenges and invites us to find new expressions. Naming God anew and realizing our inadequacy to name God properly allows us to transcend theoretical reason alone and leads us into a conscious ignorance.

Schillebeeckx never rescinded his account of the clear break with his earlier participatory metaphysics. However, the recurring attention to the theme of creation in his later writings acts as further proof of the fact that his theological hermeneutics remains intimately connected with the theological relational ontology of his early period.[100] In his 'theological testament', for instance, he explicitly reaffirms his early view of creation as 'participating in God, being in and of God', without any mention of the inadequacy of such a participatory framework of thought.[101] In view of the previous consideration, I conclude, therefore, that this participatory theological metaphysics continues to ground the practical-hermeneutical and eschatological anticipation in Schillebeeckx's theology.[102]

The fact that Schillebeeckx's hermeneutical project remains intimately connected with his metaphysics does not mean that this metaphysics has simply remained the same. Some authors have emphasized that due to Schillebeeckx's growing suspicion of metaphysics over time, his original metaphysics became a 'fundamentally negative' metaphysics.[103] Rather than emphasizing this negative element, I detect in the later Schillebeeckx an intensification of his earlier position that speculative metaphysics plays an essential, yet subordinate role within theology. His reflections on the limits of theoretical reason have strengthened his conviction that the theologian starts from the critical memory of the events of salvation history, by way of a hermeneutics of the Christian tradition and a corresponding praxis of liberation. Speculative metaphysical reflection does not become redundant, but is rather deliberately used from within a particular hermeneutical position of faith. Due to this priority, the theologian proceeds primarily inductively and only arrives at metaphysics as a conclusion, rather than taking it to be a starting point.[104] Schillebeeckx's natural theology of the contrast experience forms an example of such an *a posteriori* metaphysics.

5.2 The contrast experience as heuristics of grace

The *a posteriori* character of Schillebeeckx's metaphysics is best explained against the background of his understanding of the relationship between philosophy and

---

[100] See Schillebeeckx, *Church*, 227–43 [229–46]; Edward Schillebeeckx, 'Verlangen naar ultieme levensvervulling. Een kritische herlezing van Thomas van Aquino', *Tijdschrift voor Theologie* 42 (2002): 28–34.
[101] Edward Schillebeeckx, 'Theological Quests' [1994], in *Essays. Ongoing Theological Quests*, 124. Originally published as Edward Schillebeeckx, *Theologisch testament. Notarieel nog niet verleden* (Baarn: Nelissen, 1994).
[102] Rodenborn, *Hope in Action*, 183, similarly concludes that 'the language of anticipation represents an epistemic-apologetic development' which leaves the earlier metaphysics intact.
[103] Portier, 'Edward Schillebeeckx as Critical Theorist', 363–4; Rodenborn, *Hope in Action*, 175.
[104] Schoof, 'Masters in Israel', 952; Rodenborn, *Hope in Action*, 174.

theology. On the one hand, Schillebeeckx draws extensively from philosophical arguments in order to present faith as an existential life option that can be reasonably justified. This appreciation of philosophy is connected with his affirmation of the autonomy of the secular world and of human reason. Schillebeeckx considers Thomas to be the real initiator and inspiration of this positive view of secular philosophy.[105] On the other hand, he does not shy away from pointing out the weaknesses and shortcomings of philosophy. The critical force of theological rationality consists in the exposure of the limitations and biases of 'enlightened reason' and in the disclosure of the 'reason-transcending dimensions' of theoretical reason.[106] For Schillebeeckx, this critique is a crucial element of theology's dialogical engagement with philosophy. Over against attempts at complete theoretical rationalization, theology puts forward a concept of 'conscious unknowing'. This conscious unknowing does not negate or subject philosophical rationality, but makes us attentive of the transcendent character of human reason. Schillebeeckx elaborates on this affirmative yet critical stance with regard to philosophical reason particularly when discussing the importance of praxis. He argues that the abstract and universal reason of the Enlightenment remains entangled in personal and societal sin and, therefore, needs liberation. Over and against this theoretical universality, theology offers an account of universality as 'incarnate', 'concrete' and 'historical'.[107] This universality is realized through the faithful recollection of God's promise in Jesus Christ and through a praxis of faith. In other words, theological rationality reveals that theoretical reason must become practical in order to mediate universal truth.

> This universal liberating praxis is not a secondary superstructure upon, or merely a consequence of, a theoretical truth already recognized as universal, but it is the historical mediation of the manifestation of truth as universal truth, applying to all men and women.[108]

Hence, Schillebeeckx's appraisal of theoretical philosophy is combined with a theological criticism centred upon the importance of praxis. What consequences does this critique have for the status of metaphysics – one of the most theoretical philosophical discourses – within theology?

Schillebeeckx's sharp critique of theoretical philosophy has led some to conclude that he no longer supports the theological use of metaphysical or transcendental arguments. Martin Poulsom, for instance, summarily dismisses the suggestion that Schillebeeckx is a 'transcendental thinker', and Francis Schüssler Fiorenza argues that 'his later work has moved away from a position that could accurately be labelled "transcendental Thomism"'.[109] Anthony Godzieba too deems Schillebeeckx's

---

[105] Schillebeeckx, 'Theological Quests', 122–3; Schillebeeckx, 'Verlangen naar ultieme levensvervulling', 18–20.
[106] Schillebeeckx, 'Theological Interpretation of Faith', 67.
[107] Schillebeeckx, *Church*, 29 [29]; 167–8 [168–9].
[108] Ibid., 176 [178].
[109] Poulsom, *The Dialectics of Creation*, 7; Fiorenza, 'The New Theology and Transcendental Thomism', in *Modern Christian Thought. The Twentieth Century*, 227. Alternatively, Carsten Barwasser,

opposition to the oppressive and idolatrous force of theoretical philosophy to be problematic. Insofar as it leads to the 'wholesale dismissal of transcendental argument', it runs the risk of becoming an 'extrinsicist position where secular history and the history of salvation proceed on parallel tracks or parallel planes, with ultimately no philosophical-anthropological way to discern their connection'.[110] Alternatively, Godzieba argues that there is need for a natural theology that explores the limits of human experience in order to disclose a 'clearing' for transcendence.[111] He argues that Schillebeeckx's dismissal of transcendental arguments implies a refusal to provide one such rational argument for the possibility of transcendence and the existence of God.[112]

My analysis of the contrast experience, however, challenges this assessment. I demonstrated that Schillebeeckx renounces neither natural theology nor metaphysical or transcendental arguments. However, his natural theology is markedly different, insofar as it entails a theological metaphysics which is conscious of the limitations of theoretical reason. Schillebeeckx situates himself firmly in the Christian tradition of faith and develops, from this position, a transcendental-ontological argument that seeks to communicate a view of reality which remains ultimately inaccessible for theoretical philosophical reason alone. A closer reflection on the notion of the contrast experience helps to clarify the particular shape this theological metaphysics adopts.

It is possible to draw a parallel between Rahner's transcendental experience and Schillebeeckx's contrast experience. Both concepts fulfil a transcendental function in their respective theologies, in three distinct ways.[113] First, both concepts of experience operate as a transcendental condition of possibility. Schillebeeckx considers the givenness of trust, in and through the contrast experience, to be the condition for the possibility of the praxis of liberation, whereas for Rahner, transcendental experience forms the condition for the possibility of all human knowing and actions. Second, transcendental experience and contrast experience are developed as ontological concepts. Rahner's elaboration of transcendental experience as *Vorgriff* demonstrates how we are always with Being, without ever grasping or comprehending Being. The contrast experience similarly serves to make us attentive to the refractory dimension of reality and to the fundamental givenness of all experience. It discloses that contingent givenness contains an objective reference towards its ontological source and ground. Third, transcendental experience and contrast experience are philosophical concepts, which are used to explain the universal possibility of experiencing transcendent mystery or God. In other words, they function as a

---

Theologie der Kultur und Hermeneutik der Glaubenserfahrung, 105–86, argues that Schillebeeckx has followed the transcendental turn towards the subject in Catholic theology. In the period up until the Second Vatican Council, he develops a transcendental anthropology as the foundation for his 'theology of culture' (106).

[110] Anthony Godzieba, 'God, the Luxury of our Lives: Schillebeeckx and the Argument', in *Edward Schillebeeckx and Contemporary Theology*, 25–35 (32).
[111] Godzieba, 'God, The Luxury of our Lives', 33.
[112] Ibid., 33–5.
[113] Haight, *The Future of Christology*, 108–9, observes that Schillebeeckx's notions of basic trust and contrast experience manifest that he too uses a significant degree of transcendental analysis in order to identify universal structures of experience in human existence. See also Rodenborn, *Hope in Action*, 170, who argues that Schillebeeckx's identification of 'self-transcending hope' serves as a transcendental structure by which to make Christian faith intelligible.

heuristic to make attentive to what believers call the experience of grace and serve to make this claim of faith intelligible.[114] Crucially, it is this third heuristic function that particularly reveals the theological origin and purpose of these concepts as well as their transformative consequences.

In Chapter 5, I explained how Rahner theologically transforms philosophical transcendentality through the historicity of grace. Now, Schillebeeckx's contrast experience actually effects a similar theological transformation of philosophical metaphysics. In order to explain this, it is essential to recognize that the contrast experience has been developed from within a *theological* context, as the result of an inductive reflection on the Christian proclamation of the experience of grace in Jesus Christ. Thus, it is not a general philosophical anthropology, but rather Schillebeeckx's belief in this concrete historical experience, mediated in the Christian confession and praxis, which forms the foundation of his claim that the contrast experience is a 'basic human experience'.[115] The transcendental and metaphysical structure of human experience that Schillebeeckx articulates with the help of the contrast experience is therefore informed by a concrete theological perspective. This is a perspective that is more encompassing than theoretical philosophy, because it is based in a concrete historical experience that brings together theory and praxis, rather than in speculative reflection alone. This methodology is similar to Schillebeeckx's early theological appropriation of philosophy, which enabled him to express the theologal relation as a transcendental relation.

It must be noted, though, that Schillebeeckx himself does not always acknowledge the theological shape of his own thought. While he lays these theological cards more openly on the table when explaining the impossibility of establishing a purely philosophical proof for the existence of God, he seems to conceal his own theological position in his criticism of Protestant correlation theologians and their deduction of human questions. Schillebeeckx may have paid more attention to the commonality and differences between non-religious humanistic answers and religious answers, but his articulation of the human question in terms of the contrast experience has an unmistakeable theological pedigree. However, he is also convinced that despite these theological origins, this concept has an intelligibility that transcends intra-Christian discourse.

Now, in order to communicate this experience of grace to people who do not share the particular Christian framework, Schillebeeckx resorts to philosophy while he also goes beyond philosophy. He expresses the experience of grace philosophically, with the help of transcendental and metaphysical arguments, as the universally shared experience of contrast in the confrontation with negativity. In other words, the contrast experience is the philosophical articulation of the relational ontology of creation that is revealed in Christ. However, Schilllebeeckx also takes care to emphasize the abstract

---

[114] I derive this characterization of the contrast experience as a heuristic principle from Kennedy, *Deus Humanissimus*, 361.

[115] See also Borgman, 'Tussen theologie en universiteit', 256; Boeve, 'The Enduring Significance', 21, who similarly argues that Schillebeeckx's natural theology is 'a forceful *theological* reading of secularity, including the contrast experience'; and Kennedy, *Deus Humanissimus*, 368, who argues that the supportive role played by philosophy is characteristic for Schillebeeckx's work at large.

nature of this theoretical concept and its consequent limitations. The notion of the contrast experience is informed by the Christian interrelation of theory and praxis, but as an abstract philosophical concept it cannot be equated with a concrete religious experience. As Schillebeeckx already argued in his early career, Christian faith is not a 'supra-metaphysics'.[116] Thus, the contrast experience should not be understood as a plea for an independent natural or general religious anthropology. In developing the contrast experience, Schillebeeckx uses the argumentative force of philosophy heuristically. This theologically shaped metaphysics serves to identify a shared element within concrete experiences of contrast, which provides the religious interpretation of this element with rational plausibility.

However, this religious interpretation of experience can never be 'the conclusion of a logically or philosophically stringent argumentation', but ultimately requires a conversion.[117] Abstract theoretical metaphysical and transcendental explication is a helpful tool, but it can never prove God or convince people to believe by itself. A theological participatory metaphysics offers an insightful perspective on the concurrence of positivity and negativity in experiential confrontations with suffering, but this theoretical participatory framework remains limited and incomplete. Ultimately, a 'transfinalization' of metaphysics is required. For Schillebeeckx, this conversion involves a turn towards orthopraxis.[118] Theoretical metaphysics explains the possibility of experiencing grace, but concrete experiences of grace only occur within praxis and are, as historical experiences, anticipations of salvation at best. It is only in combination with practical anticipation that the theoretical participatory metaphysical concept of the contrast experience becomes an intelligible justification of Christian faith.[119] This plea for the theological transfinalization of metaphysics demonstrates Schillebeeckx's positive, yet critical relation to philosophical rationality. It is possible to explicate the rational intelligibility of faith, without reducing faith to a self-evident rational truth.[120] Crucially, this theological appropriation and transformation of philosophical rationality ultimately stems from his view on the relationship between nature and grace.

---

[116] Schillebeeckx, 'The New Trends', 295 [115].

[117] Schillebeeckx, 'Verlangen naar een ultieme levensvervulling', 22–3. In this article, Schillebeeckx argues that this also holds true for Thomas's five ways. With the help of these five philosophical explorations, we stumble upon a mystery. But naming this mystery as God is not possible as the result of philosophical argument. Rather, Thomas is able to make such an identification because he stands trustingly in the Christian tradition of experience.

[118] I derive this term 'transfinalization' from Schillebeeckx himself, who employs this term in *Church*, 89 to explain the relation between secular ethics and theologal praxis.

[119] Kennedy, *Deus Humanissimus*, 370, observes that this affirmation, of the necessity of orthopraxis for the experience of grace, is 'devoid of rational legitimation'. He concludes that Schillebeeckx does not sufficiently 'ground philosophically' what he 'declares theologically'. Kennedy suggests that this theoretical support could be found in the later Habermas. This suggestion, however, is put into question by Francis Schüssler Fiorenza, 'Review of *Deus Humanissimus. The Knowability of God in the Theology of Edward Schillebeeckx*, by Philip Kennedy', *The Journal of Religion* 76 (1996): 126–7, who argues that since the later Habermas moved closer to a transcendental mode of argumentation, it seems doubtful that his thought might provide the basis for a praxis-oriented theology.

[120] Schillebeeckx, *God is New Each Moment*, 104–5.

5.3 One reality in two languages

The theological vision of reality as a graced reality, always and everywhere touched by God, lies at the very heart of Schillebeeckx's theological project. 'God's grace in the sense of his saving presence among people is not a separate sector of inwardness but encompasses – in different gradations of revelational density – the entire reality in which we live and which we are'.[121] As Borgman explains, this theological vision is part of the incarnational approach of the *nouvelle théologie* that views the world and the contemporary situation at large as a *locus theologicus*: 'The world *is* God's world because it is created, whether people acknowledge it or not. History is God's history because it is redeemed, and this redemption has left its traces in human lives, whether this is confessed to or not.'[122] Roger Haight has characterized Schillebeeckx's later theology by employing the expression 'one reality in two languages'.[123] Schillebeeckx seeks to recognize that there are really different interpretative perspectives, secular or religious, but these perspectives ultimately concern the same reality. I argue that this particular view of one graced reality in two languages explains Schillebeeckx's positive view of philosophical rationality as well as his plea for a transfinalization of philosophy.

Schillebeeckx considers the upholding of the integrity and autonomy of humanist ethical praxis and secular self-understanding to be essential. This high regard for secular philosophy is reflected in the conviction that Christian faith is intelligible and open – but is not reducible – to reasonable explanation using philosophical arguments. Moreover, autonomous philosophical rationality is also able to exercise a critical function, unmasking the ideological elements of religion.[124] However, it also contains an important qualification, given that the foundation of Schillebeeckx's affirmation of the autonomy of the secular realm is ultimately theological. Ethical praxis is transfinalized and acquires a theologal dimension when viewed from within the Christian tradition. The unity of the love of neighbour and the love of God illustrates this theological transfinalization of ethics.[125] Accordingly, Schillebeeckx affirms the *relative* autonomy of secular ethics and self-understanding. In this regard, his theology remains indebted to Thomas who according to Schillebeeckx recognized the 'finite autonomy' of creation.[126] Hence, Schillebeeckx accords a clear primacy to faith and theology, his respect for humanist, philosophical, agnostic or other non-religious world views notwithstanding.[127]

---

[121] Schillebeeckx, 'Experience and Faith', 31.
[122] Erik Borgman, 'Retrieving God's Contemporary Presence: The Future of Edward Schillebeeckx's Theology of Culture', in *Edward Schillebeeckx and Contemporary Theology*, 238.
[123] Roger Haight, 'Engagement met de wereld als zaak van God. Christologie en postmoderniteit', *Tijdschrift voor Theologie* 50 (2010): 79.
[124] Schillebeeckx, *Church*, 90 [92].
[125] Ibid., 89 [92]. See Bernhard Kohl, 'Jenseits des Diskurses. Ethische Anstöße bei Edward Schillebeeckx', in *Edward Schillebeeckx. Impulse für Theologien*, 158.
[126] Schillebeeckx, 'Verlangen naar een ultieme levensvervulling', 18–20. See also Erik Borgman, 'Deus Humanissimus. Christelijk geloof als excessief humanisme bij Edward Schillebeeckx', in *Humanisme en religie. Controverses, bruggen, perspectieven*, ed. Joachim Duyndam, Marcel Poorthuis, and Theo de Wit (Delft: Eburon, 2005), 230, for this theological affirmation of humanism and its Thomistic origins. Borgman also emphasizes that Schillebeeckx's own 'Christian-religious humanism' is a 'humble humanism'.
[127] See Kennedy, 'Continuity underlying Continuity', 276.

This qualification of secular autonomy reveals that Schillebeeckx takes a more normative position than he himself sometimes acknowledges. In *Church*, he argues, for instance, that a religious interpretation 'helps' to understand this experience, instead of giving it a 'better understanding' than the non-religious interpretation.[128] However, his argument for the transfinalization of humanist ethics and his comparison between the secular and religious accounts of the objective ground of hope suggest that he does hold to their being a qualitative difference between the secular and the religious points of view. In his early work, he expressed this even more sharply, claiming that the perspective of faith provides an interpretative benefit. Faith brings us 'in the right mood to be open and receptive' for the 'objective aspects' in reality that refer us to the mystery of God.[129] Just as Rahner argues that salvation history sheds new light upon human transcendentality, thereby claiming to know more than the transcendental philosopher, Schillebeeckx claims that the religious identification of grace transforms and augments secular ontology and secular ethics. This 'more' in reality is articulated religiously by describing contingent reality as God's creation on the way to salvation.[130]

But despite this qualitative difference, both the secular philosophical 'language' and the theological 'language' are appropriate ways through which to speak about reality. The religious world view is 'at least an equally reasonable account' compared with the agnostic humanist view of the world.[131] Crucially, Schillebeeckx shares the Thomistic view on the continuity between nature and grace: *gratia non tollit naturam, sed perficit*. On the one hand, this means that philosophical humanism is not in direct competition with theology. Since the God confessed by Christians is a *Deus humanissimus*, secular ethics and philosophical discourse generally retain their validity and integrity. Neither can they be reduced to a preliminary phase of religion nor can they simply become superfluous within religious discourse. They themselves bear traces of God's grace.[132] On the other hand, religious interpretation also inwardly differentiates secular experience in a manner analogous to the transformation of nature by grace. Religious interpretation is, therefore, not a 'superstructure' that is simply imposed upon secular experience and understanding.[133] Instead, it is a transformation of the humanist perspective of horizontal transcendence, which affirms this horizontalism but also sees it as being grounded in, and pointing towards, an ultimate vertical transcendence. For the theologian, horizontal transcendence and vertical transcendence are two dimensions of the same reality.[134]

---

[128] Schillebeeckx, *Church*, 82 [84].
[129] Schillebeeckx, 'Non-Religious Humanism and Belief in God', 56–7.
[130] Schillebeeckx, *Church*, 229 [231–2]; See Edward Schillebeeckx, 'Christian Identity and Human Integrity', *Concilium* 155 (1982): 26: 'And it is with this "more" that is at stake that the theologian is concerned'.
[131] Schillebeeckx, 'Verlangen naar een ultieme levensvervulling', 28. Haight, 'Engagement met de wereld als zaak van God', 90, argues that the religious account is ultimately more satisfactory than nihilism and relativism, insofar as it offers hope for an 'absolute future'.
[132] Schillebeeckx, 'Christian Identity and Human Integrity', 29. See Borgman, *Edward Schillebeeckx*, 239–41, for the Christological and sacramental background of the notion *Deus humanissimus*.
[133] Schillebeeckx, 'Theological Quests', 124–5.
[134] Kennedy, 'Continuity underlying Discontinuity', 276; Borgman, 'Deus Humanissimus'. Christelijk geloof als excessief humanisme', 245.

As the living witness of this reality, the Christian church is 'a "sacrament" of the salvation that God brings about in the world which he has created'.[135] In other words, the Christian tradition explicitly identifies the salvific grace that is universally present in reality, including secular philosophy and ethics. As Schillebeeckx puts it in rather paradoxical terms, 'The *redundance* of religious transcendence in human ethics only becomes apparent in light of a human religious tradition.'[136] For secular philosophers and humanists alike, this theological qualification of their discourses may appear as a relativization of their autonomy. Schillebeeckx was not unaware of this delicate issue. This can be illustrated by considering his view on the concept of the 'anonymous Christian'.

5.4 Anonymous Christians: A real possibility?

Terms such as 'anonymous Christian', 'anonymous faith', 'anonymous religion' or 'implicit Christianity' occur repeatedly throughout Schillebeeckx's writings, particularly in the late 1950s and early 1960s.[137] Stephen Bullivant has suggested that Schillebeeckx was actually as important as Rahner in the introduction of this idea to modern Catholic theology.[138] However, he argues that '*unlike* Rahner, Schillebeeckx ultimately came to disown the phrase, believing an *anonymous* Christian to be a contradiction in terms'.[139] As Bullivant himself admits, his assessment is rather formal, that is merely based on Schillebeeckx's use of these terms. This is confirmed by Bullivant's attribution of the eventual terminological change to the influence of Hans Urs von Balthasar's critique of Rahner.[140] However, the more interesting question is whether or not this terminological change also implies a substantive change. Since Bullivant does not support his claim by considering Schillebeeckx's (changed) theological position, he is unable to offer an answer to this question. In this chapter, I have argued extensively that there is a significant degree of continuity in Schillebeeckx's thought. This not only gives us reason to challenge Bullivant's suggestion but also provides an alternative interpretative key for understanding Schillebeeckx's take on anonymous Christians.

To begin with, it must be noted that Schillebeeckx already signalled the problematic nature of the term 'anonymous Christian' at an early stage. In 'Non-Religious Humanism and Belief in God', he explicitly rejects the suggestion that there is any point in telling a non-believer that he or she is, in actual fact, an anonymous Christian, since this would

---

[135] Schillebeeckx, *Church*, 13. For a discussion on the sacramental role played by the Church as 'sign and instrument' of salvation, see Borgman, 'Like a Sacrament', 230–51.
[136] Schillebeeckx, 'Culture, Religion and Violence', 180.
[137] See, for instance, Edward Schillebeeckx, 'Priest and Layman in a Secular World' [1952–1953], in *God and World*, CW vol. 4, trans. N.D. Smith (London: Bloomsbury, 2014), 25–6 [32–4]; Edward Schillebeeckx, 'Church and World' [1964], in *World and Church*, 75–81 [98–107]; Edward Schillebeeckx, 'The Church and Mankind' [1965], in *World and Church*, 96–101; Schillebeeckx, 'Non-Religious Humanism and Belief in God', 75–7; Schillebeeckx, 'Life in God', 174; 209.
[138] Stephen Bullivant, 'The Myth of Rahnerian Exceptionalism', *Philosophy and Theology* 22 (2010): 339–51 (342–44). Bullivant lists several places in Schillebeeckx's early work in which he uses the adjective 'anonymous' or 'implicit'.
[139] Ibid., 349.
[140] Ibid., 343. This seems to be a rather speculative suggestion, especially because Schillebeeckx himself does not indicate this Balthasarian influence anywhere.

imply not taking this person seriously.[141] However, Schillebeeckx immediately adds that even though we must accept this non-religious self-identification, this does not mean that this interpretation cannot be challenged or criticized. Even someone who has not found God herself is still found by God.[142] A couple of years later, in 1965, Schillebeeckx writes that, given his trust in the power of grace, he considers anonymous Christianity a 'real possibility', but without wanting to claim 'that all non-Catholic people are in themselves anonymous Christians'.[143] By 1970, Schillebeeckx even states that 'it is not really possible to speak of "anonymous Christians"', since 'Christians call themselves such in an explicit, conscious and justified way'.[144] At the same time, he warns that this does not imply that non-Christians are deprived of salvation.

Following his hermeneutical turn, Schillebeeckx refrains from using the specific term 'anonymous Christian'. However, he does keep using the adjective 'anonymous' in other instances. Thus, he argues in *Christ* that the source which becomes manifest in the human experience of contingency often remains unnamed, but he considers it to be the task of believers and theologians alike 'to name this ultimate reality and not leave it in anonymity'.[145] Furthermore, he still speaks in *Church* about the 'anonymous, concealed and modest coming of God into the world'.[146] Finally, even though Schillebeeckx may have dropped the specific term 'anonymous Christian' from his lexicon, he still argues that non-religious contrast experiences may be called 'natural faith', in contradistinction to 'religious faith', insofar as Christians recognize the presence of God's grace in these concrete experiences.[147] How can this ambiguity be explained? I suggest that Schillebeeckx's growing attentiveness to hermeneutics explains the 'disowning' of the term 'anonymous Christian', but because of the prevailing influence of his metaphysics he refuses to give up the claim that grace can be present *implicitly*.

To explain this, let us consider Schillebeeckx's famous modification of the dictum '*extra ecclesiam nulla salus*' into '*extra mundum nulla salus*'.[148] Through the employment of this statement he seeks to affirm the world of human experience at large as comprising the locus of God's salvific activity. God's grace cannot be confined to the borders of the visible church or to explicitly religious domains solely.[149] Mindful of hermeneutical insights, Schillebeeckx seeks to recognize the active involvement of the subject in this encounter with grace. Hence, the universal presence of salvific grace in human experience should not be misunderstood as an '"ontological unconscious"

---

[141] Schillebeeckx, 'Non-Religious Humanism and Belief in God', in *God and Man*, 77.
[142] Ibid., 79-81. This priority of God's searching for humankind and its grounding of the human search for God, which Isaiah, St. Paul, and St. Augustine already expressed, is reiterated in Schillebeeckx, 'Verlangen naar een ultieme levensvervulling', 28.
[143] Schillebeeckx, 'The Church and Mankind', 101, n. 18.
[144] Schillebeeckx, 'Correlation between Human Question', 87 [100].
[145] Schillebeeckx, *Christ*, 42-3 [57].
[146] Ibid., 13 [14].
[147] Schillebeeckx, 'Theologie der Erfahrung', 393.
[148] Schillebeeckx, *Church*, 12 [12].
[149] Ibid. Already in *Christ*, 808 [812], Schillebeeckx has argued that God's grace is 'the whole of reality in which we live and of which we ourselves are part' rather than a 'special realm of inwardness'. Janet M. O'Meara, 'Salvation: Living Communion with God', in *The Praxis of the Reign of God*, 100, comments that in *Church* Schillebeeckx 'completes the "turn to the world"' that he initiated in *Christ*.

dimension' that is merely 'brought to "consciousness" by revelation'.[150] This view not only violates the hermeneutical insight that experience is always interpreted but also ignores the constitutive role played by praxis. Salvation needs to be appropriated – through intentional human liberation – and, therefore, always involves 'a degree of awareness'.[151] When the universal presence of grace is indeed a conscious presence, it seems inappropriate to speak of anonymous Christians. This misrepresents the self-understanding of both self-identifying Christians and non-Christians. Salvific grace does not work in spite of or below secular self-interpretation, but precisely *in* this secular interpretation and action. The non-believer has her own consciousness of the surplus of trust and hope that presents itself in contingency. This surplus does not simply remain implicit, but is always somehow given a name, even though it is not necessarily a Christian or religious name. In order to respect the variety of human responses to grace, Schillebeeckx emphasizes the distinction between salvation and revelation: 'Salvation history is not the same thing as the history of revelation; in the latter, salvation history becomes a conscious and literate experience of faith.'[152] This sheds some light on Schillebeeckx's decision to no longer use the term 'anonymous Christian'. However, this naturally leads to the question of how salvation, which is not yet revelation, should be termed.

Immediately following the emphasis placed on the conscious aspect of the human appropriation of salvation, Schillebeeckx continues by affirming the primacy of God's agency in the mediation of grace. The offer of salvation always precedes our recognition of this offer in explicitly religious terms: 'God and his initiative of salvation are a reality independent of human consciousness, and independent of our expression of God.'[153] The reality of God's salvific action extends further than the realm of human interpretation. Schillebeeckx's metaphysics of experience, with its attention to inner interpretative or pre-reflective elements, serves to explain this priority and independence of grace which precedes and escapes subjective control. The conscious appropriation of grace does not require an explicitly religious vocabulary, but takes place whenever 'good is furthered and evil is challenged' by way of the historical praxis of love.[154] He affirms squarely that 'a good human action, performed in freedom, is grace in the concrete'.[155] The response to the divine initiative and articulation of this experience, then, are dependent upon and shaped by one's specific historical context. Nonetheless, it is clear that the metaphysical Schillebeeckx chooses to maintain the possibility of there being a concealed presence of salvific grace within human self-understanding and actions, even when it is consciously non-Christian or non-religious. His hermeneutical turn has not negated his fundamental theological conviction about the intertwinement of nature and grace at the transcendental-anthropological level. As created beings, human persons are universally ordered towards grace and are capable

---

[150] Schillebeeckx, *Church*, 10 [10].
[151] Ibid., 11 [11].
[152] Ibid., 12 [12].
[153] Ibid. [13].
[154] Ibid. [12].
[155] Schillebeeckx, 'Christian Identity and Human Integrity', 24.

of consciously appropriating the offer of salvific grace, without necessarily requiring a religious framework of interpretation.[156]

In order to recognize the fact that even this concealed presence of grace presumes a conscious and practical attitude, and in view of the many misunderstandings surrounding the notion of anonymous Christians, it may be better to speak about the possibility of an 'implicit' presence of grace within non-religious or other religious experience.[157] Yet this term too implies a normative theological claim. This claim may conflict with the self-understanding of other people, but the concept of anonymous Christians is not in the first place intended for use in interreligious dialogue. Rather, it is a concept belonging to systematic theology and serves in the first place to develop the Christian understanding of God's action through grace. Schillebeeckx is convinced that theology must affirm that grace can be a reality in human life without being named as such.[158] Both his metaphysical realism and his insistence on the priority of God's offer of grace lead him to the insight that even a mistaken identification of grace can still be an appropriation of grace. For this reason, it must be concluded that Schillebeeckx ultimately continues to support the notion of implicit grace, albeit in a more hermeneutically sophisticated way.

6 Conclusion

This chapter concludes my argument that Schillebeeckx's theological method is structurally characterized by a dialectics of metaphysics and hermeneutics. I have explained how his natural theology of contrast experience effectively comprises a synchronic application of this dialectics. Following his critical-hermeneutical turn, Schillebeeckx remains convinced about the need to demonstrate the universal intelligibility of Christian faith. However, he rejects a hermeneutically naive outsider's perspective or the possibility of explaining Christian belief solely in terms of abstract metaphysical or transcendental arguments. Instead, Schillebeeckx argues that the Christian tradition offers an intelligible interpretation of human experience. Communicating the universal intelligibility of this Christian interpretation requires a combination of metaphysical and hermeneutical arguments.

---

[156] Poulsom, *The Dialectics of Creation*, 143, confirms this interrelation of nature and grace and rightly concludes that, for Schillebeeckx, there is no 'pure nature'.

[157] See also Van Erp, 'Implicit Faith', 222, who accentuates the connection between De Petter's theory of implicit intuition and Schillebeeckx's account of the experience of the absolute limit and arrives at the notion of 'implicit faith'. This implicit faith may even be present in what manifests itself as 'fully secular'. Theology must, therefore, develop a larger openness for 'new ways in which people with secular worldviews are associated with the history of an incarnate God, and are therefore connected with the people in the church'.

[158] In a letter included in *Edward Schillebeeckx and Contemporary Theology*, xiv, Schillebeeckx emphasizes that his phrase *extra mundum nulla salus* is highly theological: 'Some Christians and even some theologians misinterpret this expression because they think – wrongly – that it refers only to humanism and not to salvation by God. This is because they put the accent on *mundum* instead of *salus*. *Salus* always comes from God, but it is experienced in the world. God is always the foundation – the source of salvation – and that is the core point of the Christian religion'.

A metaphysical argument is used to explain that our encounters with the contingency and refractoriness of reality have a particular revelatory potential. Reality contains a hidden magnet that offers itself in revelation and concealment. Praxis plays a primary role in the interpretation of this revelatory aspect of reality. Contrast experiences are concentrated occasions of this dynamic between manifestation and interpretation. Encounters with suffering and evil, which elicit indignation and a practical liberating response, mediate a universal mysterious confluence of negativity and positivity. The positive perspective of the *humanum* cannot be expressed purely theoretically, but is nonetheless anticipated in the praxis that responds to suffering. Yet this praxis is sustained by a trust or hope, which is open to various interpretations.

While the hope that supports and motivates a praxis of justice is not necessarily thematized religiously, the religious interpretation contains a distinct intelligibility. I have explained that Schillebeeckx draws upon his dialectics of metaphysics and hermeneutics in order to explain the Christian interpretation. In light of the revelation in Jesus Christ, the contrast experience can be interpreted as an experience of grace – one which can be expressed theologically as a dialectics between eschatological hope and creation faith. Recognizing this mystery and naming this mystery theologically require some form of metaphysics. However, this metaphysics must be hermeneutically conscious of its own limitations in order to avoid idolatry. Insofar as Schillebeeckx's metaphysical account of experience is conscious of its theological inspiration and of its necessary incompleteness, it can be considered an *a posteriori* metaphysics.

I have explained that Schillebeeckx's use of the contrast experience as a heuristics of grace offers a revealing insight into his view on the role that philosophy plays within theology. Schillebeeckx supports the autonomy of secular philosophy and acknowledges the crucial critical force that secular thought can exert regarding theology. But he also points to the limitations of theoretical reason and to the transcendent character of reason. Basing himself on the revelation of 'concrete universality' in Jesus Christ, he advocates a transfinalization of metaphysics. Hence, from the perspective of the theologian, the autonomy of philosophy is ultimately affirmed to be relative. This theological corrective of philosophy alerts primarily to the necessity of praxis for a proper understanding of reality.

Crucially, this theologically qualified approach to philosophical rationality offers an interpretative key to the dialectics between metaphysics and hermeneutics in Schillebeeckx's theological epistemology. It provides Schillebeeckx a distinct strategy to reflect on the universality of Christian faith in a hermeneutically responsible way. For this reason, Schillebeeckx's theological method is highly relevant for contemporary fundamental theology.

Conclusion

This study has engaged in a retrieval of the fundamental theologies of Karl Rahner and Edward Schillebeeckx. The aim of this retrieval has been to rethink how theology can account for the universality of the salvific truth to which the Christian tradition bears witness. Based on the concrete revelation in Jesus Christ, Christians believe in a loving God who seeks to be in relationship with humankind. The traditional theological strategy of turning to metaphysical arguments in order to account for the universal intelligibility of Christian faith has been called into question by postmodern thinkers, who have pointed out the limitations and potential dangers of these metaphysical forms of theology. My retrieval of Rahner and Schillebeeckx challenges this postmodern verdict on the incompatibility of hermeneutical sensitivity and metaphysical reflection within theology. I have argued that these thinkers demonstrate the possibility of a dialectical interrelation between hermeneutics and metaphysics within theology. This dialectics of metaphysics and hermeneutics offers a way to think about the universal truth of Christian faith from within particularity. Crucially, the metaphysics of mystery that results from this dialectical interrelation brings out both the potentialities and the limitations of metaphysical reflection within theology.

In Chapter 1, I assessed the way in which contemporary fundamental theologians have responded to the challenges posed by postmodern critical consciousness. Francis Schüssler Fiorenza and David Tracy have turned to hermeneutics in order to take seriously the postmodern call to particularity and otherness. They have developed theological methodologies that are attentive to the fundamental influence exerted by history, cultural differences, linguistic mediation and ideological distortion on theological reflection on faith and its truth claims. However, this hermeneutical focus on particularity, and the consequent distancing from metaphysical modes of reflection, has resulted in a relative forgetfulness of the crucial universal dimension of theological truth. Together with Fiorenza and Tracy, I concluded that theology is currently in need of a reconceptualized form of metaphysical theology. Fundamental theology has to renew its attention to the universality of faith, yet it cannot forego the insights of (post)modernity. Theological reflection on universality must deal responsibly and adequately with the limitations and particularities that shape and condition every engagement with truth. I have argued for a return to the work of Rahner and Schillebeeckx as a way of bringing this theological discussion forward. By virtue of the dialectical interrelation of metaphysics and hermeneutics in their theological methods, Rahner and Schillebeeckx offer a valuable and insightful example of a modest metaphysical theology. In order to disclose and explain these hermeneutically chastised metaphysical theologies, I undertook an extensive retrieval of Rahner's and Schillebeeckx's method.

In Part I, I explained that Rahner's transcendental arguments are consistently conditioned by a hermeneutical sensitivity. Importantly, though, this attentiveness to hermeneutical conditions of transcendental reflection qualifies, rather than invalidates, the universal scope of these transcendental arguments. Chapter 2 retraced the formative influence of Thomas Aquinas, Joseph Maréchal and Martin Heidegger on Rahner's thought. Taking into account these various and different influences proved to be crucial for presenting a different picture of his transcendental theology. The misconception that Rahner merely applies Immanuel Kant's transcendental philosophy within his theology was corrected by explaining the high degree of idiosyncrasy of Rahner's transcendental method. Rahner's understanding of transcendentality revolves around three interrelated aspects: a scholastic metaphysical aspect, a critical Kantian aspect and a phenomenological-hermeneutical aspect. I argued that understanding this multifaceted background is essential to recognize the dialectical interrelation of hermeneutics and transcendentality within Rahner's theology.

The application of these three aspects was subsequently explored in Chapter 3 by examining Rahner's metaphysics of knowledge as developed in *Spirit in the World*. Taking human questioning as the starting point of metaphysics incorporates hermeneutical circularity into Rahner's transcendental-metaphysical theology. His metaphysics probes rather than resolves the tension between questionability and questionableness and is, therefore, consciously open-ended and incomplete. Rahner's incarnational metaphysics of knowledge confirms this concrete starting point. Following Aristotle's and Thomas's materialism, Rahner affirms that human beings have a transcendental openness to Being not despite, but rather by virtue of, their relation to concrete otherness. Human beings have an extraordinary capacity of self-transcendence, but only as finite spirits who are incarnated in the world. Accordingly, Rahner advocates a *categorical metaphysics* that strives to express the *a priori* in full awareness of the fact that all human reflection is hermeneutically conditioned by an *a posteriori* experience. I demonstrated that the modest shape of this metaphysics recurs in Rahner's careful delineation of the scope of human self-transcendence. Human transcendence entails a *Vorgriff* towards absolute Being, but we cannot simply objectify or grasp this horizon of transcendence. While Rahner identifies absolute Being with God, he does not claim that we can conclusively prove the existence of God. Rahner only goes as far as to claim that we can *anticipate* God in metaphysics. As a result, metaphysical knowledge of God always remains a *tenebrae ignorantiae* – an intelligible reflection in response to something which manifests itself in a dialectics of disclosure and concealment, which ultimately remains mysterious to us.

Even though Rahner elaborates his metaphysics of knowledge primarily with recourse to philosophical arguments, his emphasis on the categorical shape of metaphysics is clearly connected with the Christian conviction that the fullest disclosure of truth occurred in the historical incarnation of Jesus Christ. This historical aspect was examined in Chapter 4, in critical dialogue with theologians who dispute Rahner's hermeneutical attentiveness. In *Hearer of the Word*, Rahner seeks to explain the intelligibility of the historical revelation in Jesus Christ by developing his anthropology of 'spirit in the world' into an anthropology of 'spirit in history'. Human persons are potential hearers of the Word, equipped to discern mystery's self-revelation within their own historical experiences. This experiential mediation of revelation was examined in greater detail through a discussion of the dialectics between the transcendental and the categorical dimension of experience. The transcendental relation to mystery is mediated and conditioned, but is not determined by linguistic and contextual interpretation. Rahner expresses this dialectics of experience and interpretation with the term 'mediated immediacy'. Importantly, I demonstrated that his prioritizing of the transcendental element of experience functions hermeneutically, insofar as it impels us to review and to reconsider every interpretation of (transcendental) experience. The discussion of the unity of the love of God and the love of neighbour not only articulated Rahner's attention to inter-subjectivity but also brought the incarnate and practical dimension of the human transcendental relation more sharply into focus. The human transcendental relation to God is discovered and realized primarily through acts of love. Hence, concrete relations with human others are the key to any metaphysical, transcendental or theological conceptualizations of the relation to the transcendent Other. Finally, the discussion of Rahner's reflections on mystery has shed more light on his view of the modest role of metaphysics within theology. His positive account of the hiddenness of God puts forward a radically different model of truth. Letting go of rational clarity and control as the ideal of knowledge makes room for the recognition of the transcendent and ecstatic shape of reason. Knowing is first and foremost about being receptive to the self-offering mystery. While we have come to know this mystery as the loving God in Jesus Christ, even this revelation does not lift the veil of mystery completely. Accordingly, seeking to name God theologically, with the help of metaphysical categories, is a hermeneutical task that does not result in a comprehensive grasp of God, but is instead a *docta ignorantia*. Metaphysical theological reflection guides us to the place where knowledge has to give way and become a surrender in love to that which is beyond reason.

In Chapter 5, I explained that the dialectical interrelation between hermeneutics and transcendentality in Rahner's work is rooted in his understanding of the relationship between nature and grace, or philosophy and theology. Rahner employs transcendental and metaphysical arguments inductively in order to explain the universal salvific will revealed in the particular historical person of Jesus Christ. The notion of the supernatural existential serves to explain the concrete truth that human transcendentality is always and everywhere affected by the history of grace. As a result, the offer of divine revelation can be encountered universally throughout human history. Interpreting human transcendentality in light of the Christ event shows that the boundaries between philosophy and theology cannot be distinguished sharply. For Rahner, this porosity between philosophy and theology works in two ways. On the one hand, since grace builds on nature, theology can trust the power of reason and constructively appropriate philosophy, so as to contribute to the self-understanding of faith. On the other hand, theological insights derived from this particular history also prompt a qualified understanding of philosophy as a discipline having a relative, rather than an absolute, autonomy. Theology's concern with the historical effects of grace functions as a powerful hermeneutical reminder, warning transcendental and metaphysical forms of philosophy against the risks of forgetting their own contextual and limited character. I demonstrated that Rahner applies these insights to his own transcendental theology. Recognizing the challenges of history and pluralism, he rejects the possibility of one universal philosophy. However, being conscious of limitations and conditions is something else than letting oneself be determined and confined by these same conditions. Standing within the particular Christian tradition, Rahner advocates a modest use of transcendental arguments to convey the insight of faith that each and every human experience entails the possibility of an indirect, yet real encounter with the self-revealing God. It is his dialectical interrelation between hermeneutics and transcendentality that enables this thinking of universality from within particularity in a hermeneutically conscious and responsible way.

Retrieving the hermeneutical profile of the transcendental theologian Rahner yielded an insightful example of a fundamental theology that is attentive to the challenges of particularity, but which refuses to give up its universal outlook. However, I pointed out that Rahner's attention to the role of language and to the corrupting influence of power and ideology remains relatively underdeveloped in his work. For this reason, I complemented the retrieval of Rahner with a retrieval of Schillebeeckx in Part II. Due to his active engagement with hermeneutical and critical theory, Schillebeeckx has a keener eye for the conditioning role of language and ideology. At the same time, I argued that Schillebeeckx offers an example of a theological turn to hermeneutics that avoids shutting itself off from metaphysics. As a result, Schillebeeckx offers a pertinent complementary perspective on the dialectical interrelation of metaphysics and hermeneutics in theology.

Chapter 6 started with the retrieval of Schillebeeckx by discussing three intellectual resources that are key to understanding his theological work: the phenomenological metaphysics of Dominicus De Petter, the hermeneutical philosophy of Hans-Georg Gadamer and Paul Ricoeur, and the critical theory of Theodor Adorno and Jürgen Habermas. Contrary to Schillebeeckx's own assessment, I argued that the application of his later critical-hermeneutical insights did not negate his earlier metaphysical framework. On the contrary the fundamental level of continuity between the early and the later Schillebeeckx accounts for the dialectical interrelation of metaphysics and hermeneutics in his method. This thesis was developed over the course of the three subsequent chapters.

In Chapter 7, I retraced the origins and evolution of Schillebeeckx's theological focus on experience as the medium of revelation. Schillebeeckx argues that theology must first and foremost be oriented towards salvation history, because it is in concrete historical experiences that the mysterious living God has been revealed. Although he rejects the notion of Christian faith as a kind of supra-metaphysics, he maintains that the mystery of faith is intelligible and open to explication. For this reason, metaphysics plays a useful, albeit subordinate, role within theology. I examined how Schillebeeckx combines a Thomistic relational metaphysics of creation with De Petter's phenomenology, thereby developing a perspectival epistemology that explains how human beings have a real, yet limited access to absolute truth or God. This perspectival epistemology comprises the first indication of the dialectical interrelation of metaphysics and hermeneutics in Schillebeeckx's work. It must be noted, though, that this early theological epistemology had a rather narrow intellectualist character. Schillebeeckx's qualified use of metaphysics was explained in greater detail by looking to his incarnational anthropology. Schillebeeckx argues that the varied concrete human relations are grounded in a transcendental relation. Through relationships to the world and to other people, we encounter an experience of contingency that contains a reference to mystery. I argued that Schillebeeckx develops this incarnational account inductively, reasoning from a concrete Christian perspective, rather than through purely abstract transcendental and metaphysical analysis. The transcendental relation is an attempt to make the Christian conviction intelligible that God seeks to enter into a theologal relationship with humankind. However, the communicability of this vision of graced nature by way of metaphysical and transcendental arguments is put under pressure with Schillebeeckx's later critical-hermeneutical turn. Distancing himself from a participatory metaphysics, he elaborates an account of experience that is more attentive to the intrinsic interpretative dimension of all human experience. Since we always experience interpretatively, different cultural-historical linguistic frameworks result in different experiences. I analysed how Schillebeeckx develops his hermeneutical account of experience as a dialectics of subjective interpretation and objective givenness. While he applies his hermeneutical insights to explain the first aspect, he requires his metaphysical framework in order to account for the second aspect. I concluded, therefore, that Schillebeeckx's hermeneutical understanding of experience remains intimately connected with his metaphysics of experience.

Schillebeeckx argues that an experience can become a Christian experience when interpreted through the interpretative framework of the Christian experiential tradition. But how can we understand this tradition, made up by texts and symbols from the past, in our situation today? I explained in Chapter 8 that Schillebeeckx applies his dialectics of metaphysics and hermeneutics diachronically to address this issue. He argues that a living tradition requires a reinterpretative understanding, which involves fidelity to the past, the creative use of the present hermeneutical framework and a practical openness to the future. Especially in view of this last element, Schillebeeckx emphasizes that theoretical hermeneutics must be complemented with a hermeneutics of praxis that has particular eye for ideological distortions of understanding. While interpreting subjects have a necessary role in the process of reinterpretative understanding, it is ultimately their existential relation to mystery, initiated by God's gift of grace, that ensures a continuity of theological understanding. To explain this aspect of givenness in interpretation, Schillebeeckx theologically appropriates Heidegger's ontological understanding of language. In other words, encounters with divine mystery today form the key to understanding past encounters with mystery, and understanding these past encounters helps us to discern mystery in the present. This mutual dynamic between past and present experiences forms the basis for Schillebeeckx's reworking of correlation theology. His 'correlation of correlation' recognizes the co-constitutive role of situation in past and present experiences of grace. We can never grasp the offer of revelation directly, nor can we distil its essence from concrete articulations. Different socio-historical circumstances and acquired insights into ideological distortions require different articulations and therefore legitimate a certain discontinuity with the tradition. The only continuity possible is a *continuity in discontinuities*, which is located at the level of the proportional relation between the different socio-historical expressions of faith. While Lieven Boeve and Erik Borgman have elaborated upon this aspect of discontinuity in theological understanding, I called for a closer examination of the aspect of continuity. Schillebeeckx's hermeneutics of tradition increasingly emphasizes the particular creative role of the interpreting subject, but he needs a metaphysical argumentation to account for the possibility of proportional continuity in theological understanding. I argued that this metaphysical argumentation operates implicitly in his correlation theology and attempted to make it explicit once more with reference to his philosophy of history and his theology of revelation. This resulted in another demonstration of the dialectical interrelation of metaphysics and hermeneutics in Schillebeeckx's theology.

In Chapter 9, I explained how Schillebeeckx applies this dialectics synchronically in his theology of the contrast experience. The contrast experience is developed as a hermeneutically conscious contribution to natural theology. Importantly, this natural theology searches from *within* the particular perspective of Christian faith for a way to explain the *universal* possibility of encountering God's grace. The goal is not to establish a conclusive proof for the truth of Christian faith, but rather to develop what I called a heuristics of grace. Philosophical arguments are used to show the point at which Christian discourse becomes intelligible. Schillebeeckx focuses on the human experiential encounter with suffering and contingency, arguing that these experiences have a universal revelatory potential. Since every experience is interpretative, the contrast experience must *not* be understood as a general religious experience. Contrast experiences are open to various interpretations and only become so-called religious experiences with the help of a religious interpretative framework. Nonetheless, Schillebeeckx argues that the rich variety of variously interpreted encounters with suffering share a common element. I demonstrated that he employs a metaphysical argument in order to articulate this common element but that this metaphysical argument is kept in check by a concurrent critical-hermeneutical qualification. Schillebeeckx argues that contrast experiences mediate a glimpse of the *humanum*, which can never be comprehensively rationalized and is, therefore, merely anticipated through praxis. This forms an important break with his earlier narrow intellectualist approach to knowledge of God. Yet, despite the priority of praxis in this mediation of the *humanum*, a theoretical element remains. Practical resistance to suffering is sustained by a trust and hope. Christians interpret this trust and hope, in light of the revelation in Jesus Christ, as faith in God's abiding presence in creation. Practical anticipation, thus, presumes participatory trust, but this trust always remains conditioned by the eschatological-practical proviso. For human beings, the presence of grace is always a mediated immediacy. While we cannot remain silent when encountering this mysterious reality, our interpretative naming of this mystery is inherently limited and is constantly in danger of falling into idolatry. Arguing that Jesus Christ reveals a concrete universality, Schillebeeckx advocates a transfinalization of theoretical metaphysics through praxis that entails a theological appreciation as well as qualification of philosophy. His affirmation of the relative autonomy of philosophy is reflected in the subordinated and critical-hermeneutically conditioned role of metaphysical reflection within his theological method. Theology can employ philosophical metaphysics to explain its understanding of reality as graced reality, but it must also point beyond theoretical reason alone. It is precisely by becoming attentive to the limitations of reason that the concrete universal perspective of Christian faith comes into view.

Retrieving the dialectical interrelationship of metaphysics and hermeneutics in the work of Rahner and Schillebeeckx sheds new light on these two modern theologians. It corrects the image that a theological turn to transcendental philosophy necessarily results in a forgetfulness of history and hermeneutics. It calls the assumption into question that a sincere hermeneutical turn forces one to break entirely with metaphysics. Restoring the nuanced theological profiles of Rahner and Schillebeeckx is an important result that has occurred because of this retrieval. However, can these modern theologians also contribute to contemporary fundamental theology? In conclusion, I point to three crucial insights resulting from this study that can bring fundamental theology forward, thereby demonstrating the actual relevance of Rahner and Schillebeeckx.

The theological character of fundamental theology

The first important insight yielded by this retrieval of Rahner and Schillebeeckx concerns a renewed appreciation for the *theological* character of fundamental theology. While Rahner and Schillebeeckx extensively use philosophical insights, ranging from metaphysical and transcendental arguments to hermeneutical and critical theory, their fundamental theologies are unashamedly theological. As a result, their attempts to demonstrate the universal intelligibility of Christian faith remain closely connected to the particular and concrete shape of the Christian tradition and its account of revelation. Crucially, the persistent awareness of the fact that theology reflects on a truth that is revealed in the particular contingencies of history is translated into their modest and hermeneutically sensitive application of transcendental and metaphysical arguments. I argue that this dialectical interrelation of metaphysics and hermeneutics can be traced back to a particular application of philosophy within theology, that is in turn rooted in a theological-metaphysical view on the relation between nature and grace. Rahner and Schillebeeckx remind contemporary fundamental theology to reconsider the fundamental importance of this question of the relationship between philosophy (nature) and theology (grace).

Rahner's and Schillebeeckx's approach to fundamental theology contrasts markedly with the contemporary tendency to restrict fundamental theology to an exclusively philosophical mode of argumentation. Tracy, for instance, argues that the task of fundamental theology is finding public warrants for the truth of Christian faith. Fundamental theology must, therefore, resort to strictly philosophical arguments. His extensive reflections on the nature of systematic theology, on the other hand, make clear that every human engagement with truth is hermeneutically conditioned. However, due to his rather strict separation between philosophical fundamental theology and hermeneutical systematic theology, Tracy seems unable to apply these hermeneutical insights fruitfully to fundamental theology.[1] While he realizes that metaphysical

---

[1] See particularly Tracy, *The Analogical Imagination*, 62–9.

arguments for Christian faith must be weak and modest, he does not explore the extent to which the specific nature of theological truth itself points to ways to communicate this truth intelligibly, without falling into the trap of a hubristic rationalism. Fiorenza similarly seems to look almost exclusively to philosophical rationality in order to find an approach to universal truth that is hermeneutically conscious, but which is able to transcend particular discourses. Hence it seems that the hermeneutical turn in theology has led to, or has at least coincided with, an unfortunate separation of philosophical and theological rationalities.

In my opinion, the relative inattentiveness of hermeneutical theologians to the theological-metaphysical question of the relationship between nature and grace offers an explanation for this separation between philosophical rationality and theological rationality. This question is not merely interesting for historical theologians studying the intense debate that raged in twentieth-century theology. Quite the contrary, reconsidering this question seems to be highly relevant and urgent for contemporary fundamental theology.[2] The attempts by modern theology to overcome the neo-scholastic two-tiered understanding of nature and grace notwithstanding, there is still a widespread contemporary tendency to divide reality into a strictly secular and a strictly religious realm. Insofar as theologians like Tracy and Fiorenza keep primarily looking for purely philosophical justifications of faith, they seem to assume – at least implicitly – this strict separation between nature and grace. This separation impedes a productive confrontation between philosophical and theological rationality. Conversely, Rahner and Schillebeeckx view nature and grace as being dynamically interrelated and, therefore, approach reality as graced reality. The productive effects of this metaphysical perspective for theological epistemology can be explained with reference to a Thomistic current that informs their theological approaches.

In view of Rahner's and Schillebeeckx's respective contributions to the dialogue between traditional scholastic theology and modern thought, it should come as no surprise that their fundamental theologies bear a strong Thomistic mark. Like Thomas, they situate themselves within the concrete tradition of Christian faith and recognize the concrete and historical nature of the truth mediated by this tradition. However, they are also convinced that this incarnate and particular truth has a universal intelligibility.[3] Ascribing to Thomas's dynamic and harmonious understanding of the interrelationship between nature and grace, Rahner and Schillebeeckx advocate a constructive, albeit qualified, use of philosophy within theology. While they acknowledge that there are differences between philosophy and theology, they see no need to maintain a pure distinction between these disciplines in their own work. Thomas explains in the *Summa Theologiae* I, q. 1 a. 7 that theological enquiry is not characterized by a specific material object that it studies, for instance religious practices or religious doctrines. Instead, theology is characterized by a specific way of looking at reality. Theology examines reality under a specific formal aspect, namely '*sub ratione*

---

[2] See, for instance, Kathryn Tanner's book *Christ the Key* (Cambridge: Cambridge University Press, 2010). Tanner begins her account of a Christ-centred theological vision by explicitly considering the question of the relationship between nature and grace.
[3] See Rudi te Velde, *Aquinas on God. The 'Divine Science' of the* Summa Theologiae (Farnham: Ashgate, 2006), 4–5; 20, for this recognition of universality in particularity by Thomas Aquinas.

Dei'; it studies reality as related to and revelatory of God. Now this concept of theology invites a particular openness to philosophy. From the perspective of faith, philosophical knowledge is not opposed to or in competition with theological knowledge; both disciplines are concerned with the same material reality. For this reason, philosophy can be 'subsumed' and 'integrated' into theology, without dominating theology.[4] It is precisely this qualified understanding of the porous relation between theology and philosophy that enables Rahner and Schillebeeckx to think about universality from within particularity.

On the one hand, they fundamentally trust the capacity of reason to contribute to the understanding of faith. A transcendental analysis of human subjectivity or a phenomenological-metaphysical account of contingency can serve to demonstrate the place where the message of faith becomes intelligible. Moreover, the critical force of philosophical rationality can also contribute to the identification and correction of ideological distortions of theological understanding. This facet is tacitly present in Rahner's position on philosophy and comes much more sharply to the fore in Schillebeeckx's work, due to his dialogue with critical theory. On the other hand, these thinkers are also aware of the limitations of philosophical arguments within theology. The concrete manifestation of truth in history shows that the truth of Christian faith is ultimately beyond reason. While faith is not opposed to philosophical rationality, its intelligibility cannot be reduced to philosophical rationality. Hence, the theological appropriation of philosophical rationality also entails a relativization or transfinalization of philosophy. This qualification avoids a theocratic subjugation of philosophy though. Instead, theology 'builds' on philosophy and points to the transcendent character of reason.

By virtue of their appropriation of this specific relationship between nature and grace, Rahner and Schillebeeckx have been able to develop a theological method that opposes a purist separation of philosophy and theology.[5] As a result, philosophical and theological rationality are kept in mutually complementary and critical dialectics. Rahner and Schillebeeckx dare to probe the universal dimension of Christian truth with the help of metaphysical reflection, without losing sight of the hermeneutical limitations of any (metaphysical) explication of this concrete universal truth. Their *metaphysics of mystery* offers an exemplary attempt to account theologically for the universality of Christian truth.

The incarnational shape of hermeneutical experience

In the second instance, the retrieval of Rahner and Schillebeeckx warrants a reconsideration of the category of experience within fundamental theology. Hermen-

---

[4] Ibid., 27.
[5] For a philosophical critique of the sharp distinction between philosophy and theology and a corresponding plea for conceiving of this relationship in terms of porosity, see William Desmond, *God and the Between* (Oxford: Blackwell, 2008); and Charles Taylor, 'Reason, Faith, and Meaning', in *Faith, Rationality, and the Passions*, ed. Sarah Coakley (Malden: Wiley Blackwell, 2013), 13–27.

eutical theologians like Fiorenza and Tracy have grown suspicious of appeals to experience, fearing that these ignore the particular and concrete character of experience.[6] However, Rahner and Schillebeeckx demonstrate that theological accounts of experience as potential universal locus of encounter with divine revelation need not suffer from hermeneutical naivete. An incarnational approach to experience provides a way to attend responsibly to both its particular and its universal aspects.

Taking the particular Christian understanding of truth as their point of departure, Rahner and Schillebeeckx put forward a *realist* and *incarnational* understanding of truth. God's becoming human in Jesus Christ reveals that the divine is not encountered directly, for instance by way of intellectual intuition, but only comes into our view through concrete and particular encounters with the material world and with other people. If God can be encountered universally, it must be through the concrete mediation of the world. Hence, the human relation to theological truth is incarnational. Now, Rahner and Schillebeeckx explain this Christian incarnational understanding of truth with the help of a more general philosophical epistemology of experience. They present each a distinct account of experience as a dialectics of experience and interpretation. Crucially, these epistemologies of experience share the conviction that we can discover a non-reflective relatedness to reality within the variety of variously interpreted experiences that escapes or transcends any particular hermeneutical framework. Pointing to this non-reflective experiential element legitimately raises metaphysical questions that can function as a reference point to explain the Christian conviction that God's self-revelation can be discerned universally.

At first glance, Rahner's account of experience as a dialectics of transcendental and categorical experience seems to be marked by a clear focus on the subject. However, his transcendental analysis of human subjectivity actually starts by considering the subject's concrete relations to objective reality. Human beings know and act through their relations to the concrete otherness of the world and realize themselves most fully by loving their neighbours. As culturally historically situated beings, these concrete experiences are always hermeneutically conditioned. But for Rahner, our experience is not determined and confined by these hermeneutical conditions. Instead, it is precisely through the express recognition of our own particular hermeneutical framework that we become reflectively aware of a primordial and universal horizon that is always already unthematically present within concrete experiences. The primordial relation to this mysterious self-giving horizon grounds and enables our concrete interpretative cognitional and volitional actions. Rahner acknowledges that we only become reflectively aware of this transcendental horizon through our interpretative experiences. As such, he recognizes the hermeneutical conditions of any articulation of this unthematic horizon. However, even though our knowledge of this horizon cannot be more than an anticipation, this anticipatory manifestation still demonstrates that there is more to our particular hermeneutical frameworks than we can know and articulate at any given moment. Hence, Rahner's dialectics of transcendental and categorical experience shows a transcendence of hermeneutics through hermeneutics.

---

[6] See, especially, Fiorenza, *Foundational Theology*, 296–301; and Fiorenza, 'The Experience of Transcendence', 208–16.

While Rahner's dialectics of experience starts with human subjectivity, Schillebeeckx's dialectics remains specifically concerned with the phenomenological aspect of objective givenness in experience. The concrete and incarnate character of the human relation to truth is first developed with the help of a perspectival epistemology. His attention to the concrete and hermeneutical nature of human experience grows increasingly stronger due to his explicit engagement with hermeneutical and critical theory. As a result, Schillebeeckx's account of the interpretative and linguistic dimensions of experience is substantially more nuanced and sophisticated than Rahner's. Nevertheless, in his elaboration of the hermeneutical nature of experience Schillebeeckx keeps pointing to a non-reflective, metaphysical aspect of experience. This non-reflective element becomes particularly manifest within encounters with contingency and negativity that demonstrate our inadequacy to make hermeneutical sense of our experience. Reality presents itself within these experiences as providing its own directive and interpretative influence. Hence, our interpretative experience of the world also involves an experience of reality as a self-offering mystery that resists complete rationalization. Articulating this non-reflective element of experience is, of course, always a hermeneutically conditioned effort. Yet, Schillebeeckx maintains that this awareness of the inadequacies of any particular articulation can also be considered a conscious ignorance. Recognizing the hidden magnet in reality entails a transcendence of hermeneutics through hermeneutics.

These two dialectical accounts demonstrate that recognizing the hermeneutical conditions of experience can also legitimately raise the question of whether our interpretative experiences of reality mediate more than we can express and articulate through hermeneutics alone. In their recent book *Retrieving Realism*, Hubert Dreyfus and Charles Taylor put forward a similar argument.[7] While Dreyfus and Taylor recognize that human beings are always 'in the linguistic dimension', they want to draw attention to a 'prearticulate', 'prereflexive' or 'prelinguistic' level of our understanding of reality.[8] Inspired by Merleau-Ponty and Heidegger, they argue that our explicit conceptual knowledge of the world is preceded by an implicit and more primordial mode of knowledge that results from our bodily contact with and embeddedness in the world. At this most primitive level of contact with reality, our understanding of the world is not simply constructed or determined by the subject, but is 'co-produced' by the subject and the world.[9]

Crucially, this primordial level of understanding reality is claimed to be universally human. Accordingly, this universal openness to a shared world explains why despite the different hermeneutical frameworks that shape experience and understanding, we are not 'imprisoned in our skins or minds', but are instead capable of communicating intelligibly with each other.[10] To be sure, Dreyfus and Taylor do not dispute that a human understanding of reality in its reflective mode presumes a horizon constituted by a particular culture and a particular language. But their emphasis on the fact that

---

[7] Hubert Dreyfus and Charles Taylor, *Retrieving Realism* (Cambridge, MA: Harvard University Press, 2015).
[8] Dreyfus and Taylor, *Retrieving Realism*, 84–8.
[9] Ibid., 93–4.
[10] Ibid., 107; 147.

our understanding by way of horizon is always a response to independent reality results in an insight that seems very close to Rahner's and Schillebeeckx's dialectics of experience and interpretation:

> Our different worlds are linguistically constituted, but our languages are responding to something, trying to articulate something in the human condition. If we want to say that language or culture, in forming our worlds, mediates our contact with the universe and with our human nature, we have to add that our language doesn't exhaust this contact.[11]

Dreyfus and Taylor employ this insight to argue for what they call a 'pluralistic robust realism'.[12] On the one hand, it is possible to give a correct description of the independent reality that manifests itself in our encounters with the world. On the other hand, no description can claim to provide a view from nowhere that is beyond every partial perspective. As Dreyfus and Taylor observe, this retrieval of realism also invites us to consider interpretations of reality, such as the Christian perspective on the world.[13]

I argue that the theologies of Rahner and Schillebeeckx purport to make the same point. They do *not* reduce the variety of human experiences to one general category of limit experience or religious experience. Instead, they point out that each and every concrete and particular interpretative experience shares a general characteristic, namely a reference to independent reality that we share commonly in our various particular encounters, without ever completely grasping it. Both thinkers are in agreement that this universal feature of human experience allows for different and multiple *a posteriori* transcendental, metaphysical or theological explications and articulations. This is not to say that every account of reality is equally true. But in order to assess the coherence or plausibility of any metaphysical account, by bringing it into conversation with an alternative explication for instance, requires first the recognition that legitimate, yet limited, representations of this universal dimension of human experience are possible.

As theologians, Rahner and Schillebeeckx argue that this reference to reality can be interpreted as a trace of the hidden God. Their incarnational accounts of experience are ultimately aimed at demonstrating the plausibility of the Christian claim that God reveals Godself universally to humankind. Importantly, neither Rahner nor Schillebeeckx claims that the notion of transcendental experience or the concept of contrast experience comprises a proof of God. Instead, their incarnational accounts of experience merely seek to raise *reasonable* questions. They argue that every particular hermeneutics of experience arouses questions such as these: What is the horizon that we anticipate in our daily experiences? What grounds the radically contingent realities that constitute our world? What sustains the praxis of liberation that responds to

---

[11] Ibid., 128–9.
[12] Dreyfus and Taylor, *Retrieving Realism*, 154.
[13] Ibid., 158–9; 128. See also Charles Taylor, 'Overcoming Modern Epistemology', in *Faithful Reading. New Essays in Theology and Philosophy in Honour of Fergus Kerr, OP*, ed. Simon Oliver, Karen Kilby, and Tom O'Loughlin (London: T&T Clark, 2012), 58–9, for this 'new point of junction' between philosophical and theological discourses offered by this new epistemological and ontological framework.

situations of radical suffering? Recognizing the legitimacy of these questions makes it possible to consider the answer provided by the Christian tradition – a response that does not claim to be a demonstrable necessary truth, but rather presents itself as an intelligible and plausible response to these questions.

Rahner's and Schillebeeckx's incarnational approach demonstrates that paying proper attention to the inescapable hermeneutical aspect of experience does not foreclose questions about the universal aspect of human experience. On the contrary, a hermeneutical focus on particularity actually opens up a perspective on universality that invites a variety of metaphysical explications. For Rahner and Schillebeeckx, this is theologically relevant inasmuch as it provides a connection point to explain the Christian faith perspective on reality. At the same time, these metaphysical and theological accounts of universality remain subjected to a hermeneutical critical consciousness that points to the inherent limitations of all reflective thematizations of this universal dimension. This leads me to my third and final point.

The self-critical force of a metaphysics of mystery

Commenting on the recent revival of interest in medieval apophaticism, Denys Turner observes a tendency in contemporary theology that 'the apophatic is sheared off from its moorings in an equally ultimate cataphaticism'.[14] According to Turner, both the absolutizing of cataphaticism and the absolutizing of apophaticism are equally erroneous forms of theological epistemology. Postmodern thinkers have variously criticized theological tendencies towards the first extreme, but this radical criticism runs the risk of falling into the opposite extreme.[15] I argue that the theological epistemologies of Rahner and Schillebeeckx represent a powerful example of a theology that keeps the apophatic and the cataphatic together. My claim is grounded in the aforementioned argument that their dialectics of metaphysics and hermeneutics is rooted in the porous interrelationship between philosophy and theology. I will now detail how this specific interrelation of philosophical and theological rationalities enables a metaphysics of mystery that has its own self-critical-hermeneutical disciplining.

Rahner and Schillebeeckx seek to account for the intelligibility of the Christian claim of faith that God universally relates to humankind. By employing the argumentative force of philosophical reason, they develop transcendental and metaphysical arguments to demonstrate that ordinary experience involves an encounter with mystery. This results in the understanding of the human person as someone who stands in a receptive relationship to a self-giving mystery that challenges and invites the subject to respond. Rahner and Schillebeeckx introduce their concepts of transcendental experience and contrast experience in order to explain the Christian response to this mystery as faith

---

[14] Denys Turner, *Faith, Reason and the Existence of God* (Cambridge: Cambridge University Press, 2004), 50.
[15] For a critical discussion of philosophical negative theologies that view language as a contamination of truth or the transcendent, see Lieven Boeve, 'Theological Truth, Particularity and Incarnation. Engaging Religious Plurality and Radical Hermeneutics', in *Orthodoxy, Process and Product*, ed. Mathijs Lamberigts, Lieven Boeve and Terrence Merrigan (Leuven: Peeters, 2009), 323–48.

in God. However, they are also mindful of the impossibility of fully comprehending this divine mystery and the consequent need for continual critical correction and purification. Their firm belief in the intelligibility of Christian faith does not aim to reduce the mysterious aspect of faith. For all of their philosophical explorations and examinations, Rahner and Schillebeeckx never forget that the proper object of faith, God, is *beyond* reason. This insight fundamentally conditions their theological discourse. As Nicholas Lash aptly expresses, 'To speak appropriately of the holy mystery that makes and heals the world, but is not the world nor any item in it, is quite beyond the resources of language.'[16] Accordingly, any theological explication of mystery must remain conscious of the fact that it can never be more than a *broken language*. I argue that Rahner's and Schillebeeckx's dialectics of metaphysics and hermeneutics forms the key to such a broken language that avoids both the idolatry of onto-theology and the idolatry of silence.

The theological dialectics between metaphysics and hermeneutics in Rahner's work can be traced back to the notion of the supernatural existential and its incarnational origin. He develops this concept in response to the concrete revelatory message in Jesus Christ in order to explain its universal significance. With the supernatural existential Rahner seeks to explain that every human person can concretely relate to God's grace in everyday experiences. For this purpose, he engages in an extensive transcendental analysis of human subjectivity. Due to the theological starting point of this analysis, though, it has several inherent checks and balances which guard against an unjustified overstepping of its own limits. On the one hand, the supernatural existential is developed within the context of a metaphysical anthropology and serves to explain the universal effects of this concrete salvific event. On the other hand, this concept also functions as an important hermeneutical reminder that every theoretical reflection, no matter how strictly transcendental or metaphysical, is conditioned by history, more concretely by the history of grace. Accordingly, Rahner's account of transcendental subjectivity does not claim to be strictly *a priori*, but is more appropriately termed as having a theological *a priori* character. This theological hermeneutical conditioning of transcendental reflection comes particularly strongly to the fore in Rahner's reflections on mystery.

Rahner's transcendental analysis of human experience serves to show that every person is oriented to a mysterious horizon. This understanding of the mysterious character constantly qualifies Rahner's transcendental method and provides it with its distinctly modest character. Both his account of human subjectivity and his account of knowledge of God attest to this. Conceiving of the transcendental horizon as mystery puts the epistemological ideal of knowledge as a comprehensive and controlling grasp into question. It decentres the subject, who is no longer thought of as the shepherd of Being, but rather as standing in a responsive relation to mystery. In Rahner's opinion, this is not merely a theoretical concern but necessarily has practical

---

[16] Nicholas Lash, *Holiness, Speech and Silence. Reflections on the Question of God* (Aldershot: Ashgate, 2004), 84. See also Nicholas Lash, *A Matter of Hope. A Theologian's Reflections on the Thought of Karl Marx* (Notre Dame, IN: University of Notre Dame Press, 1982), 144: 'The only logic appropriate to theological discourse would be, if I may so put it, a "broken" logic.'

consequences. Recognizing the limitations of knowledge enables a transcendence of reason. Knowledge allows itself to be enlightened by love and surrenders itself in trust to mystery. This love of mystery is realized primarily by loving concrete neighbourly others and, thereby, strengthens the relational and decentred understanding of human subjectivity.

The understanding of God as mystery also forms the key to understanding Rahner's account of the universal knowledge of God. While he insists that we can encounter God through our concrete experiences in the world, he continually seeks to avoid reducing this horizon into to an object among objects. Rahner variously reflects on the tension between thematic knowledge and unthematic knowledge, in order to navigate between dumbfounded silence and idolatry. The argument for the *Vorgriff* aims to show that we anticipate God without ever grasping God. Instead of using philosophy to prove God, Rahner engages in a reflective exercise of conscious ignorance. He is convinced that a mystery that cannot be fully comprehended can still be explored intelligibly. While he argues that in the light of revelation, the mysterious horizon can be called God, he also emphasizes that this does not bring to an end the mysterious character of God. The perspective of faith and the light of grace do not end God's incomprehensibility but, as Thomas argues, grace instead 'joins us to him as to an unknown'.[17] Accordingly, Rahner's account of God dares to break the silence about mystery, but remains aware of its necessarily open-ended and incomplete character.

Schillebeeckx's theology similarly engages in a daring, yet careful, exploration of the intelligibility of mystery. From the very beginning of his career, he has argued that theology must primarily focus on the particular events of salvation history. But Schillebeeckx also maintains that the mystery to which these events and words attest is an intelligible one. For this reason, metaphysics can play a subordinate role within theology. This trust in the argumentative force of reason is, however, consistently combined with several critical hermeneutical correctives.

In Schillebeeckx's early work, the hermeneutical disciplining of the theological use of metaphysics is developed theoretically. The theory of implicit intuition is connected with a relational ontology of creation with the aim of defending the claim that theological concepts provide legitimate knowledge about God. Schillebeeckx, thus, appropriates a metaphysical argumentation theologically in order to justify the cataphatic character of theology. The resulting perspectival epistemology contains, tacitly at least, a lucid insight into the hermeneutical conditioning of human knowledge. Crucially, this hermeneutical awareness is not merely philosophical, but also has a distinctly theological origin. Following Thomas, Schillebeeckx argues that all of our concepts are creaturely and therefore are necessarily limited. For this reason, theological concepts do not offer a comprehending grasp of God. Instead, they provide us with what Schillebeeckx calls an intelligible 'tending' towards mystery.

This hermeneutical disciplining of metaphysical theology is continued in an eschatological-practical form after Schillebeeckx's critical-hermeneutical turn. Due to his reflections on the historicity of the revelation in Jesus Christ and the eschatological

---

[17] Thomas Aquinas, *Summa Theologiae* I, q. 12, a. 13 ad 2. See also Turner, *Thomas Aquinas*, 143, who argues that 'for Thomas, as the degrees of divine darkness rank, faith's is the deeper'.

incompleteness of history, Schillebeeckx intensifies his emphasis on the anticipatory character of human knowledge of the divine mystery. Although this does not lead to a break with any participatory metaphysics, it does bring out even more sharply the limited role of metaphysical arguments within theology. This comes clearly to the fore in his account of theological understanding as a continuity in discontinuities. Accounting for the possibility of reinterpretative understanding of faith is only possible by virtue of the self-offering gift of mystery. However, any expressing of this mystery requires the application of a hermeneutics of suspicion to older formulations of faith and the creative search for new formulations of faith. Theological understanding of faith is enabled and aided by the self-offering mystery, but finding the right words for this response remains a challenging and always incomplete task. The recognition of the co-constitutive role of context in revelation serves as a powerful warning against the metaphysical or dogmatic reification of faith.

The concept of the contrast experience comprises perhaps the clearest example of the hermeneutical disciplining of Schillebeeckx's theological use of metaphysics. The contrast experience is consciously developed from a particular perspective of Christian faith. It is a heuristic device used to point to the universally transcendent dimension of human interpretative experience, but it also recognizes that multiple particular interpretations of this mysterious transcendent dimension are possible. Schillebeeckx employs a metaphysical argumentation in order to demonstrate that experiences of negativity are effected by a hidden magnet. However, he points out that this universal feature of experience cannot be fully captured by theoretical reason alone and is primarily mediated through praxis. For Schillebeeckx, this dialectical interrelation goes back to the revelation of concrete universality in Jesus Christ. In Jesus Christ, we learn that the hope which resists suffering can be articulated as a trust and faith in God's abiding presence in creation. Through experiences of contrast we encounter God's offer of grace. At the same time, this faith in the presence of grace is revealed as an eschatological promise. No theological use of metaphysics can conclusively demonstrate that the mystery which we encounter is God's self-communication in grace. The universal truth of faith needs to be realized in a concrete praxis of liberation in order to be understood. This eschatological-practical reminder puts every theoretical expression of grace and every practical response to grace under critique. At the same time, it also recognizes that inadequate thematizations of grace are crucial to sustaining liberative practices. Because of this combination of creation faith and eschatological hope, the Christian interpretation of experience is reminded of its own brokenness and provisionality. Christians are called to explain and to practise their belief in the universal God, but in the full awareness that this mysterious God is new each moment.

Bibliography

Note on the use of sources

In this study, I refer to the English translations of the original German version of Karl Rahner's writings whenever such a translation is available. Unless stated otherwise, the references to *Spirit in the World* concern the second edition, whereas the references to *Hearer of the Word* concern the first edition. When referencing untranslated writings, I refer as much as possible to Karl Rahner's *Sämtliche Werke* published by the Karl-Rahner-Stiftung and edited by Karl Lehmann, Johann Baptist Metz, Karl-Heinz Neufeld, Albert Raffelt and Herbert Vorgrimler.

In a similar fashion, I refer to the English translations of Edward Schillebeeckx's writings wherever possible. When no translation is available, I refer to the Dutch original. A substantial amount of Edward Schillebeeckx's writings has recently been published by the Edward Schillebeeckx Foundation as the *Collected Works* (CW), edited by Ted Mark Schoof and Carl Sterkens with Erik Borgman and Robert J. Schreiter. Following the advice of the editors, when using the *Collected Works* I have not only provided the page numbers of the new translation but also added the page numbers of the old translation in square brackets.

When I refer to sources in languages other than English, the translations are my own, unless stated otherwise. All italics in quotations are as they appear in the original, unless I have indicated otherwise. Finally, a word on the use of gender-inclusive language must be mentioned. Rahner and Schillebeeckx both use primarily masculine language. When I quote directly from their work, I have kept to their specific use of language as rendered in the translations of their work. In all other instances I have opted for gender-inclusive language.

Works by Karl Rahner

Rahner, Karl. 'Anonymous Christians' [1965]. In *TI*, vol. 6, 390–8.
Rahner, Karl. 'Begleittext zu "Geist in Welt"' [1939]. In Rahner, *Sämtliche Werke Band 2*, 431–7.
Rahner, Karl. 'Bemerkungen zum Begriff der Offenbarung'. In *Offenbarung und Überlieferung*, ed. Karl Rahner and Joseph Ratzinger, 11–24. Quaestiones disputatae 25. Freiburg: Herder, 1965.
Rahner, Karl. 'Christianity and the non-Christian Religions' [1961]. In *TI*, vol. 5, trans. Karl-H. Kruger, 115–34. London: Darton, Longman and Todd, 1966.
Rahner, Karl. 'The "Commandment" of Love in relation to the other Commandments' [1961]. In *TI*, vol. 5, 439–59.
Rahner, Karl. 'Concerning the Relationship between Nature and Grace' [1950]. In *TI*, vol. 1, 297–317.

Rahner, Karl. 'The Current Relationship between Philosophy and Theology' [1972]. In *TI*, vol. 13, 61–79.
Rahner, Karl. 'The Development of Dogma' [1954]. In *TI*, vol. 1, 39–77.
Rahner, Karl. 'Einführung in den Begriff der Existentialphilosophie bei Heidegger' [1940]. In Rahner, *Sämtliche Werke Band 2*, 319–46.
Rahner, Karl. 'Erfahrungen eines katholischen Theologen' [1984]. In *Karl Rahner in Erinnerung*, ed. Albert Raffelt, 134–48. Düsseldorf: Patmos Verlag, 1994.
Rahner, Karl. 'The Eternal Significance of the Humanity of Jesus for our Relationship to God' [1953]. In TI, vol. 3, trans. Karl-H. and Boniface Kruger, 35–46. London: Darton, Longman and Todd, 1974.
Rahner, Karl. 'The Experience of God Today' [1970]. In *TI*, vol. 11, 149–65.
Rahner, Karl. 'Experience of Self and Experience of God' [1971]. In *TI*, vol. 13, 122–32.
Rahner, Karl. 'Experience of Transcendence from the Standpoint of Catholic Dogmatics' [1978]. In *TI*, vol. 18, trans. Edward Quinn, 173–88. London: Darton, Longman and Todd, 1983.
Rahner, Karl. 'Faith between Rationality and Emotion' [1973]. In *TI*, vol. 13, 60–78.
Rahner, Karl. *Faith in a Wintry Season. Conversations and interviews with Karl Rahner in the Last Years of his Life*. Trans. Harvey Egan, ed. Paul Imhof and Hubert Biallowons. New York: Crossroad, 1991.
Rahner, Karl. *Foundations of Christian Faith. An Introduction to the Idea of Christianity*. Trans. William Dych. New York: Crossroad, 1978. Original: *Grundkurs des Glaubens. Einführung in den Begriff des Christentums*. Freiburg: Herder, 1976. Included in Rahner, *Sämtliche Werke Band 26*, 1–442.
Rahner, Karl. *Glaube in winterlicher Zeit*. Edited by Paul Imhof and Hubert Biallowons. Düsseldorf: Patmos Verlag, 1986.
Rahner, Karl. *Hearer of the Word: Laying the Foundation for a Philosophy of Religion* [1941]. Trans. Joseph Donceel, ed. Andrew Tallon. New York: Continuum, 1994. Original: *Hörer des Wortes. Zur Grundlegung einer Religionsphilosophie*. München: Kösel, 19411 / 19632. Included in Rahner, *Sämtliche Werke Band 4*, 1–281.
Rahner, Karl. 'The Hiddenness of God' [1974]. In *TI*, vol. 16, 227–43.
Rahner, Karl. 'The Historicity of Theology' [1967]. In *TI*, vol. 9, 64–82.
Rahner, Karl. 'Interview: Gnade als Mitte menschlicher Existenz. Ein Gespräch mit und über Karl Rahner aus Anlaß seines 70. Geburtstages'. *Herder Korrespondenz 28*, no. 2 1974: 77–92.
Rahner, Karl. *Im Gespräch. Band 1: 1964–1977*. Ed. Paul Imhof and Hubert Biallowons. München: Kösel Verlag, 1982.
Rahner, Karl. *Im Gespräch. Band II: 1978–1982*. Ed. Paul Imhof and Hubert Biallowons. München: Kösel, 1983.
Rahner, Karl. 'An Investigation of the Incomprehensibility of God in St Thomas Aquinas' [1974]. In *TI*, vol. 16, 244–54.
Rahner, Karl. 'Liebe'. In *Sacramentum Mundi: Theologisches Lexikon für die Praxis*, vol. 3, ed. Karl Rahner and Adolf Darlap. Freiburg: Herder, 1969.
Rahner, Karl. 'Nature and Grace' [1960]. In *TI*, vol. 4, 165–88.
Rahner, Karl. 'Observations on the Doctrine of God in Catholic Dogmatics' [1966]. In *TI*, vol. 9, trans. Graham Harrison, 127–44. London: Darton, Longman and Todd, 1972.
Rahner, Karl. 'On the Concept of Mystery in Catholic Theology' [1959]. In *TI*, vol. 4, 36–73.
Rahner, Karl. 'On Recognizing the Importance of Thomas Aquinas' [1970]. In *TI*, vol. 13, 3–12.

Rahner, Karl. 'On the Theology of the Incarnation' [1958]. In *TI*, vol. 4, 105–20.
Rahner, Karl. 'Philosophy and Theology' [1962]. In *TI*, vol. 6, trans. Karl-H. and Boniface Kruger, 71–81. London: Darton, Longman and Todd, 1974.
Rahner, Karl. 'Philosophy and Philosophising in Theology' [1967]. In *TI*, vol. 9, 46–63.
Rahner, Karl. 'Pluralism in Theology and the Unity of the Creed in the Church' [1969]. In *TI*, vol. 11, trans. David Bourke, 3–23. London: Darton, Longman and Todd, 1975.
Rahner, Karl. 'Possible Courses for the Theology of the Future' [1970].]. In *TI*, vol. 13, trans. David Bourke, 32–60. London: Darton, Longman and Todd, 1975.
Rahner, Karl. 'Priest and Poet' [1956]. In *TI*, vol. 3, 294–317.
Rahner, Karl. 'Questions of Controversial Theology on Justification' [1958]. In *TI*, vol. 4, trans. Kevin Smith, 189–218. London: Darton, Longman and Todd, 1974.
Rahner, Karl. 'Reflections on the Methodology in Theology' [1970]. In *TI*, vol. 11, 68–114.
Rahner, Karl. 'Reflections on a New Task for Fundamental Theology' [1972]. In *TI*, vol. 16, trans. David Morland, 156–66. London: Darton, Longman and Todd, 1979.
Rahner, Karl. 'Reflections on the Unity of the Love of Neighbour and the Love of God' [1965]. In *TI*, vol. 6, 231–49.
Rahner, Karl. *Sämtliche Werke Band 2. Geist in Welt: philosophische Schriften*. Ed. Albert Raffelt. Soloturn – Düsseldorf: Benziger / Freiburg im Breisgau: Herder, 1995).
Rahner, Karl. *Sämtliche Werke Band 4. Hörer des Wortes. Schriften zur Religionsphilosophie und zur Grundlegung der Theologie*. Ed. Albert Raffelt. Soloturn – Düsseldorf: Benziger / Freiburg: Herder, 1997.
Rahner, Karl. *Sämtliche Werke Band 26. Grundkurs des Glaubens. Studien zum Begriff des Christentums*. Ed. Nikolaus Schwerdtfeger and Albert Raffelt. Zürich: Benziger / Freiburg: Herder, 1999.
Rahner, Karl. 'Some Implications of the Scholastic Concept of Uncreated Grace' [1939]. In *TI*, vol. 1, trans. Cornelius Ernst, 319–46. London: Darton, Longman and Todd, 1974.
Rahner, Karl. *Spirit in the World* [19391, 19572]. Trans. William Dych with a foreword by Johannes B. Metz and an introduction by Francis P. Fiorenza. New York, Continuum, 1994. Original: *Geist in Welt. Zur metaphysik der endlichen Erkenntnis bei Thomas von Aquin*. Innsbruck, Rauch, 19391 / 19572. Included in Rahner, *Sämtliche Werke Band 2*, 3–300.
Rahner, Karl. 'Theology and Anthropology' [1967]. In *TI*, vol. 9, 28–45.
Rahner, Karl. 'Theological Reflections on the Problem of Secularisation' [1967]. In *TI*, vol. 10, trans. David Bourke, 318–48. London: Darton, Longman and Todd, 1973.
Rahner, Karl. 'Thomas Aquinas on Truth' [1938]. In *TI*, vol. 13, trans. David Bourke, 13–31. London: Darton, Longman and Todd, 1975.
Rahner, Karl. 'Transcendental Theology'. In *Sacramentum Mundi: An Encyclopedia of Theology*, vol. 6, ed. Karl Rahner and Adolf Darlap. New York: Herder and Herder, 1970.
Rahner, Karl. 'Über Martin Heidegger'. In *Martin Heidegger im Gespräch*, ed. Richard Wisser, 48–9. Freiburg: Alber, 1970.
Rahner, Karl. *Wer ist dein Bruder?* Freiburg: Herder, 1981.
Rahner, Karl. 'What is a Dogmatic Statement?' [1961]. In *TI*, vol. 5, 42–66.
Rahner, Karl. 'Zum Geleit'. In *Die anthropologische Wende. Karl Rahners philosophischer Weg vom Wesen des Menschen zur personalen Existenz*, ed. Peter Eicher. Freiburg: Universitätsverlag, 1970.
Rahner, Karl, and Herbert Vorgrimler. *Theological Dictionary* [1961]. Trans. Richard Strachan, ed. Cornelius Erst. New York: Herder and Herder, 1965.

Works by Edward Schillebeeckx

Schillebeeckx, Edward. 'Arabisch-Neoplatoonse achtergrond van Thomas' opvatting over de ontvankelijkheid van de mens voor de genade'. *Bijdragen 35* (1974): 298–308.
Schillebeeckx, Edward. *Christ: The Christian Experience in the Modern World* [1977]. CW vol. 7. Trans. John Bowden. London: Bloomsbury, 2014. Original: *Gerechtigheid en liefde, genade en bevrijding*. Bloemendaal: Nelissen, 1977.
Schillebeeckx, Edward. 'Christian Identity and Human Integrity'. *Concilium 155* (1982): 23–31.
Schillebeeckx, Edward. 'The Church and Mankind' [1965]. In *World and Church*, CW 4, 89–107.
Schillebeeckx, Edward. 'Church and World' [1964]. In *World and Church*, 73–86.
Schillebeeckx, Edward. 'Christelijke identiteit, uitdagend en uitgedaagd. Over de rakelingse nabijheid van de onervaarbare God'. In *Ons Rakelings Nabij. Gedaanteveranderingen van God en geloof. Ter ere van Edward Schillebeeckx*, ed. Manuela Kalsky, André Lascaris, Leo Oosterveen, and Inez van der Spek, 13–32. Zoetermeer: Meinema, 2005.
Schillebeeckx, Edward. 'The Concept of "Truth"' [1954–1962]. In *Revelation and Theology*, 189–205.
Schillebeeckx, Edward. 'The Context and Value of Faith-Talk' [1972]. In *The Understanding of Faith*, 13–18.
Schillebeeckx, Edward. 'Correlation between Human Question and Christian Answer' [1970]. In *The Understanding of Faith*, 69–88.
Schillebeeckx, Edward. 'The Crisis in the Language of Faith as a Hermeneutical Problem'. *Concilium 5*, no. 9 (1973): 31–45.
Schillebeeckx, Edward. 'Culture, Religion and Violence' [1996]. In *Essays. Ongoing Theological Quests*, 163–82.
Schillebeeckx, Edward. 'Discontinuities in Christian Dogmas' [1994]. In *Essays. Ongoing Theological Quests*, 85–109.
Schillebeeckx, Edward. *Essays. Ongoing Theological Quests*. CW vol. 11. Trans. Marcelle Manley, Edward Fitzgerald, and Peter Tomlinson. London: Bloomsbury, 2014.
Schillebeeckx, Edward. 'Experience and Faith' [1980]. In *Essays. Ongoing Theological Quests*, 1–34.
Schillebeeckx, Edward. 'Faith Functioning in Human Self-Understanding'. In *The Word in History: The St. Xavier Symposium*, ed. T. Patrick Burke, 41–59. London: Collins, 1968.
Schillebeeckx, Edward. *God the Future of Man* [1968]. CW vol. 3. Trans. N. D. Smith. London: Bloomsbury, 2014.
Schillebeeckx, Edward. *God and Man* [1965]. Theological Soundings vol. 2. Trans. Edward Fitzgerald and Peter Tomlinson. London: Sheed and Ward, 1969. Original: *God en mens*. Theologische peilingen vol. 2. Bilthoven: Nelissen, 1965.
Schillebeeckx, Edward. *God is New Each Moment. In Conversation with Huub Oosterhuis en Piet Hoogeveen* [1982]. Trans. David Smith. Edinburgh: T&T Clark, 1983.
Schillebeeckx, Edward. *I am a Happy Theologian. Conversations with Francesco Strazzari*. Trans. John Bowden. London: SCM, 1994.
Schillebeeckx, Edward. 'Het gezag van de traditie in de theologie'. In *Jezus, een eigentijds verhaal*, ed. Maurice Bouwens, Jacobine Geel, and Frans Maas, 76–87. Zoetermeer: Meinema, 2001 In *Jezus, een eigentijds verhaal*, ed. Maurice Bouwens, Jacobine Geel and Frans Maas. Zoetermeer: Meinema, 2001.

Schillebeeckx, Edward. 'Humaniora en humaniora'. *Biekorf* (1936–1937), no. 1.
Schillebeeckx, Edward. *Interim Report on the Books Jesus and Christ* [1978]. CW vol. 8. Trans. John Bowden. London: Bloomsbury, 2014. Original: *Tussentijds verhaal over twee Jezus boeken*. Bloemendaal: Nelissen, 1978.
Schillebeeckx, Edward. *Jesus: An Experiment in Christology* [1974]. CW vol. 6. Trans. Hubert Hoskins. London: Bloomsbury, 2014. Original: *Jezus, het verhaal van een levende*. Baarn: Nelissen, 1974.
Schillebeeckx, Edward. 'Natuur en bovennatuur'. *Biekorf* (1942–1943), no. 4–5.
Schillebeeckx, Edward. 'The New Critical Theory' [1971]. In *The Understanding of Faith*, 89–107.
Schillebeeckx, Edward. 'The New Critical Theory and Theological Hermeneutics' [1971]. In *The Understanding of Faith*, 109–35.
Schillebeeckx, Edward. 'The New Image of God, Secularization and Man's Future on Earth' [1968]. In *God the Future of Man*, 101–25.
Schillebeeckx, Edward. 'The New Trends in Present-day Dogmatic Theology' [1961]. In *Revelation and Theology*, 289–320.
Schillebeeckx, Edward. 'The Non-Conceptual Intellectual Dimension in our Knowledge of God according to Aquinas' [1952]. In *Revelation and Theology*, 207–38.
Schillebeeckx, Edward. 'The Non-Conceptual Intellectual Element in the Act of Faith: A Reaction' [1963]. In *Revelation and Theology*, 239–68.
Schillebeeckx, Edward. 'Non-Religious Humanism and Belief in God' [1961]. In *God and Man*, 41–84.
Schillebeeckx, Edward. 'Priest and Layman in a Secular World' [1952–1953]. In *World and Church*, 25–57.
Schillebeeckx, Edward. 'The Problem of the Infallibility of the Church's Office. A Theological Reflection'. *Concilium* 3, no. 9 (1973): 77–94.
Schillebeeckx, Edward. 'Prologue: Human God-Talk and God's Silence'. In *The Praxis of the Reign of God: An Introduction to the Theology of Edward Schillebeeckx*, ed. Mary Catherine Hilkert and Robert J. Schreiter, ix–xviii. New York: Fordham University Press, 2002.
Schillebeeckx, Edward. 'Revelation-in-Reality and Revelation-in-Word' [1960]. In *Revelation and Theology*, 25–41.
Schillebeeckx, Edward. *Revelation and Theology* [1964]. CW vol. 2. Trans. N.D. Smith. London: Bloomsbury, 2014. Original: *Openbaring en theologie*. Theologische peilingen vol. 1. Bilthoven: Nelissen, 1964.
Schillebeeckx, Edward. 'Salvation History as the Basis of Theology: *Theologia* or *Oikonomia*' [1953]. In *Revelation and Theology*, 271–88.
Schillebeeckx, Edward. 'The Search for the Living God' [1959]. In *Essays. Ongoing Theological Quests*, 35–50.
Schillebeeckx, Edward. 'Secularization and Christian Belief in God' [1968]. In *God the Future of Man*, 31–54.
Schillebeeckx, Edward. 'Terugblik vanuit de tijd na Vaticanum II. De gebroken ideologieën van de moderniteit'. In *Tussen openheid en isolement. Het voorbeeld van de katholieke theologie in de negentiende eeuw*, ed. Erik Borgman and Anton van Harskamp, 153–72. Kampen: Kok, 1992.
Schillebeeckx, Edward. 'Theological Criteria' [1969]. In *The Understanding of Faith*, 41–68.
Schillebeeckx, Edward. 'Theologie als bevrijdingskunde. Enkele noodzakelijke beschouwingen vooraf'. *Tijdschrift voor Theologie* 24 (1984): 388–402.

Schillebeeckx, Edward. 'Theologie der Erfahrung – Sackgasse oder Weg zum Glauben? Ein Gespräch mit Prof. Edward Schillebeeckx'. *Herder Korrespondenz 32* (1978): 391–7.
Schillebeeckx, Edward. *Theologisch testament. Notarieel nog niet verleden*. Baarn: Nelissen, 1994.
Schillebeeckx, Edward. 'Theological Interpretation of Faith in 1983' [1983]. In *Essays. Theological Quests*, 51–68.
Schillebeeckx, Edward. 'Theological Quests' [1994]. In *Essays. Ongoing Theological Quests*, 111–61.
Schillebeeckx, Edward. 'Towards a Catholic Use of Hermeneutics' [1968]. In *God The Future of Man*, 1–29.
Schillebeeckx, Edward. *The Understanding of Faith* [1972]. CW vol. 5. Trans. N. D. Smith. London: Bloomsbury, 2014. Original: *Geloofsverstaan: interpretatie en kritiek*. Theologische Peilingen vol. 5. Bloemendaal: Nelissen, 1972.
Schillebeeckx, Edward. 'Verlangen naar ultieme levensvervulling. Een kritische herlezing van Thomas van Aquino'. *Tijdschrift voor Theologie 42* (2002): 15–35.
Schillebeeckx, Edward. 'What is Theology' [1958]. In *Revelation and Theology*, 65–118.
Schillebeeckx, Edward. *World and Church*. CW vol. 4. Trans. N.D. Smith. London: Bloomsbury, 2014. Original: *Wereld en kerk*. Theologische peilingen vol. 3. Bilthoven: Nelissen, 1966.

Secondary Literature

Adams, Nicholas. 'Rahner's Reception in Twentieth Century Protestant Theology'. In *The Cambridge Companion to Karl Rahner*. Cambridge: Cambridge University Press, 211–24.
Adams, Nicholas, George Pattison, and Graham Ward, eds. *The Oxford Handbook of Theology and Modern European Thought*. Oxford: Oxford University Press, 2013.
Adorno, Theodor W. *Metaphysics: Concept and Problems*. Ed. Rolf Tiedemann and trans. Edmund Jephcott. Stanford: Stanford University Press, 2001.
Adorno, Theodor W. *Negative Dialectics*. Trans. E. B. Ashton. London: Taylor and Francis, 2004.
Aquinas, Thomas. *Summa theologiae*. Latin text, English translation, introduction, notes, appendices, and glossary. Ed. Thomas Gilby. 60 volumes. London: Blackfriars and Eyre & Spottiswoode, 1964–1976.
Augustine. 'Sermon 90A'. In *The Works of Saint Augustine: A Translation for the 21st Century. Part III: Sermons. Vol. 11: Newly Discovered Sermons*. Trans. Edmund Hill. Ed. John E. Rotelle. New York: New City Press, 1997.
Bacik, James J. *Apologetics and the Eclipse of Mystery: Mystagogy According to Karl Rahner*. Notre Dame, IN: Notre Dame University Press, 1980.
Balthasar, Hans Urs von. *Cordula oder der Ernstfall*. Einsiedeln: Johannes Verlag, 1966.
Balthasar, Hans Urs von. 'Rezensionen: Karl Rahner, *Geist in Welt*'. *Zeitschrift für Katholische Theologie* 63 (1939): 375–9.
Baron, Craig. 'The Poetry of Transcendental Thomism'. In *The Presence of Transcendence: Thinking 'Sacrament' in a Postmodern Age*, ed. Lieven Boeve and John C. Ries, 43–59. Annua Nuntia Lovaniensia 42. Leuven: Peeters, 2001.
Barwasser, Carsten. *Theologie der Kultur und Hermeneutik der Glaubens-erfahrung. Zur Gottesfrage und Glaubensverantwortung bei Edward Schillebeeckx OP*. Münster: LIT Verlag, 2010.

Bateman, Terence. *Reconstructing Theology: The Contribution of Francis Schüssler Fiorenza*. Minneapolis: Fortress Press, 2014.

Batlogg, Andreas R., Paul Rulands, Walter Schmolly, Roman A. Siebenrock, Günther Wassilowsky, Arno Zahlauer, eds. *Der Denkweg Karl Rahners. Quellen – Entwicklungen – Perspektiven*. Mainz: Matthias Grünewald Verlag, 2004.

Bergin, Helen. 'Edward Schillebeeckx and the Suffering Human Being'. *International Journal of Public Theology* 4 (2010): 466–82.

Bernstein, Richard. *Beyond Objectivism and Relativism: Science, Hermeneutics, and Praxis*. Philadelphia, PA: University of Pennsylvania Press, 1983.

Beyer, Gerald J. 'Karl Rahner on the Radical Unity of the Love of God and Neighbour'. *Irish Theological Quarterly* 68 (2003): 251–90.

Bloch, Ernst. *The Principle of Hope*. Trans. Neville Plaice. Oxford: Blackwell, 1986.

Boeve, Lieven. 'The Enduring Significance and Relevance of Edward Schillebeeckx? Introducing the State of the Question in Medias Res'. In *Edward Schillebeeckx and Contemporary Theology*, ed. Lieven Boeve, Frederiek Depoortere, and Stephan van Erp, 1–22. London: T&T Clark.

Boeve, Lieven. 'Experience According to Edward Schillebeeckx: The Driving Force of Faith and Theology'. In *Divinising Experience: Essays in the History of Religious Experience from Origen to Ricoeur*, ed. Lieven Boeve and Laurence P. Hemming, 199–225. Studies in Philosophical Theology 23. Leuven: Peeters, 2004.

Boeve, Lieven. *God Interrupts History. Theology in a Time of Upheaval*. New York: Continuum, 2007.

Boeve, Lieven. *Lyotard and Theology*. London: Bloomsbury, 2014.

Boeve, Lieven. 'Revelation, Scripture and Tradition: Lessons from Vatican II's Constitution *Dei verbum* for Contemporary Theology'. *International Journal of Systematic Theology* 13 (2011): 416–33.

Boeve, Lieven. 'Systematic Theology, Truth and History: Recontextualisation'. In *Orthodoxy: Process and Product*, ed. Mathijs Lamberigts, Lieven Boeve, and Terrence Merrigan, 27–44. Leuven: Peeters.

Boeve, Lieven. 'Theological Truth, Particularity and Incarnation: Engaging Religious Plurality and Radical Hermeneutics'. In *Orthodoxy: Process and Product*, ed. Mathijs Lamberigts, Lieven Boeve, and Terrence Merrigan, 323–48. Leuven: Peeters.

Boeve, Lieven, Frederiek Depoortere, and Stephan van Erp, eds. *Edward Schillebeeckx and Contemporary Theology*. London: T&T Clark, 2010.

Bokwa, Ignacy. 'Das Verhältnis zwischen Christologie und Anthropologie als Interpretationsmodell der Theologie Karl Rahners'. In *Karl Rahner in der Diskussion. Erste und zweites Innsbrucker Karl-Rahner-Symposion*, ed. Roman A. Siebenrock, 33–43. Innsbruck: Tyrolia, 2001.

Bonsor, Jack Arthur. 'Editorial Symposium. Irreducible Pluralism: The Transcendental and Hermeneutical as Theological Options'. *Horizons* 16 (1989): 316–28.

Bonsor, Jack Arthur. *Rahner, Heidegger, and Truth: Karl Rahner's Notion of Christian Truth. The Influence of Heidegger*. Lanham, MD: University Press of America, 1987.

Borgman, Erik. 'Christelijk: een identiteit die er geen is'. In *Jezus, een eigentijds verhaal*, ed. Maurice Bouwens, Jacobine Geel, and Frans Maas, 91–5. Zoetermeer: Meinema, 2001 In *Jezus, een eigentijds verhaal*, ed. Maurice Bouwens, Jacobine Geel and Frans Maas. Zoetermeer: Meinema, 2001.

Borgman, Erik. 'Van cultuurtheologie naar theologie als onderdeel van de cultuur. De toekomst van het theologische project van Edward Schillebeeckx'. *Tijdschrift voor Theologie* 34 (1994): 335–60.

Borgman, Erik. 'Deus Humanissimus. Christelijk geloof als excessief humanisme bij Edward Schillebeeckx'. In *Humanisme en religie. Controverses, bruggen, perspectieven*, ed. Joachim Duyndam, Marcel Poorthuis, and Theo de Wit, 229–46. Delft: Eburon, 2005.

Borgman, Erik. *Edward Schillebeeckx. A Theologian in his History. Vol. 1: A Catholic Theology of Culture (1916-1965)*. Trans. John Bowden. London: Continuum, 2003.

Borgman, Erik. '… Like a Sacrament': Towards a Theological View on the Real Existing Church'. In *Edward Schillebeeckx. Impulse für Theologien im 21. Jahrhundert – Impetus Towards Theologies in the 21st Century*, ed. Thomas Eggensperger, Ulrich Engel, Angel F. Méndez Montoya, 230–51. Mainz: Matthias Grünewald Verlag, 2012.

Borgman, Erik. 'Retrieving God's Contemporary Presence: The Future of Edward Schillebeeckx's Theology of Culture'. In *Edward Schillebeeckx and Contemporary Theology*, ed. Lieven Boeve, Frederiek Depoortere, and Stephan van Erp, 235–51. London: T&T Clark.

Borgman, Erik. 'Theologie als schatbewaarder of als bedelaar? In discussie met de "Onderbroken traditie" van Lieven Boeve'. *Tijdschrift voor Geestelijk Leven* 56 (2000): 183–98.

Borgman, Erik. 'Theologie tussen universiteit en emancipatie. De weg van Edward Schillebeeckx'. *Tijdschrift voor Theologie* 26 (1986): 240–58.

Bos, Maarten van den, and Stephan van Erp. *A Happy Theologian. A Hundred Years of Edward Schillebeeckx*. Nijmegen: Valkhof Press, 2014.

Bouwens, Maurice, Jacobine Geel, and Frans Maas, eds. *Jezus, een eigentijds verhaal*. Zoetermeer: Meinema, 2001.

Bowden, John. *Edward Schillebeeckx: Portrait of a Theologian*. London: SCM, 1983.

Bradley, Denis. 'Rahner's *Spirit in the World*. Aquinas or Hegel?' *The Thomist* 41 (1977): 167–99.

Bullivant, Stephen. 'The Myth of Rahnerian Exceptionalism'. *Philosophy and Theology* 22 (2010): 339–51.

Bullivant, Stephen. *The Salvation of Atheists and Catholic Theology*. Oxford: Oxford University Press, 2012.

Burke, Patrick. *Reinterpreting Rahner: A Critical Study of His Major Themes*. New York: Fordham University Press, 2002.

Caponi, Francis J. 'Karl Rahner and the Metaphysics of Participation'. *The Thomist* 67 (2003): 375–408.

Caponi, Francis J. 'A Speechless Grace: Karl Rahner on Religious Language'. *International Journal of Systematic Theology* 9 (2007): 200–21.

Caputo, John D. 'Radical Hermeneutics and Religious Truth: The Case of Sheehan and Schillebeeckx'. In *Phenomenology of the Truth Proper to Religion*, ed. Daniel Guerrière, 146–72. Albany: State University of New York, 1990.

Carr, Anne. *The Theological Method of Karl Rahner*. Missoula, MT: Scholars Press, 1977.

Clayton, John P. *The Concept of Correlation: Paul Tillich and the Possibility of a Mediating Theology*. Berlin: De Gruyter, 1980.

Coffey, David. 'The Whole Rahner on the Supernatural Existential'. *Theological Studies* 65 (2004): 95–118.

Conlon, James J. 'Karl Rahner's Theory of Sensation'. *The Thomist* 41 (1977): 400–17.

Conway, Eamonn. *The Anonymous Christian – A Relativized Christianity? An Evaluation of Hans Urs von Balthasar's Criticisms of Karl Rahner's Theory of the Anonymous Christian*. Frankfurt am Main: Peter Lang, 1993.

Conway, Eamonn. '"So as not to Despise God's Grace": Re-assessing Rahner's Idea of the "Anonymous Christian"'. *Louvain Studies* 29 (2004): 107–30.
Conway, Pádraic, and Fáinche Ryan, eds. *Karl Rahner: Theologian for the Twenty-first Century*. Bern: Peter Lang, 2010.
Cooper, Jennifer. *Humanity in the Mystery of God: The Theological Anthropology of Edward Schillebeeckx*. London: T&T Clark, 2009.
Corduan, Winfried. 'Hegel in Rahner: A Study in Philosophical Hermeneutics'. *The Harvard Theological Review* 71 (1978): 285–98.
Coreth, Emerich. 'Philosophische Grundlagen der Theologie Karl Rahners'. *Stimmen der Zeit* 212 (1994): 525–36.
Coreth, Emerich, Walter M. Neidl, and Georg Pfligersdorffer, eds. *Christliche Philosophie im katholischen Denken des 19. und 20. Jahrhunderts. Band 2: Rückgriff auf scholastisches Erbe*. Graz: Styria Verlag, 1988.
Dalferth, Ingolf U. 'Hermeneutische Theologie – heute?'. In *Hermeneutische Theologie – heute?*, ed. Ingolf U. Dalferth, Pierre Bühler, and Andreas Hunziker, 3–38. Tübingen: Mohr Siebeck, 2013.
Dalferth, Ingolf U., and Andreas Hunziker, eds. *Gott denken – ohne Metaphysik? Zu einer aktuellen Kontroverse in Theologie und Philosophie*. Tübingen: Mohr Siebeck, 2014.
Depoorter, Annekatrien. 'Correlatie onder vuur? Bedenkingen bij de theologische methode van Paul Tillich en Edward Schillebeeckx'. *Bijdragen. International Journal in Philosophy and Theology* 66 (2005): 37–64.
Depoorter, Annekatrien. 'Orthopraxis as a Criterion for Orthodoxy? Edward Schillebeeckx' View on the Development and the Characteristic of Religious Truth'. In *Theology and the Quest for Truth. Historical- and Systematic-theological Studies*, ed. Mathijs Lambertigts, Lieven Boeve, and Terrence Merrigan, 165–80. Bibliotheca Ephemeridum Theologicarum Lovaniensium 202. Leuven: Peeters, 2006.
Depoortere, Frederiek. 'Taking Atheism Seriously: A Challenge for Theology in the 21st Century'. In *Edward Schillebeeckx and Contemporary Theology*, ed. Lieven Boeve, Frederiek Depoortere, and Stephan van Erp, 36–48. London: T&T Clark.
De Maeseneer, Yves. 'The Question of Universality. A Response to Francis Schüssler Fiorenza'. *Louvain Studies* 39 (2015–2016): 141–54.
De Petter, Dominicus Maria. 'Impliciete intuïtie'. *Tijdschrift voor Filosofie* 1 (1939): 84–105.
De Petter, Dominicus Maria. 'Zin en grond van het oordeel'. In *Begrip en werkelijkheid. Aan de overzijde van het conceptualisme*. Hilversum: Brand, 1964.
De Schrijver, Georges. 'Hertaling van het Christus-gebeuren: een onmogelijke opgave?'. In *Volgens Edward Schillebeeckx*, ed. Etienne Kuypers, 53–90. Leuven: Garant, 1991.
Desmond, William. *God and the Between*. Oxford: Blackwell, 2008.
Desmond, William. 'The Metaphysics of Modernity'. In *The Oxford Handbook of Theology and Modern European Thought*, ed. Nicholas, Adams George Pattison, and Graham Ward, 542–63. Oxford: Oxford University Press, 2013.
Desmond, William. 'Is There Metaphysics after Critique?' *International Philosophical Quarterly* 45 (2005): 221–41.
Donceel, Joseph, ed. *A Maréchal Reader*. Ed. and trans. Joseph Donceel. New York: Herder & Herder, 1970.
Donceel, Joseph, ed. 'Transcendental Thomism'. *The Monist* 58 (1974): 67–85.
Duffy, Stephen. 'Experience of Grace'. In *The Cambridge Companion to Karl Rahner*, ed. Declan Marmion and Mary E. Hines, 43–62. Cambridge: Cambridge University Press.
Duffy, Stephen. *The Graced Horizon: Nature and Grace in Modern Theological Thought*. Collegeville, MN: The Liturgical Press, 1992.

Dulles, Avery. 'Method in Fundamental Theology: Reflections on David Tracy's *Blessed Rage for Order*'. *Theological Studies* 37 (1976): 304–16.
Duns, Ryan. 'Recovering Rahner's Concept of Being in *Spirit in the World*'. *New Blackfriars* 91 (2010): 567–85.
Dupré, Louis. 'Experience and Interpretation: A Philosophical Reflection on Schillebeeckx' *Jesus* and *Christ*'. *Theological Studies* 43 (1982): 30–51.
Dupré, Louis. 'On the Natural Desire of Seeing God'. *Radical Orthodoxy: Theology, Philosophy, Politics* 1 (2012): 81–94.
Dupré, Louis. *The Other Dimension. A Search for the Meaning of Religious Attitudes*. Garden City, NY: Doubleday, 1972.
Dreyfus, Hubert, and Charles Taylor. *Retrieving Realism*. Cambridge, MA: Harvard University Press, 2015.
Eggensperger, Thomas, Ulrich Engel, Angel F. Méndez Montoya, eds. *Edward Schillebeeckx. Impulse für Theologien im 21. Jahrhundert – Impetus Towards Theologies in the 21st Century*. Mainz: Matthias Grünewald Verlag, 2012.
Eicher, Peter. *Die anthropologische Wende. Karl Rahners philosophischer Weg vom Wesen des Menschen zur personalen Existenz*. Freiburg: Universitätsverlag, 1970.
Eicher, Peter. 'Wovon spricht die transzendentale Theologie? Zur gegenwärtige Auseinandersetzung um das Denken von Karl Rahner'. *Theologische Quartalschrift* 157 (1977): 285–8.
Endean, Philip. 'Has Rahnerian Theology a Future?' In Declan Marmion and Mary E. Hines, eds. *The Cambridge Companion to Karl Rahner*. Cambridge: Cambridge University Press, 281–96.
Endean, Philip. *Karl Rahner and Ignatian Spirituality*. Oxford: Oxford University Press, 2001.
Erp, Stephan van. 'Geïmpliceerde transcendentie. De Petter's "impliciete intuïtie" als bevestiging van het zijn van de zijnden én het Zijn zelf'. In *Subliem Niemandsland. Opstellen over intersubjectiviteit, metafysica en transcendentie*, ed. W.F.C.M. Derkse, A. J. Leijen, and B. M. J. Nagel, 295–308. Best: Damon, 1997.
Erp, Stephan van. 'Implicit Faith: Philosophical Theology after Schillebeeckx'. In *Edward Schillebeeckx and Contemporary Theology*, ed. Lieven Boeve, Frederiek Depoortere, and Stephan van Erp, 209–23. London: T&T Clark.
Erp, Stephan van. 'Incarnational Theology: Systematic Theology after Schillebeeckx'. In *Edward Schillebeeckx. Impulse für Theologien im 21. Jahrhundert – Impetus Towards Theologies in the 21st Century*, ed. Thomas Eggensperger, Ulrich Engel, Angel F. Méndez Montoya, 53–66. Mainz: Matthias Grünewald Verlag, 2012.
Erp, Stephan van. 'Incessant Incarnation as the Future of Humanity: The Promise of Schillebeeckx's Sacramental Theology'. *Concilium. International Review of Theology* no. 1(2012): 92–105.
Erp, Stephan van. *De onvoltooide eeuw. Voorlopers van een katholieke cultuur*. Nijmegen: Valkhof Pers, 2015.
Erp, Stephan van. 'The Sacrament of the World: Thinking God's Presence beyond Public Theology'. *ET Studies* 6 (2015): 119–34.
Erp, Stephan van. 'Tussen traditie & situatie: Edward Schillebeeckx voor een volgende generatie'. *Tijdschrift voor Theologie* 50 (2010): 6–26.
Fabro, Cornelio. *La svolta antropologica di Karl Rahner*. Milan: Rusconi, 1974.
Feingold, Lawrence. *The Natural Desire According to St. Thomas and His Interpreters*. Washington: The Catholic University of America Press, 2004.

Fiorenza, Francis Schüssler. 'The Conflict of Hermeneutical Traditions and Christian Theology'. *Journal of Chinese Philosophy* 27 (2000): 3–31.
Fiorenza, Francis Schüssler. 'The Crisis of Hermeneutics and Christian Theology'. In *Theology at the End of Modernity*, ed. S. Greeve Davaney, 117–40. Philadelphia, PA: Trinity Press, 1991.
Fiorenza, Francis Schüssler. 'Editorial Essays. The Cosmopolitanism of Roman Catholic Theology and the Challenge of Cultural Particularity'. *Horizons* 25 (2008): 298–319.
Fiorenza, Francis Schüssler. 'Editorial Symposium. Theology: Transcendental or Hermeneutical?' *Horizons* 16 (1989): 329–41.
Fiorenza, Francis Schüssler. 'The Experience of Transcendence or the Transcendence of Experience. Negotiating the Difference'. In *Religious Experience and Contemporary Theological Epistemology*, ed. Lieven Boeve, Yves de Maeseneer, and Stijn van den Bossche, 183–218. Bibliotheca Ephemeridum Theologicarum Lovaniensium 188. Leuven: Peeters, 2005.
Fiorenza, Francis Schüssler. *Foundational Theology: Jesus and the Church*. New York: Crossroads, 1984.
Fiorenza, Francis Schüssler. 'Foundational Theology: Review Symposium – Author's Response'. *Horizons* 11 (1984): 415–23.
Fiorenza, Francis Schüssler. 'Gaudium et Spes and Human Rights: The Challenge of a Cosmopolitan World'. In *The Church and Human Freedom: Forty Years after Gaudium et Spes*, ed. D. F. Weaver, 38–65. Villanova, PA: Villanova University Press, 2006.
Fiorenza, Francis Schüssler. 'Introduction: Karl Rahner and the Kantian Problematic'. In Rahner, Spirit in the World, xix–xlv.
Fiorenza, Francis Schüssler. 'Karl Rahner: A Theologian for a Cosmopolitan Twenty-First Century'. In *In God's Hands: Essays on the Church and Ecumenism in Honour of Michael Fahey, S.J.*, ed. J. Z. Skira and M. S. Attridge, 109–35. Bibliotheca Ephemeridum Theologicarum Lovaniensium 199. Leuven: Peeters, 2007.
Fiorenza, Francis Schüssler. 'Method in Theology'. In Declan Marmion and Mary E. Hines, eds. *The Cambridge Companion to Karl Rahner*. Cambridge: Cambridge University Press, 65–82.
Fiorenza, Francis Schüssler. 'The New Theology and Transcendental Thomism'. In *Modern Christian Thought. Vol. 2: The Twentieth Century*, ed. James C. Livingston and Francis Schüssler Fiorenza, with Sarah Coakley and James H. Evans Jr., 197–232. Minneapolis: Fortress Press, 2006.
Fiorenza, Francis Schüssler. 'Pluralism: A Western Commodity or Justice for the Other?'. In *Ethical Monotheism, Past and Present: Essays in Honor of Wendell S. Dietrich*, ed. T. Vial and M. Poster, 278–306. Providence, RI: Brown Judaic Studies, 2001.
Fiorenza, Francis Schüssler. 'Political Theology and Latin American Liberation Theology'. In *Modern Christian Thought. Vol. 2: The Twentieth Century*, ed. James C. Livingston and Francis Schüssler Fiorenza, with Sarah Coakley and James H. Evans Jr., 273–308. Minneapolis: Fortress Press, 2006.
Fiorenza, Francis Schüssler. 'Political Theology as Foundational Theology'. *Proceedings of the Catholic Theological Society of America* 32 (1977): 142–77.
Fiorenza, Francis Schüssler. Review of *Deus Humanissimus. The Knowability of God in the Theology of Edward Schillebeeckx*, by Philip Kennedy. *The Journal of Religion* 76 (1996): 126–7.
Fiorenza, Francis Schüssler. 'Roundtable Discussion. The Influence of Feminist Theory on My Theological Work'. *Journal of Feminist Studies in Religion* 7 (1991): 95–105.

Fiorenza, Francis Schüssler. 'Seminar on Rahner's Ecclesiology: Jesus and the Foundation of the Church – An Analysis of the Hermeneutical Issues'. *Proceedings of the Catholic Theological Society of America* 33 (1978): 229–54.

Fiorenza, Francis Schüssler. 'Systematic Theology: Task and Methods'. In *Systematic Theology: Roman Catholic Perspectives*. 2nd ed., ed. Francis Schüssler Fiorenza and John P. Galvi, 1–74. Minneapolis: Fortress Press, 2011.

Fiorenza, Francis Schüssler, and John P. Galvin, eds. *Systematic Theology: Roman Catholic Perspectives*. 2nd ed. Minneapolis: Fortress Press, 2011.

Fodor, Jim. 'Hermeneutics'. In *The Oxford Handbook of Theology and Modern European Thought*, ed. Nicholas, Adams George Pattison, and Graham Ward, 499–521. Oxford: Oxford University Press, 2013.

Fodor, Jim. 'Postliberal Theology'. In *The Modern Theologians: An Introduction to Christian Theology Since 1918*, 3rd edition, ed. David F. Ford with Rachel Muers, 229–48. Oxford: Blackwell, 2005.

Fischer, Klaus P. *Der Mensch als Geheimnis: Die Anthropologie Karl Rahners*. Freiburg: Herder, 1974.

Fößel, Thomas. *Gott – Begriff und Geheimnis. Hansjürgen Verweyens Fundamentaltheologie und die ihr inhärente Kritik an der Philosophie und Theologie Karl Rahners*. Innsbrucker theologische Studien 70. Innsbruck: Tyrolia, 2004.

Fößel, Thomas. 'Warum ein Existential *übernatürlich* ist. Anmerkungen zur kontroversen Diskussion um Karl Rahners Theologoumenon vom "übernaturlichen Existential"'. *Theologie und Philosophie* 80 (2005): 389–411.

Frede, Dorothea. 'The Question of Being: Heidegger's Project'. In Guignon, *The Cambridge Companion to Martin Heidegger*, 42–69.

Fritz, Joseph. 'Karl Rahner Repeated in Jean-Luc Marion?' *Theological Studies* 73 (2012): 318–38.

Fritz, Joseph. *Karl Rahner's Theological Aesthetics*. Washington: The Catholic University of America Press, 2014.

Gadamer, Hans-Georg. *Truth and Method*. Revised trans. Joel Weinsheimer and Donald G. Marshall. London: Continuum, 2004.

Gadamer, Hans-Georg. 'The Universality of the Hermeneutical Problem'. In *The Hermeneutic Tradition: From Ast to Ricoeur*, ed. Gayle L. Ormiston and Alan D. Schrift, 147–58. Albany: SUNY, 1990.

Garhammer, Erich. 'Editorial'. *Lebendige Seelsorge* 64 (2013): 361.

Geldhof, Joris. 'Pascal's Double Mistake, or the Desirability of Sound Metaphysics'. *Downside Review* 128 (2008): 235–46.

Gelpi, Donald. *The Turn to Experience in Contemporary Theology*. New York: Paulist, 1994.

Godzieba, Anthony. 'God, the Luxury of Our Lives: Schillebeeckx and the Argument'. In *Edward Schillebeeckx and Contemporary Theology*, ed. Lieven Boeve, Frederiek Depoortere, and Stephan van Erp, 25–35. London: T&T Clark.

Greisch, Jean. *Hermeneutik und Metaphysik: Eine Problemgeschichte*. München: Wilhelm Fink Verlag, 1993.

Grondin, Jean. *Introduction to Metaphysics: From Parmenides to Levinas*. Trans. Lukas Soderstrom. New York: Columbia University Press, 2012.

Guarino, Thomas G. *Foundations of Systematic Theology*. London: T&T Clark, 2005.

Guarino, Thomas G. '*Philosophia Obscurans?* Six Theses on the Proper Relationship between Theology and Philosophy'. *Nova et Vetera* 12 (2014): 349–94.

Guenther, Titus F. *Rahner and Metz. Transcendental Theology as Political Theology*. Lanham, MD: University Press of America, 1994.

Guignon, Charles B., ed. *The Cambridge Companion to Martin Heidegger*. Cambridge: Cambridge University Press, 1991.

Habermas, Jürgen. *Knowledge and Human Interest*. Trans. Jeremy J. Shapiro. Cambridge: Polity Press, 1998.

Habermas, Jürgen. 'On Hermeneutics' Claim to Universality'. In *The Hermeneutics Reader: Texts of the German Tradition from the Enlightenment to the Present*, ed. Kurt Mueller-Vollmer, 293–319. Oxford: Blackwell, 1986.

Habermas, Jürgen. *Theory and Practice*. Trans. John Viertel. Cambridge: Polity Press, 1986.

Habermas, Jürgen. *The Theory of Communicative Action*. 2 vols. Trans. Thomas McCarthy. Cambridge: Polity Press, 1997–1998.

Haight, Roger. 'Engagement met de wereld als zaak van God. Christologie en postmoderniteit'. *Tijdschrift voor Theologie* 50 (2010): 73–94.

Haight, Roger. *The Future of Christology*. New York: Continuum, 2005.

Hall, Eric H., and Hartmut von Sass. *Groundless Gods: The Theological Prospects of Post-Metaphysical Thought*. Eugene, OR: Wipf and Stock, 2014.

Healy, Nicholas M. 'Indirect Methods in Theology: Karl Rahner as an Ad Hoc Apologist'. *The Thomist* 56 (1992): 613–33.

Hegel, Georg Wilhelm Friedrich. *Enzyklopädie der Philosophischen Wissenschaften im Grundrisse*. Ed. Wolfgang Bonsiepen and Hans-Christian Lucas. Hamburg: Felix Meiner Verlag, 1992.

Heidegger, Martin. *Being and Time*. Trans. John Macquarrie and Edward Robinson. Oxford: Basil Blackwell, 1962.

Heidegger, Martin. 'What is Metaphysics'. In *Martin Heidegger: Basic Writings*, trans. and ed. David Farrell Krell, 93–110. London: Routledge, 1993.

Hilkert, Mary Catherine. 'Experience and Revelation'. In Hilkert and Schreiter, *The Praxis of the Reign of God*, 59–77.

Hilkert, Mary Catherine. '"Grace-Optimism": The Spirituality at the Heart of Schillebeeckx's Theology'. *Spirituality Today* 44 (1991): 220–39.

Hilkert, Mary Catherine. 'Nieuwe paden in een oude tuin. Sacramentele theologie en antropologie'. *Tijdschrift voor Theologie* 50 (2010): 108–21.

Hilkert, Mary Catherine. 'St. Thomas and the Appeal to Experience. A Response to Kenneth L. Smith'. *CTSA Proceedings* 47 (1992): 21–5.

Hilkert, Mary Catherine. 'The Threatened *Humanum* as *Imago Dei*: Anthropology and Christian Ethics'. In *Edward Schillebeeckx and Contemporary Theology*, ed. Lieven Boeve, Frederiek Depoortere, and Stephan van Erp, 127–41. London: T&T Clark.

Hilkert, Mary Catherine, and Robert J. Schreiter, eds. *The Praxis of the Reign of God. An Introduction to the Theology of Edward Schillebeeckx*. New York: Fordham University Press, 2002.

Hill, William J. 'A Theology in Transition'. In Hilkert and Schreiter, *The Praxis of the Reign of God*, 1–18.

Hinze, Bradford E. 'Eschatology and Ethics'. In Hilkert and Schreiter, *The Praxis of the Reign of God*, 167–83.

Höffe, Otfried. *Kant's Critique of Pure Reason: The Foundation of Modern Philosophy*. Studies in German Idealism vol. 10. Dordrecht: Springer, 2010.

Hogan, Kevin. 'Entering into Otherness: The Postmodern Critique of the Subject and Karl Rahner's Theological Anthropology'. *Horizons* 25 (1998): 181–201.

Holzer, Vincent. 'Philosophy With[in] Theology: Rahner's Philosophy of Religion'. *The Heythrop Journal* 55 (2014): 584–98.

Horkheimer, Max, and Theodor W. Adorno. *Dialectic of Enlightenment. Philosophical Fragments*. Ed. Gunzelin Schmid Noerr. Trans. Edmund Jephcott. Stanford: Stanford University Press, 2002.

Hoy, David Couzens. 'Heidegger and the Hermeneutic Turn'. In Guignon, *The Cambridge Companion to Martin Heidegger*, 170–94.

Hurd, Bob. 'Being is Being-Present-to-Itself: Rahner's Key to Aquinas's Metaphysics'. *The Thomist* 52 (1988): 63–78.

Inwood, Michael. *A Hegel Dictionary*. Oxford: Blackwell, 1992.

Irlenborn, Bernd. 'Was ist eine "transzendentale Erfahrung"?' *Theologie und Philosophie* 79 (2004): 491–510.

Jeanrond, Werner G. 'Correlational Theology and the Chicago School'. In *Introduction to Christian Theology: Contemporary North American Perspectives*, ed. Roger A. Badham, 137–53. Louisville: Westminster John Knox Press, 1998.

Jeanrond, Werner G. 'Hermeneutics and Revelation'. In *Memory, Narrativity, Self and the Challenge to Think God: The Reception within Theology of the Recent Work of Paul Ricoeur*, ed. Maureen Junker-Kenny and Peter Kenny, 42–57. Münster: LIT Verlag, 2004.

Jeanrond, Werner G. 'The Problem of the Starting-Point of Theological Thinking'. In *The Possibilities of Theology: Studies in the Theology of Eberhard Jüngel in His Sixtieth Year*, ed. John Webster, 70–89. Edinburgh: T&T Clark, 1994.

Jeanrond, Werner G. *Theological Hermeneutics: Development and Significance*. London: SCM Press, 1994.

Jeanrond, Werner G. 'Theology in the Context of Pluralism and Postmodernity: David Tracy's Theological Method'. In *Postmodernism, Literature and Theology*, ed. David Jasper, 143–63. London: Macmillan Press, 1993.

Jeanrond, Werner G. *A Theology of Love*. London: T&T Clark, 2010.

Jeanrond, Werner G. 'Thinking about God Today'. In Jeanrond and Lande, *The Concept of God in Global Dialogue*, 89–97.

Jeanrond, Werner G., and Aasulv Lande, eds. *The Concept of God in Global Dialogue*. Maryknoll, NY: Orbis, 2005.

Kant, Immanuel. *Critique of Practical Reason*. Trans. Mary Gregor with an introduction by Andrew Reath. Cambridge: Cambridge University Press, 2015.

Kant, Immanuel. *Critique of Pure Reason*. Trans. and ed. Paul Guyer and Allen W. Wood. Cambridge: Cambridge University Press, 2000.

Kasper, Walter. 'Christologie von unten? Kritik und Neuansatz gegenwärtige Christologie'. In *Grundfragen der Christologie heute*, ed. Leo Scheffczyk, 141–70. Quaestiones disputatae 72. Freiburg: Herder, 1975.

Kasper, Walter. *The God of Jesus Christ*. New edition trans. Dinah Livingstone. London: Continuum, 2012.

Kasper, Walter. *Jesus the Christ*. New edition trans. Dinah Livingstone. London: Continuum, 2011.

Kasper, Walter. 'Karl Rahner. Theologe in einer Zeit des Umbruchs'. In *Walter Kasper. Theologie im Diskurs*, 401–11. Gesammelte Schriften vol. 6. Ed. George Augustin and Klaus Krämer. Freiburg: Herder, 2014.

Kennedy, Philip. 'Continuity underlying Discontinuity: Schillebeeckx's Philosophical Background'. *New Blackfriars* 70 (1989): 264–77.

Kennedy, Philip. 'God and Creation'. In Hilkert and Schreiter, *The Praxis of the Reign of God*, 37–58.

Kennedy, Philip. *Schillebeeckx*. Collegeville, MN: Liturgical Press, 1993.

Kerr, Fergus. *Immortal Longings: Versions of Transcending Humanity*. London: SPCK, 1997.
Kerr, Fergus. *Theology after Wittgenstein*. Oxford: Blackwell, 1986.
Kerr, Fergus. *Twentieth-Century Catholic Theologians: From Neo-Scholasticism to Nuptial Mystery*. Oxford: Blackwell, 2007.
Kilby, Karen. 'Balthasar and Karl Rahner'. In *The Cambridge Companion to Hans Urs von Balthasar*, ed. Edward T. Oakes and David Moss, 256–68. Cambridge: Cambridge University Press, 2004.
Kilby, Karen. *Karl Rahner: A Brief Introduction*. New York: Crossroad, 2007.
Kilby, Karen. *Karl Rahner. Theology and Philosophy*. London: Routledge, 2004.
Kim, Younhee. 'David Tracy's Postmodern Reflection on God: Towards God's Incomprehensible and Hidden Infinity'. *Louvain Studies* 30 (2005): 159–79.
Klauke, Heinrich, ed. *100 Jahre Karl Rahner. Nach Rahner post et secundum*. Cologne: Karl Rahner Akademie, 2004.
Knieps, Thomas. *Die Unvertretbarkeit von Individualität. Der wissenschafts-philosophische Ort der Theologie nach Karl Rahners 'Hörer des Wortes'*. Bonner Dogmatische Studien 19. Würzburg: Echter, 1995.
Knoepffler, Nikolaus. *Der Begriff 'transzendental' bei Karl Rahner. Zur Frage seiner Kantischen Herkunft*. Innsbrucker theologische Studien 39. Innsbruck: Tyrolia Verlag, 1993.
Kohl, Bernhard. 'Jenseits des Diskurses. Ethische Anstöße bei Edward Schillebeeckx'. In *Edward Schillebeeckx. Impulse für Theologien im 21. Jahrhundert – Impetus Towards Theologies in the 21st Century*, ed. Thomas Eggensperger, Ulrich Engel, Angel F. Méndez Montoya, 156–69. Mainz: Matthias Grünewald Verlag, 2012.
Kreutzer, Karsten. *Transzendentales versus hermeneutisches Denken. Zur Genese des religionsphilosophischen Ansatzes bei Karl Rahner und seiner Rezeption durch Johann Baptist Metz*. Regensburg: Friedrich Pustet Verlag, 2002.
Küng, Hans. 'Toward a New Consensus in Catholic (and Ecumenical) Theology'. In *Consensus in Theology? A Dialogue with Hans Küng and Edward Schillebeeckx*, ed. Leonard Swidler, 1–17. Philadelphia: The Westminster Press, 1980.
Küng, Hans, and David Tracy, eds. *Paradigm Change in Theology: A Symposium for the Future*. Trans. Margaret Kohl. Edinburgh: T&T Clark, 1990.
Lakebrink, Bernhard. *Klassische Metaphysik. Eine Auseinandersetzung mit der existentialen Anthropozentrik*. Freiburg: Rombach, 1967.
Lamb, Matthew. 'A Response to Fr. Metz'. In *Theology and Discovery: Essays in Honor of Karl Rahner, SJ*, ed. William J. Kelly, 179–83. Milwaukee, WI: Marquette University Press, 1980.
Lamberigts, Mathijs, Lieven Boeve, and Terrence Merrigan, eds. *Orthodoxy: Process and Product*. Bibliotheca Ephemeridum Theologicarum Lovaniensium 227. Leuven: Peeters, 2009.
Lash, Nicholas. *Easter in Ordinary*. Reflections on Human Experience and the Knowledge of God. London: SCM Press, 1988.
Lash, Nicholas. *Holiness, Speech and Silence. Reflections on the Question of God*. Aldershot: Ashgate, 2004.
Lash, Nicholas. *A Matter of Hope: A Theologian's Reflections on the Thought of Karl Marx*. Notre Dame, IN: University of Notre Dame Press, 1982.
Lash, Nicholas. 'Where does Holy Teaching Leave Philosophy? Questions on Milbank's Aquinas'. *Modern Theology* 15 (1999): 433–44.
Lehmann, Karl. 'Karl Rahner, ein Porträt'. In SW 2, xii–lxvii.

Lehmann, Karl. *Was bleibt von Karl Rahner? Theologische Problematik für heute und morgen*. Karl Rahner Lecture 2009. Freiburg: Universitätsbibliothek, 2009.
Lehmann, Karl. 'Philosophisches Denken im Werk Karl Rahners'. In Raffelt, *Karl Rahner in Erinnerung*, 10–27.
Lennan, Richard. *The Ecclesiology of Karl Rahner*. Oxford: Clarendon Press, 1995.
Lennan, Richard. 'The Theology of Karl Rahner: An Alternative to the *Ressourcement*?' In *Ressourcement: A Movement for Renewal in Twentieth-Century Catholic Theology*, ed. Gabriel Flynn and Paul D. Murray, 405–22. Oxford: Oxford University Press, 2012.
Lindbeck, George. *The Nature of Doctrine. Religion and Theology in a Postliberal Age*. 25th Anniversary Edition with a new introduction by Bruce D. Marshall and a new afterword by the author. Louisville, KY: Westminster John Know Press, 2009.
Livingston, James C. *Modern Christian Thought. Vol. 1: The Enlightenment and the Nineteenth Century*. 2nd edition. Minneapolis: Fortress Press, 2006.
Livingston, James C., and Francis Schüssler Fiorenza, with Sarah Coakley and James H. Evans Jr., eds. *Modern Christian Thought. Vol. 2: The Twentieth Century*. Minneapolis: Fortress Press, 2006.
Lonergan, Bernard. *Method in Theology*. New York: Herder & Herder, 1972.
Lotz, Johannes Baptist. 'Joseph Maréchal'. In Coreth, Neidl, and Pfligersdorffer, *Christliche Philosophie im katholischen Denken des 19. und 20. Jahrhunderts. Band 2*, 453–69.
Lubac, Henri de. *Surnaturel: Études historiques*. Paris: Aubier, 1946.
Lyotard, Jean-François. *The Postmodern Condition: A Report on Knowledge*. Trans. G. Bennington and B. Massumi. Foreword by F. Jameson. Minneapolis, University of Minnesota Press, 1984.
Maas, Frans. 'Stem en stilte. Waarheid en openbaring bij Schillebeeckx'. *Tijdschrift voor Theologie* 50 (2010): 51–72.
Maréchal, Joseph. *Le point de départ de la métaphysique*, 5 vols. Louvain: Éditions du Museum Lessianum, 1926–1947.
Maréchal, Joseph. *Le point de départ de la métaphysique. Cahier 5: Le Thomisme devant la Philosophie critique*. Louvain: Éditions du Museum Lessianum, 1926.
Marion, Jean-Luc. *God without Being*. 2nd edition with a foreword by David Tracy and a new preface by the author. Trans. Thomas A. Carlson. Chicago: The University of Chicago Press, 2012.
Marion, Jean-Luc. *In Excess: Studies of Saturated Phenomena*. Trans. Robyn Horner and Vincent Berraud. New York: Fordham University Press, 2002.
Marion, Jean-Luc. 'The Universality of the University'. *Communio* 40 (2013): 64–75.
Marmion, Declan. 'Rahner and His Critics: Revisiting the Dialogue'. *Irish Theological Quarterly* 68 (2003): 195–212.
Marmion, Declan. 'Theology. Spirituality, and the Role of Experience'. *Louvain Studies* 29 (2004): 49–76.
Marmion, Declan, and Mary E. Hines, eds. *The Cambridge Companion to Karl Rahner*. Cambridge: Cambridge University Press, 2005.
Marshall, Bruce D. *Christology in Conflict: The Identity of a Saviour in Rahner and Barth*. New York: Blackwell, 1987.
Masson, Robert. 'Interpreting Rahner's Metaphoric Logic'. *Theological Studies* 71 (2010): 380–409.
McCool, Gerald. *From Unity to Pluralism: The Internal Evolution of Thomism*. New York: Fordham University Press, 1989.
McCool, Gerald. 'Introduction: Rahner's Philosophical Theology'. In *A Rahner Reader*, ed. Gerald McCool, xiii–xxviii. London: Darton, Longman and Todd, 1975.

McDermott, John M. 'The Analogy of Knowing in Karl Rahner'. *International Philosophical Quarterly* 36 (1996): 201–12.
McGinn, Bernard. 'Response to Edward Schillebeeckx and Jürgen Moltmann'. In Küng and Tracy, *Paradigm Change in Theology*, 346–51.
Metz, Johann Baptist. 'Athen versus Jerusalem? Was das Christentum dem europäischen Geist schuldig geblieben ist'. In *Die Gegenwart des Holocaust. 'Erinnerung' als religionspädagogische Herausforderung*, ed. Michael Wermke, 9–17. Münster: Lit Verlag, 1997.
Metz, Johann Baptist. *Christliche Anthropozentrik. Über die Denkform des Thomas von Aquin.* München: Kösel, 1962.
Metz, Johann Baptist. 'Facing the World: A Theological and Biographical Inquiry'. *Theological Studies* 75 (2014): 23–33.
Metz, Johann Baptist. *Faith in History and Society: Toward a Practical Fundamental Theology*. Trans. J. Matthew Ashley. New York: Crossroad, 2011.
Metz, Johann Baptist. 'Fehlt uns Karl Rahner?'. In Raffelt, *Karl Rahner in Erinnerung*, 85–99.
Metz, Johann Baptist. *Glaube in Geschichte und Gesellschaft. Studien zu einer praktischen Fundamentaltheologie*. Mainz: Matthias Grünewald Verlag, 1977.
Metz, Johann Baptist. *Memoria Passionis. Ein provozierendes Gedächtnis in pluralistischer Gesellschaft*. Freiburg: Herder, 2006.
Milbank, John. *The Suspended Middle: Henri de Lubac and the Renewed Split in Modern Catholic Theology*. Grand Rapids: William B. Eerdmans, 2014.
Milbank, John. *Theology and Social Theory: Beyond Secular Reason*. London: Blackwell, 2006.
Milbank, John. *The Word Made Strange: Theology, Language, Culture*. Oxford: Blackwell, 1997.
Muck, Otto. 'Die deutschsprachige Maréchal-Schule – Transzendental-philosophie als Metaphysik: J.B. Lotz, K. Rahner, W. Brugger, E. Coreth u.a.'. In Coreth, Neidl, and Pfligersdorffer, *Christliche Philosophie im katholischen Denken des 19. und 20. Jahrhunderts*, 590–622.
Muck, Otto. 'Heidegger und Karl Rahner'. *Zeitschrift für katholische Theologie* 116 (1994): 257–69.
Muck, Otto. 'The Logical Structure of the Transcendental Method'. *International Philosophical Quarterly* 9 (1969): 342–62.
Muck, Otto. 'Thomas – Kant – Maréchal: Karl Rahner's transzendentale Methode'. In Schöndorf, *Die philosophischen Quellen der Theologie Karl Rahners*, 31–56.
Muck, Otto *The Transcendental Method*. Trans. William D. Seidensticker. New York: Herder and Herder, 1968.
Müller, Klaus. 'Der Streit um Begründungsfiguren'. In Valentin and Wendel, *Unbedingtes Verstehen?*, 9–22.
Müller, Klaus. 'Zur Verantwortung des Glaubens. Ein Aufriss fundamentallogischer Positionen im Streit um die Rolle der Philosophie in der Theologie – nach Rahner'. In Klauke, *100 Jahre Karl Rahner*, 91–113.
Murdoch, Jessica M. 'Contesting Foundations: Karl Rahner and Francis Schüssler Fiorenza's Non-Foundationalist Critique'. *Philosophy & Theology* 27 (2015): 127–52.
Murdoch, Jessica M. 'Overcoming the Foundationalist/Nonfoundationalist Divide: Karl Rahner's Transcendental Hermeneutics'. *Philosophy and Theology* 22 (2010): 373–87.
Murdoch, Jessica M. 'Transcendence and Postmodernity: A Rahnerian Reading'. *New Blackfriars* 92 (2011): 678–90.

Murray, Paul. 'The Lasting Significance of Karl Rahner for Contemporary Catholic Theology'. *Louvain Studies* 29 (2004): 8–27.
Myatt, William. 'Public Theology and "The Fragment": Duncan Forrester, David Tracy, and Walter Benjamin'. *International Journal of Public Theology* 8 (2014): 85–106.
Neufeld, Karl H. *Die Brüder Rahner: Eine Biographie*. 2nd edition. Freiburg: Herder, 2004.
Neufeld, Karl H. 'Joseph Maréchal und Karl Rahner (K. Rahner Todestag 30.3.). Vom Umgang mit Thomas von Aquin'. *Zeitschrift für katholische Theologie* 137 (2015): 127–40.
Neufeld, Karl H. *Wie "tickt" Karl Rahner?: Theologisches Erkennen und Argumentieren*, Karl Rahner Lecture 2014. Freiburg: Universitätsbibliothek, 2015.
Nieuwenhove, Rik van de. 'Karl Rahner, Theologian of the Experience of God?'. *Louvain Studies* 29 (2004): 92–106.
O'Donovan, Leo. 'Karl Rahner SJ (1904–1984). A Theologian for the Twenty-First Century'. *Theology Today* 62 (2005): 352–63.
O'Donovan, Leo. 'Orthopraxis and Theological Method: Rahner'. *Proceedings of the Catholic Theological Society of America* 35 (1980): 47–65.
O'Donovan, Leo, ed. *A World of Grace. An Introduction to the Themes and Foundations of Rahner's Theology*. New York: Crossroad, 1981.
O'Leary, Joseph S. 'Rahner and Metaphysics'. In Conway and Ryan, *Karl Rahner: Theologian for the Twenty-first Century*, 23–38.
O'Meara, Janet M. 'Salvation: Living Communion with God'. In Hilkert and Schreiter, *The Praxis of the Reign of God*, 97–116.
O'Meara, Thomas F. 'The History of Being and the History of Doctrine: An Influence of Heidegger on Theology'. *American Philosophical Quarterly* 12 (1995): 351–74.
Pascal, Blaise. *Pensées*. Trans. Martin Turnell. London: Harvill, 1962.
Pattison, George. *God & Being. An Enquiry*. Oxford: Oxford University Press, 2013.
Pattison, George. 'How Much Metaphysics Can Theology Tolerate?'. In Hall and von Sass, *Groundless Gods*, 59–74.
Peters, Tiemo Rainer. 'Karl Rahner und die neue Politische Theologie'. In Klauke, *100 Jahre Karl Rahner*, 43–50.
Portier, William. 'Edward Schillebeeckx as Critical Theorist: The Impact of Neo-Marxist Social Thought on his Recent Theology'. *The Thomist* 48 (1984): 341–67.
Portier, William. 'Schillebeeckx' Dialogue with Critical Theory'. *The Ecumenist* 21 (1982): 20–7.
Poulsom, Martin. 'Book Essay. New Resonances in Classic Motifs. Finding Schillebeeckx's Theology in Translation'. *Louvain Studies* 38 (2014): 370–81.
Poulsom, Martin. *The Dialectics of Creation. Creation and the Creator in Edward Schillebeeckx and David Burrell*. London: Bloomsbury, 2014.
Puntel, L. Bruno. 'Zu den Begriffen "transzendental" und "kategorial" bei Karl Rahner'. In Vorgrimler, *Wagnis Theologie*, 189–98.
Purcell, Michael. *Mystery and Method. The Other in Rahner and Levinas*. Milwaukee, WI: Marquette University Press, 1998.
Purcell, Michael. 'Rahner amid Modernity and Post-Modernity'. In Declan Marmion and Mary E. Hines, eds. *The Cambridge Companion to Karl Rahner*. Cambridge: Cambridge University Press, 195–210.
Raffelt, Albert. 'Editionsbericht'. In SW 2, xiii–xxxvii.
Raffelt, Albert. 'Editionsbericht'. In SW 4, xiii–xxxviii.
Raffelt, Albert. 'Geist in Welt: einige Anmerkungen zur Interpretation'. In Schöndorf, *Die philosophische Quellen der Theologie Karl Rahners*, 57–80.

Raffelt, Albert, ed. *Karl Rahner in Erinnerung*. Düsseldorf: Patmos Verlag, 1994.
Raffelt, Albert. 'Neue politische Theologie und das Werk Karl Rahners – eine Gegenrede'. In Klauke, *100 Jahre Karl Rahner*, 51–62.
Raffelt, Albert. 'Pluralismus – Ein Plädoyer für Rahner und eine Bemerkung zur Sache'. In *Hoffnung, die Gründe nennt: Zu Hansjürgen Verweyens Projekt einer erstphilosophischen Glaubensverantwortung*, ed. Gerhard Larcher, 127–38. Regensburg: Friedrich Pustet Verlag, 1996.
Raffelt, Albert, and Hansjürgen Verweyen. *Karl Rahner*. München: Beck, 1997.
Rawls, John. *A Theory of Justice*. Revised edition. Cambridge, MA: Harvard University Press, 1999.
Regan, Ethna. 'Not Merely the Cognitive Subject: Rahner's Theological Anthropology'. In Conway and Ryan, *Karl Rahner: Theologian for the Twenty-first Century*, 121–40.
Russell Reno. *The Ordinary Transformed: Karl Rahner and the Vision of Transcendence*. Grand Rapids, MI: Eerdmans, 1995.
Russell Reno. 'Rahner the Restorationist'. *First Things* May 2013: 45–51.
Ricoeur, Paul. 'Existence and Hermeneutics'. Trans. Kathleen McLaughlin. In *The Conflict of Interpretations*, ed. Don Ihde, 3–24. Evanston, IL: Northwestern University Press, 1974.
Ricoeur, Paul. 'Explanation and Understanding'. In *Interpretation Theory: Discourse and the Surplus of Meaning*, 71–95. Fort Worth, TX: Texas Christian University Press, 1976.
Ricoeur, Paul. *Freud and Philosophy: An Essay on Interpretation*. Trans. Denis Savage. New Haven: Yale University Press, 1970.
Ricoeur, Paul. 'The Hermeneutical Function of Distanciation'. In *From Text to Action: Essays in Hermeneutics, II*, trans. Kathleen Blamey and John B. Thompson, 72–85. Evanston, IL: Northwestern University Press, 1991.
Ricoeur, Paul. 'Hermeneutics and the Critique of Ideology'. In *Hermeneutics and the Human Sciences*, ed. and trans. John B. Thompson, 63–100. Cambridge: Cambridge University Press, 1981.
Ricoeur, Paul. *History and Truth*. Trans. Charles A. Kelbley. Evanston, IL: Northwestern University Press, 1965.
Ricoeur, Paul. *Oneself as Another*. Trans. Kathleen Blamey. Chicago: The University of Chicago Press, 1992.
Ricoeur, Paul. 'Response to Karl Rahner's Lecture: On the Incomprehensibility of God'. *The Journal of Religion (Supplement)* 58 (1978): 126–31.
Ricoeur, Paul. 'The Tasks of the Political Educator'. *Philosophy Today* 17 (1973): 142–152.
Ricoeur, Paul. *Time and Narrative*. Vol. 3. Trans. Kathleen Blamey and David Pellauer. Chicago: The University of Chicago Press, 1988.
Rodenborn, Steven. *Hope in Action. Subversive Eschatology in the Theology of Edward Schillebeeckx and Johann Baptist Metz*. Minneapolis: Fortress Press, 2014.
Rulands, Paul. *Menschsein unter dem An-Spruch der Gnade. Das übernatürliche Existential und der Begriff der natura pura bei Karl Rahners*. Innsbrucker theologische Studien 55. Innsbruck: Tyrolia Verlag, 2000.
Rulands, Paul. 'Selbstmitteilung Gottes in Jesus Christus: Gnadentheologie'. In Batlogg et al., *Der Denkweg Karl Rahners*, 161–96.
Sacks, Mark. 'Transcendental Constraints and Transcendental Features'. *International Journal of Philosophical Studies* 5 (1997): 164–86.
Sartre, Jean-Paul. *Being and Nothingness: An Essay on Phenomenological Ontology*. Trans. Hazel E. Barne. London: Methuen, 1958.

Sass, Hartmut von, and Eric E. Hall. 'Metaphysics, Its Critique, and Post-Metaphysical Theology. An Introductory Essay'. In Hall and Sass, *Groundless Gods*, 1–37.

Schaeffler, Richard. 'Philosophie und katholische Theologie'. In *Christliche Philosophie im katholischen Denken des 19. und 20. Jahrhunderts. Band 3 Moderne Strömungen im 20. Jahrhundert*, ed. Emerich Coreth, Walter M. Neidl, and Georg Pfligersdorffer, 49–78. Graz: Styria Verlag, 1990.

Scheffcyzk, Leo. 'Christology in the Context of Experience: On the Interpretation of Christ by E. Schillebeeckx'. *The Thomist* 48 (1984): 383–408.

Scheltens, D. 'De filosofie van p. D.M. De Petter'. *Tijdschrift voor Filosofie* 33 (1971): 439–505.

Schindler, David C. *The Catholicity of Reason*. Grand Rapids: Eerdmans, 2013.

Schindler, David C. 'On the Universality of the University: A Response to Jean-Luc Marion'. *Communio* 40 (2013): 76–98.

Schöndorf, Harald. 'Die Bedeutung der Philosophie bei Karl Rahner'. In Schöndorf, *Die philosophischen Quellen der Theologie Karl Rahners*, 13–29.

Schöndorf, Harald, ed. *Die philosophische Quellen der Theologie Karl Rahners*. Quaestiones disputatae 213. Freiburg: Herder, 2005.

Schoof, Ted Mark. 'Introduction to the New Edition "God the Future of Men"'. In Schillebeeckx, *God the Future of Men*, xiii–xv.

Schoof, Ted Mark. 'Masters in Israel: VII. The Later Theology of Edward Schillebeeckx'. *Clergy Review* 55 (1970): 943–61.

Schreiter, Robert J. 'Edward Schillebeeckx'. In *The Modern Theologians: An Introduction to Christian Theology in the Twentieth Century*, ed. David F. Ford, 152–60. 2nd edition. Oxford: Blackwell, 1997.

Schreiter, Robert J. 'Edward Schillebeeckx: His Continuing Relevance'. In Hilkert and Schreiter, *The Praxis of the Reign of God*, 185–94.

Schreiter, Robert J. 'Indicators of the Future of Theology in the Works of Edward Schillebeeckx'. In *Edward Schillebeeckx. Impulse für Theologien im 21. Jahrhundert – Impetus Towards Theologies in the 21st Century*, ed. Thomas Eggensperger, Ulrich Engel, Angel F. Méndez Montoya, 21–38. Mainz: Matthias Grünewald Verlag, 2012.

Schumann, Karl. 'Fragmentaire metafysiek. De metafysiek van D.M. De Petter'. *Tijdschrift voor Filosofie* 36 (1974): 574–84.

Schwarz-Boenneke, Bernadette. 'Die Widerständigkeit der Wirklichkeit als erstes Moment des Erfahrens'. In *Edward Schillebeeckx. Impulse für Theologien im 21. Jahrhundert – Impetus Towards Theologies in the 21st Century*, ed. Thomas Eggensperger, Ulrich Engel, Angel F. Méndez Montoya, 94–109. Mainz: Matthias Grünewald Verlag, 2012.

Schwerdtfeger, Nikolaus. *Gnade und Welt. Zum Grundgefüge von Karl Rahners Theorie der 'anonymen Christen'*. Freiburg: Herder, 1982.

Shakespeare, Steven. 'Language'. In *The Oxford Handbook of Theology and Modern European Thought*, ed. Nicholas, Adams George Pattison, and Graham Ward, 105–26. Oxford: Oxford University Press, 2013.

Sheehan, Thomas. *Karl Rahner: The Philosophical Foundations*. Athens, OH: Ohio University Press, 1987.

Sheehan, Thomas. 'Karl Rahner's Transcendental Project'. In In Declan Marmion and Mary E. Hines, eds. *The Cambridge Companion to Karl Rahner*. Cambridge: Cambridge University Press, 29–42.

Sheehan, Thomas. 'Metaphysics and Bivalence: On Karl Rahner's *Geist in Welt*'. *The Modern Schoolman* 63 (1985): 21–43.

Siebenrock, Roman. '"Draw nigh to God and He will draw nigh to you" (James 4:8) The Development of Karl Rahner's Theological Thinking in Its First Period'. *Louvain Studies* 29 (2004): 28–48.
Siebenrock, Roman. 'Glauben gibt zu denken: "Geist in Welt" und "Hörer des Wortes"'. In Batlogg et al., *Der Denkweg Karl Rahners*, 55–105.
Siebenrock, Roman. 'Transzendentale Offenbarung. Bedeutungsanalyse eines Begriffs im Spätwerk Rahners als Beispiel methodisch geleiteter Rahnerforschung'. *Zeitschrift für katholische Theologie* 126 (2004): 33–46.
Siebenrock, Roman, and Walter Schmolly. '"Der Heilswille Gottes berührt uns in Christus Jesus und der Kirche": Die erste Gnadenvorlesung'. In Batlogg et al., *Der Denkweg Karl Rahners*, 106–43.
Simon, Derek. 'Rahner and Ricoeur on Religious Experience and Language. A Reflection on the Mutuality between Experience and Language in the Transcendental and Hermeneutical Traditions'. *Église et Théologie* 28 (1997): 77–99.
Simon, Derek. 'Salvation and Liberation in the Practical-Critical Soteriology of Schillebeeckx'. *Theological Studies* 63 (2002): 494–520.
Sobrino, Jon. 'Karl Rahner and Liberation Theology'. *The Way* 43 (2004): 53–66.
Sokolowski, Robert. *Introduction to Phenomenology*. Cambridge: Cambridge University Press, 2000.
Sölle, Dorothee, and Johann Baptist Metz. *Welches Christentum hat Zukunft? Dorothee Sölle und Johann Baptist Metz im Gespräch mit Karl-Josef Kuschel*. Stuttgart: Kreuz Verlag, 1990.
Stiver, Dan R. *Ricoeur and Theology*. London: Bloomsbury, 2012.
Swidler, Leonard, ed. *Consensus in Theology? A Dialogue with Hans Küng and Edward Schillebeeckx*. Philadelphia: The Westminster Press, 1980.
Tanner, Kathryn. *Christ the Key*. Cambridge: Cambridge University Press, 2010.
Taylor, Charles. 'Overcoming Modern Epistemology'. In *Faithful Reading. New Essays in Theology and Philosophy in Honour of Fergus Kerr, OP*, ed. Simon Oliver, Karen Kilby, and Tom O'Loughlin, 43–60. London: T&T Clark, 2012.
Taylor, Charles. 'Reason, Faith, and Meaning'. In *Faith, Rationality, and the Passions*, ed. Sarah Coakley, 13–27. Malden: Wiley Blackwell, 2013.
Thiel, John. *Nonfoundationalism*. Guides to Theological Inquiry Series. Minneapolis: Fortress Press, 1994.
Thompson, Daniel Speed. 'Epistemological Frameworks in the Theology of Edward Schillebeeckx'. *Theological Studies* 15 (2003): 19–56.
Thompson, Daniel Speed. 'Schillebeeckx on the Development of Doctrine'. *Theological Studies* 62 (2001): 303–21.
Tillich, Paul. *Systematic Theology*. Vol. 1. Chicago: The University of Chicago Press, 1951.
Tillich, Paul. *Systematic Theology*. Vol. 2. Chicago: The University of Chicago Press, 1957.
Torrell, Jean-Pierre. 'Thomism'. In *Encyclopedia of Christian Theology*, vol. 3, ed. Jean-Yves Lacoste, 1578–83. London: Routledge: 2005.
Tracy, David. *The Achievement of Bernard Lonergan*. New York: Herder and Herder, 1970.
Tracy, David. *The Analogical Imagination: Christian Theology and the Culture of Pluralism*. New York: Crossroad, 1981.
Tracy, David. *Blessed Rage for Order: The New Pluralism in Theology*. 2nd edition with a new preface by the author. Chicago: The University of Chicago Press, 1996.
Tracy, David. 'Foreword'. In Jean-Luc Marion, *God Without Being*, xi–xvii.
Tracy, David. 'Form and Fragment. The Recovery of the Hidden and Incomprehensible God'. In Jeanrond and Lande, *The Concept of God in Global Dialogue*, 98–114.

Tracy, David. 'Fragments: The Spiritual Situation of our Times'. In *God, the Gift, and Postmodernism*, ed. John D. Caputo and Michael J. Scanlon, 170–84. Bloomington: Indiana University Press, 1999.
Tracy, David. 'God, Dialogue and Solidarity: A Theologian's Refrain'. *The Christian Century* 107 (1995): 900–4.
Tracy, David. 'God and Trinity. Approaching the Christian Understanding of God'. In *Systematic Theology: Roman Catholic Perspectives*. 2nd ed., ed. Francis Schüssler Fiorenza and John P. Galvi, 109–27. Minneapolis: Fortress Press, 2011
Tracy, David. 'The Hermeneutics of Naming God'. *Irish Theological Quarterly* 57 (1991): 254–64.
Tracy, David. 'A Hermeneutics of Orthodoxy'. *Concilium: International Review of Theology – English Edition*, no. 2 (2014): 71–81.
Tracy, David. 'Lindbeck's New Program for Theology: A Reflection'. *The Thomist* 49 (1985): 460–72.
Tracy, David. 'On Naming the Present'. In *On Naming the Present: Reflections on God, Hermeneutics, and Church*. Concilium Series. Maryknoll: Orbis Books, 1995.
Tracy, David. 'Particular Questions within General Consensus'. In Swidler, Consensus in Theology?, 33–9.
Tracy, David. *Plurality and Ambiguity: Hermeneutics, Religion, Hope*. Chicago: The University of Chicago Press, 1987.
Tracy, David. 'Religion im öffentlichen Bereich: Öffentliche Theologie'. In *Im Dialog. Systematische Theologie und Religionssoziologie*, ed. Ansgar Kreutzer and Franz Gruber, 189–207. Quaestiones disputatae 258. Freiburg: Herder, 2013.
Tracy, David. 'Theology and the Many Faces of Postmodernity'. *Theology Today* 51 (1994): 104–14.
Tracy, David. 'The Uneasy Alliance Reconceived: Catholic Theological Method, Modernity, and Postmodernity'. *Theological Studies* 50 (1989): 548–70.
Turner, Denys. *Faith, Reason and the Existence of God*. Cambridge: Cambridge University Press, 2004.
Turner, Denys. *Thomas Aquinas: A Portrait*. New Haven: Yale University Press, 2013.
Valentin, Joachim, and Saskia Wendel, eds. *Unbedingtes Verstehen? Fundamentaltheologie zwischen Erstphilosophie und Hermeneutik*. Regensburg: Friedrich Pustet Verlag, 2001.
Van Wyngaerden, Johan. *Voorstudie tot het denken van E. Schillebeeckx. D.M. De Petter O.P. (1905–1971): Een inleiding tot zijn leven en denken*. Unpublished licentiate thesis. Faculty of Theology, Catholic University of Leuven, 1989.
Vanhoozer, Kevin J. 'Theology and the Condition of Postmodernity: A Report on Knowledge (of God)'. In *The Cambridge Companion to Postmodern Theology*, ed. Kevin J. Vanhoozer, 3–25. Cambridge: Cambridge University Press, 2003.
Velde, Rudi te. *Aquinas on God. The 'Divine Science' of the* Summa Theologiae. Farnham: Ashgate, 2006.
Verweyen, Hansjürgen. *Gottes letztes Wort. Grundriß der Fundamentaltheologie*. Düsseldorf: Patmos Verlag, 1991.
Verweyen, Hansjürgen. 'Wie wird ein Existential übernatürlich? Zu einem Grundproblem der Anthropologie K. Rahners'. *Trierer Theologische Zeitschrift* 95 (1986): 115–31.
Vorgrimler, Herbert. 'Der Begriff der Selbsttranszendenz in der Theologie Karl Rahners'. In Vorgrimler, *Wagnis Theologie*, 242–58.
Vorgrimler, Herbert. 'Gotteserfahrung im Alltag. Der Beitrag Karl Rahners zu Spiritualität und Mystik'. In Raffelt, *Karl Rahner in Erinnerung*, 100–17.

Vorgrimler, Herbert. *Karl Rahner: Gotteserfahrung in Leben und Denken*. Darmstadt: Primus Verlag, 2004.
Vorgrimler, Herbert, ed. *Wagnis Theologie. Erfahrungen mit der Theologie Karl Rahners*. Freiburg: Herder, 1979.
Walle, Ambroos R. van de. 'Theologie over de werkelijkheid. Een betekenis van het werk van Edward Schillebeeckx'. *Tijdschrift voor Theologie* 14 (1974): 463–90.
Wendel, Saskia. 'Zum Verhältnis von christlicher Theologie und postmoderner Philosophie'. In *Fundamentaltheologie – Fluchtlinien und gegenwärtige Herausforderungen*, ed. Klaus Müller, 193–214. Regensburg: Friedrich Pustet Verlag, 1998.
Wolde, Ellen van. 'Semiotiek en haar betekenis voor de theologie'. *Tijdschrift voor Theologie* 24 (1984): 138–67.
Williams, Rowan. 'Augustinian Love'. In *Dynamics of Difference. Christianity and Alterity: A Festschrift for Werner G. Jeanrond*, ed. Ulrich Schmiedel and James M. Matarazzo Jr., 189–97. London: Bloomsbury, 2015.
Williams, Rowan. 'Balthasar and Rahner'. In *The Analogy of Beauty: The Theology of Hans Urs von Balthasar*, ed. John Riches, 11–34. Edinburgh: T&T Clark, 1986.
Wittgenstein, Ludwig. *Philosophical Investigations*. Trans. G. E. M. Anscombe. Oxford: Basil Blackwell, 1958.
Wolfe, Judith. *Heidegger and Theology*. London: Bloomsbury, 2014.

Index

Adam, Karl 199 n.97
Adams, Nicholas 103 n.24
Adorno, Theodor W. 162, 174–6, 178, 247, 248 n.35, 259, 275
Altizer, Thomas 195 n.69
Anselm of Canterbury 141
Apel, Karl Otto 34
Aquinas, Thomas 48–51, 54–5, 57–8, 66, 69–70, 73–5, 78–82, 83 n.75, 85, 86 n.94, 88–9, 91, 94–7, 99 n.2, 124, 148 n.105, 161–3, 182, 184, 188–93, 199 n.97, 238, 243, 261, 265–6, 272, 275–6, 286
Aristotle 28, 34, 75, 83, 88, 130, 163, 165, 189, 237, 272
Augustine 83 n.77, 121, 189, 238

Badiou, Alain 39
Balthasar, Hans Urs von 76–7, 101, 139, 199, 267
Baron, Craig 114 n.75
Barth, Karl 29, 77 n.40, 167, 131 n.18, 182 n.2, 243
Barwasser, Carsten 196 n.83, 257 n.96, 261 n.109
Baudrillard, Jean 8
Benjamin, Walter 99
Bernstein, Richard 19
Beyer, Gerald J. 119 n.100
Bloch, Ernst 99, 173, 176, 247, 248 n.35, 251
Blondel, Maurice 137 n.100, 185
Boeve, Lieven 10 n.37, 180, 204 n.130, 209 n.154, 212, 219 n.43, 229–32, 234–7, 263 n.115, 276
Bonaventure 83 n.77
Borgman, Erik 2, 162 n.5, 180, 194 n.69, 206 n.141, 212, 229–30, 232–6, 248 n.35, 249 n.39, 265, 276
Brunner, Emil 131 n.18

Bullivant, Stephen 137 n.100, 267
Bultmann, Rudolf 11, 167, 173, 195 n.69, 201, 215 n.19, 243

Camus, Albert 248 n.35
Caponi, Francis J. 87 n.96, 88 n.97, 114
Caputo, John 180
Cardijn, Joseph 248 n.34
Carr, Anne 64, 69 n.1
Certeau, Michel de 33 n.174
Coffey, David 135, 141 n.67
Congar, Yves 137 n.100
Conlon, James 79 n.56, 92 n.124
Conway, Eamonn 137 n.50
Cooper, Jennifer 184 n.10
Coreth, Emerich 58 n.69, 60 n.83, 105 n.34, 155

Daniélou, Jean 137 n.100
De Lubac, Henri 131, 135 n.37, 137 n.100, 139, 199
De Maeseneer, Yves 39
De Petter, Dominicus 161–6, 178, 180–2, 185–9, 191–2, 195 n.69, 201, 203, 209, 275
Depoorter, Annekatrien 231 n.116
Depoortere, Frederiek 194 n.65
Derrida, Jacques 8–9, 19, 33 n.33
Descartes, René 34, 76–8, 92, 123, 172
Desmond, William 41
Dilthey, Wilhelm 11
Dreyfus, Hubert 282–3
Duffy, Stephen 200
Duns, Ryan 86 n.93
Dupré, Louis 89, 204 n.130, 205 n.133, 206 n.141, 207 n.147, 208

Ebeling, Gerhard 11, 167, 201
Eicher, Peter 51, 64 n.108, 69 n.1, 73, 74 n.25, 82 n.72, 89 n.102
Eliade, Mircea 102, 108 n.48

Index

Endean, Philip 1, 121
Erp, Stephan van 1, 181, 189, 204 n.126, 270 n.157

Fichte, Johann Gottlieb 56, 76, 80 n.58, 178
Fiorenza, Francis Schüssler 2, 4, 11–24, 37–9, 41–2, 90 n.110, 156, 261, 264 n.119, 272, 279, 281
Fössel, Thomas 144, 147, 149 n.106, 156
Foucault, Michel 8, 19, 33 n.174
Frege, Gottlob 171
Freud, Sigmund 171
Fritz, Joseph 59, 65 n.119, 69 n.1, 77, 82 n.70, 86 n.91, 91 n.118, 97 n.147, 106 n.37, 148 n.102
Fuchs, Ernst 11, 167, 203

Gadamer, Hans-Georg 11, 15, 26, 28–30, 33 n.174, 43, 142, 156, 162, 167–70, 172–3, 176, 202, 212–13, 215, 275
Geldhof, Joris 147 n.100
Gilson, Etienne 58
Godzieba, Anthony 261–2
Grondin, Jean 52 n.27
Guarino, Thomas 7–8, 11

Habermas, Jürgen 18, 23–4, 34, 38, 43, 162, 171, 174, 176–9, 215, 264 n.119, 275
Haight, Roger 200 n.104, 262 n.113, 265, 266 n.131
Hall, Eric 40
Hartshorne, Charles 27 n.140, 34
Hauerwas, Stanley 20
Healy, Nicholas 153
Hegel, Georg Wilhelm Friedrich 32 n.168, 49–51, 74 n.26, 83 n.77, 84, 87, 93 n.130, 117 n.88, 202
Heidegger, Martin 8, 11, 15, 26, 33 n.174, 41, 48–51, 59–66, 71, 73 n.20, 77, 80 n.58, 82–6, 89 n.105, 90 n.112, 93, 94 n.133, 96, 106 n.37, 114, 134, 151 n.117, 163, 167, 170, 173 n.87, 202, 212, 216–18, 247, 272, 276, 282
Henry, Michel 80 n.58

Hilkert, Mary-Catherine 182 n.2, 202, 204 n.131, 218 n.34, 238 n.152, 252
Hogan, Kevin 77 n.43
Holzer, Vincent 80 n.58
Horkheimer, Max 174, 176
Hurd, Bob 73 n.21
Husserl, Edmund 61, 64, 80 n.58, 90 n.112, 110 n.58, 163

Irigaray, Luce 8

Jeanrond, Werner G. 20 n.92, 25, 37 n.204, 108 n.48, 119, 172
John Paul II 5–6

Kant, Immanuel 3, 17, 22–4, 32 n.168, 41, 47–58, 60, 66, 70, 83–5, 110–11, 114 n.78, 162–3, 178, 186 n.23, 187, 196, 243
Kasper, Walter 99, 101–2, 104, 117
Kennedy, Philip 161, 180, 185 n.18, 186 n.19, 190, 196 n.82, 203 n.119, 236, 247 n.30, 254 n.78, 258, 263 n.115, 264 n.119
Kerr, Fergus 75–8, 131
Kilby, Karen 51, 64 n.108, 69 n.1, 77 n.40, 81, 86 nn.91–4, 111, 145–6, 153
Kim, Younhee 25 n.128
Knoepffler, Nikolaus 71 nn.11–12, 82 n.72, 111 n.62, 155 n.139
Kreutzer, Karsten 74 n.25, 82 n.70, 86 n.94, 89 n.102, 93 n.128, 140, 149 n.106, 151 n.117
Krings, Herman 110 n.58
Kristeva, Julia 8, 33 n.174
Küng, Hans 26 n.131, 220–1, 224 n.74

Lacan, Jacques 33 n.174
Lamb, Matthew 104 n.30
Lash, Nicholas 115–18, 122, 148 n.105, 285
Lehmann, Karl 47–8, 59, 150 n.111
Lennan, Richard 130 n.10
Leo XIII 49
Lessing, Gotthold Ephraim 105
Levinas, Emmanuel 20, 93, 197
Lévi-Strauss, Claude 33 n.174
Lindbeck, George 20, 22, 99, 102–3, 115

Lonergan, Bernard   12, 16, 18, 24–5, 102
Lotz, Johannes Baptist   55 n.44, 56 n.53, 58 n.69, 59, 110 n.58
Lyotard, Jean-François   5, 9, 231 n.118

Maas, Frans   187 n.24, 209 n.158
Malebranche, Nicolas   83 n.77
Maréchal, Joseph   48, 51, 54–60, 64, 66, 71 n.11, 76 n.38, 81–2, 162–4, 178, 185–9, 272
Marion, Jean-Luc   35, 40, 64
Maritain, Jacques   58, 137 n.100
Marx, Karl   171
McCool, Gerald   56 n.53, 59 n.77
Mendelsohn, Moses   52 n.27
Merleau-Ponty, Maurice   163, 217, 282
Metz, Johann Baptist   12, 22, 69 n.1, 99–101, 104, 117, 141 n.65, 151 n.117, 179, 230 n.115, 248 n.35
Milbank, John   20, 128, 138–140, 142–3, 146–8, 152
Moltmann, Jürgen   248 n.35
Muck, Otto   56 n.53, 58 n.69
Müller, Klaus   74 n.25, 140
Müller, Max   5, 59 n.77, 105 n.34
Murdoch, Jessica   23 n.116, 123 n.128
Myatt, William   25 n.128

Newman, John Henry   17
Nietzsche, Friedrich   171

O'Donovan, Leo   108 n.51, 118 n.92
O'Leary, Joseph   75 n.31, 77 n.42
O'Meara, Janet   268 n.149
O'Meara, Thomas F.   65 n.115
Origen of Alexandria   10 n.35

Pascal, Blaise   147, 193
Pattison, George   40–1
Peirce, Charles Sanders   17
Pius X   49, 50 n.13
Pius XII   132
Plato   83–4, 164, 189
Plotinus   83 n.77
Portier, William   173 n.87, 178
Poulsom, Martin G.   178 n.110, 186 n.23, 225 n.82, 235, 252, 254 n.78, 261, 270 n.156

Pröpper, Thomas   140
Przywara, Erich   49 n.11
Puntel, Bruno   109
Purcell, Michael   64, 77–8, 92–3, 94 n.133

Quine, Willard Van Orman   14 n.55

Raffelt, Albert   54 n.42, 65 n.119, 69 n.1, 73 n.20, 93 n.130, 147, 153 n.128
Ramsey, Ian   243
Rawls, John   15
Regan, Ethna   77 n.43
Reno, Russell   1
Ricoeur, Paul   11, 26, 28, 33 n.174, 43, 102, 104 n.30, 114 n.74, 142, 156, 162, 167, 169–72, 174 n.88, 176, 202 n.114, 205, 212, 214, 216–17, 248 n.35, 275
Robinson, John T.   196 n.69
Rodenborn, Steven   176, 179, 254 n.78, 260 n.102, 262 n.113
Rorty, Richard   8, 14 n.55
Rousselot, Pierre   51, 54
Rulands, Paul   135

Sacks, Mark   22
Sartre, Jean-Paul   247, 251
Sass, Hartmut von   40
Saussure, Ferdinand de   33 n.174
Schaeffler, Richard   58, 110 n.58
Scheffczyk, Leo   180, 214 n.9
Schindler, David C.   40
Schleiermacher, Friedrich   11, 77 n.40, 151 n.120, 182 n.2, 220
Schoof, Ted   166 n.38, 219
Schreiter, Robert   1, 254 n.78
Schwarz-Boenneke, Bernadette   204 n.130, 206 n.141
Sellars, Wilfred   14 n.55
Shakespeare, Steven   114 n.78
Sheehan, Thomas   64, 67 n.124, 82 n.70, 84 n.79, 86 n.91, 90, 92, 94, 96 n.142
Siebenrock, Roman   69 n.1, 79 n.53, 136 n.45, 141 n.68
Siewerth, Gustav   59
Suárez, Francisco   49

Tanner, Kathryn 279 n.2
Taylor, Charles 282–3
Thompson, Daniel Speed 161 n.4, 230 n.110
Tillich, Paul 26, 220–1, 229, 243
Tracy, David 2, 4, 11, 24–39, 41–2, 102, 103 n.28, 156, 220, 224, 272, 278–9, 281
Turner, Denys 73, 284, 286 n.17

Verweyen, Hansjürgen 65 n.119, 73 n.20, 88, 89 n.102, 93 n.130, 128, 138, 140–3, 146–8, 149 n.106

Vincent of Lérins 7 n.17
Vorgrimler, Herbert 59 n.77, 109 n.52, 112 n.67

Welte, Bernhard 59
Wendel, Saskia 7–11
Whitehead, Alfred North 27 n.140
Williams, Rowan 76–7, 121
Wittgenstein, Ludwig 33 n.174, 75, 117, 142, 243
Wolde, Ellen van 237
Wolfe, Judith 60

www.ingramcontent.com/pod-product-compliance
Lightning Source LLC
Chambersburg PA
CBHW070015010526
44117CB00011B/1578